APR 2014   19.95

DATE DUE

	PRINTED IN U.S.A.

WITHDRAWN

W9-BZO-655

HIGHLAND PARK PUBLIC LIBRARY
494 LAUREL AVE.
HIGHLAND PARK, IL 60035-2590
847-432-0216

917.7311
T583
6th ed.
2013

Time Out Digital Ltd
Universal House
251 Tottenham Court Road
London W1T 7AB
United Kingdom
Tel: +44 (0)20 7813 3000
Fax: +44 (0)20 7813 6001
Email: guides@timeout.com
www.timeout.com

Published by Time Out Digital Ltd, a wholly owned subsidiary of Time Out Group Ltd.
Time Out and the Time Out logo are trademarks of Time Out Group Ltd.

© Time Out Group Ltd 2013
Previous editions 2000, 2002, 2004, 2007, 2009

10 9 8 7 6 5 4 3 2 1

This edition first published in Great Britain in 2013 by Ebury Publishing.
A Random House Group Company
20 Vauxhall Bridge Road, London SW1V 2SA

Random House Australia Pty Ltd 20 Alfred Street, Milsons Point, Sydney, New South Wales 2061, Australia

Random House New Zealand Ltd 18 Poland Road, Glenfield, Auckland 10, New Zealand

Random House South Africa (Pty) Ltd Isle of Houghton, Corner Boundary Road & Carse O'Gowrie, Houghton 2198, South Africa

Random House UK Limited Reg. No. 954009

Distributed in the US and Latin America by Publishers Group West (1-510-809-3700)

For further distribution details, see www.timeout.com.

ISBN: 978-1-84670-399-7

A CIP catalogue record for this book is available from the British Library.

Printed and bound by Butler Tanner & Dennis, Frome, Somerset.

The Random House Group Limited supports the Forest Stewardship Council® (FSC®), the leading international forest-certification organisation. Our books carrying the FSC label are printed on FSC®-certified paper. FSC is the only forest-certification scheme supported by the leading environmental organisations, including Greenpeace. Our paper procurement policy can be found at www.randomhouse.co.uk/environment.

While every effort has been made by the author(s) and the publisher to ensure that the information contained in this guide is accurate and up to date as as at the date of publication, they accept no responsibility or liability in contract, tort, negligence, breach of statutory duty or otherwise for any inconvenience, loss, damage, costs or expenses of any nature whatsoever incurred or suffered by anyone as a result of any advice or information contained in this guide (except to the extent that such liability may not be excluded or limited as a matter of law). Before travelling, it is advisable to check all information locally, including without limitation, information on transport, accommodation, shopping and eating out. Anyone using this guide is entirely responsible for their own health, well-being and belongings and care should always be exercised while travelling.

All rights reserved. No part of this publication may be reproduced, stored in a retrieval system, or transmitted in any form or by any means, electronic, mechanical, photocopying, recording or otherwise, without prior permission from the copyright owners.

MIX
Paper from responsible sources
FSC® C023561

Contents

ELVIS PRESLEY
JERRY LEE LEWIS
CARL PERKINS
JOHNNY CASH
MILLION DOLLAR QUARTET
Now Chicago's Longest Running Broadway Musical! Inspired by the Electrifying True Story!
APOLLO THEATER CALL 773.935.6100
TICKETMASTER.COM I GROUPS CALL 312.977.1710 I 2540 N LINCOLN AVE, CHICAGO
MILLIONDOLLARQUARTETLIVE.COM

Introduction

If journalist AJ Liebling knew in the 1950s how long his nickname for Chicago would stick, maybe he would have thought twice. Second City: a name that jabs at Chicago's weak spot – its reputed inferiority complex when compared to the real city, New York. But as any proud Chicagoan will tell you – and you'll find them in spades – Chicago stands on its own merits.

Architecturally, it's one of the most remarkable cities in the country. Between the minimalist Mies van der Rohe buildings along the lake, the cloud-skimming Willis Tower (formerly Sears Tower), the twin corncobs of Marina City and the ornate former Carson Pirie Scott building designed by Louis Sullivan, the skyline is at once unpredictable and awe-inspiring. And it's constantly improving. While Millennium Park's construction wrapped up well over budget and behind schedule, most locals agree it was well worth it. On the west side of town, the old Bloomingdale Line rail track is being transformed into a trail-cum-park.

Just as the cityscape is evolving, so too are the neighbourhoods. The South Side's Back of the Yards area, which served as inspiration for Upton Sinclair's novel about immigrant struggle, *The Jungle*, is now the backdrop for burgeoning Bridgeport, where artists and pioneering entrepreneurs are setting up shop. Logan Square, once a relatively desolate area commercially, is now buzzing with new bars and restaurants. And the historically artsy, gritty Wicker Park has not only gentrified but become the main attraction for the baby-toting, boutique-shopping and brunching set.

Culturally, the city is as vibrant as ever. Known for its improv scene, with notable training programmes and performance venues such as Second City, Chicago is still a breeding ground for young comedic talent. And with an abundance of boundary-pushing storefront venues and Broadway-bound acts from the Goodman and Steppenwolf, theatre isn't lagging far behind.

The city's culinary culture is also on the rise. We can officially bid farewell to Chicago's reputation as a meat-and-potatoes town. Sure, we still like our steakhouses and deep-dish pizza joints, but the dining scene here now fiercely rivals both coasts.

In short, for most residents Chicago is second to none – and we're pretty sure that once you've spent some time here, you'll be inclined to agree. *Jessica Herman, Editor*

CHICAGO
CityPASS.

SAVE
49%
5 famous attractions

Includes:

- Shedd Aquarium
- Skydeck Chicago Fast Pass
- The Field Museum
- Your choice of Museum of Science and Industry, Chicago, OR John Hancock Observatory Fast Pass
- Your choice of Adler Planetarium OR Art Institute of Chicago

Buy at these attractions

- Good for 9 days
- Skip most ticket lines

Connect for current pricing
citypass.com **or (888) 330-5008**

Prices and programs subject to change.

TIME OUT
SHORTLIST
GUIDES

These pocket-sized guides select the very best of each city's sightseeing, restaurants, shopping, local culture and entertainment

- **Comprehensive and easy to use**
- **Shortlist boxes highlight our top picks and tips**
- **All locations marked on maps**
- **Includes all the latest openings and suggested itineraries**

WRITTEN BY LOCAL EXPERTS
POCKET-SIZE
FROM ONLY £6.99/$11.95

London 2014

New York 2014

Paris 2014

Available at all major bookshops and from
timeout.com/shop

TIME OUT GUIDES
WRITTEN BY
LOCAL EXPERTS
visit timeout.com/shop

About the Guide

GETTING AROUND

The back of the book contains street maps of Chicago, as well as overview maps of the city and its surroundings. The maps start on page 304; on them are marked the locations of hotels (**❶**), restaurants (**❶**), and bars (**❶**). Many businesses listed in this guide are located in the areas we've mapped; the grid-square references in the listings refer to these maps.

THE ESSENTIALS

For practical information, including visas, disabled access, emergency numbers, lost property, useful websites and details of local transport, please consult the Essential Information section. It begins on page 284.

THE LISTINGS

Addresses, phone numbers, websites, transport information, hours and prices are all included in our listings, as are selected other facilities. All were checked and correct at press time. However, business owners can alter their arrangements at any time, and fluctuating economic conditions can cause prices to change rapidly.

The very best venues in the city, the must-sees and must-dos in every category, have been marked with a red star (★). In the Explore chapters, we've also marked venues with free admission with a FREE symbol.

PHONE NUMBERS

Chicago has a number of different area codes: The Loop and other downtown districts are covered by 312; the rest of the city is served by 773; and the suburbs surrounding the city are served by 630, 708 and 847. You don't need to use the area code if you're calling from a number with the same code.

From outside the US, dial your country's international access code (00 from the UK) or a '+' symbol, followed by the number as listed in this guide. So, to reach the Art Institute of Chicago, dial +1-312 443 3600. For more on phones, see p293.

FEEDBACK

We welcome feedback on this guide, both on the venues we've included and on any other locations that you'd like to see featured in future editions. Please email us at guides@timeout.com.

Time Out Guides

Founded in 1968, Time Out has grown from humble beginnings into the leading resource for anyone wanting to know what's happening in the world's greatest cities. Alongside our influential weeklies in London and New York, we publish more than 20 magazines in cities as varied as Beijing and Beirut; a range of travel books, with the City Guides now joined by the newer Shortlist series; and an information-packed website. The company remains proudly independent, still owned by Tony Elliott four decades after he launched *Time Out London*.

Written by local experts and illustrated with original photography, our books also retain their independence. No business has been featured because it has advertised, and all restaurants and bars are visited and reviewed anonymously.

ABOUT THE EDITOR

Jessica Herman came to Chicago in 2000. She's the former Associate Editor Shopping & Style at *Time Out Chicago*, author of *The HUNT Chicago*, and a co-founder of Fête, a Chicago-based food and design festival. Her writing has appeared in *Chicago Magazine*, the *Chicago Tribune*, *Slate* and other publications. A full list of the book's contributors can be found on page 13.

LOGAN SQUARE
It's a breeding ground for ambitious new restaurants, but Logan Square maintains the laid-back vibe it's had for years. Drawing everyone from moustachioed hipsters to old-timers playing backgammon on their stoops, the square is a superb people-watching spot.

WICKER PARK
While some trendsetters may gripe that Wicker Park has become too commercialised, you'll still find the original qualities – such as great dive bars and record shops – that made its name in the first place.

MAGNIFICENT MILE
With its parade of chic boutiques, designer flagships, upscale malls and big-name department stores, Michigan Avenue is the perfect spot for a serious shopping splurge.

© Copyright Time Out Group 2013

2 miles
3 km

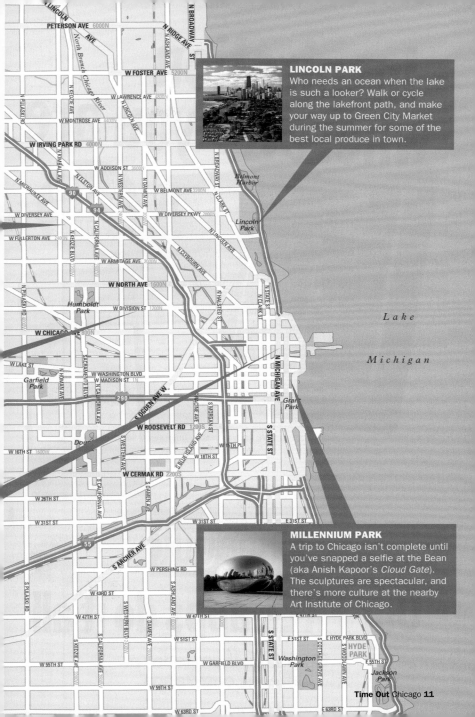

LINCOLN PARK
Who needs an ocean when the lake is such a looker? Walk or cycle along the lakefront path, and make your way up to Green City Market during the summer for some of the best local produce in town.

MILLENNIUM PARK
A trip to Chicago isn't complete until you've snapped a selfie at the Bean (aka Anish Kapoor's *Cloud Gate*). The sculptures are spectacular, and there's more culture at the nearby Art Institute of Chicago.

Lake

Michigan

Inspiration
wherever you are

**REVIEWS
TICKETS
BOOKINGS**

TimeOut

Our FREE apps do it all

Download them today at
timeout.com/apps

TimeOut Chicago

Editorial
Editor Jessica Herman
Consultant Editor Lisa Ritchie
Deputy Editor Dominic Earle
Fact Checkers Ashley Devick, Gabriel Charles Tyler
Proofreader Ros Sales
Indexer Ros Sales

Editorial Director Sarah Guy
Management Accountant Margaret Wright

Design
Senior Designer Kei Ishimaru
Designer Darryl Bell
Group Commercial Senior Designer Jason Tansley

Picture Desk
Picture Editor Jael Marschner
Deputy Picture Editor Ben Rowe
Freelance Picture Researcher Isidora O'Neill

Advertising
Sales Director St John Betteridge
Advertising Sales Noelle Auberger, Melissa Keller, Robert Ruthardt, Christy Stewart

Marketing
Senior Publishing Brand Manager Luthfa Begum
Head of Circulation Dan Collins

Production
Production Controller Katie Mulhern-Bhudia

Time Out Group
Chairman & Founder Tony Elliott
Chief Executive Officer Tim Arthur
Chief Financial Officer Matt White
MD Magazine & Guides Greg Miall
Chief Commercial Officer David Pepper
Group IT Director Simon Chappell
Group Marketing Director Carolyn Sims

Contributors
Introduction Jessica Herman. **Chicago Today** Robert K Elder. **Just for Laughs** Jason Heidemann. **Diary** Jessica Herman, Madeline Nusser. **Explore** Jessica Herman. **Restaurants** Julia Kramer, Heather Shouse, David Tamarkin. **Bars** Julia Kramer, Heather Shouse, David Tamarkin. **Shops & Services** Jessica Herman, Lauren Weinberg. **Hotels** Jessica Herman. **Children** Judy Sutton Taylor. **Film** Hank Sartin. **Gay & Lesbian** Kevin Aeh. **Nightlife** Josh Ferguson. **Performing Arts** Asimina Chremos, Brent DiCrescenzo, Jason Heidemann, Bryant Manning, Areif Sleiss-Kitain. **Sport & Fitness** Tim McCormick. **Escapes & Excursions** Ruth Welte. **History** Victoria Cunha. **Architecture** Madeline Nusser. **Esssential Information** Jessica Herman.

The Editor would like to thank all contributors to previous editions of *Time Out Chicago*, whose work forms the basis for parts of this book.

Maps john@jsgraphics.co.uk

Cover photograph Romeo Banias
Back cover photography Songquan Deng/Shutterstock.com

Photography Martha Williams, except pages 7 Songquan Deng/Shutterstock.com; 20, 23 Scott Regan; 30/31, 40, 55 photo.ua/Shutterstock.com; 28, 36 (top), 242 maxhphoto/Shutterstock.com; 43 (bottom) Richard Cavalleri/Shutterstock.com; 53, 227 Nagel Photography/Shutterstock.com; 58 Lissandra Melo/Shutterstock.com; 59 Thomas Barrat/Shutterstock.com; 87 (top), 113 (bottom), 118 (left) Erica Gannett; 99 Juhyun Baik; 108 (top), 113 (top), 135, 136, 140, 141 Jason Little; 111 Simon Brubaker; 122 Sara Mays; 126 Ben Reed; 138 Colin Beckett; 144 Tupungato/Shutterstock.com; 153 Allison Williams; 188 Cafebeanz Company/Shutterstock.com; 192 Ben Rowe; 195 REX/SNAP; 198 Theresasc75/Shutterstock.com; 199 Tim Klein; 202 Jeremy Bolen; 208 Damien Thompson; 214 Ming Tang-Evans; 216 Julien Hautcoeur/Shutterstock.com; 230 Herb Migdoll; 231 Max Herman; 233 Susan Montgomery/Shutterstock.com; 234, 237 Michael Brosilow; 238 Anna Knott; 240 Lara Goetsch; 244 David Durochik/isiphotos.com; 248/249 Thomas Barrat/Shutterstock.com; 262 Alamy; 267 Getty Images; 268 Arsen Brzostek; 272 AP/Press Association Images; 284/285 jkirsh/Shutterstock.com.

The following images were provided by the featured establishments: pages 36 (bottom), 48, 79, 132, 175, 178, 180, 182, 191, 211, 221, 228, 236, 252, 258.

© Copyright Time Out Group Ltd
All rights reserved

In Focus

Chicago Today

Change is blowing through the Windy City.

TEXT: ROBERT K ELDER

Loving Chicago, wrote Nelson Algren in his 1951 essay *Chicago: City on the Make*, is 'like loving a woman with a broken nose'. More than half a century later, Algren's words still ring true, but they could use a little modification. It might be more accurate to suggest that loving Chicago in the early 21st century is like loving a woman with a broken nose and plastic surgery. A great deal of plastic surgery.

While the recession has stalled some projects, Chicago continues to build. One possible high-profile addition to the city is Barack Obama's presidential library, which could break ground near the University of Chicago campus, where Obama taught law. Another contender is the University of Illinois at Chicago, which has formed an exploratory committee.

IF YOU BUILD IT...

For all the apparent modernity of the city's glass-and-steel skyline, much of Chicago's recent urban makeover has been a long time coming. Over the past decade, the cityscape has welcomed a number of high-profile additions: the Trump International Hotel & Tower, overlooking the Chicago River; the expansion of the Blue Cross Blue Shield Tower, close to the Aon Center; the array of Lakeshore East condo towers, in the north-east corner of the Loop. These skyscrapers have been joined by other landmarks, chief among them Millennium Park. With its shrapnel-like concert stage (designed by Frank Gehry), array of public art (Anish Kapoor's bean-shaped *Cloud Gate*, Jaume Plensa's *Crown Fountain*) and beautiful gardens, the park now rivals Navy Pier for visitor appeal and postcard popularity.

In the meantime, Hollywood has rediscovered Chicago. Director Christopher Nolan reshaped the Windy City as Gotham City in *The Dark Knight*, and Michael Bay has since blown in it up in the third and fourth *Transformers* movies. In 2013, the city provided the backdrop for *Jupiter Ascending*, a fantasy thriller from *Matrix*-makers Lana and Andy Wachowski, as well as an adaptation of Veronica Roth's dystopian teen adventure *Divergent*. Small-screen dramas such as NBC's *Chicago Fire* and spin-off *Chicago PD* will soon be joined by USA's *Sirens* and two new ABC shows, *Betrayal* and *Mind Games*.

In 2009, the Chicago Plan Commission approved a $15.5 billion proposal for downtown rejuvenation that encompasses everything from a new transport hub in the West Loop and a high-speed rail link connecting the city and its two airports to further beautification of the walkways along the Chicago River. The proposal was made under mayor Richard J Daley's administration, in the shadow of a failed bid for the Olympics. Current mayor Rahm Emanuel seems to be more focused on expanding Chicago's tech sector, dubbed the 'Silicon Prairie', and furthering the city's success as a start-up incubator and business leader. Chicago is home to GrubHub, Belly, Threadless, CareerBuilder and a slew of other high-tech ventures.

But despite these city-of-tomorrow ambitions, there have been hiccups – local hero Groupon received a blow when its stock price dipped and founder Andrew Mason was shown the door in 2013.

Growth has also strained the city's existing infrastructure. Take the century-old elevated train system – the city's brittle backbone, described by filmmaker Danny Boyle as 'the sexiest railway in the world'. The 'El' remains a reliable network, and retains an iconic status worldwide. But while some sections of the railway have been renovated in recent years – with the South Side Red line getting a major overhaul – the network continues to suffer budgetary shortfalls, with unending maintenance leading to disgruntled riders.

Wrigley Field, home of the beloved (and bedevilled) Chicago Cubs, could soon undergo a controversial revamp. Under its new owners, the Ricketts family, the century-old ballpark may get a $500 million facelift, which some have argued will ruin the old-time charm of the park. Proposed plans include an expanded clubhouse, new training facilities and an adjacent 175-room hotel. Most controversial, though, is the addition of a 5,700-square-foot Jumbotron screen, which will dwarf Wrigley's manually run scoreboard.

PLAYING HARDBALL

Although Chicago boasts two major-league baseball teams, a growing soccer presence and basketball, hockey and football franchises, the city's real sport is politics. 'Chicago isn't more corrupt than any other city,' Studs Terkel once claimed. 'We're just proud of our corruption.'

In Chicago, politics is entertainment, a three-ring circus kept in check by Mayor Emanuel. For all his power, however, he hasn't been able to stem the tide of violence – especially gang violence – that continues to plague the South and West Sides. In 2012, the city topped more than 500 homicides, the worst year since 2008. 'We've got a gang issue, specific to parts of the city, and we have a responsibility to bring a quality of life to those residents, and we are going to do it,' Mayor Emanuel told the *New York Times* in 2013.

IN FOCUS

Bags packed, milk cancelled, house raised on stilts.

You've packed the suntan lotion, the snorkel set, the stay-pressed shirts. Just one more thing left to do – your bit for climate change. In some of the world's poorest countries, changing weather patterns are destroying lives.

You can help people to deal with the extreme effects of climate change. Raising houses in flood-prone regions is just one life-saving solution.

**Climate change costs lives.
Give £5 and let's sort it *Here & Now***

www.oxfam.org.uk/climate-change

Oxfam is a registered charity in
England and Wales (No.202918)
and Scotland (SCO039042). Oxfam GB
is a member of Oxfam International.

Be Humankind **Oxfam**

From 2011 to 2012, the homicide rate rose 16 per cent, despite the efforts of the police and community organisations such as CureViolence (formerly CeaseFire), a street-level intervention group featured in Steve James' documentary *The Interrupters*. The killing of local rapper Joseph 'Lil JoJo' Coleman exacerbated Chicago's image as a violent town, particularly when fellow artist Chief Keef mocked his rival's death on Twitter.

This comes at a time when gun laws have been loosened against the will of city government by the Supreme Court's ruling on McDonald v Chicago, which decreed that permissive federal gun statutes should apply to all US states and cities. Critics fear more guns on the street as a result, and South Side pastor and activist Rev Michael Pfleger told the Associated Press that the new gun laws may make things worse, not better as gun enthusiasts argue.

'You are going to see a lot more gun fights and you are going to see people using guns as their first line of defence when they are confronted,' Pfleger said.

RACE RELATIONS

Although Chicago has been called America's most segregated big city, ethnic tensions aren't overt. In a 2013 update of its statistics, the US Census Bureau estimated the make-up of the city's 2.7 million population as 45 per cent white and 32.9 per cent black, with a booming population of Latinos (28.9 per cent) and a smaller contingent of Asians (5.5 per cent); the sum total of these figures exceeds 100 per cent as some citizens identify with more than one racial group. Within these categories lies further diversity; in particular, Chicago is home to strong Polish, Puerto Rican, Mexican and Middle Eastern populations, including a thriving enclave of Assyrians (Iraqi Christians). The northern suburb of Skokie even hosted an *Assyrian Superstar* contest via satellite TV – a kind of Middle Eastern *American Idol* for Aramaic speakers.

The city's African-American communities are mostly concentrated in the South and West Sides, following patterns established during the Great Migration of the early 20th century, yet Chicago's neighbourhoods are constantly in flux. Both black Bronzeville and largely Latino Pilsen, southwest of the Loop, have seen an influx of young hipsters seeking to establish arts communities in areas with cheaper rents. In 2012, the Manhattan Institute for Policy Research released a study that revealed a decline in segregation, though it concluded Chicago was still the most segregated urban area in the country. The study attributed the demolition of housing projects such as the Cabrini–Green high-rises as a catalyst for racial integration.

THAT TODDLIN' TOWN

President Barack Obama's two-term presidency has bolstered the already strong sense of local pride in this overwhelmingly Democratic region. A self-described 'proud Chicagoan', Obama has called his adopted hometown 'that most American of American cities… A city where the world's races and religions and nationalities all live and work and play and reach for the American Dream that brought them here; where our civic parades wave the colours of every culture; where our classrooms are filled with the sounds of the world's languages.'

Those classrooms are fewer today, as Mayor Emanuel closed some 50 schools and laid off more than 2,100 teachers and support staff in the face of a $1 billion budget deficit within Chicago Public Schools. While fighting unions and renegotiating Chicago's unpopular parking meter contract, the embattled mayor has pushed for pension reform, marriage equality and the addition of a casino in Chicago. 'You never let a serious crisis go to waste,' he famously told the *Wall Street Journal* before his mayoral run. 'And what I mean by that is it's an opportunity to do things you think you could not do before.'

Grassroots politics continue to be the currency of the land, for better or for worse, it seems. Which brings us back to Algren's line about Chicago's similarity to a woman with a broken nose. 'You may well find lovelier lovelies,' he added, 'but never a lovely so real.'

Just for Laughs

New clubs are putting stand-up back in the spotlight.

TEXT: JASON A HEIDEMANN

Junior Stopka is a bit of a local legend in comedy circles. He's an odd-looking dude with long, parted-down-the-middle hair and a perfectly round face intensely paled by more than 30 Chicago winters. His brain, meanwhile, is a chaotic web of brilliant non sequiturs that, when taken out of context, sound like the ravings of a madman. When he's killing it on stage, it's hard not to be captivated.

Theoretically, at least, he's practising his craft in the right town. Chicago has long been a world-class incubator for comic talent, thanks in part to Second City, the legendary sketch and improv theatre that has launched the careers of countless superstars such as Bill Murray, Tina Fey and Stephen Colbert, along with recent *Saturday Night Live* additions like Aidy Bryant. Throw iO and the Annoyance (whose collective alumni include Mike Myers, Amy Poehler, Jane Lynch, Andy Richter, Cecily Strong, Vanessa Bayer and others) into the mix, and it's easy to see why Chicago is America's first city for comedy.

In the world of stand-up, however, it's a different story. A guy like Stopka, for example, will frequently play the smaller rooms in town, such as the Lincoln Lodge, Chicago Underground Comedy at Beat Kitchen, the Comedy Bar and the Comedians You Should Know at Timothy O'Toole's, while featuring for touring comedians. But aside from Zanies and Bronzeville's Jokes & Notes, which for years were the only full-time stand-up comedy clubs in Chicago, local comedians like Stopka had few places left to go.

That all changed in 2012, when Second City debuted its latest venture, the UP Comedy Club, a 285-seat stand-up and cabaret-style venue that boasts unobstructed sightlines and the Booth One banquette from legendary nightspot the Pump Room, where the likes of Dan Aykroyd and John Belushi once perched. A few months later, the nearly 400-seat Laugh Factory (a local outpost of the LA-based chain whose first comedy show in 1979 featured Richard Pryor) opened in the space once occupied by another stand-up club, the Lakeshore Theater. Zanies followed suit with another Chicago-area location, in Rosemont. After years without much in the way of full-time clubs, Chicago is slowly experiencing its own stand-up renaissance. Maybe.

When I mention this to comedians, they're naturally sceptical. '[Second City] has no business being in stand-up,' says Stopka. His dismissiveness is understandable. Stand-up comedy clubs haven't flourished here in more than a decade. A nationwide club boom that crested in the 1980s and '90s included a dozen-plus Chicagoland venues such as Catch a Rising Star, the Chicago Improv (which still has a Schaumburg outpost), the Funny Firm and All Jokes Aside. But that was long ago. Thanks to the rise of comedy specials on cable TV and big-name comics moving towards stadiums and large theatres, the club scene dwindled by the mid-'90s. Lately, many national headliners have been performing in rock venues such as Schubas, the Hideout and the Vic. Part of the reason for this decline was that, as with the music industry, the model changed.

'The sound of laughter gives me more of a high than anything.'

Emerging comedians view stage time at clubs as just one part of a larger picture that also includes producing their own night in the back room of a bar, uploading clips on to YouTube and launching a podcast. 'The industry as a whole is turning away from the traditional comedy-club model,' says Chris Ritter, general manager at Mayne Stage, which features stand-up and music acts. 'It's moving away from that idea that comedy is a generic product that anybody can deliver.' Headliners like Doug Stanhope and Paul F Tompkins have argued against the comedy-club model, which pays comedians a set amount in exchange for a gruelling five or six shows a weekend in front of generic audiences, in favour of making the same amount by doing a single show in a bar packed with diehard fans who have been alerted to the show in advance via Facebook and Twitter.

Though both UP and Laugh Factory look like traditional comedy clubs, their respective owners believe they'll succeed. 'There's, like, 17 stand-up comedy clubs in New York and three in the Chicagoland area, and we're supposed to be the home of improv and comedy,' says former Second City president Diana Martinez. Second City CEO and executive producer Andrew Alexander agrees. 'I think it's a stable industry,' he says, pointing to Levity Entertainment's Improv chain, which has 35 locations nationwide and with whom UP is a partner. 'There was a lot of culling of people who just kind of got into [stand-up] and it was definitely overexposed in the '80s.' UP is not exclusively stand-up and has augmented its revenue with off-night products such as archival sketch shows, solo offerings by its vaunted alumni and live podcasts.

Laugh Factory owner Jamie Masada waxes more philosophically about the competition three North Side clubs now creates. 'Can Chicago sustain three

Time Out

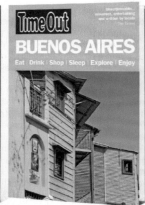

EXPLORE FROM THE INSIDE OUT

Time Out Guides
written by local experts

Our city guides are written from a unique insiders' perspective by teams of
local writers covering all you need to know about life in the world's greatest cities

visit timeout.com/store

clubs? Absolutely,' he says. 'You could give me any drugs or alcohol, but the sound of laughter gives me more [of a] high than anything.' For their part, Jokes & Notes owner Mary Lindsey, Improv manager Tony Baldino and longtime Zanies owner Bert Haas all report robust business after a dip during the recession.

For either UP or the Laugh Factory to continue to succeed, good business sense will have to win out. Large venues are costly and hard to fill, and no one I spoke to believed the influx of local comedy clubs indicates a nationwide trend. But local comedians point to the recent success stories of Chicago alumni such as Hannibal Buress, TJ Miller, Kyle Kinane, Cameron Esposito and Kumail Nanjiani, who have popped up on late-night TV or written for or appeared on shows like *SNL* and *The Colbert Report*, as proof the local scene is hot. 'If you look at the people who came out of this city, it's kind of ridiculous,' says Adam Burke, a local comic who has run several successful shows around town. 'The thing is, this has been a great stand-up town for a while in terms of alternative venues.'

The other issue is whether local comedians will find stage time at venues so big that national headliners will have to be booked often to fill seats and make ends meet. 'Most comics don't get booked anywhere, so I can't imagine they're super excited about another place that won't return their emails,' says Drew Michael, a co-founder of Comedians You Should Know. Thus far, Second City and Laugh Factory have consistently invited local comedians to take part in off-night showcases and open mics at their clubs and, more enticingly, nab hosting and feature slots on weekends. 'For the middle acts, you do need local people,' says Mike Lebovitz, another Comedians You Should Know co-founder, who has featured at Zanies. Booking locals in these slots could be good news for comedians like Lebovitz, who would like to make a living at stand-up in Chicago, though it would still require heavily working the road. Regardless, most comedians, who augment stand-up with acting and writing gigs, still see the leap

to either New York or LA as inevitable. 'There's no possible way to make a living staying in Chicago at all,' Stopka says.

As is often the case with our arts and entertainment scene, the silver lining serves to highlight the city's status as the scrappy sibling to its coastal counterparts. 'Chicago is such a good place [for comedy] because it's a healthy place to fail,' Michael says. '[Stopka] is the perfect example. He failed a million times and is now undeniably brilliant. Would he have emerged out of another place?'

To cement the city's status as a formidable training ground for emerging stand-up, Second City needs to prove it's as committed to the art form as it is to sketch comedy. So far, it continues to offer headlining acts on most weekends. Meanwhile, the Laugh Factory has made good on its promise to book local headliners, in part because it rarely books national ones.

Sure, folks like Stopka and others may bolt for the coasts eventually, but if we can take our funniest folk out of the back room of a bar and put them in front of the masses, all of Chicagoland will one day be able to brag we knew them first.

Laugh Factory owner Jamie Masada.

Diary

Even winter doesn't put a freeze on festivities in the Windy City.

During the warmer months, Windy City denizens take to the streets for a flurry of celebrations often involving fried food, fireworks and live music. Mammoth festivals fill the parks; further out, street fairs and block parties are a great way to escape the crush. And even when temperatures plunge, Chicagoans brush off the wind chill and head to an outdoor party.

For more about the city's festivals and events, check out the Arts & Entertainment section. Note that dates and other details are subject to change, so before you plan a trip around an event, it's wise to call or check online first.

You'll find comprehensive, up-to-date listings at www.timeout.com/chicago, and it's also worth checking the Friday editions of the *Chicago Tribune* and *Chicago Sun-Times,* which do their bit with regular pull-out guides. Most of the events listed in this section are free and family-friendly.

IN FOCUS

SPRING

Chicago Flower & Garden Show
Navy Pier, Streeterville (1-312 595 5400, www.chicagoflower.com). El: Red to Grand. **Date** mid Mar. **Map** p309 H11-H13.
An annual harbinger of spring, this green-fingered delight brings horticulture and flower-arranging competitions, gardening supply and landscape vendors, and life-size theme gardens to Navy Pier. Chef demos, seminars and appearances by top national gardeners are also featured.

St Patrick's Day
Columbus Drive, from E Balbo Drive to E Monroe Street, the Loop (1-312 421 1010 x12, www. chicagostpatsparade.com). El: Blue or Red to Jackson; Brown, Green, Orange, Pink or Purple to Adams/Wabash. **Date** Sat before 17 Mar. **Map** p309 H11-H13.
During election years, the candidates magically become Irish for the duration of St Patrick's Day, which is celebrated with a serious level of abandon by locals and suburbanites, regardless of whether or not they have any connection to the Emerald Isle in the first place. Downtown, the Chicago River is dyed green at 10am on the nearest Saturday to St Patrick's Day (it's best viewed from the upper level of the Michigan Avenue Bridge), before a parade rumbles through the Loop.

SUMMER

Summer in Chicago is awash with small neighbourhood festivals, block parties and other similar events. For details of these celebrated neighbourhood festivals, held just about every weekend during summer, *see p27* **Celebrate the City**.

Andersonville Midsommarfest
N Clark Street, between W Foster Avenue & W Berwyn Street, North Side (1-773 728 2995, www.andersonville.org/midsommarfest). El: Purple or Red to Berwyn. **Date** early June.
The Andersonville area was first known as a Swedish immigrant hub, then as a vibrant lesbian hangout, and more recently for its condo-dwelling urban professionals. Today, the area boasts a bit of all three, as evidenced at this weekend festival. Some 50,000 locals descend to watch maypole dancers, munch street food and generally make merry at this free summer solstice celebration.
▶ *For more on Andersonville, see p72.*

Printers Row Lit Fest
S Dearborn Street, between W Congress Parkway & W Polk Street, South Loop (1-312 527 8132, www.chicagotribune.com/entertainment/books/ printersrowlitfest). El: Blue to LaSalle; Red to Harrison. **Date** early June. **Map** p308 H13.

Pick a few books for your travels at this two-day outdoor event held in what was once the wellspring of the city's publishing prosperity. Printers Row rekindles its heritage once a year, as more than 150 booksellers hawk new, used and rare items; authors are on hand to give readings and sign copies of their works. Show up early for the best selection; but for true bargains, stroll up at closing time, when vendors weigh up the benefit of packing less. Advance tickets are available for many author appearances, which take place in tents and surrounding buildings.

Old St Pat's World's Largest Block Party

Old St Patrick's Church, 700 W Adams Street, at N Des Plaines Avenue, West Loop (1-312 648 1021, www.worldslargestblockparty.com). Bus: 8, 126, 156. **Date** late June. **Map** p311 G8-H8.
This festival has a reputation with singles, having apparently brought together more than 70 sets of spouses over the years. It probably helps that five free drinks are included with admission. Still, the friendly, open atmosphere provides visitors with a great opportunity to mingle with locals. Expect performances by local music acts.
▶ *For more on the church, see p78.*

★ Taste of Chicago

Grant Park, the Loop (1-312 744 2400, www. choosechicago.com). El: Brown, Green, Orange, Pink or Purple to Adams/Wabash; Red to Monroe. **Date** early July. **Map** pp308-309 J11-J14.
More than 35 restaurants representing every corner of the city serve more than 1.5 million food fans over five days at this, the city's largest festival. Entry is free; instead, you pay for tickets that you then exchange for either sample-sized 'taste portions' or only slightly more generous entrée servings. Large crowds at weekends and evenings make it tricky to find a seat, or even a peaceful place to stand. Entertainment comes from big-name music acts, and there are also family-friendly activities.

★ Independence Day Fireworks

Navy Pier, Streetville (1-312 595 7437, www. navypier.com/things2do/fireworks.html). El: Red to Grand. **Date** 3-4 July. **Map** p309 H11-H13.
On Independence Day and the day before, huge crowds descend on downtown to sway to live bands, before turning their eyes to the sky for a spectacular fireworks display at around 9.30pm. The display is best viewed from the Dock Stage near 600 E Grand Avenue or along the lakefront.

Dearborn Garden Walk

N Dearborn, N State, N Astor & N LaSalle Streets & N Sandburg Terrace, between W Goethe Street & W North Avenue, Gold Coast (1-312 632 1241, www.dearborngardenwalk. com). El: Red to Clark/Division. **Date** mid July. **Map** p311 G8-H8.

It's rare that common folk are afforded a peek behind the iron gates protecting Gold Coast mansion-dwellers from the outside world. This horticultural celebration – America's oldest garden walk, running since the 1950s – works its way around 20 or so luxurious homes and private gardens. Garden items and refreshments are sold en route. You'll also encounter live music and garden vignettes in some of the yards.

Venetian Night

Lake Michigan, from the Adler Planetarium to Monroe Harbor, the Loop (1-312 744 2400, www. cityofchicago.org). El: Brown, Green, Orange, Pink or Purple to Adams/Wabash; Red to Harrison. **Date** late July. **Map** pp308-309 K12-K14.
For this festival, inspired by Venice's boat parade, about 35 boat owners dress up their vessels with lights and decorations for a procession along the waterfront. Brilliant fireworks conclude the evening.

Bud Billiken Day Parade & Picnic

From 39th Street, at S King Drive, to Washington Park, at E 51st Street, Hyde Park (1-312 536 3710, www.budbillikenparade.com). El: Green to 51st or Indiana. **Date** 2nd Sat in Aug. **Map** p316 X16.

St Patrick's Day.

IN FOCUS

Chicago Air & Water Show.

This huge kid-centred parade was first launched in 1929 by Robert S Abbott, founder of African-American newspaper the *Chicago Defender*. Since then, the South Side procession has grown to include upwards of 160 floats and vehicles, marching bands, community groups and a reliable assortment of big-time politicos acting as grand marshal (Barack Obama once held the title). Drawing about 1.5 million spectators annually, it's thought to be the largest and oldest parade of its kind in the nation. The procession ends with a picnic in Washington Park.

★ Chicago Air & Water Show

North Avenue Beach, at North Avenue & from W Oak Street to W Diversey Parkway (1-312 744 2400, www.choosechicago.org). Bus: 72, 151. **Date** Aug. **Map** pp310-312 G4-H9.
If you didn't know this free event was scheduled, the sonic booms bouncing off the Gold Coast high-rises as planes soar over your head should wake you up to its existence. Don't duck for cover: instead, join about two million other people heading to the lakefront to take in the spectacular aerobatic and aquatic stunts. The roaring Navy Blue Angels and the Army Golden Knights Parachute Team are typically part of the line-up. Great views of the air show can be had from just about anywhere near the water; the boat show is best seen from the North Avenue Beach.

INSIDE TRACK
CULTURAL EVENTS

Many other cultural festivals are listed in their arts-specific chapter. For **movie festivals**, *see p196*; for **music festivals**, *see pp206-226*; and for **gay and lesbian events**, *see p198*.

AUTUMN

German-American Festival

4700 N Lincoln Avenue, at W Lawrence Avenue, Lincoln Square (1-630 653 3018, www.german day.com). El: Brown to Western. **Date** early Sept.
Held in Lincoln Square, this Oktoberfest hasn't changed much over the decades. Revellers pack the neighbourhood annually for a German-American celebration that includes generous mugs of beer, brass bands for dancing and juicy sausages. The festival coincides with the Von Steuben Day Parade down Lincoln Avenue on the Saturday.

★ Renegade Craft Fair

W Division Street, from N Hermitage Avenue to N Damen Avenue, Wicker Park (1-312 266 8654, www.renegadecraft.com). El: Blue to Division. **Date** early Sept. **Map** p309 J13.
Browse crafty handmade creations from more than 300 local and national indie designers. Showcasing everything from clothing and handbags to poster art and jewellery, Renegade Craft is a great chance to pick up one-of-a-kind gifts.

Wine Crush in Old Town and Macaroni Festival

N Wells Street, at W North Avenue, Old Town (1-773 868 3010, www.chicagoevents.com). El: Brown or Purple to Sedgwick. **Date** mid Sept. **Map** pp308-309 J11-J14.
The Wells Street Crush has expanded its offerings to include yet more food, music and laughs. The comedy element seems appropriate – famed comedy clubs Second City and Zanies are located nearby. You'll still find an art market, food from local restaurants, crafts, a music stage and plenty of wine-tasting pavilions.
▶ *For more on the comedy scene, see pp20-23.*

Celebrate the City

The 'hoods come alive in summer with block parties, bashes and blowouts.

When winter is at its fiercest and the snow feels like it'll never melt, Chicagoans go into huddled hibernation. But when warmer weather rolls around, nothing can keep them off the streets. Payback for the often vicious winters arrives around May or June, and locals hardened by the ice and snow are anxious to make the most of the sun-soaked summer months before the mercury starts to fall again.

The City of Chicago organises a number of huge summer events, most of which take over Grant Park and the lakefront. But a more charismatic window into summer in the city can be found in the city's neighbourhoods, which celebrate the sunny months with glorious enthusiasm at a variety of block parties. There are dozens of these low-key events around the city each year. Streets are blocked off for the weekend, vendors provide food and drink aplenty, and musicians of varying talent offer entertainment.

Many of these block parties reflect the neighbourhoods in which they're set. **Wicker Park Fest** (late July) features an array of indie-rock bands spread over two days, while the Near West Side's **West Fest** (mid July) is even artier. A number reflect the melting pot make-up of the city: Greektown's **Taste of Greece** (late August); the Polish-oriented **Taste of Polonia** (www.copernicusfdn.org), held each year in Jefferson Park on the first weekend in September; and August's **Ukrainian Festival** in (where else?) Ukrainian Village. But others are far more straightforward affairs: a couple of bands, a couple of kegs and a couple of cops, all combined into an opportunity for the locals to hang out and celebrate the city at its most jubilantly beautiful.

IN FOCUS

Taste of Greece.

Bank of America Chicago Marathon.

Open House Chicago

Across Chicago (1-312 922 3432, www.openhousechicago.org). **Date** Oct.
This event devoted to Chicago's architecture allows entry to explore over 150 places and spaces that aren't ordinarily accessible to the public – the mayor's rooftop garden, wetlands occupying former steel mill properties and so on. The dozens of excursions cover other special interest topics, including labour history, hidden gem restaurants and skyscrapers. The Chicago Architecture Foundation (www.architecture.org) oversees the tours; events are free and no registration is required.

★ Bank of America Chicago Marathon

Start/end: Grant Park, nr Buckingham Fountain, the Loop (1-312 904 9800, www.chicagomarathon. com). El: Blue or Red to Monroe; Brown, Green, Orange, Pink or Purple to Adams/Wabash. **Date** mid Oct. **Map** p309 J13.
The city all but shuts down as nearly 40,000 sweaty athletes race along a 26.2-mile course, one of the fastest in the world. Starting from Grant Park, runners head north via Lincoln Park to Wrigleyville, then turn on their heels to come back down through Old Town, out into the West Loop, south through Pilsen and across via Chinatown into Grant Park again to the finish line at Buckingham Fountain.

Chicago Humanities Festival

Across Chicago (1-312 661 1028, www.chicago humanities.org). **Date** 3wks Oct-Nov.
Get up close and personal with big (and small) names in literature, film and art. The programme of lectures, readings and panel discussions is vast; the festival's theme changes each year.

Day of the Dead

National Museum of Mexican Art, 1852 W 19th Street, at S Damen Avenue, Pilsen (1-312 738 1503, www.nationalmuseumofmexicanart.org). El: Blue or Pink to 18th. **Date** early Nov.
Tiny skeletons placed in colourful scenarios within shadowbox-like altars honour those gone-but-not-forgotten loved ones for this Mexican All Souls' Day tradition. The elaborate displays of macabre but oddly joyous folk art offerings to the dead are complemented by a procession that kicks off at the St Precopious School (1625 S Allport Street, at W 16th Street, Pilsen) and ends up at the museum.
▶ *For more on Pilsen's Mexican culture, see p80.*

WINTER

In addition to the events below, the City of Chicago stages a variety of events in January and February for its **Winter Delights** series; see www.choosechicago.com for details.

McDonald's Thanksgiving Parade

State Street, from Congress Parkway to Randolph Street, the Loop (1-312 781 5681, www.chicago festivals.org). El: Blue or Red to Jackson, Monroe or Washington; Brown, Green, Orange, Pink or Purple to Adams/Wabash, Madison/Wabash or Randolph/Wabash. **Date** Thanksgiving Day (4th Thur in Nov). **Map** pp309 H11-H13.

While most shops and attractions close for the big holiday, there's still fun to be had. This big parade in the Loop stars everything from monster-size floats and gigantic helium balloon characters to upbeat marching bands and countless performance groups. Events start at 8.30am and conclude by 11am.

Christmas Around the World

Museum of Science & Industry, 5700 S Lake Shore Drive, at E 57th Street, Hyde Park (1-773 684 1414, www.msichicago.org). Metra: 55th-56th-57th Street. **Date** mid Nov-early Jan. **Map** p316 Z17.

For more than 60 years, the Museum of Science & Industry has staged a seasonal exhibition on, and celebration of, the ways in which the festive season is observed all over the globe. In addition to Christmas, there are events based around Diwali, Hanukkah, Kwanzaa and Chinese New Year, with theatre, dance and music shows to jolly along the proceedings.
▶ *For more on the museum, see p96.*

★ Zoolights

Lincoln Park Zoo, 2200 N Cannon Drive, at W Webster Avenue, Lincoln Park (1-312 742 2000, www.lpzoo.org). El: Brown, Purple or Red to Fullerton. **Date** late Nov-early Jan. **Map** p312 H5.

The zoo stays open late through the holidays, and the atmosphere is dazzling. Evening visitors are guided along the winding pathways by a sprawling display of illuminated designs, many of them shaped like animals, and there's a synchronised musical light show. If the two million bulbs leave you dazed, the hot cider and chainsaw-wielding ice sculptors are sure to give you a jolt.
▶ *For more on the zoo itself, see p66.*

Christkindlmarket & Holiday Tree Lighting Ceremony

Daley Plaza, W Washington Boulevard & N Dearborn Street, the Loop (1-312 644 2662, www.christkindlmarket.com). El: Blue to Washington; Brown, Green, Orange, Pink or Purple to Randolph/Wabash; Red to Lake. **Date** late Nov-late Dec. **Map** p309 H12.

The night after Thanksgiving, usually around 4.30pm, a giant 80ft tree constructed from piles of smaller evergreens is illuminated at Daley Plaza. Four giant toy sentries tower over onlookers and an enormous toy train roams around the plaza. At around the same time, the plaza is converted into a traditional German-style market, complete with German food and handicrafts, and twinkling lights.

Small stands are packed full of gifts and culinary treats; wooden huts brim with candy, blown glass, Christmas decorations and other delights.

Winter WonderFest

Navy Pier, 600 E Grand Avenue, at Streeter Drive, Streeterville (1-312 595 7437, tickets 1-312 595 1212, www.ticketmaster.com). El: Red to Grand. **Admission** free. *Activity wristbands* $15-$20. **Date** early Dec-early Jan. **Map** p310 K10.

This seasonal wonderland of holiday-themed indoor amusements in the Pier's Festival Hall lets kids cut loose with inflatable games, a carousel, slides, a crafts area and an indoor ice-skating rink. Trees, lights and decorations set the festive mood.

Snow Days Chicago

Gateway Park, Navy Pier, Streeterville (1-312 742 4007, www.choosechicago.org). El: Brown, Green, Orange, Pink or Purple to Adams/Wabash; Red to Monroe. **Date** late Jan. **Map** pp308-309 J11-J14.

Leave it to Chicagoans to embrace the bone-chilling cold wholeheartedly. This winter festival draws all ages outdoors to frolic in the snow, check out the snow-sculpting competition, cheer on canines in dog-sled demonstrations and gasp at gravity-defying snowboarding stunts. An activities igloo keeps kids warm and engaged with crafts and games.

★ Chinatown New Year Parade

Along S Wentworth Avenue, Chinatown (1-312 326 5320, www.chicagochinatown.org). El: Red to Cermak-Chinatown. **Date** 1st Sun after Chinese New Year (early Feb). **Map** p308 H16.

The Lunar New Year is ushered in with a colourful parade that includes marching bands, floats, lion teams, the 100ft Mystical Dragon dance and a fanfare of firecrackers. Revellers would be wise to stick around Chinatown to stroll the shops and fill up at neighbourhood restaurants.

Chicago Auto Show

McCormick Place, 2301 S Lake Shore Drive, South Side (1-312 791 7000, www.chicago autoshow.com). Bus: 2, 3, X3, 4, 6, 10, 14, 21, 26, 28. **Tickets** $12; $6 reductions; free under-6s. **Date** early Feb.

Petrolheads can be among the first to check out what's new in motoring at this ten-day car showcase that's been running for more than a century. Close to 1,000 different vehicles are on display, along with accessories, collectibles and car-themed exhibits.

INSIDE TRACK
GET THE LOWDOWN

A schedule of events can be obtained from the **Department of Cultural Affairs and Special Events** (www.cityofchicago.org).

IN FOCUS

Explore

48 Hours in Chicago

Day 1 Downtown Delights

Millennium Park.

9AM Start by taking in one of the best views of the city, from the **Michigan Avenue Bridge** (*see p37*). If your appetite for architecture has been whetted, and if it's summer, it's a short hop to the pier from where you can catch the **Chicago Architecture Foundation**'s Architecture River Cruise (book in advance; *see p288*). Otherwise, walk south to **Millennium Park** (*see p34*), then move on to the **Art Institute of Chicago** (*see p36*).

NOON If you're lucky, there may be a free concert at the **Chicago Cultural Center** (*see p229*). If not, try Rick Bayless's **Frontera Fresco** on the top floor of Macy's (*see p143*) or, for something a bit more formal, nouveau-gastropub the **Gage** (*see p103*).

1.30PM Weather permitting, walk off your lunch by taking our tour of public art in the Loop (*see p38*). From here, stroll through Millennium Park and **Grant Park**, past the **Buckingham Fountain** (*see p36*) and on to **Museum Campus**. When you get here, take your pick from three fine attractions: the **Shedd Aquarium**, the **Field Museum** (for both, *see p48*) and the **Adler Planetarium** (*see p46*), from which you can get tremendous views of the Loop skyline.

5.30PM No first-time visit is complete without **riding around the Loop** on one of the elevated train lines (*see p286*). Wander across from Museum Campus and pick up the Orange line at Roosevelt, taking in Chicago's business district from this most evocative of vantage points.

7PM The Loop quietens down at night, but there are plenty of dinner options west across the river in the West Loop (try **Publican** or **Blackbird**; *see p120*) or south in **Chinatown** (*see p104*). From here, take the train or a cab to the **John Hancock Center** (*see p56*) and head up to the 95th floor for a nightcap in the **Signature Lounge**. It's pretty touristy, and you'll pay heavily for your drink. However, it'll still be better value than a ride to the observation deck. And the views, especially at night, are incomparably dramatic.

NAVIGATING THE CITY

Thanks to its grid system, Chicago is easy to navigate. Ground zero is at the corner of State and Madison Streets in the Loop. Addresses on north–south roads are numbered according to how many blocks north or south of Madison they sit; the same is true of east–west thoroughfares and State Street. A street-number range of 800 corresponds to about a mile; for example, it's roughly two miles between 1 N Clark Street and 1601 N Clark Street.

The grid system also makes it easy to pinpoint the location of any address. For instance, notable main east–west streets north of Madison include Chicago Avenue. Chicago Avenue is on the axis of 800 N, which means that street addresses close to 800 N will be near the road's intersection with Chicago (for instance, Water Tower Place at 835 N Michigan Avenue is a mere block north of Michigan and Chicago). Other notable east–west streets include Division (at 1200 North),

EXPLORE

Day 2 Exploring the City

8.30AM Start your second day in Chicago off the beaten downtown path. Start with a lush breakfast at the **Bongo Room** in Wicker Park (*see p125*), then ride the bus east along North Avenue. At the end of the line, you'll be right by the fine **Chicago History Museum** (*see p65*). But if it's a nice day, consider statue-spotting in lakeside **Lincoln Park** (*see p67*), with a detour to the **Green City Market** or the **Lincoln Park Zoo** (*see p66*).

NOON If you're here when the Chicago Cubs are playing a day game at **Wrigley Field** (*see p71 and p241*), follow lunch at the lovely **Southport Grocery & Café** (*see p117*) with an

Violet Hour.

afternoon at America's oldest ballpark before exploring **Wrigleyville** and **Lakeview** (*see pp69-73*). If they're not playing, or if baseball doesn't appeal, consider a **Chicago Greeter** tour (*see p288*): conducted by volunteer locals, they're a great way to explore the city's residential neighbourhoods. For both these options, you'll need to book in advance.

5PM With any luck, there'll be time before dinner for a little shopping. If big-name brands are your thing, head to the **Magnificent Mile** to catch more or less every big name in American retail. All the major stores remain open until 7pm; many continue trading until 8pm or even 9pm. If independents are more your bag, try the cornucopia of small stores around **Wicker Park**, dealing in fashion, books, gifts and more. For more on shops, *see pp143-166*.

8PM And if you've been shopping in Wicker Park, you'll be in a pretty good place for dinner. After a cocktail at **Violet Hour** (*see p141*), take your pick from local favourites such as **Big Star**, **Bristol** (for both, *see p125*) and **Mana Food Bar** (*see p126*).

10PM Still got energy? See if there are any worthwhile bands playing at the **Double Door** or the **Empty Bottle** (for both, *see p219*), or check out the DJs at **Danny's Tavern** (*see p139*), **Beauty Bar** or the **Debonair Social Club** (for both, *see p212*).

EXPLORE

North (1600 N), Armitage (2000 N), Fullerton (2400 N), Diversey (2800 N), Belmont (3200 N) and Addison (3600 N); notable north–south streets include Halsted (at 800 West), Racine (1200 W), Ashland (1600 W) and Damen (2000 W).

SEEING THE SIGHTS
Sightseeing in Chicago can be expensive. However, many of the big museums offer free admission one day a week; for a list of these free days, *see p57*.

PACKAGE DEALS
The **Chicago CityPass** (www.citypass.com) gives pre-paid, queue-jumping access to several big attractions: the trio at Museum Campus, plus the Willis Tower Skydeck and either the Museum of Science & Industry or Fast Pass admission to the John Hancock Observatory. The pass is valid for nine days after first use and costs $89 for adults ($79 for kids). You can buy a CityPass at www.citypass.com or at any of the participating attractions.

The Loop

Money makes this world go round.

An unmatched architectural showcase, a high-culture hot spot and the financial heart of the Midwest, the Loop is the hub around which Chicago revolves. It's named after the route carved around it by its distinctive elevated rail tracks; you can take in the area's beguiling mix of history and modernity up close from one of these 'El' trains. But the best way to see the Loop is on foot, weaving between vertical canyons of glass and steel before adjourning to the regenerated Millennium Park.

The Loop's main focus is commercial; outside of its smattering of concert halls and theatres, it slows down after 7pm. However, of late, more locals have chosen the convenience of city living over the suburbs. Condo towers and college dorms have sprung up during the past decade, and the area's character continues to evolve.

This chapter refers to many of the Loop's architectural highlights. However, the Architecture chapter contains more detail, plus a map on which more than 30 of these buildings are marked. See pp274-283.

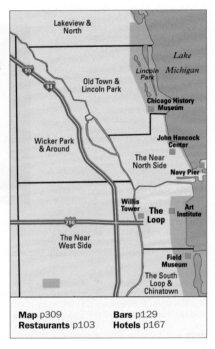

| Map p309 | Bars p129 |
| Restaurants p103 | Hotels p167 |

MILLENNIUM PARK & GRANT PARK

Millennium Park

Bordered by Randolph Street, Michigan Avenue, Monroe Street and Columbus Drive, Millennium Park was completed four years late and $300 million over budget. But as soon as the 24.5-acre project opened in 2004, on a site previously occupied by abandoned railroad tracks and parking, affection for it crushed questions about whether it violates the city's obligation to keep Grant Park 'forever open, clear and free of any buildings, or other obstruction whatever' (according to an 1836 declaration that predated the opening of the park), and whether it's big enough to contain the ego of its champion, mayor Richard M Daley. Stop by the **Welcome Center** (201 E Randolph Street, 1-312 742 2963) for maps and audio guides, or download them for free at www.millenniumpark.org.

The park's most photographed attraction is Anish Kapoor's sculpture **Cloud Gate** (aka 'the Bean'), which looms over the **McCormick Tribune Ice Rink** (*see p247*). The seams between the quarter-inch polished stainless steel plates that cover its steel support skeleton have been polished into invisibility: although it's 66 feet long and 33 feet high, the 110-ton structure appears to be as lightweight and fluid as the drop of mercury that supposedly inspired it. Its mirror finish reflects Michigan Avenue's historic 'streetwall', clouds, trees and your puzzled face, as you try to find yourself among the throng of tourists distorted in its trippy surfaces.

Jaume Plensa's **Crown Fountain** also improbably succeeds as both contemporary art and Chicago icon. Its two 50-foot towers, which contain 122,000 glass bricks, face each other across a plaza; each projects the face of one of 1,000 Chicagoans whom Plensa filmed. From time to time, the faces purse their lips and 'spit' torrents of water, to the delight of the children waiting below. The water is shut down during winter, but the striking images remain.

The *Crown Fountain* almost makes up for the hideous **Millennium Monument** at the corner of Michigan Avenue and Randolph Street, a replica of the peristyle that 'graced' the spot from 1917 to 1953. It bears a long list of 'Millennium Park founders'; basically, the rich people and corporations who provided the park's private funding. Unfortunately, you have to pass this neo-neoclassical monstrosity to reach the Welcome Center, the **Harris Theater** (*see p228*) and the **McDonald's Cycle Center** (*see p245*).

Designed by Frank Gehry, the **Jay Pritzker Pavilion** dominates the northern end of the park. Echoing the exploding-metal style Gehry perfected at the Guggenheim Bilbao,

**INSIDE TRACK
PARIS OF THE MIDWEST**

Among Chicago's multifarious nicknames was the 'Paris of the Midwest'. Even so, it's disconcerting to see one of the Paris Métro's famous art nouveau entrances at S Michigan Avenue and E Van Buren Street. Passers-by who spot the decorative sign, directing passengers to the Metra, may assume a pathetic attempt to bestow European elegance on the commuter railway. However, this is the real deal: Paris's RATP constructed the entrance's curvilinear cast-iron forms from the same moulds that Hector Guimard, their French designer, used in 1900, and donated the piece to Chicago in 2003.

the outdoor concert venue's steel flourishes curl 35 to 40 feet into the air above the 60-foot bandstand. The pavilion has room for 11,000 people: 4,000 on seats near the stage, the rest on the lawn. The steel 'trellis' that shades the grass contains a state-of-the-art sound system; the chatty picnickers who attend the (mostly free) concerts don't notice.

Gehry also designed the **BP Bridge**, which snakes east from the south-eastern corner of the Pritzker Pavilion's lawn to **Daley Bicentennial Plaza**, passing over Columbus Drive. Just south of it, the 2.5-acre **Lurie Garden** honours two periods of Chicago history through plants: the garden's 'dark plate' recreates the lakefront's natural prairie topography, while the orderly beds of perennial flowers that make up the 'light plate' evoke the city as it developed after the Chicago Fire.

To see the garden from above, take Renzo Piano's 620-foot **Nichols Bridgeway** from this end of Millennium Park over Monroe Street to the third floor of the Art Institute's Modern Wing (*see p37*). Piano claims that the shape of the slender white steel and aluminium pedestrian bridge was inspired by the hull of a boat, but it's really a life raft meant to funnel scads of tourists into the museum.

Grant Park

Millennium Park has overshadowed its less flashy neighbour to the south, which was built on landfill in the 1920s and runs to Museum Campus (*see p46*). Adding insult to injury, the Grant Park Music Festival has even decamped to the Pritzker Pavilion. Yet the 319-acre **Grant Park** retains a prominent role in the life of the city. During the summer, the park hosts popular events such as the

Millennium Park.

EXPLORE

EXPLORE

Buckingham Fountain.

The intrigue of Chicago's most noteworthy museum begins before you cross the threshold, when you meet two of the city's most beloved characters outside its Michigan Avenue entrance. Donated by Mrs Henry Field, sister-in-law to department store mogul Marshall, Edward Kemeys' two bronze lions have guarded the Art Institute of Chicago since 1894. But few locals realise that the pair aren't identical twins: the south lion is said to stand in an attitude of defiance, while the north lion is reportedly 'on the prowl'.

Past these leonine doormen lies a world-class institution, one that looks the part from the moment you reach the atrium lobby: built by Shepley, Rutan and Coolidge in 1892 for the World's Columbian Exposition the following year, it's as grand as it is large. The signage around the museum is good, and the free map is comprehensive enough for most visitors. However, the museum's sheer size can make it a daunting place; you may also want to invest in the excellent audio guide ($6), which provides an overview of the highlights.

Collections

In 2005, the museum started an ambitious project: a 264,000sq ft limestone and glass building by Italian architect Renzo Piano. Dubbed the **Modern Wing**, Piano's building was designed to hold the Art Institute's collections of modern European painting and sculpture, contemporary art, and architecture and design.

When it opened in spring 2009, the Modern Wing allowed the museum to redistribute its tightly packed collection into a more spacious and, in many ways, more logical layout. The museum's three buildings, plus the Modern Wing, each feature two to three storeys of exhibition space, making it impossible to cover the country's second largest art

Taste of Chicago (*see p25*). And on the night of 4 November 2008, a quarter of a million people joined Barack Obama to help celebrate his victory in the presidential election.

Aside from the **Art Institute of Chicago** (*see below*), Grant Park's main point of interest is the **Buckingham Fountain**, which was donated to the city in 1927 in memory of Art Institute benefactor Clarence Buckingham. Located east of Congress Parkway, the fountain is modelled on the fountain at Versailles, but is twice the size and contains more than a million gallons of water. On summer nights, crowds gather to watch the fountain's water and light shows, during which water shoots 150 feet into the air to musical accompaniment.

For a more subtle aesthetic experience, find Richard Serra's 1988 sculpture *Reading Cones*. The width of a person is all that separates its two steel arcs, which enclose intrepid viewers in an isolating chamber. It's an unexpected oasis of solitude in Chicago's 'front yard'.

★ Art Institute of Chicago

111 S Michigan Avenue, at W Adams Street (1-312 443 3600, www.artic.edu). El: Brown, Green, Orange, Pink or Purple to Adams/ Wabash. **Open** 10.30am-5pm Mon-Wed, Fri-Sun; 10.30am-8pm Thur. **Admission** $23; $12-$18 reductions; free under-12s & Illinois residents 5-8pm Thur. **Credit** AmEx, Disc, MC, V. **Map** p309 J12.

Art Institute of Chicago.

museum in a single day. However, by prioritising the Modern Wing's modern and contemporary art, and the American 1900-1950 collection in the **Rice Building**, you'll get to see many of the Art Institute's most notable works.

The Modern Wing delivers a notable succession of textbook classics. Numerous works by Salvador Dalí (room 396) sit alongside Magritte's *Time Transfixed*, Picasso's *The Old Guitarist* (391) and countless other instantly recognisable pieces. It's also home to the **Ryan Education Center**, which has dozens of drop-in classes to keep children interested. The new wing is also accessible through Millennium Park by a quick walk over the **Nichols Bridgeway**, a pedestrian bridge that leads to **Terzo Piano**, a third-floor dining area helmed by Spiaggia chef Tony Mantuano (*see also p112*). Reservations are a must.

After this stunning beginning, move on to the **Pritzker Galleries**, where you'll find many of the Art Institute's most prized canvases. The museum has managed to accumulate amazing collections of Impressionist and post-Impressionist paintings since opening in the late 19th century, and it's here that you'll find them. Look out in particular for Caillebotte's famous *Paris Street; Rainy Day* (room 201) and Seurat's *A Sunday on La Grande Jatte – 1884* (240), at which Ferris Bueller gawped on his day off, along with other notable works such as Renoir's *Acrobats at the Cirque Fernando* and Cézanne's *The Basket of Apples*.

The American 1900-1950 Collection in the nearby Rice Building is scarcely less impressive, containing such gems as Edward Hopper's *Nighthawks* (262), Grant Wood's *American Gothic* (263; also now immortalised in sculptural form by J Seward Johnson outside the Tribune Tower, *see p55*), and works by Georgia O'Keeffe (265), Winslow Homer (171) and Mary Cassatt (273).

Less celebrated but equally worthy are the new **Alsdorf Galleries of Southeast Asian Art** (140-142), also designed by Renzo Piano, and the **Medieval and Renaissance Art Collections**, all of which are of interest to more than just aficionados. And we're still not done: other diversions include a paperweight collection and the **Thorne Miniature Rooms**, a collection of scale models of American, European and oriental houses spanning four centuries.

Despite the strength of its permanent collection, the Institute stages regular temporary exhibitions. Check the website for details of what's on while you're in town.

MICHIGAN AVENUE

The mile-long stretch of Michigan Avenue that runs south of the river isn't Magnificent, like its counterpart to the north, but it's packed with buildings of artistic and architectural interest. What's more, the street offers glimpses of both

Chicago Cultural Center.

aspects of the Loop: the hard-nosed and the tranquil. To the west stands an array of tall, imposing and often historic buildings, housing hotels, businesses and cultural institutions. And to the east are the city's parks and the lake.

Start at the **Michigan Avenue Bridge**, which affords spectacular views from its northern tip. The south-west tower houses the **McCormick Bridgehouse & Chicago River Museum** (*see p39*), which celebrates the role of the river in the city's history while also providing some fantastic views. East of the bridge, along Wacker Drive towards the lake, sit the **Lakeshore East** condo towers. The most dazzling is Jeanne Gang's relatively new **Aqua**, an 82-storey building.

South of the bridge, you won't find much of interest until you reach the **Hard Rock Hotel** (no.230, at E South Water Street; *see p168*) – or rather, the **Carbide & Carbon Building**, the 1929 skyscraper it occupies. The building's distinctive green terracotta exterior is trimmed in gold leaf, and its awe-inspiring lobby is awash with marble and glass ornamentation.

More opulence awaits at the **Chicago Cultural Center** (78 E Washington Boulevard, at N Michigan Avenue, 1-312 744 6630, www.chicagoculturalcenter.org). Built in 1897 as the city's central library, complete with two stunning Tiffany stained-glass domes and marble staircase, the centre now stages free concerts and films, superlative art shows and,

EXPLORE

EXPLORE

Walk Art in the Loop

Spot some world-class sculpture as you scoot around downtown.

The prevalence of skyscrapers in the Loop means it's all too easy to walk around with your eyes to the sky. But if you snap your head back to eye level, you'll notice some striking pieces of public art. City Hall passed a groundbreaking ordinance over 30 years ago, forcing those in charge of building projects to set aside a fraction of construction costs for art. Private companies followed suit, and the result has left the Loop as a sculpture garden like no other in the country.

Start at the north-west corner of Madison and Wells.

Found under a glass-walled atrium at 200 W Madison Street (8am-7pm daily), **Louise Nelvelson**'s *Dawn Shadows* (1983) is thought to have been influenced by the design of the El. Happily, Chicago's rail system is more reliable than this monstrous black form might suggest.

Go east on Madison, north at LaSalle. The Flight of Daedelus and Icarus, **Roger Brown**'s vast mosaic above the entrance of 120 N LaSalle Street, tells of Icarus, who ignored his father's warnings and flew too close to the sun. There may be a moral in this story for the financial industry.

Continue north.

Freeform, on the façade of the Illinois State Office Building at 160 N LaSalle Street, is one of several Loop works by local artists. **Richard Hunt** has many works on display in the city, though this eye-catching abstract piece is perhaps his most prominent.

Walk back and take a left on Randolph to the Thompson Center's plaza.

Jean Dubuffet's fibreglass *Monument with Standing Beast* demands attention. Dubuffet always had affection for Chicago after a 1951 lecture he gave at the Arts Club of Chicago was rapturously received.

Move east to Dearborn and then south to Daley Plaza.

This striking piece of work is known locally only as 'the Picasso'; its creator,

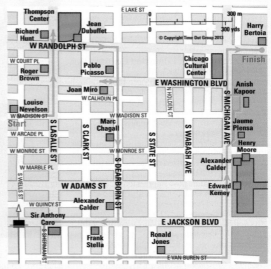

Pablo Picasso, didn't give it a title when he donated it to the city in 1967. Its lack of title helped to stoke the confusion – and, in some quarters, the contempt – that greeted its installation. It's believed to be based on the head of a woman. Or maybe a baboon.

Continue down Dearborn, then turn right into Washington.

Outside the Brunswick Building at 69 W Washington sits *Miró's Chicago*. Created by **Joan Miró** with ceramics expert Joan Artigas, it was completed in 1981.

Return to Dearborn and continue south. He may be best known for his paintings, but Chicagoans know **Marc Chagall** more as a sculptor thanks to his vibrant, 70-foot mosaic *The Four Seasons*, now under a glass cover at Bank One Plaza.

Head south to Federal Center Plaza.

Alexander Calder was once asked why he had called his vast, hooped sculpture *Flamingo*. The questioner doubtless expected an answer swamped in allusion. Said Calder, 'It was sort of pink and has a long neck.'

Cross the road and go right on Jackson. Between 1986 and 1997, **Frank Stella** created 266 works of art influenced by *Moby Dick*. Few of them are more striking than *The Town-Ho's Story*, a jarring collection of mangled metal that dominates the lobby of the Ralph H Metcalfe Federal Building.

Continue east.

The shapes that make up *Chicago Fugue*, by British sculptor **Sir Anthony Caro**, allude to musical instruments. It can be seen in the lobby of 190 S LaSalle Street.

Go left on Sherman and left again on Van Buren as far as State Street.

Pritzker Park, designed by **Ronald Jones** and completed in 1991, is less sculpture and more landscape garden. However, its highlight, an interpretation of Magritte's *The Banquet*, is worthy of a detour.

Continue to Michigan, then turn left.

Edward Kemeys' *Lions* have guarded the entrance of the Art Institute of Chicago for almost a century. North of the main entrance, in the Institute's McCormick Memorial Court, sit two more works by notable sculptors: *Flying Dragon*, another vast piece by **Alexander Calder**; and *Large Interior Form*, with three holes that distinguish it as a work by British sculptor **Henry Moore**.

Continue north to Millennium Park.

The two most popular pieces of public art in Chicago are two of the newest. The vast faces beamed on to **Jaume Plensa**'s *Crown Fountain* (*see p35*) unnerve adults but tickle kids. Everyone, though, loves **Anish Kapoor**'s *Cloud Gate* (*see p34*).

Continue north and then head east on Randolph, just above the park.

Harry Bertoia's *Sounding Sculptures* sit outside the Aon Center. Inspired by wheat swaying in the breeze on Midwestern farms, the pieces are comprised of copper tubing, which make eerie music when the wind hits them.

on some Saturdays, civil marriage ceremonies. It's also the starting point for the **Chicago Greeter** tours; *see p288*. The Randolph Street lobby contains a café with free Wi-Fi.

Further south sits **Symphony Center** (*see p230*), home to the Chicago Symphony Orchestra. Connected by a central rotunda, its three wings encompass the 1904 Orchestra Hall, a park, a shop and an education and administration wing. Down the block is the **Santa Fe Building** (224 S Michigan Avenue, at E Jackson Boulevard), designed in 1904 by Daniel Burnham (who liked it so much that he moved his own offices here). On the ground floor is the marvellous **Chicago Architecture Foundation** (www.architecture.org), best known for its tours, lectures and small-scale exhibits. The gift shop is a real treat.

The **Fine Arts Building** (410 S Michigan Avenue, at E Van Buren Street) once housed the showrooms of the Studebaker Company, which held carriages rather than cars in the late 19th century. Soon after, it was converted into a theatre at ground level and artists' studios above, and the words 'All Passes – Art Alone Endures' were carved inside the entrance. Frank Lloyd Wright had a studio here at one time; so did L Frank Baum, author of *The Wizard of Oz*.

When the **Auditorium Building** (S Michigan Avenue, at E Congress Parkway) was built by Adler and Sullivan, then dedicated in 1889 by President Benjamin Harrison, it was the tallest building in the world, housing a theatre (the first home of the Chicago Opera), a hotel and offices. After a spell of neglect, it was restored in the 1960s; for the programme, check out www.auditoriumtheatre.org. Just south are the **Spertus Institute** and the **Museum of Contemporary Photography** (for both, *see p40*).

McCormick Bridgehouse & Chicago River Museum

Southwest tower, Michigan Avenue Bridge, at E Wacker Drive (1-312 977 0227, www.bridge housemuseum.org). El: Brown, Green, Orange, Pink or Purple to State/Lake. **Open** *May-Oct* 10am-5pm Mon, Thur-Sun. **Admission** $3; free under-5s. **Credit** AmEx, MC, V. **Map** p310 J11.

The famous 1920 Michigan Avenue Bridgehouse now serves as a museum that celebrates the river's role in building Chicago into a major metropolitan city. The five-storey space might prove difficult to traverse if you're travelling with children or Grandma; however, if you make it to the top, you'll be rewarded with a unique viewpoint of the Chicago River, the bridge itself and the Trump Tower on the northern bank. The photographs, maps, newspaper articles and historical titbits are a feast for history buffs, riverphiles or anyone with a keen interest in

EXPLORE

Sounding Sculptures

EXPLORE

urban planning; the insider views of the massive gears, mechanisms and counterweights used to lift the bridge lend the place a broader appeal.

FREE Museum of Contemporary Photography

Columbia College, 600 S Michigan Avenue, at Harrison Street (1-312 663 5554, www.mocp. org). El: Green, Orange or Red to Harrison. **Open** 10am-5pm Mon-Wed, Fri, Sat; 10am-8pm Thur; noon-5pm Sun. **Admission** free. **Map** p309 J13.

Affiliated with Columbia College, the Museum of Contemporary Photography has three floors of galleries, which encompass new work in shows and exhibitions culled from the collection of 10,000 photographs and photographic objects. Work by some of the world's best photographers and video artists is on show; the Midwest Photographers Project highlights local contemporary work.

Pritzker Military Library

104 S Michigan Avenue, at E Monroe Street (1-312 374 9333, www.pritzkermilitarylibrary. org). El: Blue, Red to Monroe. **Open** 10am-6pm Tue-Thur; 10am-4pm Fri, Sat. **Admission** $5. **Map** p310 J10.

In 2003, James N Pritzker, retired National Guard colonel and member of Chicago's affluent Pritzker family, assembled this major collection of books and materials on non-partisan military history. The result is an elegant, apolitical treasure trove of books and ephemera dating back to the Revolutionary War, along with a gallery with rotating exhibitions and live events throughout the year.

FREE Spertus Institute for Jewish Learning and Leadership

610 S Michigan Avenue, at E Harrison Street (1-312 322 1700, www.spertus.edu). El: Green, Orange or Red to Harrison. **Open** 10am-5pm

Chicago Theater.

Mon-Wed, Sun; 10am-6pm Thur; 10am-3pm Fri. **Admission** free. **Credit** AmEx, Disc, MC, V. **Map** p309 J13.

Completed in late 2007 and fronted by an illuminated glass façade, the Spertus Institute's ten-storey, Kruek & Sexton-designed digs was one of the first new construction projects in decades on Michigan Avenue's 'street wall'. The building's two top floors house the museum's core collection and changing exhibitions in 8,000sq ft of exhibition space. The expanded displays detail the rich diversity of Jewish culture, with the 1,500 artefact-strong permanent Depot Display alongside new 19th- and 20th-century exhibits that stir the pot with often risqué contemporary artwork on Judaism. Lectures, screenings and performances also take place weekly, and often welcome drop-ins.

STATE STREET & AROUND

Macy's (no.111, at E Randolph Street; *see p143*) tops the long list of landmarks on 'That great street', the stuff of which songs are made. However, plenty of longtime locals defiantly call the block-long retail extravaganza by its original name: Marshall Field's. The store first opened on this site in 1868 (it was twice destroyed by fire, once in the Chicago Fire of 1871 and again six years later) and became the flagship shop in a pioneering nationwide chain.

When Macy's bought the store in 2005 and changed its name the following year (a century

---

INSIDE TRACK OFF THE WALL

Completed in 1985 and measuring a vast 90ft by 72ft, Sol LeWitt's wall relief *Lines in Four Directions* covers the western façade of 10 W Jackson Boulevard (between S Dearborn & S State Streets). Each of its four panels consists of extruded aluminium slats pointing in a single direction, forming an abstract composition designed to change with the shifting effects of sun and shadow. A small public plaza below the sculpture encourages contemplation. But to many local workers, *Lines in Four Directions* looks more like a sandblasting project gone awry.

---

after Field's death), Chicagoans were outraged, but not much has changed: the Tiffany mosaic dome (c1907) still stands high above one atrium, and the clock at State and Randolph Streets, the inspiration for a Norman Rockwell painting that made the cover of the *Saturday Evening Post* in November 1945, still keeps perfect time. (The original Rockwell work hangs near the seventh-floor visitors' centre.)

The city has tried for more than two decades to turn **Block 37**, bounded by State, Washington, Randolph and Dearborn Streets (directly opposite Macy's), into a mixed-use complex. Construction work began in 2005, and it's now a shopping hub filled with chain stores and refuelling stops such as Magnolia Bakery (108 N State Street at Washington Street, 312 346 7777).

Close by sits the lovely **Chicago Theater** (175 N State Street, at W Randolph Street). You can't miss the iconic red marquee of this former movie house, which opened in 1928 and today hosts entertainers ranging from Leonard Cohen to Bob the Builder. Opposite is the **Gene Siskel Film Center** (164 N State Street, at W Randolph Street; *see p194*), one of the best arthouse cinemas in Chicago.

The **Reliance Building** (1 W Washington Street, at N State Street) was one of Chicago's most elegant early skyscrapers when it opened in 1895, but years of neglect had left it in disrepair by the time a developer bought it in 1996. Restoration followed, after which the building reopened as the **Hotel Burnham** (*see p168*); it's named after Daniel Burnham, the building's architect.

South of Macy's sits Louis Sullivan's **Carson Pirie Scott** department store (1 S State Street, at E Madison Street), now home to Target and DSW (in addition to the Art Institute). During renovations on the store in 2008, contractors removed a metal panel from the neighbouring building at 22 S Wabash Avenue (at E Madison Street). Behind it, they found ornamental work that suggested Sullivan's hand. Having lost several Sullivan buildings to fire of late, enthusiasts were thrilled when this 'lost' Sullivan storefront was rediscovered, and further research confirmed that Sullivan had indeed created the building.

Two more notable buildings sit just off State Street on Monroe Street. To the west is the **LaSalle Bank Theatre** (22 W Monroe Street, at S State Street), built in 1905 as the Shubert Theatre and now home to some of the biggest shows to visit Chicago. And just east of State is the **Palmer House Hilton** (17 E Monroe Street, at S State Street; *see p169*), built in 1927 by Holabird & Roche with a spectacular lobby.

A couple of blocks west, the **Marquette Building** (140 S Dearborn Street, at Marble Place) shows what Holabird & Roche could do back in 1895. The building is named after the 17th-century explorer and missionary Father Jacques Marquette, who was the first European to spend the winter in Chicago. Bas-relief panels over the main entrance, and a panoply of bronze sculptures and spectacular Tiffany glass mosaics in the two-storey lobby illustrate episodes from Marquette's journey through the Midwest – and reveal a lot about 19th-century attitudes towards Native Americans.

EXPLORE

Clock at State and Randolph Streets

EXPLORE

El train in the Loop.

Due south, you'll find the world's tallest all-masonry building. When, in 1891, Daniel Burnham and partner John Root erected the 16-storey **Monadnock Building** (53 W Jackson Boulevard, at S Dearborn Street), they had to make its walls six feet thick at the base to support its weight, thinning them out as the building rose. Across the street, the **Chicago Federal Center** embodies what was cutting-edge 60 years later: the Everett McKinley Dirksen Building, the John C Kluczynski Building and the one-storey Loop Post Office were designed by Ludwig Mies van der Rohe. Mies's spare black steel and glass façades contrast with Alexander Calder's 53-foot *Flamingo*, which looks as if it could go for its own walk around the Loop at any moment.

A block south and east sits Harry Weese's **Metropolitan Correctional Center** (71 W Van Buren Street, at S Federal Street), which rises like a forbidding wedge of cheese. The top 16 floors house federal prisoners and suspects awaiting trial, which is why the windows are mere slits. Peer down on it from above and you may see some of these inmates stretching their legs in the rooftop exercise yard; rumour has it that their wives and girlfriends sometimes entertain them by dancing on the roof of a nearby parking structure.

The **Harold Washington Library Center** (400 S State Street, at W Van Buren Street, 1-312 747 4300, www.chipublib.org), which opened in 1991, is less formally innovative but more uplifting: it's a fitting tribute to the city's first African-American mayor, who appears in Jacob Lawrence's mosaic mural, *Events in the Life of Harold Washington*, which hangs in the lobby. Talks, discussions and concerts are held at the library regularly; check online for details.

RANDOLPH STREET & AROUND

Chicago government looms large on Randolph Street between LaSalle and Dearborn Streets; never larger than at the round **James R Thompson Center** on Randolph, between LaSalle and Clark Streets, named for the former Illinois governor who commissioned it. On the second floor, the **Illinois State Museum Gallery** (1-312 814 5322, www.museum.state.il.us) presents free shows that usually feature local artists.

City Hall and the adjoining **Cook County Building** sit opposite the Thompson Center, on the block bounded by Randolph, Washington, Clark and LaSalle Streets. City council meetings are held every two weeks on City Hall's second floor; call 1-312 744 5000 if you'd like to attend.

Across the street from City Hall, located on Randolph between Clark and Dearborn Streets, stands the **Daley Center**, named after former mayor Richard J Daley. Cook County's court system has its headquarters in this rust-coloured high-rise, but it's best known for the untitled Picasso sculpture that dominates Daley Plaza (*see p38* **Walk**). A Christmas tree is put up each year in the plaza, which also plays host to the largest German holiday market outside Germany, a summer farmers' market and the occasional political protest. The plaza's Eternal Flame Memorial, surrounded by a low metal fence, honours dead American soldiers. During the winter, the gas flame takes on an unexpected poignancy when pigeons huddle around it for warmth.

Rising 400 feet above ground a block south of City Hall on Washington, the **Chicago Temple** (77 W Washington Street, at N Clark Street, www.chicagotemple.org) is known as the 'Chapel in the Sky'. On an exterior first-level wall, stained-glass windows depict the history of the First United Methodist Church of Chicago. The temple's eight-storey spire is visible only from a distance.

LASALLE STREET

LaSalle Street has been the heart of the Midwest's financial industry since 1848, when a group of merchants founded the Chicago Board of Trade (CBOT) to regulate the grain futures market. In 2007, the CBOT merged with the Chicago Mercantile Exchange (CME) to form the **CME Group** (1-312 930 1000, www.cmegroup.com), the world's largest futures exchange. but security concerns have resulted

Profile Willis Tower

Despite a name change, Chicago's king pin retains its iconic status.

When it was completed in 1973, the Sears Tower received mixed reviews from the critics. For years, Sears, Roebuck & Co had trouble renting out the extra space in its behemoth, eventually abandoning it in 1992. And then, in 1998, the building finally lost its status as the world's tallest structure. However, despite all these problems, and despite the 2009 renaming of the building in honour of a London-based insurance group, the rechristened **Willis Tower** (*see p44*) has retained its status as Chicago's most iconic building.

Nine steel tubes of varying heights form the frame of the building, which is covered in black aluminium and glass. Designed by Bruce Graham from Chicago firm Skidmore, Owings & Merrill, it carries a certain grandeur, but its scale is more impressive than its appearance; the American Institute of Architects' guide to the city's buildings suggests that the

tower is 'more of a structural engineering triumph than an architectural accomplishment', which seems about right.

An annual charity event offers super-fit Chicagoans the chance to ascend the 2,109 steps between the ground floor and the Skydeck. In 1999, French daredevil Alain Robert went one better, climbing to the top in a little over an hour – from the outside. But those heading to the 103rd-floor Skydeck need not suffer such discomfort, thanks to the building's high-speed elevators.

After enduring seemingly endless queues, visitors are then faced with an overlong introductory movie and other exhibits on the building and the city. But everyone's really here for the views: on a clear day, you can see 60 miles from the Skydeck, which since 2009 has included an all-glass section that extends four feet over Wacker Drive and may leave vertigo-sufferers paralysed with fear.

In truth, the views from the John Hancock Center (*see p56*) are better, chiefly because they afford a better perspective of the Loop's skyline. The Hancock is also a more attractive building. But it's shorter. And when it comes to iconic status, at least in Chicago, size matters.

EXPLORE

VITAL STATISTICS
Completed
3 May 1973
Storeys 108
Height
1,451 feet
Weight
445 million
pounds

in the closure of the trading floor to the public. To set up a private tour, contact the public affairs office on 1-312 435 3590.

Back in the 19th century, birds nested in the run-down temporary City Hall at 209 S LaSalle Street, at W Adams Street. When Burnham and Root built a new structure there in 1888, the birds were remembered in the building's name: the **Rookery**. Two (sculpted) rooks at the LaSalle Street entrance serve as further reminders. The building's light-filled glass and marble lobby, a 1905 Frank Lloyd Wright redesign, is particularly lovely.

One Financial Place (440 S LaSalle Street, at W Congress Parkway) stands above the Eisenhower Expressway. If you're in a car, you can't miss it: traffic heading in or out of the Loop drives under the building, through arches that serve as stilts. Built in 1985 by the same architects responsible for the Willis Tower, it's home to the Chicago Stock Exchange.

W WACKER DRIVE & THE CHICAGO RIVER

The **Willis Tower** (*see right*) is Chicago's most famous landmark. However, it's far from the only notable building here. Just below, **311 S Wacker Drive** (at W Jackson Boulevard) is the tallest reinforced concrete building in the world. Its exterior of glass and pink granite is surrounded by a landscaped concourse; at night, the crown of the 65-storey structure is lit up like a Christmas tree. And to the north, Henry Cobb's curvaceous 2005 **Hyatt Center** (71 S Wacker Drive, at W Monroe Street) is one of the Loop's more feline and glamorous skyscrapers.

Home to the Lyric Opera since 1950, the 1929 **Civic Opera House** (20 N Wacker Drive, at E Madison Street; *see p227*) is centred on a lavish art deco auditorium adorned in red and orange with gold leaf accents. Its 3,500-plus capacity makes it the second-largest opera house in the country. Renovated in 1996, the building still boasts the terracotta and bronze forms of a trumpet, a lyre, and the masks of tragedy and comedy on its interior and exterior walls.

The Loop unofficially extends west over the Chicago River to encompass the **Ogilvie Transportation Center** (500 W Madison Street, at N Canal Street). Nearby **Union Station** (210 S Canal Street, at W Adams Street, 1-312-322-6777 metra information line), where Amtrak stops as well as the Metra, has much more grandeur. Don't be surprised if the station, which was built in 1925 and beautifully restored in 1992, seems familiar: the famous staircase shootout at the end of *The Untouchables* was filmed there.

Heading west, you'll enter the **West Loop** and **Greektown** (*see p77*). But before you get there, you'll run into Claes Oldenburg's 1977 **Batcolumn**, a 100-foot Cor-Ten steel baseball bat outside the **Social Security Administration Building** (600 W Madison Street, at N Jefferson Street). Critics interpret the piece as a homage to baseball, the steel industry or historical monumental columns. Still, the artist may also have been referring to the 1968 Democratic National Convention protests, where he was beaten by police.

★ **Willis Tower (formerly Sears Tower)**
233 S Wacker Drive, at W Jackson Boulevard (1-312 875 9696, www.theskydeck.com). El: Brown, Orange, Pink or Purple to Quincy/Wells. **Open** *Apr-Sept* 9am-10pm daily. *Oct-Mar* 10am-8pm daily. **Admission** $18 adults; $12 reductions; free under-3s. **Credit** AmEx, MC, V. **Map** p309 G12. *See p43* **Profile**.

Quincy station.

INSIDE TRACK
STATION RESTORATION

The Quincy/Wells CTA station boasts Victorian-style light fixtures, lustrous oak doors and mouldings, Corinthian pilasters and other neoclassical details on its sheet-metal walls. Yet despite appearances, none of these details are original. In the 1980s, the Illinois State Historic Preservation Office agreed to restore a Loop station to its 1897 appearance so the entire CTA system would be added to the United States' National Register of Historic Places. It chose Quincy/Wells because the station still retained some of its original features, including the fare booths.

The South Loop & Chinatown

High society and high rises converge in this evolving area.

While the West Loop consistently makes headlines, the South Loop has quietly been making a comeback of its own. As Chicagoans have moved back to the heart of the city, new apartment blocks have sprung up in the streets south of Congress Parkway, contributing to the gentrification of an area that had been neglected for years. Dozens of high-rise condo complexes have sprouted in the past few years; restaurants and supermarkets have joined them, giving the area something of a neighbourhood feel for the first time in decades.

The character of the South Loop can alter enormously within the space of a block or two. Apartment towers overlook tourist-packed Museum Campus, home to three of the country's finest (the Shedd Aquarium, the Adler Planetarium and the Field Museum), and the glossy McCormick Place convention centre stands just blocks from scruffy Chinatown. Change continues apace in an area that's still to fully evolve.

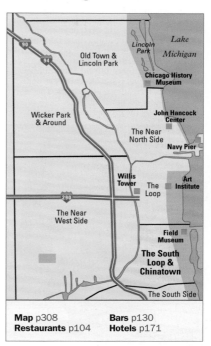

Map p308
Restaurants p104
Bars p130
Hotels p171

PRINTER'S ROW

El: Red to Harrison.

The stretch of Dearborn Street between Congress Parkway and Polk Street is pretty quiet these days, but things were considerably different a century or so ago. In the late 19th century, this stretch of Dearborn became the heart of the Midwest's printing and publishing industry: Printing House Row, it was called, a nickname later shortened to **Printer's Row**. (You'd think that with all the publishers in the area, they'd have managed to put the apostrophe in the right place.) The industry has long since scattered, but many of the old buildings remain, nowadays converted into apartments and restaurants.

At the southern end of Printer's Row, at the corner of Dearborn and Polk Streets, stands Chicago's old railway terminus. Built in 1883, **Dearborn Station** was most famous as the starting point for trains to Los Angeles, used by those who couldn't or wouldn't travel between the two cities by car on Route 66. The last train pulled out of the station in 1971 and it's now home to shops, restaurants and other businesses that lend the area a lift.

EXPLORE

MUSEUM CAMPUS

El: Green, Orange or Red to Roosevelt.

Three of the country's finest museums share the grassy plot known as **Museum Campus**, jutting out into Lake Michigan at the southern edge of Grant Park (just south of Roosevelt Road). Although they've changed hugely in the intervening years, the **Adler Planetarium** (*see right*), the **Shedd Aquarium** and the **Field Museum** (for both, *see p48*) were erected here in time for the Century of Progress World's Fair of 1933-34; each is named after the Chicago business mogul who commissioned it. Get off the Red line at Harrison, take the sidewalk that heads east from 9th Street and Michigan Avenue, and stroll between the three.

In 2005, **Northerly Island Park** (1521 S Lynn White Drive, 1-312 745 2910) was added to the area's recreational attractions. The island was previously occupied by Meigs Field, an airport used by the prosperous to jet in and

Adler Planetarium.

out of downtown. On 30 March 2003, citing post-9/11 concerns over terrorism, Mayor Daley shocked the city by bulldozing the runways in the middle of the night, instantly closing the airport (and stranding a number of aircraft). These days, the redeveloped parkland offers fishing and walking opportunities, and is home to the First Merit Bank Pavilion open-air music venue.

Just a football's throw or two from here is **Soldier Field**, home to the Chicago Bears (*see p242*). Built during the early 1920s as a memorial to America's war dead, the stadium was dramatically renovated in the early 21st century, with shiny modern grandstands effectively being dropped into the framework formed by the austere old façades. There may well be uglier buildings in the city, but you'll have to work pretty hard to find them.

★ Adler Planetarium

1300 S Lake Shore Drive, at E Solidarity Drive (1-312 922 7827, www.adlerplanetarium.org). El: Green, Orange or Red to Roosevelt. **Open** *mid June-mid Sept* 9.30am-6pm daily. *Mid Sept-mid June* 10am-4pm Mon-Fri; 10am-4.30pm Sat, Sun. **Admission** $12; $8-$10 reductions; free under-3s. *Basic Pass (incl 1 show)* $22; $18 reductions. *Premium Pass (incl 2 shows)* $28; $22 reductions. **Credit** AmEx, Disc, MC, V. **Map** p308 L14.

The name of this facility on the banks of Lake Michigan, housed in a 12-sided architectural marvel built in 1930, is only semi-appropriate: this excellent enterprise is more than just a planetarium. For a start, there are actually two planetariums here: the Definiti Space Theater and the Sky Theater, the latter offering a more traditional experience. In addition, the Universe 3D Theater showcases educational space films with whizz-bang effects that only a Pink Floyd-loving stoner could fully appreciate. Between them, they offer six shows that run in rotation all day long.

Most of the museum's permanent collection is accessible through a disorienting, mirrored walkway that sets the tone for what follows: it's interactive, interesting and kid-friendly but somehow never dumbed-down. The ground floor offers assorted nuggets of trivia (if the earth is a baseball, the moon is a ping-pong ball eight feet away), the 3-D Milky Way Theater and working replicas of Mars rovers.

Shoot for the Moon features a fully restored Gemini 12 spacecraft and more than 30 related items. Many were donated by former NASA astronaut James Lovell. In part, the exhibit tells the story of Lovell's own Apollo 13 mission, whose ill-fated return to earth prompted the Tom Hanks film of the same name.

The museum also boasts the largest collection of historic scientific instruments in the western hemisphere. Look out for the vast Dearborn telescope, the

INSIDE TRACK
VIEWS FROM THE ADLER

Even if you don't go inside the **Adler Planetarium** (*see right*) on the banks of Lake Michigan, it's still worth taking a stroll around the grounds: the grass verge outside offers one of the best landlocked, ground-level views of Chicago's stunning skyline.

Profile Field Museum

This longtime local favourite continues to expand and thrive.

The **Field Museum** (*see p48*) opened as part of the World's Columbian Exposition in 1893 as the Columbia Museum of Chicago, but was renamed after philanthropist and department store magnate Marshall Field in the early 20th century and moved to its impressive location soon afterwards. A Chicago must-see, the museum is one of the most impressive natural science centres in the world, with a vast wealth of biological and anthropological exhibits alongside world-class on-site research facilities.

One big draw here is Sue, the world's largest tyrannosaurus rex. Since she made her debut here in the late 1990s, costing the museum a cool $8.36 million at auction, Sue has become a mini-industry all by herself. Suitably awed children are normally to be found in her vicinity (near the north entrance of the museum), while parents rue the amount of Sue merchandise on sale at the well-stocked museum shops. Despite the name, its sex is unknown: it's actually named after Susan Hendrickson, who first unearthed the skeleton in North Dakota in 1990.

Popular though Sue is, she's by no means the whole story. The Field is too big to get around comfortably in a day, but pick up a map, plan your visit carefully, and you'll be rewarded. Among the standout exhibits are Evolving Planet, which starts with the world's oldest known single-cell organism and walks through a massive collection of dinosaur remains; Ancient Egypt, a life-sized tomb filled with real mummies and 14,000 artefacts; and the taxidermic libraries, which include the famed (and stuffed) lions of Tsavo.

Young families will find the museum a paradise for travel-weary kids. The Crown Family PlayLab lets really young tots hold their pace with interactive displays; while Underground Adventure, one of the museum's most amusing exhibits, shrinks viewers to the size of a bug in order to inspect the lives of tiny organisms. Try and time your visit to coincide with one of the free tours of the museum's highlights, held at 11am and 2pm (Mon-Fri).

EXPLORE

Shedd Aquarium.

largest in the world in its time; and Chicago's oldest planetarium, the 1913 Atwood Sphere, which is just 15 feet in diameter.

★ Field Museum

1400 S Lake Shore Drive, at E Roosevelt Road (1-312 922 9410, www.fieldmuseum.org). El: Green, Orange or Red to Roosevelt. **Open** 9am-5pm daily (hours may be extended in summer). **Admission** $15; $10-$12 reductions; free under-3s. **Credit** AmEx, Disc, MC, V. **Map** p308 J14. *See p47* **Profile**.

★ Shedd Aquarium

1200 S Lake Shore Drive, at E McFetridge Drive (1-312 939 2438, www.sheddaquarium. org). El: Green, Orange or Red to Roosevelt. **Open** *Summer* 9am-6pm daily. *Winter* 9am-5pm Mon-Fri; 9am-6pm Sat, Sun. **Admission** *Shedd Pass* $28.95; $19.95 reductions; free under-3s. *Total Experience Pass* $37.95; $28.95 reductions. **Credit** AmEx, Disc, MC, V. **Map** p308 K14.

Housed in a beautiful, circular 1930s building on the lake, the Shedd Aquarium holds what seems like every conceivable kind of fish and water mammal. Enter through the main lobby and you'll be greeted by a large Caribbean coral reef exhibit, spectacularly plonked in the middle of a domed hall. From this central root protrude a number of corridor-like exhibition spaces devoted to themes from the exotic (African tropical fish) to the everyday (invasive species found in the Great Lakes).

The displays are clearly labelled, and you can approach the exhibits in any order. Be sure to get a look at Granddad, the lungfish in the Waters of the World gallery. He was plucked from the waters of Australia in 1933 for the Century of Progress World's Fair; at an estimated age of 100 years, he's thought to be the oldest aquatic animal living in captivity anywhere in the world.

The aquarium more than doubled its visitorship in 1991 with the addition of the spectacular $45-million Oceanarium. Dominated by a vast tank, flooded with natural light and with great views of the lake, it features whales and dolphins swimming and performing shows daily. In 2009, it received a revamp, adding a video show and a river that runs through faux rocks and ends in a fish-filled pool. One of the Shedd's most successful programmes is the long-running Project Seahorse, which raises awareness about the potential extinction of the species.

The other always-crowded attraction is Wild Reef. This faithful re-creation of a coral reef habitat in the Philippines contains various sections devoted to the many facets of reef life, from the creatures that inhabit the shoreline surf to those that patrol the drop-off. In one spectacular spot, shark tanks create an overhead arch, giving visitors an all-consuming diver's-eye view of the fierce predators. Amid all the fun, a few little lessons on the importance of maintaining reef habitats have also been included.

The aquarium also offers 4-D Experience films, surprisingly fun 15-minute movies full of water squirts and air bursts, in the Phelps Auditorium. And don't miss *Man with Fish*, a painted bronze fountain created by German artist Stephan Balkenhol that sits just outside the aquarium. It's a humorous comment on stewardship, with an inexpressive everyman hugging a huge speckled fish.

THE PRAIRIE AVENUE HISTORIC DISTRICT

El: Red to Cermak-Chinatown.

During the late 19th century, before the city's rich and powerful moved to the North Side, the roads around 18th Street and Prairie Avenue were the grandest part of town, the centre of Chicago's high society and home to well over a hundred mansions. Only five properties from this era remain, but they provide a sense of what life must have been like among the city's privileged Victorian elite.

On the south-west corner of 18th Street and Prairie Avenue sits the **Glessner House Museum** (*see p50*), one of the key stops on a historical tour of Chicago. The property was built for John Jacob Glessner, who made his fortune in farm machinery. His neighbours were just as wealthy: among them were the train car-designing Pullmans, whose mansion has long since vanished, and the piano-making Kimballs, whose pad at 1801 S Prairie Avenue is now home to the US Soccer Federation. To the south lived both Marshall Field, Sr and Marshall Field, Jr. However, the area's oldest house is an intruder: the **Clarke House Museum** (*see below*) originally sat on 20 acres of land at 16th Street and Michigan Avenue, and was moved to the area three decades ago.

A century after the area began to fade from prominence, it's undergoing a resurgence. Old warehouses have been converted into lofts, and new apartment complexes have sprung up from nothing. It all stands in stark contrast both to the streets that run roughly four blocks west, which are drenched in impoverished public housing, and to the hulking, ugly **McCormick Place** (E 23rd Street, at S Lake Shore Drive), which sits a few blocks south-east on the other side of Lake Shore Drive. Best accessed via the Metra service from the Randolph Street station (by Millennium Park), it's a gargantuan site, with over two million square feet of meeting space. See www.mccormickplace.com or call 1-312 791 7000 for more information.

Clarke House Museum

1827 S Indiana Avenue, at E 18th Street (1-312 326-1480, www.clarkehousemuseum.org. El: Red to Cermak-Chinatown. **Open** *Tours noon, 2pm Wed-Sun.* **Admission** *$10; $6-$9 reductions; free under-5s & all Wed. Clarke & Glessner Houses $15; $8-$12 reductions. Prairie Avenue tour $15, select Sundays in summer (call for details).* **Credit** AmEx, Disc, MC, V. **Map** p308 J16.
Built in 1837 for hardware dealer Henry Clarke, this impressive property is the oldest house in Chicago. It's also the hardest place for the post office to keep track of: it's been moved twice in its long history, most recently in 1977 when the city lifted the building over a set of El tracks and on to its present home. Unlike the fortress-like Glessner House (*see p50*), this Greek revival property was built before electricity, indoor plumbing and the Chicago Plan changed the nature of architectural design in the city. Even so, the timber frame and mortise-and-tenon joints have travelled well, with ongoing restoration work enabling visitors to get a window into early upper-class life in Chicago. Tours begin at the Glessner House Museum.

Prairie Avenue.

EXPLORE

INSIDE TRACK
AMTRAK BRIDGE

Just north of Ping Tom Memorial Park
(*see right*) sits a still-functioning relic of
Chicago's industrial age. The imposing
steel **Amtrak Bridge**, built circa 1917,
is one of the few remaining vertical
lift bridges of its kind. If you're lucky
enough to be in the park at the right time,
you'll be able to watch in wonder as its
massive concrete counterweights lift the
suspension tracks 130 feet above the
water as boats pass through.

★ Glessner House Museum

*1800 S Prairie Avenue, at E 18th Street (1-312
326 1480, www.glessnerhouse.org). El: Red to
Cermak-Chinatown.* **Open** *Tours* 1pm, 3pm
Wed-Sun. **Admission** $10; $6-$9 reductions;
free under-5s & all Wed. *Clarke & Glessner
Houses* $15; $8-$12 reductions. *Prairie Avenue
tour* $15, select Sundays in summer (call for
details). **Credit** AmEx, Disc, MC, V. **Map** p308 J16.
A stroll through the Prairie Avenue Historic District
is enjoyable in its own right, but it's incomplete without a tour of this museum. The imposing stone mansion was designed by Henry Hobson Richardson
(who died in 1886, the year before it was completed).
It's dark, draughty and Victorian, yet manages to
maintain a certain cosiness, thanks to oak-panelled
walls and gold-leaf ceilings. The house was furnished
in part by local furniture-maker Isaac Scott, and covered in William Morris carpets and wallpaper.

A number of Glessner's artefacts are on display
in the house, among them a solid silver candlestick
on the concert grand and bronze casts of Abraham
Lincoln's face and hands. (The casts mysteriously
disappeared in 1992, only to reappear on the
doorstep a few days later after plenty of publicity.)
An afternoon spent in the conservatory on the top
floor, or browsing the bookshelves in the study,
would make a visit here sublime. Unfortunately, you
only get an hour in the house, tailed the entire time
by a security guard armed with three words: 'Do not
touch'. Tours begin inside the main doors on Prairie
Avenue; combination tickets are available if you've
also got time to see the nearby Clarke House.

CHINATOWN

El: Red to Cermak-Chinatown.

A century after the Chinese first arrived,
Chinatown remains modest. Intersected by
every imaginable thoroughfare – Amtrak rail
lines and the Chicago River to the west, I-55 to
the south, the El network to the north and east
– the district hasn't had much room to grow,

which explains its oft-crowded streets. Chinese
businesses dominate along Wentworth Avenue
and Cermak Road: restaurants, bakeries, and
small shops hawking everything from healing
herbs to samurai swords. To see the area at its
most vibrant, visit for the **New Year Parade**
(late Jan or early Feb; *see p29*), the **Chinatown
Summer Fair** (mid July) or the **Dragon Boat
Races** (late July), when locals race elaborately
painted wooden boats down the river to raise
funds for local charities.

The Chinatown gate just west of the Cermak-
Chinatown El station welcomes visitors to
Wentworth Avenue, the area's main drag. On
the west side of the street is the attractive **On
Leong Merchants Association Building**
(no.2216), also known as the Pui Tak Center.
The impressively frescoed three-storey building
blends styles typical of 1926, the year it was
built, with traditional Chinese design elements.
It never betrays the fact that it was designed
by a pair of Norwegian-American architects.

Other notable diversions in Chinatown
include the **Chinese-American Museum**,
which opened in 2005 (*see p51*); **Chinatown
Square** (2133 S China Pl, 1-312 808 1745), a
two-storey outdoor shopping complex erected
in 1993; and **Ping Tom Memorial Park** (300
W 19th Street), a Chinese-themed riverside park
tucked behind a new housing development.
However, most non-Chinese Chicagoans head
here for culinary reasons: the area is packed
with restaurants, including some real gems.

Chinese-American Museum of Chicago

*238 W 23rd Street, at S Wentworth Avenue
(1-312 949 1000, www.ccamuseum.org). El:
Red to Cermak-Chinatown.* **Open** 9.30am-1.30pm
Tue-Fri; 10am-5pm Sat, Sun. **Admission** $5;
$3 reductions. **Credit** (website only) AmEx,
Disc, MC, V.

Chinatown has more to offer than dim sum and
cheap gifts, as this museum of Chinese-American
history and culture proves. That said, it won't take
long to get through the two floors of exhibition
space. The rotating displays, some better curated
than others, include travelling exhibitions from
around the country, but the most fascinating shows
are those culled from the personal collections of
Chicago's own Chinese-American community. Past
topics have included a survey of traditional Chinese
furniture and clothing, an examination of Chinese
Chicagoans' role in the 1893 and 1933 World's Fairs,
and a look at the versatility of tofu.

Around Chinatown

Nearby, at State Street and Cermak Road, sits
the **Hilliard Homes** public housing complex.
Designed by Chicago's Bauhaus-trained
Bertrand Goldberg in 1966 and added to the
National Register of Historic Places 33 years
later, the estate comprises the most notable
buildings that fall under the care of the Chicago
Housing Authority. Reminiscent of Goldberg's
earlier Marina City corncobs, the honeycomb-
windowed residences were once mooted for

redevelopment into luxury homes, though
they're now mixed income housing.

There are more notable buildings nearby
on Michigan Avenue (2200-2500 blocks) and
parallel Indiana Avenue (2200-3500 blocks),
in an area informally known as **Motor Row**.
Back in the early 20th century, this was the
city's main area for car sales and repair; 116
makes of automobile were sold and repaired
along its streets. Many of the showrooms, some
of which featured rotating display areas and
elevators for the cars, occupied architecturally
significant buildings; several of them have
retained their terracotta façades.

Blues Heaven

*2120 S Michigan Avenue, between E 21st &
E 22nd Streets (1-312 808 1286, http://blues
heaven.com). El: Red to Cermak-Chinatown.* **Open**
noon-4pm Mon-Fri; noon-3pm Sat. **Admission**
$10; $5 reductions. **Credit** AmEx, Disc, MC, V.

From 1957 to 1967, this building was the home of
the legendary Chess label and Chess/Ter-Mar studios, recording and releasing records from legendary
bluesmen such as Muddy Waters, Howlin' Wolf and
Buddy Guy. It's said that when the building was sold
in the '70s, the new owners destroyed 250,000
records that had been abandoned here. Decades
later, Willie Dixon's widow purchased the site and
opened a museum and educational foundation in
1997. Today, you can tour the recording, rehearsal
and office spaces, which feature guitars, memorabilia and a bit of the original soundproofing.

EXPLORE

Chinatown.

The Near North Side

Chicago's wealthy downtown is awash with tourist treats.

The pocket of Chicago that sits directly north of the river and the Loop has long been rich in dense and fascinating contradictions. It remains so today, and is all the more interesting for its contrasts. Once an industrial hub, River North has managed to find its footing in recent years as a hub for creative types, making their homes and conducting their businesses from old warehouses and factories.

The serene piety of the area's Cathedral District is offset by the rowdy bacchanalia of many neighbouring bars and clubs. Nearby, on the Gold Coast, some of the city's oldest homes sit snuggled at the feet of soaring pioneers in Modernist design.

And then there's the most wondrous contradiction: the fact that this buzzing urbanity sits within a comfortable stroll of several lovely and unexpected beaches. For millions of tourists, the experience of visiting Chicago never extends beyond the Near North Side. It's easy to see why.

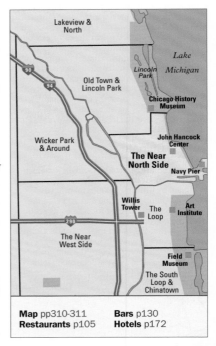

Map pp310-311   Bars p130
Restaurants p105   Hotels p172

RIVER NORTH

El: Brown or Purple to Chicago or Merchandise Mart; Red to Chicago or Grand.

These days, River North shines brightly with more than 70 upscale art galleries, a slew of smart restaurants and some of the sleekest nightclubs in town. The presence of such businesses makes it hard to believe that, before the late 1980s, locals issued visitors with stern warnings about the rampant drug trafficking and armed robberies for which the area was known. Much of the crime spilled over from nearby Cabrini-Green, one of the nation's most notorious housing projects, which used to sit just north of Chicago Avenue. But these days, the elegant neighbourhoods to the east wield more influence.

The area's first boom dates back to the industrial era of the 1890s, when most of the bigger buildings were erected. River North remained dominated by factories and warehouses until the 1970s, when, with post-industrial rust setting in, it morphed into a low-rent enclave for starving artists and other similar types. Their pioneering spirit has found a belated echo in the resurgence of the western portion of River North as a desirable business district for creative enterprises, with interior designers, dotcom start-ups, designer furniture stores and art dealers all taking leases on converted loft spaces.

The blocks bound by Chicago Avenue to the north, Wells Street to the east, Erie Street to the south and Orleans Street to the west comprise the **River North Gallery District**, home to large numbers of galleries and antiques stores

EXPLORE

(see p158). You'll also find a host of clubs, which attract both chic city dwellers and suburban weekenders; see p207. But despite the many hip, high-style clubs and galleries, the area is not without a few unabashed tourist traps, especially around the intersection of Clark Street and Ohio Street.

Towards Michigan Avenue sit a handful of notable churches, which provide solace from the hectic street life and, architecturally, some relief from the vertigo-inducing skyscrapers, malls and hotels. One is the Catholic **Holy Name Cathedral** (735 N State Street, at E Chicago Avenue, 1-312 787 8040, www.holyname cathedral.org), a Victorian Gothic edifice built in 1875. A fire in February 2009 destroyed a large section of the roof, but the church has remained open pending repairs. Nearby is the Episcopalian **St James Cathedral** (65 E Huron Street, at N Wabash Avenue, 1-312 787 7360, www.saintjamescathedral.org), the unusual interior walls of which are decorated with stencil patterns in more than 20 colours.

For all that, though, Chicagoans tend to associate the area with a former church often known as 'the Castle' (632 N Dearborn Street, at W Ontario Street). Designed by Henry Ives Cobb, architect of the Fisheries Building at the 1893 World's Fair, this red granite Romanesque revival building was for years the home of the Chicago Historical Society, but now houses the **Castle** club (see p207).

Holy Name Cathedral.

INSIDE TRACK
GANGLAND SECRETS

Holy Name Cathedral (see left) is quietly notorious as the place where Al Capone shot gangster Dion O'Banion and, later, his successor Hymee Weiss. Until his death, O'Banion operated a flower shop across the street, providing bouquets for a number of funerals for which he was personally responsible. Sadly, visitors won't be able to find any additional gang-era history in any of the city's official whitewashed tourist literature; perhaps rampant corruption hits a little too close to home in Chicago.

Close by, the **Tree Studios** (4 E Ohio Street, at N State Street) are proof that the area's association with artists is nothing new. Built by lawyer and philanthropist Lambert Tree in 1894 and later expanded, the studios were used by some of the city's best-known artists for decades, among them sculptor Albin Polasek, muralist John Warner Norton and painter Ruth van Sickle Ford. The complex was threatened by developers during the 1990s real estate boom, but – for once – the story has a happy ending: in 2001, city fathers saved the Queen Anne and Arts and Crafts buildings from the wrecking ball, allowing artists and construction crews to recreate some of the stunning architectural details from found fragments. The ground floor now houses galleries and furniture stores, among other enterprises.

For a time, artists at Tree Studios shared their space with the **Medinah Temple Association** (600 N Wabash Avenue, at Ohio Street). Built for the national Shrine fraternal organisation in 1912, the temple was considered one of the nation's finest examples of a Middle Eastern-style Shrine temple. In 2003, Bloomingdale's Home & Furniture Store took over the space; the renovation that ensued preserved much of the exterior architecture and restored the interior's former glory.

Several blocks south-west of Tree Studios stands the former nemesis of Chicago's criminal contingent: **Courthouse Place** (54 W Hubbard Street, at N Dearborn Street). The former Cook County Court building was built in 1892 as the second county court facility. Over the years, it was the site of some momentous legal wrangles, including attorney Clarence Darrow's successful bid to save convicted murderers Leopold and Loeb from the death sentence in 1924. Even more chillingly, it was also once used for hangings, and is purported to be haunted. These days, it's an office building.

EXPLORE

Magnificent Mile.

Mart for the Design Center, which boasts more than 130 showrooms of design products, and for the shopping area on the first two floors.

Richard H Driehaus Museum

40 E Erie Street, at N Wabash Avenue (1-312 482 8933, www.driehausmuseum.org). El: Red to Chicago. **Open** 10am-5pm Tue-Sun. **Admission** $20; $10-$12.50 reductions. **Credit** AmEx, Disc, MC, V. **Map** p310 H10.

Fund manager and philanthropist Driehaus opened this museum in 2008 to display his expansive collection of Louis Comfort Tiffany lamps and accessories, along with other 19th-century furnishings. Housed inside a mansion built by 19th-century liquor magnate Samuel M Nickerson, the immaculate 'marble palace' is also a shining example of building preservation.

THE MAGNIFICENT MILE & STREETERVILLE

El: Red to Chicago or Grand.

Michigan Avenue's Magnificent Mile is actually a Magnificent Three-Quarters-of-a-Mile, but few visitors let that sully their impression of the bustling commercial avenue. Every year, many of the city's 45 million visitors make it a top priority on their itineraries, spending full days collecting one rustling bag after another. While the street is a veritable Who's Who of American retail, locals have complained that the stretch of 460-plus shops is in the process of losing its unique character, with independent Chicago retailers giving way to big-name chains.

In the years after World War II, developer Arthur Rubloff christened the street the Magnificent Mile as he went about renovating old buildings and erecting new ones. At the time, there wasn't anything too magnificent about it; but in due course, the road grew into its lofty sobriquet as big shops flocked. It's at

EXPLORE

South of here, overlooking the river, stands Bertrand Goldberg's distinctive **Marina City** (300 N State Street). Its two iconic structures, nicknamed the Corncob Towers for obvious reasons, have made cameos in everything from Steve McQueen's final movie to a Wilco album cover. The top 40 storeys house trapezoid apartments, with the lower 20 storeys used for parking. The complex is also home to the **House of Blues** (*see p220*) music venue and **Hotel Sax** (*see p173*).

East of the Corncobs along the river is the **Trump International Hotel & Tower** (*see p173*), completed in 2009. At one time, the 92-storey, silvery glass curtain wall giant was slated to become the world's tallest building, but plans were scaled back due to the sagging real estate market. Instead, upon completion, the mixed-use retail/condo/hotel became Chicago's second tallest building.

Just as Trump's skyscraper stands as testament to a vibrant 21st-century economic optimism in Chicago, so the hulking riverfront building to its west pays tribute to earlier wealth and enthusiasm. Built in 1930 as showrooms and a wholesale office for Marshall Field's, the art deco **Merchandise Mart** (between N Wells and N Orleans Streets, www.merchandisemart.com) is the largest LEED-certified building in the world, boasting an astonishing 4.2 million square feet of floor space, as well as its own zip code. When the mart hit hard times in the 1940s, Field sold the building to Joseph P Kennedy, the father of JFK. It was the elder Kennedy who installed the outdoor Merchandise Mart Hall of Fame in 1953, honouring captains of industry with Romanesque bronze busts along the river. These days, visitors head to the Merchandise

---

INSIDE TRACK
AESOP'S FABLES

Tribune Tower (*see p55*) is adorned with many ornate bells and whistles that often go unnoticed by harried passers-by. One notable example is the Hall of Inscriptions, as the grand entrance to the main lobby is known: intricate carvings depict symbolic imagery from Aesop's *Fables*, famous quotes heralding the ideals of a free press and some wise words from *Tribune* founder Colonel McCormick.

its best in the run-up to Christmas, when the buildings and trees are garlanded with lights, but it's pleasant (if congested) all year round, the broad expanse of the road dotted with small flower gardens and handsome greenery.

The Magnificent Mile is best approached by walking up it from south to north, especially if you first take in the views from the southern side of the **Michigan Avenue Bridge**. After it opened in 1920, the bridge quickly became an asset to the area north of the river, making access to the Loop easier for residents and businessmen. A plaque at the south-eastern end commemorates Fort Dearborn, the military outpost from which the city developed, and four sculptures on pylons along the bridge nod to events in the city's history: the arrival of Joliet and Marquette, trader Jean Baptiste Point du Sable's settlement, the Fort Dearborn Massacre and the rebuilding following the fire of 1871.

John Howells' and Raymond Hood's Gothic design for **Tribune Tower** (435 N Michigan Avenue), the offices of the *Chicago Tribune*, was selected in 1922 by then publisher Colonel Robert McCormick from a field of international entries, and was completed to great acclaim three years later. The Gothic block houses the offices of the daily newspaper, the *Tribune*-owned WGN radio station (the letters stand for 'World's Greatest Newspaper') and CLTV, Chicago's 24-hour local news station. As you walk around the first level, look for the stones purportedly swiped by *Tribune* correspondents

from the Alamo, the Berlin Wall, the Parthenon and St Peter's Basilica, as well as a piece of steel from the World Trade Center and a moon rock.

Across the street is the stunning **Wrigley Building** (400 N Michigan Avenue). The white terracotta-clad structure was designed by Charles Beersman for Graham, Anderson, Probst & White, later also responsible for Merchandise Mart. It has stood at the base of Michigan Avenue since 1924 and remains home to Wrigley. The handsome clock tower was based on the cathedral tower in the Spanish city of Seville.

Further north, Michigan Avenue has its share of breathtaking architecture, not least the formerly exclusive (and men-only) Medinah Athletic Club building that's now home to the **Hotel InterContinental** (*see p175*). However, the main reason people flock here is for the shops. From Gap to Gucci, Apple to Armani, the Magnificent Mile is one long paean to consumerism. Some shops have their own individual premises, but many others lie within malls. For details, *see pp143-166*.

Towards the northern end of the Magnificent Mile, just across from Chicago Avenue, stand the **Water Tower** and the **Chicago Water Works** (163 E Pearson Street, at N Michigan Avenue), two of only a handful of structures to survive the Chicago Fire of 1871. Inside the Water Tower is the compact **City Gallery**, which favours Chicago-oriented exhibits; the Water Works across the street houses

EXPLORE

Wrigley Building.

a visitors' centre, a decent gift shop and the **Lookingglass Theatre Company** (*see p235*). Also right here is the **Loyola University Museum of Art** (*see right*).

The Water Tower is a handsome building, but these days it's very much in the shadow of the **John Hancock Center** (*see right*) just to the north. Towering 1,107 feet above the Magnificent Mile and the Gold Coast, it's smaller than the Willis Tower but affords more impressive views. The criss-cross braces that form the building's outer frame were designed to keep the structure from swaying in the wind. Much of the building is residential, but the lower levels and the sunken plaza are home to shops and eateries.

John Hancock Center.

Across the street from the Hancock is the impressive **Fourth Presbyterian Church** (126 E Chestnut Street, at N Michigan Avenue, 1-312 787 4570, www.fourthchurch.org), built in 1914. The interior courtyard provides a quiet contrast to the bustling din of traffic and hordes of shoppers outside. On Fridays in summer, free jazz and classical concerts take place here. A block north is the **Drake Hotel** (*see p179*), which has long been a stopover for the rich and famous. The hotel was designed to resemble a Renaissance palace: a gorgeous second-floor lobby ushers in guests, while the first floor is lined with small retail shops. This is where the **Gold Coast** (*see p59*) really begins.

★ John Hancock Center

875 N Michigan Avenue, between E Delaware Place & E Chestnut Street (1-888 875 8439, www.jhochicago.com). El: Red to Chicago. **Open** 9am-11pm daily. **Admission** $15; $9.50 reductions; free under-3s. **Credit** AmEx, Disc, MC, V. **Map** p310 J9.

Though it's a few storeys shorter than the Willis Tower, Big John offers even more astonishing views. For one thing, it's far enough north to take in the Loop's skyline, and close enough to the water to allow glimpses of boats miles out on Lake Michigan. For another, the 94th-floor Hancock Observatory has an outdoor walkway: it's not for the faint of heart, but it's guaranteed to blow away the cobwebs. Buy your ticket on the ground floor and take the ear-popping elevator ride to the observatory, where you can soak up views through floor-to-ceiling windows.

Another point in the Hancock's favour is its 96th-floor Signature Lounge. Though the restaurant below is pricey, locals like to bring out-of-town guests to the bar: even taking into account the cost, you're likely to come out ahead, as there's no admission charge and you won't have to endure the tourist kitsch of the observation deck. The secret's out, so even people arriving when the bar opens at 11am may be met with queues for the elevator, followed by queues for a table. But if you're willing to pay more than you usually would for a drink, the views are definitely worth the wait, particularly as the sun goes down.

Loyola University Museum of Art

820 N Michigan Avenue, at E Pearson Street (1-312 915 7600, www.luc.edu/luma). El: Red to Chicago. **Open** 11am-8pm Tue; 11am-6pm Wed-Sun. **Admission** $8; $2-$6 reductions; free to all Tue. **Credit** AmEx, Disc, MC, V. **Map** p310 J9.

LUMA, the art gallery for local Catholic college Loyola University, interprets its mission broadly: One of its efforts to 'illuminate… enduring spiritual questions' was an installation of fairy paintings. Shows can be rather hit-or-miss, but it's strongly committed to showing work by local Illinois artists and school kids.

EXPLORE

EXPLORE

INSIDE TRACK
FREE MUSEUM DAYS

Several museums that ordinarily charge admission set aside one or more days each week when they're free to all. Timing your visit with care could save you plenty of cash.

Art Institute of Chicago (*see p36*)
5-8pm Thur.
Chicago Children's Museum (*see p187*)
5-8pm Thur; 1st Sun of mth.
Clarke House Museum & Glessner House Museum (*see pp49-50*)
tours noon and 2pm Wed.
DuSable Museum of African American History (*see p95*) noon-5pm Sun.
Field Museum (*see p48*) check website for details.
Museum of Contemporary Art (*see right*)
10am-8pm Tue.

Streeterville

As a neighbourhood founded on a garbage heap by a lunatic, it will come as no surprise to learn that Streeterville boasts one of the city's most fascinating backstories. Loosely defined as the area south of the Hancock Center and east of Michigan Avenue, the neighbourhood takes its name from a circus-owning scoundrel who ran his steamboat aground on a sandbar near the lake shore in 1886 and claimed the area as independent territory. Huge amounts of rubble were dumped in the lake after the Great Fire of 1871; Captain George Wellington Streeter began taking the waste (and money) from contractors and managed to expand his sandbar, which he called the 'United States District of Lake Michigan', by eight million square feet. When landfill connected the island to the shore, city officials (and a wealthy industrialist) tried to stake a claim. The captain fended off the intruders with gunfire, but his mansion was finally torched by the Chicago Title & Trust Company in 1918. Two decades later, his relatives gave up the fight.

The area is now considerably calmer than in Streeter's day, when thieves, prostitutes and marauders roamed the locale. Much of the neighbourhood is given over to expensive residential property and grand hotels, though it's also home to Northwestern University's downtown campus, the Ann & Robert H Lurie Children's Hospital and, at N Columbus Drive and W Illinois Street, **NBC Tower**. Built in 1989 but designed to blend in with the 1920s and '30s art deco skyscrapers around it, the

block hosts recordings of TV shows such as *Judge Mathis* (for tickets, call 1-866 362 8447 or see http://judgemathistv.warnerbros.com).

Located along the stretch of the river that flows into Lake Michigan, **North Pier** (435 E Illinois Street, at N Lake Shore Drive, 1-312 836 4300) doesn't compare to neighbouring **Navy Pier** (*see p58*) in terms of size and the number of attractions. But it does have peace and quiet in its favour. There are plenty of places to sit outside and watch boaters heading out to the lake. At the far eastern end, you'll find the **Centennial Fountain & Arc**, which commemorates the city's Water Reclamation District. An arc of water shoots out of the fountain and into the river – and sometimes on to passing boaters – every hour, on the hour (10am-2pm, 5pm-midnight daily, May-Sept).

This little pocket has been the site of much activity in recent years, with the establishment of new residential buildings and a handful of new shops and restaurants. E Illinois Street alone is home to **AMC River East 21** cineplex (no.322; *see p192*), the flashy **Lucky Strike Lanes** (in the same building; *see p243*) and the sprawling **Fox & Obel** food market (no.401; *see p161*). Fox & Obel is housed in the **River East Art Center** (www.rivereastartcenter.com), also home to a number of galleries. However, if it's art you're after, you're better served by the temporary shows at the low-key **Arts Club of Chicago** or the rather more high-profile **Museum of Contemporary Art**.

★ Arts Club of Chicago

201 E Ontario Street, at N St Clair Street (1-312 787 3997). El: Red to Chicago. **Open** 11am-6pm Tue-Fri; 11am-3pm Sat. **Admission** free (gallery). **No credit cards. Map** p310 J10.
This art gallery might be one of the city's snootiest members-only clubs, but its first-floor exhibitions are still open to the public. Established in 1916, the club was formed by wealthy art-collectors in reaction to the very traditional exhibitions on display at the Art Institute of Chicago. The Arts Club opened to display works by avant-garde artists including a young Picasso, who'd never shown in the US, and Brancusi, whose exhibit was installed by Marcel Duchamp. This mission continues today. While the club no longer makes an effort to hang the most forward-thinking art, a solid show by a big-name contemporary artist opens every couple of months.

★ Museum of Contemporary Art

220 E Chicago Avenue, at N Mies van der Rohe Way (1-312 280 2660, www.mcachicago.org). El: Red to Chicago. **Open** 10am-8pm Tue; 10am-5pm Wed-Sun. **Admission** $12; $7 reductions; free under-12s & all Tue. **Credit** AmEx, Disc, MC, V. **Map** p310 J9.

Museum of Contemporary Art.
See p57.

While the Art Institute has a pair of lions to guard it, the MCA needs no such deterrents: the $46-million building, designed by Berlin architect Josef Paul Kleihues and opened to coincide with the MCA's 30th birthday in 1997, is imposing enough. However, while its exterior is daunting (and not universally admired), it's a different story inside: since it opened, its vast spaces have proved adaptable.

The emphasis here is on temporary shows. The MCA's scattershot approach to programming is admirable and pays plenty of dividends, both with its exhibitions and the performances that take place within its walls; there's also a sculpture garden, a Wolfgang Puck restaurant and an excellent shop hawking objects from local and international designers. The 2013-14 calendar gives some idea of the variety: The Way of the Shovel: Art as Archaeology, which traces the interest in history, archaeology and archival research, is followed by Simon Starling: Metamorphology, which explores the transformative potential of art.

Navy Pier

Mention Navy Pier and most locals will roll their eyes or let out a groan. The attraction has a pretty strong reputation as a tourist trap filled with corny theme restaurants and cheesy gift shops. For children, however, the pier is a dream come true. Little ones will be wowed by attractions such as the **Transporter FX**, a high-speed virtual reality simulator; the **IMAX Theater**, showing the latest films on enormous screens; and the whizz-bang interactive exhibits inside the **Chicago Children's Museum** (*see p187*).

There's some respite for more mature audiences too. Adults will appreciate strolling through the **Crystal Gardens'** one-acre indoor palm court, taking in a play at the **Chicago Shakespeare Theater** (*see p235*) or admiring an unbeatable vista of the skyline from atop the 150-foot Ferris wheel, the pier's best attraction. The latter is made even more magical when fireworks light up the sky on Wednesday and Saturday evenings during summer, as well as for holidays such as Independence Day.

Another top sight, one that the pier neglects to promote, is the **Smith Museum of Stained Glass Windows** (1-312 595 5024; admission free). Many of the 150-plus pieces on display were made in Chicago in the late 19th century, when the city's European immigrants made the city a hub for stained-glass artisanship.

The pier hasn't always been the glittering tourist façade it is today. It was built as a commercial shipping pier in 1916 by Charles Frost, when it had the rather plain-sounding name of Municipal Pier No.2, as one of five quays proposed six years earlier by architect Daniel Burnham (who didn't live to see it built). The pier became more or less deserted when most commercial ships were re-routed to a pier on the South Side; during the two World Wars, the 50-acre site was occupied by the US Navy, before serving as the first campus for the University of Illinois at Chicago until 1965.

Following a period of dereliction, the city renovated the pier as a leisure destination in the late 1980s, a multi-million-dollar project that was completed in 1995. Boats once again leave from here, mostly of the sightseeing variety.

EXPLORE

Just outside Navy Pier to the north, off Lake Shore Drive, is **Olive Park**, a quiet green space with room for picnicking. The small **Ohio Street Beach**, just west, contains a sculpture garden honouring **Jane Addams** (*see p80*) and offering superb views of the skyline.

THE GOLD COAST

El: Red to Chicago or Clark/Division.

The Gold Coast's 24-carat moniker seems fitting when you stroll through the mansion- and luxury high rise-lined streets near the lake. Grannies wrapped in fur coats clutch tiny yapping dogs as they dodge nannies pushing oversized strollers down the pristine sidewalks; well-dressed ladies who lunch window-shop in expensive and exclusive boutiques.

But the farther you travel from the lake, the less luxurious the scene becomes; especially the area surrounding the intersection of Division and Rush Streets, home to more restaurants and bars per square foot than any other corner of Chicago since the 1920s. On weekends, the bars on Division Street are a rowdy, booze-soaked whirlpool in which tourists, conventioneers, suburbanites and college freshmen happily drown their dignity. The 1986 film *About Last Night* was set here. Meanwhile, Rush Street is now dubbed the 'Viagra Triangle' on account of its popularity with greying men on the prowl for younger women.

The neighbourhood's upmarket reputation was established by entrepreneur Potter Palmer, founder of the grand **Palmer House Hotel** (*see p169*), when he built a $250,000 'mansion to end all mansions' in 1882 on what now equates to 1350 N Lake Shore Drive. The area had been marshland up until the hotelier's arrival, but when a string of rich and influential Chicagoans followed in his wake, the area soon came to replace **Prairie Avenue** (*see p48*) as the preferred address of Chicago's elite.

As the Gold Coast's cachet grew, it became a destination to which many Chicagoans aspired. The area attracted the Roman Catholic Church; the city archbishop resides at an expansive red-brick building on State Street (*see p62*). Just blocks away, Hugh Hefner chose the building at 1340 N State Street for his **Playboy Mansion**, though he eventually moved his headquarters and his bunnies to California. Palmer's mansion was torn down in 1950 to make room for one of

EXPLORE

Summer Lovin' Oak Street Beach

Mingle with the city's beautiful people on Chicago's riviera.

Oak Street Beach is Chicago's riviera, where the city's buff and beautiful people go to sunbathe, swim and show off. In summer, there's a flurry of activity around the volleyball nets and lakeside paths; for a beach, the pace is relentless. Pedestrian access is via underpasses located next to the Drake Hotel.

Amenities Toilets, drinking fountains, a café (summer only) and volleyball posts.
Where to eat Oak Street Beach (1-312 988 4650, www.oakstreetbeach.com) offers sustenance during summer.
Location 1000 North, Gold Coast.
More information 1-213 742 5121 or www.chicagoparkdistrict.com.

the area's multiple high-rises, some of which are of architectural merit. However, many of the Gold Coast's early stately homes have been left standing, in styles from Tudor to art deco.

Technically, the Gold Coast is bounded by Chicago and North Avenues, Clark Street and Lake Michigan. While the northern half of this area is chiefly residential, the southern block is mostly commercial.

Oak Street & around

Away from the **Oak Street Beach** (*see p59* **Summer Lovin'**), the Gold Coast's other attractions are less frenetic. Oak Street itself is the city's high-end fashion strip (*see p144*); walking west along it will lead you to within a stone's throw of **Washington Square**, a green space bound by Delaware, Walton, Dearborn and Clark Streets. Throughout its history, the square saw spirited demonstrations from all kinds of lively orators and protestors, until

Mayor Richard J Daley cracked down on it in the 1960s. These days, it's a calm place for 364 days a year. The exception is the last Sunday of July, when the square hosts the lively, politicised Bughouse Debates in tribute to the park's past life. The debates are organised by the **Newberry Library**, Chicago's research library for the humanities.

FREE Newberry Library

60 W Walton Street, between N Dearborn & N Clark Streets (1-312 943 9090, www.newberry. org). El: Red to Chicago. **Open** 8.15am-5pm Mon, Fri, Sat; 8.15am-7.30pm Tue-Thur. **Admission** free. **No credit cards. Map** p310 H9.
Neither the patrician setting nor the classic architecture of the Newberry Library, designed by Henry Ives Cobb and completed in 1893, betray its mission to bring highbrow culture to the plebs. Founded in 1887 by banker Walter L Newberry, it's not a lending library but a research centre that contains a vast variety of texts covering local history, literature,

EXPLORE

Summer Lovin' North Avenue Beach

Soak up the skyline views, if you can tear your eyes away from the beach.

Seething during the summer months with sexy singles playing beach sports and muscle-bound men on bikes, North Avenue Beach basically equates to the West Coast minus the surf. If you're not into scoping and getting scoped, you might find this strip of sand a bit run-down. Still, it's worth it for the beautiful skyline views of the city. And even if you don't play volleyball, it's worth checking out the action, which can get highly competitive.

Amenities The big boat-shaped building houses toilets, showers and a host of services (beach towel and bike rental, for instance). You'll also find a newspaper stand, a café and other temporary fixtures.
Where to eat Open in summer, Castaways Bar & Grill serves until 11pm. All the cafés and hot-dog stands close at 5pm.
Location 1600 North, Gold Coast.
More information 1-773 281-1200 or www.chicagoparkdistrict.com.

genealogy and cartography texts, along with a collection of Jefferson's letters. It's open to anyone; all you need is a reading card, which will require a photo ID, proof of address and a reason for wanting to search a specific collection. The small but exceptional exhibitions generally revolve around historical or literary themes, and are always free.

Astor Street

The grandeur of leaded-glass bay windows, elaborately carved frescoes, soaring turrets and manicured streetfront gardens make it seem as if time forgot about Astor Street. In truth, it was a 1970s Chicago Landmark designation that fought off time, engaging the street in a brutal battle between old and new.

Architecturally, Astor Street is an old-fashioned anomaly nestled among a forest of modern high-rises, many of which have not aged well. Running north from Division Street, close by the colourful and exuberant **Lake Shore Drive Synagogue** (70 E Elm Street, 1-312 337 6811, tours by request), the handsome street makes for an enjoyable and quiet stroll past magnificent mansions that, for the most part, are immaculately preserved by their current residents.

Astor Street offers a glimpse into an era when Chicago's wealthiest citizens jostled for bragging rights by engaging in a contest to build more luxurious mansions than their neighbours. It went up in the world after the Great Chicago Fire of 1871, when the city was forced to rebuild. However, the quarter-mile stretch of road didn't come into its own until the turn of the 20th century. Unlike the barn-like palaces that languished on Prairie Avenue, the mansions built on Astor Street by the likes of Cyrus McCormick and the Goodmans were more akin to overgrown townhouses. Most of the properties were built in the Queen Anne, Romanesque or Georgian Revival architectural styles, though their gaudy coats of arms, turrets and balconies were later dubbed 'Stockyard Renaissance' by one wag.

From the late 19th century until World War II, the street was home to many of the richest men and women in the city. But after the war, the lure of the North Shore put the area on the skids: many of the buildings were knocked down in the 1960s to make room for the faceless high-rise condo buildings that stud the Gold Coast. However, community protest prevailed and Landmark District status was secured in 1975, the first such area award in Chicago; the homes are now largely in excellent shape.

Even the apartment towers along Astor Street carry with them a little class. Take the pair at **no.1260** and **no.1301**, for example: built in the early 1930s by Philip B Maher,

Astor Street.

EXPLORE

they're almost identical examples of art deco luxury, the artful minimalism of their design providing a bridge between the new and old Gold Coasts. And at the same intersection (with Goethe Street) stands **Astor Tower**, no.1300, the most eye-catchingly modern building on the road. Built in 1963 by one-time Astor Street resident Bertrand Goldberg (who also built Marina City; *see p54*), the 28-storey tower sits perched on a small glass box and some precariously slender columns.

Before continuing up Astor Street, it's worth taking a stroll east to the former home of the **Three Arts Club** (1300 N Dearborn Street), built by Holabird & Root in 1914 to resemble a Tuscan villa. Before it closed in 2007, the enterprise harked back to an era when society women felt the need to protect young ladies from the 'wicked city' by giving them a refuge in which to study music, art or drama. The club sold the building several years ago with a heavy heart, after anticipated public funding for renovation failed to materialise, but it continues its mission of supporting artists via awards and fellowships.

From there, head back to Astor Street and continue north to no.1355, which is also known as **Astor Court**. This Georgian mansion was designed by Howard Van Doren Shaw in 1914 for William O Goodman, who funded the construction of the Goodman Theatre in the Loop (*see p235*) in tribute to his late playwright son. The marble archway and spiked fence give it a hint of Versailles, as does the tantalising glimpse through a gate of a lost-in-time courtyard.

Next door is one of the real landmarks on the street, the **Charnley-Persky House** (no.1365). A simple, compact building, it was built in 1892 and designed by Frank Lloyd Wright while he was still working under the auspices of Louis Sullivan's firm (he was later fired for moonlighting on his own projects). A mix of the duo's styles, combining Wright's sweeping horizontal lines and Sullivan's ornamentation, it's now the headquarters of the Society of Architectural Historians, which conducts tours of the house every Wednesday and Friday at noon and every Saturday at 10am and noon (and also at 1pm from April to November). Wednesday noon tours are free; Saturday tours cost $10 ($5-$8 reductions) and include the exterior and interior of nearby Madlener House, and an exterior walking tour of the 1400 block of North Astor Street. Call 1-312 573 1365 or see www.charnleyhouse.org.

Across the junction with Schiller Street sits the **Ryerson House** (no.1406), which was designed by David Adler in 1922 for steel magnate Joseph T Ryerson. Its look was patterned, mostly successfully, after Paris

hotels. Just beyond it stands a tall, skinny slice of art deco simplicity: completed in 1929 by the firm of Holabird & Root, the **Russell House** (no.1444) faces the world with a sleek stone façade imported from France and carved decorative panels. Opposite, the **Fortune House** (no.1451) was built in the Jacobethan style in 1910 by Howard Van Doren Shaw.

At the junction with Burton Place stands the imposing edifice of the *palazzo* that former mayor Joseph Medill built for his daughter, Mrs Robert Patterson, in 1893. The orange brick walls, terracotta trim and inviting courtyard of no.1500 have all aged well, though the property has now been divided into frighteningly exclusive condominiums. Just west off Astor Street, the thick, immovable **Madlener House** (4 W Burton Place) was built in 1902 by Richard Schmidt. Its interior can be seen as part of the Saturday tours of Charnley House (*see left*).

Its postal address is 1555 N State Parkway, but the **Archbishop's Residence** stretches an entire block along Astor Street. This 1885 Queen Anne mansion is built of red brick with sandstone trim and has 19 chimneys poking up to the sky. At the top of Astor Street, either turn right in the direction of the **International Museum of Surgical Science** or wander left along W North Avenue. At no.59 is one of the city's oldest and most expensive private schools, the **Latin School of Chicago**. Founded in 1888, it counts guitarist Roger McGuinn and sculptor Claes Oldenburg among its alumni. Just across the road is the **Chicago History Museum** (*see p65*) and the **Old Town** neighbourhood (*see p63*).

International Museum of Surgical Science

1524 N Lake Shore Drive, between E North Boulevard & E Burton Place (1-312 642 6502, www.imss.org). El: Red to Clark/Division.
Open 10am-4pm Tue-Fri; 10am-5pm Sat, Sun.
Admission $15; $8 reductions; free to all Tue.
Credit AmEx, MC, V. **Map** p311 H7.
Not everyone will appreciate the surgery-related artefacts at this unusual museum. Indeed, many will probably shudder at the sight of a 3,000-year-old Peruvian skull drill or the Civil War-era amputation kit. Still, as with a gruesome car accident, it's difficult not to at least peek. Operated by the neighbouring International College of Surgeons since 1954, the creepy International Museum of Surgical Science also houses a rare (working) iron lung; a re-created X-ray lab that includes Emil Grubbe's turn-of-the-century equipment; oddly captivating surgery-related murals by Gregorio Calvi di Bergolo; and, for the kids, a walk-in recreation of a 19th-century apothecary. If your stomach starts to turn, make a dash for outside: the façade of the lakefront mansion is also worth a look.

EXPLORE

Old Town & Lincoln Park

Laid-back living by the lake.

Similar in spirit yet nonetheless quite distinct, the adjoining residential neighbourhoods of Old Town and Lincoln Park carry broad appeal for a certain type of Chicagoan who finds River North too brash but Wicker Park too edgy. Both neighbourhoods grew increasingly affluent during the 1980s and early '90s, since when they've settled into comfortable middle age.

Old Town and Lincoln Park are dominated by handsome residential housing, with a handful of commercial drags – North Avenue and Wells Street in Old Town, Lincoln Avenue and Clark Street in Lincoln Park – giving focus to the communities. However, for visitors, the main appeal lies alongside Lake Michigan in the shape of Lincoln Park itself, which begins at North Avenue and runs five miles north along the waterfront. It's easy to lose a summer's afternoon just wandering around its vast, appealing pastures, and many locals often do.

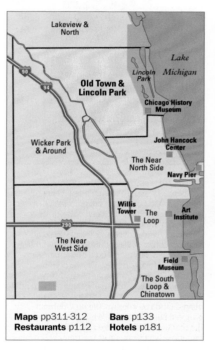

Maps pp311-312 **Bars** p133
Restaurants p112 **Hotels** p181

EXPLORE

OLD TOWN

El: Brown or Purple to Sedgwick; Red to North/Clybourn.

Once a trading spot for Indian tribes, the neighbourhood now known as Old Town was properly settled by German immigrants, who were pushed north following the Chicago Fire of 1871. At the time, the stretch of land between North Avenue, Clark Street, Armitage Avenue and Larrabee Street was little more than a patchwork of gardens and cow pastures, but it was redeveloped after the blaze; the influx

of German shops and restaurants along North Avenue earned it the moniker 'German Broadway'. After World War II, the area was finally considered venerable enough to assume its current name.

The development of the Cabrini-Green public housing project along Division Street and the collapse of industry in the area in the 1950s changed the face of Old Town's south-west corner. Home to 20,000 people, the project became a symbol of the city's neglect of its urban poor, the extremes of gang violence and the local drug trade. Ever-conscious of its public image (and aware of the escalating

EXPLORE

Crilly Court

price of real estate), the city tore down the development's main towers a few years ago and relocated its residents, a programme of enforced gentrification that's not been without its critics.

The downturn of Old Town made it financially viable territory for movers and shakers in the 1950s counterculture, who began to lend the neighbourhood a new character. During the following decade, the area became a kind of Midwestern equivalent of New York's Greenwich Village and San Francisco's Haight. The likes of Miles Davis and John Coltrane played (and recorded) at the now-defunct Plugged Nickel (1321 N Wells Street); just down the road sat Mother Blues (No.1305), a no less important music venue at the time. Folk singers also descended on the district, to the **Old Town School of Folk Music** (*see p220*) on Armitage Avenue and the Earl of Old Town pub at 1615 N Wells Street. Just opposite the latter, Mike Nichols' and Elaine May's **Second City** crew (*see p215*) went about defining modern sketch comedy after emerging from the ashes of the Compass Players troupe.

It couldn't last, and didn't. As has been the case with many such fashionable and forward-thinking neighbourhoods across the world, Old Town proved too attractive for its own good. As its reputation rose, so did the rents, and the hippies, beatniks and folkies were gradually forced to look elsewhere. The cutting-edge is conspicuous by its absence in what is now a relatively affluent and cultured part of town. Along Wells Street and Armitage Avenue sit a slew of smart restaurants and one of the city's longest string of boutiques. Still, some of the old raffishness remains in the **Old Town Ale House** (*see p133*), a glorious drinking hole that continues to draw a democratic mix of working stiffs, theatrical luvvies, rabble-rousing twentysomethings and hopeless old soaks.

Bona fide sights and attractions are largely absent from Old Town, but a wander around its confines is nonetheless an agreeable way to lose track of an afternoon. It remains a handsome place, nowhere more so than in the historic **Old Town Triangle**. Hemmed in by Wells Street to the east, North Avenue to the south and a vaguely diagonal line connecting the Lincoln Avenue/Wisconsin Street junction with the corner of North and Larrabee, this cosy district has retained many of its 19th-century cottages, built in the three decades after the Chicago Fire. It's easy to see why the locals are so proud of their neighbourhood.

One such street is **Crilly Court**, constructed by developer Daniel F Crilly in the middle of an entire block he purchased in the early 1880s. Between 1885 and 1893, Crilly built row houses on the west side of the block and four-storey apartment buildings on the east, carving the names of his four children above the doors. Some five decades later, son Edgar renovated the buildings, closing off the alleys to form a series of courtyards. The renovation was one of the first in the Old Town Triangle, and the younger Crilly is credited with leading the way in the historical preservation of the area.

Several homes near Crilly Court have their own historic significance. The residence at **216 W Menomonee Street** is believed to have been a 'fire relief cottage', built by the city following the Chicago Fire (at a cost of $75) to provide shelter for homeless residents. Just north are two other frame houses built in the 1870s for the Swiss-born Wacker brewing family. Frederick Wacker's son Charles, then a member of Chicago's planning commission and the man after whom Wacker Drive is named, lived in the carriage house at **1836 N Lincoln Park West**, while his father resided in the Swiss chalet-style residence at 1838. Down the street, the row houses at **1828-1834 N Lincoln Park West** were designed by Dankmar Adler and Louis Sullivan in 1884 and 1885. Displaying Sullivan's love of geometric ornamentation, they're rare examples of his early residential work.

One of the oldest buildings in Old Town is also one of its tallest. Built in 1869 on land donated by beer baron Michael Diversey, the Romanesque **St Michael's Church** (1633 N Cleveland Avenue, at W North Avenue, 1-312 642 2498, www.st-mikes.org) was partially gutted by the Chicago Fire, but rebuilt in next to no time by the Germans who worshipped in it. Local tradition dictates that if you can hear the ringing of the bells (the largest of which weighs an amazing 6,000lbs), you're in Old Town. The interior, open to the public, contains a carved wooden altar and stained-glass windows.

A few streets away sits the **Midwest Buddhist Temple** (435 W Menomonee Street, at N Hudson Avenue, 1-312 943 7801, www.midwestbuddhisttemple.org), a modernist structure built in the early 1970s by Japanese immigrants who began to settle in the area. The one-storey concrete base is topped by a pagoda-like roof; inside sits a sizeable gold Buddha. The congregation hosts an annual Ginza Holiday in the middle of August, celebrating Japanese culture, dance, music and food.

Heading east, it's hard to miss the enormous **Moody Church** (1609 N LaSalle Street, 1-312 327 8600, www.moodychurch.org), named after the 19th-century evangelist Dwight L Moody and completed in 1925. Directly beyond it is the southwestern corner of **Lincoln Park** (*see right*), and the excellent **Chicago History Museum** (*see below*).

★ Chicago History Museum

1601 N Clark Street, at W North Avenue (1-312 642 4600, www.chicagohistory.org). El: Brown, Purple to Sedgwick. **Open** 9.30am-4.30pm Mon-

Sat; noon-5pm Sun. **Admission** $14; $12 reductions; free under-12s. **Credit** AmEx, DC, Disc, MC, V. **Map** p311 H7.
Founded in 1852, the Chicago Historical Society is the city's oldest cultural institution. Permanent exhibitions include Facing Freedom, an examination of freedom in American history, and a collection of dioramas that demonstrate Chicago's evolution from a frontier outpost to a thriving city that hosted the World's Columbian Expo. There's also a vast collection of audio interviews, readings and musicals from Studs Terkel's tenure on WFMT Radio.

The temporary exhibitions are just as interesting and varied, taking in everything from Chicago sports memorabilia to local photography. The spruced-up building still houses a tastefully stocked gift shop; the selection of books, in particular, is impeccable. A programme of lectures, discussions and tours rounds things out nicely.

LINCOLN PARK

El: Brown or Purple to Armitage, Diversey or Fullerton; Red to Fullerton.

In the middle of the 19th century, the area around **Lincoln Park** contained little more than a smallpox hospital and a conveniently located cemetery. Today, it's one of Chicago's most desirable neighbourhoods, its popularity due in no small part to the picturesque, 1,200-acre lakefront space from which it takes its name. The park runs along Lake Michigan, from North Avenue (1600 N) up to Hollywood Avenue (5700 N) on the edge of Andersonville. The neighbourhood, however, extends only as far as Diversey Avenue (2800 N), running westwards all the way to the Chicago River.

The park

The same urban Utopian spirit that inspired the design for New York's Central Park made Lincoln Park a reality. Named after Abraham Lincoln in the wake of his 1865 assassination, the park was created on drained swampland (and the city's cemetery) over several decades. Not even the Chicago Fire put a stop to its construction, which continued into the 20th century with the addition of several of its most beloved institutions and the extension of the park far into northern Chicago. It's grown into one of the city's most cherished sites.

Lincoln Park is laced with paths that invite aimless strolling or unimpeded cycling (*see p244*), but also has facilities for other activities. There are playing fields and golf courses, tennis courts and chess tables; you can even rent a paddleboat on the South Pond, from a kiosk right by the historic **Café Brauer** (2021 N Stockton Drive, 1-312 742 2400). The park is

EXPLORE

EXPLORE

Lincoln Park.

undoubtedly at its best on weekdays during summer, when it's a relatively peaceful place. Even at weekends, though, it's not too hectic: its immense size and reach mean the crowds tend to spread out along its length.

When the city began work on the park in the 1860s, it decided to move all the bodies from the cemetery to other locations in the north of the city. Most went quietly, as one might expect dead people to go. However, the family of hotelier Ira Crouch went to court to prevent the city from shifting their beloved's corpse. Much to their surprise, and to the city's irritation, they won; as a result, the **Couch Mausoleum** stands near the junction of LaSalle and Clark Streets, not far from the world's oldest statue of the president who lends his name to the park.

The park's main attraction, and the one area that can get a little too busy in summer, is the **Lincoln Park Zoo** (*see below*), a small and much beloved operation located at around 2200 N (near Webster Avenue). Just north of the elephant house sits the **Alfred Caldwell Lily Pool**, built in 1889 and redesigned four decades later by the Prairie School architect whose name it bears.

Just north of the zoo's main entrance is the **Shakespeare Garden**, which contains a variety of flowers and plants mentioned in the Bard's plays. The garden also contains the Bates Fountain, a popular cooling destination in summer, and a bronze bust of the playwright that dates back to 1894; it's one of more than 20 sculptural monuments dating from the late 19th century, maintained with funds raised by an advocacy group (*see p67* **Bronze Age**).

The broad lawn leads to the **Lincoln Park Conservatory** (1-312 742 7736), a Victorian greenhouse erected in 1892. The four halls of the conservatory retain a variety of climates and allow plants from all over the world to flourish. The conservatory is open 9am-5pm daily, and admission is free. Just across from it is the **Notebaert Nature Museum**, which plays host to the Green City Market during the winter months.

FREE Lincoln Park Zoo
2200 N Cannon Drive, at W Webster Avenue (1-312 742 2000, www.lpzoo.org). El: Brown, Purple or Red to Fullerton. **Open** *Zoo buildings* Apr, May, Sept, Oct 10am-5pm daily. June-Aug 10am-5pm Mon-Fri; 10am-6.30pm Sat, Sun. Nov-Mar 10am-4.30pm daily. *Zoo grounds* Apr, May, Sept, Oct 7am-6pm daily. June-Aug 7am-6pm Mon-Fri; 7am-7pm Sat, Sun. Nov-Mar 7am-5pm daily. **Admission** free. **No credit cards.**
Map p312 H5.
Compared to its competitors, it's small. That said, there are few Chicagoan activities more enjoyable than strolling through Lincoln Park Zoo on a sunny

Bronze Age

Lincoln Park is awash with statues. Here are five of its finest.

ABRAHAM LINCOLN

The man after whom Lincoln Park is named is memorialised in it by *Standing Lincoln*, the work of Irish-American sculptor Augustus Saint-Gaudens. The figure, set on a plinth designed by Stanford White, was unveiled in 1885, two decades after Lincoln's death. Based in Vermont at the time, Saint-Gaudens used a local farmer named Langdon Morse as his model. Brits who think the statue looks familiar aren't dreaming – there's a replica in London's Parliament Square.
Location At the south end of the park, close to the Chicago History Museum.

JOHANN WOLFGANG VON GOETHE

The great German writer never visited Chicago before his death in 1832 at the ripe old age of 82. No matter. At the dawn of the 20th century, Chicago's community of German immigrants decided he deserved a tribute anyway. The competition to design the statue was won, appropriately, by a German, Herman Hahn, who cast Goethe in the form of a Greek god with an eagle on his knee above a plaque memorialising him as 'the mastermind of the German people'. Hahn presumably intended the figure to look heroic; through 21st-century eyes, though, he looks rather camp.
Location Near the intersection of Diversey Parkway and Stockton Drive.

ULYSSES S GRANT

Native of Galena, Illinois, Civil War hero and the 18th US president, Grant gets his tribute in the form of a suitably grand statue by Italian-American sculptor Louis Rebisso. Grant sits astride a horse, looking out across the park like he owns the place. In truth, he has a greater claim to Grant

Abraham Lincoln.

Park in the Loop, named after him and home to another dominating statue of this most dominating of men.
Location Cannon Drive, near the southern entrance to the park.

HANS CHRISTIAN ANDERSEN

Chicago's Swedish community have long been fairly prominent in the city, especially in Andersonville. Their Danish neighbours, though, are really only celebrated in the statue of their most famous storyteller. The seated bronze figure of Hans Christian Andersen in the park was created by John Gelert, an obscure sculptor better known for his monument to the police killed during the Haymarket Riots; it stands outside the Chicago Police Department HQ at 3510 S Michigan Avenue on the South Side.
Location Close to Café Brauer, around the 2000 block of N Cannon Drive.

GREENE VARDIMAN BLACK

As the inventor of a foot-powered dental drill and the first man to use nitrous oxide as a dental anaesthetic, Winchester, Illinois native Greene Vardiman Black (1836-1915) is widely regarded as the founding father of modern dentistry. Frederick C Hibbard's statue portrays him as a fairly severe-looking figure, but wisely omits any depictions of his presumably agonised patients.
Location At the intersection of North Avenue and Astor Street.

Ulysses S Grant.

EXPLORE

weekday afternoon. It opened in 1868 after the park was presented with two swans by New York's Central Park; nearly 150 years later, it's one of the oldest zoos in the country, its 35-acre site home to a thousand species.

The Kovler Lion House remains popular; so, too, does the Regenstein African Journey, which recreates an African landscape and houses a variety of species native to the continent. Another top draw is the Regenstein Center for African Apes. The zoo is a world leader in gorilla breeding, with more than 50 born here since 1970. Added in 2005, the Pritzker Family Children's Zoo features a recreated wooded environment, complete with beavers, wolves and bears. All told, it's an attractive place and it's a wonder it's still free: since 1995, it's been run not by the city but by the Lincoln Park Zoological Society, with two-thirds of its income coming from private sources.

Notebaert Nature Museum

2430 N Cannon Drive, at W Fullerton Avenue (1-773 755 5100, www.naturemuseum.org). El: Brown, Purple or Red to Fullerton. **Open** 9am-5pm Mon-Fri; 10am-5pm Sat, Sun. **Admission** $9; $6-$7 reductions; free under-3s & Illinois residents Thur. **Credit** AmEx, Disc, MC, V. **Map** p312 H5. Its location, along Lincoln Park's North Pond, is ideal. Its $31-million, 73,000sq ft building is grand. And the fanfare that greeted its opening in 1999 was enormous. Highlights in the museum include the Hands-On Habitat, which aims to teach kids about how animals live, and Birds of Chicago, a show of 100 Illinois bird specimens, some dating back to the 1900s. The temporary exhibitions also occasionally hit the mark. But the museum's main selling point is the Judy Istock Butterfly Haven, a glass-topped space populated by more than 75 species of butterfly. The most attractive parts of the museum are the outdoor pond and walkway through the artfully restored native prairie; these can be enjoyed for free, leaving the admission fee to be invested in a good lunch at North Pond (see p115), one of Chicago's finest eateries.

The neighbourhood

Lincoln Park began to take off as a residential neighbourhood in the late 1970s, after the Puerto Rican Young Lords turf gang that once rumbled around its streets began to disperse. These days, it's a sought-after address among the North Side's burgeoning population of youngish urban professionals and career-focused post-collegiates with money to burn. (This image of Lincoln Park locals has become something of a cliché, but is still grounded in truth.) As with Old Town, its neighbour to the south, Lincoln Park doesn't contain many sights per se, but it's no less appealing for that. Wide, tree-lined streets lead – if you're lucky –

to attractive corner bars and appealing shops, frequented by a mostly laid-back bunch.

The neighbourhood is anchored by **DePaul University**, the campus of which ebbs quietly out from around the intersection of Fullerton and Sheffield Avenues. The college connection is most obvious along the nearby stretches of Lincoln Avenue and Clark Street, dotted with sports bars and low-key party palaces that get flooded with people, and alcohol, on weekends. Armitage Avenue and Halsted Street are more easygoing alternatives.

Although Lincoln Park is more famous, fans of Chicago resident L Frank Baum will want to visit nearby **Oz Park** (see p188).

Over half of the buildings in Lincoln Park were built between 1880 and 1904. These days, there's a battle raging between preservationists, who want to hang on to the area's heritage, and developers, who'd prefer to tear parts of it down and start again. Quaint Victorian houses are increasingly having to fight for attention with giant new mansions, but they're winning the battle. One of the highlights is the **Francis J Dewes Mansion**, built at 503 W Wrightwood Avenue (at N Hampden Court) for a local beer baron in 1896.

Just west of the zoo (see p66) is the site of the infamous **St Valentine's Day Massacre**, where, on 14 February 1929, seven members of Bugs Moran's gang were executed against a garage wall by Al Capone's henchmen. Though Moran escaped (he'd overslept), the killings broke his resistance and cemented Capone's position at the forefront of Chicago's lucrative organised crime world. Film fans will have seen a fictional and comical version of the massacre at the beginning of Some Like it Hot. The garage, at 2122 N Clark Street, has since been replaced by a lawn. But the incident still resonates: the nearby **Chicago Pizza & Oven Grinder Company** (2121 N Clark Street, at W Dickens Avenue, 1-773 248 2570, www.chicagopizzaandovengrinder.com) tells the tale on its menus.

Several blocks north-west is the site of yet another fabled gangland killing: that of John Dillinger, a professional criminal who had escaped from police custody in Crown Point, Indiana, where he was awaiting trial for the murder of a cop. He'd been pinned as Public Enemy Number One by the FBI, who tracked him down to the **Biograph Theatre** (2433 N Lincoln Avenue, at W Fullerton Avenue) on 22 July 1934. As he left a screening of Manhattan Melodrama, police shot him dead; bystanders dipped their skirts and handkerchiefs in his blood as souvenirs. The Biograph closed as a cinema several years ago, but was recently taken over by the **Victory Gardens Theater** (see p238).

Lakeview & North

A jumble of communities compete for attention on Chicago's North Side.

The sight of 40,000 baseball fans cheering in unison, the sound of a drag queen's stiletto heels hitting the pavement, the smell of Italian, Swedish, Asian and Indian food wafting through the air, the touch of warm sand in your toes on a perfect beach day… Welcome to Lakeview, the undisputed hub of Chicago's North Side and a mecca for yuppies and guppies, swingers and singles, movers and shakers and so much more. If Lincoln Park presented a perfect snapshot of city life in the 1980s, Lakeview happily eclipsed it during the Clinton era.

But urban bliss doesn't come cheap. Many Lakeview denizens have flown the coop in the last decade, realising that lakefront living could be enjoyed at a significantly reduced price by moving north, and the area now lacks a little of the edge that it once had. Further north and west, Uptown, Edgewater, Andersonville and Ravenswood/Lincoln Square all merit attention if time allows.

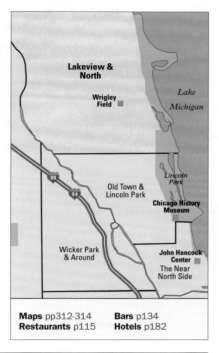

Lakeview & North

Wrigley Field

Lake Michigan

Old Town & Lincoln Park

Lincoln Park

Chicago History Museum

Wicker Park & Around

John Hancock Center

The Near North Side

Maps pp312-314   **Bars** p134
Restaurants p115   **Hotels** p182

EXPLORE

LAKEVIEW

El: Brown to Belmont, Southport or Wellington; Purple to Belmont or Wellington; Red to Addison or Belmont.

Lakeview is said to have taken its name from a hotel built in 1853 by James Rees and EE Hundley. Having completed the construction, the pair struggled to decide on a name until their friend Walter Newberry turned up to see the place. Impressed by the waterside vistas, Newberry suggested that they call it the Hotel Lake View. The name eventually carried over to the neighbourhood itself.

At the time Rees and Hundley were building, the area was countryside, farmed by European immigrants. Things changed in 1854, when cholera swept through Chicago and many locals

fled north to escape it. As there were no roads to the area from Chicago, Rees and Hundley laid down a plank thoroughfare. Lake View Plank Road, as it was plainly christened (it's since morphed into modern-day Broadway), spurred an immediate, dramatic expansion of the area.

During the following three decades, the now-incorporated Lakeview Township stretched as far north as Devon Avenue and all the way to Western Avenue in the west. In 1887, it lost its independence and was annexed by the city. The event led to the area shrinking, with its northern reaches having been absorbed into Andersonville, Edgewater, Buena Park, North Center, St Ben's, Lincoln Square and Uptown. Today, Lakeview is officially bordered by Diversey Parkway to the south, Irving Park Road to the north and Ashland Avenue to the west, with the lake as the eastern boundary.

EXPLORE

Cubs kit in Wrigleyville

In truth, Lakeview is a jumble of micro-neighbourhoods crammed into one. **Boystown** (*see p197*), the epicentre of gay life in Chicago, hugs the lakefront and stretches west to Clark Street where it turns into **Wrigleyville**, home of the Chicago Cubs and a seemingly infinite number of sports bars. Further west lies the charming **Southport Corridor**, a yuppified stretch of chic clothing shops and restaurants anchored by the historic Music Box Theater. Beyond it, **Roscoe Village** revels in self-satisfaction with its cosy Main Street feel.

For a time Lakeview had a hip cachet, and the punky shops around Belmont and Clark, such as the **Alley** (3228 N Clark Street, at W Belmont Avenue, 1-773 883 1800, www.thealley chicago.com), are testament to an edgier past. However, the district has since grown more affluent and less cutting-edge, and is nowadays visited mainly for its reliable restaurants, its baseball team and its lakefront. In summer, the park offers a multitude of activities (jogging, tennis) and inactivities (snoozing on the grass).

The hubs of Lakeview's culture, nightlife and commerce are the stretches of Clark, Halsted and Broadway Streets to the north and south of Belmont Avenue, home to an array of clothing stores, kitschy shops, and gay and straight bars and restaurants. Among the best are the **Unabridged Bookstore** (*see p147*) and **Uncle Fun** (*see p149*), which offers a selection of bizarre knick-knacks, kitsch and gag gifts.

Close at hand are two very different cinemas. The 1912 **Vic Theatre** is a former vaudeville house that stages touring rock acts alongside the rowdy Brew & View movie nights (*see p192*). Meanwhile, the more demure **Music Box** (*see p196*) is an over-the-top, Italian Renaissance-inspired spot. The main theatre, seating 750, uses trompe l'oeil paintings of garden walls to create the illusion of sitting in an outdoor courtyard, with a ceiling covered with stars and moving cloud formations.

Wrigleyville

Central Lakeview was changed forever in 1914 with the construction of **Wrigley Field** (*see p241*). On game days (the Cubs play here 81 times a year; more if they reach the play-offs), Lakeview morphs from a sedate, cultured enclave to a wild, beer-soaked bacchanal. Cubs culture rules near the junction of Clark and Addison: sports bars dominate the area. Even Boystown gets in on the act: the **North End** (3733 N Halsted Street, at W Bradley Place, 1-773 477 7999, www.thenorthendchicago.com) is a gay sports bar.

However, not every hangout around here focuses on baseball. Chief among the avoiders is the **Metro** (*see p220*), originally a Swedish community centre but now one of the country's favourite indie music venues. The adjoining **Smart Bar** (*see p210*) was a key centre in the emergence of both the industrial and house scenes. A few doors down sits the **Gingerman** (3740 N Clark Street, between W Waveland Avenue & W Grace Street, 1-773 549 2050), where the ambience is rather gentler than at the likes of **Murphy's Bleachers** (*see p135*).

Roscoe Village

West of Lakeview, around the junction of Roscoe and Damen, Roscoe Village is a handsome but slightly self-satisfied hideaway

Have a Field Day – and Night

Go for a Cubs game and stick around Wrigleyville for more food and fun.

Uncommon Ground.

11.30am Start your day with breakfast or lunch at Uncommon Ground (3800 N Clark Street, at W Grace Street, 1-773 929 3680, www.uncommonground.com). The primarily vegetarian menu is hearty, with everything from *huevos rancheros* in the morning to sweet potato fries with goat's cheese fondue later on. In line with the restaurant's boho vibe, bands play a few nights each month.

12.30pm Stop by comics and collectibles store Yesterday (1143 W Addison Street, at N Racine Avenue, 1-773 248 8087) and dust off old *Star Trek* toys, film posters, vinyl and even campaign buttons. If you're looking for something to sport on game day, find all the Cubs gear you can imagine at Wrigleyville Sports (959 W Addison Street, at N Sheffield Avenue, 1-773 883 2079, www.wrigleyvillesports.com), including onesies for fledgling Cubs fans.

1.20pm It's game time, but you don't necessarily need tickets to the field itself. Goose Island Wrigleyville (3535 N Clark Street, at W Addison Street, 1-773 832 9040, www.gooseisland.com) has 20 TVs and three projection screens. More interested in socialising than staring at a screen? Head west to ivy-covered Guthries Tavern (1300 W Addison Street, at N Lakewood Avenue, 1-773 477 2900) for a round of Battleship; the bar owns some 50 board games. Vines on Clark (3554 N Clark Street, at W Roscoe Street, 1-773 327 8572, www.vineswrigley.com) also hosts a trivia night on Thursdays and a weekly special on Fridays: half-price large pizzas and $5 'you call it' cocktails (non-game nights only).

5pm If you're looking to unwind after the game, tune out the stadium din at Moksha Yoga Center (3334 N Clark Street, at W Roscoe Street, 1-773 975 9642, www.mokshayoga.com), which offers classes every day of the week. Just imagine how Zen you'll feel walking out of a candlelit evening class while Cubs fans are roaring around the corner.

6pm Matsuya (3242 N Clark Street, at W School Street, 1-773 477 1652, www.chicagomatsuya.com) serves sushi until 11.30pm at weekends. And other than the occasional $15 'Windy City Roll', it's surprisingly cheap for fresh fish.

8pm The former stomping ground of Mike Myers and Amy Poehler, iO (3541 N Clark Street, at W Addison Street, 1-773 880 0199, www.ioimprov.com) presents some of the best improv in town with shows every night of the week. You can't go wrong with Wednesday faves TJ & Dave.

11pm Music rules at concert venue Metro (3730 N Clark Street, at W Grace Street, 1-773 549 4140, www.metrochicago.com) and its basement-level dance club, Smart Bar, which specialises in house, techno and electro. Swap your sports jersey for a scrubby shirt and you'll fit right in.

EXPLORE

Goose Island.

for soccer moms, newlyweds and other Chicagoans who can't afford to live in Lincoln Park. The area has generally stood apart from the nightlife loop, but a handful of new venues such as **Volo** wine bar (2008 W Roscoe Street, at N Damen Avenue, 1-773 348 4600, www. volorestaurant.com) have joined a smattering of funky shops in recent times. There's also great antiques shopping along Belmont Avenue, a few blocks south; and fabulous cakes at German-American bakery **Dinkel's** (3329 N Lincoln Avenue, at W Henderson Street, 1-773 281 7300, www.dinkels.com).

HEADING NORTH

El: various Red line stations north of Addison.

North of Lakeview sits **Uptown**, a district that's still finding its gritty way along the comeback trail. The dynamic of the area has changed in recent years with the arrival of exiled Lakeviewites in search of cheaper digs.

In the past, Uptown served as a playground for gangsters such as Al Capone, who appreciated the anonymity afforded by hanging out away from his native South Side in Jazz Age clubs such as the **Green Mill** (*see p226*). This fabulous old bar remains, as do other pensionable theatres: built in 1926 at a cost of $2 million, the once-spectacular, now-faded **Aragon Ballroom** (*see p218*) today serves as a rock venue, as does the slightly older, slightly smaller **Riviera Theatre** (*see p222*) and the **Annoyance Theatre** (*see p213*).

Further north, centred on N Clark Street and W Foster Avenue, sits **Andersonville**. In the past, Chicago's Swedish-American community

INSIDE TRACK
DEAD HANDSOME

At Lakeview's northern boundary sits the mighty **Graceland Cemetery** (4001 N Clark Street, at W Irving Park Road, 1-773 525 1105, www.gracelandcemetery.org), an 80-acre swatch of land purchased as a private cemetery in 1860 and designed by landscape architect Horace Cleveland. Many pillars of society are buried here, among them architects Daniel Burnham, Ludwig Mies van der Rohe, John Wellborn Root and Louis Sullivan, retail kingpin Marshall Field and railroad magnate John Pullman. But the cemetery is worth a stroll as much for its beauty as for its celebrity dead; Cleveland's landscaping prowess is almost unmatched.

called the area home; the community's story is told at the **Swedish American Museum Center** (*see p73*). But today, Andersonville is characterised more by its large gay community, which fled Boystown a decade ago in search of less ghettoised pastures. Stroll among the many furniture stores before grabbing a Belgian brew at the **Hopleaf** or a fine cup of java at the **Coffee Studio** (for both, *see p119*).

North of here but south of Evanston (*see p74*) lie some chiefly residential areas. Among them are **Rogers Park**, home to Loyola University and the unrelated but nonetheless educational **Leather Archives & Museum** (*see p73*), and **Edgewater**, complete with enviable lakefront and fine beaches.

Dinkel's.

EXPLORE

Leather Archives & Museum

*6418 N Greenview Avenue, at W Devon Avenue,
Rogers Park (1-773 761 9200, www.leather
archives.org). El: Red to Loyola.* **Open** 11am-
7pm Thur, Fri; 11am-5pm Sat, Sun. **Admission**
$10; $5 reductions. **Credit** AmEx, Disc, MC, V
Housed in a former synagogue, this museum is purportedly the only one in the US devoted to the
leather lifestyle. Visitors can thumb through 10,000
sex magazines and peruse leather whips, 19th-
century male chastity belts and common kitchen
tools used for sex play. The museum takes a serious
approach to preserving the history of leather as an
object of fetish.

Swedish American Museum Center

*5211 N Clark Street, at W Foster Street,
Andersonville (1-773 728 8111, www.samac.
org). El: Purple or Red to Berwyn.* **Open** 10am-
4pm Mon-Fri; 11am-4pm Sat, Sun. *Children's
Museum* 1-4pm Mon-Thur; 10am-4pm Fri; 11am-
4pm Sat, Sun. **Admission** $4; $3 reductions;
free under-1s & all 2nd Tue of mth. **Credit**
AmEx, Disc, MC, V.
The Museum Center enjoys healthy support in
Andersonville, an area long populated by Swedish
immigrants. The museum has gained a reputation
for its modern art exhibitions, which often feature
Swedish or Swedish-American artists working with
textiles. Classes in everything from cooking to the
Swedish language, plus screenings, round off this
excellent enterprise.

RAVENSWOOD & LINCOLN SQUARE

El: Brown to Damen or Western.

Occupying a fascinating cultural space
between Old World traditions and New World
trendiness, **Ravenswood** manages the neat
trick of being simultaneously quaint and hip.
Gentrification has arrived in this nook of the
city north-west of Roscoe Village, bringing
music and art schools, clothing and antiques
shops, and restaurants. Still, many of the
characteristics that people cherish about the
area, such as the park and the large library,
were here decades ago, back when Ravenswood
was the Germanic part of town. You can still
hear German spoken, though these days it
competes with Croatian and Spanish.

Newcomers to the area will tell you that they
live in **Lincoln Square**, although longtime
residents – like the two women who co-own the
marvellous **Café Selmarie** (4729 N Lincoln
Avenue, at W Lawrence Avenue, 1-773 989
5595, www.cafeselmarie.com) – prefer the old
title. Historically, the 'Lincoln Square' label was
reserved for a one-block prime business stretch
of Lincoln Avenue (between W Leland and

W Lawrence Avenues) in which Café Selmarie
sits dead centre, flanked by a pedestrian square.

A handful of old establishments still remain
on this stretch of Lincoln Avenue, each within
walking distance of the Western station on the
Brown line. The **Chicago Brauhaus** (No.4732,
1-773 784 4444, www.chicagobrauhaus.com),
dishes up classic German fare; it's open late
with music and dancing. However, while it was
established in 1875, the **Merz Apothecary**
(*see p163*) didn't move to the area until 1982.

The old warehouses along the Ravenswood
Avenue industrial corridor now contain some
of the city's hippest small businesses, many
around the intersection with W Montrose
Avenue (right by the Montrose station on the
Brown line). Among them are **Architectural
Artifacts** (4325 N Ravenswood Avenue, 1-773
348 0622, www.architecturalartifacts.com),
which boasts 80,000 square feet of vintage
treasures that run from old jukeboxes to
neoclassical columns; the **Lillstreet Art
Center** (4401 N Ravenswood Avenue, 1-773
769 4226, www.lillstreet.com), which contains
a gallery, a café (First Slice) and studio space;
and **Nadeau Imports** (4433 N Ravenswood
Avenue, 1-773 728 3497, www.nadeauimports.
com), which showcases bargain basement
hand-crafted wood furnishings at its giant
warehouse space.

Cultural venues dot the streets around
Lincoln Square. Housed in a former library, the
Old Town School of Folk Music (*see p220*)
retains two whimsical WPA-era murals, one of
them above the stage in the intimate concert
hall. The space is used for concerts and also
for more casual jam sessions, open to all. And
though it doesn't sport a fancy lit-up marquee,
the **Davis Theater** (*see p193*) remains a
treasure. How many other movie houses are
decorated with a framed poster of Bette Davis's
axe-wielding romp *The Anniversary*?

INSIDE TRACK PRETTY IN PINK

Ask a native Chicagoan where their
grandparents danced the night away,
and they might have a story or two about
the **Edgewater Beach Hotel** (5557 N
Sheridan Road, at W Bryn Mawr Avenue).
Built in 1916, the beachfront resort drew
a host of VIPs with its own private bathing
beach, tennis courts, two children's
playgrounds, nine-hole putting green
and variety of gardens. Most of the hotel
was demolished in the 1970s, but the
adjoining apartments (which date from
1928) remain a monstrous pink beacon
on the horizon.

EXPLORE

The North Shore

The affluent northern suburbs offer plenty of low-key diversions.

Beyond the northernmost reaches of the Red line, urban grit becomes a distant memory: the streets get a little wider and a lot quieter, and skyscrapers and taprooms are replaced by low-rise office blocks and innumerable churches. Towns such as Evanston may have more to offer residents than the few tourists who make the trek out to see them, but the North Shore is not without its attractions for visitors, including the sprawling Chicago Botanic Garden and the cultural draws of Northwestern University.

EXPLORE

EVANSTON

El: Purple to Davis.

The good-sized suburb of Evanston marks the southern end of the affluent region known as the North Shore. Bounded to the east by the lake, to the west by Skokie and to the south by Howard Street, the last stop on the Red line and the dividing line between Chicago and the North Shore, Evanston is best known as the home of **Northwestern University** (*see p75*). But thanks to a dedicated El line and decent civic amenities, it's surpassed its initial status as a mere dormitory community.

The immense mansions on Sheridan Road, along the lakefront, are among the North Shore's most handsome sights. But even inland, Evanston's streets are attractive, lined with old maples, oaks and elms thriving in the rich prairie soil amid wonderful public parks. Safe neighbourhoods, a handsome little downtown (centred on Church and Davis Street just east

of the lake), and scores of shops and eateries have all enhanced the town's desirability among those looking for a quieter life in the shadow of the big city.

While no one's likely to confuse Evanston's cultural scene with Chicago's, it's definitely a pretty decent alternative. The **Noyes Cultural Arts Center** (927 Noyes Street, at Maple Avenue, 1-847 448 8260, www.cityofevanston. org/arts-culture/noyes-cultural-arts-center) offers an array of cultural entertainments in the shape of theatrical performances and gallery exhibitions. And there's a surprising amount of live music going on here; *see p214* **The E-Town Shuffle**.

A handful of museums dot the town, all low-key affairs. The **Mitchell Museum of the American Indian** (*see below*) offers a scholarly survey of ancient American life, while the **Frances Willard House** (1730 Chicago Avenue, at Church Street, 1-847 328 7500, www.franceswillardhouse.org) pays tribute to one of the leading lights in the Temperance movement of the 19th century. It's open for tours ($10, $5 reductions) from 1pm to 4pm on the first and third Sundays of the month. Also here, and open to visitors for tours on weekends from June to September, is the **Grosse Point Lighthouse**, which was constructed in 1873 at the corner of Central Street and Sheridan Road (1-847 328 6961, www.grossepointlighthouse.net).

Mitchell Museum of the American Indian

3001 Central Street, Evanston (1-847 475 1030, www.mitchellmuseum.org). El: Purple to Central.

INSIDE TRACK SUNDAY BLUES

Evanston in the 19th century was a devout town, nicknamed **Heavenston** for the preponderance of Methodist churches. Legend has it that the ice-cream sundae was renamed in Evanston after local religious leaders objected to its original name, 'Sunday' (the dessert was reputedly invented to counteract a church ban on ice-cream sodas on the Sabbath).

Open 10am-5pm Tue, Wed, Fri, Sat; 10am-8pm Thur; noon-4pm Sun. Admission *Suggested donation* $5; $3 reductions. Credit MC, V.

An avid collector of Native American artefacts, John Mitchell founded this museum with his personal collection in 1977. Now housing more than 10,000 pieces, it features ceremonial dolls, beadwork, masks, carvings and Paleolithic-era tools from native peoples throughout the US and Canada.

Northwestern University

Since 1851, this highly selective, intellectually rigorous institution has earned a strong reputation for academic and sporting excellence. Northwestern's medical, law and business graduate schools rank as some of the most innovative in the world, and its performing and fine arts departments are deservedly respected.

The university's 240-acre campus lacks the gravitas of the University of Chicago in Hyde Park (*see p95*), but it's still a picturesque place. Unusually for a university, the campus was once considerably bigger than it is now, but the authorities were forced to sell off more than half its original 380-acre site due to financial difficulties. When the university grew in the middle of the 20th century, it needed some of this land back, but it had by then been developed into housing. The university's novel response was to expand eastwards by filling in a large chunk of Lake Michigan.

The campus, officially located at 2001 Sheridan Road (1-847 491 3741, www. northwestern.edu), is a pleasant place for a wander, its site dotted with a mix of buildings old and new. In the former category is University Hall (1897 Sheridan Road), a grand structure that was constructed in 1869 and is now the oldest remaining building on campus. In the latter is the 1975 Pick-Staiger Concert Hall (1977 S Campus Drive, on the Arts Circle, 1-847 467 4000), a combined classroom and performance facility. If it's a nice day, grab some lunch and head away to munch it in the becalmed Shakespeare Garden, perhaps via the Mary & Leigh Block Museum of Art (*see below*).

Big Ten football fans enthusiastically support the Northwestern Wildcats each autumn, if only to see the opposing teams run roughshod over the home field. Still, a festive air pervades the masses near the stadium, located on Central Avenue just west of the Purple line El stop.

FREE Mary & Leigh Block Museum of Art
Northwestern University, 40 Arts Circle Drive, Evanston (1-847 491 4000, www.blockmuseum.

northwestern.edu). El: Purple to Davis. Open 10am-5pm Tue; 10am-8pm Wed-Fri; noon-5pm Sat, Sun. Admission free. No credit cards.

The visual arts are celebrated at this multi-faceted university space, which encompasses four galleries and additional venues for screenings (*see p193*), concerts and symposia. The museum's extensive collection of works on paper includes prints, photographs and drawings spanning the 16th to the 20th centuries; exhibitions drawn from it are supplemented by interesting (if niche) temporary shows. The film programming is notable and worth the trip north as well.

FURTHER NORTH

Various stations.

Due west of Evanston sits the suburb of Skokie, a fairly unassuming part of the world that's home to the Illinois Holocaust Museum & Education Center (*see p76*). Immediately to the north of Evanston, Wilmette is best visited for the vast and amazing Bahá'í Temple House of Worship (*see p76*) or, on a more down-to-earth level, for a scrumptious apple pancake at the Walker Bros Original Pancake House (153 Green Bay Road, Wilmette, 1-847 251 6000, www.walkerbros.net). Glencoe is home to the Chicago Botanic Garden (*see p76*), which has been charming visitors for decades.

Two other North Shore spots come into their own in summer. During the warmer months, the century-old Ravinia Festival in Highland

EXPLORE

Mary & Leigh Block Museum of Art.

EXPLORE

Park (*see p231*) provides an outdoor home for fantastic classical performances, but also mixes in a variety of pop acts and always well received returning acts such as Lyle Lovett. Unlike many music festivals, the cheap seats are a big draw here, offering concertgoers a chance to spread out and picnic on the lawn (you're encouraged to bring your own food and drink). But if you want to see the musicians while you hear them, you'll need to pony up for the pavilion seats.

Further north sits **Six Flags Great America & Hurricane Harbor** (I-94/I-294 from Chicago, exit at Route 132, 1-847 249 4636, www.sixflags.com), a vast, loud and exhausting amusement park in the suburb of **Gurnee**. After a day at this thrillfest, most parents (and a fair few kids) come away sunburned, foot-weary and broke.

And still further north, not too far from the Wisconsin border at the town of **Zion**, sits **Illinois Beach State Park** (1-847 662 4811, www.dnr.state.il.us). Whether you choose overnight accommodation at a fully equipped inn or beachside camping, or just a day trip, it's not hard to take it easy at this clean and uncomplicated lakeside beach park that stretches for six miles and covers 4,000 acres. Nearby **Tempel Farms** (17000 Wadsworth Road, Wadsworth, 1-847 623 7272, www.tempelfarms.com) breeds Lipizzan horses, which give full dressage performances during the summer months.

★ FREE Bahá'í Temple House of Worship

100 Linden Avenue, at Sheridan Road, Wilmette (1-847 853 2300, www.bahai.us). El: Red, then Purple to Linden. **Open** *Auditorium* 6am-10pm daily. *Visitors' centre* 15 May-15 Sept 10am-8pm daily. 16 Sept-14 May 10am-5pm daily. **Admission** free.

No visit to the North Shore is complete without taking in this enormous whitewashed temple, which resembles nothing so much as the world's largest lemon squeezer. Inspiring prayer, devotion and countless photo ops – and visible for miles – this 164ft spiritual dome is magnificent when illuminated at night; its surrounding manicured garden adds to the beauty by day. It was completed in 1953 as a place of prayer and meditation for the Bahá'í faith, which advocates the 'oneness of God, the oneness of mankind and the oneness of religion'.

FREE Chicago Botanic Garden

1000 Lake Cook Road, at Hastings Avenue, Glencoe (1-847 835 5440, www.chicagobotanic. org). Metra: Glencoe. **Open** 8am-sunset daily. **Admission** free.

A variety of planting styles has delighted visitors to the Botanic Garden since 1972. The sprawling yet calm oasis is beautifully maintained, with trails that encourage walkers and cyclists to linger. Highlights include a walled English garden; the series of islands that make up the Japanese gardens; a 15-acre prairie; summertime concerts; and the Lenhardt Library, which houses thousands of horticulture titles, many extremely rare. There's also a pleasant restaurant, plus galleries that host rotating exhibitions of botanic-themed art. Note that although admission is free, parking costs $25 (reduced to $10 for seniors on Tuesdays); take the Metra to avoid the charges.

Illinois Holocaust Museum & Education Center

9603 Woods Drive, at Old Orchard Road, Skokie (1-847 677 4640, www.ilholocaustmuseum.org). El: Yellow to Skokie. **Open** 10am-5pm Tue, Wed, Fri; 10am-8pm Thur; 11am-4pm Sat, Sun. **Admission** $12; $6-$8 reductions; free under-5s. **Credit** AmEx, MC, V.

When a group of neo-Nazis planned to march in heavily Jewish Skokie in the 1970s, local Holocaust survivors banded together to create an educational group, the Holocaust Memorial Foundation of Illinois. After ten years of planning, the foundation opened a Stanley Tigerman-designed museum in April 2009. It houses more than 11,000 artefacts, some of which are on display in a 10,000sq ft main exhibit on the Holocaust and genocide.

Bahá'í Temple House of Worship.

The Near West Side

Art mixes with commerce in a global cultural stew.

The contrast between the rough and the new makes the Near West Side – loosely speaking, the streets due west of the Loop and due south of Ukrainian Village/West Town – one of the most dynamic areas of the city.

The area facing the greatest flux at present is the West Loop. The streets rattle with tough urban authenticity, courtesy of freeways carving their way above ground level and the rumble emanating from the Lake Street and Morgan El tracks, but they're also upscale, thanks to the frequent addition of swanky new bars and restaurants.

In an arc below the West Loop stand three neighbourhoods originally settled by immigrants: Greektown, Little Italy and Pilsen. Many of the original settlers have long since moved to the suburbs, but their replacements – some Latino, some upwardly mobile anglo – have given the area a dynamic new feel.

It's easy to explore the main streets of West Loop, Greektown, Little Italy and Pilsen on foot, and the commercial areas of each neighbourhood are increasingly busy with activity. But it's wise to keep your wits about you when venturing into the long stretches of no man's land that separate them.

| Map p314 | Bars p137 |
| Restaurants p120 | |

EXPLORE

THE WEST LOOP

El: Green or Pink to Ashland, Clinton or Morgan.

The Loop's western boundary is officially marked by the Chicago River. Unofficially, though, the area has come to extend several blocks further, as far as the twin transport hubs of **Ogilvie Transportation Centre** and **Union Station**. Trains serving both stations funnel commuters to and from the city each day; Union Station, a Beaux Arts-style building designed by Daniel Burnham, is by far the more handsome of the two.

The West Loop really begins beyond these two transport hubs, west of the Kennedy Expressway. For decades, these streets were an uninviting maze of warehouses and garment factories, but the last 15 years have seen them transformed into some of the hottest real estate in this post-industrial town, a development craze that encompasses both residential conversions and new businesses.

Along **Randolph Street** between Halsted and Racine Streets, a string of highly regarded restaurants compete for attention with bars, clubs and lounges. As they do so, old-line wholesalers such as the **Puckered Pickle Company** look on with bemusement and

Hellenic Museum & Cultural Center.

occasional irritation. Randolph also hosts a monthly antiques market between May and October, and a street festival in summer.

The **Fulton Market** area is also in flux, to say the least. During the day, the streets are full of trucks and men in white jackets working in the meatpacking industry and lunching at greasy diners. Come sundown, though, it's a nightlife hotspot with several clubs and some of the city's most talked-about fine dining establishments, such as **Publican** (*see p121*).

It's a similar story along **Lake Street** between Halsted and Morgan Streets, where meat and veg cash-and-carry outposts share the street with nightclubs and loft apartments. But, from the looks of it, the meat business is still in good shape. For a vision of the area's bone-hacking present, check out the **Peoria Packing Butcher Shop** (1300 W Lake Street, at N Elizabeth Street, 1-312 738 1800, www.peoriapacking.com), where piles of raw meat and pigs' feet are heaped in refrigerated rooms for the benefit of eager bargain hunters.

Before real estate prices spiralled, a colony of artists had discovered the West Loop; indeed, the current boom was partly brought about by their arrival and the kudos that came with it. A number of galleries remain in the district, clustered at Peoria and Washington, and in the Fulton Market area between Peoria and Racine (*see pp158-159*). There's also the sprawling **Harpo Studios** where *The Oprah Winfrey Show* used to tape.

About a mile west on Madison Street is the massive **United Center** (*see p242*). Home to the famous Chicago Bulls basketball team and the Chicago Blackhawks hockey team, it also welcomes big-time music acts and circuses (which sometimes amount to the same thing). The once-bleak blocks around the arena are sprouting with new development, but it's still not currently an area in which to linger.

GREEKTOWN

El: Blue to UIC-Halsted.

In the late 1970s, there were more than 125,000 Greeks in Chicago. It's a different story today, though you might not know it from a walk along Halsted Street from Monroe Street south to Van Buren Street – this stretch remains the Midwest's biggest Hellenic commercial area. Scattered between welcoming Greek restaurants is an eclectic array of shops selling everything from baklava and Greek pop music to candles and evil eye stones at the fabulously odd **Athenian Candle Company** (300 S Halsted Street, at W Jackson Street, 1-312 332 6988, www.atheniancandle.com). The **Hellenic Museum & Cultural Center** (*see below*) provides what remains of the community with an anchor.

On Adams Street, one block east of Halsted and across the freeway, sits the decidedly un-Greek **Old St Patrick's Church** (700 W Adams Street, at S Desplaines Street, 1-312 648 1021, www.oldstpats.org). Dating from 1856, it was one of the first churches in America built to serve Irish immigrants; having survived the Chicago Fire in 1871, it's also the oldest church building in the city. The interior is decorated with muted stained-glass windows and a mix of pagan and Christian symbols. Every summer, the church hosts the **World's Largest Block Party** (*see p25*).

Hellenic Museum & Cultural Center

333 S Halsted Street, between W Van Buren & W Jackson Street (1-312 655 1234, www. hellenicmuseum.org). El: Blue to UIC-Halsted. **Open** 10am-5pm Mon, Wed, Fri; 10am-8pm Thur; 11am-5pm Sat, Sun. **Admission** $10; $7-$8 reductions. **Credit** AmEx, MC, V. **Map** p314 F12.

This shrine to immigrant Greek culture derives many of its pieces from the collections of local Greek families, but it's not only of interest to those with Greek ancestry. The building opened at the end of 2011 with four storeys, 40,000 square feet and more than 17,000 artefacts. Recent exhibitions have covered topics ranging from the story of Greek independence to the Holocaust in Greece. Language and culture classes are open to the public.

UIC & AROUND

El: Blue to UIC-Halsted.

Stroll down Halsted Street south from Greektown and you'll soon find yourself surrounded by the brutalist architecture of the **University of Illinois at Chicago (UIC)** campus, built in the 1960s and an ever-expanding interruption to the historic neighbourhoods that surround it. The campus has been a controversial fixture since it was developed, and the passing years haven't calmed the ire of those who have long opposed it. The most contentious development in recent years has been the University Village project

of residential and retail development, in part because it's sparked further changes in the nearby Pilsen neighbourhood. Tucked away from all the fresh concrete is the **Jane Addams Hull-House Museum** (*see p80*).

A couple of blocks south of Hull-House lies the former site of **Maxwell Street Market**, where Jewish and other European merchants and traders in set up shop at the turn of the 20th century. During the Great Migration, southern blacks settled there and gave birth to the Chicago blues (*see below* **Migration Music**).

In the early 1990s, UIC got permission from Mayor Daley to raze the entire site, demolishing landmarks such as Nate's Deli (where Aretha Franklin bursts into song in *The Blues Brothers*) as the campus expanded. Bloodied but unbowed, the multi-ethnic market has since been forced to move twice; it's now on the stretch of Desplaines Street between Roosevelt and Harrison – just north, incidentally, of where Ms O'Leary's cow is reputed to have started the Great Chicago Fire. On Sundays from 7am to 3pm, you can find stalls selling everything from power tools to bootleg DVDs, plus a parade of Mexican food stands.

Migration Music

How Maxwell Street Market helped revolutionise the blues.

The Great Migration brought thousands of southern blacks to Chicago in the early 20th century. But this great movement of people would also lead to a musical revolution, as these Mississippi Delta migrants brought with them the blues.

The blues of the South was acoustic and country-style, but it found a large audience among the city's steel mills and meatpacking factories in the 1920s. Opportunities for the hustling musician were incredible, but other migrants struggled. As a result, the songs were often laments of the hard times that were endured by new arrivals in Chicago.

Blues music found a home in the city's 'black belt' of Bronzeville, but also in the immigrant-dominated Near West Side, and specifically on Maxwell Street's Sunday market day. Calling the area 'Jew Town', as it was dominated by stores owned by Jews arrived from Europe, blues musicians found that they could play to large audiences at the market and make some

decent money while they worked their way up to playing at the established clubs. After World War II, there were even fly-by-night record labels in Chicago that signed acts directly off Maxwell Street.

But the market also demanded something extra: volume. To be heard in the busy, bustling street, blues players realised they needed electric instruments, like the electric guitars made by Silvertone, and amplifiers. This new mode of performance required an alliance with the Jewish shopkeepers, who traded electricity for promoting their wares on the pavement.

In the 1940s, the louder guitar-and-amp set-ups came into vogue on Maxwell Street, in clubs and, eventually, recordings. By the '50s, Chicago's urban electrified take on the blues was in full bloom, with Muddy Waters, Little Walter, Bo Diddley and Howlin' Wolf all in their prime. It's doubtful it would have sounded quite the same without the influence of market forces.

EXPLORE

FREE **Jane Addams Hull-House Museum**
800 S Halsted Street, at W Polk Street (1-312 413 5353, www.uic.edu/jaddams/hull). El: Blue to UIC-Halsted. **Open** 10am-4pm Tue-Fri; noon-4pm Sun. **Admission** free. **Map** p314 F14.

After an 1888 visit to London's Toynbee Hall, a pioneering settlement house that provided social services for a working-class neighbourhood, a pair of young women named Jane Addams and Ellen Gates Starr returned to Chicago vowing to start something similar. A year later, Hull-House opened its doors. It began as a relatively small operation, but eventually expanded to include educational facilities, social assistance offices and the city's first swimming pool, public kitchen and gymnasium. One beneficiary of the music programme was a young Benny Goodman, who learned to play clarinet here.

The fame of Hull-House grew, inspiring other socially conscious people in the US just as Addams herself had been inspired by Toynbee Hall. She died in 1935, aged 74, but her work is commemorated in the two structures that remain of her 13-building

complex. In the original 1856 mansion (donated to Addams by Charles Hull, hence the name) sit displays of paintings that once hung at the settlement, pottery and tableware created at Addams' community art programme, and her desk. If you dial a number on your mobile phone at the house, you'll hear narratives on the collection. Next door is the dining hall, which now holds photographs, exhibits and a slide-show introduction to the American labour movement and the social problems faced by the West Side's immigrants. Enlightening and inspiring.

LITTLE ITALY

El: Blue to Polk or Racine; Pink to Polk.

Sauntering west from Halsted on Taylor Street will lead you into Little Italy. It's said that pizza first made its way from Naples to the US in this once-thriving district. However, like Greektown, it's a shadow of its formerly charismatic self, with the Italians who once lived here forced

---

EXPLORE

Neighbourhood Watch

Pilsen's many murals unite the community.

When Mexicans and Mexican Americans settled in the Pilsen neighbourhood in the 1960s, wall murals emerged as a powerful form of community expression. Influenced by the Mexican muralists of the 1910 Revolution, among them Diego Rivera and Jose Orozco, Pilsen's street painters advocated civil rights and praised the virtues of a united neighbourhood.

The landscape has altered dramatically since the 1960s. Most of the murals from the '60s and '70s have vanished, including many of the more politically charged works that bemoaned the Vietnam War and

Latino struggles. Fortunately, though, several artists from that generation are alive and well and still making murals, alongside a younger generation who've picked up the torch.

In 1994, a group headed by longtime muralist **Hector Duarte** painted a small mural entitled *Alto al desplazamiento* at 18th and Bishop Streets. In it, a claw reaches out from behind two Latino workers. The name of the mural loosely translates as 'Stop the gentrification', a sentiment still widely voiced today.

To the north of Damen station, **Juan Chavez**'s glass mosaic collage *Vida Simple* (Damen Avenue & Cullerton Street) depicts Pilsen residents atop a collage of buildings, plants and gesturing hands. The collage was co-commissioned by the Chicago Transit Authority and the city's Public Art Program.

Finally, **Francisco Mendoza**'s Orozco Community Academy mosaics (1645 W 18th Place, at S Paulina Street) include portraits of Mexican and Chicano people made from coloured bits of tile. Among them are Frida Kahlo stoically posing, and neighbourhood folk hitting the books at the library.

These are just three examples, but the area is full of them. Keep your eyes peeled as you wander through the area, and you may even see a muralist at work.

out by the construction of the Eisenhower Expressway or driven away by the the the creation of the UIC's Circle Campus. What remains is a nostalgia trip, but it's not an unenjoyable one.

Aside from the **National Italian American Sports Hall of Fame** (*see below*), the main attractions are culinary, with most of the action along Taylor Street between S Morgan Street and S Ashland Avenue. There are prime people-watching opportunities at the **Rosebud Café** (no.1500, 1-312 942 1117, www.rosebudrestaurants.com). Sandwiches and gourmet goods can be procured at the perennial **Conte di Savoia** deli (no.1438, 1-312 666 3471, www.contedisavoia.com). In summer, folk queue up for flavoured ices at **Mario's Italian Lemonade** (1068 W Taylor Street, at S Carpenter Street, no phone, closed Oct-Apr).

To the west, Little Italy has a maze of fascinating residential sidestreets that reward exploration. From Taylor, head north on Loomis to view the classic Chicago three-flats and stoops that line the street, then turn east on Lexington to enjoy the beautiful old homes that overlook **Arrigo Park**, a peaceful green that stands out amid the brick, stone and stucco.

South of Little Italy, one modern structure dominates amid a stretch of empty lots. The former **Illinois Regional Library for the Blind & Physically Handicapped** (1055 W Roosevelt Road) has been converted into a bank, but retains its 165-foot window and unique curving shape.

FREE National Italian American Sports Hall of Fame

1431 W Taylor Street, at S Bishop Street (1-312 226 5566, www.niashf.org). El: Blue to Racine. **Open** noon-4pm Mon-Sat; **Admission** $5; $3-$4 reductions. **Credit** AmEx, Disc, MC, V. **Map** p314 D14.

This Little Italy museum honours more than 200 sporting heroes with a collection that includes Mario Andretti's racing car and Rocky Marciano's championship belt. Piazza DiMaggio, a small plaza dedicated to every Italian American's favourite son, lies directly across the street and makes a convenient spot to sip an espresso from Conte di Savoia.

PILSEN

El: Blue or Pink to 18th.

Pilsen was originally settled in the 1800s by German, Czech, Polish and Yugoslavian immigrants drawn to work on the railroads. The neighbourhood's name is an echo of the Czech city of Plzen. In 1857, under orders from Mayor Wentworth, police forced Bohemians out of the Near North Side to join them. By the late 19th century, industrialisation and its

Garfield Park Conservatory. *See p82.*

concomitant social pressures had transformed the area into a hub of labour activism. But as immigrant quotas began to restrict the influx of southern and eastern Europeans in the 1920s, Pilsen's Mexican heritage took root.

Isolated to a degree by the Chicago River and railroad tracks, Pilsen is coming out of its shell. For decades, it's been a vibrant Latino cultural centre, home to the largest Mexican and Mexican-American community in the Midwest. But an influx of artists and students in recent years has brought change, and change has in turn brought strife. The conflict is not a simple matter of ethnicity; Muppies (Mexican yuppies) are among the gentrifiers. But the character of the area is shifting, and fast.

Pilsen's main commercial activity takes place on W 18th Street between S Racine Avenue and S Paulina Street, where street vendors abound and salsa music pours out of passing vehicles. Bilingual visitors can pick up Neruda in the original Spanish at **Libreria Girón** (2141 W 21st Street, at S Leavitt Street, 1-773 847 3000, www.gironbooks.com), and there's plenty of great food around here too.

A sizeable artistic community inhabits the blocks around the intersection of 18th and Halsted Streets; many artists rent from the Podmajersky family, which has supported creative entrepreneurs and historic preservation in the community for generations. Scenesters tend to congregate at **Skylark** (2149 S Halsted

Street, at W 21st Street, 1-312 948 5275, www. skylarkchicago.com), a boho bar with a fine beer selection, or blend in with the clubby and largely recycled decor at **Simone's** (960 W 18th Street, at Morgan Street; *see p137*).

Other notable buildings include the old **Schoenhofen Brewery** (W 18th Street & S Canalport Avenue), built in 1902 and a well preserved example of American architecture's movement away from revivalist styles. Designed by Richard E Schmidt and Hugh Garden, disciples of Frank Lloyd Wright, it sits on an artesian spring-fed well that's some 1,600 feet deep, and could conceivably brew again in the future. A few blocks away, the **National Museum of Mexican Art** (*see below*) provides Pilsen with a cultural focus.

It's an easy walk from the north to Pilsen, albeit a slightly grim one, but the area's southern edge is blocked off by the Chicago River and an array of shipping, storage and trucking facilities. The area is served by the El but it's notoriously hard to hail a cab out of Pilsen at night, so be sure to bring a taxi company number with you.

★ FREE **National Museum of Mexican Art**
1852 W 19th Street, at S Damen Avenue (1-312 738 1503, www.nationalmuseumof mexicanart.org). El: Blue or Pink to 18th Street. **Open** 10am-5pm Tue-Sun. **Admission** free.
This Pilsen staple remains one of Chicago's most enjoyable community museums, featuring art, religious artefacts and other ephemera. Several of the galleries are given over to temporary exhibits, such as a recent display of LA artist Chaz Bojorquez's street art or a collection by John Valdez featuring pastel depictions of the people and places of Southern California. All the exhibits come with informative and engaging captions in English and Spanish.

Call ahead for details of music, dance and other performances, especially if you're here during the annual Day of the Dead festival (*see p28*). Open all year, the crafts-packed Tienda Tzintzuntzan gift shop is one of the best museum stores in town.

EAST GARFIELD PARK

El: Green to Conservatory–Central Park Drive.

Precious little of note surrounds the district of East Garfield Park, isolated between the rapidly smartening West Loop and Oak Park. For visitors, it merits inclusion for the wonderful **Garfield Park Conservatory** (*see below*), safely accessible from its own El station. But otherwise, the area is best avoided: it's sketchy in places and downright unsafe in others.

★ FREE **Garfield Park Conservatory**
300 N Central Park Avenue, at Fulton Boulevard (1-312 746 5100, www.garfieldconservatory.org). El: Green to Conservatory/Central Park. **Open** 9am-5pm Mon, Tue, Thur-Sun; 9am-8pm Wed. **Admission** free.
The Garfield Park Conservatory was described as 'landscape art under glass' when it opened in 1908. Its contents are certainly impressive, but the architecture itself is notable too. Between the building's haystack shape and walls of stratified stonework, landscape architect Jens Jensen considered the Fern Room, with its 'prairie waterfall' to be one of his greatest achievements.

Inside, roughly 120,000 plants representing some 600 species occupy the conservatory's 1.6 acres; four times a year, flower shows herald the change in seasons. Among the various display houses are Sugar from the Sun, an exhibit on photosynthesis, which is explored through living displays (plenty of plants but a scant few text panels), and the Desert House, featuring cacti and succulents. *Photo p81.*

Czech Move

Pilsen's Bohemian past proves hard to shift.

It's easy to forget that Pilsen was founded by the Irish and Germans and then settled by Bohemian and Czech immigrants. After all, their descendants moved on a long time ago. But on 20 April 1857, migration to Pilsen was encouraged – with a billy club – when Chicago Mayor Wentworth led the 'Battle of the Sands', sending police in to the Near North Side to boot poor Bohemian families out. The Bohemians duly left, but thrived in their new home. By 1910, Pilsen had become the largest Bohemian community in the US, but it

also welcomed almost 30 European ethnic groups. The neighbourhood is now dominated by Mexican-Americans and other Latino immigrants, but a few buildings remain that illuminate the Pilsen of the past. The handsome and historic **APO Building** (1438 W 18th Street, at S Laflin Street) was a community centre for the Czech population. Today, in a sign of the changing make-up of the district, it houses the art gallery **La Casa de la Cultura Carlos Cortez** and hosts an unsuitably lively Día de los Muertos event around Halloween.

EXPLORE

Wicker Park & Around

Join the smart set in Chicago's neighbourhood du jour.

There's a downside to being cool: everyone wants a piece of you. In the 1960s, Wicker Park was one of Chicago's most notoriously unapproachable neighbourhoods. Half a century later, it's an extremely fashionable address for those wanting a faintly edgy backdrop to their property investment. Settled mainly by waves of Eastern European immigrants, Bucktown and Ukrainian Village continue to lend the area a distinctly Slavic feel. But they, too, have officially reached a state of post-gentrification.

The borders of the neighbourhoods are far from rigid. Beginning where Milwaukee Avenue meets the Kennedy Expressway, the Milwaukee Avenue corridor trails Chicago Avenue west to Western Avenue, and then follows Milwaukee north until around Armitage. The portion south of Division Street is known as West Town, and contained within the area is Ukrainian Village. Above it, bordered roughly by Division Street and Western, Ashland and Bloomingdale Avenues, is Wicker Park. And north of Wicker Park and up to Fullerton Avenue is Bucktown.

Map p315   **Bars** p137
Restaurants p125   **Hotels** p182

UKRAINIAN VILLAGE & WEST TOWN

El: Blue to Chicago or Division.

Eastern European immigrants first moved to the area now known as **Ukrainian Village** in the years after the Chicago Fire of 1871, with Ukrainians and Russians in particular developing healthy communities in the neighbourhood. Many of the area's Eastern Europeans began to resettle in the suburbs during the rapid urban expansion of the 1950s and '60s. However, a noteworthy population continues to make its homes in the area, which remains one of the city's largest east Slavic population bubbles. The Ukrainians have since been joined by Puerto Ricans and Mexicans, who first came to the streets between here and Wicker Park seeking solid blue-collar work in the then-thriving apparel industry. Many arrived too late: the jobs had begun to move overseas, and the area became something of a vacuum. But the Spanish-language billboards that dot the streets speak of a Puerto Rican and Mexican influence that still holds steady in this part of town.

Any tour of the area should begin at the south-west corner of Milwaukee Avenue and Augusta Boulevard, where you'll find the **Polish Roman Catholic Union of America**. The building is the home of the

INSIDE TRACK
RENEGADE CRAFT FAIR

The Renegade Craft Fair (www.renegade craft.com), a gathering of hundreds of craftspeople and artists from all around North America, takes place each September along Division Street. It's an inspiring place if you're in the market for handmade courier bags, silkscreen art, stuffed toys, stationery and knitted versions of just about anything.

oldest Polish fraternal organisation in the US, established in 1873; Vincent Barzynski, one of its founders, was a vital figure in the development of Chicago's Polish community. It's now home to the **Polish Museum of America** (*see p85*); established in 1935 and opened two years later, it's the country's oldest ethnic museum.

A block to the west and north stands the **Northwestern University Settlement House** (1400 W Augusta Boulevard, at N Noble Street), home base of the organisation founded by sociologist Charles Zeublin. A lesser-known cousin of Hull-House (*see p80*), it played a major role in the development of American social services. The building was designed by architect Irving K Pond, who earned a name for himself as a developer of settlement houses; it still houses several social service organisations.

To the north-west, the three-way intersection of Milwaukee, Division and Ashland marks the **Polonia Triangle**, known throughout the city's history as Polish Downtown and the one-time heart of Polish Chicago. On the west side of the corner sits a fountain dedicated to writer Nelson Algren, who lived in the area. Just to the east, at **1520 W Division Street**, is a large grey building that once housed the Polish National Alliance, the largest fraternal Polish organisation in the country.

On the corner of Evergreen and Noble stands the gigantic **St Stanislaus Kostka** (1351 W Evergreen Avenue, at N Noble Street, 1-773 278 2470, www.sanctuaryofthedivinemercy.org), completed in 1881 and home to Chicago's first Polish-Catholic congregation. Modelled after a church in Krakow, St Stanislaus boasted one of the largest congregations in the US – close to 5,000 families – at the turn of the 20th century. The church was dedicated and served by Barzynski until his death in 1899.

One block north of the church runs **Blackhawk Street**, which will take you back to Ashland. Though redevelopment has reared its ugly head, a few pre-20th century

homes remain, built at the height of the area's economic prosperity. The oldest homes are easily distinguished by the fact that they were constructed below sidewalk level, an oddity resulting from an 1850 decision by the city to raise sidewalks to facilitate better drainage.

The heart of Ukrainian Village, though, is further west. At the south-west corner of Haddon and Leavitt stands the **Holy Trinity Orthodox Cathedral** (1121 N Leavitt Street, at W Haddon Street, 1-773 486 6064, www.holytrinitycathedral.net), the first Orthodox/Greek Rite church to drop anchor in the community. Founded in 1892 by Carpatho-Ukrainian immigrants as St Vladimir's Russian Orthodox Church, it was redesigned by Louis Sullivan to resemble a Slavic church, with Tsar Nicholas II donating $4,000 towards the construction. The new church was consecrated in 1903 and was designated a cathedral by the Russian Orthodox Church two decades later. Added to the National Register of Historic Places over 30 years ago, it's open to visitors by appointment only.

A couple of blocks away, on the north-eastern corner of Oakley and Cortez, is **St Volodymyr Ukrainian Orthodox Cathedral** (2238 W Cortez Street, at N Oakley Avenue, 1-773 278 2827). Built in 1911, it marks the proper entrance to Ukrainian Village, and was the first religious institution formed by local Ukrainians in the area.

From here, head south on Oakley until you come to Rice Street. You can't miss the huge, Byzantine-styled **St Nicholas Ukrainian Catholic Cathedral** (835 N Oakley Avenue at Rice Street, 1-773 276 4537, www.stnicholas chicago.org), modelled after the Basilica of St Sophia in Kiev. Completed in 1915, it was founded by Uniate Catholics, who hailed from Galicia (on the border between Poland and Ukraine) and Carpatho-Ukraine. The interior is among Chicago's most elaborate, with ornate paintings, an enormous Greek chandelier and carpentry dominating the interior cupolas and imparting a distinctive Byzantine flavour. Call ahead to look around or show up for a service.

St Nicholas was the community centre for Ukrainians until 1968, when a split in the parish over the use of the Gregorian and Julian calendars divided the congregation and sent many to the **Sts Volodymyr & Olha Church** (2245 W Superior Street, at N Oakley Avenue, 1-312 829 5209, www.stsvo.org). The church is a modern Byzantine edifice with golden cupolas and a gigantic mosaic depicting the conversion of the Ukraine to Christianity in AD 988 by St Volodymyr. It's also a piece of living history: the Eastern Rites are still conducted here in Ukrainian. The **Ukrainian Institute of Modern Art** (*see p85*) is a block north.

St Nicholas Ukrainian Catholic Cathedral.

happy to explain the community's history and recommend one of the many Polish restaurants in Little Warsaw, further up Milwaukee Avenue.

FREE Ukrainian Institute of Modern Art

2320 W Chicago Avenue, at N Oakley Avenue (1-773 227 5522, www.uima-chicago.org). Bus: 66. **Open** *noon-4pm Wed-Sun.* **Admission** *free.* **Credit** *AmEx, Disc, MC, V.* **Map** *p315 A9.*

As its name suggests, this operation is devoted to modern and contemporary art by Ukrainian artists. One of the city's better-kept secrets, the not-for-profit organisation has a small permanent collection, which usually takes second billing to notable temporary shows on topics such as graphics and war art.

Ukrainian National Museum

2249 W Superior Street, at N Oakley Avenue (1-312 421 8020, www.ukrainiannationalmuseum. org). Bus: 49, X49, 66. **Open** *11am-4pm Thur-Sun.* **Admission** *suggested donation* $5; free under-12s. **Credit** *MC, V.*

Located in the heart of Ukrainian Village, this sweet little museum houses traditional clothing, musical instruments, agricultural tools and folk art from the Eastern European nation. A library houses some 16,000 books and periodicals, and cultural archives.

WICKER PARK & BUCKTOWN

El: Blue to Damen, Division or Western.

In centuries gone by, the main artery of Wicker Park was the road which is now known as **Milwaukee Avenue**. The route was first worn into a pathway by several tribes of Native

From here, wander east along Chicago Avenue, past an array of authentic Ukrainian and Russian businesses, towards the south-east corner of the neighbourhood. At Chicago and Ashland stands the **Goldblatt Bros** building (1609 W Chicago Avenue, at N Ashland Avenue), established as a discount department store in 1914 by two sons of Polish immigrants. From this store, Maurice and Nathan built an impressive empire that stretched to more than 40 locations by the 1970s. After years of neglect and requests from locals to spare it from demolition, the restored building now houses city workers and occasional art exhibits.

Polish Museum of America

984 N Milwaukee Avenue, at W Augusta Boulevard (1-773 384 3352, www.polish museumofamerica.org). El: Blue to Chicago. **Open** *11am-4pm Mon-Wed, Fri-Sun.* **Admission** $7; $5-$6 reductions. **Credit** *AmEx, Disc, MC, V.* **Map** *p315 D9.*

While it does a fine job of explaining the history of the city's Polish settlers, the Polish Museum of America has a colourful history in its own right. The museum opened in 1937, but its collection expanded dramatically when exhibits sent by the Polish government to New York for the 1939 World's Fair became stuck in the US after Poland was invaded. The museum purchased many of the artefacts for its archives, which grew even more when Ignacy Paderewski, noted Polish pianist and the first prime minister of a free Poland, left many personal effects to the museum in 1941. Paderewski was exiled to the US when war broke out; a plaque recognising his contribution to the city stands at the entrance of Wicker Park.

These days, the dark, dusty museum complements its permanent collection with temporary shows, most of which feature odds and ends from Chicago's Polish community. Staff are only too

---

INSIDE TRACK
PUERTO RICAN CHICAGO

The spiritual heart of Puerto Rican Chicago is not hard to find: just look for the steel Puerto Rican flag that hangs over Division Street as it heads into the neighbourhood of Humboldt Park (close to the intersection with Western Avenue). The park explodes with colourful activity in June when Puerto Ricans celebrate their heritage for six days straight. The festival roughly coincides with the feast of the patron saint of San Juan, but it has a pan-Latin appeal, attracting Dominicans, Cubans and just about anyone who enjoys salsa music in the outdoors. The musical offerings on the outdoor stages tend towards the tropical but also include Latin house DJs, reggaeton acts and plenty more besides.

EXPLORE

Americans, who used it to gain access to the game-rich outer prairies. In the mid 19th century, the area became home to industry of various stripes: first a major steelworks near Ashland and Armitage, and later an array of clothing, furniture, musical instrument and cigar manufacturers, plus a fair few breweries.

At roughly the same time that Ukrainians and Russians were moving into West Town and what became known as Ukrainian Village, the neighbourhoods to the north were also settled by immigrant communities. German immigrants, unwelcome in Anglo lakeside Chicago, built stately houses in the area around the plot of recreational land known as **Wicker Park**; directly north of there, the Poles moved into **Bucktown**. Paved after the Chicago Fire, Milwaukee Avenue (and, later, the Metropolitan West Side Elevated Railroad) connected these new European settlements with downtown.

Artists and musicians began to move to the area during the 1980s, often displacing residents even poorer than themselves. The seeds they planted for a Greenwich Village-style bohemian enclave blossomed into a vibrant music and arts scene in the '90s. But, as is usually the case with such ground-up cultural regeneration, the 'hood has since gone dramatically upscale, making it even more of a destination than ever.

Wicker Park and Bucktown are still hip, but they're also now affluent and commercial. Luxury condos house young professionals, and strollers, joggers and dog-walkers lend the district a gentrified feel. Damen, Division and Milwaukee Avenues are lined with high-end boutiques and concept bars scattered among the established outposts of bohemia – record shops, cafés and vintage stores. The creative classes still live here, and come to play here too, but there's a sense that the funky frontier lies elsewhere: in Pilsen, perhaps, or Logan Square.

Wicker Park

From the Goldblatt Bros building (*see p85*), wander north up Ashland and then north-west up Milwaukee towards the bewildering '**Six Corners**' intersection of Milwaukee, North and Damen. This is the beating heart of the Wicker Park neighbourhood, but also the junction at which the local gentrification is at its most pronounced. A liver-boggling number of clubs, bars and restaurants sit within a stone's throw.

And yet for all the moneyed development that's swept the area in the last half-decade or so, many iconic old buildings still remain – relics from previous periods of prosperity but also, at the same time, veterans of intermittent depressions and recessions. Perhaps chief

Get Your Kicks on the 606

An old rail line is being transformed into an elevated public trail.

The Bloomingdale Trail project, which has been talked about for more than a decade, finally has a name: the 606, as in the first three digits of all Chicago zip codes. Construction to turn the former rail line into a 2.7-mile elevated trail (much like New York's High Line) began in summer 2013, and the first phase is due to open in late 2014. While it will still be known as the Bloomingdale Trail, the overall project is now the 606 (www.the606.org).

The numeric designation is the brainchild of Matt Gordon, who has one of those jobs you didn't know was a job: director of naming and writing in the Chicago office of the creative agency Landor Associates. 'Through his naming work,' Gordon's bio says, 'he develops compelling names that help brands articulate their positioning to prospects, customers, employees and shareholders.' He has done work for Charles Schwab, Coors, FedEx, Microsoft and Frito-Lay. Corn chips, a new Chicago park – same difference. Gordon's ultimate

goal was to generate a name generic enough to appeal to all potential donors.

But enough with the name. The great news is that the 606 will create elevated paths for biking, running, art installations and environmental designs. It will also bring two new parks and improve the existing green spaces along Bloomingdale Avenue, and connect Bucktown, Wicker Park, Logan Square and Humboldt Park.

Northwest Tower.

actually donated by Mary L Stewart in 1870, but Charles Wicker is nevertheless commemorated by a life-size bronze statue. The figure was dedicated in 2006 and depicts the businessman, politician and developer wielding a broom, which evidently was his habit. Community activists have noticed that the statue's placement coincided with the emergence of a more sanitised neighbourhood, but few bemoan the loss of the crack dealers who once made this a dangerous corner of the city. Today, you're more likely to encounter farmers' markets and tasteful gardens.

The literary-minded should walk one block south of the park to **Evergreen Avenue**, aka Nelson Algren Honorary Boulevard. Algren, author of *The Man with the Golden Arm* and one of Chicago's most accomplished writers, lived at no.1958 from 1959 to 1975. The city erected a Historical Wicker Park monument to help the curious locate the house; a plaque commemorates his residency. Further south on Damen (at Division Street) is the **Rainbo Club** (*see p139*), formerly favoured by Algren but now a popular haunt for local hipsters.

Beer Baron Row.

EXPLORE

among these landmarks is the **Northwest Tower** (at the corner of Milwaukee and North Avenues), a 12-storey art deco building that was completed just before the Depression in 1929 by the architectural firm Holabird & Root. The one-time centre of Wicker Park's business activity, it was lying virtually empty by 1970, but a restoration plan in 1984 again filled the building with offices and businesses. Across the street from the Northwest Tower stands the two-block-long, three-storey **Flat Iron Building** (1579 Milwaukee Avenue, at W North Avenue), a less venerable structure than its neighbour and largely occupied by young artists. South of the Milwaukee–Damen–North intersection, things get a little quieter. For a glimpse into Wicker Park's history, wander along **W Pierce Avenue**, lined with large homes built by earlier German and Polish residents. The **Gingerbread House** (no.2137) was constructed in 1888 by Herman Weinhardt; across the street stands the **Paderewski House** (no.2138), built two years earlier and since renamed after the Polish pianist who once entertained a crowd from the verandah of the property. And at **no.2141** stands a house adorned with an Orthodox cross on top. Built in the late 19th century, it was once the home of the archbishop of the Russian Orthodox Holy Virgin Protection Church. There are more handsome old mansions on nearby Hoyne Avenue between Pierce and Schiller: known as **Beer Baron Row**, it was once a retreat for Chicago's prosperous brewers.

Further south along Damen Avenue, you'll find the plot of land that gives the area its name. Although it's named after German Protestants Charles and Joel Wicker, **Wicker Park** was

INSIDE TRACK BEER BARONS

German beer barons built ostentatious mansions in Wicker Park in the 1860s on what was then known as Ewing Place; some survive today along Hoyne and Pierce Avenues, an area known as Beer Baron Row. But the existence of the mansions begs the question: what happened to Chicago brewing? In short, the Chicago Fire. After the Chicago Brewery burned to the ground in 1871, Milwaukee's already robust brewing industry suddenly had a monopoly, and Wisconsin-based brewers such as Schlitz immediately increased their market share in the city. However, the city does once again boast a handful of decent breweries (*see pp129-142*).

Oak Park

Head west for Hemingway and Wright, the stars of the suburbs.

Travelling west on the Green line, you'll pass by some of the city's most deprived areas once you've crossed the Chicago River. From the window of the El train, you'll see abandoned public housing, empty warehouses, boarded-up storefronts and trash-littered vacant lots. But towards the end of the line, it's another story.

The first town over the city limits as you head west from downtown, Oak Park is one of Chicago's oldest suburbs, and one of its most handsome. The village grew up in the years following the Great Fire of Chicago and still feels slightly old-fashioned. Yet it's more than just a cute suburb. Oak Park doesn't work hard to please visitors, but it's a worthy diversion all the same.

EXPLORE

AROUND OAK PARK

El: Green to Harlem, Oak Park or Ridgeland.

Three Green line El stops serve the suburb of Oak Park, with the line itself following the east–west route of Lake Street. Ridgeland station lies at its eastern extremity, while Harlem/Lake station in downtown Oak Park is at the end of the line. Aside from the kid-oriented **Wonder Works** (*see p187*), and a smattering of shops along Harrison Street close to the junction of Ridgeland Avenue (very close to the Austin stop on the Blue line, but also an easy walk from the Ridgeland Green line station), there's not much east of Oak Park Avenue. So, to cover the most interesting parts of the town, get off at the Oak Park station and carve an anti-clockwise loop, heading north, west and south.

INSIDE TRACK VAL'S HALLA

Record stores are closing down all across the US, but **Val's Halla** (239 Harrison Street, 1-708 524 1004, www.vals hallarecords.com) remains something of an Oak Park legend. Although the store has only been on this site since 2006, Val Camilleti has been running it since 1972 and remains the consummate record-shop host.

Emerge from the train at Oak Park station and you'll be within a stone's throw of the intersection of Oak Park Avenue and Lake Street, the heart of the area's commercial activity. There are a few shops south of here on Oak Park Avenue. **Oak Park Records** (179 S Oak Park Avenue), for instance, is one of a dying breed of neighbourhood record stores. But most of the action is a touch further north. Among the bijou stores are olive-oil specialist **Olive & Well** (1-708 848 4230, www.oliveand well.com) and the family-friendly **Magic Tree Bookstore** (141 N Oak Park Avenue, 1-708 848 0770, www.magictreebooks.com).

Further north along Oak Park Avenue are the **Ernest Hemingway Birthplace & Museum** (*see p89*), a pair of buildings dedicated to one of the two famous residents to whom Oak Park owes much of its tourist appeal. Just opposite, at 211 N Oak Avenue, is a bistro apparently named after the author, but oddly spelled with two 'M's.

If you head north from here, then west on Chicago Avenue, you'll find evidence of the area's other most famous son: Frank Lloyd Wright, who got his start in Oak Park and built 25 homes around the junction of Chicago and Forest Avenues. For more on Wright, *see p90* **Profile**. After you've explored the Wright stuff, tuck into a sundae at the historic **Petersen's Ice Cream Parlor** (1100 Chicago Avenue, 1-708 386 6131, www.petersenicecream.com).

Turning left from Chicago on to Harlem Avenue will lead you towards further evidence of Oak Park's independent mindset, with a number of small, thriving local shops and even the family-owned **Lake Theatre** (1022 Lake Street, 1-708 848 9088, www.classic cinemas.com), which books art films as well as Hollywood blockbusters. From here, at the intersection of Harlem and Lake, you can catch the Green line train back to Chicago.

Ernest Hemingway Birthplace & Museum

Birthplace *339 N Oak Park Avenue, between Erie Street & Superior Street.* **Museum** *200 N Oak Park Avenue, between Ontario Street & Erie Street (1-708 848 2222, www.ehfop.org). El: Green to Oak Park.* **Both Open** 1-5pm Mon-Fri, Sun; 10am-5pm Sat. **Admission** $10; $8 reductions; free under-5s. **Credit** AmEx, Disc, MC, V.

Looked after by the Hemingway Foundation, the house where Ernie emerged has been open to the public for years. The displays include photographs, furnishings, memorabilia and the like. A museum two blocks away continues the theme with videos, books, posters and other Ernestabilia. All very well and good, of course, but the fact that Hemingway despised Oak Park, leaving as soon as he could (aged 18, for Kansas City, Missouri, and a job on a newspaper) and memorably referring to it as a place of 'wide lawns and narrow minds', is skimmed over.

Frank Lloyd Wright Home & Studio

951 Chicago Avenue, between N Forest Avenue & Woodbine Avenue, Oak Park (1-312 994 4000, www.wrightplus.org). El: Green to Oak Park. **Open** *Tours* (45-60mins) 11am, 1pm, 3pm Mon-Fri; every 20mins, 11am-3.30pm Sat, Sun. **Admission** $15; $10-$12 reductions; free under-3s. **Credit** AmEx, Disc, MC, V.

See p90 **Profile**.

Oak Park Conservatory

615 Garfield Street, between S Clarence & S East Avenues (1-708 725 2400, www.oakpark conservatory.org). El: Green to Oak Park. **Open** 2-4pm Mon; 10am-4pm Tue-Sun. **Admission** *Suggested donation* $2. **No credit cards.**

Unity Temple.

Much more than just a greenhouse, this 73-year-old glass structure contains three large themed rooms (highlighting tropical, fern and desert plants). A 5,000sq ft building provides space for social and educational events. Next door, Rehm Park has a play area for children, tennis courts and a pool.

Pleasant Home/Historical Society of Oak Park & River Forest

217 S Home Avenue, at Pleasant Street (1-708 848 6755, www.oprfhistory.org). El: Green to Oak Park. **Tours** *Mar-Nov* 12.30pm, 1.30pm, 2.30pm Thur-Sun. *Dec-Feb* 12.30pm, 1.30pm Thur-Sun. **Admission** $10; $5-$8 reductions; free under-5s & Illinois residents all day Fri. **No credit cards.**

Designed in 1897 by Prairie School architect George W Maher, Pleasant Home is used primarily for meetings and wedding receptions. However, there's also a photograph and document archive here, plus a charming little local museum with exhibits relating to long-time local resident Edgar Rice Burroughs and the ubiquitous Mr Hemingway. You can only visit the museum and home as part of a tour.

Unity Temple

875 Lake Street, at N Kenilworth Avenue (1-708 383 8873, www.utrf.org). El: Green to Oak Park. **Open** 10.30am-4.30pm Mon-Fri; 10am-2pm Sat; 1-4pm Sun. **Admission** $10; $8 reductions; free under-5s. **Credit** AmEx, MC, V.

This Unitarian Universalist church, which was designed by Lloyd Wright in 1905 and eventually completed in 1908, is notable for its striking first-floor sanctuary and community room. Also of interest are the physical expressions of Wright's notions of divinity and sacred space found throughout (for example in light fixtures, leaded glass windows and furniture); his love of music is reflected in the regular concerts that are held here. Take a self-guided tour or join a guided group any day of the week.

Also in the area

Brookfield Zoo

3300 Golf Road, at 31st Street & 1st Avenue, Brookfield (1-708 688 8000, www.brookfield zoo.org). Metra: Hollywood (Zoo Stop). **Open** *May-early Sept* 9.30am-6pm Mon-Sat; 9.30am-7.30pm Sun. *Early Sept-Apr* 10am-5pm daily. **Admission** $15; $10.50 reductions; free under-2s & all Tue-Thur Oct-Feb. **Credit** AmEx, Disc, MC, V.

Brookfield Zoo, about five miles from Oak Park, is worlds apart from its compatriot in Lincoln Park (*see p66*) in terms of geography, tone and size. Here, more than 200 acres are dedicated to more than 400 species of wildlife. Cages are largely eschewed in favour of letting the animals roam free, to the delight of the crowds. The dolphin shows in the Seven Seas Panorama are predictably popular. And, of course, everyone loves the inquisitive meerkats. Parking costs an additional $8.

EXPLORE

Profile Frank Lloyd Wright

America's most famous architect got his start in Chicagoland.

EXPLORE

The majority of eye-catching and headline-grabbing buildings in Chicago are priapic, sky-piercing affairs. Spend a mere five minutes walking around the Loop and it'll become apparent why the city is known as the home of the skyscraper. It's perhaps ironic, then, that Chicagoland's most celebrated architect made his name not by designing grandiose public buildings or flashy towers, but by constructing isolated residences for rich suburbanites, shuttered from the prying eyes of the common man. Nowadays, Frank Lloyd Wright's style is taken for granted. A century ago, it was virtually revolutionary.

Raised in Wisconsin, Wright arrived in Chicago in the years following the Great Fire and went to work in the offices of Adler and Sullivan, where he was assigned to the firm's residential design department. Eschewing the Beaux Arts style so popular at the time, Wright's residential designs reflected both his own interest in other architectural cultures and the influence of his bosses, both forward-thinking architects in their own right.

In 1893, though, Wright was fired from Adler and Sullivan for moonlighting and set up his own practice at his home in suburban Oak Park, which he shared with his wife Catherine Tobin and their six children. At his home studio, Wright spent the next decade defining what would come to be known as the Prairie Style, building more than 20 homes for his Oak Park neighbours. Miraculously, all of them survive today.

Mostly constructed of light-coloured brick and stucco, Wright's early Prairie Style homes are low, ground-hugging, rectangular structures featuring broad gabled roofs, sweeping horizontal lines and open,

Moore House.

flowing floor plans. Wright was careful that they should blend in with their surroundings, imitating the wide open and flat topography of the Midwest plains. Common features of the homes include enclosed porches, stout chimneys and overhanging eaves.

Among the more notable Wright-designed properties in Oak Park are, chronologically, the relatively early **Parker** and **Gale Houses** (1019 and 1027 W Chicago Avenue); the **Thomas House** (210 N Forest Avenue), considered Wright's first true Prairie Style home; the **Moore House** (333 N Forest Avenue), which Wright himself reworked almost three decades after its 1895 completion; the **Hills House** (313 Forest Avenue), reconstructed after a fire in 1977; and the **Gale House** (6 Elizabeth Court), one of the last homes he built in the area. None of them are open to the public, but you can admire the exteriors simply by strolling around the neighbourhood. For more insight, get an audio tour from the **Frank Lloyd Wright Home & Studio** (*see p89*) or join one of the guided tours available (booking may be required).

Wright also designed Oak Park's **Unity Temple** (*see p89*), a liberal Protestant church that recently celebrated its centenary (and is currently trying to raise funds for a much-needed restoration). Both of Wright's parents belonged to the Unitarian Church, which encourages its followers to approach religion through nature, science and art in the belief that such disciplines reveal the underlying principles of God's universe. Indeed, Wright's respect for natural elements and precise geometry is apparent in the designs of his homes and the temple.

Wright left his home studio in 1909 and sold the property in 1925. Five decades later, the building had been so abused and altered by subsequent owners that it barely resembled the architect's original design. In 1974, the Frank Lloyd Wright Home & Studio Foundation was formed to acquire the property, oversee a $3-million restoration that returned the property to its 1909 appearance, and eventually open it to the public as a museum and education centre dedicated to the architect's work. Tours of the Frank Lloyd Wright Home & Studio offer fascinating insights into Wright's early life and

Hills House.

creative influences. If you're lucky, you'll get taken around by one of the more entertaining tour guides, who won't gloss over the soapy details of Wright's philandering ways. Joint tickets are available with the guided tours of Oak Park; see www.wrightplus.org for full details of the many tours available.

One of the last designs to come out of Wright's Oak Park studio was **Robie House** (*see p98*), which is located near the University of Chicago on the city's South Side. Wright began work on the home of Chicago industrialist Frederick C Robie in 1909; the project is particularly noteworthy as the architect later proclaimed it as 'the cornerstone of modern architecture'.

When asked what his best building was, the self-aggrandising Wright always answered, 'My next one'. He may have had a point: New York City's Guggenheim Museum was the last structure he designed before his death in 1959. Although Wright went on to design notable buildings all over the country, the small town where he got his start remains a fascinating place to see has talent in action.

Thomas House.

EXPLORE

The South Side

From economic misery to academic excellence, all human life is here.

EXPLORE

Cherry-pick moments from its history, and the South Side may seem like the most important region of Chicago. Huge academic progress has been made over decades at the University of Chicago; the country's cultural history was rewritten with the emergence of the electric blues; and, in the shape of Barack Obama, Chicago's South Side delivered the country its first African-American president.

However, such landmark moments don't tell the whole story. Pockets of affluence and influence dot the South Side, most notably in collegiate Hyde Park, where the Museum of Science and Industry is one of Chicago's top attractions. But huge swathes of the sprawling South Side still suffer from serious economic decay and high crime rates, partly as a result of public housing policies enforced by the city council that were historically segregationist. There's plenty to see here, but also a number of stretches that are best avoided.

Map p316   **Bars** p142
Restaurants p128

INSIDE TRACK
SALUTE TO THE PIONEERS

Chicago's black population swelled substantially during the Great Migration, the name given to the relocation of countless thousands of African Americans from the South to northern cities during the early 1900s. Their pioneering spirit is honoured with a 15-foot bronze statue at King Drive and 26th Place. The work of LA artist Alison Saar, it depicts a man carrying a suitcase and waving goodbye; he's wearing a suit made from shoe soles, representing the hard journey endured by many who made the trek.

THE NEAR SOUTH SIDE

El: Red to Cermak-Chinatown.

The streets immediately beyond the **South Loop** and **Chinatown** (*see p45*), which end around I-55, are either uninspiring or downright shady. However, there are a few landmarks, chief among them the **Wood-Maxey-Boyd House** at 2801 S Prairie Avenue (near E 28th Street). This Queen Anne-style building was saved from demolition during the 1950s and again in 2003, when owner Alva Maxey-Boyd faced down the city and won. Her neighbours weren't as tough or as lucky: after a programme of systematic demolition, this is the only house on the block. It is currently being renovated back to its original splendour.

Given the vast amounts of ink and paper that have been expended on describing the Ludwig Mies van der Rohe buildings in the Loop and on the Near North Side, it's somewhat surprising that his designs for the main campus of the **Illinois Institute of Technology** (IIT) are generally overlooked – this is, after all, one of the more important modernist sites in the country. Guided tours of the site ($10) run at 10am (Mon-Fri) and 10.30am (Sat, Sun), with self-guided audio tours ($10) also available (10am-3pm daily). All tours depart from the ultra-postmodern **Collens Welcome Center** (3201 S State Street, at S 32nd Street), itself designed by noted Dutch architect Rem Koolhaas. The giant graphic of a head pays tribute to Mies with a wink and a nudge; the stainless steel tube around the El trains helps to reduce the noise emanating from them. For more information, call 1-312 567 7146 or see www.miessociety.org. The site is easily accessible by catching the 29 bus that runs down State Street.

BRONZEVILLE

El: Green to 35th-Bronzeville-IIT.

Taking as its approximate borders Wentworth and Cottage Grove Avenues, and 26th and 51st Streets, Bronzeville emerged as a product of racial segregation and de facto residential restrictions. The neighbourhood came to be symbolic of the Chicago Renaissance, a period

Victory Monument. *See p94.*

INSIDE TRACK
AN UNLIKELY MEMORIAL

Given his racist tendencies, it's ironic that 19th-century politician **Stephen A Douglas** once owned the land now occupied by Bronzeville. Douglas died in 1861, the year after he was defeated by Abraham Lincoln in the presidential elections; two decades later, he was commemorated at 35th Street and Cottage Grove Avenues with an ostentatious tomb – a 46-foot column topped by a statue of the man himself.

---

of African-American cultural flowering in the city, before fading under the weight of underinvestment and neglect. In recent years, it's begun to make a comeback, but this long-beleagured district still has a little way to go.

African-Americans began to settle in the area in the late 19th century, joining the Irish-Americans who already called it home. By the 1920s, the area had become a 'Black Metropolis': two major waves of migration brought some 200,000 southerners to the South Side, and the area prospered. Around this time, the area was christened Bronzeville by the *Chicago Bee*, an African-American newspaper that elected a 'mayor' for the district every year.

It didn't last. The Depression and ongoing, city-approved segregation contributed to a downturn in the area's fortunes (as chronicled by local resident Richard Wright in his 1940 novel *Native Son*). The city's response was to drop more than 30 blocks of public housing on the neighbourhood and starve it of investment and attention, two acts that essentially rubber-stamped its earlier segregationist policies and invited economic decline. The district degenerated throughout the 1970s and '80s.

Bronzeville still hasn't recovered from all these years of neglect and blight. Parts of the area remain decidedly sketchy, especially at night. However, an array of newer local businesses are trying to turn the area around. Restaurants such as **Chicago's Home of Chicken & Waffles** (3947 S King Drive at E Oakwood Boulevard, 1-773 536 3300, www.chicagoshomeofchickenandwaffles.com) see lines out the door for brunch after church on Sundays. Nearby, at the corner of 47th Street and King Drive, the old Regal Theater has been converted into the **Harold Washington Cultural Center** (4701 S King Drive, at E 47th Street, 1-773 373 1900, www.broadwayinbronzeville.com), a community-focused arts enterprise.

EXPLORE

University of Chicago.

EXPLORE

Some relics from Bronzeville's glory days have survived into the 21st century. The former **Chicago Defender Building** (3435 S Indiana Avenue, at E 35th Street) was built as a synagogue, but went on to house the newspaper that agitated for civil rights and encouraged the Great Migration. Not far away sit the offices of its former competitor, the *Chicago Bee*, now a Chicago Public Library (3647-3655 S State Street, at E 36th Street). Opposite each other at the corner of 35th Street and King Drive are the old **Supreme Life Offices**, once the home of the country's first African-American insurance agency, and the **Victory Monument** (*photo p93*), erected in 1926 to honour black soldiers who fought in World War I.

BRIDGEPORT

El: Orange to Halsted; Red to Sox-35th.

Originally and fatefully dubbed Hardscrabble, Bridgeport (south from 26th Street to Pershing Road, between Wentworth and Ashland Avenues) grew up around the Illinois–Michigan Canal as a settlement of Irish Americans willing to work for land. During the early and mid 20th century, it was known for its hostility to outsiders and for the gangs that enforced its boundaries. However, such behaviour didn't prevent it from exerting a huge influence over the development of the city; indeed, it might even have helped. For it was from here that the fabled Democratic political machine cranked into action.

Centred around Halsted Street, Bridgeport has maintained a working-class Irish character, but is now home to communities of Mexican Americans and Lithuanian Americans. And while Bridgeport remains tight-knit, an influx of condo conversions and an assortment of 'space available' signs on nearby warehouses tell their own story. The **Polo Café** (3322 S Morgan Street, at W 33rd Place, 1-773 927 7656, www.polocafe.com), a former candy shop, has become a focal point for the new district.

However, most Chicagoans visit Bridgeport to take in a Chicago White Sox baseball game at **US Cellular Field** (S Wentworth Avenue & E 35th Street; *see p241*), a hulking concrete bowl of a stadium built in the early 1990s. Aesthetically, it's not a patch on Wrigley Field, but the fans don't seem to mind too much. After all, since it opened, the Cubs haven't been a patch on the White Sox, who won the World Series in 2005.

INSIDE TRACK
UNION STOCK YARDS

For years, Bridgeport's economy was driven by meat. Opened in 1865, the **Union Stock Yards** were the centre of the country's meatpacking industry, and eventually grew to cover an area constrained by Pershing Road, Halsted Street, 47th Street and Ashland Avenue. Upton Sinclair's 1906 book *The Jungle* passed damning judgment on the slaughterhouse conditions, but the yards continued to thrive. They closed in 1971, but their presence is commemorated by the Stockyards Gate over Exchange Avenue (at Peoria Street), next to a memorial for firefighters who died in a fire here in 1910.

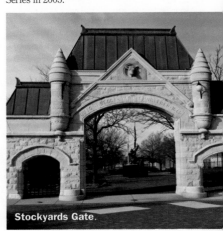

Stockyards Gate.

HYDE PARK

Metra: 55th-56th-57th Street.

With the University of Chicago as its anchor, Hyde Park enjoys a reputation as an oasis of intellectualism and community activism. The neighbourhood is much more low-key than the equivalent, college-dominated districts on the North Side; largely geared towards the middle-class families that have settled here, it has far fewer bars, restaurants and nightclubs than, for example, DePaul-dominated Lincoln Park. But its campus culture and geographic isolation – it's ringed by rather more deprived areas – also makes it feel much more self-enclosed.

The campus of the **University of Chicago** is at the heart of Hyde Park, both figuratively and literally. Many of the buildings are neo-Gothic, but several newer structures are worthy of attention. Chief among them is Cesar Pelli's flowing and airy **Gerald Ratner Athletic Center**, which houses a pool visible from the sidewalk between 55th and 56th Streets on Ellis Avenue. In addition to the **Oriental Institute** (*see p96*), the campus is home to a pair of galleries. The **Renaissance Society** (5811 S Ellis Avenue, at E 58th Street, 1-773 702 8670, www.renaissancesociety.org) offers modern art shows, while the **Smart Museum of Art** (*see p98*) boasts an enviable permanent collection. For a tour of the campus, *see p97* **Walk**.

As you might expect, the leafy streets around the college are dotted with bookstores. Close by sits **Robie House** (*see p98*), a Frank Lloyd Wright masterpiece. Other attractions sit further away. To the east, in lakefront Jackson Park, sits the **Museum of Science and Industry** (*see p96*), one of the city's premier family-friendly museums. And to the west, in Washington Park, is the **DuSable Museum of African American History** (*see below*). Both parks are ideal for enjoying pensive pauses unavailable in other parts of the city, rather like the district as a whole.

DuSable Museum of African American History

740 E 56th Place, at E 57th Street (1-773 947 0600, www.dusablemuseum.org). Metra: 55th-56th-57th Street. **Open** 10am-5pm Tue-Sat; noon-5pm Sun. **Admission** $10; $3-$7 reductions; free under-5s & all Sun. **Credit** AmEx, MC, V. **Map** p316 X17.

When the DuSable Museum opened in the early 1960s, African-American history was suffering serious neglect at the hands of the nation's cultural institutions. The seeds of change were planted when, in 1961, printmaker and schoolteacher Margaret Burroughs cleared the furniture out of her South Side home's living room, replaced it with an enviable

DuSable Museum of African American History

CHICAGO AFRICAN AMERICAN HISTORY MAKERS ®

Dr. Margaret T.G. Burroughs

collection of African-American art and artefacts, and hung a shingle outside reading 'African American Museum'. And so the DuSable was born. One of the country's first museums dedicated to black history, the DuSable is now housed in a stately former Park District building in Washington Park. Exhibitions spotlight everything from African-American entrepreneurship and the civil rights movement to Chicago's own African-American community.

★ Museum of Science & Industry

5700 S Lake Shore Drive, at 57th Street (1-773 684 1414, www.msichicago.org). Metra: 55th-56th-57th Street. **Open** *9.30am-4pm daily.* **Admission** *$18; $11-$17 reductions; free under-2s.* **Credit** *AmEx, Disc, MC, V.* **Map** *p316 Z17.*

If you're into exhibits loaded with interactive features, this expansive Hyde Park operation should be just the ticket. Built in 1893 as the Palace of Fine Arts for the World's Columbian Exposition, the building was converted to its present incarnation in the 1920s. Although it's a fair way from downtown, it's deservedly one of the city's top attractions.

The challenge for every science museum is not only to track the history of technological progress, but also to keep pace with it. While some of the whizz-bang exhibits are good – notably the Fast Forward display, which features cuisine made by inkjet printers and instant-messaged hugs – there are some real clunkers here too.

Overall, the museum's focus is broad, as witnessed by low-tech displays such as Colleen Moore's Fairy Castle (lower level), a gaudy but fabulous multi-room miniature that's just a bit too big to be called a doll's house. The long queues that form outside the Coal Mine (main floor) hide an exhibit that kids enjoy immensely, at least if they don't go mad during the boring wait on the staircase.

Of all the vehicles in the museum, the 1934 Pioneer Zephyr train (Great Hall) is one of the highlights, as is the not-to-be-missed U-505 German submarine (ground level). One of only five surviving World War II subs in the world, it has its own vast underground chamber. It's surrounded by lots of interpretative materials, short films and various artefacts that were found on board when, in June 1944, it was captured by American seamen off the coast of West Africa.

Elsewhere in the museum, young visitors in particular will be dazzled by the interactive science displays, whether whispering to a friend across the hall in the Whispering Gallery (main floor), watching Earth Revealed's NASA real-time footage of the planet from afar (main floor), or seeing a chick hatch before their eyes in the hatchery (main floor). It's easy to get disorientated, and it'll take at least a day to see anything close to all that the museum has to offer. Still, it's well worth your time.

★ Oriental Institute Museum

University of Chicago, 1155 E 58th Street, at S University Avenue (1-773 702 9520, www.oi.uchicago.edu). Metra: 55th-56th-57th Street. **Open** *10am-6pm Tue, Thur-Sat; 10am-8.30pm Wed; noon-6pm Sun.* **Admission** *free (suggested donation $10; $5 under-12s).* **Credit** *(gift shop) MC, V.* **Map** *p316 X17.*

This University of Chicago-run archaeological treasure trove thankfully avoids the current museum trend of providing hokey interactive displays that pander to the PlayStation generation's short attention span. Instead, it allows some stunning architectural finds to speak for themselves in old-fashioned glass display cases. Years ago, John D Rockefeller bankrolled the institute so archaeologist and Egyptologist James Breasted and his colleagues could lead expeditions to excavate lost civilisations.

Museum of Science & Industry.

EXPLORE

Walk Back to School

Explore the collegiate territory of Hyde Park.

*Begin at the corner of 58th Street
and Woodlawn Avenue.*

Just south of Frank Lloyd Wright's **Robie
House** (*see p98*) sits the **Charles M Harper
Center** (1101 E 58th Street). Designed
by Rafael Vinoly, it's in part a modern
reinterpretation of its Wright-designed
neighbour. Approach the Harper Center
from the south to see how the two
buildings interact. It's just a pity that
from this particular angle, Robie House is
overshadowed – literally – by the somewhat
less distinguished **McGiffert House** (5751
S Woodlawn Avenue).

*Head south down Woodlawn Avenue
until you get to the junction of Woodlawn
and 59th Street.*

It looks pretty big out front, but the churchy
Ida Noyes Hall (1212 E 59th Street) is
even bigger once inside. It was built in
1916 as a women's hall of residence;
these days, it holds a cinema and a pool.
Across the way you'll find the **Rockefeller
Memorial Chapel** (5850 S Woodlawn
Avenue, 1-773 702 2100, www.rockefeller.
uchicago.edu), named after the man whose
cash funded the building of the university.
Built to the Gothic designs of Bertram
Goodhue in 1928, the chapel is notable
for its stained glass, a surfeit of exterior
statues and its clanging carillon.

*Walk a block west, then take the next
right up University Avenue to the south-
west corner with E 57th Street.*

If you're lucky, your visit to Hyde Park will
coincide with a concert at **Mandel Hall**.
Some top-notch classical ensembles
perform in its beautiful auditorium.

*Walk north up University Avenue
for a block.*

George and William Keck designed
the three-flat, International-style **Keck-
Gottschalk-Keck Apartments** (5551 S
University Avenue) for themselves and
Professor Louis Gottschalk in 1937.
It's now a designated Chicago landmark
known for the external blinds attached
to its street-facing windows.

Turn left on to E 56th Street.

The **Smart Museum of Art** (*see p98*) is
the second university museum that you'll
come across on the walk. On the left sits
an unappealing block of residences, but
at the intersection with Ellis Avenue, your
gaze may well be drawn to the modern,
eye-catching curves of the **Gerald Ratner
Athletics Center**.

Turn left down Ellis Avenue.

A Henry Moore sculpture, **Nuclear Energy**,
stands on the site of Stagg Field, the
former football field. It was here, on
2 December 1942, that Enrico Fermi
conducted the first successful nuclear
experiment. Moore's statue was unveiled
exactly 25 years later. The **Joe & Rika
Mansueto Library**, designed by Helmut
Jahn, is located here as well.

Turn left into E 57th Street.

The Gothic **Cobb Gate** makes for a grand
entrance to the college, and made for
an equally grand exit for Billy Crystal and
Meg Ryan when they set off for New York
City from here in *When Harry Met Sally*.
Ask one of the savvy students to explain
the collegiate myth that has grown up
around the figures on the gate.

Continue south to the roundabout.

The portentous **Swift Hall** is home to
the university's Divinity School. It figures,
then, that right next to it should be the
Bond Chapel, all dark woods and studied
calm. Close by, **Cobb Hall** is the oldest
building on campus, dating back to 1892.
It takes its name from Henry Ives Cobb,
the architect who designed 18 of the
college buildings. Inside, the university
mounts exhibitions of unapologetically
modern art in the **Renaissance Society**
(*see p98*).

EXPLORE

EXPLORE

INSIDE TRACK
SOUTH SIDE LUXURY

Looming over the northern edge of Hyde Park, the **Powhatan Apartments** building (E 50th Street & S Chicago Beach Drive) is a world apart from the undistinguished and poverty-soaked high-rises that dot the South Side. It was built in the 1920s, just before the Great Depression put a lid on developers' hopes to reinvent the area. The art deco detailing is by Charles L Morgan, a graphic artist and friend of Frank Lloyd Wright.

The vast collection that resulted, which includes cuneiform tablets, mummies and larger-than-life stone statues from Egypt and the Near East, evokes all the mystery and intrigue any whip-cracking, fedora-wearing action hero could handle.

The space is divided into galleries themed around the great civilisations of Mesopotamia, Egypt and Persia, along with newer galleries that take in the Palestine and Nubia collections. Among the highlights are the hard-to-miss, 16ft solid-stone, human-headed winged bull that guarded King Sargon II's palace court more than 2,700 years ago, and the equally imposing 3,000-year-old King Tut statue that was uncovered in Thebes.

FREE Renaissance Society

5811 S Ellis Avenue, between E 58th & 59th Streets (1-773 702 8670, www.renaissancesociety. org). Metra: 55th-56th-57th Street. **Admission** free. **No credit cards. Map** p316 X17.
Despite the name, you won't find any Michelangelos here: this gallery, which isn't affiliated to the University of Chicago but inhabits a space inside its Cobb Hall, has specialised in new and cutting-edge art since it opened in 1915. The 'Ren' introduced Alexander Calder and Fernand Léger to the US and still stages some of the most daring, conceptual-heavy shows in Chicago. The gallery also sells affordable, unique editions and artists' books.

★ Robie House

5757 S Woodlawn Avenue, at E 58th Street (1-312 994 4400, www.gowright.org/visit/robie-house.html). Metra: 55th-56th-57th Street. **Tours** 11am-3pm Mon, Thur-Sun. **Admission** $15; $12 reductions. **Credit** AmEx, Disc, MC, V. **Map** p316 Y17.
If you have even a basic knowledge of the history of architecture, you'll know who's behind this place. Commissioned by Chicago industrialist Frederick C Robie and completed in 1910, this is Frank Lloyd Wright at his finest. A masterpiece of the Prairie Style, the house features dramatic horizontal lines,

cantilevered roofs, expansive stretches of glass and Wright's signature open floorplan. Tickets for some tours are available in advance.
▶ *For Wright's work in Oak Park, see pp90-91.*

FREE Smart Museum of Art

University of Chicago, 5550 S Greenwood Avenue, at E 55th Street (1-773 702 0200, www.smartmuseum.uchicago.edu). Metra: 55th-56th-57th Street. **Open** 10am-5pm Tue, Wed, Fri-Sun; 10am-8pm Thur. **Admission** free. **Map** p316 X17.
The Smart Museum of Art houses a dizzying collection of more than 10,000 objects, spanning a 5,000-year period from ancient Shang Dynasty bronzes to modern works of art. The mind reels, stepping from Shinto prints in one room to Anselm Kiefer in the next.

THE PULLMAN DISTRICT
Metra: 111th Street.

The Pullman District (roughly bounded by 104th, 115th, Cottage Grove and Langley Streets) is the preserved remains of the first model planned industrial community in the US. Tycoon George Pullman conceived a workers' Utopia to be built alongside his new railcar factory, and set about creating it on a 3,000-acre site. Erected from 1880, the 1,300 structures included houses, shops, churches, parks and a library for his employees. Sadly, Pullman's dream turned into a nightmare when worker dissatisfaction resulted in a destructive strike. As a result, the town was annexed by Chicago in 1898, though Pullman wasn't around to see it happen; he'd died a year earlier.
Much of the original town is gone, destroyed by overzealous construction workers and, in the case of the old clock tower, arsonists (it burned down in 1998). Still, the buildings that remain give a decent impression of what this community was like. The Hotel Florence, the Greenstone Church and some rowhouse-lined sidestreets are all either intact or have been restored in what is now a National Landmark District. Start your visit at the **Historic Pullman Visitor Center**.

Historic Pullman Visitor Center

11141 S Cottage Grove Avenue, at S 112th Street (1-773 785 8901, www.pullmanil.org). Metra: 111th Street. **Open** 11am-3pm Tue-Sun. **Tours** *May-Oct* 1.30pm 1st Sun of mth. Call to arrange group tour. **Admission** *Suggested donation* $5; $4 reductions; free under-6s. **Credit** AmEx, MC, V.
The Pullman Visitors Center houses historic photos and Pullman-related items, such as a buffet table from the Pullman mansion, ornamental decor from the old Hotel Florence and the 'Perfect Town' award given to Pullman.

Walk Barack's Backyard

Follow the President's path.

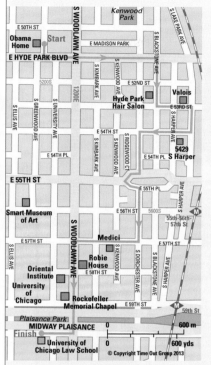

a nod – albeit under the alias Smitty's – in *Dreams from My Father*.

Continue south on Blackstone to 53rd Street and turn left.

Peer through the window of **Valois** (1518 E 53rd Street, 1-773 667 0647, www. valoisrestaurant.com), a cafeteria-style restaurant that attracts everyone from working Joes and ageing African Americans to University of Chicago profs and students, as chronicled in Mitchell Duneier's book *Slim's Table*. Obama was once a regular.

Go right on Lake Park, right on 54th Street and left on Harper.

The first apartment Obama rented as a young community organiser in the late '80s stands at **5429 S Harper Avenue**. The building's a little tattered but full of charm.

At 54th Place, turn right, then head south on Dorchester Avenue and west on 57th Street.

Another former Obama hangout, **Medici on 57th** (1327 E 57th Street, 1-773 667 7394, www.medici57.com) has grasped on to its patron's coattails. A glass case on one wall enshrines a selection of 'Obama Eats Here' T-shirts and each table has an 'Obama 2008'-engraved wood cutting board. If you ask what his favourite dishes are, though, your server might walk away mumbling something about the secret service making it hard for the president to drop in.

Continue west on 57th, then go south on Woodlawn Avenue and walk through the Midway Plaisance.

Obama taught at the **University of Chicago Law School** (1111 E 60th Street) for more than a decade, beginning in 1992.

EXPLORE

Start at 5046 S Greenwood Avenue.
The Obamas are currently making their home on Pennsylvania Avenue in DC. But in Chicago, the family calls this two-storey, red-brick mansion home. If you gawk through the evergreens too long or snap pictures from too close an angle, expect to hear the security staff guide you away with a well-rehearsed 'Please take your pictures from the other side of the street'.

Head down Hyde Park Boulevard and turn south on Blackstone Avenue.

For 20 years, Obama engaged the services of the **Hyde Park Hair Salon & Barber Shop** (5234 S Blackstone Avenue, 1-773 493 6028, www.hydeparkhairsalon.net) to keep his perfectly trimmed, close-cropped 'do looking politician-perfect. The shop has seen a spike in business since the rock star-like rise of Obama, who even gave it

Hyde Park Hair Salon & Barber Shop.

Consume

Restaurants

The world on a plate.

Residents of the City of Big Shoulders have long had famously healthy appetites. But in the last couple of decades, the dining scene has come into its own. The cosy local restaurants, ethnic eateries and comfort-cooking operations for which the city has been known have been joined by an array of high-end eateries; alongside them sit a terrific variety of mid-range spots, many offering creative and seasonally slanted reinventions of dishes from both home and abroad. Chicago now counts as one of the best cities for dining in the US, and the DIY food movement is strong – these days, a hot restaurant that doesn't make its own mayo is an oddity.

THE LOCAL SCENE

Leaders of the local food and drinks industry are no longer content to farm it out. They're roasting their own coffee, brewing their own beer, making bread and doughnuts from scratch, bottling house-made condiments and canning anything that will stand still. All this round-the-clock production has meant the typical restaurant model has shifted, so you'll find spots that triple as coffee shop, bakery and bar.

Even before a number of local chefs such as Stephanie Izard got serious street cred taking home prizes on Food Network and Bravo TV shows, ambitious chef-driven dining that goes way beyond Chicago's old meat and potatoes reputation was big news in the city. Highlights include Grant Achatz's themed restaurant **Next**; Matthias Merges' yakitori-inspired **Yusho**; and Paul Virant's seasonal farm-to-table **Perennial Virant**.

Midscale-casual restaurants such as the **Bristol**, **Avec**, **Balena** and **Lula Café** have been bringing seasonal flavours to the fore in impressive fashion. They're all democratic places, tax brackets mingling comfortably in the often-full rooms. But if you're looking to rub elbows with a few locals, the influx of

eateries offering communal dining make a great icebreaker. Whether it's over steaming bowls of noodles at **Urbanbelly**, incredible cheeseburgers at **Au Cheval** or Belgian beers at **Publican**, there's no better community organiser than great food.

Elsewhere, homesickness cures are offered in innumerable ethnic enclaves: Chinatown for Chinese food and Pilsen for Mexican eats; Greektown and Little Italy for Greek and Italian; Andersonville for Swedish fare and Lincoln Square for German cooking; and, further out, Indian cooking on Devon Avenue on the Far North Side and more Italian treats along Harlem Avenue in Elmwood Park. And that's without tackling Chicago's deep-dish pizzas and hot dogs…

Essential information

Competition for tables at some smart and/or hip restaurants can be fierce. If in doubt, book ahead, especially on weekends. Few restaurants operate a dress code, but men may be asked to don a jacket and tie in some particularly posh old-school spots downtown; call to check if you're in doubt.

Prices given throughout the chapter are for an average main course. We've used the **$** symbol to denote places offering particularly good value: restaurants with main courses for around $10 or less, plus cafés, diners and other similarly cheap operations.

New restaurants open all the time. For the latest reviews, see www.timeoutchicago.com.

> ❶ Blue numbers in this chapter correspond to the location of each restaurant on the street maps. *See pp308-316.*

THE LOOP

$ Cafecito

*26 E Congress Parkway, between S State Street
& S Wabash Avenue (1-312 922 2233, www.
cafecitochicago.com). El: Brown, Orange, Pink
or Purple to Library; Blue or Red to Jackson.*
Open 7am-9pm Mon-Fri; 10am-6pm Sat,
Sun. **Sandwich** $5. **Credit** MC, V. **Map**
p309 H13 **❶ Cuban**
There's no confusion over the star of the show here:
the Cubano's crusty bread is toasted just right, its
roast pork juicy, its pickles thick, and its mustard
and gooey cheese plentiful. And once it's devoured,
only a potent *cortadito* will keep you from slumping
on the café's comfy couch.

★ $ Do-Rite Donuts

*50 W Randolph Street, at N Dearborn Street
(1-312 488 2483, www.doritedonuts.com). El:
Red to Lake; Blue, Brown, Green, Orange, Pink
or Purple to Clark/Lake.* **Open** 6.30am-2pm
Mon-Fri; 7am-2pm Sat, Sun. **No credit cards**.
Map p309 H11 **❷ Café**
Chances are good that when you walk into this
tiny, morning-only doughnut shop from Lettuce
Entertain You, you'll find lots of people milling
about, waiting for the bacon doughnuts to be ready.
You can join them if you want, but you'll be just
as happy if you go for the yeasty, puffy cinnamon
crunch doughnuts – and you'll get your hands on
them a lot faster.

★ Gage

*24 S Michigan Avenue, at E Madison Street
(1-312 372 4243, www.thegagechicago.com).
El: Brown, Green, Orange, Pink or Purple to
Madison/Wabash.* **Open** 11am-midnight Mon;
11am-2am Tue-Fri; 10am-3am Sat; 10am-midnight
Sun. **Main courses** $30. **Credit** AmEx, Disc,
MC, V. **Map** p309 J12 **❸ Gastropub**
Owner Billy Lawless has a real hit on his hands
with this Loop take on a British gastropub. The
food is rich and aggressively flavourful, from the
perfect-for-snacking Scotch egg to the Gage burger,
served a juicy medium-rare and dripping with
melted onion marmalade and stinky Midwestern
camembert. The whisky list is lengthy, beer options
reach beyond the basics and wines are accompanied
by clever descriptions. *Photo p106.*

$ Hannah's Bretzel

*180 W Washington Street, at N Wells Street
(1-312 621 1111, www.hannahsbretzel.com).
El: Blue, Brown, Orange, Pink or Purple to
Washington.* **Open** 7am-7pm Mon-Fri; 10am-
3pm Sun. **Main courses** $9. **Credit** AmEx,
MC, V. **Map** p309 H12 **❹ Café**
This tiny Euro-chic café bills itself as an organic
carry-out restaurant, but note that the word 'healthy'
is nowhere to be found. Warm, wholegrain pretzels

– baked throughout the day on the premises – may
indeed be good for you; no doubt the organic salads
are too. Sandwiches, such as the organic grass-fed
sirloin on soft 'bretzel' bread, aren't unhealthy either.
But doctors probably wouldn't condone the wall
dedicated to chocolate, on which you'll find more
than 175 different bars.

Park Grill

*11 N Michigan Avenue, at E Madison Street
(1-312 521 7275, www.parkgrillchicago.com). El:
Blue or Red to Monroe; Brown, Green, Orange,
Pink or Purple to Madison/Wabash.* **Open** 11am-
9.30pm Mon-Thur, Sun; 11am-10.30pm Fri, Sat.
Main courses $19. **Credit** AmEx, Disc, MC, V.
Map p309 J12 **❺ Contemporary American**
Park Grill's location overlooking the Millennium
Park ice rink has its pros and cons: watching flailing
skaters is transfixing, but with food this good, you
might want to focus on your meal. Seasonal offerings may include whisper-thin beef carpaccio sprinkled with parmesan and juicy capers or jumbo lump
crab cake. The Kobe burger is also a treat, melted
gorgonzola topping thick-as-your-fist beef between
buttery brioche. Afterwards, strap on a pair of skates
to get your heart pumping again.
▶ *For more details of the Millennium Park ice
rink, see p247.*

Russian Tea Time

*77 E Adams Street, between S Michigan & S
Wabash Avenues (1-312 360 0000, www.russian
teatime.com). El: Blue or Red to Jackson; Brown,
Green, Orange, Pink or Purple to Adams/Wabash.*
Open 11am-9pm Mon-Thur, Sun; 11am-11pm
Fri, Sat. **Main courses** $24. **Credit** AmEx,
Disc, MC, V. **Map** p309 J12 **❻ Russian**
A classy choice for the symphony set and couples
looking to indulge themselves, this place proves
that excess is best. Slide into a cosy booth and start
the assault with borscht, sour cream-slathered
dumplings and caviar blini, followed by creamy beef
stroganoff or oniony, nutmeg-laced ground beef-
stuffed cabbage rolls. Be sure to order a flight of
house-infused vodkas (pineapple, ginger, coriander
and more) too.

Terzo Piano

*Art Institute of Chicago, 159 E Monroe Street,
between Michigan Avenue & Columbus Drive
(1-312 443 8650, www.terzopianochicago.com).
El: Brown, Green, Orange, Pink or Purple to
Adams.* **Main courses** $23. **Credit** AmEx,
Disc, MC, V. **Map** p309 J12 **❼ Italian**
Like the rest of the Renzo Piano-designed Modern
Wing, the restaurant at the Art Institute is a beautiful space: sleek, pristine and awash with light. The
highlights of the hyper-seasonal menu, which is
overseen by Spiaggia's Tony Mantuano, exhibit
similar simplicity and elegance. Eschew lacklustre
mains in favour of flatbreads (topped with creamy

CONSUME

CONSUME

INSIDE TRACK
SNACK ATTACKS

Running out of steam somewhere between Neiman Marcus and Bloomingdale's? Magnificent Mile shoppers should make a beeline for the *gelato* and *cannoli* at Italian deli **L'Appetito** (*see p161*) or the unusual but always delicious chocolates from **Vosges Haut-Chocolat** (*see p161*). Fight off the munchies in the Loop with a visit to **Garrett Popcorn Shop** (*see p161*).

burrata cheese and seasonal ingredients like scapes) and heaping salads (like pea shoots and crisped prosciutto), then end with a rich, indulgent salted caramel semifreddo.

Vivere
71 W Monroe Street, between S Clark & S Dearborn Streets (1-312 332 7005, www.vivere-chicago.com). El: Blue or Red to Monroe; Brown, Green, Orange, Pink or Purple to Adams/Wabash. **Open** 11.30am-2.30pm Mon-Fri; 5-10pm Mon-Thur; 5-11pm Fri, Sat. **Main courses** $20. **Credit** AmEx, Disc, MC, V. **Map** p309 H12 ❽ Italian
The best of the three restaurants that make up the multi-level Italian Village, Vivere boasts a menu as contemporary as its decor. That's quite an impressive feat, given that the room looks like an Italian Baroque version of Alice's Wonderland. The menu is a balance of classics and interesting twists applied to house-made pasta, seafood stews and grilled game. The best part about the kitchen offering half-orders of pasta is that you can get two: try the sage-scented, pheasant-filled agnolottini and the tagliatelle alla bolognese.

THE SOUTH LOOP & CHINATOWN
The South Loop

$ Epic Burger
517 S State Street, between E Congress Parkway & E Harrison Street (1-312 913 1373, www.epicburger.com). El: Red to Harrison. **Open** 10.30am-10pm Mon-Thur; 10.30am-11pm Fri, Sat; 10.30am-9pm Sun. **Main courses** $6. **Credit** AmEx, Disc, MC, V. **Map** p309 H13 ❾ American
This burger joint makes much of its Slow Food principles (beef and chicken are all-natural, hand-cut fries are cooked in trans fat-free vegetable oil)… but is the food up to much? It's pretty good. Burgers are hand-formed to almost an inch thick and cooked to a nice pinky medium. Opt for aged cheddar, bacon and egg toppings, and be sure to add the earthy, skin-on fries to your order.

$ Manny's Coffee Shop & Deli
1141 S Jefferson Street, at S Grenshaw Street (1-312 939 2855, www.mannysdeli.com). El: Blue to Clinton. **Open** 6am-8pm Mon-Sat. **Main courses** $10. **Credit** AmEx, Disc, MC, V. **Map** p308 G14 ❿ American/cafeteria
The city's most quintessential restaurant is not a steakhouse or a lab-like kitchen putting out cutting-edge cuisine. It's a cafeteria. Decide what you want before you get in line at this 66-year-old institution. You'll pass plates of Jell-O and chicken salad, but the line moves quickly. Our advice? Grab one of the oversized corned beef or pastrami sandwiches, a potato pancake on the side and a packet of Tums for dessert.

Chinatown

$ Lao Hunan
2230 S Wentworth Avenue, between W 22nd Place & W Alexander Street (1-312 842 7888, www.laohunanonline.com). El: Red to Cermak/Chinatown. **Open** 11am-9.30pm Mon-Thur, Sun; 11am-10pm Fri, Sat. **Main courses** $10. **Credit** AmEx, Disc, MC, V. Chinese
Tony Hu's Hunanese contribution to Chinatown has an eccentric Chairman Mao theme, but don't let that distract you from the food, which is intense, spicy, oily and delicious. 'Home-fed chicken' (roughly equating to free-range) is hung for two days to dry-age before it's lightly smoked over a wok filled with dry rice and spices. Chef Fada Zhang, a native of Hunan, uses the same technique for his 'famous Hunan preserved pork', smoking it over a fragrant haze of toasted dry rice, whole star anise and cinnamon bark. For contrast, order the cool, thin rectangles of jade tofu surrounded by a slick of chilli oil brightened with coriander and spring onions.

★ $ Lao Sze Chuan
2172 S Archer Avenue, between W Wentworth & W Princeton Avenues (1-312 326 5040, www.tonygourmetgroup.com). El: Red to Cermak-Chinatown. **Open** 10.30am-midnight daily. **Main courses** $10. **Credit** AmEx, Disc, MC, V. **Map** p308 H16 ⓫ Chinese/Szechuan
This place is the best spot for Szechuan cuisine in town, evident from the nightly queues of heat-seekers. The kitchen uses plenty of Szechuan pepper, dried chillis, garlic and ginger to create addictive flavours; favourites include Chengdu dumplings, crispy Chinese eggplant with ground pork, twice-cooked pork, *ma po* tofu, Szechuan prawns and 'chef's special' dry chilli chicken.

$ Three Happiness Restaurant
209 W Cermak Road, between S Wentworth & S Archer Avenues (1-312 842 1964). El: Red to Cermak-Chinatown. **Open** 24 hrs daily. **Main courses** $8. **Credit** AmEx, Disc, MC, V. Chinese

This isn't the giant Three Happiness on the corner of Wentworth Avenue; it's worth stressing this because the difference is monumental. Skip the so-so appetisers in favour of black pepper beef with rice noodles (ordered 'crispy'), stir-fried Dungeness crab in chilli-seafood XO sauce, salt-and-pepper shrimp and Cantonese-style crispy-skin chicken.

THE NEAR NORTH SIDE

River North

Bavette's
218 W Kinzie Street, between N Franklin & N Wells Streets (312 624 8154, www.
bavetteschicago.com). El: Brown, Purple to Merchandise Mart. **Open** 5-10.30pm Mon, Sun; 5-11.30pm Tue-Thur; 5pm-12.30am Fri, Sat. **Main courses** $20. **Credit** AmEx, Disc, MC, V. **Map** p310 G11 ⓰ **French**
Brendan Sodikoff's vaguely French steakhouse is a departure – or perhaps an evolution – for the restaurateur. While his other spots (Gilt Bar, Au Cheval) have their charms, the appeal of this spot, with its jazz-era decor and soundtrack, is practically universal. You don't even have to be a steak fan to get a good meal; in fact, as good as the *steak-frites* is, the fried and roasted chicken are even better. Elegant cocktails begin meals here; fabulous pies (lemon meringue, chocolate cream) end them.

Dog Days

The classic Chicago hot dog brooks no arguments.

Order a hot dog in Chicago, and you'll need to accede to time-honoured tradition. Hold the ketchup and forget the pork: you'll get a beef dog (steamed or boiled) on a poppy-seed bun, topped with mustard, relish, chopped onions, tomato wedges, a pickle spear, sport peppers and celery salt. But how these particulars came to form the classic Chicago dog is part speculation, part marketing schtick and part gossipy hearsay. And the guy who's heard most of these stories is Bruce Kraig, author of *The Hot Dog*.

'The best I got from various interviews from old-timers,' says Kraig, 'was that the Chicago dog as we know it was invented in the 1910s, and the toppings came from competition among Greek and Italian vendors, who needed to add value to their product during the Depression.' But before that, the hot dog – *sans* seven toppings – made its Chicago debut at the 1893 World's Columbian Exposition, trotted out under the Vienna name by a couple of Austrian immigrants looking to cash in on the eastern European frankfurter.

More than a century later, the Vienna company is still the main game in town, supplying franks to a vast majority of Chicago's hot-dog stands. But what of those seven toppings? As Kraig explains, it's all down to Chicago's immigration stew.

'Sausage is German in origin and so is mustard, but buns are American; Germans would eat it with bread, but not a bun. Sport peppers are basically giardiniera, as is relish, which is Italian. Dill pickles are German. Tomatoes and onions are Mediterranean, so that's Greek and Italian; these came from guys who turned their produce carts into hot-dog carts on Maxwell Street. Chicago was once a major producer of celery; celery salt became a substitute. The poppy-seed bun is Jewish and was introduced locally by Rosen's bakery. It didn't appear until after World War II.'

Makes sense, but why have locals rejected ketchup? The red line they've drawn between themselves and those who 'ruin' a dog with ketchup is so notorious that it's infiltrated the National Hot Dog & Sausage Council, whose Hot Dog Etiquette guide includes the rule, 'Don't use ketchup on your hot dog after the age of 18.'

Bob Schwartz, a senior VP at Vienna, is such a disciple of the rule he's written a book called *Never Put Ketchup on a Hot Dog*. 'The real reason is because the sweetness and acidity doesn't blend well with the other toppings,' he says.
► If you only eat one hot dog while you're here, get it from **Hot Doug's** (3324 N California Avenue, at W Roscoe Street, 1-773 279 9550, www.hotdougs.com).

CONSUME

Gage. *See p103.*

Bin 36

*339 N Dearborn Street, at W Kinzie Street
(1-312 755 9463, www.bin36.com). El: Red to
Grand.* **Open** 6.30am-11pm Mon-Wed; 6.30am-
midnight Thur; 6.30am-1am Fri; 7am-1am Sat;
7am-10pm Sun. **Main courses** $22. **Credit**
AmEx, Disc, MC, V. **Map** p310 H11 ⓭
American/wine bar

Thankfully, no dish here is getting by merely on
street cred. Lamb meatballs tossed in romesco sauce
are like Prozac in their ability to cause happiness.
Desserts are surprisingly good, too, but you'll probably never taste them when you're faced with one of
the best cheese plates in the city.

Café Iberico

*739 N LaSalle Street, between W Superior Street
& W Chicago Avenue (1-312 573 1510, www.cafe
iberico.com). El: Brown, Purple or Red to Chicago.*
Open 11am-11.30pm Mon-Thur; 11am-1.30am Fri,
Sat; 11am-11pm Sun. **Tapas** $7. **Credit** AmEx,
Disc, MC, V. **Map** p310 H10 ⓮ **Tapas**

The wait at this always-packed tapas joint can be
long, but once you get inside, things move pretty
quickly. Cheap plates of *patatas bravas* and *croque-
tas de pollo* (creamy chicken and ham fritters) arrive
at the table almost immediately, dropped like after-
thoughts by overworked servers. But with a plate of
manchego and a pitcher of sangria to tide you over,
you won't even notice the wait.

★ Chicago Chop House

*60 W Ontario Street, between N Dearborn &
N Clark Streets (1-312 787 7100, www.chicago
chophouse.com). El: Red to Grand.* **Open** 5-11pm
Mon-Thur; 5-11.30pm Fri; 4.30-11.30pm Sat;
4.30-11pm Sun. **Main courses** $30. **Credit**
AmEx, Disc, MC, V. **Map** p310 H10 ⓯ **American**

This century-old brownstone is a quintessential
Chicago steakhouse. Conventioneers and local businessmen with fat expense wallets head upstairs for
white-tablecloth service, pricey wines, and 48oz or
64oz porterhouses fit for a king. Alternatively, head
to the subterranean piano bar, where every inch of
wall is covered with vintage photos of Capone and
crew, and the high wooden tables are packed with
loud storytellers and uncompromising carnivores.

Club Lago

*331 W Superior Street, at N Orleans Street (1-312
951 2849, www.clublago.com). El: Brown or
Purple to Chicago.* **Open** 11am-10pm Mon-Thur;
11am-11pm Fri, Sat. **Main courses** $15. **Credit**
AmEx, Disc, MC, V. **Map** p310 G10 ⓰ **Italian**

Once, a chimney crashed through the ceiling and
obliterated the kitchen of this red-sauce stalwart. But
Club Lago persevered, just as it has for more than
60 years. Despite a fairly recent renovation, the place
looks exactly the same as always and many of the
staff have been there for decades. So follow suit and
regress to old habits: massive portions of lasagne,
soft roast beef on white bread, carafes of watery
Chianti, and – this is crucial – some pasta with
Lago's meat sauce.

▶ *There's more old-school Italian cooking at
nearby Gene & Georgetti; see p107.*

★ Frontera Grill

*445 N Clark Street, between W Hubbard & W
Illinois Streets (1-312 661 1434, www.rickbayless.
com). El: Brown or Purple to Merchandise Mart;
Red to Grand.* **Open** 11.30am-2.30pm, 5.20-10pm
Tue; 11.30am-2.30pm, 5-10pm Wed, Thur;
11.30am-2.30pm, 5-11pm Fri; 10.30am-2.30pm,
5-11pm Sat. **Main courses** $25. **Credit** AmEx,
Disc, MC, V. **Map** p310 H11 ⓱ **Mexican**

CONSUME

Most celeb chefs branch out to other cities, leaving the original restaurant at home to suffer. But Rick Bayless kept close to the kitchen and chose to expand in other ways (books, TV shows). Lucky Chicago. Frontera offers a vibrant slice of Mexico City, a place to chow down on ceviche, earthy *mole*, wood-grilled steak tucked into house-made tortillas and, of course, insanely good margaritas.

Fulton's on the River

315 N LaSalle Street, at Chicago River (1-312 822 0100, www.fultonsontheriver.com). El: Brown or Purple to Merchandise Mart. **Open** 11am-10pm Mon-Thur; 11am-11pm Fri; 5-11pm Sat; 5-10pm Sun. **Main courses** $40. **Credit** AmEx, Disc, MC, V. **Map** p310 H11 ⑱ **American**
Fulton's is as much about the view as it is about the food. Fortunately, both merit a visit. The menu – equal parts seafood and steak – is nothing out of the ordinary, but everything is of exquisite quality. King crab legs from the extensive raw bar are fresh and sweet, filet mignon is tender, and a side dish of Yukon Gold mashed potatoes is so decadent that you can skip dessert. Make your trip worth the price and ask for a window seat.

Gene & Georgetti

500 N Franklin Street, at W Illinois Street (1-312 527 3718, www.geneandgeorgetti.com). El: Red to Grand. **Open** 11am-11pm Mon-Thur; 11am-midnight Fri, Sat. **Main courses** $35. **Credit** AmEx MC, V. **Map** p310 G10 ⑲ **Steakhouse**
This old-school River North steakhouse has been serving steaks and Italian classics in a dimly lit, cosy restaurant since 1941. The murals on the walls are as appealing as the menu and impeccable service. Of course, a hearty, juicy steak is the main draw:

go for the filet mignon or loin. Tasty non-steak options include calf's livers, veal vesuvio and an egg-plant parmigiana (for vegetarians).

GT Fish & Oyster

531 N Wells Street, at W Grand Avenue (1-312 929 3501, www.gtoyster.com). El: Red to Grand; Brown, Purple to Merchandise Mart. **Open** 11.30am-11pm Mon-Thur; 11.30am-midnight Fri, Sun; 10am-2.30pm, 4.30pm-midnight Sat. **Main courses** $14. **Credit** AmEx MC, V. **Map** p310 H10 ⑳ **Seafood**
Girl & the Goat restaurateurs Kevin Boehm and Rob Katz are also behind this seafood spot that's raised the profile of chef Giuseppe Tentori. Sunfish ceviche sparkles with acidity but is never drowned by it, duck confit is ingeniously paired with an apple frisée salad, and the seared scallop and short rib cannelloni is masterful. If you don't want a full meal, stop by the bar for oysters and cocktails. *Photo p111.*

Hub 51

51 W Hubbard Street, at N Dearborn Street (1-312 828 0051, www.hub51chicago.com). El: Red to Grand. **Open** 11am-midnight Mon-Wed; 11am-2am Thur, Fri; 10am-3am Sat; 10am-10pm Sun. **Main courses** $20. **Credit** AmEx, Disc, MC, V. Map p310 H11 ㉑ **Contemporary American**
This mid-scale River North catch-all offers a menu ranging from an ahi tuna burger to filet mignon steak tacos. The crowd at Hub 51 is as varied as the eats – a mix of tourists, ladies who lunch and local working stiffs all rubbing elbows – and everyone seems content with the large portions and boisterous scene. Braised pork tacos with house-made tortillas are a surprise hit, and plump maki do the trick if sushi cravings hit.

CONSUME

Frontera Grill.

Chef's Selections

La Sirena Clandestina's John Manion.

PERFECT NIGHT OUT
I'd head to the bar at the **Carriage House** (1700 W Division Street, at N Paulina Street, 1-773 384 9700, www.carriage housechicago.com) for the quail and dumpling dish – the best thing I've eaten this year. Next the **Bluebird** (1749 N Damen Avenue, at W Willow Street, 1-773 486 2473, www.bluebirdchicago.com), which has a well-curated wine and beer list, and Dave Ford is doing really good things with the food. The night usually ends at **Bar Deville** (701 N Damen Avenue, at W Huron Street, 1-312 929 2349, www. bardeville.com), which is something of an industry clubhouse.

FOOD OR DRINK ADDICTION
La Colombe (955 W Randolph Street, at N Morgan Street, 1-312 733 0707, www.lacolombe.com) for either iced coffee or americano, depending on the weather. The margaritas at **Big Star** (*see p125*), the only place I know where it seems OK to back up a shot of whisky with a margarita. Tex-Mex sloppy joe from **Butcher & Larder** (1026 N Milwaukee Avenue, between W Cortez Street & W Augusta Boulevard, 1-773 687 8280, www.thebutcherandlarder. com). If I were a purveyor of sloppy joes, one single tear would roll down my cheek and I would hang up my slotted spoon forever. Also, the double cheddar char dog from **Phil's Last Stand** (2258 W Chicago Avenue, at N Oakley Boulevard, 1-773 245 3287), mustard and onions only, and the biscuits at **Bang Bang** (*see p127*).

SECRET SPOT
Teco Veloz (1745 W Chicago Avenue, between N Wood & N Hermitage Streets, 1-312 738 0363) for Mexican karaoke.

Big Star.

Japonais

600 W Chicago Avenue, at N Larrabee Street (1-312 822 9600, www.japonaischicago.com). El: Brown or Purple to Chicago. **Open** 11.30am-2.30pm, 5-10.30pm Mon-Fri; 5-10.30pm Sat; 5-10pm Sun. **Main courses** $25. **Credit** AmEx, Disc, MC, V. **Map** p310 F9 ㉒ **Japanese**

Spend more than a million bucks building a restaurant in an undeveloped stretch of town, and you too can have a spot capable of transporting Chicagoans to a distant land. The Ian Schrager-esque space is swank, sexy and vibrant, and the food is also worthwhile. The modern Japanese cuisine centres around superb-quality raw fish, presented simply as sashimi or whacked out into tasty rolls. Don't leave without having the wagyu carpaccio.

Joe's Seafood, Prime Steaks & Stone Crab

60 E Grand Avenue, at N Wabash Avenue (1-312 379 5637, www.joes.net/chicago). El: Red to Grand. **Open** 11.30am-11pm Mon-Thur; 11.30am-midnight Fri; 11am-midnight Sat; 11am-11pm Sun. **Main courses** $40. **Credit** AmEx, Disc, MC, V. **Map** p310 H10 ㉓ **American**

When you're paying through the nose for a steakhouse experience, you should be made to feel like a king. The service should be top-notch, the atmosphere should be classy and the food should be stellar. Joe's delivers on all counts. Start with one of the signature stone crabs, the sugar prawns and a delicious chopped salad that could feed two. Then go straight to the bone-in New York strip, perfect when charred medium-rare.

Naha

500 N Clark Street, at W Illinois Street (1-312 321 6242, www.naha-chicago.com). El: Red to Grand. **Open** 11.30am-2pm, 5.30-9.30pm Mon-Thur; 11.30am-2pm, 5.30-10.30pm Fri; 5.30-10.30pm Sat. **Main courses** $35. **Credit** AmEx, Disc, MC, V. **Map** p310 H10 ㉔ **Contemporary American**

Chef Carrie Nahabedian delivers an upscale experience minus the pomp, courtesy of a snazzy room, great service and a seasonal menu that reads like an encyclopaedia of regional, sustainable foods. The menu changes daily: expect anything from seasonal veggies accompanying a wild Copper River Alaskan salmon to slow-roasted salmon with morels, sugar snap peas and cipollini onions.

Quartino

626 N State Street, at W Ontario Street (1-312 698 5000, www.quartinochicago.com). El: Red to Grand. **Open** 11.30am-2am Mon-Fri; 11.30am-3am Sat; 11.30am-1am Sun. **Small plates** $9. **Credit** AmEx, Disc, MC, V. **Map** p310 H10 ㉕ **Italian**

This cavernous, rustic Italian dining room is decked out with reclaimed wood and subway tiles, vintage mirrors and mismatched chairs. To ensure authenticity on the plate, the chef produces house-made salumi such as spiced salami, spicy *soppressata* and duck prosciutto served with house-made *giardiniera* and *mostarda*. The pizza is among the better thin-crust versions in town. As the name suggests, the affordable, half-Italian, half-global wine list is offered in quarter, half and full litres.

★ Slurping Turtle

116 W Hubbard Street, between N Clark & N LaSalle Streets (1-312 464 0466, www.slurping turtle.com). El: Red to Grand; Brown or Purple to Merchandise Mart. **Open** 11.30am-3pm, 5-10pm Mon-Thur, Sun; 11.30am-3pm, 5-11.30pm Fri, Sat. **Main courses** $13. **Credit** AmEx, Disc, MC, V. **Map** p310 H11 ㉖ **Japanese**

Takashi Yagihashi's foray into River North is the chef's attempt to capture the taste of his noodle-slurping childhood in Japan. Based on the menu's highlights – *hamachi* tartare in delicate little taro-root tacos, *tan tan men* ramen weighted with herb-packed pork meatballs, fried ramen noodles you toss with a dollop of spicy mustard for a dish called Chiyan Pon, and joyful desserts such as softball-sized cream puffs – Yagihashi may have had the best childhood ever.

Sumi Robata

702 N Wells Street, between W Huron & W Superior Streets (1-312 988 7864, www.sumirobatabar.com). El: Brown or Purple to Chicago. **Open** 11.30am-2.30pm, 5-11pm Mon-Wed; 11.30am-2.30pm, 5pm-midnight Thur, Fri; 5pm-midnight Sat. **Main courses** $12. **Credit** AmEx, Disc, MC, V. **Map** p310 G10 ㉗ **Japanese**

At the heart of Gene Kato's Japanese eatery is a traditional charcoal grill, on which he cooks pitch-perfect skewers of protein such as juicy cubes of skirt steak, tender hunks of salmon, and miso-marinated lamb ribs. Appetisers are the same size as the skewers and offer wonderful complexity (tiny squares of tuna topped with avocado and crispy shallots, a sweet and earthy shaved burdock root salad). Fried chicken, Japanese sliders and chocolate-filled doughnuts all make an appearance, and they're all robust and satisfying, but ultimately this is a place where subtlety rules. *Photos p112.*

XOCO

449 N Clark Street, at W Illinois Street (1-312 334 3688, www.rickbayless.com). El: Red to Grand. **Open** 8am-9pm Tue-Thur; 8am-10pm Fri, Sat. **Main courses** $11. **Credit** AmEx, Disc, MC, V. **Map** p310 H10 ㉘ **Mexican**

Breakfast at Rick Bayless's most casual spot yet is quiet perfection: a cup of masterfully concocted hot chocolate, a flaky egg *empañada*, one hell of a sugar-and-cocoa-coated *churro*. Lunch here is no less delicious, but it's a frenzy: queues extend out

THE WORLD CAN BE AN UNJUST AND TREACHEROUS PLACE, BUT THERE ARE THOSE WHO STRIVE TO MAKE IT SAFE FOR EVERYONE.

© 2003 Human Rights Watch

Operating in some of the world's most dangerous and oppressed countries, **Human Rights Watch** conducts rigorous investigations to bring those who have been targets of abuse to the world's attention. We use strategic advocacy to push people in power to end their repressive practices. And we work for as long as it takes to see that oppressors are held accountable for their crimes.

KNOWLEDGE IS POWER. LEARN ABOUT LIFE-CHANGING EVENTS IN YOUR WORLD THAT DON'T ALWAYS MAKE THE HEADLINES AND HOW YOU CAN HELP EFFECT POSITIVE CHANGE.

Stay informed, visit HRW.org

HUMAN RIGHTS WATCH

the door for *tortas* filled with fatty, crispy pork *carnitas*. The crowds keep up at dinner, when *caldos* such as braised-short-rib soup and chicken stew with toothsome *posole* are the ideal prelude to... another *churro*.

The Magnificent Mile & Streeterville

NoMI
Park Hyatt Chicago, 800 N Michigan Avenue, between W Chicago Avenue & W Pearson Street (1-312 239 4030, www.nomirestaurant.com). El: Red to Chicago. **Open** 6.30-10.30am, 11.30am-2pm, 5.30-10pm Mon-Fri; 11.30am-2pm, 5.30-10pm Sat, Sun. **Main courses** $36. **Credit** AmEx, Disc, MC, V. **Map** p310 J9 ㉙ **French/Asian**
There are two NoMIs: the NoMI with the stunning view of the water tower, and the NoMI with the awkward view of the kitchen. Which one you get depends on where your table is, but don't sweat it too hard: Both NoMIs feature the same somewhat inconsistent menu, and therefore the same opportunity for either a great meal or a disappointing one. Chef Ryan LaRoche can generally be trusted with chicken (both the $75 poached and the cheaper roasted), steak tartare and tagliolini, but his food is so pared down that it can barely hide even minor imperfections (such as those that we found in the mushroom salad, boring crudo or tough strip steak). Desserts follow the same pattern: for a sure thing, go for the chocolate ice-cream.
▶ *For a full review of the Park Hyatt Chicago hotel, see p174.*

Pizzeria Due
619 N Wabash Avenue, between E Ohio & E Ontario Streets (1-312 943 2400, www.unos.com). El: Red to Grand. **Open** 11am-1am Mon-Thur; 11am-2am Fri, Sat; 11am-11pm Sun. **Main courses** $15. **Credit** AmEx, Disc, MC, V. **Map** p310 H10 ㉚ **Pizza**
This crowd-pleasing sister to the original Uno features a cosy dining room/bar that reeks of that 'old Chicago' feel, complete with black-and-white tiled floor and historical photos lining the walls. Knife-and-fork, deep-dish pizza is its sole *raison d'être*, with a rich crust that gets crisp from its time in a traditional black-iron pan. Tourists love it (and, secretly, so do jaded locals).
▶ *The original Pizzeria Uno is located just around the corner at 29 E Ohio Street (1-312 321 1000, www.unos.com).*

Shanghai Terrace
Peninsula Chicago, 108 E Superior Street, between N Michigan Avenue & N Rush Street (1-312 573 6744, www.peninsula.com). El: Red to Chicago. **Open** 11.30am-2pm, 5-10.30pm daily. **Main courses** $20. **Credit** AmEx, Disc, MC, V. **Map** p310 J10 ㉛ **Chinese**

GT Fish & Oyster. *See p107.*

Normally we don't condone paying through the nose for Chinese food when so many excellent Chinatown options abound, but this gorgeous fourth-floor terrace, brimming with fresh flowers and offering a view of the historic Water Tower, is hard to beat. Elevated takes on five-spiced duck, drunken baby chicken and wok-baked lobster mostly surpass expectations, but if you're looking to take advantage of the digs while keeping within budget, stick with snacking on dim sum and splurge on a fancy cocktail.

INSIDE TRACK BAR NONE

Dining alone can be one of the most relaxing ways to unwind after a hard day, provided you aren't surrounded by canoodling couples. One neat trick: eat at the bar. At places such as **Naha** (*see p109*), **Le Bouchon** (*see p125*) and **Avec** (*see p120*), you'll get the same menu as the rest of the room, but the privacy to enjoy it in peace.

The Gold Coast

★ Café des Architectes

Sofitel Chicago, 20 E Chestnut Street, at N Wabash Avenue (1-312 324 4000, www.cafedes architectes.com). El: Red to Chicago. **Open** 6am-10pm daily. **Main courses** $30. **Credit** AmEx, Disc, MC, V. **Map** p310 H9 ❷ **French**

The French vibe of the Sofitel carries over into its sun-streaked restaurant: The staff have accents, and say '*bonjour*' and '*merci*'. The waiters all look

Sumi Robata. *See p109.*

a little like Frenchmen who appear in romantic daydreams, only maybe a little bit older, but they're not whispering '*je t'aime*' into your ear. They're whispering, 'Try the truffle-poached halibut'. Or the tender guinea hen, executed with precision and plated with soft polenta and black garlic. The food is a bit heavy at times, but it all ranges from good to very good.

★ Spiaggia

980 N Michigan Avenue, between E Oak Street & E Walton Place (1-312 280 2750, www. spiaggiarestaurant.com). El: Red to Clark/Division. **Open** 6-9pm Mon-Thur, Sun; 5.30-10.30pm Fri, Sat. **Main courses** $42. **Credit** AmEx, Disc, MC, V. **Map** p310 J9 ❸ **Italian**

Want to have the best Italian fine-dining experience in town? Splurge here. Under executive chef Tony Mantuano, chef Sarah Grueneberg marries top-notch ingredients with a brilliant understanding of cuisine from the north end of 'the boot'. The wood-burning oven makes beautiful work of duck and prime rib-eye, while rosemary honey, bitter greens and aged balsamic finish the plates with Italian flair. Pasta, from pappardelle to gnocchi (served with ricotta and black truffle sauce), is made fresh every day. Add in a two-dozen-choice cheese cave and perfect service, and you've got a night that's worth blowing the budget for.

OLD TOWN & LINCOLN PARK
Old Town

★ Alinea

1723 N Halsted Street, between W North Avenue & W Willow Street (1-312 867 0110, www.alinearestaurant.com). El: Red to North/ Clybourn. **Open** 5.30-9.30pm Wed-Fri; 5-9.30pm Sat, Sun. **Tasting menu** $145. **Credit** AmEx, Disc, MC, V. **Map** p311 F7 ❸ **Contemporary American**

A few years ago, now-defunct foodie bible *Gourmet* anointed Alinea the number one restaurant in the country. So what's all the fuss? Grant Achatz's food, a well-orchestrated ride that plays with textures, temperatures and notions of 'normal' cuisine while somehow remaining grounded in season, flavour and flawless execution. Recent highlights have included 'black truffle explosion' with romaine and parmesan, and 'hot potato cold potato' served with black truffle and butter.

Perennial Virant

1800 N Lincoln Avenue, at N Clark Street (1-312 981 7070, www.perennialchicago.com). El: Brown or Purple to Sedgwick. **Open** 7-11am, 5-10pm Mon-Thur; 7-11am, 5-11pm Fri; 9am-2pm, 5-11pm Sat; 9am-2pm, 5-10pm Sun. **Main courses** $23. **Credit** AmEx, Disc, MC, V. **Map** p311 H7 ❸ **Contemporary American**

CONSUME

Chef's Selections

Ada Street's Zoë Schor.

PERFECT NIGHT OUT
An early dinner with my girlfriend at **Sapori Trattoria** (2701 N Halsted Street, between W Wrightwood & W Diversey Avenues, 1-773 832 9999), followed by the theatre, then a late-night visit to **Acre** (5308 N Clark Street, at W Summerdale Avenue, 1-773 334 7600, www.acrerestaurant.com) for dollar oysters and a glass of rosé.

FOOD OR DRINK ADDICTION
Dr Pepper, gummy bears, chicken tenders at **Konak Pizza & Grill** (5150 N Clark Street, at W Foster Avenue, 1-773 271 6688, www.konakchicago.com) and a 'Wreck' with everything from sandwich chain **Potbelly's** (www.potbellys.com).

SECRET SPOT
Whenever I can, I eat at **Itto Sushi** (2616 N Halsted Street, between W Wrightwood & W Diversey Avenues, 1-773 871 1800, www.ittosushi.com). It's the best sushi I've ever had (on any of the three coasts), and very reasonably priced. Plus, you can pick your own chopsticks and keep them there.

CONSUME

Balena. *See p114.*

INSIDE TRACK NICE BUNS

When a burger craving hits, accept no substitute. Finding the best in town depends on your type of vibe, so know that burgers at **Kuma's Corner** (*see p127*) come with a side of metal (the head-banging, tattooed kind, not steel); Mindy's **Hot Chocolate** (*see p126*) has a neighbourhood feel with its sunny-side-up farm egg-topped patty; and **Moody's** (*see p136*) can either be a beer garden party in summer or a recluse's fireside friend in winter.

Perennial Virant lives and dies by chef Paul Virant's dedication to seasonal ingredients – the urgency with which he creates some of his dishes may explain why they sometimes disappoint. But make no mistake: for every miss, there's a phenomenal success, such as a perfect ribeye, pillowy gnocchi, robust house-made sausages and basically every cocktail on the list.

Lincoln Park

★ Balena

1633 N Halsted Street, between W North Avenue & W Willow Street (1-312 867 3888, www.balena chicago.com). El: Red to North/Clybourn. **Open** 5-10pm Mon-Thur; 5-11pm Fri; 4.30-11pm Sat; 4.30-10pm Sun. **Main courses** $22. **Credit** AmEx, Disc, MC, V. **Map** p311 F7 ③ **Italian**

Between the warmth of the room and the compelling simplicity of Chris Pandel's food, there is something hugely comfortable about Balena, the first collaboration between the Bristol (*see p125*) and the BOKA Restaurant Group. Settle in with a few amaro cocktails (our pick: the Montenegro No6), share a pizza topped with ingredients such as rhubarb, pancetta, spring onion, ricotta and mint, don't miss the smoked mackerel and end on a sweet note with a bowl of *gelato*. *Photo p113.*

★ Floriole Café & Bakery

1220 W Webster Avenue, between N Racine & N Magnolia Avenues (1-773 883 1313, www.floriole.com). El: Brown, Purple, Red to Fullerton. **Open** 8am-4pm Mon, Sun; 7am-5.30pm Tue-Fri; 8am-5.30pm Sat. *Pizza nights* 6-9pm Fri, Sat. **Pastries** $4. **Credit** AmEx, Disc, MC, V. **Café**

During her years hawking French pastries at farmers' markets, chef Sandra Holl developed a passionate following, with the best croissants and fruit galettes in the city. Here, they have a permanent home, along with superb cakes, dreamy cream puffs, rustic-chic sandwiches and insane brownies. On pizza nights, you can enjoy Holl's creations with a glass of wine or beer.

Half Shell

676 W Diversey Parkway, between N Orchard & N Clark Streets (1-773 549 1773, www.half shellchicago.com). El: Brown or Purple to Diversey. **Open** 11.30am-11pm Mon-Sat; noon-11pm Sun.

Floriole Café & Bakery

Anteprima. *See p118.*

CONSUME

Main courses $16. **No credit cards.**
Map p312 F4 ❸ **Seafood**
'We close when we feel like closin'' and 'Nothin' but cash, no exceptions' are among the oh-so-perfect-for-the-setting sayings that you might be greeted with during an evening at this 40-plus-year-old subterranean restaurant. Grab a table in the tiny Christmas light-strewn room, and start out with the Mulligan stew and an order of crispy calamari. If you're looking to crack some serious crab, splurge on the massive, meaty king legs.

North Pond
2610 N Cannon Drive, between W Fullerton Parkway & N Lake Shore Drive (1-773 477 5845, www.northpondrestaurant.com). Bus: 76, 151, 156. **Open** *Oct-May* 5.30-9.30pm Tue-Sat; 10.30am-1.30pm, 5.30-9.30pm Sun. *June-Sept* 11.30am-1.30pm, 5.30-9.30pm Tue-Fri; 5.30-9.30pm Sat; 10.30am-1pm, 5.30-9.30pm Sun. **Main courses** $40. **Credit** AmEx, Disc, MC, V.
Map p312 G4 ❸ **Contemporary American**
OK, so technically you're not eating outside. But when you're only a few feet from a pond in the middle of Lincoln Park, you're as close to nature as it gets in the city. Even more so when you sample chef Bruce Sherman's elevated contemporary menu, concocted with as much locally grown organic food as he can find. Dishes might include the likes of English peas with minted goat's cheese gnocchi.

★ Riccardo Trattoria
2119 N Clark Street, between W Dickens & W Webster Avenues (1-773 549 0038, www. riccardotrattoria.com). El: Brown, Purple or Red to Fullerton. **Open** 5-10pm Mon-Thur; 5-11pm Fri, Sat; 5-9pm Sun. **Main courses** $20. **Credit** AmEx, Disc, MC, V. **Map** p312 G6 ❸ **Italian**
One of the best Italian restaurants in town isn't tucked away in Little Italy. Surprisingly, it's smack-bang in vanilla Lincoln Park. Chef Riccardo Michi's family founded the Bice restaurant empire in Milan, so he knows a thing or two about regional Italian food. Don't miss the *orecchiette* with wild-boar sausage, garlicky *rapini* and pecorino cheese or the rack of lamb. Become a regular and the Italian waiters might just cap off your meal with a slice of ricotta cheesecake.

LAKEVIEW & NORTH
Lakeview & Wrigleyville

$ Chicago Diner
3411 N Halsted Street, between W Roscoe Street & W Newport Avenue (1-773 935 6696, www. veggiediner.com/wp). El: Brown, Purple or Red to Belmont. **Open** 11am-10pm Mon-Thur; 11am-11pm Fri; 10am-11pm Sat; 10am-10pm Sun. **Main courses** $11. **Credit** AmEx, Disc, MC, V. **Map** p313 F2 ❹ **Vegetarian**

Avec. See p120.

Even staunch non-vegetarians know about the Chicago Diner. The vibe is normal, everyday, albeit with soy milk, tofu and tempeh on the giant menu. The queues for weekend brunch can get pretty painful, but rewards include flaky soy margarine biscuits and sweet blueberry-lemon muffins made with vegan egg substitute. The back patio is an outdoor oasis in summer.

$ Crisp

2940 N Broadway, between W Oakdale & W Wellington Avenues (1-877 693 8653, www.crisponline.com). El: Brown or Purple to Diversey. **Open** 11.30am-9pm daily. **Main courses** $8. **Credit** AmEx, MC, V. **Map** p313 F3 ❹ **Korean**

The chicken at Crisp is fresh, good-quality and comes slathered in a choice of three different sauces: sticky barbecue, hot buffalo or a sesame soy glaze

---

THE BEST PLACES TO BLOW THE BUDGET

For an Italian-style splurge
Spiaggia. *See p112.*

For a top-ranking meal
Alinea. *See p112.*

For a gastronomic adventure
Schwa. *See p126.*

---

dubbed 'Seoul Sassy'. The latter is a winner; but even unadorned, the chicken stands out for its juicy meat and crunchy black pepper-dotted crust. There's also a decent bibimbap and Korean-style burritos. But really, chicken is king.

Mia Francesca

3311 N Clark Street, between W Aldine Avenue & W Buckingham Place (1-773 281 3310, www. miafrancesca.com). El: Brown, Purple or Red to Belmont. **Open** 5-10pm Mon-Thur; 5-11pm Fri; 10am-11pm Sat; 10am-10pm Sun. **Main courses** $15. **Credit** AmEx, Disc, MC, V. **Map** p313 F2 ❹ **Italian**

Locals dig into huge oval platters of cool, caper-studded carpaccio; pasta tossed with lemony cream and asparagus; and the best garlic spinach in town. Couples and families happily wait at the bar, somehow oblivious to the chaos of the always-packed room and the obligatory wait even for those with a reservation. A very amiable Italian spot.

★ Mixteco Grill

1601 W Montrose Avenue, at N Ashland Avenue (1-773 868 1601, www.mixtecogrill.com). El: Brown to Montrose. **Open** 5-10pm Tue-Thur; 5-11pm Fri; 10am-2.30pm, 5-11pm Sat; 10am-2.30pm, 4-9pm Sun. **Main courses** $17. **Credit** AmEx, Disc, MC, V. **Mexican**

The *moles* here steal the show. *Sopes* get a dose of the brooding, smoky *mole rojo*, and white fish gets treated with a lighter, sprightly *mole verde*. And while it's not a *mole*, the smooth *poblano* sauce

CONSUME

pooled around perfectly grilled shrimp is so marine, there's almost no need for seafood. In fact, protein is all but superfluous when you have a bowl of *mole* and some handmade tortillas.

$ Southport Grocery & Café

3552 N Southport Avenue, between W Eddy & W Addison Streets (1-773 665 0100, www.southport grocery.com). El: Brown to Southport. **Open** 7am-4pm Mon-Fri; 8am-5pm Sat; 8am-4pm Sun. **Main courses** $9. **Credit** AmEx, Disc, MC, V. **Map** p313 D1 ❹ **Café**

Go ahead and believe the hype about the cupcakes here: They're moist, they're substantial but not heavy, and the thick, sugary icing hides deep flavours of chocolate and vanilla. For a bright start, try the sweet-and-savoury French toast with rosemary-roasted ham. Later, tuck into the albacore tuna melt with local butterkäse cheese and green olive aïoli. Eat up, but make sure you save room for one of those cupcakes.

$ TAC Quick Thai

3930 N Sheridan Road, between W Dakin Street & W Irving Park Road (1-773 327 5253, www. tacquick.net). El: Red to Sheridan. **Open** 11am-10pm Mon, Wed-Sat; 11am-9.30pm Sun. **Main courses** $8. **Credit** AmEx, MC, V. **Thai**

This once-tiny Thai joint has more than doubled in size. Luckily, the kitchen isn't having any trouble keeping up with the crowds that flood the simple

THE BEST CHEAP EATS

For a top chef's take on tacos
Big Star. *See p125.*

For badass burgers
Kuma's Corner. *See p127.*

For exceptional pies
Hoosier Mama Pie Company. *See p123.*

For a Chicago original
Al's #1 Italian Beef. *See p121.*

room. Surefire flavour explosions include tart and smoky pork-and-rice sausage; ground chicken with crispy basil and preserved eggs; wrap-ready pork meatballs served with rice papers, fierce chillis, garlic cloves, fresh basil and mint, diced banana and apple; and the best beef noodle dish in town, the brisket-packed 'boat noodles'.

Roscoe Village

Volo

2008 W Roscoe Street, between N Damen & N Seeley Avenues (1-773 348 4600, www. volorestaurant.com). Bus: 50, 77, 152. **Open** 5-10pm Mon-Thur; 5pm-midnight Fri, Sat.

CONSUME

Publican. *See p120.*

Small plates $10. **Credit** AmEx, MC, V.
Map p314 B2 ㊹ **Contemporary**
Owner Jon Young, of Kitsch'n on Roscoe and Kitsch'n River North, has teamed up with chef Stephen Dunne at this small-plates wine bar. Dunne's best dishes are the rich ones: plates such as intense duck confit leg with sweet garlic purée or roasted veal marrow bones with toast. Luckily the eclectic wine list is well thought-out and stocked with plenty of food-friendly quaffs to cut through it all.

Andersonville, Edgewater & Uptown

★ Anteprima
5316 N Clark Street, between W Berwyn & W Summerdale Avenues (1-773 506 9990, www. anteprimachicago.net). Bus: 22, 92. **Open** 5.30-10pm Mon-Thur; 5.30-11pm Fri, Sat; 5-9.30pm Sun. **Main courses** $20. **Credit** AmEx, Disc, MC, V. **Italian**

Morning Glory

For the perfect brunch, order one of these textbook classics.

EGGS BENEDICT
The smoked ham on the **Bristol**'s (*see p125*) eggs benedict is thick-cut and tender, but it's the pungent edge of the mustard hollandaise that takes the dish to new flavour heights.

EGG SANDWICH
With a pile of rocket, the morning favourite at **Sola** (3868 N Lincoln Avenue, at W Byron Street, 1-773 327 3868, www.sola-restaurant.com) feels blissfully guilt-free. Over-easy eggs are light, crispy bacon offers texture, and fluffy goat's cheese brings it all together.

DOUGHNUTS
Famed doughnut cook (yes, there is such a thing) Enoch Simpson may have left **Nightwood** (*see p121*) to open his own

Nightwood.

Bristol.

CONSUME

What's not to like about this supremely cute Andersonville bistro? Well, the veal meatballs aren't too hot; but other than that, very little. Don't miss the balsamic- and honey-laced quail, perfectly roasted so that the crispy skin gives way to juicy, well-seasoned meat; the tender, lemon-kissed grilled octopus; or the salumi plate. And make sure you save room for desserts such as vanilla bean-speckled lemon pannacotta and chocolate tart lined with a buttery hazelnut crust. *Photo p115.*

spot, **Endgrain** (1851 W Addison Street, at N Wolcott Street, 1-773 687 8191, www.endgrainrestaurant.com), but his iconic doughnuts (including the unbeatable bacon butterscotch) remain.

QUICHE
The word 'quiche' seems too pedestrian to describe the version served at **Floriole** (*see p114*): rich, smooth egg custard teamed with locally sourced vegetables, quality cheese and occasional meats (the selection changes daily). The sublime puff pastry shell crumbles into a million buttery flakes.

HUEVOS RANCHEROS
Putting the Bayless empire up against humble *taquerias* is a David and Goliath move, but at **Frontera Grill** (*see p106*) you'll side with the big guy once you taste the oh-so-soft house-made tortillas, the orange-yolked farm eggs and the beautiful blistered tomato sauce.

FRENCH TOAST
Longman & Eagle (*see p127*) puts a genius spin on the brunch standby: make your way from this brioche's crisp exterior to its custardy interior and a mass of whipped cream reveals its true identity – whipped maple syrup, melting over the hot toast.

HASH
You can keep your corned beef. The pinnacle of hashes at **Bite Café** (1039 N Western Avenue, at W Cortez Street, 1-773 395 2483, www.bitecafechicago. com) tosses Yukons, sweet potatoes, brussels sprouts and kohlrabi with tender braised pork shoulder, then adds two over-easy eggs and a pool of spicy hollandaise to round it all of.

$ Coffee Studio
5628 N Clark Street, at W Olive Avenue (1-773 271 7881, www.thecoffeestudio.com). El: Red to Bryn Mawr. **Open** 6.30am-9pm daily. **Coffee** $3. **Credit** AmEx, MC, V. **Café**
Andersonville is nuts about this coffee shop, which offers a colourful variety of organic, sustainable menu items. The quiche selection, featuring hearty wild mushroom pies, is definitely a draw, as are the handful of can't-believe-it's-vegan desserts. The smooth, expertly pulled shots of espresso and smart, mid-century modern design make this the sexiest coffee shop on the block.

★ Hopleaf
5148 N Clark Street, between W Winona Street & W Foster Avenue (1-773 334 9851, www. hopleaf.com). El: Red to Berwyn. **Open** noon-11pm Mon-Thur; noon-midnight Fri, Sat; noon-10pm Sun. **Main courses** $18. **Credit** AmEx, Disc, MC, V. **Gastropub**
Carnivores can tuck into tasty organic treats such as smoky brisket sandwich or grilled Dakota beef flank steak at this bar-restaurant, which specialises in Belgian beers. Other highlights, in season, might include roasted spring chicken with oven-roasted artichokes; and CB&J, a grilled sandwich of house-made cashew butter, fig jam and raclette cheese on sourdough bread.

$ M Henry
5707 N Clark Street, between Hollywood & Edgewater Avenues (1-773 561 1600, www. mhenry.net). El: Red to Bryn Mawr. **Open** 7am-3pm Tue-Fri; 8am-3pm Sat, Sun. **Main courses** $9. **Credit** AmEx, Disc, MC, V. **Café**
At this adorable, sunny, daytime-only café, the health food is tasty enough to eat. The owners are committed to organic ingredients and offer meat-free options, but they're OK with a little cheese, butter and sugar every now and then. Case in point: thick, dense blueberry pancakes and a vast breakfast sandwich of fried egg, gorgonzola, applewood-smoked bacon and fresh thyme. If that's too shocking for you health nuts, there's always the Vegan Epiphany, an organic tofu scramble.

THE NEAR WEST SIDE
The West Loop & Greektown

$ 9 Muses
315 S Halsted Street, between W Jackson Boulevard & W Van Buren Street (1-312 902 9922, www.9museschicago.com). El: Blue to UIC-Halsted. **Open** 11am-2am Mon-Fri; noon-3am Sat; noon-2am Sun. **Main courses** $7. **Credit** AmEx, Disc, MC, V. **Map** p314 F12 ⑮ **Greek**
It's a good sign that this trendy, clubby sort of restaurant is packed with young Greeks: their presence suggests that the Hellenic munchies, like the

CONSUME

Florina peppers (two roasted red peppers stuffed with creamy feta), *loukanika* (a pork-lamb sausage) and huge gyro platters, are on the mark. If you can stop yourself from talking by shovelling in the food, nobody will know you don't belong.

★ Au Cheval

800 W Randolph Street, at N Halsted Street (1-312 929 4580, www.aucheval.com). El: Green, Pink to Clinton. **Open** 11am-1.30am Mon-Sat; 10am-12.30am Sun. **Main courses** $17. **Credit** AmEx, Disc, MC, V. **Map** p314 F11 ⑯ **American**

You practically trip over all the perfectly executed food at Brendan Sodikoff's 'diner': exemplary matzo ball soup, devastatingly delicious chopped chicken liver, gloriously messy double-decker burgers. But there's not a lot of lighter fare to kick off a meal here. So head to Au Cheval when it will serve you best: for a burger and a beer at the bar or a plate of fried chicken after hitting the neighbourhood bars.

★ Avec

615 W Randolph Street, between N Jefferson & N Desplaines Streets (1-312 377 2002, www. avecrestaurant.com). El: Green or Pink to Clinton. **Open** 3.30pm-midnight Mon-Thur; 3.30pm-1am Fri, Sat; 11am-2pm, 3.30pm-midnight Sun. **Small plates** $10. **Credit** AmEx, Disc, MC, V. **Map** p314 F12 ⑰ **Mediterranean**

Owner Donnie Madia and chef Paul Kahan's tiny space looks like a sauna, has communal seating, doesn't take reservations and is as loud as hell. But it's a must-eat spot for foodies. Small plates such as chorizo-stuffed dates and salty brandade are superb, as are the likes of cheesy focaccia and burrata salad. *Photo p116.*

Blackbird

619 W Randolph Street, between N Jefferson & N Desplaines Streets (1-312 715 0708, www. blackbirdrestaurant.com). El: Green or Pink to Clinton. **Open** 11.30am-2pm, 5.30-10pm Mon-Thur; 11.30am-2pm, 5.30-11pm Fri; 5.30-11pm Sat; 5.30-10pm Sun. **Main courses** $33. **Credit** AmEx, Disc, MC, V. **Map** p314 F12 ⑱ **Contemporary American**

This iconic West Loop kitchen, overseen by executive chef Paul Kahan, is still one of Chicago's best. The beautiful seasonal dishes from chef de cuisine David Posey are full of surprising elements – chilled spring pea and tofu soup with paddlefish roe, perhaps, or wood-grilled sturgeon and chicken wings with kale, turnips and walnut purée – which makes for exciting and sometimes challenging eating. In the same vein, pastry chef Dana Cree aims to 'work with really familiar stuff in an unfamiliar way.'

★ Girl & the Goat

809 W Randolph Street, at N Halsted Street (1-312 492 6262, www.girlandthegoat.com).

El: Green or Pink to Clinton. **Open** 4.30-11pm Mon-Thur, Sun; 4.30pm-midnight Fri, Sat. **Main courses** $15. **Credit** AmEx, Disc, MC, V. **Map** p314 F11 ⑲ **Contemporary American**

This West Loop restaurant from Top Chef Stephanie Izard is packed to the gills with diners seeking something more than the faddy pork-and-beer route. It's refreshing that most of her menu goes the other way, with inspired vegetable and seafood dishes (and desserts) that operate on a lighter, livelier plane. When Izard tops octopus with lemon-pistachio vinaigrette, pairs green beans with a fish sauce vinaigrette, and serves bittersweet chocolate toffee alongside a shitake-caramel *gelato* for dessert, she's evolving contemporary Chicago cuisine.

★ Maude's Liquor Bar

840 W Randolph Street, between N Green & N Peoria Streets (1-312 243 9712, www.maudes liquorbar.com). El: Green or Pink to Clinton. **Open** 4.45-11.30pm Mon-Thur, Sun; 4.45pm-1am Fri, Sat. **Main courses** $12. **Credit** AmEx, Disc, MC, V. **Map** p314 F11 ㊿ **French**

Cocktailers hit Maude's around midnight, but make a point to get there earlier, when the kitchen is still open. That way you can nosh on butter-smooth chicken-liver mousse slathered on toast with shallot marmalade, smoky slabs of pork belly fanned over a pitch-perfect salad Lyonnaise, and roasted chicken *paillard*. Desserts are limited to crème brûlée or fancy chocolate squares, an audacious move that would be maddening if this hot spot wasn't so dead-on.

Next

953 W Fulton Street, between N Morgan & N Sangamon Streets (1-312 226 0858, www. nextrestaurant.com). El: Green or Pink to Clinton. **Open** times vary, check website for details. **Menus** prices vary, check website for details. **Credit** AmEx, Disc, MC, V. **Map** p314 E11 ㉛ **Contemporary American**

To dine at Grant Achatz's follow-up to Alinea (*see p112*) is a rare – and rarefied – opportunity to submit oneself to a very specific vision of what great dining might look like. That vision is a restaurant with a menu that entirely changes its concept every three months, from vegan to childhood-inspired (think foie gras frosted desserts and newfangled fruit roll-ups), and a reservation system based on tickets purchased in advance (no money is exchanged at the restaurant). Word to the wise: follow the restaurant on Facebook to find out about last-minute tickets for sale. Usually the experience is more lighthearted and lively than Alinea, but it is in no way less delicious.

★ Publican

837 W Fulton Market, between N Green & N Peoria Streets (1-312 733 9555, www.thepublican restaurant.com). El: Green or Pink to Clinton. **Open** 3.30-10.30pm Mon-Thur; 3.30-11.30pm Fri; 10am-2pm, 3.30-11.30pm Sat; 10am-2pm, 5-10pm

CONSUME

Sun. **Main courses** $19. **Credit** AmEx, Disc,
MC, V. **Map** p314 F11 ② **Gastropub**
The third project from the team behind Blackbird
(*see p120*) is a minimalist, golden-hued, beer hall-
like space. Pork is king of chef Brian Huston's menu;
to come here and not order the impeccable charcuterie is to miss the point. But non-swine entrées come
off just as well, whether in shareable plates of lightly
charred half-chicken paired with thick rounds of
summer sausage or pan-seared whole loup-de-mer
stuffed with bitter greens. The Belgian-heavy beer
merits thorough exploration. *Photos p117.*

★ La Sirena Clandestina

*954 W Fulton Street, between N Morgan &
N Sangamon Streets (1-312 226 5300, www.
lasirenachicago.com). El: Green or Pink to Morgan.*
Open 11am-1am Mon-Fri; 5pm-1am Sat; 10am-
10pm Sun. **Main courses** $18. **Credit** AmEx,
Disc, MC, V. **Map** p314 E11 ③ **Latin American**
Chef John Manion's permanent home is designed
to be a place you want to hang out in: it's dim and
sultry, and cocktails such as the caipirinha (cachaça,
muddled lime and blend of sugars) get things off to
a good start. If you order right – *moqueca*, a seafood
stew, and ceviche are standouts – you'll never want

La Sirena Clandestina.

to leave. Yes, some dishes may miss the mark (lacklustre empañadas; overly rich pork loin milenesa),
but in general the food is bright and finessed.

Little Italy & Heart of Chicago

$ Al's #1 Italian Beef

*1079 W Taylor Street, between S Carpenter
& S Aberdeen Streets (1-312 226 4017, www.
alsbeef.com). El: Blue to Racine.* **Open** 9am-11pm
Mon-Thur; 9am-midnight Fri; 10am-midnight
Sat. **Main courses** $4. **No credit cards.**
Map p314 E14 ④ **American**
Having opened in 1938, this Al's is the oldest, and
the only direct descendant of the original (a wooden
stand at Laflin and Harrison). These days, you'll find
Italian beefs all over town, but there's something
special about eating one at this surviving piece of
Little Italy. Order the six-inch bun piled with tender,
thinly sliced beef as a 'combo' (topped with char-
grilled sausage), 'dipped' in beef jus and finished
with hot giardiniera.

RoSal's

*1154 W Taylor Street, between S May Street & S
Racine Avenue (1-312 243 2357, www.rosals.com).
El: Blue to Racine.* **Open** 4-9pm Mon-Thur; 4-11pm
Fri, Sat; 3-8pm Sun. **Main courses** $18. **Credit**
AmEx, Disc, MC, V. **Map** p314 E14 ⑤ **Italian**
Typically, we'd tell the server to save the speech, but
here, it's somehow still charming when the bubbly
girl 'from da neighbourhood' explains how namesake owners Roseanne and Salvatore came to open
their Little Italy spot. Cuteness aside, the food's
among the best to be found on the Taylor Street
strip. Start with lightly charred but tender grilled
calamari; then go for the veal saltimbocca with a side
of spinach for the main event.

Pilsen

Nightwood

*2119 S Halsted Street, between 21st Street &
Cermak Road (1-312 526 3385, www.nightwood
restaurant.com). El: Orange to Halsted.* **Open**
5.30-10pm Mon-Thur; 5.30-11pm Fri, Sat; 9am-
2.30pm Sun. **Main courses** $20. **Credit** AmEx,
Disc, MC, V. **Contemporary American**
The consistently successful dishes at this understated spot from the Lula Cafe crew share two traits:
first, that fresh-from-the-garden liveliness that's won
Lula a cultish status (marinated Illinois tomatoes
with warm chorizo vinaigrette, goat's cheese and
purslane, for example). Second, a distinctive wood-
grilled flavour that gives an intoxicating aroma to
the juicy half-chicken and earthy cheeseburger. The
menu changes daily, so you'll always be treated to
the freshest ingredients. The sweet side of the menu
hits all the right notes (think mascarpone cheesecake
with rhubarb sorbet), and the dining room is so cosy
that you may want to linger over after-dinner drinks.

CONSUME

Streets Ahead

These innovative meals on wheels leave standard food trucks for dust.

Tamalespaceship.

CONSUME

5411 EMPANADAS
The three Argentines behind catering company 5411 Empanadas are also behind this baby blue truck serving up gourmet empanadas and cookies. The baked (as opposed to deep-fried) pastries are supremely flaky and come stuffed with a choice of half a dozen fillings: gently spiced ground beef, simple ham and cheese, stewed spinach and cheese, caramelised onions, barbecued chicken, and straight-up corn. Also look for the occasional guest appearance when the bakers get bored and decide to mix it up.
Twitter @5411empanadas.
Average item $2.

HUMMINGBIRD KITCHEN
You can find this truck humming around Evanston, where it takes advantage of city regulations that allow full cooking on wheels with a 12-burner stove, a fleet of fryers and enough fridge space to hold a few sides of beef. Chef Vince DiBattista (also of Evanston mainstays Union Pizzeria and Campagnola) changes his offerings on a daily basis, but highlights might include Italian-inspired riffs such as chicken-parmesan sandwiches, garlicky fries and honey *gelato* sandwiched between lavender shortbread to finish on a sweet note.
Twitter @hummingbirdtogo.
Average item $5.

THE MORE MOBILE
The city's most upscale cupcakery also has the city's most elegant food truck. It's more of a van, really, with a display window showing off the sophisticated – and devastatingly delicious – cupcakes people track it down for. The savoury cakes (BLT, bacon-maple) are what get all the press, but for our money (and these things ain't cheap) there's only one choice: valhrona, valhrona, valhrona.
Twitter @themoremobile.
Average item $4.

THE SLIDE RIDE
The side of this bright-pink truck features a waitress on wheels, evoking the classic drive-in diners of the 1950s, but don't expect burgers and fries from newcomer Nida Rodriguez: the mini-sandwiches on offer have flair. The menu is subject to change daily, but expect 'slider' options such as pork *banh mi* or southwestern black bean on a sturdy torpedo roll.
Twitter @thesliideride.
Average item $4.

THE SOUTHERN MAC
The Southern Mac is chef Cary Taylor of the Southern's mobile ode to macaroni and cheese. Taylor's four varieties rotate (and usually include bacon, blue cheese and roasted apple; smoked gouda; white cheddar with sun-dried tomatoes and caramelised onion; and a Cajun version with crawfish and andouille), and he'll continue making lunchtime stops until people's interest in mac-and-cheese or food trucks wanes – neither of which looks likely to be very soon.
Twitter @thesouthernmac.
Average item $9.

TAMALESPACESHIP
Though inspired by Mexican sci-fi movies, wrestling and the avant-garde movement known as Stridentism, Tamalli Space Charros keeps the food at its truck, Tamalespaceship, surprisingly down-to-earth. Donning *lucha libre* masks, the crew deliver flavourful concoctions such as Picturesque Tamalli (Yucatan-style pork with tomato habanero sauce).
Twitter @tamalespace101.
Average item $7.

$ Nuevo León

1515 W 18th Street, between S Laflin Street
& S Ashland Avenue (1-312 421 1517, www.
nuevoleonrestaurant.com). El: Pink to 18th.
Open 7am-midnight daily. **Main courses** $10.
No credit cards. **Mexican**
The Gutierrez family has been running this mecca
of Mexican food since 1962, starting every dinner
with an unexpected amuse-bouche. Don't fill up,
though, as there's a lot more where that came from,
such as roasted chicken pieces covered in a thick,
dark, intense *mole*, and *tacos de chorizo*. The waitresses hustling back and forth between two
rooms are cheerfully brisk but will bring anything
you ask except alcohol – you've got to bring the
mescal yourself.

WICKER PARK & AROUND
Ukrainian Village & West Town

$ Ada Street

1664 N Ada Street, between Concord Place
& Wabansia Avenue (1-773 697 7069, www.
adastreetchicago.com). Bus: 9, 72, 73. **Open**
5.30pm-1am Mon-Thur; 5.30pm-2am Fri, Sat.
Main courses $8. **Credit** AmEx, Disc, MC, V.
Gastropub
Michael Kornick and David Morton (DMK Burger
Bar, Fish Bar) have teamed up with chef Zoë Schor
for this hybrid cocktail bar-restaurant. The room is
lovely, and so is the food. Schor's deep-fried black-
eyed peas are the perfect drinking snack, and her
light touch with steak (dressed in nothing more than
brown butter), salads and even doughnuts makes
sense with the food-friendly cocktails.

★ Green Zebra

1460 W Chicago Avenue, at N Greenview Avenue
(1-312 243 7100, www.greenzebrachicago.
com). El: Blue to Chicago. **Open** 5.30-9.30pm
Mon-Thur; 5-10pm Fri, Sat; 5-9pm Sun. **Main**
courses $12. **Credit** AmEx, Disc, MC, V.
Map p315 D9 ⑤⑥ **Vegetarian**
Shawn McClain's moss-coloured, Asian-tinged house
of Zen is one of the only upscale dining experiences
Chicago vegetarians can truly call their own. This is
a great thing for dinner, but it may be an even better
thing for brunch. Here, there's no worrying that
bacon will be strewn over every plate (unless you
count shiitake bacon). Instead, tuck into treats such
as blueberry pancakes with lemon curd; and, for dinner, an organic duck egg with smoked potato purée.

★ Hoosier Mama Pie Company

1618 1/2 W Chicago Avenue, between N Ashland
& N Marshfield Avenues (1-312 243 4846,
www.hoosiermamapie.com). El: Blue to Division.
Open 8am-7pm Tue-Fri; 9am-5pm Sat; 10am-4pm
Sun. **Main courses** $4. **Credit** AmEx, MC, V.
Map p315 C9 ⑤⑦ **Bakery-café**

Ada Street.

CONSUME

Make the most of the city with Time Out

timeout.com

Former fine-dining pastry chef Paula Haney made a name for her pies at farmers' markets and coffee shops. Now she sells seasonal creations (from strawberry and rhubarb in spring to apple and pumpkin in autumn) and signature dishes (incomparable banana-cream), along with Metropolis coffee, at her tiny retro shop. The pies are, in a word, extraordinary. But while pie is Haney's thing, don't ignore the scones, especially the chocolate chip. *Photo p126.*

Paramount Room

415 N Milwaukee Avenue, between W Kinzie & W Hubbard Streets (1-312 829 6300, www. paramountroom.com). El: Blue to Grand. **Open** 11am-2am daily. **Main courses** $15. **Credit** AmEx, MC, V. **Map** p314 F11 ⑬ **Gastropub**
Chef Stephen Dunne focuses on elevated bar food at this West Town spot. Some of his food (fried pickle spears, wagyu burger) acts merely as a sponge for the impressive beer list. But the duck confit is sublime, the fish and chips are flavourful, and the crab salad is light. The ultimate beer and food pairing comes at dessert with the Black & Tan Float, a rootbeer float made with Guinness ice-cream.

★ Ruxbin

851 N Ashland Avenue, at W Pearson Street (1-312 624 8509, www.ruxbinchicago.com). El: Blue to Division. **Open** 5.30-10pm Tue-Sat; 5.30-9pm Sun. **Main courses** $26. **Credit** AmEx, MC, V. **Map** p315 C9 ⑤⑨ **Contemporary American**
Everything from movie-theatre seats to apple-juice crates is repurposed to turn this teensy BYOB into a glowing, energetic mind-funk. But chef Edward Kim takes a more understated approach to the food, levying subtle tweaks on contemporary American fare: mussels are topped with *togarashi*-dusted fries; miso-marinated tofu is sweet and crunchy in a way that even non-vegetarians couldn't resist; crisp-skinned trout over date-studded bulgar is simple and classic. Be sure to check out the upstairs bathroom – if you can figure out how to get into it.

Wicker Park & Bucktown

$ Big Star

1531 N Damen Avenue, between N Wicker Park & N Milwaukee Avenues (1-773 235 4039, www. bigstarchicago.com). El: Blue to Damen. **Open** 11.30am-2am Mon-Fri, Sun; 11.30am-3am Sat. **Main courses** $4. **No credit cards. Map** p315 B7 ⑥⓪ **Mexican**
What compelled a James Beard Award winning chef and the owners of the city's most exclusive cocktail lounge to open a divey bar that slings Tecates and whisky shots for $3 apiece? A stroke of absolute genius. Brutal crowds harsh the country-music mellow on weekends, but neighbourhood hipsters put up with it, dropping by the takeout window to grab a couple of tacos or planting themselves at the bar for a few beers or quality cocktails.

Bongo Room

1470 N Milwaukee Avenue, at W Evergreen Avenue (1-773 489 0690, www.thebongoroom.com). El: Blue to Damen. **Open** 8am-2.30pm Mon-Fri; 9am-2pm Sat, Sun. **Main courses** $10. **Credit** AmEx, Disc, MC, V. **Map** p315 C8 ⑥① **Café**
Hungover musicians, early-rising soccer moms and everybody in between flock to this bright, cheery spot for fancy morning cocktails and the outrageous sweet brunch specials: chocolate tower French toast is a creamy, luxurious pile of chocolate bread smothered in what's essentially melted banana crème brûlée. Prepare to wait in line.

Le Bouchon

1958 N Damen Avenue, between W Homer Street & W Armitage Avenue (1-773 862 6600, www.lebouchonofchicago.com). El: Blue to Damen. **Open** 11.30am-2.30pm, 5.30-10pm Mon-Thur; 11.30am-2.30pm, 5-11pm Fri, Sat. **Main courses** $20. **Credit** AmEx, Disc, MC, V. **Map** p315 B6 ⑥② **French**
It's small and crowded, and you'll have to wait at the bar even with a reservation, but Le Bouchon is the closest thing Chicago has to that adorable little bistro in Paris. Regulars have their favourites: flaky onion tart; robust onion soup with a gluttonous amount of gruyère; butter-topped steak flanked by perfectly crisp frites; simple profiteroles. Only ruder waiters could make for a more French experience.

★ Bristol

2152 N Damen Avenue, between W Shakespeare and W Webster Avenues (1-773 862 5555, www.thebristolchicago.com). El: Blue to Western. **Open** 5.30-10pm Mon-Thur; 5.30pm-midnight Fri; 10am-2pm, 5-11pm Sat; 10am-2pm, 5-10pm Sun. **Main courses** $16. **Credit** AmEx, MC, V. **Map** p315 B5 ⑥③ **Contemporary American**
After three years, this popular Bucktown restaurant is maturing well with stronger-than-ever cocktail and dessert menus. It's hard to steer away from Chris Pandel's signature dishes – such as salad of heirloom apples or devastatingly delicious egg- and ricotta-filled ravioli – but it's worth it to try the unusual, always-changing daily specials: marinated beef tendon salad, perhaps, or cold-smoked salmon with bacon-dill dumplings.

Enoteca Roma

2146 W Division Street, between N Hoyne Avenue & N Leavitt Street (1-773 342 1011, www.enotecaroma.com). El: Blue to Division. **Open** 5-10pm Mon-Thur; 5-11pm Fri, Sat; 2.30-9pm Sun. **Main courses** $16. **Credit** AmEx, Disc, MC, V. **Map** p315 B8 ⑥④ **Italian**
Cop a seat among the greenery and dive into the wine list; it's playful, varied (not limited to Italian bottles) and built for food. Topped with toothsome ingredients such as brie and honey, cannellini beans and black olive purée, the bruschetta come highly

CONSUME

Hoosier Mama Pie Company. *See p123.*

recommended, but don't overlook the Roman-style pizzas and Letizia's wonderfully soft, salty focaccia with spicy mustard.

★ Mindy's Hot Chocolate

1747 N Damen Avenue, at W Willow Street (1-773 489 1747, www.hotchocolatechicago.com). El: Blue to Damen. **Open** 5.30-10pm Tue; 11.30am-2pm, 5.30-10pm Wed, Thur; 11.30am-2pm, 5.30pm-midnight Fri; 10am-2pm, 5.30pm-midnight Sat; 10am-2pm, 5.30-10pm Sun. **Main courses** $14. **Credit** AmEx, Disc, MC, V. **Map** p315 B7 ⓺ **Contemporary American**

Mindy Segal revamped her Bucktown restaurant in 2012, making it sunnier and adding a huge garage door that can be opened up during warm weather. Segal – first and foremost a pastry chef – also revamped her approach to desserts: now, the pastry menu consists of seasonal cakes, puddings, pies and so on, and the dessert menu changes weekly. On the savoury side, little has changed. The popular pretzel, burger, mac and cheese – breathe easy, they're all still there.

Mana Food Bar

1742 W Division Street, between N Paulina & N Wood Streets (1-773 342 1742, www.manafoodbar.com). El: Blue to Division. **Open** 4-10pm Mon-Thur, Sun; 4-11pm Fri; noon-11pm Sat. **Small plates** $6. **Credit** AmEx, Disc, MC, V. **Map** p315 C8 ⓺ **Vegetarian**

Imagine a spot where vegetarian fare is gobbled up by diners lounging on chunky wood stools and in dark booths. It's not cheap – two people will have to spend around $50 to leave full – so to leave both replete and happy, choose wisely. Try the small portions of simple yellow squash 'pasta', asparagus ravioli in spicy tomato sauce, and brown rice-mushroom sliders.

Piece

1927 W North Avenue, between N Wolcott & N Winchester Avenues (1-773 772 4422, www.piecechicago.com). El: Blue to Damen. **Open** 11am-10.30pm Mon-Wed; 11am-11pm Thur; 11am-12.30am Fri, Sat; 11am-10pm Sun. **Main courses** $14. **Credit** AmEx, Disc, MC, V. **Map** p315 C7 ⓺ **Pizza**

Two things keep Piece from going the route of sports bar-beer-bong culture: it serves excellent house brews and makes expertly executed pizzas. The crispy pies hold a lot of weight, so after you choose your pizza style – red, white or New Haven-style 'plain' (red sauce, no mozzarella) – start piling on the toppings. Wash it down with a pitcher of the crisp Golden Arm, and you'll never disparagingly say 'pizza and beer joint' again.

★ Schwa

1466 N Ashland Avenue, at W Le Moyne Street (1-773 252 1466, www.schwarestaurant.com). El: Blue to Division. **Open** 5.30-9.30pm Tue-Sat. **Tasting menus** $55, $110. **Credit** AmEx, Disc, MC, V. **Map** p315 C7 ⓺ **Contemporary American**

Fewer than 30 diners can fit in this tiny restaurant at one time, and all of them must have reserved weeks in advance. The menu is more of a suggestion: Schwa serves what it wants and doesn't get into detailed descriptions about what those dishes are. You'll be treated to the likes of 'pad thai', with marinated slivers of jellyfish standing in for noodles; rich beer-cheese soup; and sumptuous venison paired with a white chocolate foam.

Smoke Daddy
1804 W Division Street, between N Wood & N Honore Streets (1-773 772 6656, www. thesmokedaddy.com). El: Blue to Division. **Open** 11am-11pm Mon-Thur; 11am-midnight Fri; 10am-midnight Sat; 11am-11pm Sun. **Main courses** $15. **Credit** AmEx, Disc, MC, V.
Map p315 C8 ⑳ **American**
Gluttony grabs hold in this kitschy kitchen, and it doesn't let go until the band plays its last bluesy rockabilly note. So skip the brisket, ignore the chicken, and resist filling up on the sweet-potato fries: instead, reserve your hunger for the Rib Sampler, a vast plate of baby back ribs, spare ribs and rib tips.

Humboldt Park & Logan Square

★ $ Bang Bang Pie Shop
2051 N California Avenue, between W Dickens & W McLean Avenues (1-773 661 9170, bangbangpie.com). El: Blue to California. **Open** 7am-7pm Mon-Fri; 9am-5pm Sat; 9am-4pm Sun. **Main courses** $5. **Credit** AmEx, Disc, MC, V. **Bakery-café**
You could say this place is a coffee shop: after all, it roasts its own beans to create bold, serious cups of hot and iced coffee, and back when the business was a food truck, it was called Bang Bang Pie and Coffee. But now, the 'coffee' has been lopped off, and it's mainly a pie shop. There's a particular charm to that – a place where you can just meet someone for a slice of pie, whether in the vintage-style interior or at a picnic table in the huge yard. Whatever you do, don't overlook the biscuits, particularly when topped with gravy.

Fat Rice
2957 W Diversey Avenue, between N Richmond Street & N Sacramento Avenue (1-773 661 9170, www.eatfatrice.com). El: Blue to Logan Square. **Open** 5.30-10pm Tue-Thur; 5.30-10.30pm Fri, Sat. **Main courses** $16. **Credit** Disc, MC, V. **Chinese**
Owners Abraham Conlon and Adrienne Lo (the duo behind supper club X-Marx) are cooking the food of Macau, a former Portuguese colony along the South China Sea. As such, their menu is heavy with influences both Portuguese (*bacalhau*) and Chinese (pot stickers), not to mention any other forays towards which Conlon, the chef, is guided. If this convergence sounds like 'fusion', what's remarkable is it certainly doesn't taste like it: the food – especially the paella-like wonder that is the signature 'fat rice' – is vibrant, personal and natural.

$ Feed
2803 W Chicago Avenue, at N California Avenue (1-773 489 4600, www.feedrestaurantchicago. com). Bus: 66. **Open** 8am-10pm Mon-Fri; 9am-10pm Sat; 9am-9pm Sun. **Main courses** $7. **No credit cards. American**

There's a fine line dividing kitsch from authenticity, and this homely chicken place sits right in the middle. Despite the crowds of gay Moby lookalikes, Starter jacket-clad teenagers and yuppie moms, Feed still looks and feels the way you'd imagine a rural Kentucky chicken shack should.

★ Kai Zan
2557 W Chicago Avenue, at N Rockwell Street (1-773 278 5776, www.eatatkaizan.com). Bus: 49, 52, 65, 66. **Open** 5-10pm Mon-Tue, Thur, Sun; 5-11pm Fri, Sat. **Sushi** $8. **Credit** AmEx, Disc, MC, V. **Japanese**
Brothers Melvin and Carlo Vizconde are masters of maki, and this 22-seat gem is their domain. From simple fried tofu makimono to elaborate sushi twists such as scallop wrapped in salmon, these are the rolls you wish every neighbourhood sushi spot was making. Omakase tasting menus (starting at $50) are a great way to cruise the offerings, but whatever route you choose, just don't show up on a weekend without a reservation.

$ Kuma's Corner
2900 W Belmont Avenue, at N Francisco Avenue (1-773 604 8769, www.kumascorner. com). El: Blue to Belmont. **Open** 11.30am-2am Mon-Fri; 11.30am-3am Sat; noon-midnight Sun. **Main courses** $10. **Credit** AmEx, Disc, MC, V. **American**
The servers here sport more ink than a Bic factory, and the metal is cranked up so loud you can't hear yourself talk, but therein lies Kuma's Corner's charm. Squeeze through the ass-to-elbow crowds and up to the long bar, where you might be in for a lengthy wait. What's the draw? The Slayer burger, for one – a pile of fries topped with a half-pound burger, chilli, pimientos, andouille sausage, onions and jack cheese, on a pretzel bun. That, and the menu of highbrow brews.

★ Longman & Eagle
2657 N Kedzie Avenue, at W Schubert Avenue (1-773 276 7110, www.longmanandeagle.com). El: Blue to Logan Square. **Open** 9am-2am Mon-Fri, Sun; 9am-3am Sat. **Main courses** $15. **Credit** AmEx, Disc, MC, V. **Gastropub**
There will be strategically scruffed dudes, waifish women in grandma sweaters, and flannel as far as the eye can see here. It is owned in part by the Empty Bottle (*see p138*) guys, after all. But these are hipsters who know hospitality and a chef (Jared Wentworth) who knows pub grub: his menu changes frequently, but we've seen him transform the quizzical texture of beef tongue into a hash alternately crisp and fatty, and deep-fry clams to perfection. Pastry chef Jeremy Brutzkus ends on the kind of indulgent notes best appreciated with a fork in one hand and whisky in the other (black sesame doughnut with coconut tapioca, black sesame purée, powdered coconut, coriander, lime and palm sugar

CONSUME

granita and coconut sorbet, anyone?). Too full to leave? Book into one of the six rooms in the high-design inn upstairs (*see p182*).

★ Lula Café

2537 N Kedzie Boulevard, between W Linden Place & W Albany Avenue (1-773 489 9554, www.lulacafe.com). El: Blue to Logan Square. **Open** 9am-2am Mon, Wed-Sun. **Main courses** $20. **Credit** AmEx, MC, V. **Café**

For more than a decade, 'consciously sourced', 'thoughtfully prepared' and 'sustainable' have been food traits that one could fairly describe as being 'so Lula'. But these days, Lula's food is more than that: the gorgeously plated dishes are greater even than the sum of their very great parts. The menu changes constantly, but rest assured that every dish (hanger steak with asparagus and young garlic crispy rice crêpes; suckling pig with sweet potatoes, roasted peanuts and flowering collards) hits the spot. Renovations have transformed the cramped entry area into an expansive, light-filled room, the defining feature of which is a gorgeous marble bar.

★ Urbanbelly

3053 N California Avenue, at W Barry Avenue (1-773 583 0500, www.urbanbellychicago.com). El: Blue to Belmont. **Open** 11am-9pm Tue-Sun. **Main courses** $12. **Credit** AmEx, Disc, MC, V. **Pan Asian**

You'd think a dish called the Urbanbelly Ramen would be this noodle bar's signature. No, the best dish is the rice-cake noodles: chewy, mini Frisbee-shaped noodles topped with a juicy, perfectly fried chicken breast and pieces of mango, which help cool the fiery, chilli-spiked broth. Like the rich lamb-and-brandy dumplings, it's the kind of dish you'll want to take your time over. But the crowds wanting your seat encourage you to eat fast and go.

★ Yusho

2853 N Kedzie Avenue, between W Diversey Avenue & W George Street (1-773 904 8558, www.yusho-chicago.com). El: Blue to Logan Square. **Open** 5-10pm Mon, Wed, Thur; 5pm-midnight Fri, Sat; noon-8pm Sun. **Main courses** $8. **Credit** AmEx, Disc, MC, V. **Japanese**

Matthias Merges left his post as Charlie Trotter's executive chef to open this casual, late-night yaki-tori-and-cocktails joint. The room has an energetic design that makes you want to drink, which isn't a problem with cocktails this superb. Still, save some room for the Japanese-inspired food: juicy chicken wings, thinly sliced beef tongue, sumptuous tofu, beautiful mushrooms topped with a poached egg.

THE SOUTH SIDE

$ Chant

1509 E 53rd Street, at S Harper Avenue (1-773 324 1999, www.chantchicago.com).

Metra: 55th-56th-57th Street. **Open** noon-10pm Mon; 11.30am-midnight Tue-Thur; 11.30am-1am Fri, Sat; noon-10pm Sun. **Main courses** $11. **Credit** AmEx, Disc, MC, V. **Map** p316 Y16 ⑩ **Asian**

Thumbs up to this Zen-oriented spot for its large menu, hip interior and full-service bar. The world tour of dishes wouldn't be complete without its take on standard drunken noodles: angel-hair pasta and vegetables soaked in Thai basil-jalapeño oil. Other culture-confused items include honey chipotle wings, and roasted red pepper and Thai basil houmous, but the curried chicken stays true to form with spicy red curry coconut cream sauce over jasmine rice.

$ Medici

1327 E 57th Street, at S Kimbark Avenue (1-773 667 7394, www.medici57.com). El: Red to 55th. **Open** 7am-10pm Mon-Thur; 7am-11pm Fri; 9am-11pm Sat; 9am-10pm Sun. **Main courses** $9. **Credit** MC, V. **Map** p316 Y17 ⑪ **American**

This University of Chicago hangout serves surprisingly good takes on typical student fare, including speciality burgers and shakes, as well as great salads; we like the simple but classic Ensalata Kimba – blue cheese, apples and pecans over crisp romaine. The restaurant also serves freshly baked pastries from its sister bakery next door.

La Petite Folie

Hyde Park Shopping Center, 1504 E 55th Street, at E 55th Place (1-773 493 1394, www.lapetite folie.com). Metra: 55th-56th-57th Street. **Open** 11.30am-2pm, 5-9.30pm Tue-Thur; 11.30am-2pm, 5-10.30pm Fri; 5-10.30pm Sat; 5-9pm Sun. **Main courses** $23. **Credit** AmEx, Disc, MC, V. **Map** p316 Y17 ⑫ **French**

A mid-life career change prompted chef Mary Mastricola to open this almost-hidden, mildly upscale restaurant. The French wine list provides affordable choices, and the trusty menu gets updated with seasonal additions every month or so. Early autumn eats might include the likes of boneless rabbit filled with truffled hazelnut mousse or monkfish paella with jumbo shrimp and trout Grenobloise.

★ $ Zaleski & Horvath Market Café

1126 E 47th Street, between S Woodlawn & S Greenwood Avenues (1-773 538 7372, www.zhmarketcafe.com). Bus: 2, 15, 47. **Open** 7am-5pm Mon-Fri; 8am-6pm Sat, Sun. **Main courses** $8. **Credit** AmEx, MC, V. **Map** p316 X15 ⑬ **Café**

A couple of Hyde Park veterans and a sandwich-maker from the suburbs joined forces to open this casual but high-quality grocery store and sandwich shop. The shelves are handsomely stocked with gourmet groceries, but the crowds tend to gather at the deli counter for the quince paste and Spanish *jamón* sandwiches.

CONSUME

Bars

Hophead or cocktail connoisseur, this city's got a drink for everyone.

Just as Chicagoans appreciate a great deep-dish pizza as much as the latest in molecular gastronomy, locals enjoy a cold PRB at a nameless dive while also embracing the revival in hand-crafted cocktails. The city's bar scene is right on the heels of the ambitious food culture. The craft-beer boom, which ignited several years ago, sees no sign of waning, and there has been a recent resurgence in local brewing – except now it's characterised by praiseworthy small-batch producers instead of the early 20th-century factories (such as Atlas and Pilsen) that churned out scores of mediocre macrobrews.

Bars and clubs in Chicago generally either have a 2am or 4am licence. All bars get an hour's extension on Saturday, which means the 2am bars close at 3am, and the 4am joints stay open until 5am. Although if you're still drinking at that time, chances are you won't care what the time is anyway.

THE LOOP

Angels & Kings
Hard Rock Hotel, N Michigan Avenue, at W Wacker Drive (1-312-334-6722, www.angels andkings.com). El: Blue, Brown, Green, Orange, Pink, Purple to Clark/Lake. **Open** 5pm-2am Mon-Fri, Sun; 5pm-3am Sat. **Credit** AmEx, Disc, MC, V. **Map** p309 J11 **❶**
This Pete Wentz-affiliated bar relocated to the first floor of the Hard Rock Hotel on Michigan Avenue a few years ago. Despite a slight refinement in the look, most attributes of the Clark Street location, such as a stage for impromptu shows and karaoke battles, were carried over. And the owners still want the attitude to be 'come as you are' – or at least, come as a Pete Wentz wannabe.

Kasey's Tavern
701 S Dearborn Street, between W Harrison & W Polk Streets (1-312 427 7992). El: Red to Harrison. **Open** 11am-2am Mon-Fri, Sun; 11am-3am Sat. **Credit** AmEx, Disc, MC, V. **Map** p309 H13 **❷**
The people-watching at Kasey's is almost as good as it is from the benches around the Printer's Row fountain, but this popular watering hole's got beer. And pizza. You'll recognise the same Irish-English pub vibe from up north, and you may spy a frat rat. But generally the crowd, like the bookish, lofty-artsy neighbourhood, is mixed, especially when it comes to baseball loyalties.

Living Room
W Chicago City Center, 172 W Adams Street, between S LaSalle & S Wells Streets (1-312 332 1200, www.wchicagocitycenter.com). El: Brown, Orange, Pink or Purple to Quincy/Wells. **Open** 11am-1am Mon-Thur; 11am-2am Fri, Sat; 11am-midnight Sun. **Credit** AmEx, Disc, MC, V. **Map** p309 H12 **❸**
The bar at the Loop's W Hotel attracts both local and visiting scenesters. Expect lounge-worthy leather chairs, models moonlighting as waitresses and sexed-up singles looking to clink cosmos. And while the well-stocked bar lives stocks dozens of whiskies, bartenders also make mean martinis and manhattans for the nostalgic set.
▶ *For a review of the hotel, see p170.*

Roof
The Wit Hotel, 201 N State Street, at E Lake Street (1-312 239 9501, www.roofonthewit.com). El: Blue, Brown, Green, Orange, Pink, Purple to

> **❶** Green numbers in this chapter correspond to the location of each bar on the street maps. *See pp308-316.*

Clark/Lake. **Open** 2pm-1am Mon-Wed; noon-2am Thur, Fri; noon-3am Sat; 2-10pm Sun. **Credit** AmEx, Disc, MC, V. **Map** p309 H11 ④
TheWit Hotel's swanky rooftop lounge offers a speciality cocktail menu, a well-curated wine list and small plates, but it's the breezy terrace-with-a-view that draws crowds, all ready to throw elbows to score tables as per the seat-yourself policy. Fireplaces and a glass enclosure mean it's almost as packed in winter.

Wine Bar at the Walnut Room

Macy's, 111 N State Street, 7th Floor, at E Washington Street (1-312 781 3125, www.macysrestaurants.com/walnut-room). El: Blue to Washington; Brown, Green, Orange, Pink or Purple to Randolph/Wabash. **Open** 11am-3pm Mon, Sun; 11am-7pm Tue-Sat. **Credit** AmEx, Disc, MC, V. **Map** p309 H12 ⑤
In reality, the Wine Bar is just a corner of the dining area. But it's a nice corner, full of the restaurant's characteristic dark wood and formal-yet-friendly service. Nicer still is the wine list, which has a staggering number of bottles under $30.
▶ *For a review of Macy's, see p143.*

THE SOUTH LOOP & CHINATOWN

Reggie's Music Joint

2105 S State Street, at E 21st Street (1-312 949 0120, www.reggieslive.com). El: Red to Cermak-Chinatown. **Open** 11am-2am Mon-Fri, Sun; 11am-3am Sat. **Credit** AmEx, Disc, MC, V. **Map** p308 H16 ⑥
In case you missed all the concert posters, the flatscreen TVs showing performance footage or the corner stage (which, more often than not, has a band on it), music is the theme of this South Side pub. But with such a good beer selection and friendly staff, you don't need to be into the tunes to enjoy the night.

THE NEAR NORTH SIDE

River North

Bull & Bear

431 N Wells Street, between W Illinois & W Hubbard Streets (1-312 527 5973, www.bullbearbar.com). El: Brown or Purple to Merchandise Mart. **Open** 11.30am-2am Mon-Fri; 10am-3am Sat; 10am-2am Sun. **Credit** AmEx, Disc, MC, V. **Map** p310 H11 ⑦
There's something ironic about a stock market-themed bar that opened in the middle of an economic crisis, complete with bottles of Dom and Cristal listed under 'Liquid Assets'. The cocktails and upscale bar food – truffle mac 'n' cheese, for instance – are well executed if you have cash to burn, but you'll need to plonk down serious dough for one of the talked-about booths with table-side beer taps.

Clark Street Ale House

742 N Clark Street, between W Superior & W Chicago Streets (1-312 642 9253, www.clarkstreetalehouse.com). El: Red to Chicago. **Open** 4pm-4am Mon-Fri; 11am-5am Sat; 11am-4am Sun. **Credit** AmEx, Disc, MC, V. **Map** p310 H10 ⑧
There are people who hang out at this dim Near North pub without ever ordering a drink, but it seems a shame to miss out on the two dozen beers on tap – mostly domestic gems, such as Great Lakes Brewing Company's Elliot Ness. So order a beer and settle down next to the friendly locals, who drop on to wooden stools just to chat with the bartender.

Fado

100 W Grand Avenue, between N Clark Street & N LaSalle Drive (1-312 836 0066, www.fadoirishpub.com). El: Red to Grand. **Open** 11.30am-2am Mon-Thur; 11.30am-3am Fri; 10am-3am Sat; 10am-2am Sun. **Credit** AmEx, Disc, MC, V. **Map** p310 H10 ⑨
Fado may be part of a chain, but don't hold that against it. All three floors of this dark, wood-filled and slightly over-stylised Irish pub are packed with young professionals busily getting sloshed and loosening their ties and their tongues. After trying the Black Velveteen, a smooth and sweet blend of Guinness and cider, you'll want to join them.

★ Green Door Tavern

678 N Orleans Street, between W Erie & W Huron Streets (1-312 664 5496, www.greendoorchicago.com). El: Brown or Purple to Chicago. **Open** 11.30am-2am Mon-Fri; 10am-3am Sat; 10am-midnight Sun. **Credit** AmEx, Disc, MC, V. **Map** p310 G12 ⑩
If you're into slick, minimalist lounges or enormous, bass-heavy clubs, you may find it hard to believe that this River North stalwart has anything to offer. But poke around and you'll find a pleasant dining room to the side, a pool room in the back and a jukebox that caters to most tastes.

Motel Bar

600 W Chicago Avenue, at N Larrabee Street (1-312 822 2900, www.themotelbar.com). Bus 66. **Open** 11am-2am Mon-Fri; 4pm-3am Sat; 4pm-2am Sun. **Credit** AmEx, MC, V. **Map** p310 F9 ⑪

THE BEST COCKTAIL BARS

For cutting-edge concoctions
Aviary. See p137.

For sparkling creations
Pops for Champagne. See p131.

For arty tipples
Whistler. See p142.

CONSUME

Bull & Bear.

This low-lit lounge is nothing like any motel you're likely to find by the highway, but the throwback classic cocktails, the 'room service' comfort food menu, the unpretentious staff and the varied jukebox (in lieu of a DJ turning it into a club) all work well. The massive outdoor patio is simple and sparse.

★ Pops for Champagne
601 N State Street, at E Ohio Street (1-312 266 7677, www.popsforchampagne.com). El: Red to Grand. **Open** 3pm-2am Mon-Fri, Sun; 1pm-2am Sat. **Credit** AmEx, Disc, MC, V. **Map** p310 H10 ⑫
This sleek, shiny bar in Tree Studios boasts – as the name suggests – the city's best selection of bubbles. Most of it doesn't come cheap (it never does), but you're not just paying for the booze – you're paying for some of the most educated bartenders in town, who can talk you through the selection of nearly 200 champagnes and sparking wines. The list of cocktails extends beyond the classics – try La Vie en Rose (brut champagne with elderflower liqueur and Peychaud's bitters). For harder concoctions, head downstairs to Pops' cocktail bar, Watershed (1-312 266 4932, www.watershedbar.com).

Redhead Piano Bar
16 W Ontario Street, between N State & N Dearborn Streets (1-312 640 1000, www.redhead pianobar.com). El: Red to Grand. **Open** 7pm-4am Mon-Fri, Sun; 7pm-5am Sat. **Credit** AmEx, Disc, MC, V. **Map** p310 H10 ⑬
For the piano-bar fiend, this underground spot hits all the right notes. Although the guys here aren't necessarily gay, they're at least dressed well: bouncers inspect outfits as well as IDs.

Rockit Bar & Grill
22 W Hubbard Street, between N State & N Dearborn Streets (1-312 645 6000, www.rockit barandgrill.com). El: Red to Grand. **Open** 11.30am-1am Mon-Wed; 11.30am-2am Thur, Fri; 10am-3am Sat; 10am-1am Sun. **Credit** AmEx, Disc, MC, V. **Map** p310 H11 ⑭

Most of the guys who go to this sporty, sceney homage to stainless steel don't seem to care what the food tastes like – it's more of a boobs-and-beer thing. But if they paid attention, they'd find that the kitchen offers gems such as lobster avocado cocktail. There's even a gluten-free menu. The bar isn't too shabby, either, with several dozen types of beer.

Sable Kitchen & Bar
505 N State Street, at Illinois Street (1-312 755-9704, www.sablechicago.com). El: Red to Grand. **Open** 11am-2am Mon-Sat; 11am-midnight Sun. **Credit** AmEx, Disc, MC, V. **Map** p310 H10 ⑮
The menu at this slick hotel spot is derivative of the gastropubby restaurants of the past decade: it's got 'flatbreads' and various incarnations of the slider, and the perennially popular bacon-wrapped date. But it's also got bartender Mike Ryan's fantastic cocktails, which are perfectly balanced and include locally sourced ingredients whenever possible.

Vertigo
Dana Hotel & Spa, 2 W Erie Street, at N State Street (1-312 202 6060, www.vertigoskylounge. com). El: Red to Grand. **Open** 4pm-1am Mon-Wed; 4pm-2am Thur, Fri; 2pm-3am Sat; 2pm-1am Sun. **Credit** AmEx, Disc, MC, V. **Map** p310 H10 ⑯
You'd think the focus of this bar, which sits on the 26th floor of the Dana Hotel, would be the view. But there's a lot more to distract drinkers – the roaring fire pit, the classic cocktails and the ice bar in winter, for starters. DJs play from time to time.

The Magnificent Mile & Streeterville

★ Bar at Peninsula Chicago
Peninsula Chicago, 108 E Superior Street, between N Michigan Avenue & N Rush Street (1-312 573 6766, www.peninsula.com). El: Red to Chicago. **Open** 4pm-1am Mon-Thur; 3pm-1am Fri, Sat; 5pm-1am Sun. **Credit** AmEx, Disc, MC, V. **Map** p310 J10 ⑰

Take a date to the Peninsula's dark, clubby cocktail bar and you probably won't go home alone. All the manly bases have been covered – a glowing fireplace, high-backed bar stools and cosy couched conversation nooks. Sip well-crafted cocktails, bubbly by the glass or whiskies from obscure distillers.

▶ *For a review of the hotel, see p175.*

Billy Goat Tavern

430 N Lower Michigan Avenue, at E Kinzie Street (1-312 222 1525, www.billygoattavern.com). El: Red to Grand. **Open** 6am-2am daily. **No credit cards**. Map p310 J11 ⑱

This subterranean tavern – there are other locations, but this is the only one worth a visit – was the inspiration for John Belushi's Olympia Café skits on *Saturday Night Live* in the '70s, and drinkers can still get a 'cheezborger' with a side of schtick. Weekends are a tourist crush, but weekday lunch offers glimpses of hungry reporters, cops and other downtown characters. Just remember: no fries, *cheeps*; no Pepsi, Coke.

C-View

MileNorth Hotel, 166 E Superior Street, between N St Clair Street & N Michigan Avenue (1-312

New Brews

These small breweries are proving to be a big hit with locals.

SOLEMN OATH

1661 Quincy Avenue, at Ogden Avenue, Naperville (1-630 995 3062, www.solemnoathbrewery.com).
The brewers Joe Barley, John Barley, Tim Marshall.
The story Maybe it was destiny that brought the Barley brothers to beer (or their serendipitous surname). More likely, it was their parents' time living in Belgium. When John Barley decided to open a brewery, he first brought in his brother Joe, then former Rock Bottom brewer Marshall. The suburban brewery has been rolling out Belgian-style beer with a distinctly American hoppiness since April 2012.
The style American (IPAs, red ales), Belgian (white ales) and Belgian-American hybrids (the Oubliette, made with Belgian malts and American hops).
Where to get it Bangers & Lace (*see p139*), Small Bar (*see p140*).

BEGYLE

1800 W Cuyler Avenue, at Ravenswood Avenue (1-773 661 6963, www.begyle brewing.com).
The brewers Brendan Blume, Kevin Cary, Matt Ritchey.
The story Small business, small footprint – that idea led college friends Cary and Ritchey to partner with Blume and turn their home-brewing passion into a community-driven, eco-friendly brewery. How? They started with a 4,000sq ft space that doubles as artists' studios. Then they invested in waste-reducing equipment and figured out how to make dog treats from used grain. Finally, they sourced ingredients from local farmers for, as Cary calls it, a distinct 'flavour of the Midwest'.

The style Farm-to-glass, American-style beers such as a pale wheat ale and hoppy IPA.
Where to get it Fountainhead (1970 W Montrose Avenue, at Damen Avenue, 1-773 697 8204, fountainheadchicago.com).

DRYHOP

3155 N Broadway Avenue, at Briar Place (1-773 857 3155, www.dryhopchicago.com).
The brewer Brant Dubovick.
The story 'I want people to feel like they're coming into a brewer's workshop,' says DryHop founder Greg Shuff. 'A place that's making [a] product that has a lot more soul than what you can get at a standard bar.' Shuff got his start homebrewing before studying beer at Chicago's Siebel Institute and the Doemens Academy in Munich. The brewpub opened in spring 2013.
The style Hoppy American beers such as single-hop pale ales and black IPAs.
Where to get it DryHop (3155 N Broadway Avenue, at Briar Place, 1-773 661 6963).

CONSUME

787-6000, www.milenorthhotel.com). El: Red to Chicago. **Open** 5pm-midnight Mon-Thur, Sun; 5pm-2am Fri, Sat. **Credit** AmEx, Disc, MC, V. **Map** p310 J10 ⑲

The namesake 29th-floor view is the thing at this tiny rooftop bar – at least, that's what everybody says. But though the patio section is nice, the view of the skyline isn't beautiful enough to fight for a seat there. Especially when you can sit at the stylish indoor bar and get just as much beauty out of the craft cocktails.

Drumbar

Raffaello Hotel, 201 E Delaware Place, at Mies van der Rohe Way (1-312 933 4805, www.drumbar.com). El: Red to Chicago. **Open** 5pm-midnight Mon-Wed; 5pm-2am Thur, Fri; 5pm-3am Sat; 2pm-2am Sun. **Credit** AmEx, Disc, MC, V. **Map** p310 J9 ⑳

Never heard of the Raffaello Hotel? Just hope nobody else has either so you can snag a seat at this 18th-floor rooftop bar overlooking the lake and Gold Coast before the hordes invade. Banquette seating lines the glass-walled perimeter of the 2,000sq ft space, and lounge chairs circle two fire pits. If you'd rather keep warm inside, step through the enormous arched doorway to the cavernous main bar, which has 20ft vaulted ceilings, cosy alcoves with an antique fireplace and two bars. Six to eight seasonally rotating cocktails focus on whisky, and small plates from the hotel's Italian restaurant, Pelago, are available inside and out.

The Gold Coast

★ Zebra Lounge

1220 N State Street, at W Division Street (1-312 642 5140). El: Red to Clark/Division. **Open** 5pm-2am Mon-Fri; 7.30pm-3am Sat, Sun. **Credit** AmEx, Disc, MC, V. **Map** p311 H8 ㉑

Around the corner from Division Street's jackass bar scene sits this cosy one-room saloon, tucked inside the Canterbury Court apartments. Singles, socialites and even sexagenarians pack in at busy weekends. The zebra theme is a bit reckless but distinctive. The ultrared lighting, on the other hand, makes you wonder if students from the Art Institute are going to emerge from behind the bar with developed film. A nightly piano player keeps the Zebra refreshingly unhip with old-school favourites.

OLD TOWN & LINCOLN PARK
Old Town

Goose Island Brew Pub

1800 N Clybourn Avenue, at W Willow Street (1-312 915 0071, www.gooseisland.com). El: Brown or Purple to Armitage; Red to North/Clybourn. **Open** 11am-midnight Mon-Fri, Sun; 11am-2am Sat. **Credit** AmEx, Disc, MC, V.

THE BEST DIVE BARS

For nostalgics
Old Town Ale House. *See below.*

For cheap beer and burgers
Carol's Pub. *See p135.*

For outdoor drinking
Happy Village. *See p138.*

The beer selection alone is enough of a draw to this amiable brewpub, where you could happily spend an afternoon nursing a malty Smoked Porter. But pair your drink of choice with a Paulina Market sausage sampler and things start to look even better. There's another branch in Wrigleyville (3535 N Clark Street, at N Addison Street, 1-773 832 9040).

★ Old Town Ale House

219 W North Avenue, at N Wieland Street (1-312 944 7020, www.theoldtownalehouse.com). El: Brown or Purple to Sedgwick. **Open** 3pm-4am Mon-Fri; noon-5am Sat; noon-4am Sun. **No credit cards. Map** p311 G7 ㉒

Among the framed drawings of regulars cluttering the wooden walls of this saloon-style staple are posters boasting that you're in *'le premiere* dive bar' of Chicago. It's hard to tell where this place gets off speaking French, but it's been around since 1958, so it's earned bragging rights. The clientele are a mix of buttoned-down yuppies and old soaks. *Photo p134.*

Lincoln Park

★ Atlas Brewing Company

2747 N Lincoln Avenue, between W Schubert Avenue & W Diversey Parkway (1-773 295 1270, www.atlasbeercompany.com). El: Brown or Purple to Diversey. **Open** 5pm-midnight Mon-Thur; 5pm-2am Fri, Sat; noon-midnight Sun. **Credit** AmEx, Disc, MC, V. **Map** p312 E4 ㉓

The folks that run this microbrewpub, named after an early 20th-century Chicago brewery, are serious about beer – so serious, in fact, that they brew it themselves, in tanks on view behind glass at the back of the room. Ten rotating taps dispense a selection of the wide variety of American, German and Belgian styles. Accompany the superior suds with gourmet variations on pub classics such as burgers, pizza and fish and chips.

★ Barrelhouse Flat

2624 N Lincoln Avenue, between W Wrightwood & W Schubert Avenues (1-773 857 0421, www.barrelhouseflat.com). El: Brown, Purple or Red to Fullerton. **Open** 6pm-2am Mon-Wed; 6pm-4am Thur, Fri; 6pm-5am Sat. **Credit** AmEx, Disc, MC, V. **Map** p312 E4 ㉔

CONSUME

Old Town Ale House. *See p133.*

You'll come for the cocktails, but stay for the food. The Barrelhouse Flat is one of the finest drinking establishments in the city, thanks to head bartender Stephen Cole's list of 70 classics that range from familiar (whisky sour) to arcane (Jimmie Roosevelt). Outstanding bar snacks include headcheese poutine and blue-cheese-and-bacon popcorn.

★ Delilah's

2771 N Lincoln Avenue, between W Schubert Avenue & W Diversey Parkway (1-773 472 2771, www.delilahschicago.com). El: Brown or Purple to Diversey. **Open** 4pm-2am Mon-Fri, Sun; 4pm-3am Sat. **Credit** AmEx, Disc, MC, V. **Map** p312 E4 ㉕

One of the city's best spots for rock 'n' roll doesn't have a stage. Instead, this Lincoln Park favourite has one of the best jukeboxes in town and brings in DJs on some nights who know their Buzzcocks from their Bauhaus. Add an insane whisky selection, more than 200 beers (Belgians, microbrews, seasonals), and you have a bar to call home.

Maeve

1325 W Wrightwood Avenue, at N Wayne Avenue (1-773 388 3333, www.maevechicago. com). El: Brown, Purple or Red to Fullerton. **Open** 4pm-2am Mon-Fri; noon-3am Sat; noon-2am Sun. **Credit** AmEx, Disc, MC, V. **Map** p312 D4 ㉖

This smallish, sports memorabilia-free spot boasts more class than most Lincoln Park watering holes: think dark woods, dim lighting and candle-topped tables. So go ahead and sip a glass of pinot grigio while you wait for a table at adjacent Rose Angelis. But skip the after-dinner martini: by that time of the night, the place will be packed to the gills with loud, horny thirtysomethings.

Sedgwick's Bar & Grill

1935 N Sedgwick Street, between W Armitage Avenue & W Wisconsin Street (1-312 337 7900, www.sedgwickschicago.com). El: Brown or Purple to Sedgwick. **Open** 5pm-2am Mon-Thur; 11am-2am Fri, Sun; 11am-3am Sat. **Credit** AmEx, Disc, MC, V. **Map** p312 G6 ㉗

On most nights, this cosy space is an after-work stopover for yuppies escaping their Old Town highrises. Brews, yummy comfort food and muted bigscreen sports highlights abound. All those things happen on Tuesdays, too, with a little euchre thrown into the fold. League play occupies most of the pool tables, but you'll always get a seat.

★ Webster's Wine Bar

1480 W Webster Avenue, between N Clybourn Avenue & N Dominick Street (1-773 868 0608, www.websterwinebar.com). Bus: 9, 74. **Open** 5pm-2am Mon-Fri; 4pm-3am Sat; 4pm-2am Sun. **Credit** AmEx, Disc, MC, V. **Map** p312 D5 ㉘

Many moviegoers, on their way to the Webster Place cinema, have stopped in here for a pre-show drink and never made it to the film. After all, when tasting wines is this affordable (and interesting), it's easy to pretend it's for educational purposes and stay all night, soaking up the dark, cultured vibe and munching on tasty cheese platters.

LAKEVIEW & NORTH
Lakeview & Wrigleyville

For reviews of gay bars in Boystown, *see pp197-205* **Gay & Lesbian**.

Hungry Brain

2319 W Belmont Avenue, between N Oakley & N Western Avenues (1-773 709 1401). El: Brown to Paulina. **Open** 8pm-2am Mon-Fri, Sun; 8pm-3am Sat. **No credit cards.**

This converted theatre retains its artsy charm with thrift-store finds galore. An old piano, sofas and a coffee table sit on the small stage (which gets occasional use for one-night shows). Art-school dropouts flank the Ms Pac-Man game and great jukebox, and friendly bartenders serve cheap beers with a smile.

INSIDE TRACK GOAL!

Whether they call it football, soccer, *futbol* or some other variant, fans from abroad need a place to cheer on their team. Happily, the city is full of expats who wouldn't dream of missing a game. European diehards find fellow supporters at **Fado** (*see p130*) and **Small Bar** (*see p140*), which screen big matches live.

Bartender's Choice

On the town with Barrelhouse Flat's Jeff Donahue.

FAVOURITE SPIRIT
Bottled in bond bourbon. The trend lately is to romanticise high-priced, small-release, hard-to-obtain whiskies, but if that were my go-to I'd be broke real quick. Bonded spirits are plentiful, always 100% proof, and typically offer a good bang for your buck.

FOOD ADDICTION
Double Fatso with cheese and fried jumbo shrimp form **Phil's Last Stand** (2258 W Chicago Avenue, at N Oakley Boulevard, 1-773 245 3287).

PERFECT NIGHT OFF
A night out in this industry is a day off, so that 'night' is probably going to begin sometime in the afternoon at **Big Star** (1530 N Damen Avenue, at W Pierce Avenue, 1-773 235 4039, www.bigstar chicago.com) for 'drunch' – tacos with lots of Lone Star and bourbon. Next, a stop by **Caffe Streets** (1750 W Division Street, between Wood Street and Hermitage Avenue, 1-773 278 2739) for the best Chemex cup of coffee in the city. Dinner could be **Fat Rice** (2957 W Diversey Avenue, at N Richmond Street, 1-773 661 9170, www.eatfatrice.com) for some of the most exciting food I've come across in Chicago this year. To keep from feeling

sluggish after dinner, dancing at **Danny's** (1951 W Dickens Avenue, at N Damen Avenue, 1-773 489 6457) is always a good choice. I'm a sucker for karaoke, so after the 2am bars close, if I'm still standing you could find me stumbling through some Creedence at **Alice's Lounge** (3556 W Belmont Avenue, between N Central Park and N Drake Avenues, 1-733 279 9382).

Murphy's Bleachers

3655 N Sheffield Street, at W Waveland Avenue (1-773 281 5356, www.murphysbleachers.com). El: Red to Addison. **Open** 11am-2am Mon-Fri, Sun; 11am-3am Sat **Credit** AmEx, Disc, MC, V. **Map** p313 E1 ㉙
Function trumps form and comfort at this woody, cavernous Cub corral and outdoor stable, er, patio behind Wrigley Field. It's packed to the gills for the Cubs' 81 home games a year, but Wrigleyville's frat-shack contingent keep it humming even in winter.

Vines on Clark

3554 N Clark Street, at N Eddy Street (1-773 327 8572, www.vineswrigley.com). El: Red to Addison. **Open** 11am-2am Mon-Fri; 11am-3am Sat; 11am-10pm Sun (opens 3hrs before Cubs games, so times vary). **Credit** AmEx, Disc, MC, V. **Map** p313 E1 ㉚
When does the combination of metal patio furniture, brick flooring and industrial-sized trash cans qualify as a popular beer garden? When your beer garden and rooftop patio are a fly ball from Wrigley Field. Beer goggles don't just make people more attractive.

Roscoe Village

Village Tap

2055 W Roscoe Street, at N Hoyne Avenue (1-773 883 0817, www.villagetap.com). Bus: 50, 77, 152. **Open** 5pm-2am Mon-Thur; 3pm-2am Fri; noon-3am Sat; noon-2am Sun. **Credit** AmEx, Disc, MC, V. **Map** p314 B2 ㉛
Roscoe Village has been gentrified for some time. Still, it's one of the best places in town to grab a beer, chat with the bartenders and test your alcohol-addled vocabulary with a game of Scrabble.

Andersonville, Edgewater & Uptown

For gay bars in Andersonville, *see p201.*

★ Carol's Pub

4659 N Clark Street, between W Wilson & W Leland Avenues (1-773 334 2402). El: Red to Wilson. **Open** 9am-2am Mon, Tue; 11am-4am Wed-Fri, Sun; 11am-5am Sat. **No credit cards**.

This honky-tonk offers $1 draughts, $2 domestics on Mondays, country karaoke on Thursdays and house band Diamondback on weekends. There's a pool table in the back, a greasy grill turning out late-night burgers and a Hank Williams-filled jukebox.

Moody's Pub

5910 N Broadway, between W Rosedale & W Thorndale Avenues (1-773 275 2696, www. moodyspub.com). El: Red to Thorndale. **Open** 11.30am-1am Mon-Fri, Sun; 11.30am-2am Sat. **Credit** Disc, MC.
This beer garden is one of the best in Chicago, but only if you can deal with ass-to-elbow crowds. Remember to bring a flashlight to read the menu: the place is dark enough that you could carry on an affair while your spouse is sitting across the room.

Lincoln Square & Ravenswood

Glunz Bavarian Haus

4128 N Lincoln Avenue, at W Warner Avenue (1-773 472 4287, www.glunzbavarianhaus.com).

El: Brown to Irving Park. **Open** 4pm-2am Tue-Fri, Sun; noon-3am Sat. **Credit** MC, V.
Deutschland takes a lot of pride in its beer. So before you get schnitzel-faced at this friendly German restaurant, be sure to sample the brews.

Ten Cat Tavern

3931 N Ashland Avenue, at W Byron Street (1-773 935 5377). El: Brown to Irving Park. **Open** 3pm-2am Mon-Fri, Sun; 3pm-3am Sat. **No credit cards. Map** p314 D0 ⑫
Drinking at the Ten Cat is a little like getting into a DeLorean and travelling back to 1955. Eclectic, mismatched furniture and a blues-heavy jukebox set the mood for kicking back or racking 'em up at the two vintage tables. Just be careful, McFly: the bartenders won't hesitate to embarrass you on the felt.

Tiny Lounge

4352 N Leavitt Street, at W Montrose Avenue (1-773 463 0396, www.tinylounge.com). El: Brown to Montrose. **Open** 4pm-2am Mon-Fri; noon-3am Sat; noon-2am Sun. **Credit** AmEx, MC, V.

CONSUME

Cocktails on Tap

Self-serve concoctions are the latest trend shaking up the bar scene.

First it was those self-service grocery store checkouts, and now this: pre-mixed cocktails, stored in barrels and poured, ready to drink, from a tap. Is this the end of bartending as we know it? Kind of. 'It's changed the demands on the bartender,' says Paul Tanguay, who is one half of the cocktail consulting team the Tippling Bros and a partner in River North's buzzy **Tavernita** tapas joint (151 E Erie Street, at Michigan Avenue, 1-312 274 1111, www.tavernita.com). The Tippling Bros put six cocktails on tap at Tavernita, easily the most ambitious programme of its kind in the city. 'It relieves the bartender from having to know the recipes,' he says.

Still, somebody's got to design the cocktails, and as far as Alex Bachman, cocktail guru at **Yusho** (*see p128*) is concerned, a cocktail gets on tap 'for one reason, and that is carbonation.' For Yusho's rotating draught cocktail, 'the booze is carbonated, the citrus is carbonated – everything's carbonated together,' Bachman says. 'It maintains the integrity of the drink.'

Of course, there's yet another benefit to putting cocktails on draft, and that's the speed with which bartenders can 'make' them. And anyone who's braved the crush at the latest hot bar can appreciate that.

Tavernita.

It's out with the old-school decor at the Tiny Lounge, and in with a look that's slick and a little mod. But sitting here with a Sazerac or a sidecar (both impeccably crafted) is so undeniably pleasant that it's hard not to believe that the changes were for the better.

THE NEAR WEST SIDE
The West Loop & Greektown

★ Aviary
955 W Fulton Street, at N Morgan Street (1-312 226 0868, www.theaviary.com). El: Green or Pink to Morgan. **Open** *6pm-1am Tue-Fri; 6pm-2am Sat.* **Credit** AmEx, Disc, MC, V. **Map** p314 E11 ⦿
The question Grant Achatz's cocktail lounge poses – intentionally or not – is this: when a cocktail is an intellectual exercise, how much does it matter how it tastes? Some of these drinks are exhilarating for their presentation (the Rooibos, a hot cocktail served in a vacuum-pot coffee brewer). But whatever strengths the individual cocktails exhibit, the outcome after drinking them is always them same: you'll never think of a cocktail in the same way again.

★ RM Champagne Salon
116 N Green Street, at W Randolph Street (1-312 243 1199, www.rmchampagnesalon.com). El: Green or Pink to Morgan. **Open** *5pm-midnight Mon-Wed, Sun; 5pm-2am Thur, Fri; 5pm-3am Sat.* **Credit** AmEx, Disc, MC, V. **Map** p314 F11 ⦿
You enter via an unmarked alleyway, glowing strings of lights leading you to a cobblestoned courtyard and ornate parlour that resemble a Parisian hideaway. You order glasses of champagne you've never heard of, gently unhinge oysters from their shells, and when dessert comes, your selection is plucked from a fanciful cart replete with bite-size macaroons, caramels and marshmallows. Heaven? Who needs it when there's RM? *Photo p138.*

Tasting Room
1415 W Randolph Street, at N Ogden Avenue (1-312 942 1313, www.thetastingroomchicago. com). El: Green or Pink to Ashland. **Open** *5pm-midnight Mon-Thur; 5pm-1am Fri, Sat.* **Credit** AmEx, Disc, MC, V. **Map** p314 D12 ⦿
Out of the way? Yeah. A tad snobby? Sometimes. Still a great wine bar? For sure. You'd be hard-pressed to find another wine bar in Chicago with a better list. And even harder pressed to find one with such a good view of the skyline.

Little Italy & Pilsen

Drum & Monkey
1435 W Taylor Street, at S Bishop Street (1-312 563 1874, www.thedrumandmonkey.com). El: Pink to Polk. **Open** *11am-2am Mon-Fri, Sun; 11am-3am Sat.* **Credit** AmEx, Disc, MC, V. **Map** p314 D14 ⦿

Tiny Lounge.

This immaculately detailed Irish pub might be the last thing you'd expect on the spaghetti strip of Taylor Street, but specials such as cheap tacos and all-you-can-eat fish and chips keep the regulars coming back every week.

★ Simone's
960 W 18th Street, at S Morgan Street (1-312 666 8601, www.simonesbar.com). El: Pink to 18th. **Open** *11.30am-2am Mon-Fri, Sun; 11.30am-3am Sat.* **Credit** AmEx, Disc, MC, V.
This hangout looks nothing like your typical Pilsen bar. Instead, the hyper-recycled materials used to outfit the establishment make it feel more akin to the inside of a pinball machine. And it's this innovative design – coupled with a better-than-average cocktail selection – that ensure you won't get bored.

★ Skylark
2149 S Halsted Street, at Cermak Road (1-312 948 5275, www.skylarkchicago.com). El: Orange to Halsted. **Open** *4pm-2am Mon-Fri, Sun; 4pm-3am Sat.* **Credit** AmEx, Disc, MC, V.
This speakeasy-style space – a vacuous room lined with booths and sprinkled with tables and chairs – is a nightly respite for local artists. The tater tots and mac 'n' cheese are greasy must-haves; wash 'em down with a $2 PBR. There's free jazz on Mondays, and don't miss the photo booth tucked in the back corner.

WICKER PARK & AROUND
Ukrainian Village & West Town

★ 694 Wine & Spirits
694 N Milwaukee Avenue, at W Huron Street (1-312 492 6620, www.694wineandspirits.com). El: Blue to Chicago. **Open** *5pm-2am Mon-Fri;*

5pm-3am Sat; 6pm-midnight Sun.
Credit AmEx, MC, V.
Unassumingly located along Milwaukee Avenue, this intimate, loungey wine bar has an impressive charcuterie selection. The decision not to specialise in spirits might annoy fancy cocktail drinkers lured in by the somewhat misleading name. Winos, on the other hand, will be perfectly content.

Empty Bottle

1035 N Western Avenue, at W Cortez Street (1-773 276 3600, www.emptybottle.com). Bus: 49, 66, 70. **Open** *5pm-2am Mon-Wed; 3pm-2am Thur, Fri; 11am-3am Sat; 11am-2am Sun.* **No credit cards. Map** p315 A9 ➐
This music venue and bar has increasingly turned to booking adventurous electronic, indie hip hop and experimental music acts. Just remember that it's more about the head-bobbing of hipsters than serious dancefloor action, so boogie at your own risk.
▶ *For a review of the music side of the operation, see p219.*

Exit

1315 W North Avenue, at N Ada Street (1-773 395 2700, www.exitchicago.com). El: Red to North/Clybourn. **Open** *9pm-4am Mon-Fri, Sun; 9pm-5am Sat.* **Credit** AmEx, MC, V.
Thursday is fetish night and Monday it's punk rock, but pretty much any evening you stumble on this haunt for the black-clad you'll see that the freaks indeed do come out after dark. Like any clique, it tends to have an insider feel, but brave souls looking for their Ministry and PBR fix have to start somewhere.

Gold Star Bar

1755 W Division Street, between N Wood Street & N Hermitage Avenue (1-773 227 8700). El: Blue to Division. **Open** *4pm-2am Mon-Fri, Sun; 4pm-3am Sat.* **No credit cards. Map** p315 C8 ➌
Truly a neighbourhood hangout, this tried-and-true East Village bar is frequented by those who appreciate the tamale guy, a jukebox that stocks both white-hot jazz and doom metal, a cheap pool table, equally cheap drinks and a crowd who really couldn't care less if you show up in sweats.

★ Happy Village

1059 N Wolcott Avenue, at W Thomas Street (1-773 486 1512, www.happyvillagebar.com). El: Blue to Division. **Open** *4pm-2am Mon-Fri; noon-2am Sat; noon-11pm Sun.* **No credit cards. Map** p315 C9 ➒
Picnic tables and a lush lawn all around make up the scene at this West Town dive. But when it rains (or at 11pm, when the garden closes, midnight on weekends), pack up the ciggies and head inside, where the smell of whisky and cheap beer hangs in the air, and the jukebox coughs out the Cars and Madonna.

Inner Town Pub

1935 W Thomas Street, at N Winchester Avenue (1-773-235-9795). El: Blue to Division. **Open** *3pm-2am Mon-Fri, Sun; 3pm-3am Sat.* **No credit cards. Map** p315 B9 ➓
This former speakeasy serves cheap booze in true dive fashion. Indie-rockers on their way to Empty Bottle (*see left*) shows take advantage of free pool, while a smattering of toothless old-timers keep it gritty with war stories and phlegmy coughs.

RM Champagne Salon. *See p137.*

CONSUME

INSIDE TRACK GETTING HIGH

There are few better ways to escape the city streets than heading to a rooftop patio for a view with your brew; most are partially enclosed for year-round use, so you can leave the parkas in the hotel. **C-View** (*see p132*), **Whiskey Sky** (at the W Lakeshore; *see p177*), **Drumbar** (*see p133*) and **Vertigo** (*see p131*) are best for see-and-be-seen swankness, while the wooden deck at the **Bottom Lounge** (*see p219*) offers an escape in case the band downstairs isn't destined for greatness.

★ Matchbox

770 N Milwaukee Avenue, between N Carpenter Street & N Ogden Avenue (1-312 666 9292, www.thesilverpalmrestaurant.com). El: Blue to Chicago. **Open** 4pm-2am Mon-Thur; 3pm-2am Fri-Sun. **Credit** AmEx, MC, V.

If the thought of being crammed in this tiny boxcar of a bar makes you nervous, relax. The patio practically doubles the capacity, and is the perfect spot in which to throw back one of the bar's margaritas, made with fresh lemon and lime juice, top-shelf liquors and powdered sugar, and poured with a heavy hand.

Rainbo Club

1150 N Damen Avenue, between W Haddon Avenue & W Division Street (1-773 489 5999). El: Blue to Division. **Open** 4pm-2am Mon-Fri, Sun; 4pm-3am Sat. **No credit cards.** **Map** p315 B8 ⓰

The bittersweet reality of many great little dives is that they lose charm when overrun by masses of hangers-on. Somehow, this Ukrainian Village spot has managed to remain an underground favourite. The local artists and musicians who frequent it hold on to terra firma with cheap drink in hand, awaiting a turn in the photo booth while nodding to everything from Aesop Rock to Black Sabbath.

Wicker Park & Bucktown

★ Bangers & Lace

1670 W Division Street, at Paulina Street (1-773 252 6499, www.bangersandlacechicago.com). El: Blue to Division. **Open** 2pm-2am Mon-Fri; 11am-3am Sat; 11am-2am Sun. **No credit cards.** **Map** p315 C8 ⓯

At this bar, from the owners of Bar DeVille, 'bangers' stand for sausages (we dig the Chicago-style Vienna beef over the fancier brat sandwiches), and 'lace' for Brussels lace (beer foam on the edge of a glass). The stellar draught selection, two-ounce sample options and knowledgeable staff draw a mix of beer geeks and neighbourhood locals. *Photo p140.*

Beachwood Inn

1415 N Wood Street, between W Beach Avenue & W Julian Street (1-773 486 9806). El: Blue to Division. **Open** 5pm-2am Mon-Thur; 4pm-2am Fri; 3pm-3am Sat; 3pm-2am Sun. **No credit cards.** **Map** p315 C8 ⓭

No hipsters, no yuppies, no class-drawing lines – just regular neighbourhood folks inhabit this one-room watering hole, taking turns on the pool table or playing Scrabble and Connect Four. The scatterbrained decor (old movie posters, sports crap, beer memorabilia) is as random as the jukebox, which offers pre-'90s tunes from the Pretenders to Michael Jackson.

★ Charleston

2076 N Hoyne Avenue, between W Charleston Street & W Dickens Avenue (1-773 489 4757). El: Blue to Western. **Open** 6pm-2am Mon-Fri, Sun; 6pm-3am Sat. **No credit cards.** **Map** p315 B6 ⓮

Hipsters, yuppies, freaks, dirty old men and bluegrass bands used to pack this beloved corner tap, which changed ownership in 2011 and underwent a bit of a personality shift. Now darker, sleeker and with more focus on DJs with underground cred, the Charleston has morphed into quite a scene. The newer Bucktown residents are as happy as clams, plonking down tens for Moscow mules, while those dirty old men have shuffled off to find the few remaining dives nearby.

★ Danny's Tavern

1951 W Dickens Avenue, between N Damen & N Winchester Avenues (1-773 489 6457). El: Blue to Damen. **Open** 6pm-2am Mon-Fri, Sun; 7pm-3am Sat. **No credit cards.** **Map** p315 C6 ⓯

The floors of this converted Bucktown house shake so much from the weight of hot-footed trendsetters that you'd think the place is seconds from caving in. Most of the dancing is set to a mix of hip hop, electro and rock on the weekends, but there are plenty of nooks and crannies to sit back, relax and people-watch if you prefer.

Debonair Social Club

1575 N Milwaukee Avenue, between W Honore Street & W North Avenue (1-773 227 7990, www.debonairsocialclub.com). El: Blue to Damen. **Open** 9pm-2am Wed-Fri; 9pm-3am Sat. **Credit** AmEx, MC, V. **Map** p315 C7 ⓰

Early in the evening at this two-level hangout, a bit like a starter club for Wicker Park's post-collegiate bar hoppers, the video art on the wall is the room's main source of light, giving off a cool, sultry cocktail lounge vibe. But it's the calm before the storm: when celebrity DJs stop by, the place gets packed with clubby scenesters and frantic bass lines. So if you're here for the quiet, enjoy it while you can.

Handlebar Bar & Grill

2311 W North Avenue, between N Oakley & N Claremont Avenues (1-773 384 9546,

CONSUME

CONSUME

Bangers & Lace. See p139.

www.handlebarchicago.com). El: Blue to Damen.
Open 10am-1am Mon-Fri; 9am-1am Sat, Sun.
Credit AmEx, Disc, MC, V. **Map** p315 A7 ⑰
The multiple bike racks at the back are packed with
every kind of two-wheeler imaginable, no matter
what the time of year. Eco-minded folks chat over
tasty vegan fare, check out each other's rides and
sample the diverse draught beers.

Lemmings
*1850 N Damen Avenue, between W Moffat &
W Cortland Streets (1-773 862 1688). El: Blue
to Damen.* **Open** 4pm-2am Mon-Fri; noon-3am
Sat; noon-2am Sun. **Credit** AmEx, Disc, MC, V.
Map p315 B6 ⑱
Don't take the name too literally: there's a nice crowd
here, but the joint isn't actually packed tight with
followers, so you can usually find a seat from which
to soak up the comforting vibe. It's still low-key, but
you'll usually find someone willing to take you on
at pool or the rotating pinball machines.

★ Map Room
*1949 N Hoyne Avenue, between W Homer
Street & W Armitage Avenue (1-773 252 7636,
www.maproom.com). El: Blue to Western.* **Open**
6.30am-2am Mon-Fri; 7.30am-3am Sat; 11am-2am
Sun. **No credit cards. Map** p315 B6 ⑲
You couldn't fit another beer on the killer list or
another Bucktown local around the pool table here
if you tried. In the morning, the place functions as
a coffee house.

Moonshine
*1824 W Division Street, between N Honore
Street & N Marion Court (1-773 862 8686,
www.moonshinechicago.com). El: Blue to Division.*
Open 5pm-2am Mon-Thur; 11am-2am Fri; 10am-
3am Sat; 10am-2am Sun. **Credit** AmEx, Disc,
MC, V. **Map** p315 C8 ㊿
True to its Prohibition-era theme, this bar serves its
beer in mason jars. But there's nothing redneck
about the seven booths decked out with individual
plasma-screen TVs. These are likely to get more use
during quieter weeknights when couples and small
groups stop in for beers, burgers and televised
games. Weekends can be a madhouse, with blaring
DJ-driven music and scoping singles taking over.

Phyllis' Musical Inn
*1800 W Division Street, at N Wood Street (1-773
486 9862). El: Blue to Division.* **Open** 5pm-2am
Mon; 4pm-2am Tue-Fri; 3pm-3am Sat; 3pm-2am
Sun. **No credit cards. Map** p315 C8 ㊿
One of Wicker Park's first spots for live music
refuses to go the way of cover bands, instead booking local acts that play original rock. They're not
always great, but the garden patio is. A scrappy mix
of chairs and tables, a basketball hoop and groups
of friends shooting the breeze over cheap drinks
make for a classic summer night.

Quencher's Saloon
*2401 N Western Avenue, at W Fullerton Avenue
(1-773 276 9730, www.quenchers.com). El: Blue
to California.* **Open** 11am-2am Mon-Fri, Sun;
noon-3am Sat. **No credit cards. Map** p315 A5 ㊿
This beer bar, which has been around for more than
two decades, has one of the most diverse crowds in
town. The well-heeled eye each other on weekends,
local beer nerds meet to taste the hundreds of choices
on weeknights and drunk punks wander in whenever. Luckily, they peacefully co-exist in two spacious rooms, all in the name of beer.

Small Bar
*2049 W Division Street, between N Damen & N
Hoyne Avenues (1-773 772 2727, www.smallbar
division.com). El: Blue to Division.* **Open** noon-
2am Mon-Fri; 10am-3am Sat; 10am-2am Sun.
Credit AmEx, Disc, MC, V. **Map** p315 B8 ㊿
This welcoming neighbourhood joint is far from
small – it's a decent-sized, airy space that opens up
on to a pavement patio. If they wanted a more literal
and descriptive name, maybe Beer Bar (named for
the extra strong beer list), Scenester Bar (it's not
Rainbo, but close) or Cash Bar (obscure beer ain't
cheap, kids) would have been more accurate.

Southern
*1840 W North Avenue, between N Honore
Street & N Wolcott Avenue (1-773 342 1840,
www.thesouthernchicago.com). El: Blue to
Damen.* **Open** 5pm-2am Mon-Thur; 2pm-2am

Fri; 11am-2am Sat, Sun. **Credit** AmEx, Disc, MC, V. **Map** p315 C7 ❸❹
This understated Bucktown tavern specialises in southern comfort food, ranging from Shiner Bock mussels to a big bad bacon salad. Classic whisky 'dranks' – manhattans, sazeracs, mint juleps and old-fashioneds – are the cocktail go-tos.

★ Violet Hour
1520 N Damen Avenue, between W Le Moyne Street & N Wicker Park Avenue (1-773 252 1500, www.theviolethour.com). El: Blue to Damen. **Open** 6pm-2am Mon-Fri, Sun; 6pm-3am Sat. **Credit** AmEx, MC, V. **Map** p315 B7 ❺❺
This cocktail lounge is exactly what you'd expect from a bar that takes its name from *The Waste Land*: pristine (the carefully constructed cocktails are excellent), pretentious (you won't find a sign on the door – just look for the long queues) and gorgeous.

Humboldt Park & Logan Square

Burlington
3425 W Fullerton Avenue, between N Bernard Street & N St Louis Avenue (1-773 384 3243, www.theburlingtonbar.com). El: Blue to Logan Square. **Open** 7pm-2am Mon-Fri, Sun; 7pm-3am Sat; **Credit** AmEx, Disc, MC, V.
Burlington's spare, dim room has plenty of hipster atmosphere (but no hipster snobbery), ample seating at a wood-panelled bar and a delicious beer on tap that you can't get anywhere else – just point to the unmarked draught handle adorned with antlers.

California Clipper
1002 N California Avenue, at Augusta Boulevard (1-773 384 2547, www.californiaclipper.com). Bus: 52, 66, 70. **Open** 8pm-2am Mon-Fri, Sun; 8pm-3am Sat. **Credit** AmEx, Disc, MC, V.

Brewers' Choice

Atlas Brewing Co brewmasters Ben & John Saller pour forth.

WHY BREWING?
Ben: It combines cooking and engineering, both of which have always appealed to me.
John: Living in Portland (Oregon) in the early 2000s gave me a great appreciation of fresh beer, and whenever I like something, I try to do it myself. Chicago took its time joining the craft beer boom, but now it's here, and I'm excited to be a part of it.

PERFECT NIGHT OUT
Ben: I'd start with dinner at **Small Bar** (*see p140*), then catch a rock show at **Ultra Lounge** (2169 N Milwaukee Avenue, at W Talman Avenue, 1-773 269 2900) or **Quencher's** (*see p140*) and end the night at **Webster's Wine Bar** (*see p134*) or **Telegraph** (2671 N Milwaukee Avenue, at N Sawyer Avenue, 1-773 292 9463).
John: I'd start with happy hour at the **Billy Goat** (*see p132*), the old one, where Mike Royko and Studs Terkel used to hang out. Then I'd have dinner at the **Publican** (*see p120*). Next I'd stop in at **Webster's** (*see p134*), the **Matchbox** (*see p139*) and **Revolution Brewing** (*see p142*). Then I'd maybe slip in a second dinner at **Taqueria Moran** (2226 N California Avenue, at Milwaukee Avenue, 1-773 235 2663) and a fun cocktail nightcap out of a Nalgene sitting in the park.

SECRET SPOT
John: It's not hidden, but our neighbours at **Paddy Long's Beer and Bacon Pub**

(1028 W Diversey Parkway, at N Kenmore Avenue, 1-773 290 6988, www.paddylongs.com) don't get mentioned enough among great beer bars. They don't have the sheer number of taps, but there are always two or three new things for me to try when I go in there, and that's rare. Also **Shan Foods** (5060 N Sheridan Road, at W Winona Street, 1-773 769 4961), in the back of a convenience store in a strip mall, has delicious, cheap Pakistani food and is open late.

CONSUME

The Clipper is just a photo booth away from exhibiting the same shabby-chic cool as Wicker Park dives such as Goldstar. Slide into one of the gorgeous old booths on a Friday, Saturday or Sunday night for no-cover country or rockabilly groups.

Revolution Brewing

2323 N Milwaukee Avenue, between Belden & Medill Avenues (1-773 227 2739, www.revbrew. com). El: Blue to California. **Open** 11am-2am Mon-Fri; 10am-2am Sat; 10am-2am Sun. **Credit** AmEx, Disc, MC, V.

You could wait up to an hour to get into one of this microbrewery's booths. Or you could simply hover around the bar and snap up a stool as soon as someone else calls it a night. Either way, remember you're here for the beer as much as the food. So pair that Workingman burger with a pint of Workingwoman brown beer. And follow that with a goblet of Bottom Up Wit and an order of sweet potato cakes.

★ Rootstock Wine & Beer Bar

954 N California Avenue, at Augusta Boulevard (1-773 292 1616, www.rootstockbar.com). Bus: 52, 65, 66, 70. **Open** 5pm-2am Mon-Sat; 11am-4pm Sun. **Credit** AmEx, Disc, MC, V.

The novella-length menu at this low-key wine bar contains loving and helpful descriptions of an impressive selection of wines and beers. And thanks to the array of small plates served until 1am, this is the kind of joint you'll never want – or need – to leave.

★ Scofflaw

3201 W Armitage Avenue, at Kedzie Avenue (1-773 252 9700, www.scofflawchicago.com). Bus: 73, 82. **Open** 5pm-2am Mon-Fri; noon-3am Sat; noon-2am Sun. **Credit** AmEx, Disc, MC, V.

Veterans of the Whistler (*see right*) and Logan Square pizza bar Boiler Room joined together to open this bar. One of the two rooms looks a lot like Violet Hour (*see p141*), which makes sense since cocktails (specifically gin cocktails) are a focus of the place. The other room is less loungey and truer to what Scofflaw is – a top-notch, friendly neighbourhood joint.

THE BEST BAR SNACKS

For superb sausages
Bangers & Lace. *See p139.*

For seasonal fare (and drinks)
Sable Kitchen & Bar. *See p131.*

For oysters and fromage
RM Champagne Salon. *See p137.*

For inventive nibbles
Barrelhouse Flat. *See p133.*

Whirlaway Lounge

3224 W Fullerton Avenue, between N Kedzie Boulevard & N Sawyer Avenue (1-773 276 6809, www.whirlaway.net). El: Blue to Logan Square. **Open** 4.30pm-2am Mon-Fri, Sun; 4.30pm-3am Sat. **No credit cards**.

This watering hole glows with charm – or is it the string of Christmas lights behind the bar? Either way, retired rock stars put away beers next to their disciples under the soft lights, snapshots of regulars and the warm smile of the owner-bartender Maria.

★ Whistler

2421 N Milwaukee Avenue, between W Fullerton Avenue & W Richmond Street (1-773 227 3530, www.whistlerchicago.com). El: Blue to California. **Open** 6pm-2am Mon-Thur; 5pm-2am Fri; 5pm-3am Sat; 5pm-2am Sun. **Credit** AmEx, MC, V.

From the outside, this place looks like a gallery (which, technically, it partially is). On the inside, it's open and loftlike, with a permanent stage for live music. Behind the bar, a bartender skilfully prepares cocktails such as a rosemary collins. One sip and you'll be hooked.

THE SOUTH SIDE

Cove Lounge

1750 E 55th Street, between S Hyde Park Boulevard & S Everett Avenue (1-773 684 1013, www.thecovelounge.com). Bus: 6, 55, X55. **Open** 10am-2am Mon-Fri; 11am-2am Sat, Sun. **Credit** AmEx, Disc, MC, V. **Map** p316 Z17 ⑤⑥

The payoff from the nautical theme hinted at by this blue-collar hangout's name is decidedly small. Aside from a light fixture made from a ship's wheel and anchor-shaped coat hooks, this is your standard shot-and-a-beer dive.

Schaller's Pump

3714 S Halsted Street, at W 37th Street (1-773 376 6332). El: Red to Sox-35th. **Open** 11am-2am Mon-Fri; 4pm-3am Sat; 3pm-9pm Sun. **No credit cards**.

There's no better place to cheer on your team than this down-home institution near US Cellular Field. Arrive at least half an hour before game time to tuck into the home-style dishes. Add doting servers, cheap beer and a living room-like atmosphere, and you've got the best sports experience short of front-row seats.

Woodlawn Tap

1172 E 55th Street, between S University & S Woodlawn Avenues (1-773 643 5516). Bus: 28, 55. **Open** 11am-2am Mon-Fri, Sun; 11am-3am Sat. **No credit cards. Map** p316 X17 ⑤⑦

Just off the University of Chicago campus, Jimmy's (after dearly departed original owner Jimmy Wilson) is the favoured spot for scholars to rub elbows with undergrads and working-class regulars. Cheap burgers are washed down with even cheaper beer.

Shops & Services

Stock up on and off the Magnificent Mile.

Throughout its proudly blue-collar history, Chicago has occasionally lacked a little high style. But, reflecting the changes in the city as a whole, it has now become something of a fashion hub. Impressive flagships from Barneys New York and Burberry, coupled with highly anticipated recent openings from the likes of Christian Louboutin, are luring fashionistas into the major shopping districts (*see p144* Where to Shop), while a bevy of boutiques continues to show off the local retail talent. And there's plenty to appeal to non-fashionistas, from great vintage record shops to upscale spas. Indeed, the only downer comes courtesy of the sales tax: at 9.25 per cent, it's one of the highest in the US.

General

DEPARTMENT STORES

★ Barneys New York
15 E Oak Street, Gold Coast (1-312 587 1700, www.barneys.com). El: Red to Clark/Division.
Open 10am-7pm Mon-Sat; 11am-6pm Sun.
Credit AmEx, MC, V. **Map** p310 H9.
Barneys has been offering Chicago shoppers its New York City sophistication for years, and in the spring of 2009 it offered even more by moving across the street from its old location and doubling in size. Professionals and socialites with deep pockets head here for top designer and private-label apparel: clothing, jewellery, bags, shoes and accessories, spread over 90,000sq ft of sleek retail space.

Bloomingdale's
900 N Michigan Shops, 900 N Michigan Avenue, at E Walton Street, Magnificent Mile (1-312 440 4460, www.bloomingdales.com). El: Red to Chicago. **Open** 10am-8pm Mon-Sat; 11am-7pm Sun. **Credit** AmEx, MC, V. **Map** p313 J9.
On a Magnificent Mile that's awash with tradition, Bloomies is all about having fun. A must for the younger shopper, its six levels are packed with fashions for the free-spirited; in particular, don't miss the often surprisingly well-stocked clearance racks.
▶ *There's also a Bloomingdale's Home & Furniture Store in River North (600 N Wabash Avenue, between W Ontario & W Ohio Streets, 1-312 324 7500).*

Macy's
111 N State Street, at E Randolph Street, the Loop (1-312 781 1000, www.macys.com). El: Blue to Washington; Brown, Green, Orange, Pink or Purple to Randolph/Wabash; Red to Lake. **Open** 10am-8pm Mon-Sat; 11am-6pm Sun.
Credit AmEx, Disc, MC, V. **Map** p309 H12.
It's been a few years since this chain took over the beloved Marshall Field's name, and Chicagoans finally seem at peace with the change. After all, they can still enjoy the nine levels of this landmark department store, impressively stocked with clothes, furniture, iPods (sold from vending machines) and everything in between. Sample the Frango mints, gaze at the Tiffany-domed atrium and check the various stores-within-a-store, including Lush.
▶ *The seventh floor is home to several decent eating options; see p130.*

INSIDE TRACK
MACY'S MAKE-UP

Visit the Fresh counter at **Macy's** (*see above*) on N State Street for a gratis facial a few Thursdays each month. The aesthetician whisks you away into a candlelit back room for 30 to 45 minutes, treating your skin to a bevy of Fresh products. And it's all no strings attached: you don't have to pay a penny for a product (unless you want to). Aim to book a week in advance.

CONSUME

Neiman Marcus

737 N Michigan Avenue, at E Chicago Avenue, Magnificent Mile (1-312 642 5900, www.neiman marcus.com). El: Red to Chicago. **Open** 10am-7pm Mon-Sat; noon-6pm Sun. **Credit** AmEx, Disc, MC, V. **Map** p310 J10.

Neiman Marcus woos shoppers with a refreshingly airy interior, *haute* fashions from Chanel to up-and-comers, luxurious accessories and tempting baked goods. Money is generally no object for the wealthy folks who shop here, resulting in a pricing structure that's led wags to nickname it 'Needless Markup'.

Nordstrom

55 E Grand Avenue, at N Michigan Avenue, Magnificent Mile (1-312 464 1515, www. nordstrom.com). El: Red to Grand. **Open** 10am-9pm Mon-Sat; 11am-7pm Sun. **Credit** AmEx, Disc, MC, V. **Map** p310 J10.

Nordstrom is known for its wide range of fashions, particularly in the footwear department, and its attentive customer service. If you happen to be in town during one of its famous half-yearly sales, be prepared to spend at least a full afternoon here – check in your bags with the store concierge and get power-shopping. The in-store café is perfect for a lunchtime wind-down.

▶ *Prices are lower at Nordstrom Rack, the store's discount offshoot (24 N State Street, at W Washington Street, the Loop, 1-312 377 5500).*

Saks Fifth Avenue

Chicago Place, 700 N Michigan Avenue, at E Superior Street, Magnificent Mile (1-312 944 6500, www.saksfifthavenue.com). El: Red to Chicago. **Open** 10am-7pm Mon-Wed; 10am-8pm Thur-Sat; 11am-7pm Sun. **Credit** AmEx, Disc, MC, V. **Map** p310 J10.

Where to Shop

A brief guide to Chicago's best shopping neighbourhoods.

THE LOOP
There's not much notable retail activity in the Loop beyond Block 37 (*see p145*), but bargain-hunters should hightail it to **State Street**, where a number of department stores and clothing shops offer steals.

OLD TOWN & LINCOLN PARK
In the village-like streets of these two smartening neighbourhoods, independent clothing boutiques happily coexist next to outposts of national niche brands. Fertile shopping drags include **Clark Street**.

NEAR NORTH SIDE
Between the Chicago River and Water Tower Place, **Michigan Avenue** – aka the Magnificent Mile – is a consumer paradise, packed with enormous department stores and multi-level flagships for countless big-ticket brands. As you might expect, it's packed on weekends.

The nearby **Gold Coast** isn't named for the colour of shoppers' credit cards but it might as well be. The boutiques on **Oak Street** sell the poshest clothes that money can buy.

LAKEVIEW & AROUND
The chains that have encroached upon Lincoln Park haven't all made it up to Lakeview, which is still dominated by interesting independent stores. **Clark Street** contains its fair share of stores, especially north of Belmont.

WICKER PARK & AROUND
This part of town is awash with arty stores selling cool clothing, high-design home decor and funky accessories, plus a handful of great bookstores and music shops. Much of the action is around the three-way junction of **Damen, North** and **Milwaukee Avenues**.

Magnificent Mile.

CONSUME

Favoured by Chicago's upper crust since 1929, five years after it first opened in New York City, Saks Fifth Avenue favours traditional fashions over the wilder trends. Expect to find a wide range of high-quality apparel for women and children, supplemented with stylish accessories.

► *Just across the street sits Saks' equally classy menswear store (no.717).*

Sears
2 N State Street, at W Madison Street, the Loop (1-312 373 6000, www.sears.com). El: Blue to Washington; Brown, Green, Orange, Pink or Purple to Randolph/Wabash; Red to Lake. **Open** 10am-8pm Mon-Fri; 10am-6pm Sat; 11am-5pm Sun. **Credit** AmEx, Disc, MC, V. **Map** p309 H12.
Although it's hardly a style destination, Sears offers affordable fashions for men, women and children, with regular bargains on wardrobe staples such as Levi's 501s. What it lacks in exciting clothes, the department store makes up for with its wide selection of products including washing machines and kitchen curtains.
Other locations throughout the city.

MALLS

900 Shops
900 N Michigan Avenue, at E Walton Street, Magnificent Mile (1-312 915 3916, www.shop 900.com). El: Red to Chicago. **Open** 10am-7pm Mon-Sat; noon-6pm Sun. **Map** p310 J9.
The six-floor 900 N Michigan mall is a relatively upscale operation, offering the city's only full-scale Bloomingdale's (*see p143*) alongside branches of Gucci (1-312 664 5504, www.gucci.com), J.Crew (1-312 751 2739, www.jcrew.com), Club Monaco (1-312 787 8757, www.clubmonaco.com) and a handsome Michael Kors boutique (1-312 640 1122, www.michaelkors.com).

Block 37
108 N State Street, between W Randolph Street and E Washington Boulevard, the Loop (1-312 261 4700, www.block37.com). El: Brown, Green, Orange, Pink, Purple to Randolph/Wabash. **Open** 10am-8pm Mon-Sat; 11am-6pm Sun. **Map** p309 H12.
Located in the heart of the Loop, this mall features everything from clothing chains like Anthropologie and Eileen Fisher to bath and beauty stores such as Sabon and Sephora. For a sweet mid-shop pick-me-up, stop in and sample Magnolia Bakery's banana pudding.

Century Shopping Center
2828 N Clark Street, between W Diversey Parkway & W Surf Street, Lakeview (1-773 929 8100, www.centuryshoppingcentre.com). El: Brown or Purple to Diversey. **Open** 10am-9pm Mon-Fri; 10am-6pm Sat; noon-6pm Sun. **Map** p312 F4.

This small neighbourhood mall includes an indie cinema, a branch of LA Fitness (1-773 929 6900, www.lafitness.com), plus outposts of Aveda (1-773 883 1560, www.aveda.com) and Victoria's Secret (1-773 549 7405, www.victoriassecret.com).

Shops at North Bridge
520 N Michigan Avenue, at E Grand Avenue, Magnificent Mile (1-312 327 2300, www. theshopsatnorthbridge.com). El: Red to Grand. **Open** 10am-9pm Mon-Sat; 11am-7pm Sun. **Map** p310 J10.
Nordstrom (*see p144*) is the flagship at this 100-store development on Magnificent Mile. But there are plenty of other stores to tempt a largely tourist crowd, such as Hugo Boss (1-312 321 0700, www. hugoboss.com), Kiehl's (1-312 321 3601, www. kiehls.com), jeweller Erwin Pearl (1-312 321 1445, www.erwinpearl.com) and Sephora (1-312 494 9598, www.sephora.com).

Water Tower Place
835 N Michigan Avenue, at E Chestnut Street, Magnificent Mile (1-312 440 3166, www.shop watertower.com). El: Red to Chicago. **Open** 10am-9pm Mon- Sat; 11am-6pm Sun. **Map** p310 J9.
American Girl Place (1-312 943 9400, www.american girl.com) moved into this shopping centre a few years ago, but Water Tower Place isn't just full of little girls clutching dolls. It's also a destination for fashionistas, who frequent the likes of Hendri Bendel (1-312 951 1928, www.hendribendel.com) and Canadian retailer Aritzia (1-312 867 9230, www.aritzia.ca), as well as Banana Republic (1-312 642 7667, www.banana republic.com) and Abercrombie & Fitch (1-312 787 8825, www.abercrombie.com). *Photos p146.*

Westfield Old Orchard
4999 Old Orchard Center, off Route 41 (via I-94), Skokie (1-847 673 6800,www.westfield. com/oldorchard). **Open** 10am-9pm Mon-Fri; 11am-6pm Sun.
As suburban malls go, this one's more pleasing than most, with branches of the Apple Store (1-847 983 9230, www.apple.com), Aveda (1-847 679 1863, www.aveda.com), Madewell (1-847 679 2486, www.madewell.com), Sephora (1-847 329 1494, www.sephora.com) and Abercrombie & Fitch (1-847 679 6372, www.abercrombie.com).

Woodfield Shopping Center
5 Woodfield Mall, off Route 53 S (exit at Woodfield Road), via I-90, Schaumburg (1-847 330 1537, www.shopwoodfield.com). **Open** 10am-9pm Mon-Sat; 11am-6pm Sun.
Five department stores, including Sears (1-847 330 2356, www.sears.com) and Nordstrom (1-847 605 2121, www.nordstrom.com), are joined by Crate & Barrel (1-847 619 4200, www.crateandbarrel.com) and an Apple Store (1-630 237 2160, www.apple.com). This was once the largest mall in the country.

Water Tower Place. See p145.

Outlet malls

Chicago Premium Outlets

1650 Premium Outlets Boulevard, off I-88 (exit at Aurora, Farnsworth Avenue North), Aurora (1-630 585 2200, www.premiumoutlets.com/chicago). **Open** 10am-9pm Mon-Sat; 10am-7pm Sun.
Drive about an hour outside the city limits to shop at 100-odd outlet stores, from posh brands such as DKNY (1-630 236 8900, www.dkny.com) to hipster favourites such as Diesel (1-630 236 5514, www.diesel.com) and Converse (1-630 820 7085, www.converse.com), via big-name chains including Gap (1-630 499 5068, www.gap.com) and Banana Republic (1-630 851 5135, www.bananarepublic.com).

Gurnee Mills

6170 W Grand Avenue, off I-94/I-294 (exit at Route 132, W Grand Avenue), Gurnee (1-847 263 7500, www.gurneemillsmall.com). **Open** 10am-9pm Mon-Fri; 10am-9.30pm Sat; 11am-7pm Sun.
A Nike Factory Store (1-847 855 0857, www.nike.com) and TJ Maxx (1-847 855 0146, www.tjmaxx.com) draw in the bargain hunters to this not terribly pleasant mall, which also includes a Disney Outlet (1-847 856 8239, www.disney.com) among the stores.

Specialist

BOOKS & MAGAZINES

General

See p148 **After-Words New & Used Books**.

★ Barbara's Bookstore

111 N State Street, between W Randolph & Washington Streets, the Loop (1-312 781 3033, www.barbarasbookstore.com). El: Blue, Brown, Green, Orange, Pink, Purple to Clark/Lake. **Open** 10am-8pm Mon-Sat; 11am-6pm Sun. **Credit** AmEx, Disc, MC, V. **Map** p310 H9.
This small chain originally opened up in Old Town in the early 1960s. Since then, it's expanded to a handful of locations around the city, including this Macy's outpost in 2003. The solid stock is complemented by author appearances.
Other locations Willis Tower (*see p44*); 201 E Huron Street, Streeterville (1-312 926 2665).

Barnes & Noble

1130 N State Street, at E Elm Street, Gold Coast (1-312 280 8155, www.barnesandnoble.com). El: Red to Clark/Division. **Open** 9am-9pm Mon-Sat; 10am-9pm Sun. **Credit** AmEx, Disc, MC, V. **Map** p310 H9.
The on-the-ball staffers at this spacious store often make a genuine effort to find the book you're looking for. The magazine section is large and varied.
Other locations 1 E Jackson Boulevard at S State Street, the Loop (1-312 362 8792); 1441 W Webster Avenue, at N Clybourn Avenue, Lincoln Park (1-773 871 3610).

★ Book Cellar

4736 N Lincoln Avenue, between W Lawrence & W Leland Avenues, Lincoln Square (1-773 293 2665, www.bookcellarinc.com). El: Brown to Western. **Open** 10am-10pm Mon, Wed-Sat; 10am-6pm Tue, Sun. **Credit** AmEx, Disc, MC, V.

When it comes to bookstores, this place is a class apart. Not only can you browse books while sipping wine, but the staff recommendations are usually just what you want them to be: varied and idiosyncratic. Catch young area writers here on the third Thursday of the month at Local Author Night.

★ City Lit Books

2523 N Kedzie Boulevard, between N Linden Place & W Altgeld Street, Logan Square (1-773 235 2523, www.citylitbooks.com). El: Blue to Logan Square. **Open** 11am-8pm Tue-Fri; 10am-7pm Sat; 10am-5pm Sun. **Credit** AmEx, Disc, MC, V.
Until recently, Logan Square was a literary desert, but City Lit Books owner Teresa Kirschbraun had faith that Logan Square residents wanted a general-interest bookstore. The simple interior features kids' and Spanish-language sections, a fantastic cookbook choice, and even a fireplace for curling up in winter.

Powell's

1501 E 57th Street, between S Harper & S Lake Park Avenues, Hyde Park (1-773 955 7780, www.powellschicago.com). Metra: 55th-56th-57th Street. **Open** 9am-11pm daily. **Credit** MC, V. **Map** p316 Y17.
The three branches of this chain offer an agreeably browsable selection of remaindered books and second-hand stock. The Hyde Park and South Loop locations, both about as big as each other, have strong academic collections, while the Lakeview branch has a large art and photography selection. **Other locations** 2850 N Lincoln Avenue, at W Wolfram Street, Lakeview (1-773 248 1444); 1218 S Halsted Street, University Village (1-312 243 9070).

Seminary Cooperative Bookstore

5751 S Woodlawn Avenue, between E 57th & E 58th Streets, Hyde Park (1-773 752 4381, www.semcoop.com). Metra: 59th Street. **Open** 8.30am-8pm Mon-Fri; 10am-6pm Sat; noon-6pm Sun. **Credit** AmEx, Disc, MC, V. **Map** p316 X12.
The Seminary Coop is revered by local academics, but general readers are sure to find something unusual and inspiring to read on its impeccably stocked shelves. There are obscure texts galore, leaving even the most intrepid bookworm happy. The 57th Street location offers a slightly smaller selection in a slightly airier location.
Other locations Newberry Library Bookstore, 60 W Walton Street, at N Dearborn Street, Gold Coast (1-312 255 3520); 57th Street Books, 1301 E 57th Street, at S Kimbark Avenue, Hyde Park (1-773 684 1300).

Unabridged Bookstore

3251 N Broadway Street, between W Melrose Street & W Aldine Avenue, Lakeview (1-773 883 9119, www.unabridgedbookstore.com). El: Brown, Purple or Red to Belmont. **Open** 10am-9pm Mon-Fri; 10am-7pm Sat, Sun. **Credit** AmEx, Disc, MC, V. **Map** p313 F2.
This indie bookstore largely reflects the make-up of the neighbourhood in which it sits: it's particularly strong on gay and lesbian literature. You'll find a large selection of hard-to-find LBGT magazines, as well as autographed copies of books by writers such as David Sedaris and Augusten Burroughs.

Specialist

Quimby's Bookstore

1854 W North Avenue, at N Wolcott Avenue, Wicker Park (1-773 342 0910, www.quimbys. com). El: Blue to Damen. **Open** noon-9pm Mon-Thur; noon-10pm Fri; 11am-10pm Sat; noon-7pm Sun. **Credit** AmEx, Disc, MC, V. **Map** p315 B7.
Find the newest in small press, underground and self-published magazines at this Wicker Park staple, or check out the comics and books. *Photo p148.*

INSIDE TRACK
LAND OF LINCOLN

American history buffs shouldn't miss the **Abraham Lincoln Book Shop** (357 W Chicago Avenue, at N Orleans Street, River North, 1-312 944 3085, www. alincolnbookshop.com), a dealer in Lincolnabilia and Civil War lore, including books, autographs and photos, since the 1930s. The store was the founding site of the Civil War Round Table, a discussion group that keeps alive stories of the blue and the grey.

CONSUME

★ Women & Children First

*5233 N Clark Street, at W Foster Avenue,
Andersonville (1-773 769 9299, www.womenand
childrenfirst.com). El: Red to Berwyn.* **Open** 11am-
7pm Mon, Tue; 11am-9pm Wed-Fri; 10am-7pm
Sat; 11am-6pm Sun. **Credit** AmEx, Disc, MC, V.
This welcoming, gay-friendly spot is as much a community meeting place as it is a bookstore. Readings,
for women and children alike, draw established
authors and up-and-coming activists.

Used & antiquarian

After-Words New & Used Books

*23 E Illinois Street, between N State Street & N
Wabash Avenue, River North (1-312 464 1110,
www.after-wordschicago.com). El: Red to Grand.*
Open 10.30am-10pm Mon-Thur; 10.30am-11pm
Fri; 10am-11pm Sat; noon-7pm Sun. **Credit**
AmEx, MC, V. **Map** p310 H11.
This two-storey shop offers new, used and out-of-
print volumes. Customers can access the internet by
the hour using store computers, and are even able to
order customised stationery.

★ Myopic Books

*1564 N Milwaukee Avenue, at N Damen Avenue,
Wicker Park (1-773 862 4882, www.myopic
bookstore.com). El: Blue to Damen.* **Open** 9am-
11pm daily. **Credit** MC, V. **Map** p315 C7.
Staff at this three-storey shop are serious about the
no mobile phones policy, which makes for a quiet
environment. Everything from foreign fiction to
cookbooks is represented. Prices are fair, staff are
tremendous and the shop is open late every day.

CHILDREN

Fashion

Gap Kids can be found within the four-storey
Gap flagship store (555 N Michigan Avenue,
1-312 494 8580, www.gap.com).

★ Perchance Kids

*1205 W Webster Avenue, at Racine Avenue,
Wicker Park (1-773 244 1300, www.perchance
kids.com). El: Brown, Purple, Red to Fullerton.*
Open 9am-5pm Mon-Fri; 10am-4pm Sat;
11am-4pm Sun. **Credit** AmEx, Disc, MC, V.
While there are two grown-up versions of Perchance
in Gold Coast and Lakeview, the mini-me version is
just as fashion-forward. Find mini trenchcoats,
tiered dresses and preppy elbow-patched sweaters
for tots and pre-teens, plus tons and tons of adorable
baby styles.

Psychobaby

*1657 W Division Street, at N Paulina Street,
Wicker Park (1-773 772 2815, www.psychobaby
online.com). El: Blue to Damen.* **Open** 10am-6pm
Mon-Wed, Fri, Sat; 10am-8pm Thur; 11am-5pm
Sun. **Credit** AmEx, Disc, MC, V. **Map** p315 B7.
Tots and toddlers get kitted out in funky fashions
at this Wicker Park store, where the clothes are a
real antidote to traditional frilly togs. Shoes, books
and educational toys round out the selection.

Toys & games

For **Lego Store**, *see p145* Water Tower Place.

Quimby's Bookstore. *See p147.*

Quake

*4628 N Lincoln Avenue, at W Eastwood Avenue,
Uptown (1-773 878 4288, www.quakechicago.com).
El: Red to Lawrence.* **Open** 1-6pm Mon, Wed-Fri;
noon-6pm Sat; noon-5pm Sun. **Credit** MC, V.
The place to find that elusive Mystery Date game or
that *Nightmare Before Christmas* figurine, along
with retro lunchboxes, *Star Wars* swag and board
games from the 1960s and '70s.

★ Rotofugi

*2780 N Lincoln Avenue, at W Diversey
Parkway, Lincoln Park (1-773 868 3308,
www.rotofugi.com). El: Brown to Diversey.*
Open 11am-7pm daily. **Credit** AmEx, Disc,
MC, V. **Map** p315 B10.
Grown-up kids rush to this Japanese-inspired toy
shop to pick up limited-edition vinyl dolls, plush toys
and poseable figures. There's almost always a cool
art exhibition going on.

Timeless Toys

*4749 N Lincoln Avenue, at W Lawrence Avenue,
Lincoln Square (1-773 334 4445, www.timeless
toyschicago.com). El: Brown to Western.* **Open**
10am-6pm Mon-Wed, Sat; 10am-7pm Thur, Fri;
10am-5pm Sun. **Credit** AmEx, Disc, MC, V.
Angelina Jolie helped put this years-old toyshop in
the pages of national gossip mags when the
paparazzi photographed her shopping here while in
town shooting a movie. Its inventory is comprised
of classic (wooden trains, puzzles), educational (science kits) and imaginative (costumes, puppets).

★ Uncle Fun

*1338 W Belmont Avenue, at N Southport Avenue,
Lakeview (1-773 477 8223, www.unclefunchicago.
com). El: Brown, Purple or Red to Belmont.* **Open**
noon-7pm Mon-Fri; 11am-7pm Sat; 11am-5pm Sun.
Credit AmEx, MC, V. **Map** p313 D2.
Children young and old will love digging through
drawers jammed full of plastic squirt cameras, fake
puke and other novelty toys from the 1970s and '80s,
all at fairly reasonable prices.

ELECTRONICS & PHOTOGRAPHY

The Magnificent Mile is home to an **Apple
Store** (no.679, at E Erie Street, 1-312 981 4104,
www.apple.com). Nearby, there's also a branch
of **Bang & Olufsen** (609 N State Street, 1-312
787 6006, www.bang-olufsen.com).

★ Central Camera

*230 S Wabash Avenue, at E Jackson Boulevard,
the Loop (1-312 427 5580, www.centralcamera.
com). El: Blue or Red to Jackson; Brown, Green,
Orange, Pink or Purple to Adams/Wabash.*
Open 8.30am-5.30pm Mon-Fri; 8.30am-5pm
Sat. **Credit** AmEx, Disc, MC, V. **Map** p309 H12.

The knowledgeable service and lack of appealing
decor haven't changed a great deal during Central
Camera's century in business, but the stock certainly
has: these days, it's packed with digital imaging
equipment, as well as more old-fashioned gear. The
repair service is a valued extra.

Saturday Audio Exchange

*1021 W Belmont Avenue, at N Kenmore Avenue,
Lakeview (1-773 935 4434, www.saturdayaudio.
com). El: Brown, Purple or Red to Belmont.*
Open 5.30-9pm Thur; 10.30am-5.30pm Sat;
noon-4pm Sun. **Credit** AmEx, Disc, MC, V.
Map p313 E2.
Thanks to great prices and smart, unpushy staff,
this local fave thrives despite the fact that it's only
open three days a week. Brands include Denon,
Musical Fidelity and Blu-ray; stock is a mix of new
and used equipment.

FASHION

Designer

A stroll down the fashionable pavement
of E Oak Street between State Street and
Michigan Avenue turns up big designer
names, among them **Hermès** (no.25, 1-312
787 8175, www.hermes.com), **Jil Sander**
(no.48, 1-312 335 0006, www.jilsander.com),
Kate Spade (no.56, 1-312 654 8853, www.
katespade.com) and **Prada** (no.30, 1-312 951
1113, www.prada.com).

The north end of N Michigan Avenue,
between Superior and Oak Streets, is another
important fashionista destination, not least
as it is home to the world's largest **Ralph
Lauren** (no.750, 1-312 280 1655, www.polo.
com), plus **Giorgio Armani** (no.800, 1-312
751 2244, www.armani.com), **Gucci** (in the
900 N Michigan Shops, 1-312 664 5504, www.
gucci.com), and **Chanel** (no.935, 1-312 787
5500, www.chanel.com).

Head to the now gentrified Wicker Park/
Bucktown area for another designer invasion,
with **Marc by Marc Jacobs** (1714 N Damen
Avenue, 1-773 276 2998, www.marcjacobs.com),
Nanette Lepore (1623 N Damen Avenue,
1-773 489 4500, www.nanettelepore.com),
Chicago native **Cynthia Rowley** (1653 N
Damen Avenue, 1-773 276 9209, www.cynthia
rowley.com; *photos p151*) and neighbourhood
newbie **GANT Rugger** (1702 N Damen
Avenue, www.us.gant.com).

Atelier Azza

*Level 3, 520 N Michigan Avenue, at E Grand
Avenue, Magnificent Mile (1-312 245 0733,
www.atelierazza.com). El: Red to Grand.*
Open 10am-9pm Mon-Sat; 11am-7pm Sun.
Credit AmEx, Disc, MC, V. **Map** p310 J10.

CONSUME

Breakout local designer Azeeza Khan continues to dominate the Chicago fashion scene with her first boutique. The Mag Mile shop, located within the Shops at North Bridge, features the designer's jewel-tone shift dresses, embroidered blazers and other colourful clothing with a modern Indian twist. Prices start at around $79.

Blake

212 W Chicago Avenue, between N Wells & N Franklin Streets, River North (1-312 202 0047). El: Brown or Purple to Chicago. **Open** 10.30am-7pm Mon-Fri; 10.30am-6.30pm Sat. **Credit** AmEx, Disc, MC, V. **Map** p310 G10.

You'll need to be buzzed in to browse the pricey frocks from Dries Van Noten, Marni and others, but the selection is worth the initial awkwardness. That said, the easily intimidated may prefer to head elsewhere, as the staff's attitude can be just as chilly as the shop's stark interior.

★ Edith Hart

1917 N Damen Avenue, between W Cortland & W Homer Streets, Bucktown (1-773 252 3350, www.edithhart.com). El: Blue to Damen. **Open** 11am-6pm Tue-Sat; noon-5pm Sun. **Credit** AmEx, Disc, MC, V. **Map** p315 B6.

Formerly known as the Edit, Edith Hart is named after store founder Morgan Gutterman's glamorous grandma. The shop offers a focused selection of women's clothing and accessories, including pieces from Stylestalker and Sass & Bide, plus cool jewellery on the relatively cheap.

★ Eskell

1509 N Milwaukee Avenue, at N Honore Street, Wicker Park (1-773 486 0830, www.eskell.com). El: Blue to Damen. **Open** 11am-7pm Tue-Sat; 11am-5pm Sun. **Credit** AmEx, Disc, MC, V. **Map** p312 E5.

Young, arty types depend on Eskell to find rare designer labels, many from New York's hippest enclaves. The house line displays beautiful use of pattern and texture in its rock'n'roll-meets-hippie dresses and separates.

Helen Yi

1725 N Damen Avenue, at W St Paul Avenue, Wicker Park (1-773 252 3838, www.helenyi.com). El: Blue to Damen. **Open** 11am-7pm Mon-Sat; noon-5pm Sun. **Credit** AmEx, MC, V. **Map** p315 B7.

Make sure your credit card balance is in good shape when you visit this spacious women's boutique. After you've seen the lovely clothes from Chloé and others, you'll struggle not to splurge.

★ Ikram

15 E Huron Street, between N Wabash & N State Streets, River North (1-312 587 1000, www.ikram.com). El: Red to Chicago. **Open** 10am-6pm Mon-Sat. **Credit** AmEx, Disc, MC, V. **Map** p310 J10.

Ikram Goldman learned the rag trade at Ultimo before opening her boutique. The global scope of the high-end fashions, flirty footwear and jewellery found in this shop are fresh off the pages of *Vogue*.

P.45

1643 N Damen Avenue, at W North Avenue, Wicker Park (1-773 862 4523, www.p45.com). El: Blue to Damen. **Open** 11am-7pm Mon-Fri; 11am-6pm Sat; noon-5pm Sun. **Credit** AmEx, Disc, MC, V. **Map** p315 B7.

This super-hip shop, which features a wonderful sweeping interior by famous local designer Suhail, is a piece of Soho in Chicago. The young proprietresses of the industrial-chic space buy exclusive designs from local and New York up-and-comers, which they sell at hefty prices.

★ Robin Richman

2108 N Damen Avenue, at W Charleston Street, Bucktown (1-773 278 6150, www.robinrichman.com). El: Blue (O'Hare branch) to Western. **Open** 11am-6pm Tue-Sat; noon-5pm Sun. **Credit** AmEx, Disc, MC, V. **Map** p315 B5.

A shopping pioneer in Bucktown for hip women's clothing. Antique-looking items (handsome bags, semi-precious jewellery and the like) make the atmosphere both rustic and ravishing.

★ Roslyn

2035 N Damen Avenue, between W McLean & W Dickens Avenues, Bucktown (1-773 489 1311, www.roslynboutique.com). El: Blue to Damen. **Open** 11am-7pm Tue-Fri; 11am-6pm Sat; noon-5pm Sun. **Credit** AmEx, Disc, MC, V. **Map** p315 B6.

At Roslyn, the racks of women's clothes are organised by label, each accompanied by a biography. You'll appreciate the nuance: most of the pricey pieces are by rising (read: just-out-of-school) designers.

Sarca

710 N Wabash Avenue, between W Huron & W Superior Streets, Streeterville (1-312 255 0900, www.shopsarca.com). El: Red to Chicago. **Open** 10am-6pm Mon-Sat. **Credit** AmEx, Disc, MC, V. **Map** p310 H10.

This upscale women's clothing shop is packed with exclusive lines from all over the world. You'll also find accessory and jewellery lines from British designers Jane Carr and Bex Rox, as well as one-off vintage pieces from New Yorker Randy Clare.

Scoop

1702 N Milwaukee Avenue, at W Wabansia Avenue, Wicker Park (1-773 227 9930, www.scoopnyc.com). El: Blue to Damen. **Open** 11am-7pm Mon-Sat; noon-6pm Sun. **Credit** AmEx, Disc, MC, V. **Map** p315 B7.

Cynthia Rowley. *See p149.*

There's something for the whole fashionable family here, including Jimmy Choo slingbacks, Earnest Sewn denim for kids and John Varvatos sweaters for men. Prices aren't cheap, but there's often a good selection of items on sale.

Sir & Madame

938 N Damen Avenue, between W Augusta Boulevard & W Walton Street, Ukrainian Village (1-773 489 6660, www.sirandmadame.com). Bus 50. **Open** 11am-7pm Mon-Sat; noon-5pm Sun. **Credit** AmEx, Disc, MC, V. **Map** p315 B7.
In addition to stocking designer duds for men and women, the couple behind this Ukie Village shop sell a collection of sturdy bags and cool accessories such as handkerchiefs.

Sofia

100 E Walton Street, between N Michigan Avenue and N State Street, Gold Coast (1-312 640 0878, www.sofialivelovely.com). El: Red to Clark/Division. **Open** 11am-7pm Mon-Sat; noon-5pm Sun. **Credit** AmEx, Disc, MC, V. **Map** p310 J9.
The third location for this womenswear shop, which started in 2009 as an appointment-only vintage showroom, just might be the last. Thanks to remarkable styling advice from the staff and a knockout selection of casual to cocktail-appropriate clothing (but no vintage any more), it's not only a favourite among locals. The clientele includes plenty of celebs who've famously autographed the walls of the former Sofia storefront.

General

Many of the country's familiar chains are down on Michigan Avenue, among them cheap-chic staple **H&M** (no.840, at E Chicago Avenue, 1-312 640 0060, www.hm.com), preppy **Banana Republic** (no.744, at E Chicago Avenue, 1-312 642 0020, www.bananarepublic.com) and **Gap** (no.555, at W Grand Avenue, 1-312 494 8580, www.gap.com). Cheap and cheerful **Old Navy** has a store in the Loop (35 N State Street, at W Washington Street, 1-312 578 8077, www.oldnavy.com).

The Gold Coast is home to high-concept, mid-priced chains **Anthropologie** (111 E Chicago Avenue, between N Rush Street and N Michigan Avenue, 1-312 255 1848, www.anthropologie.com), **Ugg** (909 N Rush Street, 1-312 255 1280, www.uggaustralia.com), **Original Penguin** (901 N Rush Street, at E Delaware Place, 1-312 475 0792, www.originalpenguin.com) and **Diesel** (923 N Rush Street, at E Walton Street, 1-312 255 0157, www.diesel.com). Wicker Park, meanwhile, contains branches of **Urban Outfitters** (1521 N Milwaukee Avenue, at N Damen Avenue, 1-773 772 8550, www.urbanoutfitters.com), a **Levi's Store** (1552 N Milwaukee Avenue,

CONSUME

at W North Avenue, 1-773 486 3900, www. levi.com) and the ubiquitous **American Apparel** (1563 N Milwaukee Avenue, at N Damen Avenue, 1-773 235 6778, www.americanapparel.net).

Akira
1814 W North Avenue, at N Honore Street, Wicker Park (1-773 489 0818, www.shopakira. com). El: Blue to Damen. **Open** 11am-9pm Mon-Sat; 11am-7pm Sun. **Credit** AmEx, Disc, MC, V. **Map** p315 C7.
Covetable designer togs at high prices? Welcome to 21st-century Wicker Park, where Akira draws loyal crowds. This is the women's store; there's also a men's shop (no.1910) and shoe store (no.1849) on North Avenue.

Alcala's Western Wear
1733 W Chicago Avenue, at N Ashland Avenue, West Town (1-312 226 0152, www.alcalas.com). Bus 66. **Open** 9.30am-7pm Mon, Thur-Sat; 9.30am-6pm Tue, Wed; 9.30am-5pm Sun. **Credit** AmEx, Disc, MC, V. **Map** p315 C9.
Wanna rodeo? Slip on the stetson to wallow in this shop's selections of jeans, hats and cowboy boots (some 10,000 pairs). Menswear predominates, with a smattering of shirts and jackets for cowgirls.
► *When you're all cowboyed up, head over for happy hour at the Empty Bottle on Fridays and catch excellent local honky-tonk act the Hoyle Brothers; see p138.*

Apartment No.9
1804 N Damen Avenue, at W Churchill Street, Bucktown (1-773 395 2999, www.apartment number9.com). El: Blue to Damen. **Open** 11am-7pm Tue-Fri; 11am-6pm Sat; noon-5pm Sun. **Credit** AmEx, Disc, MC, V. **Map** p315 B7.
It's virtually impossible to look bad after shopping here, so stylish and timeless are the clothes. Staff specialise in helping men who need fashion guidance. The back room generally has great discounts on pieces by the likes of Rogan and Paul Smith.

Belmont Army
1318 N Milwaukee Avenue, at N Paulina Street, Wicker Park (1-773 384 8448). El: Blue to Division. **Open** 11am-8pm Mon-Sat; noon-6pm Sun. **Credit** AmEx, Disc, MC, V. **Map** p315 C8.
You can dress like a soldier if you like, but most shoppers at this bright, tidy store prefer to choose from the selection of cool trainers and youthful streetwear by the likes of Ben Sherman and Diesel. **Other locations** 855 W Belmont Avenue, at N Clark Street, Lakeview (1-773 549 1038).

Brooklyn Industries
1426 N Milwaukee Avenue, at W Evergreen Avenue, Bucktown (1-773 360 8182, www. brooklynindustries.com). El: Blue to Damen. **Open** 11am-8pm Mon-Sat; noon-7pm Sun. **Credit** AmEx, Disc, MC, V. **Map** p315 C8.
Just like its NYC outposts, the first Brooklyn Industries to open outside the Big Apple offers messenger bags, graphic T-shirts, hoodies and more, all at reasonable prices.

Independence
2nd Floor, 47 E Oak Street, between N Michigan Avenue & N State Street, Gold Coast (1-312 675 2105, www.independence-chicago.com). El: Red to Clark/Division. **Open** 11am-7pm Mon-Sat; noon-5pm Sun. **Credit** AmEx, Disc, MC, V. **Map** p310 H9.
The name of George Vlagos's shop has many layers of meaning. Not only does it reference the independent nature of all the lines this men's store carries – from Imogene + Willie denim to tops and bottoms from Engineered Garments – it also points to the overarching theme of the shop: everything in the store is manufactured in the US. Independence doubles as Oak Street Bootmakers' flagship and the store features the entire shoe line, plus occasional one-offs.

Joe's Jeans
1715 N Damen Avenue, at W St Paul Avenue, Bucktown (1-773 252 1715, www.joesjeans.com). El: Blue to Damen. Bus 50, 56, 72. **Open** noon-7pm Mon-Thur; 11am-7pm Fri, Sat; 11am-6pm Sun. **Credit** AmEx, Disc, MC, V. **Map** p315 B7.
This hip denim label chose Chicago as the location for its first retail space. In addition to the aforementioned jeans, you'll find vintage coffee table books, jewellery and beauty treats scattered throughout the sleek interior.

Krista K Boutique
3458 N Southport Avenue, at W Cornelia Avenue, Wrigleyville (1-773 248 1967, www.kristak.com). El: Brown to Southport. **Open** 11am-7pm Mon-Fri; 10am-6pm Sat; noon-5pm Sun. **Credit** AmEx, Disc, MC, V. **Map** p313 D2.
Neighbourhood gals rely heavily on Krista K for its all-occasion sensibilities. There's a little bit of everything for sale here, from jeans and dresses to suits.

★ Penelope's
1913 W Division Street, at N Damen Avenue, Wicker Park (1-773 395 2351, www.shop penelopes.com). El: Blue to Division. **Open** 11am-7pm Mon-Sat; noon-6pm Sun. **Credit** AmEx, MC, V. **Map** p315 B8.
Recovering indie rockers swarm to this adorable store, where guys and girls get their fill of slightly mod clothes, shoes and accessories.

space519
900 N Michigan Avenue, between E Walton Street & E Delaware Place, Magnificent Mile (1-312 751 1519, www.space519.com). El: Red to Chicago. **Open** 10am-7pm Mon-Sat; noon-6pm Sun. **Credit** AmEx, Disc, MC, V. **Map** p310 J9.

CONSUME

Straight from Stock

Local company Stock Mfg. Co. is a one-stop spot for US designers.

Kickstarter has taught us a couple of things: Veronica Mars has a lot of fans, and if enough people want something it will get made. It's the latter idea that inspired Stock Mfg. Co., a local online clothing and accessories company. Consumers are curators, assisting in the selection of wearable lines of high-style, good-quality and well-priced designs. Basically, if you (and enough other people) like it, want it and click to buy it, Stock will make sure that item gets made in its Garfield Park warehouse and will ship to your home. Designers submit patterns and, if accepted, the site hosts their product for a run of about two weeks. No up-front costs are required from the designers, just the hope that pre-orders meet quota, typically a minimum of 25, and then production moves forward. The success of sales then determines whether the goods remain limited editions or become stock.

The idea of manufacturing to a more user-friendly fashion industry by selling 'straight from stock', as Stock's CEO, Jim Snediker, refers to it, grew out of the backgrounds and entrepreneurial spirit of the company's five partners. Snediker and his colleague Jason Morgan started an indie shopping site called Left of Trend; Mike Morarity and Tim Tierney ran their own menswear label, Vagrant Nobility; and Areill Ives was at the helm of his family's clothing factory in Chicago. The men pooled their resources and desire for American-made premium goods – minus the retail mark-ups. By offering a one-stop spot for designers, Stock Mfg. Co. provides the space, staff and support for the entire process, from fabrication to PR and marketing to sales. 'We want to create jobs in Chicago on many levels,' Snediker says. That goal extends to both up-and-coming names and established designers looking to try out new projects.

In spring 2013, local Columbia College graduate Shelby Steiner debuted her layered chiffon maxi-skirt. Another addition was a Montauk tie named after the Hamptons retreat, presented in a preppy linen seersucker combo by Artfully Disheveled. Stock Mfg. Co.'s pool of talent is not limited to Chicago; the company only requires its designers to be US-based. Dixon Rand, a label by Abe Voytek, who is originally from San Diego, debuted a triple-pocket day-to-night grey blazer featuring old-school tailoring details. Each article of clothing on the homepage is accompanied by a short designer bio and video montage incorporating the look into everyday settings.

Selling alongside these guest designers is Stock's own brand of ready-to-wear. As for what's next, the company plans to expand and improve its machinery, and is turning to Kickstarter to help fund those projects as well. 'The more we expand and improve,' Snediker says, 'the more diverse our offerings can get.'

CONSUME

Threadless.

CONSUME

One of the most expertly curated shops in the city, space519 carries some of the finest beauty lines (Rodin face oils), an excellent selection of coffee table books, Baldwin denim for guys, plus fantastic womenswear and accessories.

★ Threadless

3011 N Broadway, between W Wellington & W Barry Avenues, Lakeview (1-773 525 8640, www.threadless.com). El: Red, Brown or Purple to Belmont. **Open** 11am-7pm Mon-Fri; 11am-5pm Sat, Sun. **Credit** AmEx, Disc, MC, V. **Map** p313 F3.

The first floor of this two-storey shop is full of artist-designed T-shirts and hoodies, while upstairs there's a gallery space featuring artwork from Threadless.com designers.

Vive la Femme

2048 N Damen Avenue, between W Dickens & W McLean Avenues, Bucktown (1-773 772 7429, www.vivelafemme.com). El: Blue to Damen. **Open** 11am-7pm Tue-Fri; 10am-5pm Sat, Sun. **Credit** AmEx, Disc, MC, V. **Map** p315 B6.

Plus-sized women don't deserve frumpy frocks, which is why this big-girl boutique is a must-visit if you're a size 12 (UK size 14) or larger. The styles here complement curves rather than hide them; size-two twiglets often envy the designs.

Used & vintage

Beatnix

3400 N Halsted Street, between W Roscoe Street & W Newport Avenue, Wrigleyville (1-773 281 6933, www.beatnixclothing.com). El: Brown,

Purple or Red to Belmont. **Open** 10am-10pm Mon-Thur; 10am-midnight Fri, Sat. **Credit** MC, V. **Map** p313 F2.

This colourful Boystown bazaar has outfits and accessories, both new and used, to keep club kids, drag queens and muscle boys all looking their best. If you head on past the 'pimp shoes' at the back you'll find a great collection of wigs.

★ Dovetail

1452 W Chicago Avenue, between N Bishop Street & N Greenview Avenue, Ukrainian Village (1-312 308 3398, www.dovetailchicago.com). El: Blue to Chicago. **Open** noon-7pm Mon-Fri; 11am-6pm Sat; 11am-5pm Sun. **Credit** MC, V.

This shop demonstrates how to marry modern and vintage for a timeless look. There's a solid local designer representation, too, among the new stuff and reasonably regular trunk shows.

Hollywood Mirror

812 W Belmont Avenue, at N Halsted Street, Lakeview (1-773 404 2044, www.hollywood mirror.com). El: Brown, Purple or Red to Belmont. **Open** 11am-8pm Mon-Thur; 11am-9pm Fri, Sat; 11am-7pm Sun. **Credit** AmEx, Disc, MC, V. **Map** p313 F2.

This retro shop has a huge selection of weathered jeans, bowling shirts and jackets, plus old-school furniture on the lower level and a wide array of nostalgic items upstairs.

★ Knee Deep Vintage

1425 W 18th Street, at S Bishop Street, Pilsen (1-312 850 2510, www.kneedeepvintage.com). El: Pink to 18th Street. **Open** noon-8pm

Mon-Thur; 11am-9pm Fri, Sat; noon-6pm Sun. **Credit** AmEx, Disc, MC, V.

The co-owners of this fine shop, which is pretty representative of Pilsen's changing face, scour the country and local thrift shops for the best men's and womens's vintage finds and keep the mark-ups at very reasonable levels.

Kokorokoko

1323 N Milwaukee Ave at N Paulina Street, Wicker Park (1-773 252 6996, www.kokorokoko vintage.com). El: Blue to Division. **Open** noon-7pm Mon-Sat; noon-6pm Sun. **Credit** MC, V. **Map** p315 C8.

This off-the-beaten-path vintage shop stocks plenty of looks from the 1970s and beyond. All resale items are priced under $100, including a decent selection of cowboy boots.

★ LuLu's at the Belle Kay

3862 N Lincoln Avenue, between W Byron Street & W Berenice Avenue, Lakeview (1-773 404 5858, www.lulusbellekay.com). El: Brown to Addison. **Open** 11am-6pm Tue-Fri; 11am-5pm Sat; noon-5pm Sun. **Credit** AmEx, MC, V. **Map** p314 C1.

An elegant fainting couch completes the salon setting for LuLu's neatly arranged vintage handbags, furs, couture clothing and jewellery.

★ Luxury Garage Sale

1658 N Wells Street, between W Eugenie Street & W North Avenue, Old Town (1-312 291 9126,

INSIDE TRACK
LATE-NIGHT SHOPPING

Spending a late night in Pilsen? Stop by **Knee Deep Vintage** (*see p154*) for some great after-dinner deals. The shop holds 'midnight sales' the second Friday of each month, when clothing is usually discounted by 25 to 50 per cent.

www.luxurygaragesale.com). El: Brown to Sedgwick. **Open** 10am-7pm Mon-Fri; 10am-6pm Sat; 11am-5pm Sun. **Credit** AmEx, Disc, MC, V. **Map** p311 G7.

Childhood friends and co-owners Lindsay Segal and Brielle Buchberg made a name for themselves first with a high-end vintage consignment business, picking up pieces from clients' homes. Their new shop is packed with knockout designer vintage and an incredible collection of shoes, handbags and costume jewellery. But it's not all vintage: a third of the inventory is deeply discounted overstock from shops around the country.

Silver Moon

1721 W North Avenue, at N Wood Street, Wicker Park (1-773 235 5797, www.silvermoonvintage. com). El: Blue to Damen. **Open** 11am-6pm Thur-Sat. **Credit** MC, V. **Map** p315 C7.

This shop features an exquisite collection of men's and women's clothes, some of them dating back to

CONSUME

Knee Deep Vintage.

Akira State Street.

CONSUME

the 1890s. Coming more into the modern era, there's a heavy focus on Vivienne Westwood items, and everything is in immaculate condition.

FASHION ACCESSORIES & SERVICES

Cleaning & repairs

Brooks Shoe Service

Suite 610, 29 E Madison Street, between N State Street & S Wabash Avenue, the Loop (1-312 704 6805, www.brooksshoeservice.com). El: Brown, Green, Orange, Pink or Purple to Madison/ Wabash; Blue or Red to Monroe. **Open** *June-Aug* 8am-5.30pm Mon-Fri. *Sept-May* 8am-5.30pm Mon-Fri; 10am-3pm Sat. **Credit** AmEx, Disc, MC, V. **Map** p309 J12.

The third generation of the Morelli family is still here at this Loop staple, repairing footwear for socialites, retailers and everyday Joes. They're also experts at restoring vintage shoes and bags. A delivery service is also available.

Greener Cleaner

1522 N Damen Avenue, at N Milwaukee Avenue, Wicker Park (1-773 784 8429, www.greener cleaner.net). El: Blue to Damen. **Open** 7am-8pm Mon-Fri; 8am-7pm Sat; 10am-5pm Sun. **Credit** MC, V. **Map** p315 B7.

As the name suggests, this dry-cleaner is strictly eco-friendly. A delivery service is available.

Hats

Hats Plus

4706 W Irving Park Road, between N Milwaukee & N Kilpatrick Avenues, Irving Park (1-773 286 5577, www.hats-plus.com). El: Blue to Irving Park. **Open** 10am-6pm Mon-Wed, Fri, Sat; 10am-8pm Thur; 11am-5pm Sun. **Credit** AmEx, Disc, MC, V.

It's a hike from downtown, but men who take their headgear seriously will want to venture north for the city's largest choice in felt, fur, wool, straw and more. There's a small women's department.

Optimo Hats

320 S Dearborn Street, between W Jackson Boulevard and W Van Buren Street, the Loop (1-312 922 2999, www.optimohats.com). El: Brown, Orange, Pink, Purple to Library. **Open** 10am-5pm Mon-Sat. **Credit** AmEx, Disc, MC, V. **Map** p309 H13.

The Monadnock Building in the Loop and Optimo Hats make the perfect match. The clean-lined, late 19th-century building is home to a collection of yesteryear businesses: a shoe 'hospital', a barbershop and this widely renowned, high-end bespoke hat shop.

Jewellery

For salt-of-the-earth shopping, hit Jeweler's Row, a strip of jewellery stores on S Wabash Avenue between Washington and Jackson in the Loop. In particular, try the **Jeweler's Center**

(5 S Wabash Street, at E Washington Street, 1-312 424 2664, www.jewelerscenter.com), home to 150 jewellers. On a rather grander note, **Tiffany & Co** (no.730, at E Superior Street, 1-312 944 7500, www.tiffany.com) and **Cartier** (no.630, at E Ontario Street, 1-312 266 7440, www.cartier.com) both have shops on the Magnificent Mile.

★ Helen Ficalora

2014 N Halsted Street, between W Armitage & W Dickens Avenues, Lincoln Park (1-773 883 2014, www.helenficalora.com). El: Brown or Purple to Armitage. **Open** 11am-7pm Mon-Fri; 11am-5pm Sat. **Credit** AmEx, MC, V. **Map** p311 F6.

New York-based Ficalora was one of the pioneers of the alphabet-charm craze and has opened shops in SoHo, Beverly Hills and Palm Beach. The Lincoln Park outpost features letter charms, as well as chains and rings inspired by nature.

K Amato Designs

1229 W Diversey Avenue, at N Magnolia Avenue, Lakeview (1-312 882 1366, www.k-amato.com). El: Blue to Diversey. **Open** by appointment only. **Credit** AmEx, Disc, MC, V. **Map** p312 E4.

This local jewellery designer's huge workspace doubles as a 'by appointment' boutique. The line ($30-$100) includes strands of beads, delicate chokers and golden chains with adornments, as well as dangling earrings and matching bracelets.

Left Bank

1155 W Webster Avenue, between N Racine & N Clifton Avenues, Lincoln Park (1-773 929 7422, www.leftbankjewelry.com). El: Brown, Purple or Red to Fullerton. **Open** 9am-5pm Mon; noon-7pm Tue-Fri; noon-6pm Sat; noon-5pm Sun. **Credit** Disc, MC, V. **Map** p312 E5.

The owner specialises in jewellery made in France, as well as unique gift items with that Parisian *je ne sais quoi*. This romantic boutique also features dazzling, bejewelled bridal tiaras and custom veils.

Silver Room

1442 N Milwaukee Avenue, between W Evergreen Avenue & N Honore Street, Wicker Park (1-773 278 7130, www.thesilverroom.com). El: Blue to Damen. **Open** 11am-8pm Mon-Sat; 11am-6pm Sun. **Credit** AmEx, Disc, MC, V. **Map** p315 C8.

The weekend DJ says it all really: this is one style-conscious shop. Specialising in semi-precious jewellery, the Silver Room also sells hats and sunnies.

Lingerie

There are five **Victoria's Secret** (www.victoriassecret.com) stores in Chicago, including two branches on Michigan Avenue (no.830 and no.845), at North and Clybourn Avenues and in the Century Shopping Center (*see p145*).

G Boutique

2131 N Damen Avenue, between W Charleston Street & W Shakespeare Avenue, Wicker Park (1-773 235 1234, www.boutiqueg.com). El: Blue to Damen. **Open** 11am-7pm Mon-Wed, Fri, Sat; 11am-9pm Thur; noon-5pm Sun. **Credit** AmEx, MC, V. **Map** p315 B6.

One look at the bright pink façade of this underwear boutique and you know what's in store: frills, lace, and sauciness. Cosabella thongs share space with sumptuous French underthings; if you're feeling naughty, pick up a vibrating rubber duckie.

Luggage

Flight 001

1133 N State Street, at W Division Street, Gold Coast (1-312 944 1001, www.flight001.com). El: Red to Clark/Division. **Open** 11am-7pm Mon-Sat; 11am-6pm Sun. **Credit** AmEx, DC, Disc, MC, V. **Map** p310 H9.

The interior of this shop, part of a small nationwide chain, resembles an aeroplane from the days when flying was glamorous, and stocks everything from luggage and carry-on goods to in-flight gadgets.

Shoes

Nordstrom (*see p144*) and **Bloomingdale's** (*see p143*) are famous for women's shoes.

Akira State Street

122 S State Street, between E Monroe & E Adams Streets, the Loop (1-312 346 3034, www.shopakira.com). El: Red to Monroe. **Open** 11am-8pm Mon-Sat; 11am-6pm Sun. **Credit** AmEx, Disc, MC, V. **Map** p309 H11.

Ladies who work in the Loop often spend at least one lunch break a week here, scooping up deals on trendy and sexy, yet affordable shoes.

★ City Soles

2001 W North Avenue, at N Damen Avenue, Wicker Park (1-773 489 2001, www.citysoles.com). El: Blue to Damen. **Open** 10am-7pm Mon-Wed; 10am-8pm Thur-Sat; 10am-6pm Sun. **Credit** AmEx, Disc, MC, V. **Map** p315 B7.

Step into this emporium for beautifully crafted designer heels and cool loafers for guys. Many of the kicks are eco-friendly.

★ Haberdash EDC

611 N State Street, between W Ohio & W Ontario Streets, River North (1-312 646 7870, www.shophaberdash.com). El: Red to Grand. **Open** 10am-7pm Mon-Sat; noon-6pm Sun. **Credit** AmEx, Disc, MC, V. **Map** p310 H10.

While men can pick up their basics at the neighbouring Haberdash (607 N State Street), this store is in the business of footwear – brands such as Alden, Wolverine and Red Wing – and accessories, hence

Art Supplies

Fancy a brush with Chicago's gallery scene? Follow our guide to the city's best.

Carl Hammer Gallery.

Chicago is a rare city where galleries don't make you feel unwelcome – even in the event that you have no intention of dropping tens of thousands on an artwork your mother wouldn't understand. Many of the emerging artists whose work you'll see here recently graduated from prestigious masters programmes at the School of the Art Institute of Chicago (SAIC), Columbia College or University of Illinois at Chicago (UIC). The West Loop is your safest bet for a satisfying art walk, but slightly more staid River North (near the intersection of Superior and Franklin Streets) always has several worthwhile shows at any one time. Check out www.timeoutchicago.com/art for more on the local scene. *Chicago Gallery News* (www.chicagogallerynews. com), a free glossy available at many galleries, offers helpful maps of the city's various art districts.

Gallery hours often change; call ahead to check. New shows usually open with public receptions on Friday or Saturday nights, which are a blast and often attended by the artists.

RIVER NORTH

Start at 311 W Superior Street, at Orleans Street. Run by the former director of the Milwaukee Art Museum, **Russell Bowman Art Advisory** (Suite 115, 1-312 751 9500, www.bowmanart.com, by appointment Tue, Wed, 10am-5.30pm Thur-Sat) presents the cream of the mid-century to contemporary

crop. It hosted Kiki Smith's first solo show in Chicago, with life-sized bronze sculpture and nature-oriented prints. Also here is **Printworks** (Suite 105, 1-312 664 9407, www.printworkschicago.com, 11am-5pm Tue-Sat), which carries prints and other works on paper by artists at all stages of their careers.

Across the street at 300 W Superior Street, **David Weinberg Gallery** (Suite 203, 1-312 529 5090, www.davidweinberg gallery.com, 10am-5pm Mon-Sat) runs solid exhibitions of contemporary photography and painting; **Catherine Edelman Gallery** (1-312 266 2350, www.edelmangallery. com, 10am-5.30pm Tue-Sat) is a reliable source of intriguing photography; and **Judy Saslow** (1-312 943 0530, www.jsaslow gallery.com, 11am-6pm Tue-Fri, 11am-5pm Sat) specialises in self-taught or 'outsider' artists, especially popular in Chicago. For such a well-heeled address, **Zg Gallery** (1-312 654 9900, www.zggallery.com, 10am-5.30pm Tue-Sat) comes off as unusually young and cheeky.

Just down the block, at 230 W Superior, is **Stephen Daiter** (4th Floor, 1-312 787 3350, www.stephendaitergallery.com, 11am-5pm Wed-Sat), which specialises in documentary photography.

A few blocks north-east, **Roy Boyd Gallery** (739 N Wells Street, at W Chicago Avenue, 1-312 642 1606, www.royboyd gallery.com, by appointment Mon, 10am-5.30pm Tue-Sat) mainly focuses on

CONSUME

abstract painting and sculptures, both local and worldwide. The exceptional roster of 20th-century and contemporary artists at the nearby **Carl Hammer Gallery** (740 N Wells Street, at W Chicago Avenue, 1-312 266 8512, www.hammergallery.com, 11am-6pm Tue-Fri, 11am-5pm Sat) ranges from forgotten outsiders to icons such as local cartoonist Chris Ware, who lives in Oak Park.

THE WEST LOOP

Start at 835 W Washington Street, just west of Halsted Street. While the group shows at **Carrie Secrist** (1-312 491 0917, www.secristgallery.com, 10.30am-6pm Tue-Fri, 11am-5pm Sat) tend to include almost every medium, the **McCormick Gallery** (1-312 226 6800, www.thomas mccormick.com, 10am-5pm Tue-Fri, 11am-5pm Sat) focuses on Abstract Expressionist painting. The paintings, videos and installations on display at **Kavi Gupta Gallery** (1-312 432 0708, www.kavigupta.com, 10am-6pm Tue-Fri, 11am-5pm Sat) are some of the hippest the US and Europe have to offer. **Andrew Rafacz Gallery** (1-312 404 9188, www. andrewrafacz.com, 11am-6pm Tue-Fri, 11am-5pm Sat) also shows a cool mix of young artists, many from Chicago.

At 845 W Washington Street, **Western Exhibitions** (1-312 480 8390, www. westernexhibitions.com, 11am-6pm Wed-Sat) and **Tony Wight Gallery** (1-312 492 7261, www.tonywightgallery.com, open by appointment) focus on young and mid-career avant-garde artists working in painting, printmaking and video.

Just north of Washington Boulevard, there's plenty to see at 118 N Peoria Street. **Rhona Hoffman** (1-312 455 1990, www.rhoffmangallery.com, 10am-5.30pm Tue-Fri & by appointment) shows excellent work by 20th-century masters such as Sol Lewitt and Fred Sandback, plus pieces by breakout stars like Mickalene Thomas. And the **Peter Miller Gallery** (1-312 951 1700, www.petermillergallery.com, 10am-5.30pm Tue-Sat) presents a broad range of contemporary art – mostly painting – from around the country.

Across the street at 119 N Peoria, the not-for-profit **ThreeWalls** (Suite 2C, 1-312 432 3972, www.three-walls.org, 11am-5pm

Tue-Sat) alternates edgy group shows and solo residencies. Not sated yet? Walk to **Thomas Robertello** (27 N Morgan Street, at W Madison Street, www.thomasrobertello. com, noon-6pm Wed-Sat) and **Packer Schopf** (942 W Lake Street, at Morgan Street, 1-312 226 8984, www.packer gallery.com, 11am-5.30pm Tue-Sat). Both specialise in contemporary American art, as do nearby **Kasia Kay** (215 N Aberdeen Street, at Fulton Street, 1-312 944-0408, www.kasiakaygallery.com, by appointment only) and **Linda Warren Gallery** (327 N Aberdeen Street, at W Carroll Avenue, 1-312 432 9500, www.lindawarren gallery.com, 11am-5pm Tue-Sat & by appointment).

WEST TOWN & WICKER PARK

A number of not-for-profit galleries dot the neighbourhoods north of the West Loop scene. West Town's **Woman Made Gallery** (685 N Milwaukee Avenue, at Erie Street, 1-312 738 0400, www.woman made.org, noon-7pm Wed-Fri, noon-4pm Sat, Sun) is of a feminist bent. The subversive **Heaven Gallery** (1550 N Milwaukee Avenue, at W North Avenue, 1-773 342 4597, www.heavengallery. com, 1-5pm Sat & by appointment) is a Wicker Park institution.

The area's commercial galleries share their neighbours' commitment to strong work; take **Corbett vs Dempsey** (3rd floor, 1120 N Ashland Avenue, at W Haddon Avenue, 1-312 278 1664, www.corbettvsdempsey.com, 10am-5pm Tue-Sat & by appointment), which unearths neglected 20th-century artists with a Chicago connection. Fine contemporary art is always on view at **Shane Campbell** (673 N Milwaukee Avenue, at N Sangamon Street, 1-312 226 2223, www.shane campbellgallery.com, noon-6pm Wed-Sat).

The nearby neighbourhood of East Garfield Park marks the new frontier of Chicago's ever-changing art scene. **Devening Projects + Editions** (3039 W Carroll Avenue, at N Whipple Street, 1-312 420 4720, www.deveningprojects. com, noon-6pm Sat & by appointment) makes the trek to its desolate industrial block worthwhile, with thoughtful exhibitions, most frequently of prints and other works on paper.

CONSUME

the name EDC (every day carry). The shelves are filled with items such as Victorinox watches and Portland-made Tanner Supply Co belts. There's even a vintage barber's chair if you're after a shave.

Lori's Designer Shoes
824 W Armitage Avenue, at N Dayton Street, Lincoln Park (1-773 281 5655, www.lorisdesigner shoes.com). El: Brown or Purple to Armitage. **Open** 11am-7pm Mon-Thur; 11am-6pm Fri; 10am-6pm Sat; noon-5pm Sun. **Credit** AmEx, Disc, MC, V. **Map** p312 F6.

A favourite with the shoe-crazed woman, Lori's has one of the city's largest ranges of designer shoes and boots, all at between 10% and 30% less than department store prices. Great bags too.

FOOD & DRINK

Bakeries

Bang Bang Pie Shop
2051 N California Avenue, between Dickens & McLean Avenues, Logan Square (1-773 276 8888, www.bangbangpie.com). El: Blue to California. **Open** 7am-7pm Tue-Fri; 9am-5pm Sat; 9am-4pm Sun. **Credit** MC, V.

There's a particular charm to a place where you can just meet someone for a slice of pie, whether in the vintage-style interior or at a picnic table in the huge yard. Whatever you do, don't overlook the biscuits, particularly when topped with gravy.

Bittersweet
1114 W Belmont Avenue, between N Seminary & N Clifton Avenues, Lakeview (1-773 929 1100, www.bittersweetpastry. com). El: Brown, Purple or Red to Belmont. **Open** 7am-7pm Tue-Fri; 8am-7pm Sat; 8am-6pm Sun. **Credit** MC, V. **Map** p313 E2.

Pastry chef Judy Contino's café-bakery is a charming spot in which to linger over a salad, quiche or other bistro fare. The scones, cakes, croissants, tarts and cookies practically fly out of the store.

Lovely
1130 N Milwaukee Avenue, between W Haddon Avenue & W Thomas Street, Wicker Park (1-773 572 4766, www.lovelybakeshop.com). El: Blue to Division. **Open** 7am-6pm Mon-Fri; 9am-6pm Sat; 9am-4pm Sun. **Credit** MC, V. **Map** p315 D9.

From cakey, star-shaped muffins to flaky *pains au chocolat*, the pastries are just as sweet and delicious as they should be. The welcoming shop also sports a small selection of baking-inspired gifts.

★ Hoosier Mama Pie Company
1618 1/2 W Chicago Avenue, between Ashland & Marshfield Avenues, East Village (1-312 243 4846, www.hoosiermamapie.com). El: Blue to Division. **Open** 8am-7pm Tue-Fri; 9am-5pm Sat; 10am-4pm Sun. **Credit** MC, V.

Former fine-dining pastry chef Paula Haney made a name for her pies at farmers' markets and coffee shops. Now she sells seasonal creations (from strawberry and rhubarb in spring to apple and pumpkin in autumn) alongside signature pies such as sublime banana-cream, plus Metropolis coffee, at her tiny, retro shop. The pies are, in a word, extraordinary.

Molly's Cupcakes
2536 N Clark Street, between W Wrightwood Avenue & W Deming Place, Lincoln Park (1-773 883 7220, www.mollyscupcakes.com). El: Brown, Purple or Red to Fullerton. **Open** noon-10pm Mon; 8am-10pm Tue-Thur, Sun; 8am-midnight Fri, Sat. **Credit** AmEx, Disc, MC, V. **Map** p312 G4.

The owner named this sweet spot after his beloved grade-school teacher. Snag a spot on the large wooden swing near the counter and enjoy the ever-changing array of cupcakes.

Swedish Bakery
5348 N Clark Street, at W Summerdale Avenue, Andersonville (1-773 561 8919, www.swedish bakery.com). El: Red to Berwyn. **Open** 6.30am-6.30pm Mon-Fri; 6.30am-5pm Sat. **Credit** AmEx, Disc, MC, V.

You'll have to fight through a throng to get to the tantalising array of cookies, breads and pastries at this 70-year-old classic, which is why there's always free coffee on tap while you're waiting.

▶ *There's more fine Swedish fare on offer at nearby Svea (5236 N Clark Street, at W Farragut Avenue, 1-773 275 7738).*

Drinks

House of Glunz
1206 N Wells Street, at W Division Street, Gold Coast (1-312 642 3000, www.thehouseofglunz. com). El: Red to Clark/Division. **Open** 10am-8pm Mon-Fri; 10am-7pm Sat; 2-5pm Sun. **Credit** AmEx, MC, V. **Map** p311 H8.

The House of Glunz is the city's oldest wine shop. So it should come as no surprise that it harbours some of the world's oldest wines: several vintages date back as far as the early 1800s.

General

Jewel Food Stores, a basic supermarket, has numerous locations, including a 24-hour Gold Coast store (1210 N Clark Street, at W Division Street, 1-312 944 6950). Local favourite **Dominick's**, another general supermarket, also has many branches around town, including a 24-hour store in the South Loop (1340 S Canal Street, at W Roosevelt Street, 1-312 850 3915).

On a more exotic level, the city contains several branches of **Whole Foods Market**, the wildly popular (and often wildly expensive) organic supermarket chain, the most central of

CONSUME

Garrett Popcorn Shop.

which is in River North (50 W Huron Street, at N Dearborn Street, 1-312 932 9600). All are open 8am-10pm daily. Cheery (and more affordable) health food chain **Trader Joe's** also has five Chicago locations, including one in River North (44 E Ontario Street, at N Wabash Avenue, 1-312 951 6369) that opens 9am-10pm daily.

Fox & Obel
401 E Illinois Street, at N Fairbanks Court, Streeterville (1-312 410 7301, www.fox-obel. com). El: Red to Grand. **Open** *6am-10pm daily.* **Credit** *AmEx, Disc, MC, V.* **Map** *p310 J11.*
Just what Chicago really needs: a gourmet food emporium (cheeses, just-baked goods, fresh fish and so on) with an in-store café. Get a healthy snack here instead of opting for something fried at Navy Pier.

Provenance Food & Wine
2528 N California Avenue, at W Logan Boulevard, Logan Square (1-773 384 0699, www.provenancefoodandwine.com). El: Blue to California. **Open** *11am-8pm Mon; 11am-9pm Tue-Sat; 11am-7pm Sun.* **Credit** *AmEx, Disc, MC, V.*
Everything you need for a perfect picnic in the park can be found inside this friendly gourmet shop. Sample wine from boutique vintners, then pick up some wonderfully stinky cheese and Red Hen bread. **Other locations** 2312 W Leland Avenue, at N Lincoln Avenue, Lincoln Square (1-773 784 2314).

Specialist

Aji Ichiban
2117-A S China Place, Chinatown Square, Chinatown (1-312 328 9998). El: Red to Cermak-Chinatown. **Open** *10am-8pm daily.* **Credit** *MC, V.* **Map** *p308 G16.*

Feeling like a food adventure? Head here for obscure Japanese gummy candies, seaweed-hugged crackers and, inexplicably, a knitting shop in the back.

Garrett Popcorn Shop
4 E Madison Street, between N State Street & N Wabash Avenue, the Loop (1-888 476 7267, www.garrettpopcorn.com). El: Green, Orange, Pink or Purple to Madison/Wabash. **Open** *10am-8pm Mon-Thur, Sun; 10am-9pm Fri, Sat.* **Credit** *AmEx, MC, V.* **Map** *p310 J10.*
At all hours, customers craving Garrett's caramel corn form a line outside its small storefronts, lured by the sugary aroma that wafts down the block. Try the Chicago mix – caramel and cheese.
Other locations 2 W Jackson Boulevard, at N State Street, the Loop; 26 W Randolph Street, at N State Street, the Loop.

L'Appetito
30 E Huron Street, at N Wabash Avenue, River North (1-312 787 9881, www.lappetito.com). El: Red to Grand. **Open** *7.30am-6.30pm Mon-Fri; 8.30am-6.30pm Sat.* **Credit** *AmEx, MC, V.* **Map** *p310 H10.*
A great Italian grocery store with imported meats, cheeses and pastas, plus the best submarine sandwiches in the city.
Other locations John Hancock Center, 875 N Michigan Avenue, at E Chestnut Street, Magnificent Mile (1-312 337 0691).

Vosges Haut-Chocolat
Shops at North Bridge, 520 N Michigan Avenue, at E Grand Avenue, Magnificent Mile (1-312 644 9450, www.vosgeschocolate.com). El: Red to Grand. **Open** *10am-8pm Mon-Sat; 11am-7pm Sun.* **Credit** *AmEx, Disc, MC, V.* **Map** *p310 H10.*

CONSUME

Two childhood friends run this gourmet chocolatier, which specialises in truffles but also turns out chocs accented with rare spices and flowers: the Aztec hot chocolate contains cinnamon and chipotle powder, and tastes better than it sounds.

Other locations 951 W Armitage Avenue, between N Sheffield Avenue & N Bissell Street, Lincoln Park (1-773 296 9866).

GIFTS & SOUVENIRS

Chicago's museums conveniently offer some of the best souvenirs. Fun, funky objets d'art are available at the **Chicago Architecture Foundation** (*see p39*), while the **Museum of Contemporary Art** (*see p57*) features plenty of unusual items, and the **Art Institute of Chicago** (*see p36*) sells gifts and art books. The store at **Symphony Center** (*see p39*) has a range of high-culture souvenirs. Many of the gift shops located in the city's hotels offer the usual goods (postcards, T-shirts), but both **W** locations (*see p170 & p177*) add some luxe items to the mix.

★ Art Effect

934 W Armitage Avenue, at N Bissell Street (1-773 929 3600, www.shoparteffect.com). El: Brown or Purple to Armitage. **Open** 11am-7pm Mon-Thur; 11am-6pm Fri; 10am-6pm Sat; noon-5pm Sun. **Credit** AmEx, MC, V. **Map** p312 E6.

This fun, airy shop has loads of nifty gift items: tiny calculators, antique brooches, Jonathan Adler pottery and vintage-style toy robots, plus thoroughly cool, casual clothing (for women and children) and wonderful jewellery.

Paper Doll

2027 W Division Street, at N Damen Avenue, Wicker Park (1-773 227 6950, www.paperdoll chicago.com). El: Blue to Damen. **Open** 11am-7pm Tue-Fri; 11am-6pm Sat; 11am-5pm Sun. **Credit** Disc, MC, V. **Map** p315 B8.

House pug Maude welcomes you to this treasure trove of fantastic and funky items you don't really need but simply have to have. It'll be difficult to tear yourself away from the cool letterpress stationery, journals and quirky knick-knacks.

RR#1

814 N Ashland Avenue, at W Chicago Avenue, West Town (1-312 421 9079, www.rr1chicago. com). Bus 9, 66. **Open** 11am-7pm Mon-Sat; noon-5pm Sun. **Credit** AmEx, Disc, MC, V. **Map** p315 C9.

Set in a 1930s apothecary, this dimly lit but brilliantly stocked store has something for everyone. Along with a selection of hard-to-find natural bodycare lines, it also carries fun items and postcards with an international bent.

HEALTH & BEAUTY
Complementary medicine

Cortiva Institute

5th Floor, 17 N State Street, the Loop (1-312 253 3313, www.cortiva.com). El: Brown, Green, Orange, Pink or Purple to Madison/Wabash; Blue or Red to Monroe. **Open** 9am-9pm Mon-Fri; 9am-5pm Sat, Sun. **Credit** AmEx, Disc, MC, V. **Map** p309 J12.

Massage-therapy students offer low-priced massages in this spa-like environment. A small retail area in the lobby sells healing massage oils, neck supports and other homeopathic remedies.

Ruby Room

1743-1745 W Division Street, at N Wood Street, Wicker Park (1-773 235 2323, www.rubyroom. com). El: Blue to Damen. **Open** 10am-7pm Mon-Fri, Sun; 9am-7pm Sat. **Credit** AmEx, MC, V. **Map** p315 C8.

This enormous yet cosy 'healing sanctuary' has guides to help visitors select crystals, traditional Chinese medicine herbs and flower essences. The vibe is slightly New Age, but the luxurious environment and fees are far from earthy.

Hairdressers & barbers

Art + Science

1971 N Halsted Street, at W Armitage Avenue, Lincoln Park (1-312 787 4247). El: Brown or Purple to Armitage. **Open** 10am-9pm Tue-Thur; 10am-8pm Fri; 9am-6pm Sat. **Credit** Disc, MC, V. **Map** p312 F6.

Trendsetters are loathe to give up the secrets to their hip haircuts, but this place is almost always the source. The glass-fronted location is something of a see-and-be-seen place.

Other locations 1554 N Milwaukee Avenue, at N Damen Avenue, Wicker Park (1-773 227 4247).

State Street Barbers

1151 W Webster Avenue, at N Racine Street, Lincoln Park (1-773 477 7721, www.statestreet barbers.com). El: Brown or Purple to Armitage. **Open** 8am-9pm Mon-Thur; 10am-7pm Fri; 8am-5pm Sat; 9am-5pm Sun. **Credit** MC, V. **Map** p312 E5.

An inviting, old-fashioned barbershop that provides haircuts and hot lather shaves, as well as shoe shines and repairs. Make sure you ask about the first-visit discount.

Other locations 1547 N Wells Street, at W North Avenue, Old Town (1-312 787 7722).

Opticians

In the Loop, **Macy's** (*see p143*) and **Sears** (*see p145*) have optical counters.

Eye Want

1431 N Milwaukee Avenue, at W Evergreen Avenue, Wicker Park (1-773 782 1744, www. eyewanteyewear.com). El: Blue to Damen. **Open** noon-7pm Mon-Fri; noon-5pm Sat. **Credit** AmEx, Disc, MC, V. **Map** p315 B7.

The high-end styles on offer at this laid-back Wicker Park eye store are made for fashionistas. There's also an optometrist on site.

Pharmacies

You're never far from one of two chain pharmacies. **Walgreens** (www.walgreens.com) has 24-hour branches on the Magnificent Mile (757 N Michigan Avenue, at E Chicago Avenue, 1-312 664 8686) and in River North (641 N Clark Street, at W Ontario Street, 1-312 587 1416), while **CVS** (www.cvs.com) has 24-hour stores on the Gold Coast (1201 N State Street, at W Division Street, 1-312 640 2842) and in Lincoln Park (1714 N Sheffield Avenue, at N Clybourn Avenue, 1-312 640 5160).

★ Merz Apothecary

4716 N Lincoln Avenue, at W Lawrence Avenue, Lincoln Square (1-773 989 0900, www.merz apothecary.com). El: Brown to Western. **Open** 9am-6pm Mon-Sat. **Credit** AmEx, Disc, MC, V.

This classic apothecary attracts a diverse crowd to its Lincoln Square store, with a wide range of mind- and body-friendly products, including organic tooth-paste, aromatherapy kits and all-natural soaps. **Other location** 17 E Monroe Street (1-312 781 6900).

Shops

Benefit

852 W Armitage Avenue, at N Halsted Street, Lincoln Park (1-773 880 9192, www.benefit cosmetics.com). El: Brown or Purple to Armitage. **Open** 10am-7pm Mon-Fri; noon-6pm Sat, Sun. **Credit** AmEx, MC, V. **Map** p312 F6.

Drop in for a brow wax at this retro beauty spot. Its cosmetics counter majors in smart solutions for common problems such as puffy eyes and fine lines. **Other location** 1616 N Damen Avenue (1-773 342 8860).

MAC Pro

910 W Armitage Avenue, at N Fremont Street, Lincoln Park (1-773 327 4902, www.macpro. com). El: Brown or Purple to Armitage. **Open** 11am-7pm Mon-Fri; 10am-7pm Sat; noon-6pm Sun. **Credit** AmEx, Disc, MC, V. **Map** p312 F6.

In addition to core products such as foundation and lipstick, this location also carries the PRO collection. It's tailored for TV and theatrical use, meaning any-one can prepare for that high-def close-up. **Other locations** throughout the city.

Ulta

114 S State Street, between W Adams & W Monroe Streets, the Loop (1-312 279 5081, www.ulta.com). El: Red to Monroe. **Open** 10am-9pm Mon-Sat; 11am-5pm Sun. **Credit** AmEx, Disc, MC, V. **Map** p309 H12.

A large selection of high-end and drugstore cosmet-ics and fragrances fill this multi-storey cosmetic shop. The salon on the top level provides haircuts and facials.

Other locations throughout the city.

Spas

For hotel spas, *see p176 …***And, Relax**.

Asha Gold Coast

1135 N State Street, between E Elm & E Cedar Streets, Gold Coast (1-312 664 1600, www. ashasalonspa.com). El: Red to Clark/Division. **Open** 9am-9pm Mon-Fri; 8am-7pm Sat; 10am-6pm Sun. **Credit** AmEx, Disc, MC, V. **Map** p310 H9.

This spa boasts 5,000sq ft dedicated entirely to pam-pering. The exotic menu of massages ($50-$160), facials (from $65) and waxes ($15-$135) are carried out in six spa rooms decorated with bamboo. Most luxurious is the enclosed slate-tile steam shower room with heated floors, in which you can customise your rain shower with aromatherapy.

Avanti Skin Centers

409 W North Avenue, at N Sedgwick Street, Old Town (1-312 574 3138, www.avanticenters.com). El: Brown to Sedgwick. **Open** 10am-8pm Tue; 9am-8pm Wed, Thur; 9am-6pm Fri; 9am-5pm Sat; 11am-4pm Sun. **Credit** AmEx, MC, V. **Map** p311 G7.

You won't find day-spa luxuries such as gourmet nibbles and gratis wine at Avanti. But what you will find makes up for the lack of frills: thorough facials, medical-grade chemical peels and surprisingly gen-tle microdermabrasion provide all the essentials needed for beautiful skin.

★ Exhale

945 N State Street, at E Oak Street, Gold Coast (1-312 753 6500). El: Red to Chicago. **Open** 6.30am-9pm Mon, Wed, Thur; 5.30am-9pm Tue, Fri; 8am-8pm Sat, Sun. **Credit** AmEx, MC, V. **Map** p310 H9.

This Gold Coast spa is all about luxury. The spin is spa treatments and fitness education that focus on healing: acupuncture, Thai massage and drop-in core fusion classes are among the options.

John Allan's

111 W Jackson Boulevard, at S Clark Street, the Loop (1-312 663 4600, www.johnallans.com). El: Blue to Jackson; Orange, Pink, Brown or Purple to Quincy/Wells. **Open** 10am-6pm Mon-Thur; 10am-7pm Fri. **Credit** AmEx, Disc, MC, V. **Map** p309 H13.

CONSUME

Situated on the top floor of a high-rise adjoining the Chicago Board of Trade, this gentlemen's grooming club features a bar, pool table, TVs and an outdoor terrace. Of course, the real reason for hanging out here is to take advantage of the services, which include facials ($78) and pedicures ($49).

Kaya

112 N May Street, between W Randolph Street & W Washington Boulevard, West Loop (1-312 243 5292, www.kayadayspa.com). El: Green or Pink to Ashland. **Open** 9am-7pm Tue, Wed, Fri; 9am-9pm Thur; 9am-5pm Sat; 11am-5pm Sun. **Credit** AmEx, Disc, MC, V. **Map** p314 E11.

Pampering options at Kaya range from green tea facials to an 'East Meets West' body wrap designed to make skin tighter and fresher. Hydrotherapy and massage offerings are also on the menu.

Massage Envy

345 E Ohio Street, between N McClurg & N Fairbanks Courts, Streeterville (1-312 222 0808, www.massageenvy.com). El: Red to Grand. **Open** 8am-10pm daily. **Credit** AmEx, Disc, MC, V. **Map** p310 J10.

The downtown branch of this massage parlour chain specialises in rubdowns for under $100. **Other locations** throughout the city.

★ Sir Spa

5151 N Clark Street, between W Winona Street & W Foster Avenue, Andersonville (1-773 271 7000, www.sirspa.com). El: Red to Berwyn. **Open** 11am-9pm Mon- Fri; 10am-8pm Sat; noon-8pm Sun. **Credit** AmEx, MC, V.

At this lads' spa in Andersonville, foot treatments are performed from the comfort of a barber's chair and facials address specific problems of testosterone-buffeted skin.

Urban Oasis

12 W Maple Street, between N State & N Dearborn Streets, Gold Coast (1-312 587 3500, www.urbanoasismassage.com). El: Red to Clark/Division. **Open** noon-8pm Mon; 10am-8pm Tue-Thur; 9am-7pm Fri; 9am-6pm Sat; 10am-5pm Sun. **Credit** AmEx, Disc, MC, V. **Map** p310 H9.

Every massage (from $65) on the map is offered at Urban Oasis, including reflexology, deep tissue, sport, hot stone and pregnancy. The Oasis salon offers aromatherapy wraps and yoga classes.

Tattoos & piercings

Deluxe Tattoo

1459 W Irving Park Road, at N Greenview Avenue, Lakeview (1-773 549 1594, www.deluxe

Long Play

Good news for vinyl junkies: Chicago still has record stores galore.

Chicago has long been a cradle for crate-digging. Japanese collectors, Ibiza DJs and Northern Soul junkies from far and wide have long hunted through used vinyl stores searching for rare platters, and the digital era still hasn't managed to kill off all the city's mom-and-pop record stores. For new records, head to the three **Reckless Records** locations (*see p166*), **Permanent Records** (*see p166*) and **Gramaphone Records** (2843 N Clark Street, at W Diversey Parkway, Lakeview, 1-773 472 3683, www.gramaphonerecords.com), which caters to the techno set. Those in search of vintage vinyl also have a sound selection, stretching from **Record Dugout** (*see p166*) to a host of other operations.

The rarest funky stuff is at **Dusty Groove** (1120 N Ashland Avenue, at W Haddon Street, West Town, 1-773 342 5800, www.dustygroove.com), where a clean, unassuming layout belies a vast quantity of soul, jazz, reggae and Latin reissues. While some scour the globe for obscure Serge Gainsbourg and Caetano Veloso records, the smart ones just cut to the chase and

shop here. On a typical weekday, just a few souls wander in to **Mr Peabody's** (11832 S Western Avenue, at W 119th Street, Mount Hope, 1-773 881 9299, www.mrpeabody records.blogspot.com), down on the South Side. But this is perhaps the best place in the Midwest to get boogie and disco records – especially rare, original pressings and independent releases.

For rare classic rock, new wave, psych and mod LPs, try **Vintage Vinyl** (925 Davis Street, at Maple Avenue, Evanston, 1-847 328 2899, www.vvmo.com). Sheltered under the Metra station, the shop keeps only a fraction of its stock in the tidy front room. If you can't find that Stones bootleg you need, just ask: it's probably in the back. Prices are steep but the records are always mint.

Jazz hounds, meanwhile, are directed to **Jazz Record Mart** (27 E Illinois Street, at N Wabash Avenue, River North, 1-312 222 1467, www.jazzrecordmart.com). It's cluttered and dusty, with the requisite air of chaos about the place. But the range of rare jazz vinyl is unmatched in the Midwest.

tattoo.com). El: Brown to Irving Park. **Open** noon-8pm daily. **Credit** AmEx, Disc, MC, V.

Tribal tats, trompe l'oeil, 3-D layering and pin-up girls are the specialities at this in-demand shop.

Jade Dragon Tattoo

5331 W Belmont Avenue, at N Lockwood Avenue, Northwest Side (1-773 736 6960, www.jade dragontattoo.com). Bus 77. **Open** noon-2am daily. **Credit** AmEx, Disc, MC, V.

Fat Joe heads up this ink shop, which draws thousands of locals (and, reputedly, DMX and Kid Rock). The emphasis is on safety, and staff are welcoming.

HOUSE & HOME
Antiques

Andersonville, especially Clark Street between Foster and Bryn Mawr, has become the city's unofficial home decor district. Chicagoland is also home to a number of regular antiques markets, the most central of which is the **Randolph Street Market** (www.randolph streetmarket.com). Held from 10am to 5pm on the last Saturday and Sunday of the month around the junction of W Randolph Street and N Ogden Avenue, West Loop, the market draws hundreds of dealers.

Broadway Antiques Market

6130 N Broadway Street, at W Hood Avenue, Rogers Park (1-773 743 5444, www.bamchicago. com). El: Red to Granville. **Open** 11am-7pm Mon-Sat; noon-6pm Sun. **Credit** AmEx, Disc, MC, V.

This two-level antiques mall represents 75 dealers, showcasing everything from Victoriana to '70s collectibles. There's an emphasis on art deco, Arts and Crafts, and modern movements.

Salvage One

1840 W Hubbard Street, at N Wood Street, West Town (1-312 733 0098, www.salvageone. com). El: Green or Pink to Ashland. **Open** 11am-6pm Fri; 9am-5pm Sat; noon-5pm Sun. **Credit** AmEx, Disc, MC, V.

Love the thrill of the dig? Take a tour of this massive three-floor warehouse, which is filled to the rafters with beautiful and unusual furniture.

Scout

5221 N Clark Street, at Farragut Avenue, Andersonville (1-773 275 5700, www.scout chicago.com). El: Red to Berwyn. **Open** 11am-6pm Tue, Wed; noon-7pm Thur, Fri; 11am-6pm Sat; noon-5pm Sun. **Credit** AmEx, Disc, MC, V.

It's fair to say that Scout owner Larry Vodak was a pioneer of Andersonville, helping to turn the North Side 'hood into the vintage design mecca that it's now become. His shop offers an impeccable selection of vintage furniture and accessories in great condition.

Urban Remains

1850 W Grand Avenue, at S Wolcott Street, West Town (1-312 492 6254, www.urbanremains chicago.com). Bus 65. **Open** 11am-6pm Mon-Fri; noon-5pm Sat, Sun. **Credit** MC, V. **Map** p314 C11.

Housed in a former turn-of-the-century bottling company, this unconventional shop stocks architectural artefacts and antiques. You might find Victorian-era doorknobs, sconces from the Chicago Board of Trade or the owner's series of old-time photographs – a steal at just $25.

General

ID

3337 N Halsted Street, between W Roscoe Street & W Buckingham Place, Wrigleyville (1-773 755 4343, www.idchicago.com). El: Brown, Purple or Red to Belmont. **Open** 11am-7pm Tue-Thur; 11am-6pm Fri-Sun. **Credit** AmEx, Disc, MC, V. **Map** p313 F2.

This über-minimalist home accessories store features expertly selected gadgets, exquisite Swedish furniture, bath products, stylish eyewear and a small range of unusual wooden clutch bags.

★ Sprout Home

745 N Damen Avenue, at W Chicago Avenue, West Town (1-312 226 5950/www.sprouthome. com). Bus 50, 66. **Open** 9am-8pm daily. **Credit** AmEx, Disc, MC, V. **Map** p315 B10.

You'll find clever modern design pieces for the home at Sprout, including some interesting mod-print plates and stick-on decals for walls. During the warmer months, an outside garden is filled with beautiful plants and trees.

MUSIC & ENTERTAINMENT
CDs & records

K-Starke

1109 N Western Avenue, between W Haddon Avenue & W Thomas Street, Wicker Park (1-773 772 4880). El: Blue to Division. **Open** noon-8pm Mon-Sat; noon-5pm Sun. **Credit** MC, V. **Map** p315 A9.

Specialising in rare vinyl and hard-to-find 45s, this off-the-beaten-path shop draws hunter-gatherer DJs with its selections of obscure house, jazz, soul, reggae, Italo disco and punk wax. If what you're looking for is underground, it may well be available here. Enthusiastic and knowledgeable staff are on hand.

Laurie's Planet of Sound

4639 N Lincoln Avenue, between W Eastwood & W Leland Avenues, Lincoln Square (1-773 271 3569, www.lauriesplanetofsound.blogspot. com). El: Brown to Western. **Open** 11am-9pm Mon-Fri; 11am-10pm Sat; 11am-7pm Sun. **Credit** AmEx, Disc, MC, V.

CONSUME

Apart from the usual records and CDs, Laurie's sells pop culture items such as Johnny Cash action figures, Alf stuffed animals and even a little Social Distortion skeleton guy.

Permanent Records

1914 W Chicago Avenue, between N Wolcott & N Winchester Avenues, Ukrainian Village (1-773 278 1744, www.permanentrecordschicago.com). **Bus** 66. **Open** 11am-9pm daily. **Credit** AmEx, Disc, MC, V. **Map** p315 C10.

Permanent is as much a record label as it is a shop, and in fact the tiny room doesn't have a huge variety of stock. But it's a cordial cool-kids hangout, with frequent, free in-store performances. Even Zaireeka, the cat, seems to dig the sounds of the underground.

★ Reckless Records

1532 N Milwaukee Avenue, at N Damen Avenue, Wicker Park (1-773 235 3727, www.reckless. com). El: Blue to Damen. **Open** 10am-10pm Mon-Sat; 10am-8pm Sun. **Credit** AmEx, Disc, MC, V. **Map** p315 B9.

Perhaps the most well-used CD all-rounder in the city, the Wicker Park branch of Reckless has decent selections of CDs in more or less all genres.

Other locations 26 E Madison Avenue, at S Wabash Avenue, the Loop (1-312 795 0878); 3126 N Broadway Street, at W Belmont Avenue, Lakeview (1-773 404 5080).

Record Dugout

6053 W 63rd Street, between S McVicker Street & S Meade Avenue, South Side (1-773 586 1206). El: Red to 63rd. **Open** noon-7pm daily. **No credit cards.**

Vinyl geeks sift through the breathtakingly large piles of used records at this South Side hangout, hunting for hyper-rare rock, pop, soul and R&B singles. A must-visit.

SPORTS & FITNESS

Nike Chicago (669 N Michigan Avenue, between E Huron & E Erie Streets, 1-312 642 6363, www.nike.com), located on the Magnificent Mile, is something of a tourist trap but a great one. It offers just about everything from Nike's collection, including an entire section dedicated to Nike ID, and the shop is stuffed full of Chicago flair.

Lululemon Athletica

2104 N Halsted Street, at W Dickens Avenue, Lincoln Park (1-773 883 8860, www.lululemon. com). El: Brown or Purple to Armitage. **Open** 10am-7pm Mon-Sat; noon-6pm Sun. **Credit** AmEx, MC, V. **Map** p312 F6.

Super-stylish yoga gear, from mats to clothing, draws a crowd that insists on looking alluring while doing downward dog poses.

NTC Lincoln Park

833 W Armitage Avenue, at N Dayton Street, Lincoln Park (1-773 294 8121, www.gonike.me/ NTCLP). El: Brown, Purple or Red to Fullerton. **Open** 10am-7pm Mon-Sat; 10am-6pm Sun. **Credit** AmEx, MC, V. **Map** p312 F6.

This two-storey Lincoln Park shop is the first of its kind in the country, exclusively showcasing Nike's ladies' footwear, apparel and accessories on the first floor with a fitness studio on the second. The women-only classes are free (with an RSVP) and include yoga, barre and NTC (Nike Training Club) full-body training experiences.

Sports Authority

620 N LaSalle Street, at W Ontario Street, River North (1-312 337 6151, www.sportsauthority. com). El: Red to Grand. **Open** 9am-10pm Mon-Sat; 9am-9pm Sun. **Credit** AmEx, Disc, MC, V. **Map** p310 H10.

This eight-storey flagship store has entire floors given over to virtually every athletic pursuit. Watch out for the busloads of tourists who create a frenzy over the pro sports memorabilia.

Other locations 3134 N Clark Street, at W Belmont Avenue, Lakeview (1-773 871 8501).

Viking Ski Shop

3422 W Fullerton Avenue, between N Kimball Avenue & N Bernard Street, Logan Square (1-773 276 1222/www.vikingskishop.com). El: Blue to Logan Square. **Open** *May-Sept* 10am-5pm Sat; call to book an appointment or for more details. *Oct-Apr* 11am-9pm Mon, Tue, Thur, Fri; 11am-6pm Wed; 10am-5pm Sat; 11am-5pm Sun. **Credit** AmEx, Disc, MC, V.

Arguably *the* destination for skiers in the Midwest, Viking has more than 30 years' experience of fitting out the entire family with ski equipment and general cold-weather gear.

TICKETS

Discounted theatre tickets are available for same-day and advance performances at **Hot Tix**, situated inside the Chicago Tourism Center at 72 E Randolph Street. Hot Tix is also at Water Works Visitor Center, 163 E Pearson Street, at N Michigan Avenue. Half-price tickets are also sold online through www.chicagoplays. com. Check with theatres for rush tickets – discounted seats sometimes sold at box offices an hour before curtain up. Most other tickets can be purchased at www.ticketmaster.com.

TRAVELLERS' NEEDS

If you need to rent a mobile phone during your stay, try **Cellhire** (www.cellhire.com), which can deliver a phone to your hotel in advance of your stay. For more on mobile phones, *see p293.*

CONSUME

Hotels

Heritage luxury or 21st-century chic? It's your call in Chicago.

For more than a century, a handful of grand old hotels such as the Blackstone, Drake and Palmer House gave Chicago's well-heeled visitors somewhere suitably smart to drop their bags. Over the last decade, though, the hotel sector has played catch-up with the old-timers, adding new style to a once-tired scene. Familiar names and long-time favourites, such as the Hard Rock and the popular Kimpton Group hotels, have been joined in the city by bright newer operations such as the Thompson Chicago and the Langham, and hip boutique spots Hotel Lincoln and Longman & Eagle. And, happily, some of the vintage gems have been given a new lease of life with sensitive restorations.

INFORMATION & PRICES

Accommodation in this chapter has been organised by price level to give you an idea of what you can expect to pay at a given hotel, but note that rates can vary wildly according to season or room category within a single property. At peak season and during major conventions, bargains may be hard to find. Conversely, though, great deals are often available at quieter times. Note that all prices provided by hotels on their own websites will exclude the city's crippling tax of 15.4 per cent.

Before booking, always check the hotels' own websites, where many of the best deals are exclusively available. It may be worth building a little flexibility into your schedule: by arriving a day later, for instance, you could save money on the same room at the same hotel. It's also worth checking online systems such as www.hotels.com, www.priceline.com, www.lastminute.com, www.expedia.com and Chicago-based **Hot Rooms** (1-773 468 7666, www.hotrooms.com), all of which offer regular deals. However you book, always ask about cancellation policies before paying up.

We've listed a selection of services for each hotel at the bottom of the review, detailing everything from in-room entertainment options to the cost of parking. Prices for internet access and parking are for any given 24-hour period unless stated.

We've listed only those hotels within a reasonable distance of downtown. Other chain hotels can be found further out, especially around O'Hare. For a list of the main hotel chains, *see p169* **The Chain Gang**.

The Loop

Deluxe

Fairmont Chicago

200 N Columbus Drive, at E Lake Street, IL 60601 (1-866 540 4409, 1-312 565 8000, www.fairmont.com). El: Brown, Green, Orange, Pink or Purple to State/Lake; Red to Lake.
Rooms 687. **Credit** AmEx, Disc, MC, V.
Map p309 J11 ❶
A feeling of refined romance pervades in these cushy digs: oversized bathrooms, separate dressing rooms, fluffy robes and in-room spa services complete with champagne and chocolate-covered strawberries. From standards to suites, all 687 rooms offer ample space and an organic, modern feel; if you sign up for the Gold floor, you'll also gain access to a private lobby. At the end of the evening, settle down in the lobby's wine, chocolate and cheese lounge, the Eno Wine Room, for a nightcap. Extra cash allows for a hot stone massage in the spa.

❶ Red numbers in this chapter correspond to the location of each hotel as marked on the street maps. *See pp308-316.*

CONSUME

Bar. Business centre. Concierge. Disabled-adapted rooms. Gym. Internet (wireless & cable, $13.95/day). Parking ($65/day). Restaurant. Room service. Spa. TV (pay movies).

Expensive

Hard Rock Hotel

230 N Michigan Avenue, at E South Water Street, IL 60601 (1-866 966 5166, 1-312 345 1000, www.hardrock.com). El: Brown, Green, Orange, Pink or Purple to State/Lake; Red to Lake. **Rooms** 351. **Credit** AmEx, Disc, MC, V. **Map** p309 J11 ❷

The Hard Rock delivers the company's expected blend of upscale hotel chic and baby boomer-friendly rock 'n' roll graverobbing. The rooms are slick and appealing, if expensive; customers are a democratic mix of business travellers and weekending style mavens. Despite the modernity, the hotel does have strong ties to the city's past: it's housed within the Carbon & Carbide Building, an art deco landmark built in 1929 by the sons of Daniel Burnham. The building's exterior colours, so the story goes, are designed to mimic a dark green champagne bottle with gold foil.

Bar. Business centre. Concierge. Disabled-adapted rooms. Gym. Internet (wireless, $13.50/day). Parking ($60/day). Restaurant. Room service. TV (DVD, pay movies).

Hotel Allegro

171 W Randolph Street, at N LaSalle Street, IL 60601 (1-800 643 1500, 1-312 236 0123, www.allegrochicago.com). El: Blue, Brown, Green, Orange, Pink or Purple to Clark; Red to Lake. **Rooms** 483. **Credit** AmEx, Disc, MC, V. **Map** p309 H12 ❸

One of a few Kimpton hotels in the Loop (the others are the Monaco and the Burnham; see below), the Allegro offers a faintly retro chic vibe with the brand's trademark modern style. As at the other hotels in the chain, guests enjoy a daily wine hour in the lobby (5-6pm) and an in-room yoga channel. Staff are both charming and well-drilled. The hotel restaurant, 312 Chicago, offers Italian-American specialities, with the Encore Lunch Club & Liquid Lounge dealing in food and cocktails.

Bar. Business centre. Concierge. Disabled-adapted rooms. Gym. Internet (wireless, $11.99/day). Parking ($38 self, $56 valet/day). Restaurants (2). Room service. TV (DVD, pay movies).

★ Hotel Burnham

1 W Washington Street, at N State Street, IL 60602 (1-877 294 9712, 1-312 782 1111, www.burnhamhotel.com). El: Blue to Washington; Brown, Green, Orange, Pink or Purple to Randolph/Wabash; Red to Lake. **Rooms** 122. **Credit** AmEx, Disc, MC, V. **Map** p309 H12 ❹

This architectural treasure morphed several years ago from the Reliance Building into the Hotel Burnham, named in honour of the architect whose firm created it. The restoration job was beautiful (this is a National Historic Landmark, after all), but it didn't leave the building stuck in the 19th century. The Kimpton Group has brought its usual exuberance to the design of the guestrooms and suites, decking them out with rich indigo blue and gold fabrics mixed with mischievous cherubs and musical figures. Grab a pavement table for some tasty fare at Café Atwood, above-par as these things go.

Bar. Business centre. Concierge. Disabled-adapted rooms. Gym. Internet (wireless, $11.99/day). Parking ($54/day). Restaurant. Room service. TV (pay movies).

Hotel Monaco

225 N Wabash Avenue, at E Wacker Drive, IL 60601 (1-866 610 0081, 1-312 960 8500, www.monaco-chicago.com). El: Brown, Green, Orange, Pink or Purple to State/Lake; Red to Lake. **Rooms** 191. **Credit** AmEx, Disc, MC, V. **Map** p309 H11 ❺

Its facilities and location have made it popular with business travellers, but this funky Kimpton hotel rewards those who are just here to relax. Guests let go of their stress with the help of complimentary wine (5-6pm), served nightly around a limestone fireplace in the lobby. Serenity also beckons in the 191 stylishly decorated rooms, where windowsills filled with plush pillows are referred to as 'meditation stations'. Another nice gimmick: guests are offered a 'pet' goldfish for the duration of their stay. The South Water Kitchen dishes up comfort food.

Hotel Allegro.

The Chain Gang

Hotel chains with additional branches around Chicagoland.

EXPENSIVE & MODERATE
Hilton 1-800 445 8667, www.hilton.com.
Hyatt 1-800 233 1234, www.hyatt.com.
Marriott 1-888 236 2427,
www.marriott.com.
Radisson 1-888 201 1718,
www.radisson.com.
Ramada 1-800 272 6232,
www.ramada.com.
Sheraton 1-800 325 3535,
www.starwoodhotels.com.

BUDGET
Best Western 1-800 780 7234,
www.bestwestern.com.
Comfort Inn 1-877 424 6423,
www.comfortinn.com
Holiday Inn 1-800 465 4329,
www.holidayinn.com.
Motel 6 1-800 466 8356,
www.motel6.com.
Travelodge 1-800 578 7878,
www.travelodge.com.

Bar. Business centre. Concierge. Disabled-adapted rooms. Gym. Internet (wireless, $11.99/day). Parking ($56/day). Restaurant. Room service. TV (pay movies).

JW Marriott Chicago
151 W Adams Street, at S LaSalle Street, IL 60604 (1-312 660 8200, www.jwmarriott chicago.com). El: Blue, Red to Monroe. **Rooms** 610. **Credit** AmEx, Disc, MC, V. **Map** p309 H12 ❻

While there are a handful of Marriott hotels in Chicago, there's only one JW Marriott here. This luxury Loop hotel occupies the first 12 floors of the Continental & Commercial National Bank Building and has 610 guestrooms, including 29 corner suites, all of which feature dark wood and luxe standalone marble tubs. The hotel also features a VALEO wellness centre, which offers a workout area, large lap pool and spa services such as manicures, pedicures and its signature GEMassage.
Bar. Business centre. Concierge. Disabled-adapted rooms. Gym. Internet (wireless, $14.95/day). Parking ($60/day). Pool (indoor). Restaurant. Room service. Spa. TV (pay movies).

Palmer House Hilton
17 E Monroe Street, at S State Street, IL 60603 (1-800 445 8667, 1-312 726 7500, www.hilton. com). El: Blue or Red to Monroe; Brown, Green, Orange, Pink or Purple to Madison/Wabash. **Rooms** 1,641. **Credit** AmEx, Disc, MC, V. **Map** p309 J12 ❼

The Palmer House burned to the ground in the fire of 1871 just two weeks after opening. Undaunted, Potter Palmer rebuilt the place; it was back in business by 1873, and is now the longest continuously operating hotel in America. The Beaux Arts lobby remains a showpiece, with frescoes worthy of a museum, a ceiling by 19th-century muralist Louis Pierre Rigal and some tremendous people-watching potential. The smallish standard rooms can't compete but they're in good shape. *Photo p170.*

Bar. Business centre. Concierge. Disabled-adapted rooms. Gym. Internet (wireless, $14.95). Parking ($45 self, $69 valet/day). Pool (indoor). Restaurant. Room service. Spa. TV (pay movies).

Radisson Blu Aqua Hotel
221 N Columbus Drive, at E South Water Street, IL 60601 (1-312 565 5258, www.radissonblu. com). El: Brown, Green, Orange, Pink or Purple to State/Lake; Red to Lake. **Rooms** 334. **Credit** AmEx, Disc, MC, V. **Map** p309 J11 ❽

European hotel chain Radisson Blu bestowed Chicago with its first branch in Jeanne Gang's famed Aqua Tower. The lower-level lobby greets guests with a 50ft fireplace, and in-house restaurant Felini serves up classic Italian fare, plus an extensive wine selection and cocktails. Those staying at the hotel can meditate or practise yoga in a Zen garden, and even work up a sweat running on a track on the third floor. Roof deck barbecue grills on the third floor keep travellers from getting eat-out fatigue (bring your own food and cook it up at your leisure), and it's hard to deny the pleasure of the rooftop pool in the warmer months. As for the rooms, they're sleek and modern with wood-panelled floors, rich blue carpeting and simple decor.
Bar. Business centre. Concierge. Disabled-adapted rooms. Gym. Internet (wireless & cable, free). Parking ($47 self, $62 valet/day). Restaurant. Room service. Spa. TV (pay movies).

Renaissance Chicago Hotel
1 W Wacker Drive, at N State Street, IL 60601 (1-800 468 3571, 1-312 372 7200, www. renaissancehotel.com). El: Brown, Green, Orange, Pink or Purple to State/Lake; Red to Lake. **Rooms** 553. **Credit** AmEx, Disc, MC, V. **Map** p310 H11 ❾

In this 27-storey hotel, some of the 36 sprawling suites are bigger than many condos. Neutral colours and standard furnishings give guestrooms a tasteful yet generic feel; the bay windows provide impressive views of the skyline, river and Lake Michigan.

CONSUME

A funky fountain and textured wall hanging add some interest to the public areas. The location is perfect for the restaurants of River North, but those who prefer to eat in are well served by the contemporary American fare in Great Street.

Bar. Business centre. Concierge. Disabled-adapted rooms. Gym. Internet (wireless, free in public spaces; $14.95/day in rooms). Parking ($62/ day). Pool. Restaurants (2). Room service. Spa. TV (pay movies).

Swissôtel

323 E Wacker Drive, at N Columbus Drive, IL 60601 (1-800 654 7263, 1-312 565 0565, www.chicago.swissotel.com). El: Brown, Green, Orange, Pink or Purple to State/Lake; Red to Lake. **Rooms** 661. **Credit** AmEx, Disc, MC, V. **Map** p310 J11 ⑩

Though not quite as Swiss as it once was, this outpost of the global chain still offers European-style breakfasts in Geneva, its breakfast-only eaterie. Otherwise, the hotel is a high-tech operation, from the ergonomically designed furniture to the 42nd-floor fitness spa complete with jaw-dropping lake views. Even the building is modern: the hotel occupies a triangular glass high-rise.

Bar. Business centre. Concierge. Disabled-adapted rooms. Gym ($15/day). Internet (wireless & cable, $14.95/day). Parking ($65/day). Pool (indoor). Restaurants (2). Room service. TV (pay movies).

W Chicago City Center

172 W Adams Street, between S LaSalle & S Wells Streets, IL 60603 (1-877 946 8357, 1-312 332 1200, www.wchicagocitycenter.com). El: Brown, Orange, Pink or Purple to Quincy/ Wells. **Rooms** 403. **Credit** AmEx, Disc, MC, V. **Map** p309 H12 ⑪

One glance at the glamorous two-storey lobby inside this Beaux Arts building, and it's obvious that this is a see-and-be-seen kind of setting. Cocktail waitresses in short black skirts serve seasonal drinks to guests lounging on white leather banquettes beneath spinning disco balls, while a DJ provides an upbeat loungey soundtrack. Although this W lacks the heavenly Bliss day spa, guests still get a taste of spa-like pampering thanks to Bliss products in the bathrooms.

Palmer House Hilton. *See p169.*

Bar. Business centre. Concierge. Disabled-adapted rooms. Gym. Internet (wireless, $14.95/day). Parking ($60/day). Restaurant. Room service. TV (DVD, pay movies).

Wyndham Grand Chicago Riverfront

71 E Wacker Drive, between N Wabash & N Michigan Avenues, IL 60601 (1-312 346 7100, www.hotel71.com). El: Brown, Green, Orange, Pink or Purple to State/Lake; Red to Lake. **Rooms** 334. **Credit** AmEx, Disc, MC, V. **Map** p309 J11 ⑫

With more than 300 rooms, this skyscraper formerly known as Hotel 71 boasts generously sized rooms and a low-key modern look: the colours are muted and the furniture and fixtures are comfortable yet unremarkable. That said, who needs to spend much time looking around the room when you can enjoy a panorama of the city and a view of the river? Hoyt's offers breakfast, lunch and dinner, serving up classic American fare.

Business centre. Concierge. Disabled-adapted rooms. Gym. Internet (wireless, free). Parking ($60/day). Restaurant. Room service. TV (pay movies).

Moderate

Silversmith

10 S Wabash Drive, at E Madison Street, IL 60603 (1-877 227 6963, 1-312 372 7696, www.silversmithchicagohotel.com). El: Blue or Red to Monroe; Brown, Green, Orange, Pink or Purple to Madison/Wabash. **Rooms** 143. **Credit** AmEx, Disc, MC, V. **Map** p309 H12 ⑬

CONSUME

**THE BEST
HISTORIC BUILDINGS**

For starchitect clout
Langham Chicago. *See p172.*

For updated opulence
Hotel Burnham. *See p168.*

For a stately stay
Wheeler Mansion. *See p172.*

This 143-room hotel on Jewelers Row has a rather weary design aesthetic. The building's exterior is handsomely clad in dark green, highly glazed terracotta, and was built to house silversmiths (hence the name) and jewellers. Inside, though, it's all a bit grey, the olive and brown decor not enhanced by the lack of natural light in many of the rooms.
Bar. Business centre. Concierge. Disabled-adapted rooms. Gym. Internet (cable, free). Parking ($56/day). Restaurant. Room service. TV (pay movies).

★ TheWit
201 N State Street, at E Lake Street, IL 60601 (1-312 467 0200, www.thewithotel.com). El: Brown, Green, Orange, Pink or Purple to State/Lake; Red to Lake. **Rooms** 310. **Credit** AmEx, Disc, MC, V. **Map** p309 H12 ⓭

TheWit falls under the Doubletree umbrella, but don't be fooled by its corporate identity: this is one of the city's finer affordably priced hotels. The drama starts in the airy open-plan lobby; from the covetable tables directly above the front desk, you can peek at the trains running around the Loop. The rooms are attractive and modern, decorated with playful touches and high-tech amenities (HD TVs and touchscreen phones). Best of all are the views from the vast windows in all the rooms – from some corner suites and the spectacular 27th-floor Roof lounge, you can see both the lake and the river.
Bars (2). Business centre. Concierge. Disabled-adapted rooms. Gym. Internet (wireless & cable, $11.95-$19.95/day). Parking ($56/day). Restaurants (2). Room service. Spa. TV (pay movies).

★ Wyndham Blake Chicago
500 S Dearborn Street, at E Congress Parkway, IL 60605 (1-312 986 1234, www.hotelblake.com). El: Blue or Red to Jackson; Brown, Green, Orange, Pink or Purple to Library. **Rooms** 162. **Credit** AmEx, Disc, MC, V. **Map** p309 H13 ⓯

Housed in the 19th-century former headquarters of the Morton Salt Company in the heart of Printer's Row, the Blake has a historic exterior that belies the chic, contemporary digs that lie within its walls. The 162 spacious rooms have retained their crown moulding but have otherwise been brought gently up to date with casually handsome furnishings and high-tech fittings. Other attractions include a 24-hour complimentary business centre and gym.
Bar. Business centre. Concierge. Disabled-adapted rooms. Gym. Internet (wireless, free). Parking ($47/day). Restaurant. Room service. TV (pay movies).

Budget

Central Loop Hotel
111 W Adams Street, at S Clark Street, IL 60603 (1-866 744 2333, 1-312 601 3525, www.centralloophotel.com). El: Blue to Monroe. **Rooms** 429. **Credit** AmEx, Disc, MC, V. **Map** p309 H12 ⓰

Tucked away next to the Elephant & Castle pub-restaurant, this slightly unusual operation lacks the high-concept design-school charisma that defines many of its nearby competitors. However, it's a tidy little spot, and the price is most definitely right. It's basically a frill-free business hotel (the rooms are smallish, for instance, as are the TVs and the bathrooms). But everything is kept in perfect condition, all the rooms have desks, wireless is free (as is laundry) and the rates are very much on the low side for the area. Worth considering.
Bar. Business centre. Concierge. Disabled-adapted rooms. Gym. Internet (wireless & cable, free). Parking ($22 self, $41 valet/day). Restaurant. Room service. TV (pay movies).

The South Loop & Chinatown

THE SOUTH LOOP
Expensive

Hilton Chicago
720 S Michigan Avenue, at E Balbo Drive, IL 60605 (1-800 445 8667, 1-312 922 4400, www.chicagohilton.com). El: Red to Harrison. **Rooms** 1,544. **Credit** AmEx, Disc, MC, V. **Map** p309 J13 ⓱

Back in 1927, the Stevens was the largest hotel in the world. Although it's gone through countless changes since then, not least in name, it remains something of a beast. The vast public spaces are decorated with fine art, flowers and plush carpets; an executive floor in the tower has its own check-in and levels of pampering consistent with the prices. Thanks to a staff exchange programme with Ireland, its pub, Kitty O'Shea's, has at least a hint of authenticity.
Bars (2). Business centre. Concierge. Disabled-adapted rooms. Gym ($15/day). Internet (lobby, free; wireless, $12.95/day). Parking ($49 self, $64 valet/day). Pool (indoor). Restaurants (2). Room service. Spa. TV (pay movies).

★ Renaissance Blackstone
636 S Michigan Avenue, at E Balbo Avenue, IL 60605 (1-800 468 3571, 1-312 447 0955, www.blackstonerenaissance.com). El: Red to Harrison. **Rooms**: 332. **Credit** AmEx, Disc, MC, V. **Map** p309 J13 ⓲

Built more than a century ago, this hotel was long one of the grandest in Chicago. By the late 1990s, though, it had fallen into disrepair, but the Marriott group embarked on a comprehensive programme of renovations that reimagined the hotel's former glory for a 21st-century audience. The rooms are capacious and modern, but not inappropriately so, and the luxury is tastefully done throughout. The beautiful, antique-packed suite 915 is a little different

CONSUME

from the others: this is the 'smoke-filled room' of US political legend, where a group of senators met in secret to settle on the nomination of Warren Harding as president. There are plenty of nods to history elsewhere in the building (check out the artworks on the wall), but the Mercat de la Planxa restaurant is resolutely modern.

Bar. Business centre. Concierge. Disabled-adapted rooms. Internet (wireless, $12.95/day). Parking ($60/day). Restaurant. Room service. TV (pay movies).

Budget

Essex Inn
800 S Michigan Avenue, at E 8th Street, IL 60605 (1-800 621 6909, 1-312 939 2800, www.essexinn.com). El: Red to Harrison. **Rooms** 254. **Credit** AmEx, Disc, MC, V. **Map** p308 J14 ⑲
Located in the shadow of the hulking Hilton, this 1970s hotel falls squarely in the 'best bargain' category, although the bland interior and frontage aren't likely to win any design awards. The hotel shuttles guests free of charge to the Magnificent Mile, but the key attraction here is the wonderful indoor pool with a retractable glass roof, offering million-dollar views of Lake Michigan, Museum Campus and Soldier Field.
Bar. Business centre. Concierge. Disabled-adapted rooms. Gym. Internet (wireless, free). Parking ($48 valet/day). Pool (indoor). Restaurant. TV.

CHINATOWN & AROUND

Expensive

Wheeler Mansion
2020 S Calumet Avenue, at E Cullerton Street, IL 60616 (1-312 945 2020, www.wheelermansion.com). El: Red to Cermak-Chinatown. **Rooms** 11. **Credit** AmEx, Disc, MC, V. **Map** p308 J16 ⑳
One of the few mansions to survive the Chicago Fire, the Wheeler is typical of the elegant residences that once housed the city's elite. Built in 1870 for Calvin T Wheeler, the president of the Chicago Board of Trade, this opulent mansion had fallen on hard times and was slated to become a parking lot until preservationists snapped it up in 1999 and turned it into a classy B&B. A five-minute walk from McCormick Place, the 11-room inn is an intimate alternative to convention-centre lodging. Daily gourmet breakfasts are included, along with Egyptian cotton linen.
Concierge. Internet (wireless, free). Parking (free). TV.

Moderate

Hyatt Regency McCormick Place
2233 S Martin Luther King Drive, at E Cermak Road, IL 60616 (1-800 633 7313, 1-312 567 1234, www.mccormickplace.hyatt.com). El: Red to Cermak-Chinatown. **Rooms** 1,259. **Credit** AmEx, Disc, MC, V.

Trump Chicago.

The only hotel adjoining McCormick Place, this Hyatt offers 1,259 rooms to convention-going patrons. The convenience to conventioneers is obvious; while the hotel is somewhat removed from the city, prices are fair. Chinatown is a short taxi ride away, and an hourly shuttle is available for downtown access. Although the Cermak-Chinatown El train stop looks close, it's not an enjoyable walk, especially at night. There's a more central Hyatt Regency in the Loop, with a massive 2,019 rooms (151 E Wacker Drive, at N Michigan Avenue, 1-800 233 1234, 1-312 565 1234).
Bar. Business centre. Concierge. Disabled-adapted rooms. Gym. Internet (wireless, $9.95/day). Parking ($59 valet/day). Restaurant. Room service. TV (pay movies).

The Near North Side

RIVER NORTH

Deluxe

★ Langham Chicago
330 N Wabash Avenue, at E Kinzie Street, IL 60611 (1-312 923 9988, www.chicago.langham hotels.com). El: Red to Grand. **Rooms** 316. **Credit** AmEx, Disc, MC, V. **Map** p310 H11 ㉑
This new luxury hotel is the only one in the world located in a Mies van der Rohe building. If the elegant flourishes, sky-high ceilings and plush rooms don't make you feel pampered enough (though they should for the price), you'll definitely want to take a trip to the Eastern-inspired Chuan Spa. The bathing ritual alone – a 'natural water journey' offered to every guest before any spa treatment – just might change your life.

Concierge. Bar. Disabled-adapted rooms. Gym.
Internet (wireless, free). Parking ($69/day).
Pool (indoor). Restaurant. Room service. Spa.
TV (DVD, pay movies).

★ Trump Chicago

401 N Wabash Avenue, between Kinzie &
Hubbard Streets, IL 60611 (1-877 458 7867,
1-312 588 8000, www.trumpchicagohotel.com).
El: *Red to Grand.* **Rooms** 354. **Credit** AmEx,
Disc, MC, V. **Map** p310 H11 ㉒

Donald Trump originally hoped that his first
Chicago skyscraper would be the world's tallest
building. A post-9/11 change of plan capped the
design at a more manageable height, but it's still a
dominant sight along the Chicago River. The hotel
is every bit as luxurious as you'd imagine from a
Trump property, with all mod cons present and
correct in the rooms, but it's perhaps a little more
understated than you might expect. The rooms, the
bar and the 16th-floor restaurant are all fairly sober.
Still, given the amazing views, they don't need to be
too showy. There's also a lovely spa.

Bars (2). Concierge. Disabled-adapted rooms.
Gym. Internet (wireless, free). Parking ($54
self, $69 valet/day). Pool (indoor). Restaurant.
Room service. Spa. TV (DVD, pay movies).

Expensive

Dana

660 N State Street, at W Erie Street, IL 60654
(1-888 301 3262, 1-312 202 6000, www.dana
hotelandspa.com). **El**: *Red to Chicago.* **Rooms** 216.
Credit AmEx, Disc, MC, V. **Map** p310 H10 ㉓

This new-build hotel opened in 2008, offering resolutely up-to-the-minute facilities leavened with a little quasi-spiritual attitude (the hotel literature
suggests that its name translates from Sanskrit as
'the pleasure of giving'). The rooms aren't huge but
they are appealing, with crisp modern decor set off
by enormous TVs, glass-walled bathrooms (with
fantastically powerful showers) and, higher up, great
views. The hotel is topped by the Vertigo lounge,
which occasionally hosts DJs; the restaurant downstairs, Freestyle Food + Drink, serves up global
twists on American classics. Further appeal is provided by the handsome spa.

Bars (2). Gym. Internet (wireless & cable,
free). Parking ($44/day). Restaurant. Spa.
TV (pay movies).

★ Hotel Felix

111 W Huron Street, at N Clark Street,
IL 60654 (1-877 848 4040, 1-312 447 3440,
www.hotelfelixchicago.com). **El**: *Red to Chicago.*
Rooms 225. **Credit** AmEx, Disc, MC, V.
Map p310 H11 ㉔

Open since 2009, the Felix brings a green sensibility
to a building that opened in 1926 but had fallen on
hard times. The structure's exterior remains from

Dana.

the old school; inside, though, it's all change, from
the spa and low-key lobby (highlighted by a handsome water feature and a fireplace) to the crisp and
appealing guestrooms. Environmental friendliness
covers the water-saving showers, but doesn't preclude against modern convenience.

Bar. Business centre. Concierge. Disabled-adapted
rooms. Gym. Internet (wireless & cable, free).
Parking ($49/day). Restaurant. Room service.
Spa. TV (pay movies).

Hotel Palomar

505 N State Street, at W Illinois Street, IL 60654
(1-312 755 9703, www.hotelpalomar-chicago.com).
El: *Red to Grand.* **Rooms** 261. **Credit** AmEx,
Disc, MC, V. **Map** p310 H10 ㉕

Amorous couples will find one particularly memorable aspect of a night at the Kimpton hotel chain's
freshly minted Palomar: the Fuji bathtub large
enough to easily accommodate two chummy bathers
(available in every room except the Deluxe category).
If it weren't for the neutral palette (mostly tan, cream
and caramel), the deep rouge floral carpeting and
zebra- and leopard-print robes might appear out-
landish, but the place keeps decorative flourishes to
a minimum. Artwork pays tribute to the city's history, with images from the Chicago World's Fair.
Guests can stop by the lobby for complimentary
morning coffee (6-9am), and every evening starts
with an hour of free-flowing wine. *Photo p175.*

Bar. Concierge. Disabled-adapted rooms. Gym.
Internet (wireless & cable, $10/day). Parking ($58/
day). Restaurant. Room service. TV (pay movies).

Hotel Sax

333 N Dearborn Street, at W Carroll Avenue,
IL 60610 (1-877-569-3742, 1-312 245 0333,
www.hotelsaxchicago.com). **El**: *Red to Grand.*

CONSUME

Rates $229-$300 double. **Rooms** 353. **Credit** AmEx, Disc, MC, V. **Map** p310 H11 ㉖

Familiar to some previous visitors as the House of Blues, this hotel, in the shadow of the Marina City towers, has been reinvented with a new but still faintly musical name. (The House of Blues music venue, incidentally, remains open.) The rooms are done up in an appealing mix of light and dark shades, supplemented by the obligatory flatscreen TVs and other high-tech amenities. Set back from the rather awkward lobby is the Crimson Lounge, a multi-purpose bar-restaurant-club.

Bar. Business centre. Concierge. Disabled-adapted rooms. Gym. Internet (wireless, $15/day). Parking ($65/day). Restaurant. Room service. TV (pay movies).

Kinzie Hotel

20 W Kinzie Street, at N State Street, IL 60610 (1-877 262 5341, 1-312 395 9000, www.kinzie hotel.com). El: Red to Grand. **Rooms** 215. **Credit** AmEx, Disc, MC, V. **Map** p309 H11 ㉗

The 215-room Kinzie Hotel welcomes guests by sitting them down at an individual check-in desk with a personal concierge, who might suggest a complimentary cocktail in the Ravello lounge. Affectations aside, a stay here is loaded with plenty of value-added amenities, such as a nightly reception with complimentary drinks. The Kinzie Hotel also delivers on comfort, with Egyptian cotton sheets, pillow-top mattresses, plush terry robes and slippers.

Business centre. Concierge. Disabled-adapted rooms. Gym. Internet (wireless, free). Parking ($56/day). Room service. TV (DVD).

Moderate

Acme Hotel

15 E Ohio Street, between N State & N Wabash Streets, IL 60611 (1-888 775 9223, 1-312 894 0900, www.acmehotelcompany.com). El: Red to Grand. **Rooms** 130. **Credit** AmEx, Disc, MC, V. **Map** p310 H10 ㉘

Located just off of Michigan Avenue, this hip rock 'n' roll hotel, which until recently was a Comfort Inn, is full of vibrant colours and bold decor choices, from the album covers lining the lift to bright orange chairs and industrial pipe light fixtures in the rooms. The tech set will enjoy the fancy wireless audio systems and LED TVs that plug into your laptop for internet streaming.

Concierge. Disabled-adapted rooms. Gym. Internet (wireless, free). Parking ($35/day). TV (pay movies).

Hilton Garden Inn

10 E Grand Avenue, at N State Street, IL 60611 (1-800 445 8667, 1-312 595 0000, www.chicago downtownnorth.gardeninn.com). El: Red to Grand. **Rooms** 357. **Credit** AmEx, Disc, MC, V. **Map** p310 H10 ㉙

THE BEST AFFORDABLE HOTELS

For a post-spa snooze
Ruby Room. *See p183.*

For the scene
Longman & Eagle. *See p182.*

For city views
TheWit. *See p171.*

North America's largest Hilton Garden Inn offers spacious if somewhat colourless guestrooms at prices that are pretty low for the area. All the rooms have refrigerators and microwaves, and a 24-hour pantry in the lobby stocks microwaveable meals if you can't be bothered to leave the building.

Internet (wireless & cable, free). Parking ($45 self, $61 valet/day). Room service.

▶ *There's also a Hilton Suites in the shadow of the John Hancock Center on the Gold Coast (198 E Delaware Place, at N Mies van der Rohe Way, 1-800 445 8667, 1-312 664 1100).*

Budget

Ohio House

600 N LaSalle Street, at W Ontario Street, IL 60610 (1-866 601 6446, 1-312 943 6000, www.ohiohousemotel.com). El: Red to Grand. **Rooms** 50. **Credit** AmEx, Disc, MC, V. **Map** p310 H10 ㉚

This timeworn motel feels like it's straight from a 1960s movie set, offering no-frills rooms at budget rates in a desirable location. The motel does indeed date back to the '60s and is still going strong, though the attached greasy spoon diner/coffeeshop finally closed in 2013, hopefully for the better. Hip restaurateurs Matt Eisler and Kevin Heisner, of Bangers & Lace (*see p139*) acclaim, have taken over the spot with plans to keep the diner feel intact. If you're travelling with the family in tow, a large room above the office – the management calls it a 'suite' – includes a refrigerator, microwave and sofabed, and could conceivably sleep five or six.

Internet (wireless, free). Parking (free).

THE MAGNIFICENT MILE & STREETERVILLE

Deluxe

Park Hyatt Chicago

800 N Michigan Avenue, at W Chicago Avenue, IL 60611 (1-800 778 7477, 1-312 335 1234, www.parkchicago.hyatt.com). El: Red to Chicago. **Rooms** 198. **Credit** AmEx, Disc, MC, V. **Map** p310 J10 ㉛

CONSUME

Little expense has been spared at this Magnificent Mile property, housed in the lower third of a slender, 67-storey residential tower. Guests enjoy black leather Eames chairs and posh linens. NoMI's garden terrace is a happening place on summer nights; at other times, the lounge is an ideal spot to rub Rolexes with the out-crowd.

Bar. Business centre. Concierge. Disabled-adapted rooms. Gym. Internet (wireless, free). Parking ($62/day). Pool (indoor). Restaurant. Room service. Spa. TV (DVD, pay movies).

★ Peninsula Chicago
108 E Superior Street, at N Michigan Avenue, IL 60611 (1-866 288 8889/1-312 337 2888, www.chicago.peninsula). El: Red to Chicago. **Rooms** 339. **Credit** AmEx, Disc, MC, V. **Map** p310 J10 ㉜

This swanky icon is less about gaudy frills than extreme comfort: high-tech bedside control panels mean guests don't need to get up to draw the curtains or adjust the temperature. Afternoon tea in the sun-drenched lobby is a refined treat, while the G&T brigade gathers nightly around the fireplaces in the bar. Grab dim sum at Shanghai Terrace, a modern version of a 1930s Shanghai supper club.

Bar. Business centre. Concierge. Disabled-adapted rooms. Gym. Internet (wireless, free). Parking ($65/day). Pool (indoor). Restaurants (4). Room service. Spa. TV (DVD, pay movies).

Expensive

Conrad Chicago
521 N Rush Street, at E Ohio Street, IL 60611 (1-800 266 7237, 1-312 645 1500, www.conrad chicago.com). El: Red to Grand. **Rooms** 311. **Credit** AmEx, Disc, MC, V. **Map** p310 J10 ㉝

Shopaholics will appreciate the location of this Hilton-operated player, perched above the Shops at North Bridge mall. Each guestroom is decked out with a flatscreen TV, a state-of-the-art sound system and Pratesi linens; guests get to choose their pillows from an extensive menu. In warm weather, kick back on the smart outdoor sofas on the hotel's terrace, while sipping a cocktail or tucking into some tapas. Movies play in the background on Sunday nights.

Bars (2). Business centre. Concierge. Disabled-adapted rooms. Gym. Internet (wireless & cable, free). Parking ($45 self, $61 valet/day). Restaurants (3). Room service. TV (DVD, pay movies).

InterContinental Chicago
505 N Michigan Avenue, at E Grand Avenue, IL 60611 (1-800 972 2492, 1-312 944 4100, www.icchicagohotel.com). El: Red to Grand. **Rooms** 792. **Credit** AmEx, Disc, MC, V. **Map** p310 J10 ㉞

A dramatic four-storey rotunda greets guests entering this architectural showpiece, which started out in 1929 as the Medinah Athletic Club. The stock market crash put an end to its first incarnation (the opulent pool, where Johnny Weissmuller trained, has survived), before the property reopened in 1944 as a hotel. But although it hangs on to its history, the place is constantly upgrading: witness the emergence of Eno, where patrons can indulge in flights of wine, cheese and chocolate. The 792 guestrooms are suitably luxurious.

Bars (2). Business centre. Concierge. Disabled-adapted rooms. Gym. Internet (wireless, $14.95/day). Parking ($63.50/day). Pool (indoor). Restaurant. Room service. TV (pay movies).

★ James Chicago
55 E Ontario Street, at N Rush Street, IL 60611 (1-877 526 3755, 1-312 337 1000, www.james hotels.com). El: Red to Grand. **Rooms** 297. **Credit** AmEx, Disc, MC, V. **Map** p310 H10 ㉟

CONSUME

Hotel Palomar. See p173.

CONSUME

...And Relax

Hotel spas offer plenty of ways to forget your cares and worries... at a price.

There's luxury. And then there's the sort of sybaritic unlocking of your body's stress centres that you'll enjoy at Chicago's best spas, many of which are inside hotels.

It's no surprise that the sprawling **Spa at Trump Chicago** (*see p173*) raised the bar for pampering in Chicago. High-rollers will want to book a 90-minute Gem Stone treatment, during which you'll be massaged with a sapphire-, ruby- or diamond-infused organic oil. Signature-treatment guests are greeted by a personal concierge who oversees every moment of their visit. Book a 60-minute treatment and you'll get free access to the Trump's gym.

At the **James**'s **Spa by Asha** (*see p175*) guests are encouraged to come early so they can enjoy an aromatherapy foot bath in the dimly lit lounge. While you soak your peds, a therapist will wrap a heated pillow around your neck and massage your feet and calves. The pre-treatment ritual is so relaxing, it's almost a buzz-kill to have to get up for your scheduled treatment. Almost.

Spa By Asha.

The **Fairmont Chicago**'s **mySpa** (*see p167*) also has a taste for aromatherapy. The chi-chi AromaHarmony massage uses seven scented oils to balance your chakras and energise your body. When you're done being rubbed and oiled, you can count on walking out looking as good as you feel; staff in the dressing room offer quick, complimentary make-up touch-ups.

Bliss at the **W Chicago City Center** (*see p170*) is a spa in the sky with 16 treatment rooms, four movie-while-you-manicure stations with DVD players and a full slate of massage, nail and body treatments. Try the signature triple layer oxygen facial, said to clean, calm, hydrate and illuminate. Sure, prices are as lofty as the lake views, but how often can you say you've had your feet filed with a diamond dust-covered paddle?

And just for the guys, even if you're not staying at the **Waldorf Astoria** (*see p178*), the Men's Atelier at the hotel's **Elysian Spa** is worth a visit: the spa shaves are sublime.

One of the most fashionable hotels in the city continues to draw the crowds several years after its opening: to Primehouse David Burke, its all-conquering steakhouse, and the newly opened Jimmy Bar. The 297 sleek, fashionable rooms all come with large-screen TVs, stereo systems and good-sized bathrooms; the roll call of amenities is led by an impressive gym and spa. And all this just a block from Michigan Avenue.
Bars (2). Business centre. Concierge. Disabled-adapted rooms. Gym. Internet (wireless, free). Parking ($42 self, $52 valet/day). Restaurant. Room service. Spa. TV (DVD, pay movies).

Omni Chicago
676 N Michigan Avenue, at E Huron Street, IL 60611 (1-800 843 6664, 1-312 944 6664, www.omnihotels.com). El: Red to Chicago. **Rooms** 347. **Credit** AmEx, Disc, MC, V. **Map** p310 J10 ❸❻
This 347-suite property offers a variety of spacious suites, a 'get fit kit' available on request and a refreshment centre stocked with healthy snacks; all rooms come with plush robes, plasma TVs, wet bars

and, a rarity, windows that open. Sun worshippers can take advantage of two fifth-floor sundecks. The 676 restaurant and bar serves steak and seafood.
Bar. Business centre. Concierge. Disabled-adapted rooms. Gym. Internet (wireless, $9.95/day). Parking ($59/day). Pool (indoor). Restaurant. Room service. Spa. TV (DVD, pay movies).

Sheraton Chicago Hotel & Towers
301 E North Water Street, at N Columbus Drive, IL 60611 (1-877 242 2558, 1-312 464 1000, www.sheratonchicago.com). El: Red to Grand. **Rooms** 1,214. **Credit** AmEx, Disc, MC, V. **Map** p310 J11 ❸❼
This darling of the convention circuit is a behemoth, boasting more than 1,200 rooms and a massive ballroom. An equally spacious lobby with imported marble and rich wood accents has huge picture windows overlooking the river, making it a sedate spot in which to sip a cup of coffee. For something stronger, head to the stylish Fountainview Room, which has views of the Centennial Fountain that throws arcs of water across the river in summer.

Bar. Business centre. Concierge. Disabled-adapted rooms. Gym. Internet (wireless, $13.95/day). Parking ($49 self, $58 valet/day). Pool (indoor). Restaurants (3). Room service. TV (pay movies).

W Chicago Lakeshore

644 N Lake Shore Drive, at E Ohio Street, IL 60611 (1-877 946 8357, 1-312 943 9200, www.starwoodhotels.com). El: Red to Grand. **Rooms** 520. **Credit** AmEx, Disc, MC, V. **Map** p310 K10 ㊳
The city's second W hotel has come a long way from its previous incarnation as a Days Inn. At these prices, so it should have. If you've stayed at a W before, the cool vibe and sleek, casually expensive decor will be familiar. An indoor pool adjoins the outdoor sundeck, and the Bliss Spa provides pampering from head to toe. The Asian-influenced look has the young urban professional crowd swarming to both its lobby bar and lofty lounge.
Bars (2). Business centre. Concierge. Disabled-adapted rooms. Gym. Internet (wireless, $14.95/day). Parking ($60/day). Pool (indoor). Restaurant. Room service. Spa. TV (DVD, pay movies).

Moderate

★ Allerton

701 N Michigan Avenue, at E Huron Street, IL 60611 (1-877 701 8111, 1-312 440 1500, www.theallertonhotel.com). El: Red to Chicago. **Rooms** 443. **Credit** AmEx, Disc, MC, V. **Map** p310 J10 ㊴
Travellers visiting Chicago after a long absence may be in for a serious bout of déjà vu when they catch sight of this historic 443-room hotel. Built in 1924 as Michigan Avenue's first high-rise, the hotel had its brickwork restored as part of a major refurbishment. The interior was also overhauled in 2008, lending a handsome new look to decor that had grown tired over the years. The hotel's famous 'Tip Top Tap' sign still glows from its roof. It's a slight shame that the M Avenue Restaurant and Lounge are somewhat less impressive.
Bar. Business centre. Concierge. Disabled-adapted rooms. Gym. Internet (wireless, $9.95/day). Parking ($60/day). Restaurant. Room service. TV (DVD, pay movies).

Courtyard by Marriott

165 E Ontario Street, at N St Clair Street, IL 60611 (1-800 321-2211, 1-312 573 0800, www.marriott.com). El: Red to Grand. **Rooms** 306. **Credit** AmEx, DC, Disc, MC, V. **Map** p310 J10 ㊵
While other Streeterville hotels have been painstakingly renovated of late, this sleek 24-storey property was recently built from scratch to recall the art deco style of 1930s Michigan Avenue. The lobby features warm crimsons and cherry wood accented with granite and brushed chrome, as well as a chandelier of fluted blown-glass tubes.

Bar. Business centre. Concierge. Disabled-adapted rooms. Gym. Internet (cable in rooms, free). Parking ($43 self, $62 valet/day). Pool (indoor). Restaurant. Room service.

Doubletree

300 E Ohio Street, at N Fairbanks Court, IL 60611 (1-866 778 8536, 1-312 787 6100, www.doubletreemagmile.com). El: Red to Grand. **Rooms** 500. **Credit** AmEx, Disc, MC, V. **Map** p310 J10 ㊶
Guests who stayed in this hotel a few years ago when it was a Holiday Inn won't recognise the place since its makeover. Sure, the lobby still feels a tad dated, but notable details – signature cookies on arrival and the Markethouse restaurant – compensate for the lack of style.
Bar. Business centre. Disabled-adapted rooms. Gym. Internet (wireless, $9.95/day). Parking ($50/day). Pool. Restaurant. Room service. TV (pay movies).

Embassy Suites Chicago Downtown Lakefront

511 N Columbus Drive, at E Ohio Street, IL 60611 (1-888 903 8884, 1-312 836 5900, www.chicagoembassy.com). El: Red to Grand. **Rooms** 455. **Credit** AmEx, Disc, MC, V. **Map** p310 J10 ㊷
A signature atrium soaring up 17 storeys lends a wide-open feel to this all-suites hotel. Room rates include cooked-to-order breakfasts and complimentary early-evening cocktails. You can stretch your budget further by taking advantage of the suite's tiny 'kitchen' (a mini-fridge and microwave). During the week, the hotel is popular with business travellers and those who oversee their expense accounts; on weekends, economy-minded families take over. There's a sister operation on State Street (no.600, at E Ohio Street, 1-800 362 1779, 1-312 943 3800).
Bar. Business centre. Concierge. Disabled-adapted rooms. Gym. Internet (wireless & cable, $14.95/day). Parking ($39 self, $58 valet/day). Pool (indoor). Restaurant. Room service. TV (pay movies).

Inn of Chicago

162 E Ohio Street, at N St Clair Street, IL 60611 (1-800 557 2378, 1-312 787 3100, www.innofchicago.com). El: Red to Grand. **Rooms** 359. **Credit** AmEx, Disc, MC, V. **Map** p310 J10 ㊸
The dreary name belies a surprisingly handsome hotel – especially the hip and loungey lobby, replete with chocolate brown and zebra print seating, gold forest-themed wallpaper and glass bead window embellishments. The 359 rooms don't offer many frills, but they do feel fresh and clean and feature a soothing blue, green and brown colour scheme. Guests can work out in the small, stuffy fitness room; and, handily, there's free Wi-Fi on tap in the lobby.

Waldorf Astoria Chicago.

Bar. Business centre. Concierge. Disabled-adapted rooms. Gym. Internet (wireless, $5.95/day). Parking ($46 self, $52 valet/day). TV (pay movies).

Budget

Red Roof Inn
162 E Ontario Street, at N St Clair Street, IL 60611 (1-800 733 7663, 1-312 787 3580, www.redroof-chicago-downtown.com). El: Red to Grand. **Rooms** 195. **Credit** AmEx, Disc, MC, V. **Map** p310 J10 ㊹

You'll usually find this economy lodging chain along the nation's highways or tucked away in the far-flung suburbs. But here's one in the heart of the city: just a block east of fashionable Boul Mich, and perhaps the only Red Roof Inn with chandeliers in the lobby. The rooms are clean, comfortable, cheap and devoid of any individuality. Adjoining the hotel is the Coco Pazzo Café, a branch of the fine Coco Pazzo mini-chain.
Bar. Disabled-adapted rooms. Internet (wireless, free). Parking ($44/day). Restaurant. TV (pay movies).

THE GOLD COAST
Deluxe

Four Seasons
120 E Delaware Place, at N Michigan Avenue, IL 60611 (1-800 332 3442, 1-312 280 8800, www.fourseasons.com). El: Red to Chicago. **Rooms** 347. **Credit** AmEx, Disc, MC, V. **Map** p310 J9 ㊺

You can practically smell the money at this opulent hotel. The public spaces are decked out with Italian marble, glittering crystal and exquisite woodwork; rooms and suites come with classy furnishings, high-end toiletries and twice-daily maid service. Those in search of food and drink will find ample refreshment at Seasons, complete with a lounge with a fireplace,

a waterfall and views of the Magnificent Mile. The swimming pool is covered by a skylight and surrounded by Romanesque columns.
Bar. Business centre. Concierge. Disabled-adapted rooms. Gym. Internet (wireless, free). Parking ($44 self, $58 valet/day). Pool (indoor). Restaurants (3). Room service. Spa. TV (DVD, pay movies).

Ritz-Carlton Chicago
160 E Pearson Street, at N Michigan Avenue, IL 60611 (1-800 621 6906, www.fourseasons.com/chicagorc). El: Red to Chicago. **Rooms** 464. **Credit** AmEx, Disc, MC, V. **Map** p310 J9 ㊻

While the lavish lobby gains an ethereal quality thanks to a gushing fountain and massive skylight, upholstered sofas and chairs lend a slightly stuffy vibe (a facelift is on the way). Happily, the 464 richly appointed rooms, which take up the top 15 floors of Water Tower Place, look brand new after a recent renovation: leather-lined cabinetry, modern graphic wallpaper, silk chaises longues and more. Leave room in your toiletry case to snag some extra bottles of L'Occitane shower products. The Spa at the Carlton Club offers plenty of luxurious treatments.
Bar. Business centre. Concierge. Disabled-adapted rooms. Gym. Internet (wireless, free). Parking ($38 self, $65 valet/day). Pool (indoor). Restaurants (2). Room service. Spa. TV (DVD, pay movies).

Waldorf Astoria Chicago
11 E Walton Street, at N State Street, IL 60601 (1-312 646 1300, www.waldorfastoria.com). El: Red to Chicago. **Rooms** 188. **Credit** AmEx, Disc, MC, V. **Map** p310 H9 ㊼

Tucked behind a charming courtyard, the 60-storey Waldorf Astoria Chicago (formerly the Elysian) sits quietly out of sight in the heart of the Gold Coast. But upon entering the lobby, expect to be wowed – from the white marble floors to the blown-glass-and-metal chandelier hanging from the sky-high ceiling and the massive Grecian-style busts near the entrance. A simple palette of black, white, slate grey

and chocolate brown (with a few pops of pink) lends a sleek, modern air, but warm touches such as velvet sofas, silk pillows and gas fireplaces make every room feel just like home (well, in fantasyland). Take a seat at the stunning bar at Balsan, the hotel's artisanal, seasonally inspired restaurant, or Bernard's Bar for a classic cocktail. And don't miss a trip to the spa. Even if you're just there to work out in one of the weights rooms, you'll feel pampered freshening up in the locker room outfitted with a sauna, eucalyptus-scented steam room and whirlpool.
Bar. Disabled-adapted rooms. Internet (wireless, free). Parking ($55/day). Restaurant. Room service. TV.

Expensive

Drake
140 E Walton Place, at N Michigan Avenue, IL 60611 (1-800 553 7253, 1-312 787 2200, www.thedrakehotel.com). El: Red to Chicago. **Rooms** 535. **Credit** AmEx, Disc, MC, V. **Map** p310 J9 ㊽
A traditional old-money stomping ground favoured by Chicago socialites, this stately icon exudes old-school style, with velvet seats in the lifts, enormous chandeliers and a spectacular flower arrangement in the picturesque lobby. A stay in one of the guestrooms, which have been accommodating celebrities and heads of state since 1920, feels a bit like crashing a rich aunt's downtown condo. Make a point of meeting your ladies for high tea at the classic Palm Court or take a worthy date for a martini at the Coq d'Or downstairs; if you're lucky, you'll catch the slick lounge singer exercising his vocal cords.
Bars (4). Business centre. Concierge. Disabled-adapted rooms. Gym. Internet (cable, $12.95/day). Parking ($42 self, $55 valet/day). Restaurants (4). Room service. TV (pay movies).

Hotel Indigo
1244 N Dearborn Parkway, at W Goethe Street, IL 60610 (1-800 972 2494, 1-312 787 4980, www.ihg.com/hotelindigo). El: Red to Clark/ Division. **Rooms** 165. **Credit** AmEx, Disc, MC, V. **Map** p311 H8 ㊾
Original artwork from Chicago neo-Impressionist Bill Olendorf is the only remnant held over from the renovation of this 1929 hotel, formerly the Claridge. Whimsical wall murals, hardwood floors and a bold colour palette make for a refreshing change from standard hotel decor. The colourful, cheery tone is set by the inviting lobby, filled with well-stuffed chairs. The impressively equipped fitness centre and window-front bar are further bonuses.
Bar. Business centre. Concierge. Disabled-adapted rooms. Gym. Internet (wireless, free). Parking ($45/day). Restaurant. Room service. Spa. TV (DVD, pay movies).

★ MileNorth
166 E Superior Street, at N Michigan Avenue, IL 60611 (1-866 233 4642, 1-312 787 6000, www.milenorthhotel.com). El: Red to Chicago. **Rooms** 213. **Credit** AmEx, Disc, MC, V. **Map** p310 J10 ㊿
Formerly one of the Affinia hotels, the MileNorth is a tidy reinvention of a previously tired Streeterville operation called the Fitzgerald. The generous-sized rooms and suites come with a cultured look, dark carpets set off by pleasing accessories and, in the bathroom, love-it-or-hate-it shiny red wallpaper. At the top of the hotel is C-View, a pleasant bar with an appealing open-air deck; there's a restaurant just off the lobby.
Bars (2). Concierge. Disabled-adapted rooms. Gym. Internet (wireless, free). Parking ($57/ day). Restaurant. Room service. TV (DVD, pay movies).

Make Yourself At Home
Get a taste of local life – and more space – in your own pad.

If money's tight on your trip to town, or the thought of eating out for every meal sounds more like a penance than a pleasure, then renting an apartment might be your saving grace. But finance and food aren't the only reasons to consider staying in an apartment instead of a hotel. Renting a place in a new city, even if only for a long weekend, can bring you a little closer to the experience of actually living there.
Vacation Rentals by Owner (www.vrbo. com) and **Airbnb** (www.airbnb.com) are both good places to start your search. But if you'd like your accommodation pre-vetted, one Chicago-based company offers an ample supply of properties all over town. There are plenty of pictures online for every property, so you'll have a fairly good idea of where you'll be staying before you book. **At Home Inn Chicago** (1-312 640 1050, www.athomeinn.com) rents about 65 privately owned apartments; most are between the Loop and the Gold Coast, but some are as far north as Rogers Park. Rates for a studio start from $165 per night, and go all the way up to $325 a night for a four-bedroom place in Lincoln Park. The minimum stay is three nights, though busy weekends may require a four-night commitment.

CONSUME

Millennium Knickerbocker

163 E Walton Place, at N Michigan Avenue,
IL 60611 (1-866 866 8086, 1-312 751 8100,
www.knickerbockerhotel.com). El: Red to Chicago.
Rooms 306. **Credit** AmEx, Disc, MC, V.
Map p310 J9 🖸

Formerly Hugh Hefner's Playboy Towers, this regal property now caters to a more refined crowd. Guests and locals fill the ruby-coloured velvet bar stools in the two-storey lobby bar, which features a pianist five nights a week. Even if you're not invited to the party, pop into the lobby-level ballroom to check out the lit-up dancefloor beneath the dripping chandelier and gilded ceiling. Thanks to a recent refit, all the guestrooms come with a contemporary look in a warm, neutral palette with pops of pink, modern amenities and rainshower heads in the bathroom.
Bar. Business centre. Concierge. Disabled-adapted rooms. Gym. Internet (wireless in public spaces, free; wireless in rooms, $9.95/day). Parking ($63/day). Restaurant. TV (pay movies).

Public Hotel

1301 N State Parkway, at W Goethe Street
(1-312 787 3700, www.publichotels.com).
El: Red to Clark/Division. **Rooms** 285. **Credit**
AmEx, Disc, MC, V. **Map** p311 H8 🖸

Glam-connoisseur Ian Schrager gave the 1920s Ambassador building a major overhaul, starting with concrete to replace the green marble floors and glistening white walls in the lobby. But it's the ethereal lanterns hanging at varying heights throughout the historic Pump Room restaurant that will stop you in your tracks. On weekends around 8.30pm, the lights dim and the place fills to capacity – you're lucky if you can land a reservation three weeks in advance. Two lobbies – dubbed the Living Room and the Library – offer communal tables with electrical outlets and free Wi-Fi, as convenient for guests as for locals who want a spot to plonk down with a laptop and cup of coffee. Rooms are sleek and modern, with sheepskins draped over the back of desk chairs, a neutral white and beige palette, and barren walls save for black-and-white portraits of cows, a clock and flatscreen TV.
Bar. Business Centre, Concierge. Disabled-adapted rooms. Gym. Internet (free). Parking ($52/day). Room service. TV (pay movies).

Raffaello

201 E Delaware Place, at N Seneca Street, IL
60611 (1-800 983 7870, 1-312 943 5000, www.
chicagoraffaello.com). El: Red to Chicago. **Rooms**
173. **Credit** AmEx, Disc, MC, V. **Map** p310 J9 🖸

The opulent lobby has Mediterranean touches, and the rooftop Drumbar (*see p133*) features an open-air patio with fire pits, comfy booths and lush greenery during the warmer months. The hotel boasts a Michelin chef, two outdoor decks with city views, and spacious guestrooms with rainfall showers and high-end bath products.

Business centre. Disabled-adapted rooms. Gym.
Internet (cable & wireless, $9.95/day). Parking
($34 self, $59 valet/day). Restaurant. Room
service. Spa. TV (DVD).

Sofitel Chicago Water Tower

20 E Chestnut Street, at N Wabash Avenue,
IL 60611 (1-877 813 7700, 1-312 324 4000,
www.sofitel.com). El: Red to Chicago. **Rooms** 415.
Credit AmEx, Disc, MC, V. **Map** p310 H9 🖸

The radical prism-shaped design of this 32-storey building by French architect Jean-Paul Viguier is a striking addition to the Chicago skyline. The hotel opened in a plum Gold Coast location in 2002, with 415 sleekly designed rooms featuring spacious marble bathrooms. As French as the croissants baked daily on the premises, the Sofitel offers haute cuisine in a cool, modern setting at the Café des Architectes.
Bars (2). Business centre (2). Concierge. Disabled-adapted rooms. Gym. Internet (wireless & cable, free). Parking ($63/day). Restaurant. Room service. TV (pay movies).

Talbott Hotel

20 E Delaware Place, at N Rush Street, IL 60611
(1-800 825 2688, 1-312 944 4970, www.talbott
hotel.com). El: Red to Chicago. **Rooms** 149.
Credit AmEx, Disc, MC, V. **Map** p310 J9 🖸

Quite possibly the only hotel in the world with a life-sized cow mounted on its frontage (a remnant of the city's bovine-themed public art display a few years back), this boutique hotel is reminiscent of a small, upmarket European inn. The classically furnished guestrooms (with canopied beds) and the granite and marble lobby had a huge renovation in 2006. Guests get complimentary passes to a nearby health club.
Bar. Business centre. Concierge. Disabled-adapted rooms. Internet (wireless, free). Parking ($40 self, $58 valet/day). Restaurant. Room service. TV (DVD).

Thompson Chicago

21 E Bellevue Place, at N Rush Street, IL 60611
(1-312 266 2100, www.thompsonhotels.com).
El: Red to Chicago. **Rooms** 247. **Credit** AmEx,
Disc, MC, V. **Map** p310 H9 🖸

Ask any Chicagoan who fancies himself as a foodie what his favourite restaurant is in the city, and chances are high he'll stick with Avec, Publican, Blackbird or Big Star in his top five. So the fact that One Off Hospitality, the restaurant group behind these hugely popular spots, is in charge of the Thompson's Italian restaurant, NICO, is a major feather in this new hotel's cap. Designed by British designer Tara Bernerd, who created the interiors for the chain's London property, the space makes a strong statement, with bold colours and textures coupled with sleek but inviting furnishings.
Bar. Business centre. Concierge. Internet (wireless, $11.95/day). Parking ($58 valet/day). Restaurant. Room service. TV (pay movies).

Hotel Lincoln.

Westin

*909 N Michigan Avenue, at E Delaware Place,
IL 60611 (1-800 228 3000, 1-312 943 7200,
www.westin.com). El: Red to Chicago.* **Rooms** 752.
Credit AmEx, Disc, MC, V. **Map** p310 J9 ⑤⑦

Hotels are basically in the business of selling
sleep. Acknowledging this, the nationwide Westin
group equips its hotel rooms with what it calls the
Heavenly Bed, which by and large lives up to its
name. The 752 guestrooms here include 23 suites,
and if you can manage to drag yourself out of
bed, steaks and seafood are served up in the 300-seat
Grill on the Alley.

*Bar. Business Centre, Concierge. Disabled-adapted
rooms. Gym. Internet (wireless in public spaces,
free; wireless & cable in rooms, $12.95/day).
Parking ($67/day). Room service. TV.*

▶ *The other Westin in Chicago, the Westin River
North (320 N Dearborn Street, 1-800 937 8461,
1-312 744 1900), offers more of the same.*

Moderate

Whitehall Hotel

*107 E Delaware Place, at N Michigan Avenue,
IL 60611 (1-800 948 4255, 1-312 944 6300,
www.thewhitehallhotel.com). El: Red to Chicago.*
Rooms 222. **Credit** AmEx, Disc, MC, V.
Map p310 J9 ⑤⑧

The 222-room Whitehall occupies a landmark building, developed in 1928 to house luxury apartments.
The recently renovated lobby has retained its
English-Oriental look, but a stylish Italian eaterie,
Fornetto Mei, has supplanted the private dining club
that used to be here. It's a great place for people-
watching in this moneyed neighbourhood. The
handsome guestrooms feature mahogany furniture
and Chippendale desks.

*Bar. Business centre. Concierge. Disabled-adapted
rooms. Gym. Internet (wireless & cable, $9.95/day).
Parking ($57/day). Restaurant (2). Room service.
TV (pay movies).*

Old Town & Lincoln Park

Moderate

Hotel Lincoln

*1816 N Clark Street, at N Wells Street, IL 60614
(1-888 378 7994, 1-312 254 4700, www.hotel
lincolnchicago.com). Bus: 22, 36.* **Rooms** 184.
Credit AmEx, Disc, MC, V. **Map** p311 H7 ⑤⑨

The complete overhaul of this 12-storey hotel (formerly a Days Inn) has been years in the making, and
it looks as if it's been worth the wait. Boutique hotel
group Joie de Vivre's first Chicago property offers
colourful, spacious guestrooms with stunning views
of Lincoln Park and the lake, clever artwork (quirky
paintings on a lobby wall were sourced from Lincoln
Park yard sales), room service from seasonally
focused restaurant Perennial Virant, and Elaine's
coffee shop featuring La Colombe java. Best of all,
enjoy even better views of the park and skyline from
the rooftop bar. Bonus: guests can take a spin on one
of the Heritage Bicycle bikes free of charge, as long
as they're available.

*Bar. Concierge. Internet (wireless, free). Parking
($49/day). Restaurant. TV.*

Budget

Days Inn Chicago

*644 W Diversey Parkway, at N Clark Street,
IL 60614 (1-888 576 3297, 1-773 525 7010,
www.daysinnchicago.net). El: Brown or Purple
to Diversey.* **Rooms** 133. **Credit** AmEx, Disc,
MC, V. **Map** p312 F4 ⑥⓪

Belying its parent company's longstanding reputation
for midmarket blandness, the main Days Inn location
in Chicago is a handsome place, kept in fine fettle after
a renovation several years ago. The lobby offers
guests a bright entrance, and the good-looking rooms

CONSUME

CONSUME

are well kept and relatively spacious. Best of all, though, is the plum location, at the busy intersection of Broadway, Clark and Diversey on the cusp of Lincoln Park and Lakeview.
Disabled-adapted rooms. Internet (wireless, free). Parking ($26/day). TV (pay movies).

Lakeview & Around

LAKEVIEW
Budget

City Suites Chicago
933 W Belmont Avenue, at N Sheffield Avenue, IL 60657 (1-800 248 9108, 1-773 404 3400, www.chicagocitysuites.com). El: Brown, Purple or Red to Belmont. **Rooms** 45. **Credit** AmEx, Disc, MC, V. **Map** p313 E3 ⑥
This 45-room boutique hotel in a part-gentrified, part-bohemian neighbourhood is right next to the Belmont El station, from where it's a 15-minute train ride to downtown. Walk four blocks north, meanwhile, and you'll be at Wrigley Field. The hotel itself has an appealing art deco feel; its suites include sofabeds, armchairs and spacious workstations with Wi-Fi. A continental breakfast is included, but Ann Sather (909 W Belmont Avenue, between N Clark Street and N Sheffield Avenue, 1-773 348 2378, www.annsather.com) and its peerless Swedish pancakes and cinnamon rolls are temptingly close by.
Concierge. Internet (wireless, free). Parking ($22/day). TV.

Majestic
528 W Brompton Avenue, at N Lake Shore Drive, IL 60657 (1-800 727 5108, 1-773 404 3499, www.majestic-chicago.com). Bus: 145, 146, 151. **Rooms** 52. **Credit** AmEx, Disc, MC, V. **Map** p313 G1 ⑥
Set on a quiet, tree-lined residential street within walking distance of Lincoln Park Zoo, the Majestic is housed in a building dating from the 1920s, and has 29 rooms and 24 suites fitted out with microwaves and wet bars. It's not especially handy for the El, but buses along nearby Lake Shore Drive get you to the Magnificent Mile in about 15 minutes. Guests are greeted each morning with complimentary breakfast.
Concierge. Internet (wireless, free). Parking ($22/day). TV.

Willows
555 W Surf Street, at N Broadway, IL 60657 (1-800 787 3108, 1-773 528 8400, www.willowshotelchicago.com). El: Brown or Purple to Diversey. **Rooms** 55. **Credit** AmEx, Disc, MC, V. **Map** p313 G3 ⑥
This quaint, 55-room hotel near the busy intersection of Clark and Diversey has an old-fashioned French country feel. Fans of minor hotel curiosities (and, for that matter, vintage private-eye movies) will enjoy

Longman & Eagle.

riding in the original 1920s Otis elevator, creaks and all. Room rates include a continental breakfast and complimentary cookies every afternoon. Good value.
Concierge. Internet (wireless, free). Parking ($22/day). TV.

FURTHER NORTH
Budget

House 5863
5863 N Glenwood Avenue, at W Ardmore Avenue, Uptown, IL 60660 (773-682-5217, www.house5863.com). El: Red to Thorndale. **Rooms** 5. **Credit** AmEx, Disc, MC, V.
This B&B fits right in with its surrounding hip but down-to-earth North Side neighbourhood. From the dark red-brick exterior to the plasma-screen TV in the lobby and the modern design of the guestrooms, the place eschews that stale vibe some older B&Bs exude. Relax in the garden or take a walk to the lake.
Business centre. Internet (wireless, free). Parking ($30/day).

Wicker Park & Around

WICKER PARK, BUCKTOWN & LOGAN SQUARE
Moderate

★ Longman & Eagle
2657 N Kedzie Avenue, at W Schubert Avenue, IL 60647 (1-773 276 7110, www.longman

andeagle.com). El: Blue to Logan Square.

Rooms 6. **Credit** AmEx, Disc, MC, V.

Logan Square's relatively new, impeccably designed inn is perhaps the closest Chicago has come to an Ace Hotel, attached to a wildly popular restaurant. Guest perks include free drink tokens and the chance to book a coveted table at the eponymous no-reservations eatery. Enjoy works by local artists on the walls and a flatscreen TV when you need a distraction from the crowd of hipsters in the 'hood. The smaller rooms are a bit tight, but every room features site-specific pieces by local artists, exposed brick walls, custom-wood furniture (made by the in-house designers, who are also co-owners), Apple TV and even an analogue cassette tape console with accompanying mix tapes. Best of all, you have access to the great Logan neighbourhood.

Bar. Internet (wireless, free). Restaurant. Room service. TV (pay movies).

★ Ruby Room

1743-1745 W Division Street, at N Wood Street, IL 60622 (1-773 235 2323, www.rubyroom.com). El: Blue to Division. **Rooms** 8. **Credit** AmEx, MC, V, Disc. **Map** p315 C8 ㉔

The steam shower alone warrants a splurge on one of the Ruby Deluxe suites at this spa's neighbouring B&B, but the king-size beds, topped with pillow mattresses and feather beds, and minimalist yet inviting aesthetic lend a sense of luxury to each of the eight rooms. You won't find a phone or TV in this joint; a stack of books (think: a primer on healing crystals), a CD player and Wi-Fi access provide the only in-room entertainment. It's bring your own everything as far as food goes, but don't worry: the area is full of restaurants, cafés and bars, and staff can provide plenty of recommendations. Stop next door at the spa for a haircut, crystal energy healing treatment or massage.

Internet (wireless, free). Spa.

Budget

House of Two Urns B&B

1239 N Greenview Avenue, at W Division Street, IL 60622 (1-877 896 8767, 1-773 235 1408, www.twourns.com). El: Blue to Division. **Rooms** 9. **Credit** Disc, MC, V. **Map** p315 D8 ㉕

Wicker Park's reputation as an artistic enclave fits perfectly with this friendly, off-beat B&B. Named after the urn motif found in the stained-glass window and façade, this 1912 brownstone has rooms with eccentric themes such as European antique plates or the tale of the Princess and the Pea (some of the rooms have shared baths). Sweet smells still fill this former Polish bakery in the morning, when the owner whips up a full breakfast for guests. Those looking for more privacy can book one of two apartments across the street.

Business centre. Concierge. Internet (wireless, free). Parking (free). TV (DVD).

Ray's Bucktown B&B

2144 N Leavitt Street, at W Webster Avenue, IL 60622 (1-800 355 2324, 1-773 384 3245, www.raysbucktownbandb.com). El: Blue to Western. **Rooms** 11. **Credit** AmEx, Disc, MC, V. **Map** p315 B5 ㉖

A world away from traditional B&B chintz, Ray Reiss's Bucktown operation is a B&B for the 21st century with relatively modern facilities: aside from Wi-Fi throughout the building, rooms have DVR-equipped televisions, and there's even a photographic studio available to rent. In addition to a good night's sleep, your stay includes a complimentary cooked-to-order breakfast with daily specials and access to a sauna and steam room on the garden level. A two-night minimum is usually in effect, though one-night stays can sometimes be accommodated.

Internet (wireless, free). Parking (free). TV (DVD).

Wicker Park Inn

1329 N Wicker Park Avenue, at W Wolcott Avenue, IL 60622 (1-773 486 2743, www.wickerparkinn.com). El: Blue to Damen. **Rooms** 6. **Credit** AmEx, MC, V. **Map** p315 C8 ㉗

You won't find the usual frilly curtains and old-fashioned furniture at this modern B&B, located on a tree-lined street of turn-of-the-century row houses in one of the city's hipper 'hoods. The six guestrooms each have private bath, TV and free wireless internet access. Wake up to a shot of espresso and a continental breakfast buffet brought in fresh from a nearby bakery.

Internet (wireless, free). Parking (free). TV.

Children

Midwest for minis.

Whether you're travelling with junior culture vultures, pint-sized sports fans, little foodies or bored babies, Chicago is a tremendously family-friendly place. The city offers a rich blend of world-class museums and performance groups, parks and beaches, hot-dog stands and gourmet restaurants with high chairs. Along with the laid-back, friendly Midwest attitude, it's a combination that makes Chicago a perfect destination for parents and kids. For details of family-friendly events in the city, make sure you check out www.timeoutchicagokids.com.

SIGHTSEEING
Museums & attractions

Kiddie culture is a serious business in Chicago. Almost all the city's museums and cultural institutions acknowledge young visitors, and many do considerably more than that – a few museums are even aimed purely at youngsters. However, for kid-friendliness, five of the city's big attractions stand out from the pack.

In 2006, *Child* magazine named the **Art Institute of Chicago** (*see p36*) the best art museum in the US for children. Since then, things have only improved. Most of the superb kids' programming is centred around the Ryan Education Center, which expanded with the opening of the Modern Wing in 2009. The multi-purpose space, now with its own entrance, has a teacher resource area and a larger space where families can get hands-on with arts, crafts and other activities (see the website for event details).

The **Field Museum** (*see p48*) is home to Sue, the world's largest T-rex; as such, it's perpetually packed with bands of little dino-lovers. If the kids tire of Sue's charms, lead them to the Crown Family Play Lab, a sizeable permanent exhibit for kids aged up to 12. The play areas are each linked to other parts of the museum and include a woodland area, a dinosaur field station and an art studio. Little ones can make fossil rubbings, 'harvest' corn and enjoy the 'safe zones' for crawlers.

The **Spertus Institute** (*see p40*), the city's Jewish museum, occupies a spectacular space in Michigan Avenue and contains the Gray Children's Center, designed to present a universally appealing look at Judaism through displays that bring to life ancient folk tales about water, the alphabet and other subjects. Kids can climb though tunnels to get to the middle of a doughnut-shaped aquarium, make Hebrew letters in an art studio, and basically run, skip and jump their way through the space.

Like their grown-up counterparts, kids can get lost for days in the **Museum of Science & Industry** (*see p96*), where they flock to the genetics exhibit to watch as chicks break from their shells, and to the model railroads of the Great Train Story. The submarine *U505*, captured in battle during World War II, is another fave, but the famous coal mine tends to have the longest queues. Make time, too, for Colleen Moore's fairy castle.

The superb **Shedd Aquarium** (*see p48*) can keep kids happy for hours. The Wild Reef section displays a coral reef habitat, from the shoreline surf to deeper waters, with the creatures that lurk there. Kids can view

---

INSIDE TRACK GOING UP...

Kids love a tall building, but the cost of getting the whole family to the top of a skyscraper can reach stratospheric proportions. Instead of paying for the entire gang to visit the **John Hancock Observatory** (*see p56*; $28; $22 reductions; free under-3s), instead stump up for drinks or snacks at the **Signature Room** on the 95th, just one floor below.

---

anaconda and piranhas in Amazon Rising; the Oceanarium affords improved views of dolphins, sea otters, harbour seals and whales (including a baby beluga born in July 2006). The Polar Play Zone in the Oceanarium gives kids a chance to explore extremes (cold to warm, smooth to scaley) via touch pools, dressing-up areas and a play submarine.

Bronzeville Children's Museum

9301 S Stony Island Avenue, at 93rd Street, Bronzeville (1-773 721 9301, www.bronzeville childrensmuseum.com). Bus 14. **Open** *10am-2pm Tue-Sat.* **Admission** $5. **No credit cards**.
The first African-American children's museum in the country resides in a historic section of the city's South Side. In this area, African Americans who migrated to Chicago from the South created a booming business, cultural, political and residential centre known first as Black Metropolis and later as Bronzeville. Tours are conducted hourly from 10am to 2pm.

★ Chicago Children's Museum

700 E Grand Avenue, at Navy Pier, Streeterville (1-312 527 1000, www.chichildrensmuseum.org). El: Red to Grand. **Open** *June-Sept* 10am-6pm Mon-Wed, Sun; 10am-8pm Thur-Sat. *Sept-May* 10am-5pm Mon-Wed, Fri-Sun; 10am-8pm Thur. **Admission** $14; $13 reductions; free under-1s; families 5-8pm Thur & under-15s 1st Sun of mth. **Credit** AmEx, Disc, MC, V. **Map** p310 K10.
Kids will have a blast at this Navy Pier museum dedicated to under-11s, but they might also learn something via the 15 permanent exhibits and one or two touring shows usually on display in the massive, three-floor space. Aspiring archaeologists can dig for dinosaur bones in a replica excavation pit; cooped-up urban kids can get a dose of green space in the indoor Big Backyard, which combines technology and art to create a fantastical Chicago backyard that changes with the seasons.

Kohl Children's Museum

2100 Patriot Boulevard, Glenview (1-847 832 6600, www.kohlchildrensmuseum.org). Metra: North Glenview. **Open** *June-Aug* 9.30am-5pm Mon-Sat; noon-5pm Sun. *Sept-May* 9.30am-noon Mon; 9.30am-5pm Tue-Sat; noon-5pm Sun.* **Admission** $9.50; $8.50 reductions; free under-1s. **Credit** AmEx, Disc, MC, V.
Catering to kids aged eight and under, the state-of-the-art, eco-friendly Kohl has plenty of indoor exhibition space, including a pint-sized grocery store and a water play area where budding seafarers can design their own boats and control their movement with water and air jets (clothes dryers are available free of charge). Habitat Park, the museum's two acres of outdoor exhibition space, provides year-round access to the outdoors in a fenced-off site with a sculpture trail, interactive climbing structures and a sensory garden to encourage kids to connect with the environment – in other words, get good and dirty for the ride back home.

Wonder Works

6445 W North Avenue, at Elmwood Avenue, Oak Park (1-708 383 4815, www.wonder-works.org). El: Green to Oak Park/Bus 72. **Open** *10am-5pm Wed-Sat; noon-5pm Sun.* **Admission** $6; free under-1s. **Credit** AmEx, Disc, MC, V.

Chicago Children's Museum.

INSIDE TRACK ALFRESCO ART

Give kids an education in the arts while they run themselves ragged by visiting one of Chicago's many outdoor sculptures. A couple of our faves: Picasso's very climbable untitled piece in Daley Plaza, and Anish Kapoor's kidney bean-shaped *Cloud Gate* in Millennium Park (the mirrored surface is perfect for making silly faces). For both, *see p38* **Walk**.

Oak Park's Wonder Works is a small museum that feels more like a big playroom, with an emphasis on exhibits that encourage learning through creative play. There's something for kids of all ages: at Lights, Camera, Action!, young 'uns can dress up and act on stage, while North Avenue Art Works is an art studio where creative types can work with paint, crayons and other crafty tools.

Parks & gardens

Over in **Millennium Park** (*see p34*), kids get a kick out of kicking off their shoes and frolicking in the water around the two 50ft glass-brick towers that face one another at Crown Fountain. The faces of 1,000 Chicagoans flash continually across screens on the towers;

Crown Fountain at Millennium Park.

periodically, one will purse their lips and water will spout out, making it seem like the person is spitting on the crowd below.

The highlight of a visit to **Lincoln Park** (*see p65*) for many kids is a wander around the **Lincoln Park Zoo**. The Children's Zoo offers an up-close-and-personal view of more than a dozen species of North American animals in a wooded landscape and throws in a crash course on conservation, while the Farm-in-the-Zoo is a working replica of a Midwestern farm, complete with red barns housing cows, sheep and horses. There's also a carousel, children's train ride and safari ride. Best of all, admission is free.

Not far from Lincoln Park sits **Oz Park**, famous for its silver statue of the Tin Man from *The Wizard of Oz* (the story's author, L Frank Baum, lived in Chicago), along with later additions of the Cowardly Lion, the Scarecrow, Dorothy and Toto. Facilities here include basketball, volleyball and tennis courts, and everyone loves following the requisite yellow brick road.

If the rug rats still have some leftover energy you'd like them to expend, head to the 185-acre **Garfield Park** (*see p82*), about four miles west of the Loop, where you'll find a playground, baseball diamonds, soccer fields, basketball and tennis courts. The conservatory (*see p82*) is a delightful spot when it's gloomy outside. The children's garden is open 365 days a year and contains a tube slide through the trees and lots of climbable sculptures. The conservatory hosts all kinds of free, drop-in activities for little nature lovers; check the online calendar.

CONSUME

Restaurants

Children are welcome at all but the smartest spots in town. Here are a few family favourites.

★ Big Bowl

60 E Ohio Street, at N Wabash Avenue, River North (1-312 951 1888, www.bigbowl.com). El: Red to Grand. **Open** 11.30am-10pm Mon-Thur, Sun; 11.30am-11pm Fri, Sat. **Main courses** $8-$18. **Credit** AmEx, Disc, MC, V. **Map** p310 H10. Looking to expand Junior's culinary repertoire beyond chicken nuggets and fries? Try this Chinese-Thai restaurant, where the kids' menu lists steamed dumplings, satays and stir-fries, and is printed with games that go beyond the usual mazes and word-searches. The restaurant is especially festive around Chinese New Year, when young guests receive red envelopes with crisp dollar bills and 'feed' oranges to dragons that dance their way through the room. **Other location** 6 E Cedar Street, at N State Street, Gold Coast (1-312 640 8888).

Margie's Candies.

Eleven City Diner
1112 S Wabash Avenue, at 11th Street, South Loop (1-312 212 1112, www.elevencitydiner.com). El: Green to Roosevelt. **Open** 8am-9.30pm Mon-Thur; 8am-10.30pm Fri; 8.30am-10.30pm Sat; 8.30am-9pm Sun. **Main courses** $9-$13. **Credit** AmEx, Disc, MC, V. **Map** p308 H14.

Old-fashioned egg creams, penny candies, soul-soothing chicken soup and hearty sandwiches are all on the menu at the South Loop's Eleven City Diner. The Jewish-style deli has cushy booths and an easy-going retro feel. Kids especially love that you can order breakfast all day and follow it up with a banana split. Placemats printed with kids' activities were created with the help of the owner's young son, so they pass muster with the quiz-and-maze set.

★ Foodlife
Water Tower Place, 835 N Michigan Avenue, at E Pearson Street, Magnificent Mile (1-312 335 3663, www.foodlifechicago.com). El: Red to Chicago. **Open** 8am-9pm Mon-Thur; 8am-9.30pm Fri, Sat; 8am-8pm Sun. **Main courses** $7-$10. **Credit** AmEx, Disc, MC, V. **Map** p310 J9.

Your suddenly-vegan teenager and her burger-loving little brother will both find meals to please at this fun and festive food court on the mezzanine level of Water Tower Place. The kiosks offer everything from barbecue and made-to-order Mexican fare to Asian noodles and wheatgrass smoothies.
► *For more on the mall, see p145.*

★ Margie's Candies
1960 N Western Avenue, at W Armitage Avenue, Bucktown (1-773 384 1035, www.margiesfine candies.com). El: Blue to Western. **Open** 9am-midnight daily. **Main courses** $4-$8. **Credit** AmEx, Disc, MC, V. **Map** p315 A6.

The slightly surly waiters are as old as the decor at this soda fountain, here since 1921, but that's all part of the charm. The other part is the ice-cream, served in an array of tempting sundae, milkshake and malted combinations. Little ones love the saucer of hot fudge served next to their dish of ice-cream, along with a couple of wafer cookies. Margie's also makes its own boxed chocolates and candies, so you can keep the kids' sugar highs going after you leave. **Other location** 1813 W Montrose Avenue, at Ravenswood Avenue (1-773 348 0400).

Shops

For children's shops, *see p148.*

ARTS & ENTERTAINMENT

In addition to the venues listed below, the touristy but fun **Navy Pier** (*see p58; photos p190*) offers plenty for the young 'uns, including an IMAX cinema, the Chicago Children's Museum, a Ferris wheel and a massive maze. Seasonal entertainment includes the **Winter WonderFest** (*see p29*).

Dave & Buster's
1030 N Clark Street, at W Oak Street, Gold Coast (1-312 943 5151, www.daveandbusters.com). El: Red to Clark/Division. **Open** 4-11pm Mon, Tue; 11.30am-11pm Wed, Thur, Sun; 11.30am-2am Fri, Sat. **Admission** $5 after 10pm Fri, Sat. **Credit** AmEx, Disc, MC, V. **Map** p310 H9.

INSIDE TRACK PEDAL PUPPETS

Puppet Bike, a mobile playhouse built on the back of a cargo tricycle, tours around Chicago neighbourhoods performing short street shows. The puppeteers and their characters have developed something of a cult following around the city; visit www.puppetbike.com to see where they're playing while you're in town.

Navy Pier. *See p189.*

Although the focus is on arcade games, Dave & Buster's offers everything from shuffleboard to high-tech virtual reality kits. Frazzled adults can take the edge off things with a cocktail. School groups, birthday parties and the like frequent the space during the day, but at night and during big sporting events, it turns into more of a grown-up party space.

Different Strummer

4544 N Lincoln Avenue, at W Wilson Avenue, Lincoln Square (1-773 751 3398, www.old townschool.org). El: Brown to Western. **Open** 10.30am-8.30pm Mon-Thur; 10.30am-5pm Fri-Sun. **Credit** AmEx, Disc, MC, V.

The Different Strummer store, part of the Old Town School of Folk Music, offers plenty for the budding musician: CDs, videos and toy instruments, as well as real ones made especially for younger players. Check out the school's concert schedule for kids' performances by lauded local artists.

WhirlyBall

1880 W Fullerton Avenue, at N Wolcott Avenue, Wicker Park (1-773 486 7777, www.whirlyball. com). Bus 50, 74. **Open** 11am-midnight Mon-Thur, Sun; 11am-2am Fri; 11am-3am Sat. **Admission** *Walk-ins (per person, min 4 players)* $15/30mins. *Pre-bookings (up to 10 players)* $200 for the 1st hour, then $180 per hour Mon-Thur; $220 for the 1st hour, then $200 per hour Fri-Sun. **Credit** AmEx, Disc, MC, V. **Map** p315 C5.

Two teams spin around a 4,000sq ft court, attempting to scoop up a ball and whip it at a backboard. Think polo in bumper cars that go at an average of 3-5mph. Kids must be aged 12 or over and at least 54in tall. After 5pm, it's strictly 21 and over for folks without reservations.

Theatre

There's no shortage of musicals and plays for kids in Chicago, thanks to a host of professional children's theatre companies (and a few grown-up ones that also put on stellar shows for younger audiences). **Chicago Shakespeare Theater** (www.chicagoshakes.com) offers the Bard to babes with its Family Series; productions have included *MacHomer*, with Homer Simpson as the tragic King Macbeth.

★ Chicago Children's Theatre

Ruth Page Center for the Arts, 1016 N Dearborn Street, between W Oak & W Maple Streets, Gold Coast (1-773 227 0180, www.chicagochildrens theatre.org). **Tickets** $7.50-$35. **Credit** AmEx, Disc, MC, V. **Map** p310 H9.

This multi-million-dollar venture launched in 2006 with the aim of bringing high-end children's productions to young theatregoers. The company doesn't yet have a home of its own, and instead stages shows

A New Way to Play

Emerald City Theatre takes a fresh approach to creating kids' shows.

It's no secret that plenty of parents, and even some kids, get a sinking feeling at the thought of having to sit through a children's theatre production. Karen Cardarelli, executive director of **Emerald City Theatre** (*see below*) knows this first-hand, as she's always struggling to find fresh works that meet the theatre's high standards for both entertainment and educational value. 'The quality of scripts available for young theatregoers,' she admits, 'is nowhere near the calibre of what's out there for adults.'

When several works by the Lincoln Park children's company were commissioned by eight other theatre groups in the US and Canada, Cardarelli realised Emerald City wasn't alone in looking for better scripts. However, she also felt that the company was in a position to help change things. 'We want to address both the community and industry needs, and feel we can do that in a city with so much amazing writing talent.'

The newest addition to the Emerald City Theatre skews to an even younger set: in late 2013, the company produced its first ever show for under-fives. About 45 minutes in length, with gentle sound and lighting effects, the production builds on audience participation and repetition. 'It's a natural extension of our current work,' says Cardarelli. 'Often I watch younger siblings, babies and toddlers, tagging along to the theatre, loving what they see, but constrained by the experience of a traditional show and facilities meant for adults. Those children will now have their own place to experience theatre in a way that's perfect for them.'

at the Ruth Page Center for the Arts. Productions have ranged from a musical version of the book *Go, Dog. Go!* in a big top tent in Grant Park, to *The Selfish Giant* with the help of huge papier-mâché puppets.

Emerald City Theatre
Various venues (1-773 935 6100, www.emerald citytheatre.com). **Tickets** $15; $12 reductions. **Credit** AmEx, Disc, MC, V.
Performances from this top-notch kids' theatre company take place at the Apollo Theater in Lincoln Park, the Broadway Playhouse in Downtown Chicago and Emerald City's Little Theatre in Lakeview. Expect productions of everything from children's favourites such as *James and the Giant Peach* to modern, multicultural takes on classics such as *Cinderella* and *The Nutcracker*. The audience gets to ask questions and interact with the cast after each performance.

Lookingglass Theatre
Water Tower Water Works, 821 N Michigan Avenue, at E Pearson Street, Magnificent Mile (1-312 337 0665, www.lookingglasstheatre.org). El: Red to Chicago. **Tickets** $30-$60. **Credit** AmEx, Disc, MC, V. **Map** p310 J9.

Young and old watch in awe as this company performs daring acrobatic interpretations of everything from Greek myths such as *Hephaestus* to funky airy tales (*Lookingglass Alice*) in a space carved from the pipes within the Water Tower Water Works building. During selected Sunday matinée performances, parents can drop off kids aged five to 14 for classes while they take in the show.

DIRECTORY
Babysitting & childcare

Your hotel may be able to arrange childcare; ask the front desk staff or concierge.

North Shore Nannies
1-847 864 2424, www.northshorenannies.com.
This suburban service is regarded as one of the best for temporary and permanent childcare throughout Chicagoland. North Shore Nannies rates range from $14 to $20 per hour (bear in mind there's a four-hour minimum) plus parking, plus $5 per night for each additional child. You also need to factor in a $30 agency fee. It's advisable to book ahead, especially for weekends.

Film

Celluloid city.

Chicago has a long and celebrated movie history, both on and off screen. It was the centre of film production during the silent era, and for decades Chicago controlled the distribution side of the business. The cityscape itself has also lured filmmakers with its screen-friendly architecture and gritty landscape, playing in everything from *Call Northside 777* and *Ferris Bueller's Day Off* to *The Fugitive* and *The Dark Knight*.

The city once boasted some of the country's finest picture palaces downtown, and intimate neighbourhood mini-palaces all across the city. Regrettably, though, the downtown palaces have been shuttered or repurposed as theatre venues, while the Music Box is one of only a few surviving mini-palaces still showing films. But the city still scores highly, offering a variety of idiosyncratic alternatives to the multiplex experience – you can watch movies in galleries, bars and museums, and even in an old bank.

ARTS & ENTERTAINMENT

CINEMAS

Weekly film listings are available at www.timeoutchicago.com, as well as in the *Chicago Tribune*, the *Chicago Sun-Times*, *RedEye* and the *Chicago Reader*. To buy tickets in advance, either visit the theatre in person, call the numbers listed below or visit the theatre's website. Parents should note that many Chicago movie theatres won't admit children under six years old after 6pm.

INSIDE TRACK
SIP WHILE YOU WATCH

Some movies are best seen with a stiff drink in hand. Alas, most movie theatres in Chicago aren't allowed to serve alcohol, but a few do have dispensation. **Brew & View at the Vic** (*see p194*) is the most obvious place to quaff while you watch, particularly for budget boozers. For something more highbrow, venture down to the classy **Gene Siskel Film Center** (*see p194*), which has a liquor licence: buy a beer at the concession stand and drink through some of the finest examples in world cinema.

Mainstream & first-run

There are multiplexes galore dotted around the Chicagoland region; those listed below are among the best. The **Century 12** in Evanston is favoured by purists (the sound quality is excellent) and drivers (there's free parking across the street as long as you validate your parking ticket within a four-hour time frame).

AMC Loews 600 N Michigan

N Michigan Avenue, entrance at N Rush Street & E Ohio Street, Magnificent Mile (1-312 255 9347, www.amctheatres.com). El: Red to Grand. **Tickets** $10.50; $8.50 before 6pm Mon-Thur, before 4pm Fri-Sun; $7.50-$9.50 reductions. **Credit** AmEx, Disc, MC, V. **Map** p310 J10.

★ AMC River East 21

322 E Illinois Street, at N Columbus Drive, Streeterville (1-312 596 0333, www.amctheatres. com). El: Red to Grand. **Tickets** $10.50; $8.50 before 6pm Mon-Thur, before 4pm Fri-Sun; $7.50-$9.50 reductions. **Credit** AmEx, Disc, MC, V. **Map** p310 J11.

★ Century 12 Evanston & CinéArts 6

1715 Maple Avenue, at Church Street, Evanston (1-847 491 9751, www.cinemark.com). El: Purple to Davis. **Tickets** $9.50-$10; $6.75 before 6pm

Mon-Fri, before 2pm Sat, Sun; $5.50-$8.50 reductions. **Credit** MC, V.

Davis Theater
4614 N Lincoln Avenue, at W Montrose Avenue, Lincoln Square (1-773 784 0893, www.davis theater.com). El: Brown to Montrose. **Tickets** $8.25; $5.75 before 6pm; $5.75 reductions. **Credit** AmEx, Disc, MC, V.

Kerasotes Webster Place 11
1471 W Webster Avenue, at N Clybourn Avenue, Lincoln Park (1-773 327 3100, www.kerasotes. com). El: Brown, Purple or Red to Fullerton. **Tickets** $10.75; $8.75 before 6pm Mon-Thur, before 4pm Fri-Sun; $5 before noon Fri-Sun; $7.50-$9.75 reductions. **Credit** AmEx, Disc, MC, V. **Map** p312 D5.

★ Kerasotes Showplace Icon at Roosevelt Collection with Icon-X
1011 S Delano Court East, at Roosevelt Road, South Loop (1-312 386 7440, www.showplace

icon.com). El: Green, Orange, Red to Roosevelt. **Tickets** $18 (VIP), $13 (Regular); $9-$12 reductions. **Credit** AmEx, Disc, MC, V. **Map** p308 H14.

Indie & revival

In addition to the theatres listed below, there are also regular screenings at venues as varied as the **Skokie Public Library** (www.skokielibrary.info) and the **Center on Halsted** (www.centeronhalsted.org).

Block Cinema
Mary & Leigh Block Museum of Art, Northwestern University, 1967 S Campus Drive, Evanston (1-847 491 2448, www.block museum.northwestern.edu). El: Purple to Davis. **Tickets** $6; $4 reductions. **Credit** MC, V. This campus series screens an interesting mix of classic and contemporary films from around the world in a small but state-of-the-art facility. Programming is sometimes tied to art exhibits in the

Gene Siskel Film Center. *See p194.*

museum, and some screenings are introduced by Northwestern scholars. In summer, weather permitting, the series moves outdoors.

Brew & View at the Vic

3145 N Sheffield Avenue, at W Belmont Avenue, Lakeview (1-773 929 6713, www.brewview.com). El: Brown, Purple or Red to Belmont. **Tickets** $5. **Credit** AmEx, Disc, MC, V. **Map** p313 E3.

Some movies are better seen with a few drinks under your belt, and that's the mission at Brew & View. Screenings of newish movies and older flicks cost five bucks, and pitchers of beer are cheap. If the mood takes you, follow the drunken crowd and start yelling retorts at the screen. The best seats are up on the balcony.

Chicago Filmmakers

5243 N Clark Street, at W Berwyn Avenue, Andersonville (1-773 293 1447, www.chicago filmmakers.org). El: Purple or Red to Berwyn. **Tickets** $8; $7 reductions. **Credit** AmEx, Disc, MC, V.

This Andersonville set-up, one of two operations run by the not-for-profit Chicago Filmmakers enterprise, screens a selection of experimental films a few times a month (often with the filmmaker in attendance), with occasional screenings at other venues such as the Cinema Borealis in Wicker Park. The group also stages classes and workshops, and provides behind-the-scenes support for local moviemakers.

★ Doc Films, University of Chicago

Max Palevsky Cinema, Ida Noyes Hall, 1212 E 59th Street, at S Woodlawn Avenue, Hyde Park (1-773 702 8575, www.docfilms.uchicago.edu). Metra: 55th-56th-57th Street. **Tickets** $5. **No credit cards. Map** p316 Y18.

For serious film buffs, no trip to the city is complete without a pilgrimage to Hyde Park to catch a flick presented by Doc Films, where the eclectic programming is all over the cinematic map. 'Doc' is short for 'documentary', reflecting this film society's origins as the International House Documentary Film Group; founded in 1940 but with its origins eight years earlier, it's purportedly the longest-running student film society in the country. These days, the programme is wider: the range of titles, screened every night of the academic year at the 490-seat Max Palevsky Cinema, is a shrewdly selected mix of arthouse, cult and classic work during the week, balanced by more popular fare on weekends.

▶ *For more on the University of Chicago, see p95.*

Facets Multimedia

1517 W Fullerton Avenue, at N Ashland Avenue, Lincoln Park (1-773 281 4114, www.facets. org). El: Brown, Purple or Red to Fullerton. **Tickets** $9. **Credit** AmEx, Disc, MC, V. **Map** p312 D5.

This no-nonsense, not-for-profit Lincoln Park venue has always been the place to go for low-budget American indies and foreign revivals, but it's recently shifted its focus to include more documentaries. The seats are a little hard on the back, but cinephiles don't mind putting up with a little discomfort to see movies that would never get screened at bigger venues. Many of the 40,000-plus titles housed in this esteemed DVD library are all but impossible to find elsewhere.

Film Row Cinema

Columbia College, 1104 S Wabash Avenue, at W 11th Street, South Loop (1-312 369 6815, www.colum.edu/film). El: Green, Orange or Red to Roosevelt. **Tickets** free. **No credit cards. Map** p308 H14.

Columbia has been working hard to make its shiny new facility a destination, with novelties such as the Cinema Slapdown, in which two 'experts' are brought in to argue pros and cons for cult films such as *Bad Santa*. Screenings aren't on a set schedule, but it's worth checking Columbia's website – you never know when something amazing will appear, whether it's an advance screening of a new indie with the director in attendance or a revival of a rare experimental work.

★ Gene Siskel Film Center

164 N State Street, at W Randolph Street, the Loop (show times 1-312 846 2800, office 1-312 846 2600, www.siskelfilmcenter.org). El: Brown, Green, Orange, Pink or Purple to State; Red to Lake. **Tickets** $11; $4-$7 reductions. **Credit** AmEx, MC, V. **Map** p309 H12.

The Siskel Center is named for the former *Tribune* critic who found national fame when TV producers paired him with the late *Sun-Times* critic Roger Ebert. Though Siskel died in 1999, his spirit lives on in this refined, modern complex. The two state-of-the-art theatres, with some of the best projection equipment in the country outside New York and LA, feature experimental American work, new foreign movies, classic revivals, themed retrospectives and other festivals. *Photos p193.*

★ Landmark's Century Centre Cinema

2828 N Clark Street, at W Diversey Parkway, Lakeview (1-773 509 4949, www.landmark theatres.com). El: Brown, Purple or Red to Belmont. **Tickets** $11.50; $9 before 5pm Mon-Fri, 1st show Sat, Sun; $9 reductions. **Credit** AmEx, MC, V. **Map** p312 F4.

Though it's located in a yuppie shopping mall, this seven-screen cinema concentrates on films at the artier end of the spectrum, and does a great job of screening them. Upon purchasing your ticket, ask one of the disillusioned but very funny and friendly punk-rock staff their opinion of the movie you're about to see.

ARTS & ENTERTAINMENT

Essential Chicago Films

The city has a starring role in some fantastic flicks.

The Untouchables.

ARTS & ENTERTAINMENT

THE UNTOUCHABLES
BRIAN DE PALMA
(1987)

Robert De Niro stars as Al Capone and Sean Connery as world-weary cop Malone in David Mamet's memorable film about the infamous Chicago gangster's power over the city and its liquor supplies. As Eliot Ness, Kevin Costner is the unloveably upright counterpoint to the iconic tough guys.

HOME ALONE
CHRIS COLUMBUS
(1990)

Every year at Christmas you can bet there's a parade of cars driving past the Winnetka mansion where *Home Alone* was shot. This classic film about a kid (Macaulay Culkin) whose family accidentally leave him behind when they go off for the holidays is full of wildly creative pranks as two burglars try to outsmart the young smartypants.

THE BLUES BROTHERS
JOHN LANDIS (1980)

John Belushi and Dan Aykroyd made musical comedy history as Jake and Elwood Blues, characters originally developed for a *Saturday Night Live* sketch. In addition to absolute hilarity and epic car chases around Chicago, the movie features numbers by several musical legends, including Ray Charles, Aretha Franklin and John Lee Hooker.

FERRIS BUELLER'S
DAY OFF
JOHN HUGHES (1986)

Chicago is shown off magnificently as the dream playground for an irresponsible teen hero: Ferris (Matthew Broderick) drags his friends to Wrigley Field and the Art Institute, high up the Sears Tower – and even to the front of the Von Steuben Day Parade. Writer-director John Hughes, a local, called the movie his love letter to the city.

PUBLIC ENEMIES
MICHAEL MANN (2009)

Johnny Depp stars in this high-def retelling of the Depression-era exploits of bank robber John Dillinger. Michael Mann's vision of the Depression makes use of some great Chicago locations, including the Biograph Theater, where the gangster was gunned down by the FBI. Of note: Depp's fantastic fedoras come from renowned local hat-maker Optimo Hats.

HIGH FIDELITY
STEPHEN FREARS
(2000)

Wicker Park locals are proud to claim Brit writer Nick Hornby's novel was shot in their 'hood just as it was hitting its hipster stride. Audiophile Rob Gordon (John Cusack) whiles away his days at a record shop before heading out on a quest to understand women and where he's gone wrong with them in his past.

Logan Theatre

2646 N Milwaukee Avenue, between Sawyer & Kedzie Avenues, Logan Square (1-773 342 5555, www.thelogantheatre.com). El: Blue to Logan Square. **Tickets** $7; $5.50-$6.50 reductions. **Credit** AmEx, MC, V.

Originally opened in the early 1900s as a single cinema theatre, Logan recently reopened, screening new and classic old flicks. Additionally, the lounge offers weekly trivia nights and open mic nights.

★ Music Box

3733 N Southport Avenue, at W Waveland Avenue, Wrigleyville (1-773 871 6604, www. musicboxtheatre.com). El: Brown to Southport. **Tickets** $9.25; $8.25 1st show Mon-Thur; $7.25 11.30am Sat, Sun. **Credit** MC, V. **Map** p313 D1.

The darling of Chicago movie houses, Music Box has two intimate theatres screening first-run arthouse and foreign films, supplemented by matinée and midnight screenings of everything from Marx Brothers classics to cheesy 1970s 3D porn. But the vintage organ (sometimes employed to accompany silent films) and Moorish meets Tinseltown decor are even more memorable, with stars twinkling in the ceiling and projected clouds rolling by. The midnight shows offer old chestnuts of the midnight circuit (*Rocky Horror*, *The Warriors*) mixed with popular recent titles.

Navy Pier IMAX Theatre

600 E Grand Avenue, at Lake Michigan, Streeterville (1-312 595 5629, www.imax.com). El: Red to Grand. **Tickets** *IMAX films* $12; $9-$10 reductions. *Other* $15; $13-$14 reductions. **Credit** AmEx, MC, V. **Map** p310 K10.

When it comes to cinema, bigger doesn't always equal better – the projection is great, but this theatre can feel a little soulless. Still, this IMAX set-up persists in its programme of large-format movies, some of which can be spectacular. Alongside the obligatory nature films and high-budget animations, the cinema also screens occasional 35mm blockbusters.
► *The Omnimax Cinema at the Museum of Science & Industry (see p96) offers similar fare.*

FILM FESTIVALS

As befits a city with such a long cinematic history, Chicago abounds with film festivals of all stripes. The biggest and the best are detailed below, in chronological order. However, there are many others throughout the year, including a plethora of outdoor screenings in the summer. Check *Time Out Chicago* each week for details.

European Union Film Festival

Gene Siskel Film Center; for venue details, see p194. **Date** Mar.

This expertly vetted showcase of new European works runs for a good portion of March each year.

Chicago Underground Film Festival

Logan Theatre; for venue details, see left (www.cuff.org). **Date** Mar.

Transgression, subversion and complete indifference to mainstream production values are the order of the day at this hard-partying film and video fest.

Chicago Latino Film Festival

Various venues (1-312 431 1330, http://chicago latinofilmfestival.org). **Date** Apr.

Established in 1984, the two-week CLFF is usually the strongest of the city's ethnic film festivals.

Chicago Asian American Showcase

Gene Siskel Film Center; for venue details, see p194 (www.faaim.org). **Date** May.

This two-week event offers an eclectic selection of features, docs and films by or about Asian Americans.

Black Harvest International Festival of Film & Video

Gene Siskel Film Center; for venue details, see p194. **Date** Aug.

Filmmakers and artists attend screenings at Chicago's annual two-week showcase for films that explore or celebrate black culture around the world.

Onion City Experimental Film & Video Festival

Various venues (1-773 293 1447, www.chicago filmmakers.org/onion_fest/). **Date** early Sept.

Sponsored by Chicago Filmmakers (*see p194*), this weekend-long event is a bit more earnest and cerebral than its psychotronic cousin, the Chicago Underground Film Festival (*see above*).

★ Chicago International Film Festival

AMC River East 21; for venue details, see p192 (1-312 683 0121, www.chicagofilmfestival.com). **Date** Oct.

Truly international in scope, the oldest competitive film festival in North America programmes over 100 features and documentaries, making it an appealing compromise between the dauntingly comprehensive Toronto International Film Festival and the hyperexclusive New York Film Festival.

Chicago International Children's Film Festival

Facets Multimedia; for venue details, see p194 (1-773 281 9075, www.cicff.org). **Date** Oct-Nov.

Presented annually by Facets but with regular screenings further afield, this ten-day event is the largest children's film festival in North America.

Reeling: Chicago LGBT International Film Festival

Various venues (1-773 293 1447, www.reeling filmfestival.org). **Date** Nov.

Chicago Filmmakers' ten-day production is the second-oldest gay film festival in the US.

Gay & Lesbian

Good times abound in Boystown and beyond.

To the casual queer observer, miles upon miles of cornfields may not look like they lead to very much. But when those barren interstates lead to a thriving, thumping metropolis that's home to more than 400,000 corn-fed homos, the pancake-flat prairie suddenly doesn't seem so bad after all. Chicago continues to be a 'mo mecca for people in the LGBT community seeking escape from the conservative confines of middle America, as well as coastal queers wanting the comforts of urban life in an attitude-free zone.

And why wouldn't they? Chicago's own Boystown contains more than 20 nightlife venues within a five-block radius; mega-watt festivals such as International Mr Leather and Northalsted Market Days continue to draw thousands from all over the world; and the city's benevolent dictator – Mr Rahm Emanuel – proudly caters to his LGBT constituents by giving full support to same-sex marriage.

GAY NEIGHBOURHOODS

A subsection of Lakeview bordered by Addison Street to the north, Broadway to the east, Belmont Avenue to the south and Halsted Street to the west, **Boystown** is the city's out-and-proud, feather boa-wearin' gaybourhood; indeed, the name is now officially recognised by the city. Broadway is best for shopping and dining, while Halsted Street's bar scene delivers a host of party palaces.

Andersonville, an old Swedish enclave to the north, is Chicago's other key gay area. The queer scene here has its origins in the 1990s, when lesbians dug it for its low-key vibe and cheap rents. The boys soon followed, and today it's a laid-back if slightly smug enclave of trendy restaurants, gay hangouts and furniture stores, all centered along Clark Street.

While Boystown and Andersonville scream 'queer', gay life thrives all over town. Wicker Park, Ukrainian Village and Pilsen all attract alterna-queers who eschew gay-specific bars in favour of metrosexual hipster hangouts, while an older crowd can be found in River North and Lincoln Park. Muggings sometimes occur and homophobia still exists outside the gay enclaves, but most problems are verbal and generated by out-of-towners.

Cruising is common in Chicago. Popular haunts include Lincoln Park (the park itself,

not the yuppie neighbourhood); you can also score pretty much anywhere from Montrose Harbour up to the Hollywood Beach (also an excellent gay beach by day). If a car flashes its lights at you or a furtive glance is cast your way, you're in business. But the Chicago police are no fools: either head somewhere else with your new-found friend or make sure that you conduct yourselves with discretion.

LESBIAN LIFE

The easiest way for girls to come out of the closet is to walk into the **Closet** (*see p201*) on Broadway, or to take the Red line to Berwyn and head into Andersonville. There are many bars to choose from, but classy dykes should try lesbian wine bar **Joie de Vine** (*see p201*). Another lady-centric spot worth checking out is **Parlour** (www.parlourbarchicago.com), just north of Andersonville in the Rogers Park area.

In general, though, you'll fare better at the city's weekly and monthly events. **FKA at Big Chicks** (*see p201*) brings in hot ladies and trans men on the first Thursday of the month for a sweaty night of drinking and dancing. Chances, a queer dance party at the **Hideout** (1354 W Wabansia Avenue, 1-773 227 4433, www.hideoutchicago.com), draws a pretty even male/female mix, as does its sibling party Off-Chances at **Danny's Tavern** (*see p139*).

The monthly girlie-heavy Slo 'Mo party at the **Whistler** (2421 N Milwaukee Avenue, 1-773 227 3530, www.whistlerchicago.com) is worth a look, as is Femistry Fridays, which is a monthly party aimed at black women (see www.bblyss.com).

QUEER CALENDAR

Gays, straights and more or less everyone in between jam Boystown during the first two weekends in June for **Pride** (www.chicagopride calendar.org). The whole month is dotted with Pride-related events, leading up to a weekend of partying and Sunday's huge Pride Parade.

Six weeks later, the largest street festival in the Midwest rolls into Boystown: **Northalsted Market Days** (www.northalsted.com), staged over the first weekend in August on Halsted Street, between Belmont Avenue and Addison Street. It's basically a two-day outdoor gay bar with bands, DJs and street vendors galore.

For information about **Reeling**, the annual gay film festival, *see p196*.

INFORMATION & MEDIA

Timeout.com/chicago lists plenty of gay events each week. In addition, the any eaterie or meeterie in Andersonville and Boystown will have high-rise stacks of gay freesheets.

The *Windy City Times* delves into local and national issues, and also includes all-important nightlife information. *Nightspots*, with its compact map and addresses of manjoints, fits snugly into a back pocket. *Boi* contains listings, fluff pieces and occasional articles on abs or amphetamines. *Grab* has full listings. Finally, quarterly *Pink* magazine is the glossiest of

INSIDE TRACK PARTY PEOPLE

In Chicago, finding the coolest queer parties is all about knowing who the best promoters are. While you're in town, check out the Twitter feeds of Scott Cramer (@scottycramer), Bobby Pins (@bpins) and Sissy Spastik (@sissyspastik), who'll keep you up to date on the latest parties.

them all, supplementing generally well-written articles with a queer business directory.

Online, the city has become a hotbed of queer podcasting: check out the wildly popular Feast of Fun (www.feastoffun.com), comedy podcast Foul Monkeys (www.foulmonkeys.com) and the Daily Purge (www.thedailypurge.com), among others.

RESTAURANTS & CAFES

Andersonville

★ **Anteprima**

5316 N Clark Street, between W Summerdale Avenue & W Berwyn Avenue (1-773 506 9990, www.anteprimachicago.net). El: Red to Berwyn. **Open** 5.30-10pm Mon-Thur; 5.30-11pm Fri, Sat; 5-9.30pm Sun. **Main courses** $20. **Credit** AmEx, Disc, MC, V.
Anteprima is a favourite neighbourhood restaurant, thanks to rustic, reasonably priced home-style dishes and refreshingly attentive waitstaff. Local homos come here to impress their visiting friends and relatives.

Pride.

Francesca's Bryn Mawr

1039 W Bryn Mawr Avenue, at N Sheridan Road (1-773 506 9261, www.miafrancesca.com). El: Red to Bryn Mawr. **Open** 11.30am-9pm Mon; 11.30am-9.30pm Tue-Thur; 11.30am-10.30pm Fri; 10am-10.30pm Sat; 10am-9pm Sun. **Main courses** $22. **Credit** AmEx, Disc, MC, V.

There are a dozen or so versions of this hip Italian hangout in Chicagoland, but only this one is nick-named Mancesca's. You can barely swing a fettuc-cini noodle without hitting same-sex couples chowing down on good pasta, or (less frequently) large parties of guppies ordering tons of vino and checking out both the daily specials and the handsome waitstaff.

Hamburger Mary's

5400 N Clark Street, at W Balmoral Avenue (1-773 784 6969, www.hamburgermarys.com/ chicago). El: Red to Bryn Mawr. **Open** 11.30am-11pm Mon-Fri; 10.30am-11pm Sat, Sun. **Main courses** $10. **Credit** AmEx, Disc, MC, V.

Chicago's very own version of the queer hamburger chain. The burgers come in every combination of ingredients (Buffy the Hamburger Slayer, anyone?) and are pretty tasty. Supplement them with beer, before your bill arrives in a high heel.

▶ *Upstairs, Mary's Attic is a casual cocktail spot. And next door, Mary's Rec Room features major sports events on HD TVs.*

Jin Ju

5203 N Clark Street, at W Foster Avenue (1-773 334 6377, www.jinjurestaurant.com). El: Red to Berwyn. **Open** 5-9.30pm Tue, Wed; 5-10pm Thur; 5-11pm Fri, Sat; 5-9.30pm Sun. **Main courses** $15. **Credit** AmEx, Disc, MC, V.

Brick walls and a subdued sexiness draw a mixed crowd, who nibble on fiery spare ribs (a must) and sip Sojutinis, crafted with a Korean grain liquor that's made from sweet potatoes (another must). Finish with the ginger ice cream.

★ M Henry

5707 N Clark Street, at W Hollywood Street (1-773 561 1600, www.mhenry.net). El: Red to Bryn Mawr. **Open** 7am-3pm Tue-Fri; 8am-3pm Sat, Sun. **Main courses** $10. **Credit** AmEx, MC, V.

Come the weekend, you can barely get through the door here. However, you'll still want to try, simply to taste the signature Bliss Cakes – two delicious hot-cakes layered with warm blackberries and vanilla mascarpone cream, then topped with brown sugar and oat crust. The wait can be long, but it's a friendly queue full of attractive possibilities.

Ombra

5310 N Clark Street, between Berwyn & Summerdale Avenues (1-773 506 8600, www. barombra.com). El: Red to Berwyn. **Open**

Hamburger Mary's.

5-11pm Mon-Fri; 3-11pm Sat, Sun. **Cicchetti** $7. **Credit** AmEx, MC, V.

Cicchetti – the cold and room-temperature snacks common in Venetian bars – dominate the menu at this cosy restaurant. They're meant to be eaten casually alongside drinks, so grab a seat at the bar and make sure to order the *baccala fritte* (fried balls of salt cod) and a few oysters while you flirt with the cute waitstaff.

Tweet

5020 N Sheridan Road, at W Argyle Avenue (1-773 728 5576, www.tweet.biz). El: Red to Argyle. **Open** 9am-3pm daily. **Main courses** $10. **No credit cards**.

Michelle Fire's Uptown brunch spot serves up slam-min' helpings of breakfast favourites, with a won-derful coffee cake *amuse-bouche* to start. Most of the food is made with organically grown and locally pro-duced ingredients, and the clientele is über-queer.

Boystown

Ann Sather

909 W Belmont Avenue, between N Clark Street & N Sheffield Avenue (1-773 348 2378, www. annsather.com). El: Brown, Purple or Red to Belmont. **Open** 7am-3pm Mon-Fri; 7am-4pm Sat, Sun. **Main courses** $10. **Credit** AmEx, MC, V. **Map** p313 E2.

Known for its sticky buns, this hospitable, gay-run Swedish enclave has been around for half a century. The place is cheap, cosy and, despite its Nordic roots,

emphatically all-American in its cuisine. Ann Sather's owner, Tom Tunney, was elected as the city's first openly gay alderman in 2003.
Other locations 3411 N Broadway, Boystown (1-773 305 0024); 1147 W Granville, Edgewater (1-773 274 0557); 5207 N Clark Street, Andersonville (1-773 271 6677).

Caribou Coffee
3300 N Broadway, at W Aldine Avenue (1-773 477 3695, www.cariboucoffee.com). El: Brown, Purple or Red to Belmont. **Open** 5.30am-9.30pm Mon-Fri; 6.30am-10pm Sat; 7am-9.30pm Sun. **Credit** AmEx, Disc, MC, V. **Map** p313 F2.
This branch of the coffee shop chain – aka Cruisabou – is in the heart of Boystown. Come here to chat with your mates, but look elsewhere if you're looking to... well, look elsewhere.

Halsted's
3441 N Halsted Street, at W Newport Avenue (1-773 348 9696, www.halstedschicago.com). El: Red to Addison. **Open** 5-11pm Mon-Thur; 5pm-midnight Fri; 11am-midnight Sat; 11am-11pm Sun. **Main courses** $15. **Credit** AmEx, Disc, MC, V. **Map** p313 F2.
The servers here are flighty and the hours are pretty erratic. But on the plus side, multiple TV screens mean you can watch the newest Beyoncé video, the football game and CNN while simultaneously eating respectable bar food. As an added bonus, the backyard patio is a brilliant spot to hang out when the weather's warm.

Home Bistro Chicago
3404 N Halsted Street, between W Roscoe Street & W Newport Avenue (1-773 661 0299, www. homebistrochicago.com). El: Red to Addison. **Open** 5.30-10pm Tue-Thur; 5-10.30pm Fri, Sat; 5-9pm Sun. **Main courses** $20. **Credit** AmEx, Disc, MC, V. **Map** p313 F1.
There's almost nothing but tables for two in this cramped Boystown spot. Just make sure that you manage to bag the seat facing the window, so your partner has his eyes on you and not the boys on Halsted. Dig into new American dishes such as the house-smoked chicken thighs or smoked pork jowl sandwich. A decent $33 three-course prix fixe is offered on Wednesdays.

Intelligentsia
3123 N Broadway, between W Barry Street & W Briar Place (1-773 348 8058, www.intelligentsia coffee.com). El: Brown, Purple or Red to Belmont. **Open** 6.30am-9pm Mon-Thur; 6.30am-10pm Fri; 7am-10pm Sat; 7am-9pm Sun. **Credit** AmEx, Disc, MC, V. **Map** p313 F3.
It's Boystown's very own independent coffeehouse, popular with the anti-Starbucks crowd who prefer a hand-crafted cup of joe.
Other locations throughout the city.

Kit Kat Lounge & Supper Club
3700 N Halsted Street, at W Waveland Avenue (1-773 525 1111, www.kitkatchicago.com). El: Red to Addison. **Open** 5.30pm-2am Mon-Fri; 11am-2am Sat, Sun. **Main courses** $20. **Credit** AmEx, Disc, MC, V. **Map** p313 F1.
Get ready for diva overload at Boystown's boisterous cocktail joint. The martini list is exhaustive, and on Sundays, Tuesdays, Wednesdays and Thursdays they're all half-price. But it's the ebullient female impersonators that make this a favourite among gays, bachelorettes and even straight dudes. The pavement patio is among the best in B-town.

Melrose
3233 N Broadway, at W Melrose Street (1-773 327 2060). El: Brown, Purple or Red to Belmont. **Open** 24hrs daily. **Main courses** $10. **Credit** MC, V. **Map** p313 F2.
It's 4am, you're mid-hangover, and there's a frighteningly tall pile of greasy food staring you in the face. It really doesn't get much better than this. Besides, the Melrose is your last chance to decide if that bar pick-up sitting across from you is really worth the trouble of taking home.

Pillow Talk

Where to hit the hay in gay Chicago.

Provincetown this ain't. But if you're looking to stay gay on the third coast, you do have a few options. In the heart of Boystown, the **Villa Toscana** (3447 N Halsted Street, at W Cornelia Avenue, 1-773 404-2643, www.thevillatoscana. com) offers an unbeatable location smack in the middle of the 'hood; enjoy breakfast on the sundeck during the summer months while the city hums around you. Also in the area, neither the **Best Western Hawthorne Terrace** (3434 N Broadway, at W Hawthorne Place, 1-773 244 3434, www.hawthorne terrace.com), nor **City Suites** (*see p182*) are exclusively gay, but proximity to the attractions of Boystown guarantees a homo-heavy clientele.

And to the west, the five-room **Ashland Arms** (6408 N Clark Street, at W Devon Avenue, 1-312 498 9979, www.ashlandarms.com) entices the fetish and kink community with themed guestrooms, including leather, bunk and rubber rooms. It's located above Jackhammer bar (*see p203*) and Mephistor Leathers, and the owners go out of their way to make sure guests have all the fetish gear they desire.

ARTS & ENTERTAINMENT

Nookies Tree

3334 N Halsted Street, at W Buckingham Place
(1-773 248 9888, www.nookiesrestaurant.net).
El: Brown, Purple or Red to Belmont. **Open** 7am-
midnight Mon-Thur, Sun; 24hrs Fri, Sat. **Main**
courses $10. **Credit** MC, V. **Map** p313 F2.
March in here for munchies, brunches and grilled
American cheese sandwiches. It's an inevitable, even
obligatory stop right on the Boystown strip; pretty
well everybody goes there, night and day, and so
should you. There are three other branches, but this
one's got the gaydar.
Other locations Nookies, 1746 N Wells Street,
at W St Paul Avenue, Old Town (1-312 337 2454);
Nookies Too, 2114 N Halsted Street, at W Dickens
Avenue, Lincoln Park (1-773 327 1400); Nookies
Edgewater, 1110 W Bryn Mawr Avenue,
Edgewater (1-773 516 4188).

★ Ping Pong

3322 N Broadway, at W Buckingham Place
(1-773 281 7575, www.pingpongrestaurant.com).
El: Brown, Purple or Red to Belmont. **Open**
5pm-midnight daily. **Main courses** $15.
Credit AmEx, Disc, MC, V. **Map** p313 F2.
Several years ago, restaurateur Henry Chang doubled the size of his pint-sized Asian eatery. Since
then, it's been the most happening restaurant on
Broadway. Every gay in town heads here with a date
or a group of mates to chow down on succulent
Chinese classics and an ever-evolving cocktail menu
(BYOB is also allowed, with corkage fee).
▶ *If you're not in the mood to stand and model*
for A-list gays, check out Chang's impressive
sushi joint Wakamono across the street.

Wood

3335 N Halsted Street, at W Buckingham Place
(1-773 935 9663, www.woodchicago.com). El:
Brown, Purple or Red to Belmont. **Open** 5pm-
midnight Mon, Tue; 5pm-2am Wed-Fri; 5pm-3am
Sat; 10am-midnight Sun. **Main courses** $22.
Credit MC, V. **Map** p313 F2.
It's hard to pick a favourite dish at Wood because,
truth is, all the dishes at this fancier Boystown
eatery are good, from the lightly battered soft-shell
crab to the country ham flatbread to the Skuna Bay
salmon. Cocktails such as the Double Cross vodka-
based Nouveau Riche are tasty, too, but there's
enough drinking in this neighbourhood – Wood is a
reminder that, hey, Boystown's gotta eat too.

BARS

Andersonville

★ Big Chicks

5024 N Sheridan Road, at W Argyle Avenue
(1-773 728 5511, www.bigchicks.com). El: Red to
Argyle. **Open** 4pm-2am Mon-Fri; 10am-3am Sat;
9am-2am Sun. **No credit cards**.

INSIDE TRACK
SCREEN QUEENS

Indie queer cinema thrives in the
Windy City. Hosted monthly at Chicago
Filmmakers (*see p194*), Dyke Delicious
offers lesbian moviemaking; head to
Landmark's Century Centre Cinema
(*see p194*) to catch more mainstream
indie fare. And don't miss Reeling
(www.reelingfilmfestival.org), the city's
annual festival of gay and lesbian cinema.

This charming speakeasy-style saloon is more akin
to an East Village hangout than a Chicago joint.
Owner Michelle Fire doles out shots at midnight and
rolls out an all-you-can-eat Sunday buffet at no
charge. The clientele is a mixed bag of scruffy neighbourhood locals, relaxed twentysomethings and lesbians on the loose. Everyone gets along, especially
on the tiny, packed dancefloor.

Joie de Vine

1744 W Balmoral Avenue, at N Ravenswood
Avenue (1-773 989 6846). Bus 22. **Open** 5pm-
2am Mon-Fri, Sun; 5pm-3am Sat. **Credit** AmEx,
Disc, MC, V.
Romantics will quickly fall in love with this lesbian
wine bar, where flickering candles and soft house
music are combined with international wines and
light bites. Most nights, it's just a regular bar, popular with oenophiles of all orientations. But on weekends, it looks like a casting call for *The L Word*.

Marty's

1511 W Balmoral Avenue, at N Clark Street
(1-773 454 0161, www.martysmartinibar.com).
El: Red to Berwyn. **Open** 5pm-2am Mon-Fri,
Sun; 5pm-3am Sat. **Credit** MC, V.
Sure, it's tiny, but the fortysomething crowd can't
get enough of this classic cocktail joint. No thumping
music, no whiny youngsters: just some good old-
fashioned martinis. The bar staff are handsome,
attentive and know everybody's name.

Boystown

★ Closet

3325 N Broadway Street, at W Buckingham Place
(1-773 477 8533, www.theclosetchicago.com).
El: Brown, Purple or Red to Belmont. **Open**
4pm-4am Mon-Fri; noon-5am Sat; noon-4am
Sun. **No credit cards**. **Map** p313 F2.
This Lilliputian bar, a safe stone's throw away from
Halsted Street, is the perfect place to have a beer with
the ladies while watching the straight folk push their
strollers down Broadway. Things really get rolling
after 2am on weekends, when boys and girls mix as
easily as a vanilla-chocolate swirl ice-cream.

ARTS & ENTERTAINMENT

Sidetrack

ARTS & ENTERTAINMENT

Elixir

*3452 N Halsted Street, between Newport &
Cornelia Avenues (1-773 975 9244, www.elixir
chicago.com). El: Red to Addison.* **Open** 6pm-2am
Mon-Wed; 6pm-3am Thur; 6pm-4am Fri; 6pm-
5am Sat; 6pm-midnight Sun. **Credit** AmEx,
Disc, MC, V.

At this shoebox of a cocktail bar, the drinks are skill-
fully prepared, the crowd is kept to a minimum by
the doorman, and the music never gets so loud that
it drowns out your insights on Jean Genet. There's
a decent mix of ages and everyone is on their best
behaviour, which makes for a far more sophisticated
and adult experience than Elixir's next-door sister,
Hydrate (*see p205*).

Minibar

*3341 N Halsted Street, between W Roscoe
Street & W Buckingham Place (1-773 871
6227, www.minibarchicago.com). El: Red to
Addison.* **Open** 5pm-2am Tue-Fri; 5pm-3am
Sat; 11am-2am Sun. **Credit** AmEx, Disc, MC, V.
Map p313 F2.

Hold your martini glass and your nose up in the air
at this jet-set lounge for the pretentious and beautiful.
Music is kept to a low roar, which enables conversation, and bar staff are beautiful. Penny-pinchers
should head elsewhere.

▶ *While you're here, check out the wine bar and
tasting lounge next door.*

Progress Bar

*3359 N Halsted Street, between W Roscoe Street
& W Buckingham Place (1-773 697 9268, www.
progressbarchicago.com). El: Brown, Purple or Red
to Belmont.* **Open** 4pm-2am Mon-Thur; 3pm-2am

Fri; 2pm-3am Sat; 1pm-2am Sun. **Credit** AmEx,
Disc, MC, V. **Map** p313 F2.

Opened in June 2013 in the former Cocktail space at
the heart of the 'hood, this newcomer to the
Boystown scene boasts a cloud-like overhead sculpture installation made up of 19,000 twinkling light
bulbs. It also offers a better selection of craft beers
on tap than most bars on the Halsted strip, pouring
elixirs like Magic Hat #9 and local brew Hopothesis
IPA. The vibe seems laid-back – no sign yet of
Cocktail's ubiquitous go-go dancers (though we'll
keep our eye out).

Roscoe's

*3356 N Halsted Street, at W Roscoe Street (1-773
281 3355, www.roscoes.com). El: Red to Addison.*
Open 2pm-2am Mon-Thur; noon-2am Fri; noon-
3am Sat; 11am-2am Sun. **Admission** $5 after
10pm Sat. **Credit** Disc, MC, V. **Map** p313 F2.

This horny Gen-Y romper room has everything a
queer kid could ask for, including drinks specials,
loads of cute boys and plenty of entertainment courtesy of Chicago's 'finest' drag queens. It's a lovely
tavern, with loads of exposed brick, a cosy outdoor
patio, and plenty of nooks and crannies for making
out in. Expect queues on weekends.

★ Scarlet Bar

*3320 N Halsted Street, at W Buckingham Place
(1-773 348 1053, www.scarletbarchicago.com) El:
Brown, Purple or Red to Belmont.* **Open** 6pm-2am
Mon-Wed; 4pm-2am Thur, Fri, Sun; 4pm-3am Sat.
Credit AmEx, Disc, MC, V. **Map** p313 F2.

Visiting the 'hood on a Thursday night? Stop by
Scarlet for the insanely popular Frat Boy Thursday,
where you can play drinking games and drink huge

beers with boys who don't mind staying out late on a school night. But really, the adorable staff here make every night at Scarlet feel like a fun party.

★ Sidetrack

3349 N Halsted Street, at W Roscoe Street (1-773 477 9189, www.sidetrackchicago.com). El: Red to Addison. **Open** 2pm-2am Wed-Fri, Sun; 3pm-3am Sat. **Credit** AmEx, Disc, MC, V. **Map** p313 F2.

This juggernaut of a bar is famous not just in Boystown but across the US. Stare at videos or stare at men in any number of rooms, including the cavernous glass bar, the sparkling roof deck or a new addition that the locals are affectionately calling 'new bar'. Showtune nights (Mon, Sun) are legendary – and participatory, so be warned. Girls are welcome, but will find themselves in the minority.

Wangs

3317 N Broadway, between Aldine Avenue & Buckingham Place (1-773 296 6960). El: Red to Addison. **Open** 5pm-midnight Mon-Thur, Sun; 5pm-2am Fri, Sat. **No credit cards.**

This intimate cocktail bar is highly stylised, employing lush, floral wallpaper and woodwork the likes of which you've seen only in an opium den. A secret side room is a recent addition, and is home to dance parties on the weekends. Make sure to check out the, uh, graphic art in the bathroom.

Elsewhere

Crew Bar & Grill

4804 N Broadway Street, between W Lawrence Avenue & W Gunnison Street, Uptown (1-773 784 2739, www.worldsgreatestbar.com). El: Red to Lawrence. **Open** 11.30am-midnight Mon, Tue; 11.30am-2am Wed-Fri; 11am-2am Sat; 11am-midnight Sun. **Credit** MC, V.

Sports bar Crew has broken away from the Boystown pack with a novel Uptown location, a crowd that's welcoming to men and women, and fun weekly events such as trivia on Mondays and karaoke on Thursdays.

Downtown Bar & Lounge

440 N State Street, between Hubbard and Illinois Streets, River North (1-312 464 1400, www. downtownbarandlounge.com). El: Red to Grand. **Open** 3pm-2am Mon-Fri, Sun; 3pm-3am Sat. **Credit** MC, V.

This place attracts one of the more diverse gay crowds in the city, and it's also the closest queer enclave to the Loop.

★ Jackhammer

6406 N Clark Street, between W Devon Avenue & W Schreiber Avenue, Rogers Park (1-773 743 5772). Bus 22. **Open** 5pm-4am Mon-Thur; 5pm-5am Fri, Sat; 2pm-4am Sun. **Credit** AmEx, MC, V.

This sprawling bar and dance club draws a mix of adventurous Boystowners, leather folk and thirtysomethings on the prowl. The main room is dominated by a dancefloor; once a month, it hosts Flesh Hungry Dog Show, a queer rock cabaret. The upstairs lounge is all about kicking back with a beer; the downstairs Hole bar devotes itself to hardcore cruising and most nights there's a dress code.

Manhandler Saloon

1948 N Halsted Street, between W Armitage Avenue & W Wisconsin Street, Old Town (1-773 871 3339). El: Brown or Purple to Armitage. **Open** noon-4am Mon-Thur, Sat, Sun; noon-5am Fri. **No credit cards. Map** p312 F6.

If someone had managed to cryogenically freeze 1970s gay life and then defrost it in the 21st century, it would look a lot like this place. Located amid aromatherapy shops and yuppie bistros, Manhandler Saloon is a dimly lit watering hole that is the kind of place where old men stare at you too long. Still, it's nice to come here to imagine those heady days of gay lib when moustaches and short shorts ruled.

SHOPS & SERVICES

Andersonville

Early to Bed

5044 N Clark Street, at Winnemac Avenue (1-773 271 1219, www.early2bed.com). El: Red to Berwyn. **Open** noon-7pm Tue; noon-8pm Wed-Sat; noon-6pm Sun. **Credit** AmEx, Disc, MC, V.

Chicago would be full of grumpy and undersexed queer (and straight) ladies if not for this local institution. Stock up on all your favourite harnesses, dildos and battery-operated goodies, and feel free to ask the staff anything while you're at it.

Women & Children First

5233 N Clark Street, between Foster & Berwyn Avenues (1-773 769 9299, www.womenand childrenfirst.com). El: Red to Berwyn. **Open** 11am-7pm Mon, Tue; 11am-9pm Wed-Fri; 10am-7pm Sat; 11am-6pm Sun. **Credit** AmEx, Disc, MC, V.

Don't be fooled by this bookstore's name; though the Andersonville shop has a definite feminist slant, any and all can find something here.

BOYSTOWN

For the **Unabridged Bookstore**, which stocks gay and lesbian literature, *see p147.*

Batteries Not Included

3420 N Halsted Street, between W Roscoe Street & W Newport Avenue (1-773 935 9900, www.bachelorettepartystore.com). El: Brown, Purple or Red to Belmont. **Open** 11am-midnight Mon-Thur, Sun; 11am-1am Fri; 10am-2am Sat. **Credit** AmEx, MC, V. **Map** p313 F2.

They don't call Batteries Not Included bachelorette party headquarters for nothing. This cheerful adult toy store and novelty shop rules with ladies, but its Boystown location ensures that boys make a mad dash here when they're out of condoms and lube.

Beatnix
3400 N Halsted Street, at W Roscoe Street (1-773 281 6933, www.beatnixclothing.com). El: Red to Addison. **Open** noon-10pm Mon-Thur; 11am-midnight Fri, Sat; noon-9pm Sun. **Credit** MC, V. **Map** p313 F2.
This vast vintage store in the middle of Boystown is a favourite clothes closet for club kids, drag queens, bull dykes and muscle boys. It offers a sexy selection of tuxes (the queers must cater, you know) and a cute vortex in the corner devoted to wigs.

Gay Mart
3457 N Halsted Street, at W Cornelia Avenue (1-773 929 4272, www.chicagosgaymart.com). El: Red to Addison. **Open** 11am-7.30pm Mon-Sat; noon-6pm Sun. **Credit** Disc, MC, V. **Map** p313 F2.
The gaudy and goofy rooms here are overflowing with gay-themed cards, novelties, jewellery and stuff adorned with rainbows and schlongs. Shop 'til you drop your inhibitions and then cross over to Hydrate (*see p205*) for a drink.

BATHHOUSES & BOOTHSTORES
Andersonville

Man's Country
5017 N Clark Street, at W Argyle Street (1-773 878 2069, www.manscountrychicago.com). El: Red to Argyle. **Open** 24hrs daily. **Admission** $10 lifetime member. **No credit cards**.
This Andersonville bathhouse, which bills itself as 'more fun than a barrel of hunkies', contains three floors of nakedness, with a range of singles, doubles and fantasy rooms.

INSIDE TRACK SOUTH SIDE

Andersonville and Boystown tend to hog the spotlight, but there's also a queer scene on Chicago's massive South Side. Both **InnExile** (5758 W 65th Street, at S Menard Avenue, 1-773 582 3510, www.innexilechicago.com) and **Jeffrey Pub** (7041 S Jeffery Boulevard, at E 71st Street, 1-773 363 8555) are aimed at the African-American crowd. And just over in Blue Island, **Club Krave** (13126 Western Avenue, 1-708 597 8379) caters to South Siders and suburbanites with retro dance parties, barbecues and bingo nights.

Boystown

Steamworks
3246 N Halsted Street, between W Belmont Avenue & W Melrose Street (1-773 929 6080, www.steamworksonline.com). El: Brown, Purple or Red to Belmont. **Open** 24hrs daily. **Admission** $6 (one-month membership); $15-$19 lockers; $25-$60 room rentals. **Credit** AmEx, MC, V. **Map** p313 F2.
Some 70 private rooms, a gym, a sauna, gang showers, a jacuzzi and hot hunks galore. The attitude quotient can be high, especially on weekends, but furry guys are in vogue during the monthly Bears, Bath & Beyond party.

Elsewhere

Bijou Theater
1349 N Wells Street, at W Evergreen Avenue, Old Town (1-312 943 5397, www.bijoutheaterchicago. com). El: Brown or Purple to Sedgwick; Red to Clark/Division. **Admission** $18 ($10 special Mon). **Open** 24hrs daily. **No credit cards**. **Map** p311 H8.
Owned and operated by porn producer Steven Toushin since 1970, this pioneering establishment screens dirty movies in a Victorian townhouse. It sounds slightly quaint, until the hardcore flicks and exotic dancers unreel and undress.

NIGHTCLUBS
The venues below are specifically gay-oriented, but many other clubs are also big with queers; chief among them is **Berlin** (www.berlinchicago. com), a huge part of the local scene. Queues are long at weekends and Sundays are buzzing.

Boystown

Charlie's
3726 N Broadway, at W Waveland Avenue (1-773 871 8887, www.charlieschicago.com). El: Red to Addison. **Open** 3pm-4am Mon-Fri, Sun; 3pm-5am Sat. **Admission** free-$20. **Credit** AmEx, MC, V. **Map** p313 F1.
If you don't know how to dance country-style, head down to Charlie's – lessons are held several nights a week. But it's not homos doin' the hoedown that pack this queer country club: it's the circuit queens and the style-conscious who join the queues around 2am, when the crowds ditch their cowboy hats in exchange for some high-energy fun.

Circuit
3641 N Halsted Street, at W Addison Street (1-773 325 2233, www.circuitnightclubchicago.com). El: Red to Addison. **Open** 9pm-4am Thur, Fri; 10pm-5am Sat; 7pm-4am Sun. **Admission** $5-$15. **Credit** AmEx, Disc, MC, V. **Map** p313 F1.
This venerable club has had its fair share of woes, including a dispute with local condo dwellers that

Spin.

gave it a bruising some years back, but it still knows how to churn out a late-night dance party. Latin men dish and dance together most of the week, but bach-elorettes flock to the club on Saturday nights for the all-male revues and Fridays are hip hop nights.

Hydrate

3458 N Halsted Street, between W Cornelia Avenue & W Newport Avenue (1-773 975 9244, www.hydratechicago.com). El: Brown, Purple or Red to Belmont. **Open** 8pm-4am Mon-Fri, Sun; 8pm-5am Sat. **Admission** $3-$10 Fri, Sat. **Credit** MC, V. **Map** p313 F2.

Hydrate manages to lure some of the city's best DJs for its wildly busy after-hours scene, but there's plenty going on here every night, including the Hy-drag review on Wednesdays, a Latin night on Tuesdays and a lube-wrestling contest the first Friday of every month.

Spin

800 W Belmont Avenue, at N Halsted Street (1-773 327 7711, www.spin-nightclub.com). El: Brown, Purple or Red to Belmont. **Open** 4pm-2am Mon-Fri; 2pm-3am Sat; 2pm-2am Sun. **Admission** free-$5. **Credit** MC, V. **Map** p309 F2.

This video bar and dance club was looking a little worn until it bought the building next door and transformed itself into a mega-watt dance club and lounge. The new space is pumping out high-energy dance music on weekends, while the dollar drink night on Wednesdays is nearly an institution.

Theatre & piano bars

For **Jackhammer**, which hosts queer-oriented indie-rock night Flesh Hungry Dog Show on the third Friday of each month, *see p203.*

Baton Lounge

436 N Clark Street, between W Illinois Street & W Hubbard Street, River North (1-312 644 5269, www.thebatonshowlounge.com). El: Brown or Purple to Merchandise Mart; Red to Grand. **Shows** 8.30pm, 10.30pm, 12.30am Wed-Sun. **Admission** $10-$15 (min 2 drinks). **Credit** Disc, MC, V. **Map** p310 H10.

Chicago's prime drag venue allows only pre-ops to perform; these quasi-queens are so strut-alicious that straight men, as well as gay men's moms, have been known to swoon. Clap your mitts for Mimi Marks, the Marilyn Monroe-esque belle of the circuit ball.

Davenport's Piano Bar and Cabaret

1383 N Milwaukee Avenue, between Wood & Paulina Streets, Wicker Park (1-773 278 1830, www.davenportspianobar.com). El: Blue to Division. **Open** 7pm-midnight Mon, Wed, Thur; 7pm-2am Fri, Sat; 7pm-11pm Sun.

Wicker Park's only piano bar has been around since 1998, when most area sippers were still in school. Karaoke is a big part of the place: the back room bursts with would-be crooners on Friday nights. And on the other nights? Professionals – replete with boas and dirty jokes – show them how it's really done.

Homolatte

Big Chicks, 5024 N Sheridan Road, between Argyle Street & W Carmen Avenue, Uptown (1-773 728 5511, www.homolatte.com). El: Red to Argyle. **Open** 1st & 3rd Tue of mth. **Admission** free. **No credit cards.**

With performances by, for and about word-hungry queers, this twice-monthly showcase of gay, lesbian and transgendered musicians and writers is hosted by Scott Free, the angry, talented one-time falsetto soprano for the Lavender Light Gospel Choir.

Nightlife

Home of house, improv and the blues, Chicago rocks after dark.

As the birthplace of house music, Chicago will always have a place in the hearts of clubbers. Four-to-the-floor electronic beats were first interwoven with disco by Frankie Knuckles at the legendary, long-departed Warehouse club in the late 1970s. Older clubbers sometimes obsess about a lack of respect on the local scene for Chicago's original DJs. But, in reality, the city does an incredible job to accommodate all-comers, from underground club kids at the Mid to glamour-loving party people at Studio Paris.

Comedy has been synonomous with improv in Chicago ever since the 1950s, when the (now defunct) Compass Players improvised their performances based on audience suggestions. Iconic venue Second City nurtured the likes of Tina Fey and Steve Carell, and is still going strong. Though improv dominates the scene, stand-up is on the rise with the arrival of venues such as Laugh Factory and UP.

The Pitchfork Music Festival and Lollapalooza, now established fixtures on the summer calendar, have put Chicago on the map as a rock and indie music mecca. But venues such as the Empty Bottle, Lincoln Hall, the Hideout and Logan Square Auditorium also do an outstanding year-round job of attracting popular and up-and-coming touring acts from around the country. The blues is a tourist industry in its own right, while jazz fans can bask in the atmosphere of historic haunts such as Green Mill.

Clubs

River North remains the hottest and most densely concentrated nightlife district. The area still favours velvet ropes, high covers, pricey bottle service and strict dress codes; long lines preclude club-hopping. But despite the stilettos and bouncers, the tone is more naughty than haughty. Stars of European techno and minimal house can be found at **Spy Bar** (*see p207*); **Crimson Lounge** in the Hotel Sax (*see p173*) and **Angels & Kings** in the Hard Rock Hotel (*see p168*) have upped the celeb and youth factors respectively.

In the West Loop, the **Fulton Market** area is simmering but not yet boiling over, while pockets of the **Lake Street** nightlife corridor have been troubled by violence. Police are keeping an eye on the area. The real action is further north in **Ukrainian Village** and **Wicker Park**, both dotted with mid-sized spots that vie for locals' attention. Slightly lighter on cover charges but higher on edgy attitude is **Debonair Social Club** (*see p212*). Further north, in **Logan Square**, low-key and looser DJ bars such as the **Burlington** (*see p141*) and **Whistler** (*see p142*) are following in the footsteps of **Danny's Tavern** (*see p139*), a perennial bohemian hangout with a weekend soundtrack of hip hop, electro and rock.

INFORMATION & TICKETS

Check stores such as **Reckless** (*see p166*), **Gramaphone** (*see p164*), **Borderline** (3333 N Broadway Street, at W Buckingham Place, Lakeview, 1-773 975 9533, www.borderline music.com) and **K-Starke** (*see p165*) for flyers. You'll also find events listed at www.deep housepage.com and www.5chicago.com.

Tickets for **Smart Bar** and **Spy Bar** and some other venues are sold in advance via their own websites. For some clubs, you can call or email ahead (or sign up with a promoter) to get on a list offering cheaper admission, often dependent on early arrival. The city's public transport system runs all night but doesn't cover every corner of town; always carry a cab number or download the Uber app. For more on getting around town, *see pp286-288*.

THE NEAR NORTH SIDE
River North

Bodi
873 N Orleans Street, between W Chestnut & W Locust Streets (www.bodichicago.com). El: Red to Chicago. **Open** midnight-4am Tue, Thur; 10pm-4am Fri, Sun; 10pm-5am Sat. **Admission** $20. **Credit** AmEx, Disc, MC, V. **Map** p310 G9.
This self-described 'Zen liquor lounge' has settled into its role as a compact, high-end destination for style-conscious River North clubbers. It fills up quickly on the weekends and has a great rep for Tuesday nights. DJs spin hip hop most evenings, except for Thursdays when promoter Funky Couture turns the place over to house.

Castle
640 N Dearborn Street, at W Ohio Street (1-312 266 1944, www.excaliburchicago.com). El: Red to Grand. **Open** 5pm-4am Wed-Fri; 7pm-5am Sat. **Admission** *Wed* free. *Thur-Sat* $9-$20. **Credit** AmEx, Disc, MC, V. **Map** p310 H10.
Housed in a historic castle-like building (hence the name), this multifaceted mega-club is big enough to be many things at once: cabaret, pub, and fashion, music and high-tech hub. Late-night yuppies, suburbanites and tourists rub shoulders with trance, house and techno heads. Its sound system can rattle your cartilage, with sets from globe-trotting big names in progressive and electro, hip hop and bhangra.

Enclave
220 W Chicago Avenue, between N Wells & N Franklin Streets (1-312 654 0234, www.enclave chicago.com). El: Brown or Purple to Chicago. **Open** 10pm-2am Thur, Fri; 10pm-3am Sat. **Admission** free-$20. **Credit** AmEx, Disc, MC, V. **Map** p310 G10.
The classy loft appearance of this spacious River North club balances out the sexed-up, usually hip hop-fuelled parties at Enclave. Big-name radio DJs, celebrity appearances, platform dancers and MCs keep things lively.

Ontourage
157 W Ontario Street, between N Wells Street & N LaSalle Drive (1-312 573 1470, www.ontourage chicago.com). El: Brown or Purple to Merchandise Mart. **Open** 10pm-5am Sat. **Admission** $10-$30. **Credit** AmEx, MC, V. **Map** p310 H10.
Ontourage caters to a big-night-out crowd from the 'burbs with money to burn. The two-level club, bathed in pink and blue light, has two dancefloors, both packed to the limit for glossy hip hop and club remixes. Occasional special events spice things up.

Sound-Bar
226 W Ontario Street, at N Franklin Street (1-312 787 4480, www.sound-bar.com). El: Brown or Purple to Chicago. **Open** 10pm-4am Thur, Fri, Sun; 10pm-5am Sat. **Admission** $20. **Credit** AmEx, Disc, MC, V. **Map** p310 G10.
After opening in the early noughties, the sleek, modern Sound-Bar quickly became a prime Chicago venue in which to hear big-name DJs spinning techno and house. It's since turned to more Miami-style beats, but some of its biggest nights have been bhangra blowouts, while hip hop always dominates downstairs. Each of the three rooms, including the VIP-only round bar, features a DJ.

Spy Bar
646 N Franklin Street, at W Erie Street (1-312 337 2191, www.spybarchicago.com). El: Brown or Purple to Chicago. **Open** 10pm-4am Wed-Fri, Sun; 10pm-5am Sat. **Admission** $10-$30. **Credit** AmEx, Disc, MC, V. **Map** p310 G10.
At least once a week, the underground Spy Bar brings in headline-grabbing DJ talent with the latest in techno, progressive and house. On the whole, it's moderate on attitude and high on intimacy, but don't let the photogenic crowd intimidate you – this is one of the city's best clubs.

★ Studio Paris
2nd Floor, 59 W Hubbard Street, between Dearborn & Clark Streets (1-312 595 0800, www.parisclubchicago.com). El: Red to Grand.

INSIDE TRACK
JOIN THE INDUSTRY

Looking for an eclectic mix of people, cheap admission and cheaper drinks? Chicago insiders and savvy party people go where the pros go: industry nights. The concept – a weekly low- or no-cover party on a night when business would otherwise be slow – isn't original to Chicago, but it's on a firm footing. 'Industry' can refer to nightlife and dining staffers who don't have weekends off, but it also includes folks from the music, fashion and salon trades. DJs tend to be local and the atmosphere's usually extra-lively. To find out about industry nights, visit club websites or ask a club bartender.

ARTS & ENTERTAINMENT

Soul of the City

How to find Chicago's soul flame flickering in the shadows.

Chicago's association with the music genres that it spawned – house, electric blues, gospel – is so strong that its contribution to soul history tends to be neglected. Yet soul stars such as Sam Cooke, the Impressions and the Chi-Lites called the city home, as did the influential Brunswick label (in the 1449 S Michigan Avenue building that was formerly home to blues and R&B imprint Vee Jay). And with retro-style soul back in the charts, Chicago again has a lot for soul lovers to love, even if the scene isn't exactly groomed for music tourism – this is, after all, a city that can't seem to get a proper blues museum open.

Even before soul came back into fashion across the country as a whole, Chicago was ahead of the curve. Held at Danny's Tavern (*see p139*), **Soul Night** is the longest-running monthly soul party in Chicago. On the first Wednesday of every month, Dante Carfanga and Courtland Green spin all-original vinyl 45s of vintage soul and funk, plus a sprinkling of whatever else works on the dancefloor. Also worth a look are the **East of Edens Soul Express** DJ team, which drops the needle regularly at the Hideout (*see p220*) and also plays other sessions in town, and the **Windy City Soul Club**

(www.windycitysoulclub.com), which is a regular at the Empty Bottle (*see p219*).

Hearing live soul music is an all too rare event in Chicago, though it has been sneaking into North Side venues through the garage rock and retro funk circles. Down at **Lee's Unleaded Blues** (*see p225*), there are often fine soul singers on the bill. It's also worth keeping an eye on the line-ups at the **Chicago Blues Festival** (*see p225*), which often has soul acts in the mix.

There's more of Chicago's soul history on the radio. Tune in to **V-103** (WVAZ, 102.7 FM) on Saturday (8am-noon) and Sunday (noon-7pm) and you'll find Herb Kent (aka 'the Cool Gent'), who's been on the air since 1949. Kent's known for spinning 'love dusties', and he was mixing Motown and Stax with a call for civil rights before everyone else.

Failing all that, there's one more way to sample Chicago soul: through the stomach. While the city is often modest about its soul food offerings, **Pearls' Place** (3901 S Michigan Avenue at Pershing Road, Bronzeville, 1-773 285 1700, www.pearls placerestaurant.com) excels with incredibly juicy fried chicken, fragrant sweet-potato pie and pork-studded collard greens.

Soul Night.

Debonair Social Club. *See p212.*

Open 9pm-2am Wed-Fri; 9pm-3am Sat. **Bottle service** from $250. **Credit** AmEx, MC, Disc, V. **Map** p309 H11.

RJ and Jerrod Melman raised the bar with the opening of this nightclub above their French restaurant, Paris Club. Tables can only be secured with bottle-service reservations. Resident and guest DJs spin while roving photographers snap black-and-whites of the scene. In warm weather, a retractable roof turns the room into an open-air deck.

Sub 51

Lower Level, 51 W Hubbard Street, at N Dearborn Street (1-312 828 0051, www.sub51.com). El: Brown or Purple to Merchandise Mart; Red to Grand. **Open** 10.30pm-2am Tue; 9pm-2am Fri; 9pm-3am Sat. **Admission** prices vary. **Credit** AmEx, Disc, MC, V. **Map** p310 H11.

Sub 51 is the clubby portion of Hub 51 (*see p107*), the first dining venture from the Melman brothers, and it's about as exclusive as it gets (table reservations are essential). It's hired some of the most shameless, young, in-the-know party DJs to play upstairs and down, so the sonics are in good hands.

Underground

56 W Illinois Street, at N Dearborn Street (1-312 943 7600, www.theundergroundchicago.com). El: Red to Grand. **Open** 10pm-4am Thur, Fri, Sun; 9pm-5am Sat. **Admission** $20. **Credit** AmEx, Disc, MC, V. **Map** p310 H10.

With a military bunker theme and waitresses in form-fitting khaki, Billy Dec's below-street-level venture might seem a tad absurd. Its door policy, which often overloads the place with females, certainly can be. But it boasts the most congenial bar service and

drink pours in the neighbourhood, which, combined with star drop-ins from the pop, MTV and hip hop world, make it a major player in River North.

★ Y Bar

224 W Ontario Street, at N Franklin Street (1-312 787 2355, www.ychicago.com). El: Red to Grand. **Open** 10pm-4am Thur, Fri; 10pm-5am Sat. **Admission** $20. **Credit** AmEx, Disc, MC, V. **Map** p310 G10.

The upmarket sibling to the nearby Sound-Bar plays up the bottle service angle with luxury seating and model-like bartenders. But with the aid of a big sound system that pumps out house and hip hop, the designer-clad clientele raises the temperature.

The Gold Coast

★ Primary

5 W Division Street, at N State Street (www. primarychi.com). El: Red to Clark/Division. **Open** 10pm-4am Wed-Fri; 10pm-5am Sat. **Credit** AmEx, Disc, MC, V. **Map** p311 H8.

Between its oversized dancefloor, massive LED wall, 30ft bar and craft cocktail programme, Primary is swiftly becoming the envy of its Gold Coast neighbours. Owned by a posse of nightlife veterans with their ears to the sound of now, it's a hip alternative to clubs near the 'triangle' that have been coasting with the same formula. Look for some of the city's top up-and-coming DJs, alongside the occasional global talent, spinning house, electro, dubstep, underground disco and indie dance. What do real clubbers crave? An intimate, music-focused but stylish night out free of bullshit. This NKOTB puts it all on a top sound system.

ARTS & ENTERTAINMENT

OLD TOWN & LINCOLN PARK

Lincoln Park

Dolphin

2200 N Ashland Avenue, at Webster Avenue
(1-773 750 8090, www.dolphinchicago.com).
Bus: 9, 73. **Open** 10pm-4am Thur, Fri, Sun;
10pm-5am Sat. **Credit** AmEx, Disc, MC, V.
Map p315 C5.
After a recent revamp, one-time jazz club Green
Dolphin Street has been reimagined as this posh
Sin City hangout with multiple rooms and an opu-
lent outdoor patio complete with cabanas. DJs spin
dance music through the weekend.

MaxBar

2247 N Lincoln Avenue, between W Belden
& W Webster Avenues (1-773 549 5884, www.
maxbarchicago.com). El: Brown, Purple or Red
to Fullerton. **Open** 9pm-4am Thur; 10pm-
4am Fri; 10pm-5am Sat. **Admission** free-$5.
Credit AmEx, Disc, MC, V. **Map** p312 F5.
This entry-level club in Lincoln Park benefits from
the post-collegiate and young professional crowd
bored with bars and pubs. It looks like a classy bar
up front, but the back room has a Miami hot-spot
vibe, with DJs spinning surefire hip hop party music
to fun-loving youngsters. You can't hear or see the
clubbing from the well-designed front bar, leaving
you free to enjoy your gin and tonic in peace.

Neo

2350 N Clark Street, bwtween W Fullerton
& W Belden Avenues (1-773 528 2622). El:
Brown, Purple or Red to Fullerton. **Open** 10pm-
4am Wed-Fri, Sun; 10pm-5am Sat. **Admission**
free-$5. **No credit cards**. **Map** p312 G5.
Break out the ten-hole Doc Martens and the hair
products for this goth-punk outpost that hasn't
changed much since, well, before you were born. Neo
has a small dancefloor and a calendar crammed with
DJs specialising in everything from metal and industrial to new wave and electro.

LAKEVIEW & AROUND

For reviews of gay nightclubs in **Boystown**,
see p204.

Berlin

954 W Belmont Avenue, at N Sheffield Avenue
(1-773 348 4975, www.berlinchicago.com).
El: Brown, Purple or Red to Belmont. 10pm-
4am Tue; 5pm-4am Wed-Fri, Sun; 5pm-5am
Sat. **Admission** free-$5. **No credit cards**.
Map p313 E2.
This freak-friendly dance destination in Lakeview
built its reputation back in the mid 1980s with a
heady mix of German new-wave music, art installations and even transvestite shows. These days,
it's still quirky but more retro, with Prince tribute,
disco and '80s nostalgia nights. Goths and gays
are extra welcome, but the scene here is made up of
almost everyone.

★ Smart Bar

3730 N Clark Street, between W Waveland
& W Racine Avenues (1-773 549 0203, www.
smartbarchicago.com). El: Red to Addison.
Open 10pm-4am Wed-Fri, Sun; 10pm-5am Sat.
Admission free-$20. **Credit** AmEx, MC, V.
Map p313 E1.
Cutting-edge DJs from Europe, Detroit and Chicago
form the bulk of the house, techno, nu disco, dubstep
and electro bookings, but local mash-up, industrial
and indie jocks rule on bargain weeknights.
► *Smart Bar is twinned with Metro; see p220.*

THE NEAR WEST SIDE

The West Loop

★ Funky Buddha Lounge

728 W Grand Avenue, at N Halsted Street
(1-312 666 1695, www.funkybuddha.com).
El: Blue to Grand. **Open** 10pm-2am Wed;
9pm-2am Fri, 9pm-3am Sat. **Admission**
$10-$20. **Credit** Disc, MC, V. **Map** p310 F10.
The vivid colours and exotic look of this cosy establishment have weathered to ridiculous kitsch, but
the spirit at this venerable venue is strong.
Weekends are jammed with crunkers, sitters and
sippers. Mid-week, Top 40 hip-hoppers and underground R&B divas sometimes drop in for live sets.

★ Lumen

839 W Fulton Market Street, between N Green
Street & N Peoria Street (1-312 733 2222,
www.lumen-chicago.com). El: Green or Pink to
Clinton. **Open** 10pm-2am Thur, Fri; 10pm-3am
Sat. **Admission** $10-$20. **Credit** AmEx, Disc,
MC, V. **Map** p314 F11.
The emphasis is on space at this after-work lounge
that turns clubby later. An interesting LED lighting
fixture captures the theme, while some of Chicago's
harder-hustling disco and electro DJs man the booth.

★ Mid

306 N Halsted Street, at Wayman Street (1-312
265 3990, www.themidchicago.com). El: Green,
Pink to Clinton. **Open** 10pm-4am Thur, Fri;
10pm-5am Sat. **Admission** prices vary.
Credit AmEx, Disc, MC, V. **Map** p310 F11.
Launched by some of Chicago's biggest promoters,
this Fulton Market area upstart has taken just a few
years to rise to the top. It now nabs many of the big-
name bookings swinging through town – which can
mean huge queues to get in. Two levels allow for
dancing and drinking on weekends, but on other
nights the main floor showcases everything from
indie bands to up-and-coming DJs.

Sketching Out Your Week

Our night-by-night guide to Chicago comedy.

With dozens of sketch comedy troupes appearing on stages all over town each week, it's nearly impossible to figure out which shows are worth seeing, especially since so many are here today and gone tomorrow. But some shows have garnered enough belly laughs to become permanent fixtures on the scene. Here are our picks.

On Monday, many theatres go dark, but the long-running **Armando Diaz Experience** at iO Chicago (*see p213*) sheds a little light on the city's scene. Each week, a single monologist recalls stories from his or her childhood based on an audience suggestion, while improvisers create scenes around these monologues to mesmerising effect.

On Tuesday, you can choose between **Chicagoland** at the Annoyance (*see p213*) or **Cook County Social Club** at iO (*see p213*). The former features a handful of the city's veteran improvisers; and the boys at Cook County aren't afraid to rock the boat with bold on-stage moves and untraditional scenic transitions.

When Wednesday rolls around, don't miss **TJ & Dave** at iO (*see p213*). Master improvisers TJ Jagodowski and David Pasquesi perfect the art of long-form improvisation in what many regard as the best show in town. Wednesday also offers a night of social-political satire on the **Second City Main Stage** (*see p215*), attended mostly by locals.

Devote your Thursday night to **Messing with a Friend** at the Annoyance (*see p213*). In this two-person show, Susan Messing invites a different improviser to perform a set with her each week. Messing's limitless bag of characters is reminiscent of a more disciplined Amy Sedaris; it's exciting – and rare – to see a show in which a female improviser dominates.

Hit the Apollo Theater (2540 N Lincoln Avenue, at Lill Avenue, Lincoln Park, 1-773 935 6100, www.apollochicago.com) on Fridays for the fully improvised musical **Baby Wants Candy**. Improvisers perform a full-length musical (no joke) and results are often hugely impressive. Alternatively, hit the Chemically Imbalanced Theater (1422 W Irving Park, between N Janssen & N Southport Avenues, Wrigleyville, 1-773 865 7731, www.cicomedy.com) for **Pimprov**, improv with a gigolo twist.

The best improv on Saturday is **Whirled News Tonight** at iO (*see p213*): top-notch improvisers perform intelligent scenes based on news clippings ripped straight out of daily newspapers. If you're travelling with youngsters, the family-friendly comedy at the **ComedySportz** (*see p213*) includes early shows on Saturday night.

Save some comic appetite for the Sabbath. **Your Sunday's Best** at Schubas (*see p222*), ordinarily a music venue, is a fast-paced open-mic night frequented mostly by local stand-ups. Some are mediocre but others are amazing.

iO.

ARTS & ENTERTAINMENT

Rednofive
*440 N Halsted Street, at W Hubbard Street
(1-312 421 1239, www.rednofive.com). El: Blue
to Grand.* **Open** 10pm-2am Fri; 10pm-3am Sat.
Admission $10-$30. **Credit** AmEx, Disc,
MC, V. **Map** p310/p314 F11.
A decade ago, this joint was raver HQ, but it's since
been transformed several times over. It features an
old world luxury feel, stunning bartenders and a
glamorous, bottle service-loving crowd. Upstairs,
DJs accompanied by live percussion and tantalising
platformed dancers create a seductive if familiar
playlist of hip hop grinders.

WICKER PARK & AROUND
Ukrainian Village

Every boho's favourite DJ bar, **Danny's
Tavern** (*see p139*) has been kicking it since
the grunge era with little sign of losing its cool.

Beauty Bar
*1444 W Chicago Ave, between Greenview
Avenue & Bishop Street (1-312 226 8828,
www.thebeautybar.com). El: Blue to Chicago.*
Open 5pm-2am Mon-Fri, Sun; 5pm-3am Sat.
Admission prices vary. **Credit** AmEx, Disc,
MC, V. **Map** p315 D9.
It already has outposts in New York, San Francisco,
Austin and Portland, so Chicago seemed like the

Lincoln Lodge. *See p215.*

next logical location for the kitsch-happy Beauty Bar
concept. Retrofitted into the old Sonotheque space,
the bar carried over the sound system but otherwise
got a complete facelift. Sparkling glitter paint adorns
the walls, 1960s beauty salon furniture acts as seating, and the back-room dancefloor is completed with
a shimmering disco ball. The music stays obscure
and mostly dusty during the week, but DJs turn it
into an electro dance party most weekends.

Wicker Park & Bucktown

★ Debonair Social Club
*1575 N Milwaukee Avenue, at W North Avenue
(1-773 227 7990, www.debonairsocialclub.com).
El: Blue to Damen.* **Open** 9pm-2am Wed-Sat;
9pm-3am Sat. **Admission** free-$5. **Credit**
AmEx, MC, V. **Map** p315 B7.
Debonair combines star-quality bookings (Tommie
Sunshine and Steve Aoki among them) with dark,
modern design. Video art screens on an upstairs
wall; downstairs comes with an illicit red-light
district vibe, as DJs play electro, rock and club hits
to frisky hipsters making out on the dancefloor.
It's usually jam packed with young folks sporting
magazine-ready looks. *Photo p209.*

Evil Olive
*1551 W Division Street, at N Ashland Avenue
(1-773 235 9100, www.evil-olive.com). El: Blue
to Division.* **Open** 10pm-4am Mon, Fri; 11pm-4am
Wed-Thur; 10pm-5am Sat. **Admission** free-$20.
Credit AmEx, Disc, MC, V. **Map** p315 D8.

Laugh Factory. *See p215.*

This spot may have changed names more than any other venue in the 'hood, but it's become an unlikely young hipster hangout thanks to long-standing weekend dance parties hosted by local jocks Zebo, Marco Morales, Johnny Walker, and the Porn and Chicken posse. It's making serious inroads into weekdays as well thanks to the over-the-top exploits of Monday throwdown Porn and Chicken and Thursday's Let's Get Weird. No one really loves the Evil Olive space, but through sheer force of party will and audacity (and porn, and fried chicken) it's the joint.

THE SOUTH SIDE

The Shrine
2109 S Wabash Avenue, between 21st Street & Cermak Road (1-312 753 5700, www.theshrine chicago.com). El: Red to Cermak/Chinatown. **Open** 7pm-2am Tue; 9pm-2am Wed-Fri, Sun; 9pm-3am Sat. **Admission** prices vary. **Credit** AmEx, Disc, MC, V. **Map** p308 H16.
Channelling the spirit of the late, great Fela Kuti, this South Loop nightspot serves as an ideal place of worship for musicheads and lovers of everything from house to hip hop and soul to Afrobeat. It houses two DJ booths, a live stage, and cosy seating for those who trade in dancefloor exploits for bottle-service boozing. Joe Russo's vision of a DJ-driven club with an Afrocentric vibe has blossomed. It's also a legit venue for touring rap and funk acts.

Comedy

Improv is performed most visibly at the **Annoyance Theatre**, **Gorilla Tango Theater**, **Playground Theater** and **ComedySportz**, while local and touring stand-up comics are in the spotlight at **Zanies**, the **Lincoln Lodge**, **Jokes & Notes**, **UP** and the **Laugh Factory**, plus many local taprooms around town.

Tickets can be bought directly from theatre box offices. Some improv troupes don't perform in a set location; check listings for details of their movements.

COMEDY VENUES

★ Annoyance Theatre & Bar
Annoyance Theatre, 851 W Belmont Avenue, at N Clark Street, Lakeview (1-773 561 4665, www.annoyanceproductions.com). El: Red to Belmont. **Shows** 8pm, 9.30pm Tue, Wed, Sun; 8pm, 9pm, 10.30pm Thur; 8pm, 10pm, midnight Fri, Sat. **Tickets** $5-$20. **Credit** Disc, MC, V. **Map** p313 F3.
The ever-irreverent Annoyance sits alone on a particular echelon of respectability in Chicago's comedy scene, mostly because performers love to curse and offend (the theatre rose to fame with a musical

entitled *Co-ed Prison Sluts*). However, the shows are better than that description might indicate: behind the in-your-face bombast lies some of the city's best improv and sketch comedy writing. Mick Napier, one of the founders, is held up as something of a comedy guru. As such, the shows he directs are often the most reliable, although Susan Messing's *Messing with a Friend* is not to be missed.

ComedySportz of Chicago
929 W Belmont Avenue, between N Clark Street & N Sheffield Avenue, Lakeview (1-773 549 8080, www.comedysportzchicago.com). El: Brown, Purple or Red to Belmont. **Shows** 8pm Thur; 8pm, 10pm Fri; 6pm, 8pm, 10pm Sat. **Tickets** $22. **Credit** AmEx, Disc, MC, V. **Map** p313 E2.
ComedySportz is the Starbucks of its field, though it's no surprise that Chicago hosts one of its stronger franchises. The schtick is simple: two teams battle each other at improv games, complete with a scoreboard. The performers are generally talented, but the place is aimed more at providing PG-rated fun for the masses than pushing the boundaries. That said, the filth is allowed to fly every now and then, especially at late-night shows such as 'The Hot Karl'.

Gorilla Tango Theater
1919 N Milwaukee Avenue, at N Western Avenue, Bucktown (1-773 598 4549, www.gorillatango. com). El: Blue to Western. **Shows** 7.30pm, 9pm Mon-Thur; 7.30pm, 9pm, 10.30pm, midnight Fri, Sat; 2pm, 4pm, 6pm, 8pm Sun (schedule subject to change, check website). **Tickets** $10-$35. **Credit** AmEx, Disc, MC, V. **Map** p315 A6.
A little like the Lakeview's Playground Theater (*see p215*), Gorilla Tango is the place to see high-energy youngsters eagerly making their mark (and making it big). There's a lot of untrained talent running around, but occasionally a bunch of up-and-comers break away from the pack with genuinely solid improv and sketch material. Two to three troupes perform a night.

★ iO Chicago
3541 N Clark Street, at W Addison Street, Wrigleyville (1-773 880 0199, www.ioimprov.com).

> ## INSIDE TRACK
> ## GOING UNDERGROUND
>
> One of the best places in town to uncover up-and-coming local comics is actually a music venue: the **Beat Kitchen** (*see p218*). The intimate Lakeview joint majors in music but gives over Tuesdays to Chicago Underground Comedy (www. chicagoundergroundcomedy.com), a cheap-ass smörgåsbord of rising-star joke-throwers that always entertains.

The E-Town Shuffle

Musical youths, vinyl vaults and jazzers make Evanston worth the trip.

Threaded by the Purple Line, on the northern tip of the CTA, and a quick 20-minute ride up Metra's Union Pacific North line, Evanston is Chicago's nearest lakeside suburb. Though home to Northwestern University, the city hardly fits the notion of a college town. Prohibition laws kept the town dry up until the late 1970s, which explains the proliferation of liquor stores just over the Chicago border in neighbouring Rogers Park. Fret not, however, as the taps now flow with copious suds and the condensed, quaint downtown area offers a surprisingly well-rounded musical microscene.

Just off the CTA Dempster stop, **2nd Hand Tunes** (800 Dempster Street, at Sherman Avenue, 1-847 491 1690, www.2ndhandtunes.com) has been a purveyor of used vinyl for decades. There's often a whiff of garage sale about the titles on hand, but it's a great place to rediscover that album you regretfully lent to an ex. And, despite the name, the store stocks new releases on wax. A block down the street, a gutted old car dealership

holds **SPACE** (1245 Chicago Avenue, at Dempster Street, 1-847 492 8860, www.evanstonspace.com). Sleek, modern and attached to a joint selling delicious wood-fired pizzas, the club books a wide range of bigger acts, as well as some hip indie gigs with the help of student radio station WNUR.

A quick jog north gets you to the heart of the city, just off the CTA and Metra Davis stations. Before settling on to a bar stool, pop into **Vintage Vinyl** (*see p164* **Long Play**) to peruse the killer assortment of immaculately kept LPs and 45s. A fraction of its collection of classic rock, new wave, psych and mod LPs is kept in the tidy front room. If you can't find that Stones bootleg you need, just ask; it's probably out back.

Nearby, **Pete Miller's** (1557 Sherman Avenue, at Grove Street, 1-847 328 0399, www.petemillers.com) serves up steaks – and equally sizzlin' jazz – from Tuesday to Saturday. Acts range from the jumping ragtime of the Joel Paterson Trio to Green Mill regulars Deep Blue Organ Trio. There's no cover charge.

El: Red to Addison. **Shows** times vary. **Tickets** free-$14. **Credit** Disc, MC, V. **Map** p313 E1.

The most respected Chicago venue for hardcore improv (alumni include Andy Richter, Tim Meadows and founder Charna Halpern), iO Chicago takes as its house speciality a long-form style called the Harold. Created by Del Close, it features improvising teams creating fluid acts that loosely revolve around a single audience suggestion. However, it's just one of numerous shows at this two-space venue, busy every night with a young, party-hearty crowd. The name? It was formerly called the ImprovOlympic, but the International Olympic Committee felt violated.

Jokes & Notes

4641 S King Drive, at E 46th Place, Bronzeville (1-773 373 3390, www.jokesandnotes.com). El: Green to 47th Street. **Shows** 8.30pm Wed; 8.30pm, 10.30pm Thur-Sat (check website for Sun). **Tickets** $5-$20 (2-drink min). **Credit** MC, V.

In the 1940s, Bronzeville was the centre of Chicago's black culture, a hotbed of jazz musicians, writers and others of an artistic bent. Six decades later, Jokes & Notes is helping to return the neighbourhood to the primacy of its glory days by putting African-American comics front and centre. National acts swing through all the time, but owner Mary Lindsey honours hometown talent by offering top billing to local joke-makers.

★ Laugh Factory

3175 N Broadway Street, at W Belmont Avenue, Lakeview (1 773 327 3175, www.laughfactory. com). El: Brown, Purple, Red to Belmont. **Shows** 8pm Wed, Thur, Sun; 8pm, 10pm Fri, Sat. **Tickets** from $20. **Credit** MC, V. **Map** p313 F3.

The LA-based chain has been around since the late 1970s, but opened its Chicago outpost only in the last few years. The stakes are high, considering the Laugh Factory's history and longstanding reputation as one of the best comedy clubs in the country, and considering that it moved into the nearly 400-seat Lakeview Theater only after a multi-million dollar renovation, hopes are high too. Performers vary from week to week and include crowd-drawing headliners and weekly open mic nights. *Photo p212.*

★ Lincoln Lodge

4008 N Lincoln Avenue, at W Irving Park Avenue, Lincoln Square (1-773 251 1539, www. thelincolnlodge.com). El: Brown to Irving Park. **Shows** 9pm Fri (check website for other shows). **Tickets** $10. **Credit** Disc, MC, V. **Map** p314 B0.

Perhaps *the* place to see locally grown stand-up comedy, Lincoln Lodge has gained a cult following. Shows routinely sell out (reservations can be made in advance, but are only guaranteed until 8.45pm), and comedians are encouraged to perform their edgiest material. Located in the back of the Lincoln Restaurant, the room itself feels like a second-tier

supper club, complete with old-time waitresses who call you 'honey'. Performers vary week to week, but you're guaranteed a few good sets. *Photo p212.*

Playground Theater

3209 N Halsted Street, at W Belmont Avenue, Lakeview (1-773 871 3793, www.the-playground. com). El: Brown, Purple or Red to Belmont. **Shows** times vary. **Tickets** free-$15. **Credit** Disc, MC, V. **Map** p313 F3.

This improv specialist features plenty of nascent troupes and even hosts something called the Incubator, where lonely improvisers pay a small fee to meet each other. Purely in terms of entertainment, it's a little hit-and-miss. That said, on a typical night you can catch three or four different troupes each performing 30-minute long-form acts, one of which is bound to be funny. There are usually two shows each night.

★ Second City

1616 N Wells Street, at W North Avenue, Old Town (1-312 337 3992, www.secondcity. com). El: Brown or Purple to Sedgwick. **Shows** *Main stage* 8pm Tue-Thur; 8pm, 11pm Fri, Sat; 7pm Sun. *Etc stage* 8pm Thur; 8pm, 11pm Fri, Sat; 7pm Sun. *Donny's Skybox* times vary. **Tickets** *Main stage & Etc stage* $12-$25. *Donny's Skybox* $6-$16. **Credit** AmEx, Disc, MC, V. **Map** p311 G7.

The grandaddy of all comedy theatres and a temple of social-political satire, Second City is the brand name for funny business. Founded in 1959, it's a well-polished machine and a top tourist attraction. The city's top improvisers perform here, waiting to be snatched away by *Saturday Night Live* or *Mad TV*, but the humour is still cutting-edge. A different and often gutsier revue plays on the Etc stage, with Donny's Skybox given over to student shows. Get there early on weekends or book ahead, as most shows sell out.

▶ *Mere steps away, the Old Town Ale House (see p133) has hosted countless Second City comics. Portraits of many alumni line the walls; you might find their successors at the bar post-show.*

UP Comedy Club

230 W North Avenue, at N Wells Street, Old Town (1-312 662 4562, www.upcomedyclub. com). El: Brown or Purple to Sedgwick. **Shows** 8pm Mon, Wed; 8pm, 10.30pm Fri; 4pm, 8pm, 10.30pm Sat; 4pm, 7pm Sun. **Tickets** $15-$30. **Credit** AmEx, Disc, MC, V. **Map** p311 G7.

Located in the former digs of the long-standing *Tony 'n' Tina's Wedding*, this cabaret-style 285-seater venue has no obstructed sightlines (a significant feat in a city full of wonky storefront theatres), and it's also a Second City production. The calendar features seven nights a week of stand-up comedy improv and full-length shows. Dinner reservations come with preferred seating for the show.

ARTS & ENTERTAINMENT

Jay Pritzker Pavilion

Zanies

1548 N Wells Street, at W North Avenue, Old Town (1-312 337 4027, www.zanies.com). El: Brown or Purple to Sedgwick. **Shows** 8.30pm Mon-Thur, Sun; 8.30pm, 10.30pm Fri; 7pm, 9pm, 11.15pm Sat. **Tickets** $20-$25 (2-drink min). **Credit** MC, V. **Map** p311 G7.

Imagine a stand-up room and Zanies is what springs to mind – 'old school' suitably describes this local institution. Still, this oldie's still a goodie, booking a mix of established local comics and touring giants.

Music
ROCK, POP & ROOTS

These days, 2120 S Michigan Avenue, the former home of Chess Records, houses nothing more than a memorial and gift shop (*see p51*).

INSIDE TRACK
COVER TO COVER

Take an album-cover tour of the city. Riverside complex Marina City graced the cover of *Yankee Hotel Foxtrot*, the revered 2002 album from local brainy roots rockers **Wilco**, having earlier cropped up on the sleeve of the **Revolting Cocks**' *Big Sexy Land*. The Art Institute (*see p36*) houses a couple of Gerhard Richter's candle paintings, made famous by **Sonic Youth** on *Daydream Nation*, while the Museum of Contemporary Art (*see p57*) holds water stills from photographer Hiroshi Sugimoto (**U2**'s *No Line on the Horizon*) and an ink work from Raymond Pettibon, designer of **Black Flag**'s logo and **Sonic Youth**'s *Goo* album.

The same brand of harmonica-fuelled electric shuffle that kick-started rock 'n' roll continues to thrive in countless clubs around town – but the latter-day rock scene is even more vital.

The 1980s saw the emergence from the city of such disparate styles as industrial metal (courtesy of Ministry and the Wax Trax label), and house (which takes its name from the now-defunct Warehouse club), while the 1990s spawned post-rock and an insurgent country scene that continues to thrive under the banner of Bloodshot Records.

At the other end of the spectrum, Kanye West and Common gave local hip hop international currency, while a new wave of MCs, like Kid Sister and the Cool Kids, are donning '80s threads and splashing Day-Glo paint on a scene that continues to evolve.

Information & tickets

For reviews and listings of the latest concerts and events, see www.timeout.com/chicago.

In giant venues such as the Allstate Arena and the United Center, shows keep regular hours, starting around 7.30pm and wrapping up by 10.30pm. The smaller clubs, up to the size of Metro or even House of Blues, run later: gigs start about 9pm and finish between midnight and 1am, with everything an hour later on Fridays and Saturdays. Shows not designated 'all-ages' are only open to those over the age of 21. Always carry a photo ID.

Tickets for many club shows are available at the door. Tickets for bigger bands are sold in advance, either through the venue or via an agency such as **Ticketmaster** (1-312 902 1500, www.ticketmaster.com), while smaller clubs such as the Bottom Lounge and Empty Bottle peddle admission through **Ticketweb** (www.ticketweb.com). Abbey Pub uses TicketFly.Com.

Major arenas & stadiums

In addition to the venues listed below, several major sporting venues host occasional rock and pop gigs. **Soldier Field** (*see p242*), home of the Chicago Bears, welcomes the likes of the Rolling Stones or Fall Out Boy when it's not too cold, while the University of Illinois at Chicago's **UIC Pavilion** (525 S Racine Avenue, at W Congress Parkway, West Loop, 1-312 413 5700, www.uicpavilion.com) occasionally stages big-name indie acts when not holding home games for its fightin' Flames. On the South Side, the Chicago Fire's **Toyota Park** (*see p243*) also presents large-scale gigs, while the **Sears Centre** (www.searscentre.com) draws middle-aged arena-fillers and country superstars to the north-west suburbs. Multi-band summer extravaganzas such as Warped Tour and jam bands often roll into the **First Midwest Bank Amphitheatre** (19100 S Ridgeland Avenue, at Flossmoor Road, 1-708 614 1616, www.livenation.com) in Tinley Park.

Other outdoor venues include **Charter One Pavilion at Northerly Island** (1300 S Lynn White Drive, 1-312 540 2000, www.livenation.com), which hosts a handful of concerts, and the **Skyline Stage at Navy Pier** (www.navypier.com). The **Jay Pritzker**

INSIDE TRACK
RAINBO COALITION

The cheap suds at the **Rainbo Club** (*see p139*) have drawn starving artists for decades. Liz Phair shot the cover of her seminal album *Exile in Guyville* inside the bar's infamous photobooth. Sidle up to the bar, next to one of Chicago's indie rock heroes... or get served by one.

Pavilion in Millennium Park (*see p35*) and the **Petrillo Music Shell** in Grant Park stage free shows in summer, and the **Ravinia Festival** (*see p231*) supplements its classical line-up with pop and jazz shows.

Allstate Arena

6920 Mannheim Road, Rosemont (1-847 635 6601, www.allstatearena.com). El: Blue to Rosemont, then Pace bus 223 or 250. **Box office** 11am-7pm Mon-Fri; noon-5pm Sat. **Tickets** prices vary. **Credit** AmEx, Disc, MC, V. The venue known to many longtime locals as the Rosemont Horizon attracts mainstream star power, from Queen to Justin Timberlake, as well as Latin, country and world music acts.

Ravinia Festival.

ARTS & ENTERTAINMENT

Bottom Lounge.

ARTS & ENTERTAINMENT

United Center

1901 W Madison Street, between S Damon Avenue & S Wood Street, West Loop (1-312 455 4500, www.unitedcenter.com). El: Green or Pink to Ashland-Lake. **Tickets** prices vary. **Credit** AmEx, Disc, MC, V. **Map** p314 C12.
When the city's NBA and NHL franchises hit the road, this comfortable cavern lures the likes of Madonna, U2 and Jay-Z. The upper tier is so steep that even the cheap seats offer decent views.

Rock, pop & roots venues

Several major theatres stage gigs, among them the **Chicago Theatre** (175 N State Street, at W Lake Street, the Loop, 1-312 462 6300, www.thechicagotheatre.com), the **Auditorium Theatre** (50 E Congress Parkway, at S Wabash Avenue, the Loop, 1-312 341 2310, www.auditoriumtheatre.org) and the more casual **Vic Theatre** (*see p194*). There are also art-rock and laptop shows at the **Museum of Contemporary Art** (*see p57*) and free gigs at the **Chicago Cultural Center** (*see p229*).

Abbey Pub

3420 W Grace Avenue, at N Elston Avenue, Avondale (1-773 478 4408, www.abbeypub.com). El: Blue to Addision. **Tickets** free-$25. **Credit** AmEx, Disc, MC, V.

There are two sides, literally, to this spot on the city's Northwest Side. One is a small Irish pub that hosts energetic folk and traditional performances most nights, while the other is one of the city's premier venues for independent hip hop. Indie rock and electro pop acts also stop by.

Aragon Ballroom

1106 W Lawrence Avenue, at N Winthrop Avenue, Uptown (1-773 561 9500, www.aragon. com). El: Red to Lawrence. **Tickets** $30-$50. **Credit** AmEx, MC, V.
This beautiful, ornate and capacious space opened as a ballroom in 1926. These days, though, it serves as one of the biggest music venues within the city limits. The 4,500-capacity room hosts acts such as Morrissey and Beck, as well as Spanish-language gigs.

★ Beat Kitchen

2100 W Belmont Avenue, at N Hoyne Avenue, Lakeview (1-773 281 4444, www.beatkitchen. com). Bus 50, 77. **Tickets** $5-$20. **Credit** AmEx, MC, V.
This tidy little corner bar in the north of the city has hosted innumerable debut shows, many of them of the punk, garage and power-pop variety. However, it also stages gigs from more well-known acts such as a residency from bubblegrunge heroes Local H.
▶ *Beat Kitchen also hosts Chicago Underground Comedy on Tuesday nights; see p213.*

Bottom Lounge

1375 W Lake Street, at N Loomis Street, West Loop (1-312 666 6775, www.bottomlounge.com). El: Green or Pink to Ashland. **Tickets** $5-$30. **Credit** AmEx, Disc, MC, V. **Map** p314 D11.

Forced to relocate from its old train-side home due to mass transit expansion, the Bottom Lounge has risen again as a swank two-storey club, with a killer sound system and some of the most consistently solid rock 'n' roll bills in town. Everyone from local chicano kraut-popper Allá to blog-buzzing hypes such as Glasvegas have played here, helping the venue give Metro (*see p220*) competition for the city's top rock spot. A tiki bar slings rum upstairs, with an immense patio overlooking the skyline.
▶ *The alcoholic side of the operation is run by Mike Miller of rock 'n' roll bar Delilah's; see p134.*

Congress Theater

2135 N Milwaukee Avenue, between W Maplewood Avenue & W Rockwell Street, Humboldt Park (1-773 360 8162, www.congresschicago.com). El: Blue to Western. **Tickets** $20-$50. **Credit** AmEx, Disc, MC, V.

This sizeable, slightly oddball venue hosts a diverse range of shows, with everyone from mainstream alt-rockers to nationally known Latino groups and even hip hop and techno acts.

Empty Bottle.

INSIDE TRACK
EMPTY, NEVER FULL

The **Empty Bottle** (*see below*) never truly sells out before showtime. If a listing says 'sold out' online, get to the gig before the doors open and, nine times out of ten, they'll let you in.

Double Door

1572 N Milwaukee Avenue, at N Damen Avenue, Wicker Park (1-773 489 3160, www.doubledoor. com). El: Blue to Damen. **Tickets** $5-$20. **Credit** AmEx, Disc, MC, V. **Map** p315 B7.

Located in the heart of the nightlife action in Wicker Park, the Double Door is essentially the little brother to the Metro (*see p220*). Many older local bands play here, leaning towards the tattooed set, alongside turns from touring groups. With a pool room downstairs and a small cocktail balcony, the venue offers respite from noisome opening acts.

Elbo Room

2871 N Lincoln Avenue, between W George Street & W Diversey Parkway, Lakeview (1-773 549 5549, www.elboroomchicago.com). El: Brown or Purple to Diversey. **Tickets** $5-$10. **Credit** AmEx, Disc, MC, V. **Map** p313 D3.

The music may be played in the basement, but don't mistake the Elbo Room for a dive. With a rotating roster of usually undiscovered rock bands, and comfortable eye-level sightlines, there might not be a better place to find out that the homegrown alt-rock scene offers some low-key appeal.

★ Empty Bottle

1035 N Western Avenue, at W Cortez Street, Wicker Park (1-773 276 3600, www.empty bottle.com). Bus 49, 70. **Tickets** free-$20. **Credit** AmEx, Disc, MC, V. **Map** p315 A8.

Don't be fooled by its unassuming storefront: this is Chicago's premier indie rock club, hosting cutting-edge bands from home and abroad. If you need to get away from the noise for a while, the club has a comfortable front room, complete with a pool table and a friendly cat curled up on the couch. *See also above* **Inside Track**.

FitzGerald's

6615 W Roosevelt Road, at East Avenue, Berwyn (1-708 788 2118, www.fitzgeraldsnightclub.com). El: Blue to Oak Park. **Tickets** free-$25. **Credit** AmEx, Disc, MC, V.

Perhaps Chicago's premier roots music showcase, this homey haunt out in Berwyn – it's about 20 minutes from the Loop on the Blue line – features an array of zydeco, country, rockabilly and blues acts, alongside occasional big-band jazz of the deeply nostalgic variety. All-acoustic country bands

ARTS & ENTERTAINMENT

perform in a side bar. Good food comes courtesy of barbecue specialists Wishbone; it can deliver your dishes to the venue from its stand next door.

Heartland Café
7000 N Glenwood Avenue, at W Lunt Avenue, Rogers Park (1-773 465 8005, www.heartland cafe.com). El: Red to Morse. **Tickets** free-$5. **Credit** Disc, MC, V.
This Rogers Park restaurant offers acoustic entertainment of a country/folk bent. Local regulars the Long Gone Lonesome Boys are typical of the kind of thing you can expect, though the venue also features a weekly open-mic poetry and music night on Wednesdays, as well as a Saturday radio show broadcast on WLUW 88.7 FM.
▶ *Adjacent to the venue (and sharing the same fantastic kitchen), the Red Line Tap (1-773 274 5463) books small-time but usually endearing rock, folk, country and punk bands.*

★ Hideout
1354 W Wabansia Avenue, between Elston Avenue & Throop Street, Wicker Park (1-773 227 4433, www.hideoutchicago.com). Bus 72. **Tickets** free-$10. **Credit** AmEx, Disc, MC, V.
Appropriately named (it's tucked away in an industrial corridor), the Hideout serves as both an unpretentious, friendly local bar and a don't-miss roots venue. Some of the city's best alt-country acts got their start in the backroom, which also plays host to rock groups, readings and other non-music events. Its block party is always a blast. *Photo p222.*

House of Blues
329 N Dearborn Street, at W Kinzie Street, River North (1-312 923 2000, www.hob.com). El: Red to Grand. **Tickets** $10-$60. **Credit** Disc, MC, V. **Map** p310 H11.
Presenting some of the best national and international touring acts through one of the city's finest sound systems, the Chicago edition of this chain is especially beautiful (check out the lush bathrooms). Purists scorn the place, but any venue that runs the gamut from gospel to Katy Perry to Hanson must have something going for it. The majority of bands on the smaller Back Porch stage are blues acts, playing in a well-lit setting meant to look like a juke joint but actually resembling a modern art museum. Every Sunday, the venue hosts a Gospel Brunch.

Lincoln Hall
2424 N Lincoln Avenue, between W Fullerton Avenue & W Montana Street, Lincoln Park (1-773 525 2508, www.lincolnhallchicago.com). El: Brown, Purple or Red to Fullerton. **Tickets** $5-$60. **Credit** AmEx, Disc, MC, V. **Map** p312 F5.
If you've ever forgotten to go into a show at Schubas (*see p222*) because of how immensely comfortable the front bar is, you might want to consider tying a string around your finger at the Schuba brothers'

newer venue. The design is sleeker and more modern than its Lakeview sibling, but the fresh-ground burgers and big booths are just as inviting. Acts range from a night with columnist Dan Savage to shows by national touring acts and local darlings.

Logan Square Auditorium
2539 N Kedzie Boulevard, at W Albany Avenue, Logan Square (1-773 252 6179, www.logansquare auditorium.com). El: Blue to Logan Square. **Tickets** $10-$30. **No credit cards.**
This all-ages, 750-capacity Logan Square spot resembles nothing so much as a high-school gym – it's no wonder local radio station WLUW hosts its annual indie rock prom here. The acoustics leave much to be desired, but some of the gigs (many booked by the team at the Empty Bottle; *see p219*) really are can't-miss.

Martyrs'
3855 N Lincoln Avenue, at W Berenice Avenue, Lakeview (1-773 404 9494, www.martyrslive.com). El: Brown to Irving Park. **Tickets** free-$30. **Credit** Disc, MC, V.
This plain, mid-sized space has hosted big names such as Wilco and Bernie Worrell in the past, but in recent years has exposed Chicago to a welter of jazz-fusion, world music and jam acts. On first Thursdays, it stages the Big C Jamboree, Chicago's only all-rockabilly showcase and open mic night.

Metro
3730 N Clark Street, between W Waveland & W Racine Avenues, Lakeview (1-773 549 4140, www.metrochicago.com). El: Red to Addison. **Tickets** $5-$35. **Credit** AmEx, MC, V. **Map** p313 E1.
This two-level room, one of the city's older and more famous clubs, hosts a variety of mid-sized touring acts of all genres, from metal and mainstream indie to emo and electronica; mascara-wearing band members are likely to draw screaming teens. It's also known for hosting larger showcases of local bands, especially budding one-hit-wonders from the suburbs.
▶ *Downstairs, you'll find excellent DJs at the Smart Bar; see p210.*

★ Old Town School of Folk Music
4544 N Lincoln Avenue, between W Sunnyside & W Wilson Avenues, Ravenswood (1-773 728 6000, www.oldtownschool.org). El: Brown to Western. **Tickets** $10-$50. **Credit** AmEx, Disc, MC, V.
There are some shows at the Old Town School's Old Town location (909 W Armitage Avenue). However, the bigger concerts staged by this loveable local institution, featuring folk, blues, country and world music acts, are held up in the roomier Ravenswood space. Take in everything from Senegalese hip hop to Tropicalia for little to no cost on World Music Wednesdays, and don't miss the annual Old Town

Essential Chicago Albums

The perfect Second City soundtrack.

THE COLLEGE DROPOUT
KANYE WEST (2004)

Recorded over the course of four years, the Oak Lawn native's debut album showcased his tremendous promise as a soulful and dedicated hip hop artist. He'd already made a name for himself as a producer, but *Dropout* went multi-platinum and has sold more than three million copies.

YANKEE HOTEL
FOXTROT
WILCO (2002)

Chicago-based alt-rock band Wilco's fourth album was completed in 2001 and streamed live for free on their site before it was officially released for sale in 2002. It also secured a spot on *Rolling Stone*'s 500 Greatest Albums of All Time list in 2012.

THE CHESS BOX
MUDDY WATERS
(1989)

This 72-song, three-CD definitive collection box set spans 25 years of Muddy's slide-guitar glory. It's a great way to get acquainted with the father of modern Chicago blues (real name McKinley Morganfield), who died in 1983 at the age of 68.

ISLES
WILD BELLE (2013)

Brother-sister band Wild Belle (Natalie and Elliot Bergman), who grew up in and around Chicago, left quite an impression with their debut hit single 'Keep You'. They promptly signed to Columbia and released this album, and the buzz for the Jamaican-dusted brand of summery pop hasn't dissipated one little bit.

SUPER FLY
CURTIS MAYFIELD
(1972)

Soul and funk artist Curtis Mayfield was well acquainted with the serious inner-city grit captured on this album as he grew up in the now-defunct Cabrini-Green projects. It was released as the soundtrack for the blaxploitation film of the same name, but Mayfield's music was the real success story.

THE COMPLETE HOT
FIVE AND HOT SEVEN
RECORDINGS
LOUIS ARMSTRONG
(2000)

The Hot Five, a New Orleans-style jazz band, was Amstrong's first recording band under his own name, formed after he moved to the Windy City in 1922. The recordings resulted in some of the most important early jazz pieces during the mid to late 1920s.

ARTS & ENTERTAINMENT

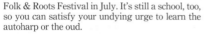

Hideout. *See p220*.

Folk & Roots Festival in July. It's still a school, too, so you can satisfy your undying urge to learn the autoharp or the oud.

★ Park West
322 W Armitage Avenue, at N Clark Street, Lincoln Park (1-773 929 1322, www.parkwest chicago.com). El: Brown or Purple to Armitage. **Tickets** $15-$50. **Credit** AmEx, MC, V. **Map** p312 G6.
This smarter-than-average venue in Lincoln Park books anyone from Over the Rhine to Sharon Jones & the Dap Kings. Note that it's a 15-minute walk from Armitage station; if you can't be bothered, the 11 or 22 buses will drop you closer.

Reggie's
2109 S State Street, at E 21st Street, Chinatown (1-312 949 0121, www.reggieslive.com). El: Red to Cermak-Chinatown. **Tickets** free-$25. **Credit** AmEx, Disc, MC, V. **Map** p308 H16.
This punk sanctuary draws the youngest crowds into its two distinct rooms, Reggie's Music Joint and Reggie's Rock Club. The latter is heir to the much-loved, now-deceased Fireside Bowl (the same dude books the gigs here now), and regularly offers all-ages shows.

Riviera Theatre
4746 N Racine Avenue, at N Broadway Street, Uptown (1-773 275 6800, www.rivieratheatre. com). El: Red to Lawrence. **Tickets** $20-$50. **No credit cards**.
The Riv is generally considered to be the sister rock club to the Aragon (*see p218*), a few blocks away. With a capacity of around 2,500, the jazz-age theatre

isn't quite as big as its neighbour, but the acoustics are much better. Those afraid of heights should probably give the steep balcony seating a miss.

★ Schubas Tavern
3159 N Southport Avenue, at W Belmont Avenue, Lakeview (1-773 525 2508, www. schubas.com). El: Brown, Purple or Red to Belmont. **Tickets** free-$18. **Credit** AmEx, Disc, MC, V. **Map** p309 D3.
This small club books some of the best indie touring acts around but also leans toward the acoustic singer-songwriter end of the spectrum, and offers month-long residencies from local groups with a national profile. You can hang out in the front bar area without paying cover for the shows; if you're under 21, go straight to the back room, which stages plenty of all-ages and over-18 shows. The Harmony Grill serves up a mean brunch at weekends.

Subterranean
2011 W North Avenue, at N Damen Avenue, Wicker Park (1-773 278 6600, www.subt.net). El: Blue to Damen. **Tickets** $5-$20. **Credit** AmEx, Disc, MC, V. **Map** p315 B7.
This upstairs club (pity the drummers lugging gear up the stairs) rarely disappoints sound-wise. There's a lofty balcony high above the stage for those who don't want to rub shoulders with the crowd, which packs in to see typically heavy rock and hip hop.

Uncommon Ground
3800 N Clark Street, at W Grace Street, Lakeview (1-773 929 3680, www.uncommonground.com). El: Red to Addison. **Suggested donation** $5-$15. **Credit** AmEx, Disc, MC, V. **Map** p313 E1.

One of Chicago's most beloved coffeehouses hosts the city's best weekly open-mic night alongside shows from folk artists. Nodding to a much-ballyhooed set by the then-unknown Jeff Buckley in 1994, the cosy shop holds a tribute to the late singer-songwriter in November that draws big crowds.
► *A second location on the Far North Side (1401 W Devon Avenue, at N Glenwood Avenue) focuses on reggae, jazz and bluegrass.*

Festivals

In addition to the festivals below, you can catch seemingly every working band in the biz at the proliferation of neighbourhood festivals and block parties around the city each summer (*see p27* **Celebrate the City**). While they still don't compare to Pitchfork, the line-ups at the **Do Division Street Fest** (www.do-division streetfest.com) and **Wicker Park Fest** (www.wickerparkfest.com) are nothing to shake a stick at. There's also music staged as part of the **Taste of Chicago** (*see p25*).

Chicago World Music Festival
www.cityofchicago.org. **Date** Sept.
This week-long wing-ding allows Chicagoans to travel the globe without leaving town via a sprawling bill of more than 40 artists from across the world. Events are held everywhere from Millennium Park to the Empty Bottle; check online for details.

Lollapalooza
www.lollapalooza.com. **Date** Aug.
Having started life as an alt-rock travelling show in the 1990s, Lollapalooza has now made Chicago its

permanent home, at least until 2018. Big names play a variety of stages over three days. A three-day pass costs around $230.

Hideout Block Party
www.hideoutchicago.com. **Date** wknd in Sept.
The tiny dive's reputation shines at its annual Block Party (tickets around $35/day), when diverse headlining acts choose to bypass larger events in favour of playing a strip of pavement in an industrial quarter of town.

Pitchfork Music Festival
www.pitchforkmusicfestival.com. **Date** July.
The locally based but globally known online tastemaker stages a three-day festival each year in Union Park. Expect to see the blog-hyped likes of Killer Mike alongside wildly popular acts like R Kelley and M.I.A. and a horde of the tragically hip.

Blues, Jazz and R&B

Without Chicago, the blues wouldn't be the same. And without the blues, Chicago would be a different town. From the 1910s to the '50s, African-Americans from the south flocked to the city in what became known as the Great Migration. A handful plugged in their guitars and invented the Chicago blues, an electrified, energetic take on traditional Delta sounds. The reverberations of Muddy Waters, Howlin' Wolf and Bo Diddley bounced around the world, influencing the likes of the Rolling Stones. Many clubs in Chicago cater to tourists these days, but you can still find musicians playing with the passion of their predecessors.

ARTS & ENTERTAINMENT

New Checkerboard Lounge. *See p225.*

INSIDE TRACK NUMERO UNO

In a basement just blocks from the Cook County Department of Corrections, a handful of treasure-hunting record geeks are giving new life to forgotten soul gems as the **Numero Group** (www.numerogroup. com). The reissue label has dug up several Chicago has-beens, from the Final Solution, a group of commercial jingle singers who scored a never-made blaxploitation flick, to Twi-Night and Bandit Records, two wanna-be Motowns that never made it out of the South Side. Most releases can be found at Dusty Groove America (*see p166* **Long Play**).

The jazz scene here is vibrant, too, with international touring acts supplementing a vibrant local scene. The **Association for the Advancement of Creative Musicians** (http://aacmchicago.org), which stages shows at the Velvet Lounge (*see p226*), is a powerhouse of African-American jazz.

Few club shows start before 9pm; many kick off nearer 10pm. At many jazz venues, the band will play two sets, wrapping up at 1am or later. A few clubs sell tickets or accept reservations in advance, especially for bigger-name acts (Buddy Guy at Buddy Guy's Legends, for example). If in doubt, call ahead or check online.

BLUES & R&B

Blues fans should also check the line-ups at the **Chicago Cultural Center** (*see p229*), the **Old Town School of Folk Music** (*see p220*) and the **Red Line Tap** (*see p220* **Heartland Café**), all of which regularly feature 2blues acts on their rosters. In addition, the 4,200-capacity **Arie Crown Theatre** (2301 S Lake Shore Drive, 1-312 791 6190, www.ariecrown.com) often hosts shows by middle-of-the-road blues and R&B acts.

Venues

B.L.U.E.S.

2519 N Halsted Street, between W Altgeld Street & W Lill Avenue (1-773 528 1012, www.chicago bluesbar.com). El: Brown, Purple or Red to Fullerton. **Tickets** $5-$8. **Credit** AmEx, Disc, MC, V. **Map** p312 F5.
The 'other' popular Lincoln Park blues club is more traditional and down-home than Kingston Mines (*see p225*). Popular acts include local stalwarts such as Vance 'Guitar' Kelly.

Blue Chicago

536 N Clark Street, at W Ohio Street (1-312 661 0010, www.bluechicago.com). El: Brown or Purple to Merchandise Mart; Red to Grand. **Tickets** $8-$10. **Credit** AmEx, MC, V. **Map** p310 H10.
Focuses on local female blues vocalists and draws a tourist-heavy crowd.

Jazz Showcase. *See p226.*

★ Buddy Guy's Legends

754 S Wabash Avenue, at E 8th Street, South Loop (1-312 427 1190, www.buddyguys.com). El: Red to Harrison. **Tickets** $10-$20. **Credit** AmEx, Disc, MC, V. **Map** p309 H13.

If you want to see Guy perform at his own club, stop by in January when he takes over the schedules. If you show up the other 11 months of the year, you may see him sitting at the bar, overseeing the whole operation. If you like Louisiana cuisine, the kitchen has just what you need.

Kingston Mines

2548 N Halsted Street, at W Wrightwood Avenue, Lincoln Park (1-773 477 4647, www.kingston mines.com). El: Brown, Purple or Red to Fullerton. **Tickets** $12-$15. **Credit** AmEx, Disc, MC, V. **Map** p312 F4.

This polite Lincoln Park club has an unusual set-up – two different bands in two different rooms on two different stages. Expect to find local bands that lean in a rock direction while playing the standards, though the club occasionally hooks out-of-town acts.

★ Lee's Unleaded Blues

7401 S South Chicago Avenue, at E 74th Street, South Side (1-773 493 3477, www. leesunleadedblues.com). Bus 30, 71, 75. **Tickets** $5. **No credit cards.**

Since the demise of the original Checkerboard, Lee's has inherited the title of the South Side's leading blues bar, and with good reason. The unassuming brick house, across from an auto wrecker in the shadow of the I-90 overpass, books a variety of local acts for seasoned regulars ready to hop. Perhaps the last truly authentic juke joint in the city.

New Checkerboard Lounge

5201 S Harper Court, at 52nd Street, Hyde Park (1-773 684 1472). Metra: 55th-56th-57th Street. **Tickets** $5. **No credit cards.** **Map** p316 Y16.

Opened in the 1970s, the original lounge was forced out of its old Bronzeville digs a while back. The blues club now holds court in a rather swankier home in a Hyde Park strip mall. *Photo p223.*

Rosa's Lounge

3420 W Armitage Avenue, at N Kimball Avenue, Logan Square (1-773 342 0452, www.rosas lounge.com). Bus: 73. **Tickets** $5-$20. **Credit** AmEx, Disc, MC, V.

Located in a working-class West Side neighbourhood, this family-run spot is owned by fine local drummer Tony Mangiullo and his mother, after whom the place is named. The schedule mixes local musicians and underground out-of-town acts with growing reputations. A full crowd makes Rosa's seem cosy rather than congested.

Festivals

Chicago Blues Festival

www.chicagofestivals.net. **Date** June.

Held over three days in early June, the Chicago Blues Festival is the biggest of all the city's free music festivals, attracting more than half a million visitors

ARTS & ENTERTAINMENT

each year. The biggest names play at the Petrillo Music Shell in Grant Park. Even if corporate sponsorship has led to goofy side stage names such as the Zone Perfect All-Natural Nutrition Bars Route 66 Roadhouse, it's hard to deny the authenticity and draw of headliners like BB King and Koko Taylor.

Chicago Gospel Festival
www.cityofchicago.org. **Date** June.
Big-name performers show up at this four-day free event that takes place in three locations, including Ellis Park in Bronzeville.

JAZZ & EXPERIMENTAL MUSIC

The **Chicago Cultural Center** (*see p229*) regularly presents free jazz shows both at lunchtime and occasionally in the evening. On Wednesdays, the **Hideout** (*see p220*) stages an ambitious programme led by local treasure Ken Vandermark, spotlighting local cats and cutting-edge improvisers. Thursdays finds similar programming at Logan Square performance space **Elastic Arts Foundation** (2830 N Milwaukee Avenue, at W Diversey, www.elasticrevolution.com). Sundays see experimental musicians play over at the **Hungry Brain** (*see p134*).

Venues

Andy's
11 E Hubbard Street, at N State Street, River North (1-312 642 6805, www.andysjazzclub. com). El: *Red to Grand.* **Tickets** $5-$15. **Credit** AmEx, MC, V. **Map** p310 H11.
This mainstream jazz haven runs regular, low-key residencies with some of Chicago's most respected scene elders, Von Freeman and Mike Smith among them. It's a comfortable, intimate space; on top of the music, the restaurant boasts a respectable menu that tempts jazzheads to make an evening of it.

Davenport's
1383 N Milwaukee Avenue, at W Wolcott Avenue, Wicker Park (1-773 278 1830, www.davenports pianobar.com). El: *Blue to Division.* **Tickets** $10-$20 (2-drink min). **Credit** AmEx, Disc, MC, V. **Map** p315 C8.
On the edge of Wicker Park's vibrant nightlife quarter, Davenport's specialises in old-fashioned cabaret reinterpreted by younger, hipper performers. The venue itself is colourful and modern, a far cry from what you might expect given the line-ups. There's often more than one show on any given night.
▶ *For other piano bars, see p205.*

★ Green Mill
4802 N Broadway, at W Lawrence Avenue, Uptown (1-773 878 5552, www.greenmilljazz.com).

El: *Red to Lawrence.* **Tickets** free-$15. **Credit** MC, V.
Al Capone used to hang here in the 1920s, but these days it's all about the music: mainstream jazz in a variety of stripes, from the idiosyncratic vocal jazz of Patricia Barber (Mondays) to the Alan Gresik Swing Shift Orchestra (Thursdays). Come early, as it's often understandably busy.

★ Jazz Showcase
806 S Plymouth Court, at W Polk Street, South Loop (1-312 360 0234, www.jazzshowcase.com). El: *Red to Harrison.* **Tickets** $10-$20. **Map** p308 H14.
Long heralded as Chicago's leading jazz venue, this venerable club has been forced to move more than once since its inception in 1947. However, since relocating to swanky new digs in 2008, the Showcase has re-established its reputation for bringing in top-shelf talent. *Photos p224.*

Katerina's
1920 W Irving Park Road, between N Wolcott & N Damen Avenues, Lakeview (1-773 348 7592, www.katerinas.com). El: *Brown to Irving Park.* **Tickets** free-$20. **Credit** AmEx, MC, V.
Den mother Katerina supports local jazz and world music like few others in the city of Chicago. Inside her cosy venue, you can catch gypsy violinist Alfonso Ponticelli, jazz chanteuse Typhanie Monique, sporadic world music gigs and, occasionally, local jam bands.

Pops for Champagne
601 N State Street, at E Ohio Street, River North (1-312 266 7677, www.popsforchampagne.com). El: *Red to Grand.* **Tickets** free. **Credit** AmEx, Disc, MC, V. **Map** p310 H10.
This spot has a tradition of showing high-quality mainstream jazz in a very upmarket setting. Even if you're not a champagne type, it's still worth a look, thanks to jazz performances every week from Sunday to Tuesday.

Velvet Lounge
67 E Cermak Road, between E Michigan & E Wabash Avenues, Chinatown (1-312 794 5904). El: *Red to Cermak-Chinatown.* **Tickets** free-$10. **No credit cards.**
Run by veteran saxophonist Fred Anderson, the Velvet Lounge concentrates on free jazz with a roster of high-calibre guests.

Festivals

Chicago Jazz Festival
www.chicagojazzfestival.org. **Date** Sept.
Held over the Labor Day weekend, this three-day festival welcomes many big names to Millennium Park and a number of smaller acts all around town. Admission is free.

Performing Arts

Book a big-ticket show or explore the thriving fringe scene.

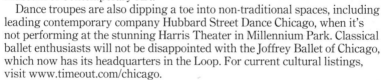

Chicago has a longstanding reputation as the breeding ground for eager, ambitious thespians, and there are plenty of opportunities to see them in action at dozens of storefront theatres across the city. Land a pair of tickets for one of the major main stages in town (Steppenwolf, Goodman, Lookingglass), and chances are high you'll catch a production that's making its way to Broadway.

Although Chi-Town is most famous for jazz and blues, it also has a lot to offer classical music aficionados, from the Riccardo Muti-directed Chicago Symphony Orchestra to the avant-garde International Contemporary Ensemble, which often takes to the stage at the Museum of Contemporary Art.

Dance troupes are also dipping a toe into non-traditional spaces, including leading contemporary company Hubbard Street Dance Chicago, when it's not performing at the stunning Harris Theater in Millennium Park. Classical ballet enthusiasts will not be disappointed with the Joffrey Ballet of Chicago, which now has its headquarters in the Loop. For current cultural listings, visit www.timeout.com/chicago.

Classical Music & Opera

The **Chicago Symphony Orchestra** and the **Lyric Opera of Chicago** both have stellar national reputations and draw enormous crowds, but there's more to the scene than these two big players. The wealth of smaller ensembles includes **Music of the Baroque** (www.baroque.org) and **Eighth Blackbird** (www.eighthblackbird.com), which join the cutting-edge **Chicago Opera Theater** (www.chicagooperatheater.org); the **Chicago Sinfonietta** (www.chicagosinfonietta.org); and the all-female **Orion Ensemble** (www.orionensemble.org) and **Chicago Chamber Musicians** (www.chicagochambermusic.org), which stage imaginative chamber music shows. Contemporary music has a strong following thanks to the likes of **Dal Niente** (www.dalniente.om), **Spektral Quartet** (www.spektralquartet.com), the **International Contemporary Ensemble** (www.iceorg.org) and the CSO's MusicNOW series, which allows ticketholders to mingle with performers.

INFORMATION & TICKETS

Tickets for the CSO, Lyric Opera and Ravinia are sold at their respective box offices and via **Ticketmaster** (*see p166*); try to book ahead, as many concerts are part of subscription series and sell out ahead of time. Tickets may not be sold in advance for smaller chamber concerts. The selection of free and cheap events is rich throughout the year, especially at the Chicago Cultural Center.

VENUES

★ Civic Opera House

20 N Wacker Drive, at E Madison Street, the Loop (1-312 332 2244, www.lyricopera.org). El: *Brown, Green, Orange or Purple to Washington.* **Box office** noon-6pm Mon-Sat. *Performance days* noon-first interval Mon-Sat; 11am-first interval Sun. **Tickets** $34-$244. **Credit** AmEx, Disc, MC, V. **Map** p309 G12.

As soon as you clap eyes on the elegant architecture and opulent lobby, built by Samuel Insull in 1929, you'll realise that subtlety isn't the order of the day at the Civic Opera House. The prestigious Lyric Opera of Chicago has made its home here since 1954,

Civic Opera House. *See p227.*

and now presents eight productions each season. It regularly ranks as one of the top opera companies in the country, boasting a talented stable of singers alongside an excellent orchestra under the musical direction of Sir Andrew Davis (formerly of the BBC Symphony Orchestra), and is also seen as one of the most traditional in both repertoire and style of production. The numbers speak for themselves: on average the house is 90 per cent full, no mean feat in a room that holds 3,500.

Ganz Hall at Roosevelt University

430 S Michigan Avenue, at E Van Buren Street, the Loop (1-312 341 3780, www.roosevelt.edu). El: Blue or Red to Jackson; Brown, Orange, Pink or Purple to Library. **Tickets** free. **Map** p309 J13.
Formerly a hotel banqueting hall and a masonic lodge, this impressive space now stages recitals by student and faculty members at Roosevelt's Chicago College of Performing Arts, alongside regular concerts by visiting soloists and ensembles. The acoustics lend every instrument a rich resonance.

★ Harris Theater

Millennium Park, 205 E Randolph Drive, between Michigan Avenue & N Columbus Drive, the Loop (1-312 334 7777, www.harristheaterchicago.com). El: Brown, Green, Orange, Pink, Purple to Randolph/Wabash. **Box office** noon-6pm Mon-Fri. **Tickets** $25-$90. **Credit** AmEx, Disc, MC, V. **Map** p309 J12.
The sleek Harris Theater prides itself on being the area's least pretentious theatre for brand-name acts. The home of numerous forward-thinking new music groups, the Harris is the city's best mainstream-alternative hall, if that's not a contradiction in terms. The theatre's mostly underground design means concertgoers have to walk up and down several flights of stairs to enter and leave, though the hard-to-find elevators do provide an alternative.

▶ *The Harris also hosts dance and ballet troupes such as Hubbard Street Dance Chicago and Garth Fagan Dance; see p231.*

Lyon & Healy Hall

168 N Ogden Avenue, at W Randolph Street, West Loop (1-800 595 4849, www.lyonhealy/hall.com/hall). El: Green or Pink to Ashland. **Box office** from 6.45pm on performance days. **Tickets** $30. **Credit** AmEx, Disc, MC, V. **Map** p314 D11.
A 200-capacity hall housed in (and run by) the Lyon & Healy harp factory stands out for its unusual design: the stage is backed by a huge window that affords breathtaking views of downtown. The music's pretty good too: L&H's own recitals series includes some impressive names, and many local musicians stage their own independent concerts.

Mandel Hall

1131 E 57th Street, at S University Avenue, Hyde Park (1-773 702 8069, http://music.uchicago.edu). Metra: 55th-56th-57th Street. **Box office** times vary. **Tickets** prices vary. **No credit cards.** **Map** p316 X17.
Part of the University of Chicago, the distinguished, century-old Mandel Hall plays host to internationally recognised string quartets, opera singers (in recital) and early music groups. Many of today's classical stars, among them violinist Hilary Hahn, made their Chicago debuts here.

Merit School of Music, Gottlieb Concert Hall

38 S Peoria Street, between W Monroe & W Madison Streets, West Loop (1-312 786 9428, www.meritmusic.org). El: Blue to UIC-Halsted. **Box office** times vary. **Tickets** free. **Credit** AmEx, Disc, MC, V. **Map** p314 F12.

This cosy 372-seat hall has been embraced by the city's chamber ensembles: the Rembrandt Chamber Players, Chicago a cappella and the Chicago Chamber Musicians have all played here in recent times. The near-downtown location is a boon for musicians and concertgoers.

Pick-Staiger Concert Hall

50 Arts Circle Drive, Evanston (1-847 491 5411, www.pickstaiger.com). El: Purple to Davis. **Box office** 10am-6pm Mon-Fri; noon-3pm Sat. **Tickets** $7-$24. **Credit** AmEx, MC, V.

This somewhat sterile mid-1970s structure on the campus of Northwestern University all the way up in Evanston provides good sightlines, a sunlit lobby, and warm acoustics for its local and international acts. The annual Winter Chamber Music Festival, Segovia Classical Guitar Series and opera productions are star attractions; local ensembles such as the Chicago Chamber Musicians, Chicago Philharmonic and Evanston Symphony Orchestra regularly rent the space. The theatre also doubles as a performance and rehearsal space for the university's acclaimed School of Music; senior and doctoral recitals are free and open to the public.

▶ *For more on Northwestern University, see p75.*

Preston Bradley Hall at the Chicago Cultural Center

78 E Washington Boulevard, at N Michigan Avenue, the Loop (1-312 744 6630, www.city ofchicago.org). El: Blue to Washington; Brown,

---

INSIDE TRACK HALLELUJAH!

Every December, the Harris Theater (*see p228*) hosts the **Do-It-Yourself Messiah**, a Chicago tradition in which have-a-go locals join an orchestra of amateurs in a rendition of Handel's classic. Tickets are $10, but you'll need to book in advance.

Green, Orange, Pink or Purple to Randolph/ Wabash; Red to Lake. **Box office** 9am-7pm Mon-Thur; 9am-6pm Fri, Sat; 10am-6pm Sun. **Tickets** free. **No credit cards. Map** p309 J12.

The original site of Chicago's public library hosts regular concerts under the world's largest (and, for that matter, most expensive) Tiffany dome. Any number of classical music events are staged here, with musicians from the nearby Chicago Symphony often among the artists. You're guaranteed to find free classical performances at 12.15pm every Monday (as part of the hall's LunchBreak series) and Wednesday (in the Dame Myra Hess Memorial Concert Series).

▶ *For details of other activities at the Chicago Cultural Center, see p37.*

Sherwood Conservatory of Music, Columbia College

1312 S Michigan Avenue, at E 13th Street, South Loop (1-312 369 1000, www.colum.edu/

ARTS & ENTERTAINMENT

Harris Theater.

Joffrey Ballet of Chicago. *See p232.*

sherwood_conservatory). El: Green, Orange or Red to Roosevelt. **Tickets** *free.* **No credit cards. Map** p308 J15.

The Sherwood Conservatory is home to the PianoForte Salon Series, broadcast live on WFMT. The hall, with its no-frills decor, also hosts a variety of educational music programmes that feature musicians of all ages and experience.

★ Symphony Center

220 S Michigan Avenue, at E Adams Street, the Loop (1-312 294 3000, www.cso.org). El: Blue or Red to Jackson; Brown, Green, Orange, Pink or Purple to Adams. **Box office** *11am-6pm Mon-Sat; 11am-3pm Sun.* **Tickets** *$10-$200.* **Credit** *AmEx, Disc, MC, V.* **Map** p309 J12.

As the architectural centrepiece in Chicago's classical music landscape, the Symphony Center is appropriately multifunctional. Its primary role, of course, is as the home of the Chicago Symphony Orchestra, directed by Riccardo Muti since 2010 and performing in Orchestra Hall every weekend from autumn to early summer.

The CSO's main programme is supplemented by occasional visits from touring soloists, small ensembles and orchestras; Saturday morning family concerts; sporadic pop and jazz shows; and occasional concerts from the Civic Orchestra of Chicago (the CSO's training orchestra for young musicians) and the Chicago Youth Symphony Orchestra (www. cyso.org). Also on site is the Buntrock Hall, an auxiliary space for chamber music; the elegant Grainger Ballroom, which stages lectures and small ensemble performances; plus a learning centre and a shop selling gifts and CDs, including many from the CSO's own Resound label.

▶ *The Art Institute of Chicago (see p36), just a 30-second walk across the street, gives Symphony Center its ideal cultural companion.*

FESTIVALS

In addition to the major events below, look out for the **Winter Chamber Music Festival** at Northwestern University's Pick-Staiger Hall (Dec & Jan; www.pickstaiger.org); and March's **Four Score Festival** at the Music Institute of Chicago in Evanston (www.musicinst.org), a four-day multimedia celebration with concerts, lectures, exhibitions and workshops.

Grant Park Music Festival

Jay Pritzker Pavilion, Millennium Park, the Loop (www.grantparkmusicfestival.com). El: Blue to Washington; Brown, Green, Orange, Pink or Purple to Randolph/Wabash; Red to Lake. **Date** *June-Aug.*

The Grant Park Music Festival has been around for more than 75 years and continues to attract some of the industry's most notable soloists to perform with its resident Grant Park Orchestra at Frank Gehry's handsome Jay Pritzker Pavilion in Millennium Park. The pavilion has room for 11,000 concertgoers, 4,000 on permanent seating and the rest camped out on the lawn, and the acoustic set-up is astonishing: the trellis that loops over the lawn carries a crystal-clear sound system.

★ Ravinia Festival
Ravinia Park, Green Bay Road, Highland Park (www.ravinia.org). Metra: Ravinia Park. **Date** June-Aug.
The oldest outdoor music festival in North America keeps the classical music scene hopping in the otherwise dog days of summer. The biggest and most famous of the three stages is the Ravinia Pavilion, which presents concerts by the Chicago Symphony alongside occasional big-name galas, concert performances of popular operas and pop gigs. The 3,200 covered seats at the pavilion are supplemented by a huge expanse of picnic-friendly lawn; tickets run from pocket change up to three-figure sums. Also on site, the 850-seat Martin Theatre hosts concerts by chamber groups, and the smaller Bennett-Gordon Hall features a variety of college-age performers. Ravinia's Steans Institute trains young musicians, and the concerts feature plenty of top-notch talent.

Dance

Whether you're looking for an experimental show or traditional ballet, flamenco or bharata natyam, you can find pretty much whatever takes your fancy on Chicago's diverse dance scene, particularly if you visit when the season is at its height (Sept-May). Find up-to-date listings at www.timeout.com/chicago or use the searchable calendar at www.seechicago dance.com. For tickets, contact the theatres, **Ticketmaster** (*see p166*) or **Ticketweb** (www.ticketweb.com).

MAJOR COMPANIES

★ Hubbard Street Dance Chicago
Information & tickets 1-312 850 9744, www.hubbardstreetdance.com.
Founded in 1977 by jazz-dance choreographer Lou Conte, Hubbard Street has built up a deserved reputation as Chicago's premier dance company. Under the leadership and vision of artistic director Glenn Edgerton and executive director Jason Palmquist, the company not only performs a repertoire of works by renowned choreographers, but it also collaborates with local institutions, such as the Art Institute of Chicago and tech start-up hub 1871. The group is often away on tour, but performs annually at the Harris Theater.

ARTS & ENTERTAINMENT

Athenaeum Theatre. *See p232.*

★ Joffrey Ballet of Chicago

*Information 1-312 739 0120, tickets 1-312
386 8905, www.joffrey.com.*
One of the major US ballet companies, Joffrey emigrated to Chicago from New York in 1995. It's now
resident at the Auditorium Theatre, but also has a
glamorous offstage headquarters: the high-rise
Joffrey Tower on the north-east corner of State and
Randolph. The troupe's eclectic repertoire is strong
on American choreographers and reconstructions of
Ballet Russe-era works. *Photo p230.*

Muntu Dance Theatre of Chicago

Information 1-773 241 6080, www.muntu.com.
This dynamic group is strongly connected to its
South Side community, but also keeps ties with
dancers and musicians in Africa. The company
draws on traditional African and African-American
dance and music to create new works, and is in the
midst of a project to build its own arts centre.

River North Dance Chicago

*Information 1-312 944 2888,
www.rivernorthchicago.com.*
For more than 20 years, this hip, sexy touring troupe
has created a trademark breezy style combining
jazz and modern dance with a strong emphasis on
accessibility. The current repertoire includes works
by artistic director Frank Chaves, among others.

VENUES

★ Athenaeum Theatre

*2936 N Southport Avenue, at W Oakdale
Avenue, Lakeview (information 1-773 935 6875,
Ticketmaster 1-312 902 1500, www.athenaeum
theatre.com). El: Brown or Purple to Wellington.*
Box office *Theatre* noon-final curtain Wed-Sun.
Ovationtix 24hrs daily. **Tickets** prices vary.
Credit *Ticketmaster* AmEx, Disc, MC, V
Built in 1911 as a recreation centre for the German
community, the 900-seat Athenaeum features red velvet seats and a gilded ceiling with allegorical paintings. However, the rest of the building recalls one of
its past lives as a girls' high school. *Photo p231.*
▶ *The main stage of the Athenaeum is used
for the annual Dance Chicago in November
($17-$30). See p233.*

Auditorium Theatre

*50 E Congress Parkway, at S Wabash Avenue,
the Loop (1-312 341 2310, www.auditorium
theatre.org). El: Blue or Red to Jackson; Brown,
Orange, Pink or Purple to Library.* **Box office**
10am-6pm Mon, Thur; noon-6pm Tue, Wed, Fri.
Tickets $25-$130. **Credit** AmEx, Disc, MC, V.
Map p309 J13.
This gorgeous palace (*see p39*) is home to the Joffrey
Ballet (*see above*), but also hosts an international
dance series that includes world-class companies
such as the Kirov Ballet. Depending on your cash

flow and connections, you can find yourself sitting
pretty in the orchestra or communing with the gods
near the golden ceiling.

Dance Center of Columbia College

*1306 S Michigan Avenue, at W 13th Street,
South Loop (information 1-312 369 8300, tickets
1-312 369 8330, www.colum.edu/dance_center).
El: Green, Orange or Red to Roosevelt.* **Box
office** noon-5pm Mon-Fri. **Tickets** $21-$30.
Credit AmEx, Disc, MC, V. **Map** p308 H15.
The only dance-dedicated theatre in Chicago is managed by the dance department of Columbia College,
the city's most progressive centre for dance education. The programming reflects this, with appearances by touring and national artists mixed in with
performances by local choreographers, faculty programmes and student workshops.

★ Harris Theater

For listings, see p228.
Completed in 2003 as part of the Millennium Park
complex, this ultra-modern 1,500-seater can house
large productions. The interior is pared-down and
white, with Dan Flavin-esque neon lighting. Inside
the vast theatre itself, sightlines are excellent. Most
of Chicago's major dance companies perform here.

★ Links Hall

*3111 N Western Avenue, between Belmont &
Barry Avenues, Logan Square (1-773 281 0824,
www.linkshall.org). Bus: 49, 77.* **Box office** 9am-
5pm Mon-Fri. **Tickets** $5-$25. **Credit** AmEx,
MC, V. **Map** p313 E2.
Founded in 1979 by a group of choreographers, this
studio/theatre offers multidisciplinary programming
that takes in a healthy portion of experimental dance
by local and international artists.

Museum of Contemporary Art

*220 E Chicago Avenue, at N Mies van der Rohe
Way, Streeterville (1-312 280 2660/www.mca
chicago.org). El: Red to Chicago.* **Box office**
10am-8pm Tue; 10am-5pm Wed-Sun. **Tickets**
$18-$50. **Credit** AmEx, MC, V. **Map** p310 J10.
The MCA's elegant theatre is set up perfectly for
viewing dance: the 300-odd seats are arranged on a
deep slope, starting at the same level as the stage
and rising to look down on it. The programming is
excellent: the MCA is one of the city's most important theatres for touring companies.
▶ *For more on the museum, see p57.*

Ruth Page Center for the Arts

*1016 N Dearborn Avenue, at W Oak Street,
Gold Coast (1-312 337 6543, www.ruthpage.org).
El: Red to Clark/Division.* **Box office** 9am-5pm
daily. **Tickets** $15-$40. **Credit** AmEx, Disc,
MC, V. **Map** p310 H9.
Heiress, dancer and choreographer Ruth Page
established this home for dance in the middle of the

swanky Gold Coast. In addition to studios and a dance library, the building houses a 200-seat theatre, which is rented out to small- or medium-sized dance companies and independent choreographers.

FRINGE COMPANIES

Chicago has hundreds of smaller troupes that together make up a healthy fringe scene. Some aspire to the aesthetic of the more established companies, while others represent cultural diversity and/or artistic experimentation. All perform off the beaten path in smaller theatres; a few stage shows in unconventional locations.

Roving contemporary companies include the dancer-run collective **Same Planet Different World Dance Theatre** (www.spdwdance.org), which boasts a repertory of works by edgy young choreographers; **Thodos Dance Chicago** (www.thodosdancechicago.org), which showcases the talents of choreographer Melissa Thodos and develops its members' talents through its New Dances programme; and **Lucky Plush** (www.luckyplush.com), which features original, lush choreography with compelling imagery by artistic director Julia Rhoads and other interdisciplinary collaborators.

Molly Shanahan (www.madshak.com) is one of the city's most compelling experimental choreographers; her solos, duets and works for small ensembles have gained recognition in Montreal and New York. **The Seldoms** (www.theseldoms.org), led by Carrie Hanson, offer intellectually stimulating dance-theatre with multidisciplinary components. And for something different, **Natya Dance Theatre** (www.natya.com) brings classical Indian bharata natyam into a contemporary context.

INSIDE TRACK
WHAT'S IN A NAME?

It sounds dainty, but **A Red Orchid Theatre** takes its name from *Naked Lunch* by anything-but-dainty Beat writer William Burroughs. When one of the book's characters shoots up heroin into the arm of another, Burroughs describes the blood sucked into the vial as 'a red orchid'.

FESTIVALS

The big event on the calendar is **Dance Chicago** (www.dancechicago.com). Founded in 1995, the festival aims to highlight the quality and variety of local dance, and features local companies performing throughout November at the Athenaeum Theatre (*see p232*). Tickets for the festival are available from the Athenaeum box office.

During the summer months, members of the public are invited to dig out their dancing shoes for **Chicago SummerDance**, a free festival held in a number of city parks (on a rotating basis) that invites the public to trip the light fantastic through a variety of dance styles. One-hour lessons in everything from ballroom dancing to Irish step-dance are followed by two hours of hoofing, often with an accompanying live band. For those who prefer to watch, **Chicago Dancing Festival** (www.chicagodancingfestival.com) is a summer extravaganza featuring nationally recognised companies with several free events taking place at Millennium Park in August.

ARTS & ENTERTAINMENT

Chicago SummerDance.

Theatre

Since the days of Maurice Brown's Little Theatre movement at the turn of the 20th century, Chicago has been a real hotbed of independent theatrical innovation. A longstanding tradition in performance arts, a vibrant ethnic mix and strong educational programmes have made it a great place for hopeful visionaries to try and make their mark.

The city's theatrical alumni include blazing mavericks (David Mamet, John Malkovich), comfort TV stars (Laurie Metcalf, David Schwimmer) and acting titans (Brian Dennehy, Joan Allen), most of whom cut their teeth in the storefront scene. The majority of these scrappy enterprises – along with those, like Steppenwolf, that have grown into institutions – demonstrate Chicago's commitment to actor-centred takes on contemporary and canonical plays. But the scene today has space for all kinds of visions, from experimental spectacles to Broadway glitz.

INFORMATION & TICKETS

Many Chicago theatres, especially the small ones, stage performances only from Thursday to Sunday. On Fridays and Saturdays, late-night shows typically begin around 11pm. It's generally best to buy tickets directly from theatre box offices in order to avoid surcharges; however, most shows also sell seats via **Ticketmaster** (*see p166*), with smaller companies preferring **Ticketweb** (www.ticketweb.com). Prices are all over the map, from $10-$20 at fringe venues to $60 or more at big theatres.

Many theatres sell half-price tickets for that day's performance through the LCT's three **Hot Tix** booths: in the Loop (72 E Randolph Street, at N Michigan Avenue) and at Block 37 (108 N State Street, at E Randolph Street), and at the **Water Works** (163 E Pearson Street, at N Michigan Avenue). All are open from 10am to 6pm Tuesday to Saturday, and 11am to 4pm on Sunday. Each morning, a list of shows with cheap seats available is posted at www.hottix.org. Some theatres list shows several days in advance, which allows you to buy, say, half-price tickets for Saturday's show on a Thursday.

American Theater Company.

MAJOR COMPANIES & VENUES

There are so many theatres in Chicago that what follows is a necessarily selective list. Check www.timeout.com/chicago.com for reviews of the latest shows when you're in town. Note that the box office hours listed in this section apply when there is no performance at the specified theatre. On days when there's a scheduled show, hours are generally extended until showtime and occasionally beyond.

★ American Theater Company

1909 W Byron Street, at N Lincoln Avenue, Irving Park (1-773 409 4125, www.atcweb.org). El: Blue to Irving Park. **Box office** noon-6pm Mon-Fri; 1-8pm Sat; noon-5pm Sun. **Tickets** $10-$40. **Credit** AmEx, MC, V. **Map** p314 C0.
The American Theatre Company has a long track record of straightforward productions of classic and occasionally new American plays. Recent productions have included everything from *Hair* to *It's a Wonderful Life: The Radio Play*.

Apollo Theater

2540 N Lincoln Avenue, at Lill Street, Lincoln Park (773 935 6100, www.apollochicago.com). El: Brown, Purple, Red to Fullerton. **Box office** 10am-6pm Mon, Tue; 10am-8pm Wed-Fri; 10am-8pm Sat; 11am-6pm Sun. **Credit** AmEx, MC, V. **Map** p312 E4.
Built in the late 1970s and renovated twice, this 440-seat commercial house in Lincoln Park has a rich history, having showcased everything from David Mamet's *Sexual Perversity in Chicago* to the Midwest premiere of *The Vagina Monologues*. The theatre tends to schedule long runs, and since 2008 has hosted the wildly popular rock icons of Million Dollar Quartet. It is also home to the kid-centric Emerald City Theatre Company (*see p191*).

Chicago Shakespeare Theater

800 E Grand Avenue, at Navy Pier, Streeterville (1-312 595 5600, www.chicagoshakes.com). El: Red to Grand. **Box office** noon-5pm Tue-Sat; noon-4pm Sun. **Tickets** $23-$70. **Credit** AmEx, Disc, MC, V. **Map** p310 K10.
Bardolators of all stripes will want to check out the lavish digs that CST has secured amid the Ferris wheels and peel-and-eat shrimp of Navy Pier. Artistic director Barbara Gaines's solid crew of journeyman actors deliver rousing performances in productions that tend towards the crowd-pleasing. Visiting international productions spice up proceedings, and the CST Family Series offers the Bard abridged for youngsters.

Congo Square Theatre Company

2936 N Southport Avenue, Lakeview (1-773 296 1108, www.congosquaretheatre.org). El: Brown to Southport. **Box office** 10am-4pm Mon-Fri. **Tickets** $20-$30. **Credit** AmEx, Disc, MC, V.
Derrick Sanders, Congo Square's founding artistic director, was a protégé of the late American playwright August Wilson, and Congo Square follows Wilson in its commitment to a regional theatre

centred on the African-American experience. The company has produced several of Wilson's plays, as well as work by up-and-coming writers. Its commitment to emerging writers sometimes leads to uneven scripts, but the company boasts consistently sharp performances, direction and design.

Court Theatre

5535 S Ellis Avenue, at E 55th Street, Hyde Park (1-773 753 4472, www.courttheatre.org). Metra: 55th-56th-57th Street. **Box office** 10am-5pm Mon-Fri; noon-5pm Sat. **Tickets** $35-$65. **Credit** AmEx, Disc, MC, V. **Map** p316 X17.
Fitting in with its Hyde Park location, the Court delivers meticulous productions of plays by the likes of Stoppard, Ionesco and Beckett. Big-name productions in past years have included Tony Kushner's *Angels in America* and an adaptation of Virginia Woolf's *Orlando*. *Photo p237.*

Gift Theatre Company

4802 N Milwaukee Avenue, at W Lawrence Avenue, Jefferson Park (1-773 283 7071, www. thegifttheatre.org). El: Blue to Jefferson Park. **Box office** times vary. **Tickets** $20-$30. **Credit** AmEx, Disc, MC, V.
The Gift is almost an archetypal Chicago storefront theatre. Packed into an impossibly intimate performance space, audience members practically share the stage with the company's young, dynamic performers. It's the acting and directing talent that sets the Gift apart: actors such as Paul D'Addario, Brendan Donaldson and Mary Fons throw themselves into roles with abandon, and director Michael Patrick Thornton has a stellar reputation.

Goodman Theatre

170 N Dearborn Street, at W Randolph Street, the Loop (1-312 443 3800, www.goodmantheatre. org). El: Blue, Brown, Green, Orange, Pink or Purple to Clark/Lake; Red to Lake. **Box office** noon-5pm daily. **Tickets** *Albert Theatre* $25-$125. *Owen Theatre* $10-$40. **Credit** AmEx, Disc, MC, V. **Map** p309 H12.
The Goodman has long stood as one of the country's leading theatrical destinations outside New York, and an anchor of Chicago's serious dramatic scene. Artistic director Robert Falls favours lush, star-studded productions of the classic American repertory (Brian Dennehy's a repeat performer), though the theatre's offerings are puckishly unpredictable.

Lookingglass Theatre Company

Water Tower Water Works, 821 N Michigan Avenue, at E Pearson Street, Magnificent Mile (1-312 337 0665, www.lookingglasstheatre.org). El: Red to Chicago. **Box office** 10am-6pm Tue-Fri; noon-7.30pm Sat, Sun. **Tickets** $22-$68. **Credit** Disc, MC, V. **Map** p310 J9.
You may not associate David Schwimmer – or *Boston Public*'s Joey Slotnik, for that matter – with

circus-flavoured productions of *The Arabian Nights*, Dickens and Dostoyevsky, but they're both ensemble members of the Lookingglass company, which blends an interest in literary adaptation with spectacular physical theatre. The troupe also includes Mary Zimmerman, maybe the most influential Chicago theatrical export since David Mamet; her gorgeously precise approach to visual design has earned her plaudits, including a Tony and a MacArthur 'genius grant'.

★ Neo-Futurists

Neo-Futurarium, 5153 N Ashland Avenue, between W Winona Street & W Foster Avenue, Andersonville (1-773 275 5255, www.neofuturists. org). El: Red to Berwyn. **Box office** 11am-6pm Mon-Fri. **Tickets** $10-$20. **Credit** AmEx, Disc, MC, V.
See p238 **Midnight Madness**.

Next Theatre

927 Noyes Street, at Ridge Avenue, Evanston (1-847 475 1875 ext 2, www.nexttheatre.org). El: Purple to Noyes. **Box office** noon-6pm Mon-Fri; 2-8pm Sat; noon-4pm Sun; from 2hrs prior to show Mon, Sun. **Tickets** $25-$35; $7-$17.50 reductions. **Credit** AmEx, Disc, MC, V.
Over the last decade or so, Evanston's Next Theatre has built a reputation as a leading destination for new, intellectually challenging and theatrically exploratory plays. As a result, it puts on regional premières of work by many of the country's most adventurous playwrights, including John Patrick Shanley and Christopher Shinn.

★ Profiles Theatre

4147 N Broadway Street, at W Gordon Terrace, Lakeview (1-773 549 1815, www.profilestheatre. org). El: Red to Sheridan. **Box office** 1pm-showtime daily. **Tickets** $20-$40. **Credit** AmEx, Disc, MC, V.
Profiles works very much in the Chicago tough-guy tradition pioneered by Mamet. Edgy works by the likes of Neil LaBute, Adam Rapp and Rebecca Gilman tend to exploit the tension inherent in the theatre's close-quarters space.

★ A Red Orchid Theatre

1531 N Wells Street, at W North Avenue, Old Town (1-312 943 8722, www.aredorchid theatre.org). El: Brown or Purple to Sedgwick. **Box office** noon-5pm Mon-Fri. **Tickets** $20-$55. **Credit** AmEx, Disc, MC, V. **Map** p311 G7.
A Red Orchid mixes the contemporary and classical: bang-up productions of Ionesco work sit alongside the work of Brett Neveu, one of Chicago's hottest writing talents and an ensemble member.

Redmoon Theater

2120 S Jefferson Street, at W 21st Street (1-312 850 8440, www.redmoon.org). El: Red to Cermak; Blue to Halsted; Pink to 18th Street or Western. **Box office** 9am-5pm Mon-Fri. **Tickets** free-$30. **Credit** AmEx, MC, V. **Map** p314 D11.
They build puppets; they organise massive pageants (for years, their Hallowe'en parade was an annual highlight in Logan Square); they're as likely to put on a performance in a park as in a traditional theatre space. There's nothing quite like Redmoon Theater

Profiles Theatre.

Court Theatre. *See p235.*

in Chicago, and its commitment to large-scale spectacle has made it a significant influence on a younger generation of artists.

Side Project

1439 W Jarvis Avenue, at N Greenview Avenue, Rogers Park (1-773 340 0140, www.theside project.net). El: Red to Jarvis. **Box office** times vary. **Tickets** $15-$20. **Credit** AmEx, Disc, MC, V.

Occupying a very intimate space, the Side Project has had a solid decade of potent and edgy productions. The group specialises in premièring new plays by writers such as Sean Graney, but has also had success with festivals of shorter works. With consistently solid direction and acting, it's a reliable venue for seeking out contemporary theatre's bleeding edge.

★ Steppenwolf Theatre Company

1650 N Halsted Street, at W North Avenue, Lincoln Park (1-312 335 1650, www.steppenwolf. org). El: Red to North/Clybourn. **Box office** 11am-5pm Mon; 11am-7.30pm Tue-Sat; 1-7.30pm Sun. **Tickets** *Main theatre* $20-$82. *The Garage* $20. **Credit** AmEx, Disc, MC, V. **Map** p311 F7.

There was a period when it was starting to look as though the legacy of Malkovich and Sinise, of John Mahoney and Joan Allen and Laurie Metcalf, was mostly resting on its laurels. But the company can thank Tracy Letts for ushering in a revitalised Steppenwolf with *August: Osage County*, which garnered a Pulitzer and a Tony after moving to Broadway. The company continues to offer a repertoire balancing the classic and the contemporary.

Strawdog Theatre Company

3829 N Broadway Street, at W Grace Street, Lakeview (1-773 528 9696, www.strawdog. org). El: Red to Sheridan. **Box office** from 1hr before show. **Tickets** $15-$28. **Credit** Disc, MC, V. **Map** p313 F1.

The sizeable ensemble at this storefront stalwart gets put to use mainly for staging stripped-down versions of the classics, but it has also mounted original productions. The cabaret space next door allows for abundant post-show fun.

TimeLine Theatre Company

615 W Wellington Avenue, at N Broadway Street, Lakeview (1-773 281 8463, www.timeline theatre.com). El: Brown or Purple to Wellington. **Box office** noon-5pm Tue-Fri; noon-8pm Sat (performance days); noon-3pm Sun (performance days). **Tickets** $22-$35; $5-$10 reductions. **Credit** MC, V. **Map** p313 F3.

Up in tony Lincoln Park, TimeLine Theatre Company mounts productions dedicated to exploring historical themes. The educational mission is reflected in the extensive programme notes and dramaturgical displays accompanying the plays. TimeLine has one of the more seasoned ensembles working the Chicago storefront scene. *Photo p240.*

Trap Door Theatre

1655 W Cortland Street, at N Paulina Street, Bucktown (1-773 384 0494, www.trapdoor theatre.com). Bus: 9X. **Box office** times vary, see website for details. **Tickets** $20. **Credit** AmEx, Disc, MC, V.

Given the mazelike walkway one has to navigate to get to this cosy space, Trap Door's name seems appropriate. Inside, artistic director Beata Pilch and associates devote themselves to plays centred on the eastern European avant garde. Expect to see some diatribes against the soullessness of modern life, maybe accompanied by scantily clad ingénues.

Victory Gardens Theater
2433 N Lincoln Avenue, at W Fullerton Avenue, Lincoln Park (1-773 871 3000, www.victory

gardens.org). El: Brown, Purple or Red to Fullerton. **Box office** noon-8pm Tue-Sat; noon-4pm Sun. **Tickets** $35-$65. **Credit** AmEx, Disc, MC, V. **Map** p312 F5.
Lincoln Park's Biograph Theater remains best known as the spot where notorious bank robber John Dillinger drew his last breath. However, its occupant for the last few years, theatre company Victory Gardens, has some claims to fame of its own, supporting emerging and established playwrights through residencies and stand-alone productions –

Midnight Madness

After two raucous decades of after-hours theatre, the Neo-Futurists still reign.

From an evolutionary standpoint, natural selection should have killed off the **Neo-Futurists** (*see p236*) long ago. The ragtag fleet of performers isn't exactly famous for being organised. Or mainstream. Or well funded. Yet, remarkably, the group's show *Too Much Light Makes the Baby Go Blind* celebrated its 25th anniversary in 2013. Featuring a game if somewhat scrappy ensemble of writer-performers attempting to perform 30 miniature plays in 60 minutes, it's part block party and part accessible performance art. Strangely populist yet also resolutely underground, the show has produced multiple generations of hard-working writer-performers and won untold legions of fans, many of them non-traditional theatregoers.

Too Much Light started as an experiment at the old Stage Left Theatre in Lakeview, made a brief stop at Live Bait Theater and eventually moved north to pre-gentrified Andersonville in 1992. There, in a space above a funeral parlour, the Neo-Futurists and *Too Much Light...* carved themselves a perfectly unusual niche.

The show was originally a hit with suburban punks who came into the city craving alternative culture, lining up around the block in the dead of winter to score a seat. But its frenzied party energy and up-to-the-minute commentary on politics and pop culture helped secure the show a permanent place in Chicago theatre.

With only a quicksilver moment in the national spotlight – the Broadway musical *Urinetown*, which had a darkly comic Neo-Futurist point of view, won a 2002 best-book Tony for Neo-Futurist alumnus Greg Kotis and earned a Tony nomination for ensemble actor Spencer Kayden – the company has somehow kept itself under the radar. But without the charismatic

accessibility these hard-driving artists have shared with generations of first-time theatre patrons, Chicago wouldn't have half the scene it has today.

Bookings aren't accepted; show up by 10.30pm if you want to get in. (If the show sells out, they'll order a pizza for the entire audience.) Tickets cost $9 plus whatever number shows up when you roll a dice; roll a five, for example, and you'll pay 14 bucks. The company also produces full-length shows, more notable for their goofy charm and political sensibility than for their polish. But it's *Too Much Light...* that continues to draw the crowds.

and nurturing talent via its training centre. The work here isn't always groundbreaking, but the level of professionalism is high.

OTHER VENUES

Athenaeum Theatre

For listings, see p232.

This antiquated, cathedral-like building was once an annex to a mammoth neighbouring church. Now it has several studio theatres and a large proscenium main stage; between them they play landlord to shows of all shapes and sizes, including dance and performance art. Prices vary, but most of the performances cost less than $25.

Briar Street Theatre

3133 N Halsted Street, at W Belmont Avenue, Lakeview (1-773 348 4000, www.blueman.com). El: Brown, Purple or Red to Belmont. **Box office** 10am-6pm Mon-Wed; 10am-8pm Thur, Fri; 10am-10pm Sat; noon-4pm Sun. **Tickets** $49-$99. **Credit** AmEx, Disc, MC, V. **Map** p313 F3.

This bigger-than-it-looks theatre might appear rather prosaic from the outside. Most nights, though, it's packed to the hilt with crowds who thrill to the colourful techno antics of Blue Man Group, which has occupied the space for years (and shows no signs of vacating soon).

Broadway in Chicago

Bank of America Theatre *18 W Monroe Street, between S State & S Dearborn Streets, the Loop. El: Blue or Red to Monroe; Brown, Green, Orange, Pink or Purple to Madison/ Wabash.* **Map** p309 H12.
Cadillac Palace Theatre *151 W Randolph Street, at N LaSalle Street, the Loop. El: Blue, Brown, Green, Orange, Pink or Purple to Clark/Lake; Red to Lake.* **Map** p309 H12.
Drury Lane Theatre *Water Tower Place, 175 E Chestnut Street, at N Michigan Avenue, Magnificent Mile. El: Red to Chicago.* **Map** p310 J9.
Ford Center for the Performing Arts Oriental Theatre *24 W Randolph Street, between N State & N Dearborn Streets. El: Blue, Brown, Green, Orange, Pink or Purple to Clark/ Lake; Red to Lake.* **Map** p309 H12.
All venues *Information 1-312 977 1700, Ticketmaster 1-312 902 1400, www.broadway inchicago.com.* **Box office** *Ticketmaster* 24hrs daily. **Tickets** vary. **Credit** AmEx, Disc, MC, V.

Three of the Loop's glorious old theatres have received a new lease of life courtesy of Broadway in Chicago, which uses them as a roadhouse for big-ticket touring shows. Gorgeous and resplendent, the 1926 **Cadillac Palace** retains the opulence of Golden-era vaudeville palaces, and now stages large-scale productions. The spectacularly renovated

INSIDE TRACK OPEN BAR

For small Chicago theatres, liquor licences are famously difficult to secure, which is why so many storefront operations can sell you nothing stronger than a Dr Pepper. One exception is Wicker Park's **Chopin Theatre** (*see below*), which not only plays host to many of Chicago's best young companies but also has a bar to boot.

Bank of America Theatre (formerly the Majestic Theatre) is the cosiest of the trio, and mixes touring shows with pre-Broadway try-outs of productions such as *Jersey Boys*. The ornate **Oriental Theatre**, former longtime home of *Wicked*, plays host to a rotating crop of crowd-pleasers. Broadway in Chicago also looks after the **Drury Lane Theatre**, at Water Tower Place, which features a variety of light musical fare.

★ Chopin Theatre

1543 W Division Street, at N Ashland Avenue, Wicker Park (1-773 278 1500, www.chopin theatre.com). El: Blue to Division. **Box office** 10am-8pm daily. **Tickets** $20-$45. **Credit** varies by show. **Map** p315 C8.

The home base for some of the city's most dynamic storefront troupes, Wicker Park's Chopin is a resolutely funky venue that consistently draws young audiences. In addition to a rotating door for visiting European companies, many of them Polish, the Chopin regularly hosts innovative companies such as Tuta, a Chicago-based ensemble with strong European ties, and the House Theatre (*see p240*).

Greenhouse Theater Center

2257 N Lincoln Avenue, at W Webster Avenue, Lincoln Park (1-773 871 3000, www.greenhouse theater.org). El: Brown, Purple or Red to Fullerton. **Box office** noon-8pm Wed-Sat; noon-4pm Sun. **Tickets** $15-$25. **Credit** AmEx, Disc, MC, V. **Map** p312 F5.

Once home to the Tony-winning Victory Gardens company (*see p238*), this facility now simply serves as a rental house, with four theatres of varying sizes. Among the many dependable companies that call it home are the Eclipse Theatre, which devotes each of its seasons to a single American playwright; Shattered Globe, a long-standing producer of mostly middle-class dramas; Remy Bumppo, a dapper and intelligent company producing high-minded literary classics; MPAACT, which produces new and non-traditional African-American works; and the Latino-themed Teatro Vista (*see p240*).

Royal George Theatre

1641 N Halsted Street, at W North Avenue, Old Town (1-312 988 9000, www.theroyal

ARTS & ENTERTAINMENT

georgetheatre.com). El: Red to North/Clybourn.
Box office 10am-6pm Mon-Sat; noon-3pm
Sun. **Tickets** $31-$60. **Credit** AmEx, MC, V.
Map p311 F7.
This dependable and tourist-friendly outlet is
located across the street from Steppenwolf (*see
p237*). The main stage favours light comedy and
musicals. Those looking to relive Catholic school
days should make a beeline for the Great Room's
sweetly satirical *Late Nite Catechism*.

Stage 773

*1225 W Belmont Avenue, at N Southport Avenue,
Lakeview (1-773 327 5252, www.stage773.com).
El: Brown, Purple or Red to Belmont.* **Box office**
1pm-showtime Wed-Sun. **Tickets** $5-$45. **Credit**
AmEx, Disc, MC, V. **Map** p313 D3.
Since the 1970s, this three-stage rental house has
been the incubator for countless storefront companies. Some feature the city's top-shelf Equity actors,
while others are produced on very tight budgets;
in other words, the reviewers are your friends.
And as the bartenders never tire of reminding you,
you can bring your drinks into the theatre. The
resident company regularly produces workshops
and new musicals.

Theatre on the Lake

*2400 N Lake Shore Drive, at W Fullerton Avenue,
Lincoln Park (1-312 742 7529, www.chicago
parkdistrict.com). Bus: 151.* **Box office** mid
June-mid Aug. **Tickets** $18. **Credit** MC, V.
Map p312 H5.
Offering a selection of the season's best storefront
plays, the Theatre on the Lake is a decades-old
summer tradition for Chicago families. The partially
open-air space on Lake Michigan changes the feel of
many of the plays from their original venues; the
drafty acoustics and sea-salt air can feel like a day
at the docks. But, miraculously, more troupes overcome it than not, and the variety of the plays makes
this a terrific sampler of the local scene.

ITINERANT COMPANIES

House Theatre of Chicago

*Information 1-773 769 3832, tickets 1-773
251 2195, www.thehousetheatre.com.*
It's a staple of theatre coverage to bemoan the lack
of interest in theatre among under-40s, but the people at House have no such worries: their formula of
visual spectacle, rock soundtracks and pop-culture
obsession has made them a destination for hipsters
and hipster-haters alike. The group's home base is
the Chopin Theatre (*see p239*) in Wicker Park.

Hypocrites

1-773 525 5991, www.the-hypocrites.com.
Artistic director Sean Graney has developed a theatrical language one part Artaud, one part David
Lynch, and several parts his own disturbing and
strangely moving vision. The Hypocrites have
staged several original pieces, but they're best
known for their skewed takes on works from the
classic and contemporary canon.

Porchlight Music Theatre

1-773 327 5252, www.porchlightmusictheatre.org.
Porchlight's not the place to find mind-blowing spectacle. However, it does reliably offer emotionally
nuanced and heartfelt versions of some underper-
formed gems by the likes of Stephen Sondheim and
William Finn, and its commitment to supporting
new musical works helps keep this vital American
form from going completely Hollywood.

Teatro Vista

1-773 599 9280, www.teatrovista.org.
Teatro Vista ('Theatre with a View') regularly premières new plays and translations by Latino drama-
tists, from inside America's borders and out. Its
productions have included adaptations of Garcia
Lorca and *Our Lady of the Underpass*. In addition to
the fine work it produces solo, the company often
gangs up with other local groups for co-productions.

TimeLine Theatre Company.
See p237.

Sport & Fitness

Chicago is a city on the move.

Even though a few of the local pro teams leave their fans perpetually hungry, you'd be hard-pressed to find a more sports-mad city in the US than Chicago. But don't be fooled into thinking the sporting life is solely enjoyed from the sidelines. Thanks to a great lake and an emerald necklace of parks, the citizens of Chicago are almost always on the move. Biking, swimming, jogging and in-line skating are just a few ways to see the city, its lakefront and its people. While spring and summer are the best times to enjoy the great outdoors, Chicagoans stay active through the year, as the city's winter ice-skaters (and lake-jumpers) can attest.

SPECTATOR SPORTS
Baseball

Chicago is home to two major league baseball teams, and the locals make the most of the rivalry. The two teams play in different leagues, but the six inter-league games they play against one another every year are raucous occasions. And when the teams stay on their own sides of town, the division remains strong – in many ways, no single characteristic says more about a longtime Chicagoan than whether they root for the Cubs or the White Sox.

Despite winning the National League Central Division several times in recent years, the **Chicago Cubs** are destined to disappoint fans every year until they win the World Series, breaking a losing streak that dates to 1908. Still, they have one great asset: Wrigley Field (*photo p242*). Built in 1914, the old ballpark is a bit rough around the edges but is still a terrific stadium, especially for afternoon games. Many games sell out, so book far ahead. And if you don't score tickets, vibrant, boozy Wrigleyville on game day is still worth a visit.

The rivalry between the North Side Cubs and the **Chicago White Sox**, who play in the American League Central Division to a devoted South Side fanbase, only intensified after the White Sox won the 2005 World Series. US Cellular Field, the Sox's ballpark, isn't as characterful as Wrigley, but it's a pretty good place to see a game. What's more, tickets are cheaper than at Wrigley, and far fewer games

sell out. The baseball season runs from the start of April to the end of September. The best teams in each league enter October's play-offs.

Chicago Cubs
Wrigley Field, 1060 W Addison Street, at N Clark Street, Wrigleyville (1-773 404 2827, www.chicago. cubs.mlb.com). El: Red to Addison. **Tickets** $9-$350. **Credit** AmEx, Disc, MC, V. **Map** p313 E1.

Chicago White Sox
US Cellular Field, 333 W 35th Street, between S Stewart & S Wentworth Avenues, Bridgeport (1-312 674 1000, 1-866 769 4263, www.chicago. whitesox.mlb.com). El: Red to Sox-35th. **Tickets** $9.50-$67. **Credit** AmEx, Disc, MC, V.

INSIDE TRACK
JUST THE TICKET

If you're after tickets for a sold-out Cubs, White Sox or Bears game, avoid the usual scalpers and ticket brokers – especially around Wrigley Field, where prices can be absurdly high – and head instead for **www.stubhub.com**. The site is an online marketplace for game tickets, sold by their original purchasers at prices they set themselves. You'll usually pay more than face value but far less than you might elsewhere, and StubHub guarantees the legitimacy of every ticket sold through its site, so you won't be left out in the cold.

Wrigley Field. See p241.

Basketball

The **Chicago Bulls** dominated the NBA in the 1990s, but when Michael Jordan, arguably the greatest player ever to step on to a court, quit in 1997, the team fell apart. Now another star has arrived on the scene: home-grown Derrick Rose. With many of the building blocks in place, tickets at the United Center are getting harder to come by as fans see another championship looming. The NBA regular season runs from November to mid April, with the best teams competing in the play-offs until June.

Chicago Bulls

United Center, 1901 W Madison Street, at N Damen Avenue, West Town (1-312 462 2849, www.nba.com/bulls). El: Blue to Medical Center. **Tickets** $44-$220. **Credit** AmEx, Disc, MC, V. **Map** p314 C12.

Football

After pulling the strings on a trade that brought Jay Cutler to Soldier Field, the **Chicago Bears** are aiming to stop leaning on their defence in a bid to bring home some wins. For some fans, the glory days in the mid 1980s under Mike Ditka were the pinnacle. But if the team can find some success through the air, Cutler & co just might make some memories of their own.

The team plays at Soldier Field, a Chicago institution built in the 1920s as a monument to America's war dead but brutalised by renovations a few years ago. The NFL season

runs from September to December, with the play-offs leading up to the Super Bowl on the first Sunday in February.

Chicago Bears

Soldier Field, 425 E McFetridge Place, at S Lake Shore Drive, Museum Campus (1-847 615 2327, www.chicagobears.com). El: Green, Orange or Red to Roosevelt. **Tickets** Pre-season $79-$395. *Regular season* $104-$420. **Credit** AmEx, DC, Disc, MC, V. **Map** p308 J15.

Hockey

Ever since 'Dollar' Bill Wirtz, the former owner of the **Chicago Blackhawks**, died in 2007, his son Rocky has been battling to make Chicago a hockey town once more. Just like the Bulls, with whom they share the United Center, the Hawks are banking on a core of young studs for titles. Keep an eye out for the annual Blackhawks Fest, where fans can get up close and personal with their hockey heroes. The season runs from October to April, with the play-offs until June.

Chicago Blackhawks

United Center, 1901 W Madison Street, at N Damen Avenue, West Town (1-312 943 4295, www.chicagoblackhawks.com). El: Blue to Medical Center. **Tickets** $34-$400. **Credit** AmEx, Disc, MC, V. **Map** p314 C12.

Soccer

Despite the large numbers of people playing the sport, soccer will never be more than a marginal interest in the United States. However, the **Chicago Fire** have found themselves a tidy little market in Chicago, drawing crowds of more than 10,000 to the games each year. The regular season runs from April to November, followed by the play-offs.

Chicago Fire

Toyota Park, 7000 S Harlem Avenue, at W 71st Street, Bridgeview (1-888 657 3473, www.chicago.fire.mlsnet.com). El: Orange to Midway, then shuttle bus. **Tickets** $20-$45. **Credit** AmEx, Disc, MC, V.

ACTIVE SPORTS & FITNESS

Sure, Chicago has spring, summer, autumn and winter like everywhere else. But there are really only two seasons here as far as sports lovers are concerned: when it's warm enough to leave the house and when it isn't.

While Chicago's weather is notorious, recent years have seen a succession of relatively mild winters, and the sight of people jogging by the water in February is not as unusual or odd as it once was. But summer is when the city really goes berserk. The **Lakefront Trail** (*see p244*) gets packed with skaters, cyclists and runners during warmer weather, all competing for the best views over the city. A ride or a jog along this stretch is one of the finest sightseeing bargains in town.

Many sporting facilities are found in locations administered by the **Chicago Park District** (1-312 742 7529, www.chicagopark district.com); see its website for full details.

Basketball

The **Chicago Park District** (*see left*) maintains more than 1,000 basketball courts in the city. Many are in fine nick, while others are in disrepair. Regardless of condition, though, almost all are packed on sunny summer afternoons.

Bowling

For whatever reason, Chicagoans love to bowl. The city is dotted with alleys of every stripe, from the ragged **Timber Lanes** via the wilfully old-school **Southport Lanes** (where the pins are manually reset) to the slick, shiny **Lucky Strike Lanes**.

Lucky Strike Lanes

322 E Illinois Street, at N Columbus Drive, Streeterville (1-312 245 8331, www.bowllucky strike.com). El: Red to Grand. **Open** 11.30am-midnight Mon-Thur; 11.30am-2am Fri; 11am-2am Sat; 11am-midnight Sun. **Rates** *Per game* $4.95-$6.95. *Per lane* $45-$65/hr. *Shoes* $3.95. 21+ after 8pm daily. **Credit** AmEx, Disc, MC, V. **Map** p310 J10.

Southport Lanes

3325 N Southport Avenue, at W Henderson Street, Lakeview (1-773 472 6600, www. southportlanes.com). El: Brown to Southport. **Open** noon-1am Mon-Fri, Sun; noon-3am Sat. **Rates** *Per lane* $35/hr. *Shoes* $3. 21+ daily. **Credit** AmEx, DC, Disc, MC, V. **Map** p313 D2.

ARTS & ENTERTAINMENT

Soldier Field.

ARTS & ENTERTAINMENT

Woman's World

Chicago's female athletes bring home the medals.

If women skating around a track and bashing each other is your thing – and, judging by their popularity, it's quite a lot of people's thing – then the **Windy City Rollers** (www.windycityrollers.com), the local roller derby team, are for you. There's action just about all year, with the hot and heavy part of the season taking place from January to June at the University of Illinois-Chicago Pavilion. The team was only founded in 2005, but they've already been ranked pretty high in the country.

Another squad on the rise is the **Chicago Force** (www.chicagoforcefootball.com) – the city's women's tackle football team and the 2013 WFA national champions. The season runs from April to June at the Holmgren Athletic Complex on the campus of North Park University.

In women's pro soccer, the **Chicago Red Stars** (www.chicagoredstars.com) share Toyota Park field with the Chicago Fire, battling it out from April to August.

If you really want to get the blood pumping, **Fleet Feet Sports**, a local outfitter for all your active needs, hosts women's fun runs on Tuesday nights (1620 N Wells Street, at W North Avenue, Old Town, 1-312 587 3338), Wednesday nights (4555 N Lincoln Avenue, at W Wilson Avenue, Lincoln Square, 1-773 271 3338) and Thursday nights (Roosevelt Collection, 150 W Roosevelt Road, South Loop, 1-312 788 3338). Expect three- to five-mile runs with talks on everything from wine to breast cancer afterwards in the store. For more information, see www.fleetfeetsports.com.

Chicago Red Stars.

Timber Lanes

1851 W Irving Park Road, between N Ravenswood & N Wolcott Avenues, North Side (1-773 549 9770, www.timberlanesbowl. com). El: Brown to Irving Park. **Open** 11am-2am Mon-Thur; 11am-3am Fri; 9am-2am Sat; 10am-2am Sun. **Rates** *Per game* $2.50-$3. *Per lane $20/hr. Shoes $3. 21+ after 9pm Fri, Sat.* **No credit cards. Map** p314 C0.

Cycling

If you're used to riding in big cities, cycling around Chicago should be straightforward and, if it's not too cold, enjoyable. Few US cities are as bike-friendly as Chicago: the roads are wide, straight and flat, and drivers generally pay attention to cyclists and to the increasingly impressive network of bike lanes. What's more, cycling is just about the best way to get views of the lake and the city's famous skyline. As usual in a big city, though, be sure to use a sturdy lock if you want to retain your steed.

Dedicated bike lanes and trails are springing up around the city all the time. The best route in town is one of the oldest: the 18-mile **Lakefront Trail**, which runs between Kathy Osterman Beach near Andersonville and 71st Street on the South Side. Whether you choose to do all or part of the trail, it's an easy and often beautiful ride, especially if you steer clear of busy summer weekends (watch out for in-line skaters). Finding the path is as easy as riding a bike: head for the lake (east of wherever you are, unless you're swimming in it), and look for the yellow lines.

For more on riding around Chicago, get in contact with the **Active Transportation Alliance** (1-312 427 3325, www.activetrans. org), which publishes the excellent Chicagoland Bike Map of local bike trails ($10 for non-members). There's more useful information at www.chicagocompletestreets.org.

Chicago's **Critical Mass** rides (www.chicagocriticalmass.org) ensure a large group setting where cyclists take over the streets, if only for a few hours. Taking place on the last Friday of the month, the outings have fun themes to ensure an enjoyable time and a safe ride.

Find rental bike stations from Chicago's new bike sharing programme **Divvy** (1-855 553 4889, www.divvybikes.com) all around town. Bike rentals are also available from **On the Route**, a Lakeview specialist store; **Bike Chicago** is a touristy operation with branches in Millennium Park. It's part of the McDonald's Cycle Center, which also offers repairs and secure bike parking (www.chicago bikestation.com) at Navy Pier, and the Ohio Street, Oak Street, North Avenue and Foster Avenue Beaches. You could also try **Bobby's Bike Hike** (*see p288*). However, the best deals are offered at the **Working Bikes Cooperative**, a charitable organisation that sells serviceable bikes at knockdown prices (*see below* **Inside Track**).

The town is also awash with bike stores. Among the best are **Irv's Bikes** in Pilsen (1725 S Racine Avenue, at W 18th Street, 1-312 226 6330, www.irvsbikeshop.com), **Rapid Transit** in Wicker Park (with two branches, the most central of which is its flagship at 1900 W North Avenue, at N Wolcott Avenue, 1-773 227 2288, www.rapidtransitcycles.com), and **Johnny Sprockets** (with two branches, the most central of which is at 3001 N Broadway, at W Wellington Avenue, 1-773 244 1079, www.johnnysprockets.com).

Bike Chicago

McDonald's Cycle Center, Millennium Park, the Loop (1-888 245 3929, www.bikechicago.com). El: Blue to Washington; Brown, Green, Orange, Pink or Purple to Randolph; Red to Lake. **Open** *Summer* 6.30am-8pm Mon-Fri; 8am-8pm Sat, Sun. *Spring, autumn* 6.30am-7pm Mon-Fri; 9am-7pm Sat, Sun. *Winter* 6.30am-6.30pm Mon-Fri. **Rates** $8-$59/hr; $25-$69/day. **Credit** AmEx, Disc, MC, V. **Map** p310 K10.
Other locations throughout the city.

Critical Mass.

On the Route

3144 N Lincoln Avenue, at N Ashland Avenue, Lakeview (1-773 477 5066, www.ontheroute. com). El: Brown to Southport. **Open** 11am-8pm Mon-Thur; 11am-7pm Fri; 10am-6pm Sat; 11am-5pm Sun. **Rates** $35-$50/day; $125-$195/week. **Credit** AmEx, Disc, MC, V. **Map** p313 D3.

Fishing

The easiest fish to catch in Lake Michigan are alewives, which float to the shore in summer. Dead. A whiff of defunct alewife, and you'll know to leave 'em be. Thankfully, most of the alewives have now been eaten by the Pacific salmon that in turn spawned a huge charter fishing industry. The lake also boasts many other live fish: perch are the most sought-after catch among pier anglers, while the smelt fishing season is a sight to behold.

You'll need a licence to fish legally in Illinois; they're available to over-16s at bait stores, sporting goods stores, currency exchanges or the City Clerk's office. The **Illinois Department of Natural Resources** (1-312 814 2070, www.dnr.illinois.gov) offers guides on where to fish. For starters, try Chicago's parks (details from the **Chicago Park District**; *see p243*); the **Forest Preserve District of Cook County** (1-800 870 3666, www.fpdcc.com); and, of course, Lake Michigan. You can cast off the shore at

---

INSIDE TRACK RIDE FOR LIFE

The **Working Bikes Cooperative** salvages Chicago's discarded and unwanted bikes, which are then revived by volunteer mechanics. Roughly 5,000 such bikes are shipped from Chicago to developing countries each year, but the WBC also sells bikes to Chicagoans for $50-$100 from its store (2434 S Western Avenue, at W 24th Place, 1-773 847 5440, www. workingbikes.org). If you fancy cycling around town, you could do worse than buy a WBC bike, ride it during your stay, then donate it when you leave – the price may be lower than a standard rental, and it's all in a good cause.

ARTS & ENTERTAINMENT

INSIDE TRACK
RUN WITH THE LOCALS

Most travellers throw their exercise regime out the window when on holiday. But you don't have to if you join the **Chicago Hash House Harriers** (www.chicagohash.com), the self-proclaimed 'running club with a drinking problem', for its weekly runs that always finish at a local watering hole.

Belmont Harbor (3200 North, 1-312 742 7673), **Diversey Harbor** (2800 North, 1-312 742 7762), **Monroe Harbor** (100 South, 1-312 742 7643) or **Burnham Harbor** (1600 South, 1-312 742 7009); for all of the above, check out www.chicagoharbors.info.

Fitness clubs

Many hotels have a fitness facility on site or offer an 'in' at a nearby club. However, if yours doesn't, there are plenty of options. Among the more popular clubs are **LA Fitness** (55 E Randolph Street, the Loop, 1-312 281 0113, www.lafitness.com), a chain with numerous local branches, or **Lakeshore Sports & Fitness** (1320 W Fullerton, Lincoln Park, 1-773 348 6377, www.lakeshoresf.com).

Golf

The **Chicago Park District** (see p243) runs half a dozen courses around the city, details of which can be found at www.cpdgolf.com.

Cog Hill Golf & Country Club

12294 Archer Avenue, at W 123rd Street, Lemont (1-866 264 4455, www.coghillgolf.com). Metra Lemont. **Open** *Summer* 6am-9pm daily. *Winter* 6am-5pm daily. **Rates** $37-$155. **Credit** Disc, MC, V.
A series of no fewer than four 18-hole courses out in Lemont. The most expensive and most impressive is Dubsdread, the on-again, off-again home to the BMW Championship in September, but the other three offer a decent challenge. Call for details of afternoon and twilight rates.

Jackson Park

6401 S Richards Drive, at E Maruette Drive, South Side (1-312 245 0909, www.cpdgolf.com). Metra: 63rd Street. **Open** sunrise-sunset daily. **Rates** *Non-residents* $23-$30. **Credit** MC, V. **Map** p315 Z18.
The Chicago Park District's (and the city's) only 18-holer runs down by the lakefront on the South Side, and should challenge even low handicappers. Club rental is available.

Sydney R Marovitz Course

3600 N Recreation Drive, in Lincoln Park (1-312 245 0909, www.cpdgolf.com). El: Red to Addison. **Open** sunrise-sunset daily. **Rates** *Non-residents* $25-$28. **Credit** MC, V. **Map** p313 G1.
This nine-hole Lincoln Park course enjoys a fantastic setting alongside the lake. The course is good, too, but you'll need to book ahead (allow up to 14 days in advance).

In-line skating

Chicago drivers tend not to notice skaters until one slams against the hood of their car. However, there's safety in numbers at the **Road Rave**, a summer skate similar to the Friday Night Skate events held in other cities around the world. The skate leaves from Daley Plaza (corner of Dearborn and Washington Streets in the Loop) at 7.30pm on the first Friday of the month from May to October, and is suitable for skaters of all grades. Experienced street skaters can also join a longer Road Rave event on the third Friday of the month (May to September).

Off the road, the **Lakefront Trail** (see p244) is a pleasant way to while away an afternoon in the company of cyclists and runners. Skates can be hired from **Bike Chicago** (see p245).

Pool

In many Chicago bars, the unspoken pool-table rule is that the winner keeps the table. However, you can rent a table by the hour at Chris's Billiards, which is one of the town's better pool halls.

Chris's Billiards

4637 N Milwaukee Avenue, at W Lawrence Avenue, Jefferson Park (1-773 286 4714). El: Blue to Jefferson Park. **Open** 9.30am-2am daily. **Rates** $5-$8/hr. **Credit** AmEx, Disc, MC, V.
Sequences for *The Color of Money* were filmed at this BYOB North Side joint, which has been drawing pool hounds and sharks for years.

Running

The **Chicago Area Runners Association** (1-312 666 9836, www.cararuns.org) has details on races and running routes, though you might be fine just jogging along the **Lakefront Trail** (see p244) or with the **Chicago Hash House Harriers** (see left **Inside Track**).

Good road surfaces, amenable weather and a pancake-flat landscape combine to make the **Chicago Marathon** one of the fastest marathons in the world. The race draws plenty of international runners.

Lakeside volleyball.

ARTS & ENTERTAINMENT

Soccer

Given Chicago's large Latino population, it's no surprise that the beautiful game is popular in the city. Some of the best action happens just off the lake at Montrose Avenue. For details of local games, contact the **Illinois Soccer Association** (1-312 226 7920, www.illinoissoccer.org) or the **National Soccer League of Chicago** (1-708 589 5599, www.nslchicago.org). If you just want to watch your team from back home, visit one of the city's soccer-friendly bars; *see pp129-142*.

Swimming

In summer, thick-skinned aquanauts swim from Navy Pier north towards the Oak Street Beach. Buoys protect swimmers from boats, at least theoretically. The season runs from Memorial Day to Labor Day, but some beaches are sporadically closed due to high water toxicity.

The **Chicago Park District** (*see p243*) operates numerous indoor swimming pools that are both free and, on the whole, well maintained. Among the best is **Welles Park**, a full-size pool in a great Lincoln Square building (2333 W Sunnyside Avenue, at N Western Avenue, 1-312 742 7511).

Tennis

With more than 600 courts around Chicago, it's easier to find a net than a partner. If you prefer to play indoors, there are courts at a few health clubs in the city. The most central public court is along the lakefront; for others, call the **Chicago Park District** (*see p243*).

Volleyball

Along the lake, there are pick-up games galore. Try **Foster Beach** (at Foster Avenue), **Montrose Beach** (at Montrose Avenue), and the **North Avenue Beach** (at North Avenue), the Centre Court of Chicago beach volleyball. *See also p60* **Summer Lovin'**.

Skating & sledding

Wintertime visitors can sled courtesy of the **Chicago Park District** (*see p243*), which operates a number of toboggan runs with wooden chutes. City-run rinks, such as those in **Millennium Park** and at **Daley Bicentennial Plaza**, are generally open from late November to mid March. From December until early January, there's also a fairly expensive ice rink on **Navy Pier**.

McCormick Tribune Ice Skating Rink at Millennium Park
McCormick Tribune Plaza, Millennium Park, 55 N Michigan Avenue, at E Randolph Street, the Loop (1-312 742 5222, www.millenniumpark.org). El: Blue to Washington; Brown, Green, Orange, Pink or Purple to Randolph; Red to Lake. **Open** *late Nov-mid Mar* times vary. **Admission** free. *Skate rental* $10. **Map** p309 J12.
This 16,000sq ft outdoor winter skating rink is free. But there's a catch: skate rental costs $10.

Rink at Wrigley
Corner of N Clark Street and W Waveland Avenue, Wrigleyville (1-773 525 1638, www.chicagocubs.com). El: Red to Addison. **Open** *Nov-Mar* 2-8pm Mon-Thur; 2-10pm Fri; noon-10pm Sat; 10am-8pm Sun. **Admission** $5-$10 (plus $5-$10 skate rental); $3-$6 (plus $3 skate rental) reductions.
This Cubs parking lot is transformed into a full-size skating rink during winter. Buy admission tickets on site for morning, afternoon or evening sessions. The rink can close when temperature rises too high.

INSIDE TRACK LAKE PLACID

Although it helps, you don't have to be Donald Trump to enjoy Lake Michigan up close and personal. Several organisations offer sailing lessons, among them the **Chicago Sailing Club** (Belmont Harbor, 1-773 871 7245, www.chicagosailingclub.com). And the lake's relative calm makes it a good place for novices to take to the water.

Escapes & Excursions

Escapes & Excursions

Head out of the Windy City for a breath of fresh air.

Simple geography makes Chicago an excellent base for touring the Midwest. Drive south-east from the Loop and within half an hour you can be in Indiana; in an hour you're in Michigan. Wisconsin is only an hour's drive north, with Milwaukee just 90 minutes away.

Shared by Illinois, Indiana, Michigan and Wisconsin, Lake Michigan is a great source of recreation. Day trips to the Indiana Dunes and Michigan's Harbor Country offer plenty of fun ways to enjoy this great inland sea, whether you're fishing, boating or just watching the waves roll in while you daydream.

Although Amtrak (*see p286*) runs services to several places listed in this chapter, you'll need a car to reach most of them. Bring a handful of single-dollar bills and plenty of change with you: tolls range from 30 cents to $4, and some unmanned tollbooths don't offer change.

Illinois

SMALL-TOWN CHARM

Galena

Welcome to presidential country: Grant, Lincoln and Reagan all took root here. Driving the back roads east of Galena over the rolling terrain of one of the few hilly regions in prairie-flat Illinois, you may encounter a bright red stagecoach pulled by a pair of brown Belgian draught horses. An authentic reproduction of a 19th-century Concord stagecoach, it's one of many living history experiences that await in Galena, the quintessential time-warp town.

Established in the 1820s, Galena grew into a lead-mining boomtown at a time when Chicago was no more than a tiny military outpost on the swampy lake shore. Today, the quaint little town is calmer, but does offer a tourist-friendly motherlode of arts and crafts, antiques shops, winery tours, stylish bistros and about 40 B&Bs. More than 85 per cent of its buildings appear on the National Register of Historic Places.

Housed in an 1858 Italianate mansion, the **Galena/Jo Daviess County Historical Society & Museum** (211 S Bench Street, 1-815 777 9129, www.galenahistorymuseum.

org) takes visitors back to the time when Galena was the richest port north of St Louis, attracting more than 350 steamboats a year. It offers an audiovisual presentation and a peek into the original shaft of one of the lead mines to which Galena owes its existence.

You can soak up more history at the **Ulysses S Grant Home State Historic Site** (500 Bouthillier Street, 1-815 777 3310, www.granthome.com), a reminder of the day (18 August 1865) when, with a jubilant procession, speeches and fireworks, proud citizens welcomed home their returning Civil War hero. Before going to war, Grant had worked at a Galena store owned by his father and run by his younger brothers. Upon his return, Grant was presented with a handsome, two-storey furnished brick mansion on Bouthillier Street, purchased for $2,500 by a group of wealthy Republicans a few months prior to his homecoming. Following his death, his children bequeathed the mansion to the city of Galena in 1904, which later turned it over to the state of Illinois. The house has since been restored to the way it appeared in drawings published in an 1868 edition of Frank Leslie's *Illustrated Newspaper*, with the addition of assorted Grantabilia.

Take time to wander away from touristy Main Street to discover the 'Artists' Row' section of Spring Street, dotted with a wide variety of one-of-a-kind shops, galleries and B&Bs. A few minutes from Main Street, you'll also find a chunk of Ireland. The **Irish Cottage & Frank O'Dowd's Irish Pub** (9853 US Route 20 W, 1-815 776 0707, www. theirishcottageboutiquehotel.com) is nestled on a 20-acre site, containing a 75-room inn, and an Irish-themed pub and restaurant created by two first cousins from Ireland.

Galena is tucked away in Illinois's north-west corner, where Iowa, Wisconsin and Illinois converge near the Mississippi. A ten-minute drive north-east takes you to spectacular views from Charles Mound, the highest point in what is otherwise a monotonously flat state.

Getting there
Galena is 165 miles north-west of Chicago. By car, take I-90 (Northwest Tollway) to Rockford, then take US 20.

LAND OF LINCOLN
Springfield

Let's be honest: the reason to visit Springfield is Abraham Lincoln – he lived, worked and raised a family there from 1837 until 1861, when he was inaugurated as the 16th President of the United States. The town is chock-full of Lincoln sites, from the humble (his home) to the grand (his tomb). And Springfield has recently

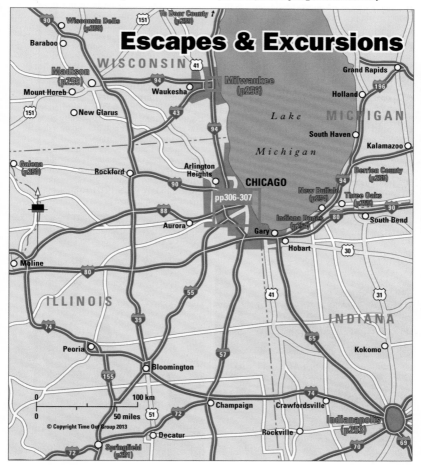

Escapes & Excursions

INSIDE TRACK
LUCKY HORSESHOE

If you ask after local delicacies in Springfield, locals will insist you partake of a 'horseshoe' sandwich, an open-faced sandwich on toasted sourdough bread with a hamburger patty or ham, topped with french fries and cheese sauce. It's every bit as messy as it sounds. The best version can be found at **D'Arcy's Pint** (661 W Stanford Avenue, 1-217 492 8800, www.darcyspintonline.com).

acquired a little more presidential polish, as the former stomping ground of then-state senator, now-commander-in-chief, Barack Obama.

You can get a personal glimpse of Lincoln's life at his home: located in a leafy neighbourhood, the house is operated by the National Park Service as the **Lincoln's Home National Historic Site** (426 S 7th Street, 1-217 492 4241, www.nps.gov/liho) with guided tours by park rangers.

For a more Disneyfied take on America's greatest president, hit the fantastic **Abraham Lincoln Presidential Library & Museum** (212 N 6th Street, 1-800 610 2094, www.alplm. org) for its memorabilia, high-end exhibits and immersive presentations. In particular, check out 'Lincoln's Eyes', where smoke machines and 3-D projection are used, and the seats actually shake (to mimic a cannon's boom) during a Civil War retelling.

The **Old State Capitol** (1 SW Old State Capitol Plaza, 1-217 785 9363, www.illinois history.gov/hs/old_capitol.htm), built in 1837, is a fine example of Greek revival architecture. Lincoln made his 'house divided' speech on slavery here in 1858; a scant seven years later, the body of the slain president lay in state in the same building. More recently, Obama announced his candidacy for the US presidency on the steps of the Old State Capitol.

Across from the Old State Capitol are the **Lincoln-Herndon Law Offices** (Adams Street, between 5th & 6th Streets, 1-217 785 7289, www.illinoishistory.gov/hs/lincoln_ herndon.htm), where Lincoln practised law. Cases were tried in the federal court below; Lincoln would sometimes lie on the office floor and observe courtroom proceedings through a peephole in the floorboards.

Springfield's most moving site is surely **Lincoln's Tomb** (1500 Monument Avenue, 1-217 782 2717, closed Sun & Mon). Most Tuesday evenings at 7pm between June and August (call ahead to confirm), a retreat ceremony is held in front of the tomb, with a drill, musket firing and the haunting sound of 'Taps' played by a bugler. Captured in an inscription are the words spoken by Secretary of War Edwin M Stanton at Lincoln's death: 'Now he belongs to the ages.'

Although Lincoln is Springfield's most famous citizen (and Obama its most famous visiting legislator), another of Springfield's native sons had an international reputation. Vachel Lindsay (1879-1931) was one of America's best-known poets during the early

Lincoln's Tomb.

Indianapolis.

decades of the 20th century, and the **Vachel Lindsay Home** (603 S 5th Street, 1-217 524 0901) has been restored as a State Historic Site.

Getting there

Springfield is 200 miles south-west of Chicago. Take I-55 from Chicago to Springfield, exit 98-B (Clearlake).

Indiana
WINDY CITY TO INDY CITY
Indianapolis

Indianapolis buzzes with a cosmopolitan vibe mixed with a classically Midwestern warmth, providing sights and sounds that can only be found here. Diagonal Massachusetts Avenue, or Mass Ave (www.discovermassave.com), is the artsy section; shops such as **Silver in the City** (434 Massachusetts Avenue, 1-317 955 9925, www.silverinthecity.com) feature city-smart designs at small-town prices. Catch music at the **Chatterbox Jazz Club** (435 Massachusetts Avenue, 1-317 636 0584, www.chatterboxjazz.com) or rub elbows with artists and sports fans at the **Lockerbie Pub** (631 E Michigan Street, 1-317 631 9545).

Mass Ave borders **Lockerbie Square** (www.lockerbiesquare.org), a quaint collection of cobbled streets and historic homes. The **Fountain Square** neighbourhood (www.discoverfountainsquare.com), on the south-east side of town, is anchored by the architecturally impressive **Fountain Square Theatre Building** (1105 Prospect Street, 1-317 686 6010, www.fountainsquareindy. com), which contains a vintage 1950s soda fountain and diner, a rooftop restaurant and two duckpin bowling alleys (a regional version of bowling).

Plenty more heady delights are available too. The intriguing **Eiteljorg Museum of American Indians and Western Art** (500 W Washington Street, 1-317 636 9378, www.eiteljorg.org) boasts a couple of minor O'Keeffes and an impressive collection of photography from indigenous peoples. While you're there, don't miss the scenic White River Canal Walk, which winds through ten and a half blocks between 11th and Washington Streets, linking the Eiteljorg Museum, the **NCAA Hall of Champions** and the **Indiana State Museum**. Jog along the paved walkways, or rent a paddleboat and cruise down the river.

The city boasts one of the best kids' museums in the country: the **Children's Museum of Indianapolis** (3000 N Meridian Street, 1-317 334 3322, www.childrensmuseum. org). Wee naturalists can peer into a real freshwater pond and backyard daredevils can scale a 20-foot climbing wall.

The works of Georges Seurat and a number of other neo-Impressionists are among the 50,000-plus pieces in the permanent collection at the striking **Indianapolis Museum of Art** (4000 Michigan Road, 1-317 923 1331, www.imamuseum.org), founded all the way back in 1883. The museum sits on an

**INSIDE TRACK
GAMBLING ON INDIANA**

A trip to the dunes isn't complete without a stop at one of the area's clutch of riverboat casinos, the king of which is **Hammond's Horseshoe Casino** (777 Casino Center Drive, Hammond, 1-866 711 7463, www.horseshoe.com). It's one of the closest casinos to the city: you can't miss its massive sign from the Chicago Skyway.

ESCAPES & EXCURSIONS

impressive 152-acre site; be sure to save some time at the end to meander through the handsome park and gardens.

A gastro mecca Indy isn't, so skip the newfangled and head straight for the classics. Steamy hot bagels and pastrami sandwiches stacked higher than Indy's tallest building rule at **Shapiro's** (808 S Meridian Street, 1-317 631 4041, www.shapiros.com), an old-school Jewish deli and cafeteria on the south side of town. Foamy beer and schnitzels are mainstay items at the near-legendary **Rathskeller** (401 E Michigan Street, 1-317 636 0396, www. rathskeller.com), a German restaurant and brewpub with an outstanding beer garden that's open in the warmer months.

Getting there
Indianapolis is 185 miles south-east of Chicago. Take the I-90 East tollway toward Indiana, then merge on to I-65 South that goes directly to Indianapolis.

THE GREAT OUTDOORS
Indiana Dunes & vicinity

Just as Easterners cherish a trip to 'the shore', thousands of Chicagoans grow up looking forward to visiting 'the dunes'. Located along Indiana's north-western corner, this beach playground offers swimming, bodysurfing and the exhilaration of a romp down steep, sandy slopes after a leg-wearying climb up to the summit. On a clear day, the Chicago skyline is visible from the shore, shimmering on the horizon.

The sloping white expanses of the dunes encompass the **Indiana Dunes State Park** (1600 North CR-25 E, Chesterton, 1-219 926 1952, www.in.gov/dnr/parklake/2980.htm), Chicago's closest beach getaway and just an hour's drive from the city. Relax along the park's three miles of Lake Michigan-hugging shoreline or explore more than 15,000 acres of dunes, bogs, marshes and prairie grounds in the surrounding **Indiana Dunes National Lakeshore** (Highway 12 & County Line Road, Chesterton, 1-219 926 7561, www.nps.gov/indu). The federal nature reserve spans 15 miles of shoreline and offers canoeing, hiking and other outdoor activities.

If you're up for a little more exertion than lying around on the beach, take a hike along the Mount Baldy Trail (Highway 12, Michigan City). It's less than a mile long, but hiking a sand dune isn't easy and you'll definitely feel it the next day. But the pay-off is well worth it, particularly at sunset: a spectacular view of the Chicago skyline from an entirely new vantage point. Less adventurous types can take a flatter

path around the 126-foot 'mountain' of sand, but be sure to snag a map at the **Dorothy Buell Memorial Visitor Center** (1215 N State Road 49, Porter, 1-219 395 8914). The centre boasts several interactive exhibits about the surrounding terrain, as well as a pleasant bookstore.

Getting there
By car, take the Chicago Skyway and I-80/90 and I-94 to Highway 49. By train, the Chicago South Shore & South Bend Railroad follows the curve of the Lake Michigan shoreline into Indiana and makes several stops in Lake and Porter Counties. Trains leave from Randolph Street station in the Loop.

Michigan
HARBOR COUNTRY

Just an hour and a half's drive from the city, Michigan's Harbor Country is a pretty amalgam of shabby-chic shops, bucolic B&Bs, tree-shaded paths and white-sand beaches. Here are three ways to experience it.

New Buffalo & vicinity

Red Arrow Highway, which runs through the heart of Harbor Country, connects dozens of tiny beach towns that come to life during Michigan's balmy summer. The largest and most central destination is New Buffalo (population 1,800), which is roughly an hour's drive from the Loop. It's a sweet place and well worth a wander.

Stroll down Whittaker Street towards the centre of town. Lined with a few chic clothing shops, Whittaker is home to the **Stray Dog Bar & Grill** (245 N Whittaker Street, 1-269 469 2727, www.thestraydog.com), packed in summer with locals vying for a spot on its rooftop deck. Continue down the block to the New Buffalo Beach, which offers casual surfing and an outpost of the popular Oink's ice-cream chain. After working up an appetite in the outdoors, head to **Redamak's** (616 E Buffalo Street, 1-269 469 4522, www.redamaks.com), where the tasty, no-frills burgers and fries have been satisfying locals since 1975.

About 20 miles up the road, at **Warren Dunes State Park** (12032 Red Arrow Highway, Sawyer, 1-269 426 4013), giant piles of sand, some nearly 250 feet high, make a perfect perch from which to take in the lake. The surrounding woods provide more than six miles of trails, making it a great place to spot wood ducks, opossum, foxes and all sorts of woodland creatures.

Getting there

New Buffalo is approximately 60 miles east of Chicago. Take I-90 east to the La Porte exit IN-39 (La Porte Road).

Berrien County wineries

The tri-county south-west region of Michigan has been designated an American Viticultural Area by the name of 'Lake Michigan Shore'. Tucked into the rolling hills and fertile valleys of Berrien County, little more than an hour's drive from the Loop, nearly a dozen wineries take advantage of the micro-climate, producing a range of wines that are sold locally and nationally. Visitors are generally welcome.

Among the best of the bunch is **Tabor Hill Winery** (185 Mount Tabor Road, Buchanan, 1-800 283 3363, www.taborhill.com), which attracts couples in search of fine dining and romantic sunsets. Windows look out over the vineyards; on the horizon sit the dark, brooding humps of the dune ridges along Lake Michigan.

Rick Moersch was a winemaker at Tabor Hill for 14 years before he opened the **Round Barn Winery, Distillery & Brewery** (10983 Hills Road, Baroda, 1-800 716 9463, www.roundbarnwinery.com) in 1992. Wine, beer and vodka tastings are conducted in the eponymous round Amish barn. Discovered in northern Indiana, it was dismantled, transported 90 miles to this site and rebuilt by Amish craftsmen. A crescent-shaped copper bar features matching wall sconces decorated with alchemical symbols from the Middle Ages.

Family-owned and family-oriented **Lemon Creek Fruit Farm & Winery** (533 East Lemon Creek Road, Berrien Springs, 1-269 471 1321, www.lemoncreekwinery.com) is a vast working farm with a fruit stand, pick-your-own orchards, tractor rides for children and abundant wildlife, including deer, foxes, hawks and owls, plus waterfowl that settle on a five-acre pond. The vineyards produce white wines ranging from dry chardonnay to sweet vidal blanc, reds that include an award-winning cabernet sauvignon, grape and raspberry sparkling wines, and three non-alcoholic sparkling juices. Just down the road is the **Domaine Berrien Cellars & Winery** (398 E Lemon Creek Road, Berrien Springs, 1-269 473 9463, www.domaineberrien.com), a popular picnic venue. The winery was opened in 2001 by Wally Maurer.

The best of the bunch is **St Julian Winery** (716 S Kalamazoo Street, Paw Paw, 1-269 657 5568, www.stjulian.com), established in 1921 and Michigan's oldest winery by far. Located in Paw Paw, St Julian also has a tasting room at downtown Union Pier (9145 Union Pier Road, Union Pier, 1-269 469 3150), with a selection of fairly priced favourites.

Getting there

At the heart of the Lake Michigan Shore viticultural region is St Joseph, approximately 95 miles north-east of Chicago. Take I-94 east to the Stevensville exit. The winery exits are posted along I-94. Amtrak runs a service from Chicago to St Joseph.

Three Oaks

Modest in comparison to its neighbouring beach towns, Three Oaks (population 1,600) is a cultured gem amid the cluster of tourist destinations along the lake. A second home for many Chicagoans, the town provides big-city comforts – fine dining, arts and entertainment – on a small-town scale.

New Buffalo.

Every October, hundreds of visitors descend on the place for the annual Manhattan Short Film Festival at the restored, turn-of-the-century **Vickers Theatre** (6 N Elm Street, 1-269 756 3522, www.vickerstheatre.com). The Vickers sponsors live music in the town's Dewey Cannon Park during the summer, and screens indie and arthouse films all year round. Down the street is the **Acorn Theater** (107 Generations Drive, 1-269 756 3879, www.acorntheater.com), a beautifully updated performance space located in the town's historic featherbone factory.

Three Oaks is also known for its visual arts and antiques. **Ipso Facto** (1 W Ash Street, 1-269 756 3404, www.ipsofactoantiques.com) concentrates on accessories, artefacts, and vintage-modern and antique finds.

A handful of popular dining establishments are worth the quick drive from the lakeshore. **Froehlich's** (26 N Elm Street, 1-269 756 6002, www.shopfroehlichs.com), pronounced 'fray-licks', oozes small-town charm. Nibble on delicious breads, sandwiches, cheeses, home-canned jams and other delights at this gourmet deli and bakery. Housed in a 100-year-old storefront, the heart-stoppingly cute **Viola** (102 N Elm Street, 1-269 756 9420, www.violacafe.com) serves breakfast, lunch and afternoon tea.

Getting there

Three Oaks is approximately 80 miles east of Chicago. Take I-94 east to the US-12 E exit 4A to Three Oaks/Niles.

Wisconsin

THE SECOND CITY'S SECOND CITY

Milwaukee

Milwaukee is as traditional as the oompah bands that it trots out periodically to celebrate its German heritage, and as contemporary as the experimental theatre that flourishes in the revitalised downtown historic districts. It has big-city assets: museums, galleries, orchestra, opera and ballet companies, lively nightlife, plenty of parkland and major league sports. Yet it's also quiet enough to please families, and compact enough to reward the day tripper up from its rival city to the south: the 90-minute commute from Chicago is well worth the effort, whether for an afternoon of art or a Friday night fish-fry.

While Milwaukee's German roots have ensured its reputation as a mecca for beer (Pabst, Schlitz, Blatz and, most famously,

INSIDE TRACK CUSTARD CRAZE

Roadfood, Jane and Michael Stern's invaluable guide to diners, mom-and-pop joints and other low-key, high-reward local eateries across the US, contains a huge array of recommendations for Milwaukee. If you only have time for one, make it an order of frozen custard from **Leon's Frozen Custard Drive-In** (3131 S 27th Street, 1-414 383 1784), which reputedly acted as the inspiration for Arnold's Drive-In in *Happy Days*.

Miller were all started in Milwaukee by German families), it's recently become known for its architecture. Chief among the town's marvels is the **Milwaukee Art Museum** (700 N Art Museum Drive, 1-414 224 3200, www.mam.org; *photo p258*). The original building has a showy extension designed by renowned architect Santiago Calatrava. The extension was inspired by the museum's lakeside location: check out the cabled pedestrian bridge with a mast suggested by the form of a sailing boat, the curving single-storey galleria reminiscent of a wave and, most strikingly, the moving steel louvres, which pay homage to the wings of a bird. It's a credit to the museum's nearly 25,000 works, including a significant number by Milwaukee native Georgia O'Keeffe, that the art itself isn't overshadowed.

In addition to its growing architectural reputation, Milwaukee's beer legacy remains. Although Miller is Milwaukee's only surviving megabrewery, it's complemented by several microbreweries that have started up over the past decade. At the same time, swathes of the admittedly small downtown area have been redeveloped to pleasing effect, most notably the Historic Third Ward, and new businesses are springing up around the city.

Much of the town's prosperity is mirrored in a recent downtown renaissance, especially on the RiverWalk along the Milwaukee River, which the city hopes will bring in more visitors. A prime example of the city's revitalisation and flourishing performing arts scene is the 4,100-seat **Milwaukee Theatre** (Wisconsin Center District, 400 W Wisconsin Avenue, 1-414 908 6000, www.milwaukeetheatre.com), a $32 million makeover of the historic Milwaukee Auditorium. The theatre features an elegant domed rotunda lobby and reception area, and hosts a range of Broadway shows as part of its programme of entertainment.

Culturally, Milwaukee's on the up. Aside from festivals, the biggest of which is late

June's **Summerfest** (1-414 273-2680, www.
summerfest.com), the **Milwaukee Symphony
Orchestra** (1101 N Market Street, 1-414 291
7605, www.mso.org) draws the crowds, and a
number of theatre groups push drama further
up the town's agenda. Don't get the **Marcus
Center for the Performing Arts** (929 N
Water Street, 1-414 273 7206, www.marcus
center.org), downtown's main entertainment
venue, confused with **Art's Performing
Center** (144 E Juneau Avenue, 1-414 271
8288), a creatively named strip joint nearby.

Families love the **Milwaukee Public
Museum** (800 W Wells Street, 1-414 278
2728, www.mpm.edu), a three-floor natural
history museum that holds some six million
exhibits, but there are other attractions
nearby; not for nothing is the area known
informally as Museum Center. **Discovery
World** (500 N Harbor Drive, 1-414 765 9966,
www.discoveryworld.org) is full of interactive

exhibits; the **Humphrey IMAX Dome
Theater** (800 W Wells Street, 1-414 319 4629,
www.mpm.edu) boasts a six-storey high screen
and a 12,000-watt sound system.

The town's real must-see is the **Milwaukee
County Zoo** (10001 W Bluemound Road, 1-414
256-5412, www.milwaukeezoo.org). With 3,000
animals across 200 acres, it's one of the nation's
largest and best zoos. Elsewhere, **Betty Brinn
Children's Museum** (929 E Wisconsin
Avenue, 1-414 390 5437, www.bbcmkids.org)
is an interactive place designed for under-tens,
while one of Milwaukee's most fascinating
museums, the **Eisner American Museum
of Advertising & Design** (208 N Water
Street, 1-414 847 3290, www.theeisner.com)
provides colourful, interactive exhibits on how
advertising effects our culture. And there's
always the **Harley-Davidson Museum**
(400 Canal Street, 1-414 287-2789, www.
h-dmuseum.com). The huge, sleek, industrial-

style exhibition space features more motorcycles than you can shake a stick at, and is part of a sprawling new complex set in 20 park-like acres along the river.

For a chance to soak up Brew City's history, along with some suds, head to the **Miller Brewing Co** (4251 W State Street, 1-414 931 2337, www.millercoors.com), which is open for free (albeit self-aggrandising) tours. Learn how the brewery churns out six gazillion bottles of Miller Lite a minute and how Miller has five of the top ten selling beers in the US. Gratis beers are a fitting end to the brisk tour. Beer connoisseurs (as opposed to beer guzzlers) might prefer a trip to the **Lakefront Brewery** (1872 N Commerce Street, 1-414 372 8800, www.lakefrontbrewery.com). The tour includes a souvenir pint glass, four pours of (good) beer and a coupon for another free beer at various local bars.

Shoppers and diners will be charmed by the Historic Third Ward, where a range of boho boutiques, gastropubs and posh eateries line the refurbished blocks. In the heart of the district sits the **Milwaukee Public Market** (400 N Water Street, 1-414 336 1111, www.milwaukeepublicmarket.org), built in autumn 2005 in an effort to preserve the neighbourhood's history as a public market-place. Here you'll find dozens of vendors selling gourmet and organic produce, seafood from around the world, baked goods, flowers, and pounds and pounds of cheese.

Getting there

By car, Milwaukee is approximately 90 miles north of Chicago on I-94. Milwaukee is a 90-minute train ride from Chicago's Union Station; services are frequent.

WATER WORLD
The Wisconsin Dells

Dispensing Hoopla with a capital 'H', the Wisconsin Dells remains one of the Midwest's great child-pleasers. Adventure parks and video arcades, helicopter rides and go-kart races, minigolf and hot dogs… The Dells is the place to head when the kids whine about wanting something to do.

The Dells is forever reinventing itself, adding new attractions every season. None, though, has had as much impact as the indoor waterparks that have popped up all over town; indeed, the place now touts itself as the 'Waterpark Capital of the World'. Among the biggest and best are the elegant **Kalahari Resort & Convention Center** (1305 Kalahari Drive, 1-608 254 5466 ,www.kalahariresort.com); the golfer-friendly **Wilderness Hotel & Golf Resort** (511

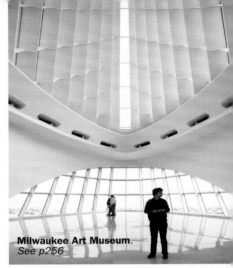

Milwaukee Art Museum.
See p256

E Adams Street, 1-608 253 9729, www. wildernessterritory.com); and the enormous **Mt Olympus Water & Theme Park** (1701 Wisconsin Dells Parkway, (1-800 800 4997, www.mtolympusthemepark.com), which boasts several outdoor theme-park rides in addition to its few dozen waterslides, floating rivers, water basketball and shallow play areas. These wet and wild destinations have helped to transform the Dells from a strictly seasonal resort into a year-round tourist hub.

Despite its brash, noisy front, the Dells somehow remains the scenic destination it was back when 19th-century photographer Henry Hamilton Bennett first set out to capture the landscape. The towering sandstone cliffs and cool, fern-filled gullies remain unspoiled, and a tour of the upper and lower rivers by boat or aboard an amphibious 'duck', a World War II landing craft, make for enjoyable outings; try **Wisconsin Ducks** (1-608 254 8751, www.wisconsinducktours.com). To experience the Dells as Bennett saw them, visit the **HH Bennett Studio & History Center** (215 Broadway, 1-608 253 3523, www.hh bennett.wisconsinhistory.org).

A number of shows keep children on their toes. The famous **Tommy Bartlett Thrill Show** (560 Wisconsin Dells Parkway, 1-608 254 2525, www.tommybartlett.com) has been entertaining visitors for a while; magician **Rick Wilcox** (1666 Wisconsin Dells Parkway, 1-608 254 5511, www.rickwilcox.com) is also a popular figure here.

Getting there

Wisconsin Dells is 188 miles north-west of Chicago. Take I-90 from Chicago to Dells exits 92, 89, 87, 85 (the best exit for downtown is 87).

LITTLE TOWN ON THE PRAIRIE
Madison

Every Saturday, 20,000 locals and tourists flock to the square around Wisconsin's neoclassical Capitol building. Although the building dates from 1917 and boasts a quite singular granite dome, it's neither history nor architecture that attract the crowds. This is the **Dane County Farmers' Market** (www.dcfm.org), awash with the aroma of freshly brewed coffee, the sweet scent of basil and the distinctive tang of handmade cheeses.

This weekly ritual illustrates why Madison is so highly regarded by those who live here and those who visit. Built on an isthmus bordered by Lake Monona and Lake Mendota, it's a beautiful town. Five lakes, 13 public beaches, 50 miles of bike paths and more than 200 parks draw the crowds in summer for cycling, hiking, fishing and canoeing. But Madison has a full calendar of events and activities all year round. Winter sees the locals ice-skating, ice-fishing, skiing and sledding.

Culturally, Madison punches above its weight, with a resident orchestra, a theatre and a full performing arts schedule at the University of Wisconsin at Madison. It keeps improving too: the **Overture Center for the Arts** (201 State Street, 1-608 258 4177, www.overturecenter.com), added in 2004, focuses on local artists in a multitude of disciplines.

Downtown's 'Museum Mile' includes the **Madison Children's Museum** (100 N Hamilton Street, 1-608 256 6445, www.madisonchildrensmuseum.org); the **Madison Museum of Contemporary Art** (227 State Street, 1-608 257 0158, www.mmoca.org); the **University of Wisconsin-Madison's Chazen Museum of Art** (750 University Avenue, 1-608 263 2246, www.chazen.wisc.edu); the **Wisconsin Historical Museum** (30 N Carroll Street, 1-608 264 6555, http://historicalmuseum.wisconsinhistory.org); and the **Wisconsin Veterans' Museum** (30 W Mifflin Street, 1-608 267 1799, http://wisvetsmuseum.com).

The **Monona Terrace Community & Convention Center** (1 John Nolen Drive, 1-608 261 4000, www.mononaterrace.com), located on the shores of Lake Monona, was conceived by Frank Lloyd Wright more than 60 years ago, but wasn't completed until 1997 after decades of architectural and civic controversy. This world-class, five-level facility hosts conventions, meetings and special events; tours are offered daily (1pm, $2-$3).

Elsewhere, clusters of boutiques, speciality shops and restaurants on King, Monroe and Williamson Streets capture the city's eclectic character. The antiquarian bookstores around State Street draw collectors from Chicago and beyond in search of rare first editions.

Getting there
Madison is 145 miles north-west of Chicago. Take I-90 to Beltline Highway (US 12/18); follow signs to downtown (look for the Capitol dome symbol).

BACK TO NATURE
Door County

Those who say the Midwest is landlocked have clearly never ventured to Door County, the long, elegant peninsula that's home to a serenely isolated cluster of communities anchored along Lake Michigan's westernmost dip into Wisconsin. Including about a dozen towns and numerous tiny villages on either side of the peninsula, and many surrounding islands, this 300-mile curved stretch of shoreline is popular in summer for sailing, fishing, hiking, canoeing and other water-based activities, but also serves as a peaceful winter getaway.

Door County's mainland peninsula has two sides – literally. The west side faces mild **Green Bay**, where winding roads connect tourist towns such as **Egg Harbor**, **Fish Creek** and **Ephraim**. The county's first inhabitants developed the sweeping **Sturgeon Bay** on the Lake Michigan (east) side of the land, the peninsula's county seat and only real city.

Travel north a few miles along the peninsula for a real escape. Just south of the town of **Jacksonport**, you'll find **Cave Point and Whitefish Dunes State Park** (3275 Clarks Lake Road, Sturgeon Bay, 1-920 823 2400, http://dnr.wi.gov/topic/parks/name/whitefish), which is know for its limestone caves.

For those in search of island life with all the amenities, **Washington Island** (www.washingtonisland.com), Door County's largest, offers an easy respite from the main peninsula's bustle. After arriving in Detroit Harbor, relaxed recreation awaits: Washington Island plays host to arts and gallery scenes, as well as a handful of museums, shopping districts and a first-rate golf course, the **Deer Run Golf Course & Resort** (1885 Michigan Road, 1-920 847 2017). Take it all in from **Mountain Park**. Or if you're visiting during summer, stick around for a performance by the **Peninsula Players** (W4351 Peninsula Players Road, Fish Creek, 1-920 868 3287, www.peninsulaplayers.com), when top-notch actors perform in an open-air theatre tucked into the woods.

Getting there
By car, Door County is 250 miles north of Chicago. Take I-94 to Milwaukee, then I-43 to Green Bay.

ESCAPES & EXCURSIONS

In Context

History

Life by the lake.

TEXT: VICTORIA CUNHA & WILL FULFORD-JONES

The location, a boggy swampland on the edge of Lake Michigan, was far from ideal. But the efforts of those who chose to settle in what eventually became Chicago turned its geographical circumstance from a potential curse into an undoubted blessing. Ever since a Haitian traveller made his home here in the 1770s, successive residents have fought tooth and nail to turn their town into a major player. Indeed, 21st-century Chicago can only be explained by a look at the 250 years that preceded it.

EARLY SETTLERS

Missionary Father Jacques Marquette and cartographer Louis Jolliet were the first Europeans to explore the lower Lake Michigan region. In 1673, chartered and funded by the governor of New France (now Quebec), the pair attempted to follow the Mississippi and its tributaries as far as possible to the north-east. After travelling to the native village of Kaskaskia (near what is now the town of North Utica) on the Illinois River, the intrepid duo proceeded north-east on the Des Plaines River.

When they reached what the local Native Americans called 'Checagou' (believed to translate as 'wild onion', which grew in the area), Marquette and Jolliet's party floated down the Chicago River to Lake Michigan before heading north to Green Bay in autumn 1673. The trip was deemed a success, so much so that Marquette returned to the area in 1674 and spent the winter in what would later become known as Chicago before heading back to Kaskaskia in the spring. Jolliet never again visited the area.

The first permanent non-native resident of Chicago, Haitian pioneer Jean-Baptiste Point du Sable, came to the area almost exactly a century later. The black Du Sable is believed to have established a fur trading post at the mouth of the Chicago River as early as 1772, marrying a Potawatomie native named Catherine around the same time. More than two decades later, Du Sable sold his property on to a fur trapper, who in turn sold it almost immediately to a trader named John Kinzie. The area's first permanent white settler, Kinzie eventually came to be known as 'the Father of Chicago'. However, it's the more unassuming Du Sable who deserves the nickname.

THEY FORT THE LAW

Fearful of further trouble after the War of Independence, the government decided a military presence was necessary, and so Fort Dearborn was built in 1803 at what is now the south end of the Michigan Avenue Bridge. Then the major western US Army garrison in the country, it occupied a strategic point near the southern end of Lake Michigan on the south side of the Chicago River, just across from the cabin built by Du Sable. Sure enough, the US was soon once more battling the British; by the summer of 1812, tensions between soldiers and natives, who were bought off by the British, were at an all-time high.

Despite efforts to appease the Potawatomie leaders, Captain Nathaniel Heald decided that safety concerns were so great, Fort Dearborn should be evacuated. Accompanied by an escort of friendly Miami natives from Indiana, the garrison began its journey along the lake, but was ambushed by natives. Heald and his wife were taken prisoner, but almost all the others who were attempting to leave the fort were executed; in all, 53 settlers and natives died. The Potawatomies returned three days later and burnt the fort.

After the war was over, trading once more began to take place in the area. Having fled during the massacre, Kinzie came back in 1816 and resumed his business activities. His descendants continued to make themselves known through their various civic and industrial ventures in the remaining years of the 19th century; his son, John H Kinzie, even stood for mayor in 1834. Today's Kinzie Street, which is located just north of the Chicago River, stands as testimony to his influence.

Gurdon Hubbard, another early settler, arrived from Montreal in 1818, the same year Illinois joined the union, and quickly established a fur trade route from Danville, Illinois, to Chicago. A decade later, he bought the Illinois branch of the massively profitable American Fur Company franchise; in so doing, he cemented his position on the trading ladder and set the stage for the city's future expansion. By the time Chicago was incorporated as a town in 1833, Hubbard had begun to diversify into meatpacking, shipping, insurance and real estate, while also campaigning for the construction of the Illinois–Michigan Canal. For the next three decades, his own prosperity mirrored that of his adopted home town.

IN CONTEXT

PIONEER CHECKPOINT

When the Erie Canal opened in 1825, it linked the Hudson River – and, thus, the East Coast – with Buffalo, New York (on Lake Erie). The canal opened up Illinois to travel and commerce, a great boon to the pioneers who were arriving from more populous areas in the east. A prime example was William Ogden, a transplanted Yankee who came west in 1835 and, two years later, became mayor of Chicago.

Meatpacking mogul Philip Armour also moved to Chicago (from Milwaukee) after the Civil War ended, and earned millions selling barrels of pork. Armour employed refrigerated train cars for shipping fresh meat, expanded the use of animal by-products, and diversified into other businesses. Meanwhile, Cyrus McCormick found Chicago to be just as hospitable to his Virginia-bred sensibilities, even borrowing money from Ogden to build the factory that would produce the mechanical reapers he had invented. During his time in Chicago, the belligerent McCormick became active in Democratic politics, and ran for Congress in 1864. Today, he's commemorated in the name of the city's convention centre.

However, few outsiders went on to have as much influence over the growth of Chicago as 'Long' John Wentworth, whose appetites for food, drink and good living matched his stature (he stood six feet six inches tall and weighed more than 300 pounds). After arriving in 1836 at the age of 21, Wentworth became the managing editor and, later, the owner-publisher of the *Chicago Democrat*, the city's first newspaper. He closed the newspaper in 1861, effectively merging it with the *Tribune* (which had been founded in 1847), but at the time, he had bigger fish to fry: having served five terms in the House of Representatives as a Democrat, Wentworth had been elected as the city's Republican mayor in 1857.

TRAINS AND BOATS AND PLAINS

An economic depression that swept the country in 1837, known as the Panic, threatened to put a lid on Chicago's growth. However, the Panic coincided with Chicago achieving city status, and things were quick to pick up after the worst had passed. In 1848, two projects were completed that between them signalled the start of Chicago's immense growth: the first telegraph line reached the city, radically improving communications, and the Illinois–Michigan Canal was finally completed almost two decades after work on it had begun, offering the city a connection to and from the Atlantic via the Great Lakes.

Because of its central location and existing trade connections, Chicago became a crucial checkpoint for railway commerce in the US. Soon, livestock, timber, grain and other goods were transported speedily through the city in previously unheard-of quantities. More and more industries established their headquarters on the south-western shores of Lake Michigan rather than at the rival St Louis, roughly 300 miles away in Missouri. By 1856, Chicago had become the largest railroad centre in the country.

Chicago's steel industry was boosted by the unmatched transport links. Situated along the banks of Lake Michigan at the mouth of the Calumet River, South Chicago became home to a number of blast furnaces. By the turn of the century, steel production in the area accounted for 50 per cent of the entire domestic output.

The use of unskilled immigrant labour in the city's steel mills was a major factor in the growth of Chicago's south-east neighbourhoods. By 1870, more than half of Chicago's 300,000-strong population was foreign-born, with Germans, Irish, Bohemians and Scandinavians representing the majority of the city's new arrivals. The rapid population growth led, by necessity, to the construction of cheap, wooden buildings – at the time, timber was both cheap and easy to obtain. Fires sprang up around Chicago from time to time, but few imagined the horror that lay just around the corner.

FIRE AND RAIN

On 8 October 1871, a fire broke out adjacent to an immigrant neighbourhood that bordered the central business district. Spreading to the north-east, the blaze gained momentum, and didn't slow even upon reaching the south branch of the Chicago River. A dry summer, a concentration of wooden constructions (including roadways), and the presence of convection whirls (nicknamed 'fire devils', they enabled the blazes to leap over rivers) all stoked the inferno.

By the time it finally burned itself out in Lincoln Park, several miles north of where it had started, the blaze had carved an unprecedented trail of destruction. Over an area from Taylor Street north to Fullerton and from the river east to Lake Michigan, 17,000 buildings were destroyed, 98,000 people were left homeless and more than 300 lives were lost.

But the city's efforts to regenerate itself in the wake of the disaster were every bit as spectacular as the fire itself. Relief efforts soon gave way to rebuilding ventures; the downtown merchants wasted no time in obtaining loans and hiring crews to construct new, fireproof buildings. A mere 12 months on, 300 new structures had been erected; a few years down the line, taller, fireproof buildings stood proudly in place of the shambolic wooden structures that once made up downtown Chicago. Attracted by a blank canvas, and motivated by the enthusiasms of the city fathers, architects began to develop the extant elevator buildings into what were later termed 'skyscrapers'. The ultimate result of the fire was what remains, to this day, the finest collection of urban architecture in the US.

Another elemental problem, that of water, also needed to be addressed. Despite the seemingly unlimited supply of freshwater provided by Lake Michigan, the vast quantities of polluting matter dumped into the Chicago River were in danger of permanently befouling the city's water supplies. The eventual solution to the problem affected not only city residents but also those from downstate, since the plan involved forcing the river to run not towards but away from the lake. The sewage that had previously flowed into the clear waters of Lake Michigan would be redirected to the Mississippi by means

of a channel built to extend as far as a tributary in Lockport, Illinois. This channel, later known as the Sanitary & Ship Canal, was commissioned in 1889 and opened 11 years later.

RIOT AND REFORM

But for all the successful regenerative efforts, not everything went smoothly. A nationwide railroad strike in the 1870s affected Chicago more than most, pitting out-of-work rioters against state militia units. The mayor issued warnings to those not affected by the walkout to stay at home, away from the out-of-control mobs, but not everyone heeded them. A number of protesters and civilians died in the violence.

The Haymarket Square riot of 1886 was a watershed in the struggle between self-described 'anarchist' workers and their bosses. On the night of 4 May, a public gathering to protest against the treatment of workers at Cyrus McCormick's factory turned violent when a bomb was thrown at the police. Eight officers and three protestors died in the riots, yet only eight men stood trial. Four were executed for their part in the demonstrations, but three were pardoned. The 'Haymarket martyrs', as they came to be known, inspired the socialist celebrations of ordinary workers that continue around the world each May Day.

Throughout this period, immigrants continued to descend on Chicago, the majority from Poland, Germany, Italy and Ireland. Not all of them immediately found work, and many of those who did were forced to live in abject poverty. Jane Addams and Ellen Gates Starr decided to do something about it. The twenty-something duo, who'd met as teenagers at Rockford Female Seminary (now Rockford College), returned in 1888 from a tour of Europe inspired by what they'd seen at Toynbee Hall in London. The following year, in a mansion on Halsted Street donated by Charles Hull, they founded Hull-House to provide social services to deprived locals. One of the first such settlement houses in the US, Hull-House proved immensely influential in the late 19th- and early 20th-century

IN CONTEXT

push for social reform in America. In 1931, Addams' work led to her being awarded the Nobel Peace Prize.

The year after Addams and Starr opened Hull-House, the wheels were set in motion for the creation of a different but equally important Chicago institution. Founded (and, for the most part, funded) by John D Rockefeller, the University of Chicago held its first classes in 1892 on a parcel of land at 57th Street and Ellis Avenue.

Something of a progressive figure, university president William Rainey Harper envisioned his institution offering an equal education for both male and female students, operating a press in order to disseminate its teachings throughout the country, and using a then-novel 'quarter' system to allow for greater flexibility in the schedules of faculty and staff. However, the university is now best known for the role it played in the development of nuclear energy when, in 1942, a team led by Enrico Fermi built the first ever nuclear reactor. The event led to the Manhattan Project and the creation of the world's first atomic bomb.

FAIR'S FARE

Held just 22 years after the Chicago Fire, the World's Columbian Exposition of 1893 was a perfect opportunity for Chicago to showcase its growth. A team of planners and designers led by Daniel Burnham and Frederick Law Olmsted created a series of grand attractions in a specially created 'White City', with 46 nations providing 250,000 displays. The first ever Ferris wheel, standing 250 feet tall and kitted out with 36 cars, was built for the fair. However, the 'Streets in Cairo' section was the fair's most profitable attraction, due in no small part to the cavortings of an exotic dancer named Little Egypt.

More than 25 million visitors came to the city during the six months the fair was in place, putting Chicago back on the map in the eyes of outsiders who'd written it off after the fire. However, it also kicked off a more general renaissance of popular entertainment in the city that lasted long after the fair had ended. Dance halls, movie palaces, nightclubs and vaudeville

shows all sprang up around the time of the event and in the years immediately after it, greatly expanding the array of cultural options available to locals.

SIN CITY

Around the time of the Columbian Exposition, the Levee district in Chicago's First Ward took corruption and decadence to levels previously unmatched in the city's already fairly rich history. Centred around State and 22nd Streets, close to modern-day Chinatown, the area was flooded with gamblers, drunks and prostitutes. The latter plied their trade in an astonishing 200 brothels, revelling in such colourful names as the Everleigh Club (run by sisters Minna and Ada), Freiberg's Dance Hall, the Library and the Opium Den.

For such activity to flourish, favours had to be granted and eyes had to look the other way. The politicos in charge of the area were only too happy to oblige. Colourfully nicknamed Chicago aldermen Michael 'Hinky Dink' Kenna and 'Bathhouse' John Coughlin got into the habit of lining their pockets with lucre from businesses grateful for their support; the duo then used some of this cash to buy votes in First Ward elections. The pair were even said to have run an unofficial office out of Freiberg's Dance Hall.

One of the beneficiaries of Kenna's and Coughlin's largesse was Charles Tyson Yerkes, who settled in Chicago in the 1880s and began to buy favours from the aldermen in a bid to gain control of the city's streetcar lines. The brash Yerkes expanded his activities into ownership of trolley cars and elevated train car lines. But eventually, the 'Traction King', as Yerkes was known, went too far when he inspired his political cohorts to introduce a bill that would extend his transit franchise for another 50 years without any compensation to the city. Although the bill was passed in 1895, it was repealed after two years of protest. Yerkes moved to New York in 1899; 48 years after his departure, the Chicago Transit Authority (CTA) was created as a municipal agency to oversee the city's mass transit.

CENTURY OF PROGRESS
I WILL
333 1933
COME!
CHICAGO
WORLD'S FAIR

However, for all his entrepreneurial spirit, the stubborn, starchy Insull's true passion was for opera. So much so, in fact, that he proposed building a new opera house for the town that would be financially supported by offices within its building (much like Adler and Sullivan's Auditorium Building, completed in 1889). Insull soon had the support of the major arts patrons, but insisted on looking after the entire project himself, hiring the firm of Graham, Anderson, Probst and White to design the structure.

Upon its completion, the Civic Opera House was acclaimed as a magnificent building, fêted by the city fathers who'd help fund its construction. Unfortunately, its completion came in 1929, shortly after the stock market crashed. After losing all of his companies, Insull travelled to Europe for a brief respite, before returning to the States to face court proceedings relating to fraud and embezzlement. He was acquitted, but his reputation and his finances never recovered. He died in 1938, suffering a heart attack on the Paris *métro*.

FATHER AND SON
The mayoral legacies of Carter Harrison senior and junior, which dated back to the 1870s, left large shoes to fill. The 24th mayor of Chicago (he went on to win five terms in office), the elder Harrison took charge in 1879 and presided over much of the rebuilding that followed the Chicago Fire; he later served as mayor during the World's Columbian Exposition, but was murdered in his home just three days before it ended.

The younger Harrison – elected in 1897 as the 30th mayor of Chicago, but the first born in the city – proved to be even more reform-minded than his father. Also winning five terms in office, he was known for his fair dealings with immigrant and minority groups, and was one of the driving forces behind the moral clean-up in the Levee during the early 1910s.

By 1915, Harrison Jr's star had started to wane. He was defeated in the Democratic primary by Robert Sweitzer, who in turn was roundly thrashed at the mayoral elections by William Hale

Eventually, a Vice Commission appointed by the mayor enabled enforcers to shut down brothels in the First Ward. After the Everleigh closed its doors in 1911, the rest of the Levee's bordellos, saloons and gambling houses were systematically raided until both patrons and proprietors wearied of the law's interference. A few later reopened under a cloak of darkness, but the area never again flourished.

SAM'S THE MAN
After emigrating from Britain to the US in 1881 to work as Thomas Edison's assistant, Samuel Insull proved his worth in business by increasing Edison's domestic business fourfold, before becoming president of the Chicago Edison Company in 1892. Insull was also one of the forces behind the creation of the railroad system that connects Chicago to its suburbs, now known as Metra.

IN CONTEXT

Thompson. The scion of a real estate business family and a powerful friend to the likes of Al Capone, 'Big Bill' was not a clever man, but his belligerence suited the mood of the city, desperate to escape a recession.

While Thompson was an enthusiastic recipient of many minority votes, his passivity during the Chicago Race Riots that same year hurt his chances of re-election. In the summer of 1919, an isolated incident on one of Chicago's beaches set off five days of rioting between whites and blacks that left more than 35 people dead and hundreds more injured. Things escalated further with the death of black teenager Eugene Williams, who drowned at the segregated 29th Street beach on 27 July 1919 after a confrontation between blacks and whites reputedly prevented him from coming ashore.

Williams' death was the spark that set alight a series of violent racial battles. When word got out about it, the story soon changed: rumours spread that Williams had been stoned to death, prompting fury in the black community. After several attempts to quell the violence without force, Mayor Thompson

IN CONTEXT

Freedom Fighters

Five protesters from the '68 Democratic Convention on their legacy.

The 1968 Democratic Convention protesters changed the way the media covered news, increased awareness of political, military and social issues and led to changes in the way primaries impact general elections. Here, five protesters discuss the legacy of the events of 1968.

Michael James, then a campaigner, now owner of the Heartland Café in Rogers Park
Marilyn Katz, then head of security for the National Mobilization Committee to End the War in Vietnam (MOBE), now president of MK Communications
Nancy Kurshan, then a co-founder and member of the Yippies, now a retired social worker
Abe Peck, then a journalist, now professor emeritus-in-service at Northwestern University

Don Rose, then press secretary for MOBE, now a political consultant and a columnist for the *Chicago Daily Observer*

What were you hoping to accomplish?
Rose It began as an anti-Democratic Party move. The fear that we were not necessarily physically violent but destructive of what [the party was] about was quite correct. We were not demonstrators trying to say, 'Look, give us healthcare planks.' We didn't want planks; we wanted to end the war.
James I remember really wanting to have a good time... to get the kids talking about the revolution and peace, the war... smoke some dope in the park. We did have a good time until the police came into Lincoln Park. That sent us into Old Town, breaking windows, hiding in gangways, police chasing us.

asked the governor of Illinois for the assistance of state troops and 5,000 men were summoned to keep the peace. Coupled with his pro-German stance during World War I, the reasons for Thompson's fall from grace become obvious. He failed to win re-election in 1923.

PROHIBITION AND THE MOB

The Prohibition era in the US began when, on 16 January 1920, Congress ratified the 18th Amendment banning the manufacture and sale of alcohol. Chicago's involvement in the days prior to the amendment came chiefly through Evanston's Frances Willard, president of the Women's Christian Temperance Union for four decades.

Spurred on by the WCTU, the temperance movement gained momentum in the years after World War I: alcohol restrictions were first enacted at the community and state levels, and then across the country. However, the ideals of the 18th Amendment created hypocrisy within American society, corruption within government, and a vast increase in organised crime. Chicago was in the thick of the action.

IN CONTEXT

Peck We were a group of people trying to live our lives in a peaceful, communal way. We were trying to demonstrate... that there was a better way of living in a culture of greed.

What did you accomplish?
Katz We have a congressional delegation that was forged out of '68. It was the ending of an illusion that all of us children of the '50s grew up with: that the US was a total democracy and that our foreign policy was benign. It changed the way power was shared and policy was forged in this country.
Kurshan I think that '68... did make it more difficult for the US to militarily move wherever it wanted in the world. Our goal was really to make sure that there wouldn't be another Vietnam, and we have not succeeded in doing that, clearly. So on the one hand, I feel like we were able to put a brake on. On the other hand, we're still dealing with the same nefariousness.

What was the most memorable incident?
Rose The Tuesday night in front of the Hilton where the police lined up along the park to 'protect' the hotel from demonstrators – and the police were replaced by armed National Guardsmen who emerged from these Jeeps covered with barbed wire.
Katz The first [night] in Lincoln Park, when the phalanx of tear gas-loaded fire trucks and police came west across the park, aiming their full force at the unprepared revellers.

Knowing what you know now, what might you have done differently?
Katz Nothing!
Rose I cannot look back at '68 and say we made a tactical mistake or something I should have known to do differently. It didn't turn out exactly the way I wanted, but I can't say it was due to a mistake on our part.

Were people more passionate then?
Rose If the times seemed more intense during Vietnam, I would attribute it to a more deadly war, plus the existence of the draft.
Katz I don't think the issue was passion, but a sense of possibility. We felt very empowered in the '60s, that what we did would or could make a difference. I think today there is a greater sense of desperation.
Peck Many today are passionate; we were in the crucible.

Mayor William Dever, who'd replaced Thompson in 1923, was in favour of Prohibition, and made every effort to enforce it. But then, as now, Chicago was a drinking city: Dever's attitudes were less than popular with the electorate, and opened the door to competition at the mayoral election in 1927. Opposing him was the indefatigable Thompson; raucous in his condemnation of Prohibition, he promised to reopen bars that Dever had closed. There was more to Thompson's pro-alcohol stance than social liberalism. Under Prohibition, the Mob controlled the city's alcohol supply. During his first two terms in office, it was said that Thompson was in the pockets of the town's gangsters: first Johnny Torrio and then Al Capone. Dever was incorruptible, but Torrio and Capone were both careful to keep Thompson sweet even after he lost office in 1923. For his part, Thompson enjoyed the Mob support, not least as it helped him defeat Dever in 1927.

THE GREAT DEPRESSION

During the late 1920s and early 1930s, according to some historians, the Depression itself acted as a force for the repeal of the 18th Amendment, due to the changes it had produced within American society. In 1933, with the 21st Amendment that repealed Prohibition, it was clear that individual states would again take control of the regulation and taxation of alcohol, and that the sale of 'demon rum' would be legal once more.

During the Depression, the city's immigrant population base altered once more, a shift dramatically reflected in Chicago politics. The changes began to take hold when Thompson was defeated in 1931 by Anton 'Tony' Cermak, a coal-miner's son and street vendor who had emigrated to the US from Bohemia as a child in the 1870s. It was Cermak who set in motion the type of machine politics that typified Chicago government for much of the rest of the 20th century, but he didn't get long to act out his plans. On 15 February 1933 in Miami, Cermak was struck by an assassin's bullet apparently intended for President FD Roosevelt. The wound eventually proved fatal.

Cermak didn't live long enough to see Chicago's second World's Fair. Entitled the 'Century of Progress', it was held 40 years after the Columbian Exposition and stayed open for two summers, 1933 and 1934. While not as influential as its predecessor, it proved both popular and profitable. Money raised aided the arts organisations involved in preserving the fair's exhibits, including the Museum of Science & Industry, Adler Planetarium and South Park Corporation (later taken over by the Chicago Park District).

After World War II, Chicago benefited from a huge boom. In 1950, its population topped 3.6 million; affluence was everywhere, as people began to move from the city to the suburbs. Five years later, the city was to reach a turning point with the election of one of the most famous US city mayors of the century.

DEUS EX MACHINE

In 1955, Richard J Daley won the first of six straight terms as mayor. Skilled in the machine politics tradition through his chairmanship of the Cook County Democratic Organization, Daley was an Irish American Democrat who gained the trust of minority and working-class voters with a get-the-job-done attitude. He reigned more or less unchallenged for his first decade in office, aided in no small part by the patronage system, his mettle was tested by spiralling crime and racial tensions, epitomised in the civil unrest triggered by the assassination of Dr Martin Luther King, Jr.

King had come to Chicago several times during the 1960s. With each visit, he flagged up more of the problems faced by minority communities: poor housing, job discrimination, poverty, illiteracy and so on. However, he was greeted with scorn by white Chicagoans, even after several meetings with Daley in a bid to set up a Citizens Advisory Committee that could address racial tensions.

When King announced his intention to take up residence in a Lawndale slum building, the owners of the structure took him to court. Various rallies and marches led by King in white neighbourhoods led to police intervention, which in turn set the stage for the widespread burning and looting of white-owned businesses that occurred mainly in black neighbourhoods on the West Side immediately following King's death in April 1968. To stem the chaos, Daley called in the National Guard, but it was only the beginning of a turbulent year, which culminated in a national PR disaster for the mayor.

THERE'S A RIOT GOIN' ON

The Democratic National Convention of 1968 was meant to be a celebration of Chicago, as the party descended on the city to choose its candidate for the upcoming presidential election. However, with both party and country split over the Vietnam War, it proved far tougher than Daley had anticipated.

When they arrived in late August, the Democrats were joined in the city by anti-war protesters. Encouraged by a group of counter-cultural mischief-makers known as the Yippies, the protestors had descended on Chicago in their hundreds to celebrate what they called the Festival of Life. Daley settled on a hard line approach to their presence, denying them permission to gather in a number of apparently sensitive locations.

At first, the Yippies' protests passed quietly. But at the first sign of trouble, the 12,000-strong Chicago police force – supplemented, at Daley's request, by 15,000 troops from the National Guard and US Army – waded in with nightsticks and tear gas, meeting mild dissent with fearsome violence. In the disarray, a number of journalists were gassed, beaten and arrested as they attempted to cover the melées; many disturbances were broadcast live on national TV. Daley stuck with his tougher-than-tough approach, but few Democrats stood alongside him. He, and his city, were humiliated.

The subsequent scapegoating of several protesters, in what became known as the 'Chicago Eight' trial, prolonged the embarrassment. A handful of the charges stuck at the chaotic, entertaining 100-day trial, presided over by Judge Julius Hoffman, but not for long: all the convictions were quashed on appeal in 1972. Three years later, it was established that the FBI, with the complicity of Judge Hoffman, had bugged the offices of the defendants' lawyers.

Further confrontations between police and radicals occurred in 1969 with the 'Days of Rage', during which members of the Black Panther-inspired radical group the Weathermen vandalised property and attacked police in the Loop, the Gold Coast and beyond. By the time the violence had ceased, dozens of police and demonstrators had been injured. Neither side came out of it well; indeed, it was symbolic that Fred Hampton, the leader of the Chicago chapter of the Black Panthers, died in a police raid that same December. What's more, racial problems in the city continued well into the next decade, and many white residents chose to leave for the suburbs in a phenomenon termed 'white flight'.

ONWARDS AND UPWARDS

During the 1970s, the Loop was turned into a financial centre as never before, skyscrapers such as the Sears Tower springing up as testament to its economic virility. But on the whole, it was a difficult decade for Chicago, much as it was for most of the Midwest. Daley retained office, but struggled to galvanise his electorate as he had in previous decades; still in office, he died of a heart attack in 1976. In the face of economic instability, the city battled gamely on until the winter of 1978-79, when it was essentially closed by an amazing 82 inches of snow. Otherwise popular mayor Michael Bilandic was blamed by the electorate for the city's slow reaction to the blizzard, and was replaced in office the same year by Daley protégée Jane Byrne.

As they had with Bilandic, Chicago voters quickly tired of the strident Byrne, who excelled at headline-grabbing gestures but proved less skilled at negotiating the machine politicians who still dominated the council. Chicago's first female mayor was then replaced by its first black mayor, as Harold Washington snuck through to win in a three-way heat for the Democratic nomination in 1983. But after winning office, Washington was left a lame duck when the council split into two camps: the reformers, led by Washington, and the old-school machine politicians, led by Edward Vrdolyak.

After Washington was re-elected in 1987, things improved. The 29, as the machine politicians had become known, no longer wielded the power they once did, and Washington was able to make progress at last. After his sudden death (like Daley, he suffered a heart attack while in office), former alderman Eugene Sawyer continued with many of his reforms. But he was defeated in the 1989 mayoral primary by one Richard M Daley, who proved to be very much his father's son.

BACK TO THE FUTURE

Over the last two decades, the machine politics tradition that Byrne and Washington tried to eradicate seems to have returned in earnest. But there's little doubt that the city has improved under Daley's and now Rahm Emanuel's watch.

The Loop continued to grow ever more powerful and influential during the 1990s, while the city's convention industry expanded to unprecedented levels. Daley threw money at city beautification schemes, in turn encouraging huge private investment in new commercial buildings and residential space. The numbers of tourists travelling to the city has also risen, attracted by measures such as the redevelopment of Navy Pier and and the cherished Millennium Park.

Its reputation for hosting a corrupt administration has remained as well, and who's to say whether Emanuel will turn the tide. Daley often let financial muscle get in the way of sentiment: witness the demolition in 1994 of the Maxwell Street Market, breeding ground for several generations of blues musicians. The city remains one of the most racially divided in the US, a legacy of the separatorist housing policies enacted by Daley Sr in the 1950s and '60s and not remedied by his successors. And then there's the curious incident of the airport in the night-time. Daley had long argued that Meigs Field airport, which occupied a prime piece of real estate just south of the Adler Planetarium, should be turned into a public park. Even so, the city was astonished when, around midnight on 30 March 2003, Daley sent bulldozers into the airfield to destroy its runways.

Yet for all the deep-cut problems that still exist in a city largely split along racial lines, Chicagoans in all corners of the city go about their business much as ever. The resilience that characterised Chicago in the days of Kinzie and Wentworth is still present today; indeed, given the difficulties the city has had to overcome (and has yet to address), it remains the town's dominant characteristic.

Barack Obama's 2008 victory speech in Grant Park.

Key Events

Chicago in brief.

1673 Father Jacques Marquette and Louis Jolliet discover what later becomes Chicago.
1779 Jean Baptiste Point du Sable becomes the first permanent resident of the area.
1812 53 settlers are killed by natives in the Fort Dearborn Massacre.
1837 Chicago incorporates as a city.
1847 The Chicago River & Harbor Convention promotes commerce.
1848 The Illinois–Michigan Canal is built; the Chicago Board of Trade is established.
1871 The Chicago Fire destroys the city and claims 300 lives.
1879 The Chicago Academy of Fine Arts (later the Art Institute of Chicago) is incorporated.
1886 The Haymarket Square labour riot takes place; 11 people are killed.
1889 Jane Addams opens Hull-House; architect Frank Lloyd Wright builds his own residence in Oak Park.
1891 The Chicago Orchestra, later the Chicago Symphony Orchestra, is set up.
1892 The first elevated train service is opened to commuters.
1893 The World's Columbian Exposition opens on the South Side.
1894 Pullman train employees strike for improved working conditions.
1909 Daniel Burnham unveils his park-filled Plan of Chicago.
1915 The Eastland pleasure boat capsizes, killing 812.
1919 Race riots rage in July; 38 die.
1920 Eight Chicago White Sox players are banned from baseball after fixing the 1919 World Series.
1929 Seven bootleggers are executed in the St Valentine's Day Massacre.
1933 The Century of Progress World's Fair opens, as does the Museum of Science & Industry; Mayor Anton Cermak is killed in Miami by a gunman apparently intending to shoot President-elect Franklin D Roosevelt.

1934 John Dillinger is shot and killed at the Biograph movie theatre in Lincoln Park.
1942 Enrico Fermi conducts successful nuclear chain reaction experiments at the University of Chicago.
1953 Hugh Hefner publishes the inaugural monthly issue of *Playboy*.
1955 Richard J Daley is elected mayor; O'Hare International Airport opens.
1968 Riots take place after the murder of Martin Luther King, Jr; the Democratic National Convention is marred by violence.
1969 The Chicago Seven trial takes place; two radicals die in a Black Panther raid.
1971 The Union Stockyards close after 105 years of continuous trading.
1973 The Sears Tower opens.
1976 Mayor Richard J Daley dies while still in office.
1979 *The Blues Brothers* is filmed in the city.
1987 Mayor Harold Washington dies while still in office.
1989 Richard M Daley, son of Richard J Daley, is elected mayor of Chicago.
1992 Chicago River floods underground tunnels, causing $1 billion of damage.
1995 Temperatures top 100 degrees for five straight days in July, killing more than 500 people.
1996 Michael Jordan and the Chicago Bulls win their sixth NBA championship.
2004 Four years late, Millennium Park opens to the public.
2005 The White Sox win the World Series for the first time since 1917.
2006 Federal investigators launch a probe into corruption at City Hall.
2008 Illinois senator Barack Obama is elected President of the US.
2010 Chicago Blackhawks win the Stanley Cup.
2011 Rahm Emanuel elected mayor.
2013 Chicago Blackhawks win the Stanley Cup again.

IN CONTEXT

Architecture

Out of disaster rose a dazzling town.

TEXT: MADELINE NUSSER

In 1871, fire wreaked havoc on Chicago, mowing it to the ground. In the months following the blaze, architects, engineers and landscapers descended on the city, then little more than a flat marsh covered in fire debris. And on this unpromising, empty landscape, a revolution was fomented.

The city's flatness spurred these architects to develop both the skyscraper and the diametrically opposed Prairie School, whose buildings were as flat as the towers were high. Alongside these new developments, architects imported other styles, from the Paris-inspired parkways set out in Daniel Burnham's 1909 vision for the city to the excessively embellished art deco style.

In the latter half of the 20th century, the revolution slowed. Mies van der Rohe's edifices grabbed headlines, as did the famously tall likes of the Sears Tower (now the Willis Tower), but the city no longer set the pace. And in the 21st century, its ambitions have all but stalled. But Chicago's skyline remains a wonder, preserved and cherished by a city that's proud of what it's given the world.

BURNING AMBITIONS

The story of Chicago's ascent from ramshackle Midwestern burg to world-class architectural showcase began in 1871, although it must have seemed like the end for those who lived in the city at the time. On the night of 8 October, a fire broke out in the barn behind the home of Patrick and Catherine O'Leary on the city's Near West Side, and raced north and east. When the blaze finally burned itself out two days later, much of the city had been reduced to smouldering ruins.

Many theories exist about the cause of the fire, from Mrs O'Leary's cow to a fiery meteorite, but most agree that poor urban planning was ultimately to blame for the way it spread. At the time, Chicago was a tinderbox: two-thirds of its 60,000 buildings were made of timber, and most of the city's 60 miles of paved streets were covered with wooden planks. In hindsight, disaster seems inevitable. But while its impact was catastrophic, the blaze inspired Chicago to rebuild as no city had done before.

THE CHICAGO SCHOOL

Refusing to be defeated by the tragedy, the city was determined to re-emerge with a daring, original vision. Once the charred buildings were cleared away, scores of architects converged on the city, drawn by the idea of working with a clean slate.

Born and educated in Boston, Louis Sullivan arrived in Chicago in 1873 and went to work for Dankmar Adler, a German émigré with a firmly established architectural practice. Despite their differences in personality, the two worked well together, Sullivan's erratic moods and artistic hauteur tempered by Adler's

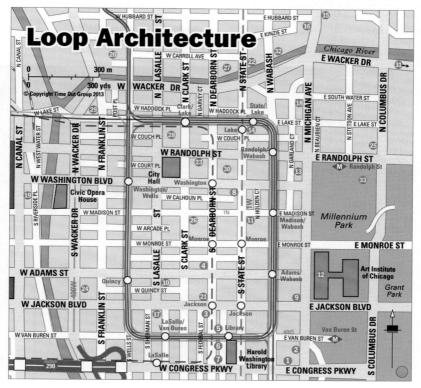

sober professionalism. Along with a handful of contemporaries, among them William LeBaron Jenney and Daniel Burnham, Sullivan would help define what came to be known as the Chicago School.

The Chicago School's biggest innovation was the use of an interior steel structure to distribute the weight of a building. Previously, constructing taller buildings meant thickening the load-bearing exterior masonry walls to support the weight of the upper floors. Particularly notable among such structures is Adler and Sullivan's **Auditorium Building** (50 E Congress Parkway, at S Wabash Avenue; map ❶), which combined a 4,200-seat theatre with offices and a hotel when it was completed in 1889. Owned by Roosevelt University since 1946, it remains in use as a theatre and music venue. Catch a performance by the Joffrey Ballet in order to see the spectacular interior.

The **Fine Arts Building** (410 S Michigan Avenue, at E Van Buren Street; map ❷), constructed by Solon Spencer Beman in 1885 as a showroom for Studebaker carriages, is another classic example of load-bearing masonry construction. So, too, is Burnham and John Wellborn Root's **Monadnock Building** (53 W Jackson Street, at S Dearborn Street; map ❸), completed in 1891 and the last skyscraper to be built from solid masonry construction. More than 120 years later, it remains an impressive sight.

BUILDING UP

Most experts agree that the first official 'skyscraper' to use a steel skeletal frame was the **Home Insurance Building**, constructed in 1885 by Jenney at LaSalle and Adams Streets (and demolished in 1931). Perhaps the most attractive of the steel-framed constructions still standing in the Loop is the **Marquette Building** (140 S Dearborn Street, at W Adams Street; map ❹), built by William Holabird and Martin Roche in 1895. Continuing south along Dearborn, you'll pass three other excellent examples: Burnham's 1896 **Fisher Building**

IN CONTEXT

Chicago Public Library.

(No.343; map **5**), Holabird and Roche's 1894 **Old Colony Building** (No.407; map **6**) and Jenney's 1891 **Manhattan Building** (No.431; map **7**).

Chicago School buildings are tall and rectangular with flat roofs, and are often made up of three distinct elements: base, rise and capital. Their grid-like steel structure is often recognisable on the structure's outer surfaces. With the steel frame taking care of the heavy lifting, the exterior walls are opened up for windows and other non-load-bearing materials, most often light-coloured terracotta. The buildings tend to avoid ornamentation in favour of utilitarian simplicity; it was Chicago School heavy-hitter Sullivan, after all, who declared, 'form follows function'.

The **Reliance Building**, located at the south-west corner of State Street and Washington Boulevard (map **8**), is a classic example of Chicago School innovations. Completed in 1895 by Charles Atwood and Burnham using foundations laid four years earlier by Root, the elegant Reliance makes use of a Chicago School mainstay: the oriel window, a protruding bay window that runs the length of the building and underscores its soaring verticality. With its abundance of large plate glass windows, the Reliance presaged the future of the modern-day skyscraper. It's now home to the **Hotel Burnham** (*see p168*).

Other Loop buildings are just as typical of the style. Take the **Santa Fe Center** (née the Railway Exchange Building; 224 S Michigan Avenue, at E Jackson Boulevard; map **9**): when it was completed in 1904, Burnham was so proud of it that he moved his own offices there. Appropriately, it's now home to the **Chicago Architecture Foundation** (*see p288*). And don't miss Burnham and Root's majestic 1888 **Rookery** (209 S Lasalle Street, at W Adams Street; map **10**), named for the birds that once inhabited it, or Sullivan's turn-of-the-century **Carson Pirie Scott Building** (1 S State Street, at Madison Street; map **11**), which makes use of another common design element: the Chicago Window, a large pane of glass which is flanked by two smaller opening windows.

'I don't want to be interesting,' Mies once commented. 'I want to be good.'

THE WHITE CITY

When the World's Columbian Exposition (aka the World's Fair) came to Chicago in 1893, Burnham oversaw the construction of the buildings in which the exhibits were to be housed. But the popularity of his gleaming white Beaux Arts classical constructions changed the course of architecture in the early 20th century, effectively – and ironically – outmoding the reigning Chicago School in the process.

Burnham's White City was levelled when the Columbian Exposition ended in order to make way for Meigs Field airstrip. Yet its influence remains in three classic Chicago landmarks: Shepley, Rutan and Coolidge's **Art Institute of Chicago** (111 S Michigan Avenue, at W Adams Street; map **12**), completed in 1893; the ostentatious **Chicago Public Library** (78 E Washington Boulevard, at N Michigan Avenue; map **13**), built by the same firm in 1897 and now the **Chicago Cultural Center** (*see p37*); and Rapp and Rapp's restored **Chicago Theater** (175 N State Street, at E Lake Street; map **14**). Of a similar period, too, is Cyrus Eidlitz's beautiful Romanesque Revival **Dearborn Station** (47 W Polk Street, at Dearborn Street), completed in 1885 as one of the city's first train stations.

Burnham is now best remembered for a contribution that lasted a little longer: the 1909 Chicago Plan, which mapped out the city's development. In addition to the introduction of traffic-relieving bi-level thoroughfares around downtown (such as Wacker Drive), Burnham's plan minimised lakefront development, a shrewd move that resulted in the expansive lakefront parks that stretch from the South Side to the northern suburbs.

Despite Burnham's prominence and influence, some designers remained unimpressed by the Beaux Arts aesthetic,

IN CONTEXT

with one Wisconsin-born architect making a particular impact. Frank Lloyd Wright began his career at Adler and Sullivan, but set up his own practice in Oak Park after being fired for moonlighting. It was here that he formulated what would become known as the Prairie Style of architecture; a walk around the neighbourhood, in which he built 25 homes, remains an enlightening experience. For more on Wright, *see p90* **Profile**; for his **Robie House** in Hyde Park, *see p98*.

TOWARDS MODERNISM

The Chicago School had become old hat by the 1920s, and architects began to look elsewhere for inspiration. The result was a 20-year period during which architects didn't concentrate on one style but toyed with many. Designs in a panoply of styles were submitted to a competition staged by the *Chicago Tribune* newspaper in 1922, as they searched for an architect to design their new offices. The winner was John Mead Howells and Raymond Hood's limestone-clad 456-foot **Tribune Tower** (435 N Michigan Avenue, at E Hubbard Street; map ⑮), a Gothic tower with flying buttresses at its ornate crown. Embedded in the walls around the entrance are artefacts from structures around the world, among them the Great Pyramids at Cheops and Notre-Dame Cathedral. Their presence was designed to draw attention to the paper's global reach, but they also nod to the growing eclecticism of architectural fashion.

Just across the street is Charles Beersman's **Wrigley Building** (400 N Michigan Avenue, at E Kinzie Street; map ⑯), a hulk of a building – completed in 1924 – that rises majestically over the Chicago River. The white terracotta that covers the building is cream-coloured at street level, but gets lighter towards the top. At night, when the façade is lit up by giant floodlights, the trompe l'oeil gives the building a glorious, glowing aspect.

The American fashion for art deco never developed in Chicago, but a few buildings in the style were constructed. Chief among them is Holabird and Root's **Chicago Board of Trade Building** (141 W Jackson Boulevard, at S LaSalle Street;

Tribune Tower.

map ⑰), completed in 1930 (and dramatically extended a half-century later). Approach it along Lasalle for the full, dramatic effect; look up to see the crowning statue of Ceres, 45 storeys above street level. Other art deco buildings include the **Carbide & Carbon Building** (230 N Michigan Avenue, at E Lake Street; map ⑱), now the **Hard Rock Hotel** (*see p168*), and two further Holabird and Root productions: the former **Palmolive Building** (919 N Michigan Avenue, at E Walton Street), later the offices of *Playboy*; and **2 Riverside Plaza**, (400 W Madison Street, at N Canal Street; map ⑲), formerly home to the *Chicago Daily News*.

And then there's the huge, art deco-styled **Merchandise Mart** (Chicago River, between N Wells & N Orleans Streets; map ⑳) the largest building in the world when it was completed in 1930. Designed by the firm of Graham, Anderson, Probst & White, the building's dramatic waterfall-style limestone façade rises 25 storeys above the river; busts of some of America's leading merchants, among them Marshall Field, A Montgomery Ward and Frank W Woolworth, line the esplanade. Commissioned by Marshall

IN CONTEXT

Field to house the wholesale operation of his department store, it was sold to the Kennedy family in the years following the Depression. A 1991 renovation created a mall for interior design businesses on the first two floors.

GLASS AND STEEL

Despite all the local innovation, it took an outsider to kick off arguably the most striking period in Chicago's architectural history. Ludwig Mies van der Rohe arrived in the city in 1938, bringing with him the International Style. The aesthetic had its roots in the architect's native Germany but borrowed heavily from the strident simplicity of the Chicago School, ultimately carrying it to new extremes.

Buildings in the International Style feature cubic shapes, long horizontal bands of glass called 'ribbon windows', low, flat roofs, and open floorplans divided by movable screen walls. Usually constructed from glass, steel and concrete, the structures are devoid of any ornamentation and regional characteristics. The emphasis is on the horizontal plane, even – perhaps perversely – in skyscrapers.

After serving as director of the Bauhaus in the early 1930s, Mies came to the US in 1937 at the relatively advanced age of 51, settling first in Wyoming before, a year later, moving to Chicago to take up a professorship at the Armour Institute (later renamed the **Illinois Institute of Technology**). In 1939, he set about redesigning the South Side campus, creating a handful of striking buildings that demonstrated his affection for steel-framed glass and cubic abstraction. These are functional buildings, their lack of frills deliberate. 'I don't want to be interesting,' Mies once commented. 'I want to be good.'

Upon their completion in 1951, the stunning, state-of-the-art **Lake Shore Drive Apartments** (860-880 N Lake Shore Drive, at E Chestnut Street) were light years ahead of their time. An indelibly classic example of the International Style, the 26-storey twin towers were an instant commercial and critical success. A few years later, Mies turned his talents to

the **Federal Center**, the unofficial name of a grouping of buildings constructed between 1959 and 1974 in the Loop (200 S Dearborn Street, at W Adams Street; map ㉑). You'll immediately recognise his signature curtain wall of glass, supported by steel black I-beams that support individual panes, emphasising the building's internal skeletal structure (and, in the process, almost turning it inside out). The grey granite used to pave the plaza continues uninterrupted into the lobby, creating a feeling of openness.

Mies lavished careful attention on every aspect of his creations, even going so far as to design their furniture. Take the 52-storey **330 N Wabash Building** (formerly **IBM Plaza**; 330 N Wabash Avenue, at E Wacker Drive; map ㉒), begun in 1969 and, after Mies's death the same year, completed in 1971 by one of the architect's associates. The building's voluminous glass-walled lobby, a Mies

Wrigley Building.

staple, is decorated with his chrome and leather Barcelona chairs, designed for an exposition in 1929.

But perhaps the most spectacular local building designed by Mies sits two hours south-west of downtown in the small town of Plano, Illinois: the **Farnsworth House** (14520 River Road, Plano, 1-866 811 4111, www.farnsworthhouse.org), completed in 1951 for Dr Edith Farnsworth (reputedly the architect's lover). This one-room, box-like house on stilts was designed by Mies to be decorated only with travertine marble floors, wooden cabinets and a rustic fireplace, and walled from the outside by mere sheets of glass. Situated on the wooded banks of the Fox River, the structure sits in striking contrast with its natural surroundings. Tours from April to November.

MOVING ON UP

Mies's influence over his contemporaries and successors is visible in a number of buildings downtown. The most notable is perhaps the **Richard J Daley Center** (55 W Randolph Street, at N Dearborn Street;

Marina City.

Willis Tower.

map ㉓), completed as the Chicago Civic Center in 1965 to designs by Jacques Brownson of CF Murphy Associates.

Designed by Bruce Graham of Skidmore, Owings & Merrill and towering 1,127 feet above the Magnificent Mile, the Mies-influenced **John Hancock Center** (875 N Michigan Avenue, at E Chestnut Street) became the city's tallest building when it was completed in 1969. Vaguely pyramid-shaped, the structure tapers from street level to its top floor, its visible X-shaped structural supports distributing the building's weight and helping it resist the tremendous forces of wind at higher elevations. The Hancock's lower floors are occupied by retail outlets and restaurants, with office space and apartments further up. It's topped by a bar/restaurant and an observatory (see p56).

Five years after the Hancock Center was completed, the doors opened on a second Mies-influenced, Graham-designed monster: the **Willis Tower** (originally Sears Tower; 233 S Wacker Drive, at W Adams Street; map ㉔), then became the world's tallest building (a title it relinquished two decades later). Standing

IN CONTEXT

a ludicrous 1,454 feet tall, the aluminium and amber glass tower owes a debt to the International Style with its chunky, cubist proportions. Although it's not a dynamic structure, it's easier on the eye than other cloudbusters from the same era, such as the 1,136-foot **Aon Center**, completed in 1973 as the Standard Oil Building (200 E Randolph Street, at N Columbus Drive; map 25), and the 859-foot **Water Tower Place** (845 N Michigan Avenue, at E Pearson Street). However, it lacks the easy elegance of the nearby **Chase Tower**, built in 1969 as the First National Bank of Chicago Building (21 N Clark Street, at W Madison Street; map 26).

ALTERNATIVE VIEWS

Not everyone took to Mies's aesthetic, something apparent from the two 61-storey 'corncob' towers of Bertrand Goldberg's **Marina City** apartment complex (map 27) on the north bank of the river. Constructed of reinforced concrete, the towers were completed in 1967 and could hardly be more distinctive: the floors are cantilevered out from the main core, which houses lift shafts and rubbish chutes. A theatre built between the two towers in 1966 is now occupied by the **House of Blues** (see p220).

While Mies's Federal Center pushed the boundaries of what a government building should look like, Helmut Jahn's dome-shaped **James R Thompson Center** (formerly the **State of Illinois Center**; 100 W Randolph Street, at N Clark Street; map 28) blew away critics when it was completed in 1985. Despite its stridently modern appearance, it pays homage to traditional government buildings, with its abstract suggestion of the classic cupola. The main attraction, though, is the 230-foot atrium created by the rotunda: ample lighting, exposed lift shafts and mechanics, and reflective surfaces give the space a vibrant sense of movement.

Another attention-grabbingly curvaceous modern building sits a few blocks west on the banks of the Chicago River. William

Jay Pritzker Pavilion. *See p283.*

IN CONTEXT

Tall Stories

For 150 years, Chicago has been reaching for the skies.

John Hancock Center.

IN CONTEXT

During its first decades, Chicago was always runner-up to Miss New York in measures of greatness. Perhaps as a result, the locals decided on an architectural strategy to prove their worth. 'Big?' went the rhetorical question. 'Bigger than yours!'

As in Europe, Chicago's earliest tall buildings were sacred sites. **Holy Name Cathedral** (733 N State Street), built in 1854, and **St Michael's Church** (1633 N Cleveland Avenue; ❶), constructed 15 years later, were two early sky-piercers, reaching 245 feet and 290 feet respectively. Reaching high towards the heavens, the spires seemed to declare a greater connection to the divine.

The next building to assume the mantle of Chicago's tallest was the first structure constructed specifically to house the **Chicago Board of Trade**

(141 W Jackson Street; ❷). But when the owners removed its clock tower due to structural instability, the title passed to Burnham & Root's long-since-demolished **Masonic Temple** (at State & Randolph Streets). Its 302 feet made it officially the world's tallest building, but its 22 floors didn't hold the record for long: New York seized back the title in 1894 when the Manhattan Life Insurance Building was completed.

The 394-foot **Montgomery Ward Building** (6 N Michigan Avenue; ❸), built in 1899, was topped in 1922 by the **Wrigley Building** (400 N Michigan Avenue; ❹), which still looms 438 feet over the Chicago River. Two years later, it was beaten by the **Chicago Temple** (77 W Washington Street; ❺), which in turn was defeated in 1930 by the 605-foot art deco monument designed to house the **Chicago Board of Trade** (141 W Jackson Street; ❻).

A futher building boom in the 1960s and '70s raised the bar once more. Built in 1965, the 648-foot Chicago Civic Center (now the **Daley Center**; 50 W Washington Street; ❼) was made to look feeble with the 1969 arrival of the now-iconic **John Hancock Center** (875 N Michigan Avenue; ❽), towering 1,127 feet over the Magnificent Mile. The Standard Oil Building (now the **Aon Center**, 200 E

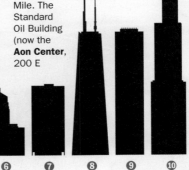

❶ ❷ ❸ ❹ ❺ ❻ ❼ ❽ ❾ ❿

E Pedersen's **333 W Wacker Drive** (map ㉙) was built between 1979 and 1983 on the bend of the river, and its curved frontage echoes the shape of the waterway in spectacular fashion. Look at it from the opposite bank or – better still – from a moving boat.

NEW HEIGHTS

Aside from the long-running saga surrounding **Block 37** in the Loop (map ㉚) – a long-dormant block hemmed in by State, Washington, Dearborn and Randolph Streets that was at last developed (*see p41*) – the most high-profile project has been the 28-acre **Lakeshore East** (map ㉛), a riverfront development on a site east of the Michigan Avenue Bridge. The first few condo towers completed as part of the development aren't memorable, but they're nonetheless notable in the way they illustrate a 21st-century Chicago trend: how young professionals have returned to make their homes in the centre of the city.

Another high-profile tower has been constructed just along the river. Donald Trump's plans to build the world's tallest building fell by the wayside in the wake of 9/11. However, after a brief delay, Trump commissioned Skidmore, Owings & Merrill to construct the shorter-than-planned but nonetheless skyscraping **Trump International Hotel & Tower** (401 N Wabash Avenue, at E Kinzie Street; map ㉜; *see p173*).

For all the skyscrapers downtown, some impressive developments keep their extremities closer to ground level. Located east of Michigan Avenue between Randolph and Monroe Streets and unveiled in 2004, the 24-acre **Millennium Park** (*see p34*) was four years late, and, at nearly $500 million, way over budget. However, Chicagoans have taken to the completed park with great enthusiasm, and especially to Frank Gehry's **Jay Pritzker Pavilion** (map ㉝).

Millennium Park may have been late in arriving, but at least it was completed. Other projects haven't been so lucky. Santiago Calatrava's **Chicago Spire** never even saw the light of day.

Randolph Street; ⑨) squeaked nine feet above it in 1973. But then the very next year, Chicago reclaimed the World's Tallest title from New York thanks to the 1,451 feet of the Sears Tower, which was renamed in 2009 as the **Willis Tower** (233 S Wacker Drive; ⑩).

The fun ended when the Council on Tall Buildings sided with some Kuala Lumpur yahoos. The Petronas Towers didn't have quite as many inhabitable floors as the Sears Tower; however, its spires counted while the Sears' antenna didn't. And with the demise of Calatrava's plans for the Chicago Spire, the Willis Tower looks set to remain the city's king pin for a little while yet.

Aon Center.

IN CONTEXT

Essential Information

Getting Around

ESSENTIAL INFORMATION

ARRIVING & LEAVING

By air

Chicago is served by two airports.

O'Hare International
1-773 686 2200,
www.flychicago.com.
O'Hare (ORD) is one of the busiest airports in the world. All domestic flights and international departures by domestic airlines use Terminals 1, 2 and 3. Non-US international airlines use T5, with two exceptions: Lufthansa and Iberia, which arrive at T5 but depart from T1 and T3 respectively. The terminals are linked by an airport train system.

The CTA provides a 24-hour **El** service on its Blue line between O'Hare and downtown. The journey takes 45-50mins, plus 15-20mins to travel between the station and the airport. Follow signs marked 'Trains to the city'. A one-way trip from the airport towards the Loop will cost $5, but like all CTA fares, the fare is $2.25 to the airport.

The next cheapest option for getting into town is by **shuttle bus**. Continental Airport Express (1-888 284 3826, www.airport express.com), which has a booth in the baggage reclaim area, charges $32 for the journey downtown (a round-trip ticket costs $60). Students attending universities in Chicago and visitors staying at specific hotels downtown or attending conventions may receive discounted prices. Visit the website for more information on discounts and a complete list of hotels and conventions that apply.

There's a **taxi** rank outside the baggage reclaim area of each terminal. The fare to downtown should come to about $35-$40 plus tip. Note that traffic on I-90 can extend the half-hour travel time, and the fare, at busy times. Money can be saved by using the Shared Ride scheme: up to four passengers can share a cab from O'Hare to downtown (as far north as Fullerton Avenue and as far south as McCormick Place) for $22 per person. From O'Hare to Midway a shared ride will come to $35 per person. During quiet spells, it can take time to assemble a shared ride.

Midway International
1-773 686 2200,
www.flychicago.com.
Smaller than O'Hare, Midway (MDW) is used mostly by lower-cost airlines. However, it's also closer to the Loop, and easier to negotiate than sprawling O'Hare.

Travelling to and from town on the El is easy on the Orange line, which runs to the Loop. The journey time is around 35mins, and the fare is the standard $2.25.

As with O'Hare, Continental Airport Express (1-888 284 3826, www.airportexpress.com) operates a **shuttle bus** into the city. The firm has a booth in the baggage reclaim; it costs $27 for a single or $50 for a round-trip ticket.

The **taxi** ride to downtown from Midway should cost around $28-$30 plus tip and will take 20-25mins. The Shared Ride scheme allows for a flat fee of $16 per person, unless you are heading to O'Hare, which will be a flat fee of $35 per person.

By bus

Greyhound services (1-800 231 2222, www.greyhound.com) use the city's main bus station (630 W Harrison Street, at S Desplaines Street, West Loop, 1-312 408 5821).

By rail

Amtrak trains (1-800 872 7245, www.amtrak.com) pull into **Union Station** (225 S Canal Street, at W Jackson Street, the Loop).

PUBLIC TRANSPORT

Chicagoland transport is overseen by the **Regional Transportation Authority (RTA)**. The service is split between the **Chicago Transit Authority (CTA)**, which runs buses and the elevated/subway train system (aka the 'El') in the city; the **Metra** rail network, which links the city to its suburbs; and **Pace**, a suburban bus system.

CTA
567 W Lake Street, IL 60661
(1-888 968 7282, 1-312 664 7200, www.transitchicago.com).
Open *By phone* 8am-4.30pm Mon-Fri.

Metra
547 W Jackson Boulevard, IL 60661 (1-312 322 6777, www. metrarail.com). **Open** *By phone* 8am-5pm Mon-Fri.
Pace
550 W Algonquin Road, Arlington Heights, IL 60005 (1-847 364 7223, www.pacebus.com). **Open** *By phone* 8am-5pm Mon-Fri.
RTA
Suite 1550, 175 W Jackson Boulevard, IL 60604 (1-312 913 3200, www.rtachicago.com). **Open** *By phone* 4.45am-1am daily.

CTA fares & tickets

The CTA operates a simple fare structure across its network of buses and trains, but prices vary depending on how you pay.

Short-term visitors might be best off with a **Visitor Pass**, which allows unlimited travel across the El and bus network for a flat fee. A one-day pass costs $10, with a three-day ticket priced at $20 and a seven-day pass retailing at $28 for the CTA only or $33 for access to the CTA and Pace. Tickets are valid for 24, 72 or 168 hours from the first time the card is used, and are available from O'Hare (Blue line), Midway (Orange) and Chicago (Red) El stations, Union Station, the Chicago Cultural Center (*see p294*), the Water Works Visitor Center (*see p294*) and a number of other locations (including many drugstores but excluding all other stations). For a full list of locations, see www.transitchicago.com.

Visitors planning to travel less often should consider a **Transit Card**, which bills travellers on a per-journey basis. The customer decides how much value to add to their card, available from vending machines at all El stations; when the money runs out or runs low, cards can be recharged at any machine. The flat fare of $2.25 is deducted when passengers pass the card through the reader on entering each bus or station. If you make another journey within two hours, you'll be charged a 'transfer' rate of 25¢; a further transfer is free.

The **Chicago Card** and **Chicago Card Plus** are electronic passes valid on El trains and on

CTA and Pace buses (UK residents may recognise the technology as similar to that of London's Oyster card.) When money runs low, it's topped up through a debit system tied to the user's credit or debit card. Fares cost $2.25 on the El and $2 on the bus. For short-term visitors, the disadvantages are that the card costs $5 and is less widely available than other tickets (you can apply online, by mail, by phone or in person from selected locations; see www.chicago-card.com).

If you don't have a ticket, you can pay with cash on buses, but the $2.25 fare doesn't allow for any transfers.

CTA trains

The CTA's elevated/subway train system, or the 'El', consists of eight colour-coded lines. It's generally fast and reliable, if a little creaky. For a map of the network, *see p320*.

Most lines run every 5-15mins, between 4.30-5am and 12.30-1.30am daily. The main exceptions are the Red and Blue lines, which run 24hrs a day (every 15-20mins in the dead of night), and the Purple line, which runs south of Howard only in rush hours (roughly 6-10am and 3-7pm). Care should be taken late at night. Destinations are shown on the front and side of trains, and on platforms.

Several El stations share a name. For instance, there are three different stations called 'Chicago' (on the Red, Purple/Brown and Blue lines). For clarity, our listings include each station's parent line.

There are plenty of El stations in the Loop: in the area bounded by Wells Street, W Wacker Drive, Michigan Avenue and Van Buren Street, 48 blocks square, there are no fewer than 16 stops. We've listed the nearest one or two stations to each venue, but if you're travelling between two points within the Loop, it may be quicker to walk.

CTA buses

CTA bus stops are marked by white signs listing the names and numbers of the routes they serve. Most routes run every 10-15mins from dawn until at least 10.30pm daily. Night buses ('Night Owls') run every half-hour on some routes, from approximately midnight to 5am.

Most routes stick to one north-south or east-west street, unless they're forced off it by one-way systems. Some of the more popular and useful routes are listed below.

6: Jackson Park Express
The Jackson Park Express is useful for visitors wanting to travel between the Loop/Museum Campus and Hyde Park. Southbound, it runs down State Street between the river and Balbo Drive, then turns east on Balbo and heads south to Museum Campus at 11th and Columbus. From here, the bus runs non-stop down Lake Shore Drive as far as 47th; here, it resumes a stopping service along Lake Park Avenue and Hyde Park Boulevard to 57th Street by the Museum of Science & Industry, then continues south. The bus follows the same route north until Balbo, where it heads north up Michigan Avenue to Wacker Drive rather than State.

20: Madison
Westbound, the 20 runs on Madison from Michigan Avenue to Austin Boulevard in Oak Park. Eastbound, it turns on to Washington at Halsted Street, then terminates at Washington and Michigan. In rush hours, its route is extended to the Illinois Center.

22: Clark
Southbound, the 22 runs on Clark between the far North Side and Polk Street in the Loop. The northbound route runs up Dearborn from Polk Street to Washington Square, where it joins Clark Street.

29: State
The 29 runs up State Street from the far South Side to Illinois Street, where it turns east and heads to Navy Pier. The return journey follows the same route, but leaves Navy Pier along Grand Avenue until it connects with State.

36: Broadway
Southbound, the 36 runs from the far North Side down Broadway to Diversey, then heads south on Clark before joining State Street at Division and continuing south to Harrison and Wells. Northbound, it runs up Dearborn from Congress to Illinois Street where it joins State. At Division, it joins Clark; at Diversey, it joins Broadway and heads north.

56: Milwaukee
Northbound, the 56 runs west on Madison from Michigan to Jefferson, then north on Jefferson, west on Fulton and north-east on Milwaukee through Wicker Park. Southbound, it runs on Milwaukee to Desplaines, then east to the Loop on Washington.

66: Chicago
The eastbound 66 runs on Chicago Avenue between the far West Side and Fairbanks Court in Streeterville, then heads south on

Fairbanks to Illinois Street and then east to Navy Pier. The westbound route is near-identical, but leaves Navy Pier along Grand Avenue instead of Illinois.

72: North
The 72 runs along North Avenue between Lincoln Park and the far West Side.

Metra rail

The Metra is an 11-line rail system that serves 243 stations in Illinois and parts of Indiana. The termini, all in the Loop or West Loop, are **LaSalle Station** (414 S LaSalle Street, at E Congress Parkway); **Millennium Station** (E Randolph Street, at N Michigan Avenue); the **Ogilvie Transportation Center** (500 W Madison Street, at S Canal Street); and **Union Station** (*see p286*). Fares run from single-route fares to a $7 ticket that allows unlimited weekend travel.

Pace buses

Pace buses serve the suburbs. A regular fare costs $1.75, with premium fares (on four routes that serve the Loop) at $4. Reduced-price fares are available for 7-11s; under-7s ride free. CTA Chicago Cards are valid on all Pace routes; Transit Cards are accepted on most services. Pace also offers a number of reduced-rate passes; among them is the Pace/CTA Seven-Day Pass ($33).

TAXIS

Taxis are prevalent in most areas covered in this guide, and can be hailed on the street. Further out, and on the South Side, you'd be better off booking a taxi; staff in bars and restaurants can help. Downloading the Uber app (www.uber.com) or the Hailo app (www.hailocab.com) are also good ideas for easy taxi booking.

Meters start at $3.25, rising by 20¢ for every one-ninth of a mile or 36 seconds of waiting time. The first extra passenger (aged 12-65) is charged $1, with additional passengers adding a further 50¢ to the fare. Journeys to or from either airport incur an additional $1 charge. There is no fee for baggage. Tipping is optional, but expected.

Taxis are usually safe and reliable. If you have a complaint, call the **Department of Consumer Services** on 1-312 744 6060 or on 311. Four taxi firms are listed below.

ESSENTIAL INFORMATION

American United
1-773 248 7600.
Checker Cab
1-312 243 2537.
Flash Cab
1-773 561 4444,
www.flashcab.com.
Yellow Cab
1-312 829 4222,
www.yellowcabchicago.com.

DRIVING

Traffic in Chicago can be tiresome, especially in the Loop and River North. The city's grid system makes it easy to negotiate, but if you're staying in the centre of town there's no point in hiring a car.

The **American Automobile Association (AAA)** offers maps, guides and other perks to members of affiliated organisations, such as the British AA. See www.aaa.com or call 1-866 968 7222.

Parking

Parking in Chicago is expensive. Street parking is limited and meter-controlled; parking in a car park costs upwards of $15 per day, at least twice that at hotels. If you're towed, call the police on 311 or 1-312 744 4000. You'll end up paying the cost of retrieving your car from the car pound plus a separate fine.

Car hire

Some firms will rent cars to over-21s, but you'll usually need to be 25 or older. Tax is 16 per cent.

Renters will be offered liability insurance and a collision-damage waiver. If you're not covered by your home policy, take both. UK travellers should note that while deals struck with the UK offices of the major firms include insurance, it's often cheaper for long rentals to rent the car from the US operation and rely for insurance on the good-value, year-long policy available from www.insurance4carhire.com.

All major firms have outlets at O'Hare; most are also at Midway.

Alamo
US: 1-800 462 5266, www.
alamo.com. UK: 0870 400
4562, www.alamo.co.uk.
Avis
US: 1-800 331 1212, www.
avis.com. UK: 0870 606 0100,
www.avis.co.uk.
Budget
US: 1-800 527 0700, www.
budget.com. UK: 0844 581
2231, www.budget.co.uk.

Dollar
US: 1-800 800 3665, www.
dollar.com. UK: 0808 234
7524, www.dollar.co.uk.
Enterprise
US: 1-800 261 7331, www.
enterprise.com. UK: 0870
350 3000, www.enterprise.co.uk.
Hertz
US: 1-800 654 3131, www.
hertz.com. UK: 0870 844
8844, www.hertz.co.uk.
National
US: 1-800 227 7368. UK:
0870 400 4581. Both: www.
nationalcar.com.
Thrifty
US: 1-800 847 4389, www.
thrifty.com. UK: 0808 234
7642, www.thrifty.co.uk.

CYCLING

Chicago is very bike-friendly, with plenty of wide roads and bike lanes. *See also p244.*

Divvy Bikes (1-855 553 4889, www.divvybikes.com), the city's bike-sharing system, are available at docking stations all over the city. Find information on the website. Annual memberships and 24-hour passes are available.

The **CTA** and **Metra** allow bikes on trains outside of weekday rush hours (7-9am and 4-6pm on CTA; trains arriving in Chicago before 9.30am and departing 3-7pm on Metra). Bikes can be transported on the front of all CTA buses.

WATER TRANSPORT

During summer, **Chicago Water Taxi** (1-312 337 1446, www.chicago watertaxi.com) runs a taxi service on the river, linking Michigan Avenue, LaSalle Street, Madison Avenue and Chinatown. Single rides are $3-$5; an all-day pass costs $8 and $10 on weekends.

From May to August, **Shoreline Sightseeing** (1-312 222 9328, www.shorelinesightseeing.com) operates water taxi services that link Navy Pier with the Shedd Aquarium and Sears Tower.

Lake cruises

Numerous operators offer cruises on the lake from Navy Pier, including **Shoreline Sightseeing** (*see above*), **Mystic Blue** (1-877 299 7783, www.mysticbluecruises. com) and **Seadog** (1-888 636 7737, www.seadogcruises.com/chicago). An alternative is provided by the 150ft schooner **Windy** (1-312 595 5555, www.tallshipwindy.com).

GUIDED TOURS

Bobby's Bike Hike
1-312 915 0995, www.bobbys
bikehike.com. **Tours** *Late May-*
early Sept 9am, 1pm, 7pm daily.
Apr-late May, early Sept-Nov
10am, 1pm Mon-Fri, Sun; 10am,
1pm, 7pm Sat. **Tickets** $10-$35.
Credit AmEx, MC, V.
A selection of non-strenuous bike tours, exploring central districts and the lakefront. Tours leave from Bobby's office at 465 N McClurg Court; rates include bike hire. Bobby's also offers bike rentals ($14-$50/half-day, $23-$65/day).

Chicago Architecture Foundation
Information 1-312 922 3432,
tickets 1-312 902 1500,
www.architecture.org. **Tours**
times vary. **Tickets** prices vary.
Credit AmEx, DC, Disc, MC, V.
The most popular of the CAF's huge range of excellent tours is the Architecture River Cruise (mid April-mid Nov; $37.85 plus tax), the best of the city's water cruises; other itineraries are conducted on foot, by coach and by bike. Book ahead for the River Cruise.

Chicago Greeter
1-312 945 4231,www.chicago
greeter.com. **Tours** by
appointment. *InstaGreeter*
10am-3pm Fri-Sun. **Tickets** free.
See the city through the eyes of volunteer locals, who guide guests through their neighbourhoods with personal anecdotes. You need to register at least 7-10 business days in advance; if not, try the walk-up InstaGreeter tours of the Loop. Tours leave from the Chicago Cultural Center (*see p294*).

Chicago Hauntings
1-888 446 7891, www.chicago
hauntings.com. **Tours** 7pm Tue-
Thur, Sun; 7pm, 10pm Fri, Sat.
Tickets $28; $20 reductions.
Credit AmEx, MC, V.
Kicking off at the Rock 'n' Roll McDonald's (Clark & Ohio Streets), noted historian, author and parapsychology enthusiast Ursula Bielski and her staff of guides visit haunted spots in Chicago.

Chicago Trolley Company
1-773 648 5000, www.coachusa.
com/chicagotrolley. **Tours** *mid*
Mar-Oct 9am-6.30pm (last pick-up
5pm) daily. *Nov-mid Mar* 9am-5pm
(last pick-up 4pm) daily. **Tickets**
1-day $45; $17-$40 reductions.
Credit AmEx, DC, Disc, MC, V.
This hop-on/hop-off service trawls landmarks in the Loop and the Near North Side. There's a route map online, where rates are 10% lower.

Resources A-Z

TRAVEL ADVICE

For up-to-date information on travel to a specific country – including the latest on safety and security, health issues, local laws and customs – contact your home country government's department of foreign affairs. Most have websites with useful advice for would-be travellers.

AUSTRALIA
www.smarttraveller.gov.au

CANADA
www.voyage.gc.ca

NEW ZEALAND
www.safetravel.govt.nz

REPUBLIC OF IRELAND
foreignaffairs.gov.ie

UK
www.fco.gov.uk/travel

USA
www.state.gov/travel

ADDRESSES

Addresses follow the standard US format. The room and/or suite number appears after the street address, followed on the next line by the city name and the relevant zip code.

AGE RESTRICTIONS

Buying/drinking alcohol 21.
Driving 16.
Sex (hetero- & homosexual) 17.
Smoking 18.

ATTITUDE & ETIQUETTE

Chicago is a buzzing metropolis, but it's also in the Midwest, and comes with all the relaxed good manners that characterise its location. Some high-end restaurants will insist on jacket or jacket and tie (call to check), while some clubs operate a dress code (no gym shoes, baggy jeans or sports gear). But mostly, casual clothes are fine.

BUSINESS

Chicago's central location, not to mention its natural and man-made travel links, has long made it attractive to industry and business. It's still an economic powerhouse: the city is visited by millions of business travellers each year, many of whom are here for a convention.

Conventions

The majority of Chicago's conventions occur at the vast **McCormick Place**: 2.2 million square feet of exhibition space, 170,000 square feet of banqueting, ballroom and meeting room space, spread over 27 acres. It's so large

that you'll need to factor journey time into your appointments. The facilities are modern, but there's nothing to do within several blocks of the centre.

Two other venues also stage conventions and exhibitions: **Festival Hall** at Navy Pier, and the **Donald E Stephens Convention Center** in Rosemont.

Donald E Stephens Convention Center *5555 N River Road (near O'Hare Airport), Rosemont (1-847 692 2220, www.rosemont.com).*
Festival Hall *Navy Pier, 600 E Grand Avenue, at Lake Michigan, Near North (1-312 595 5300, www.navypier.com). El: Red to Grand.* **Map** p310 K10.
McCormick Place Convention Complex *2301 S Lake Shore Drive, at E 23rd Street, South Side (1-312 791 7000, www.mccormickplace. com). Metra: 23rd Street.*

Couriers & shippers

DHL *1-800 225 5345, www.dhl.com.* **Credit** AmEx, Disc, MC, V.
FedEx *1-800 463 3339, www.fedex.com/us.* **Credit** AmEx, Disc, MC, V.
UPS *1-800 742 5877 (US), 1-800 782 7892 (international), www.ups.com.* **Credit** AmEx, Disc, MC, V.

Office services

All of the companies listed below have branches around the city; check online for others.

AlphaGraphics *Suite 1400, 70 W Madison Street, between N Clark & N Dearborn Streets, the Loop (1-312 226 3900, www.alpha graphics.com). El: Brown, Orange, Pink or Purple to Washington/Wells;*

Blue to Washington. **Open** 8am-6pm Mon-Fri. **Credit** AmEx, Disc, MC, V. **Map** p309 H12.
FedEx Kinko's *720 S Michigan Avenue, at E Balbo Drive, South Loop (1-312 663 1149, www.fedex. com) El: Red to Harrison.* **Open** 7am-7pm Mon-Fri; 8am-5pm Sat, Sun. **Credit** AmEx, DC, Disc, MC, V. **Map** p309 J13.
Office Depot *6 S State Street, at W Madison Street (1-312 781 0570, www.officedepot.com). El: Blue or Red to Monroe; Brown, Green, Orange, Pink or Purple to Madison/Wabash.* **Open** 7am-8pm Mon-Fri; 10am-8pm Sat; 11am-5pm Sun. **Credit** AmEx, Disc, MC, V. **Map** p309 H12.

Useful organisations

For **libraries**, *see p291.*

CONSULATES

Foreign embassies are located in Washington, DC, but many countries also have a consulate in Chicago.

British Consulate General *Suite 1300, Wrigley Building, 625 N Michigan Avenue, at E Ontario Street, Magnificent Mile (1-312 970 3800, www.britainusa.com/ chicago). El: Red to Grand.* **Open** 8.30am-5pm Mon-Fri. **Map** p310 J11.
Canadian Consulate General *Suite 2400, Two Prudential Plaza, 180 N Stetson Avenue, at E Lake Street, the Loop (1-312 616 1860, www.chicago.gc.ca). El: Brown, Green, Orange, Pink or Purple to State/Lake; Red to Lake.* **Open** 8.30am-12.30pm, 1-4.30pm Mon-Fri. **Map** p309 J11.
Irish Consulate *Suite 1820, 1 E Upper Wacker Drive, at N State*

Street, the Loop (1-312 337 2700, www.irishconsulate.org). El: Red to State/Lake. **Open** 10am-noon Mon-Fri. **Map** p309 H11.

CONSUMER

For complaints about shops, cabs, restaurants and the like, you should contact the **City of Chicago Department of Consumer Services** on 1-312 744 6060 or 311, or see www.cityofchicago.org/consumerservices.

CUSTOMS

International travellers go through Customs directly after Immigration. Give the official the filled-in white form you were given on the plane.

Foreign visitors can import the following goods duty-free: 200 cigarettes or 50 cigars (not Cuban; over-18s) or 2kg of tobacco; one litre of wine or spirits (over-21s); and up to $100 in gifts ($800 for returning Americans). You must declare and maybe forfeit plants or foodstuffs. Check **US Customs** for details (www.cbp.gov/xp/cgov/travel).

UK Customs & Excise allows returning travellers to bring in up to £145 worth of goods.

DISABLED

Chicago is reasonably accessible to disabled visitors: a lot of the buses are fitted with lifts, there are lifts on elevated CTA platforms and the sidewalks have ramps. However, it's always wise to call ahead to check accessibility.

The **Mayor's Office for People with Disabilities** (1-312 744 7050, TTY 1-312 744 4964, www.cityofchicago.org) is a good source of information about all aspects of disabled access. Try the **RTA** (1-312 836 7000, TTY 1-312 836 4949, www.rtachicago. com) or the **CTA** (1-888 968 7282, TTY 1-888 282 8891, www.transit chicago.com) for information on public travel, or contact **Special Services** on 1-800 606 1282 well in advance of your trip to arrange accessible transportation.

DRUGS

A visit to any local bar brings home how strict the local authorities are about drugs: if they're going to be that wary about serving beers to under-21s, then drugs must be policed with caution. Foreigners caught in possession of anything illegal may be treated harshly.

ELECTRICITY

US electricity voltage is 110-120V 60-cycle AC. Except for dual-voltage, flat-pin shavers, foreign appliances will need an adaptor.

EMERGENCIES

For helplines, *see right*. For police, *see p292*. For hospitals, *see below*.

Ambulance, fire, police *911*. **Illinois Poison Control** *1-800 222 1222*.

GAY & LESBIAN

For more gay and lesbian resources, *see pp197-205*.

Chicago Area Gay & Lesbian Chamber of Commerce *3179 N ClarkStreet, at W Belmont Avenue, Lakeview (1-773 303 0167, www.glchamber.org)*.
Gerber-Hart Library *6500 N Clark Street, Edgewater (1-773 381 8030, www.gerberhart.org). Bus: 22 Clark to Arthur.* **Admission** *Membership $40; $25 for full-time students, seniors or people with low incomes.* A gay and lesbian archive (closed until remodelling is complete; see website for more details).

HEALTH

Accident & emergency

Foreign visitors should ensure they have full travel insurance: medical treatment can be pricey. Call the emergency number on your insurance before seeking treatment; staff should be able to direct you to a hospital that deals with your insurance company.

For information, call **Advocate Health** (1-800 323 8622, www. advocatehealth.com), which can connect you to a hospital. There are 24-hour emergency rooms at the locations below.

Northwestern Memorial Hospital *251 E Huron Street, at N Fairbanks Court, Streeterville (1-312 926 2000, www.nmh.org). El: Red to Chicago.* **Map** p310 J10.
Rush University Medical Center *1653 W Congress Parkway, at S Ashland Avenue, West Loop (1-312 942 5000, www.rush.edu). El: Blue to Medical Center.* **Map** p314 D13.
Stroger Cook County Hospital *1900 W Polk Street, at S Wood Street, West Loop (1-312 864 6000, www.ccbh.org). El: Blue to Medical Center.* **Map** p314 C14.

University of Chicago Hospital *5841 S Maryland Avenue, at E 58th Street, Hyde Park (1-773 702 1000, www.uchospitals.edu). Metra: 59th Street.* **Map** p316 X17.

Contraception & abortion

Planned Parenthood *6th floor, 18 S Michigan Avenue, at E Madison Street, the Loop (1-312 592 6700, www.plannedparenthood.org). El: Blue or Red to Monroe; Brown, Green, Orange, Pink or Purple to Madison/Wabash.* **Open** 11.45am-4.45pm Thur. **Map** p309 H13.
A non-profit organisation that can supply contraception, treat STDs and perform abortions. **Other locations** around the city.

Dentists

For referrals, call 1-800 577 7322.

Hospitals

See left **Accident & emergency**.

Opticians

For opticians, *see p162*.

Pharmacies

For pharmacies, *see p163*.

STDs, HIV & AIDS

Howard Brown Health Center *4025 N Sheridan Road, at W Irving Park Road, Lakeview (1-773 388 1600, www.howardbrown.org). El: Red to Sheridan.* **Open** 9am-8pm Mon-Thur; 9am-5pm Fri; 9am-1pm Sat.
Comprehensive health services for the gay community, including primary care, HIV testing, support groups and research, as well as supplies of free condoms.

HELPLINES

Alcoholics Anonymous *1-312 346 1475, www.chicagoaa.org.*
Illinois HIV/STD Hotline *1-312 814 2608, www.idph.state.il.us.*
LGBT Info Line *1-773 929 4357, www.centeronhalsted.org.*
Narcotics Anonymous *1-708 848 4884, www.chicagona.org.*
Rape Crisis *1-888 293 2080, www.rapevictimadvocates.org*

ID

If you're planning on drinking in Chicago, then carry photo ID that contains your date of birth

ESSENTIAL INFORMATION

(a driving licence, say): you'll be carded if staff think there's even a tiny chance that you're under 21.

INSURANCE

Non-nationals should arrange baggage, trip-cancellation and medical insurance before they leave home. US citizens should consider doing the same. Read the small print: consequences of security scares, including cancelled flights, may not be covered.

INTERNET

Travellers with laptops should find it easy to get a Wi-Fi hook-up. There are few internet cafés here, but all branches of the Chicago Public Library have terminals. The **Harold Washington Library Center** (*see below*) has 78 terminals on which anyone can sign up for a free one-hour session, and 18 terminals for 15-minute sessions.

LEFT LUGGAGE

O'Hare and Midway don't offer any luggage storage facilities. However, you can leave bags in lockers at Union Station (*see p286*).

LEGAL HELP

Your first call in any serious legal embroilment should be to your insurance company or your consulate (*see p289*). The **Chicago Bar Association** offers a lawyer referrals service; call 1-312 554 2001.

LIBRARIES

In addition to the **Harold Washington Library Center**, the Chicago Public Library has branches on the **Near North Side** (310 W Division Street, at N Wells Street, 1-312 744 0991), in **Lincoln Park** (1150 W Fullerton Avenue, at N Racine Avenue, 1-312 744 1926) and in **Lakeview** (644 W Belmont Avenue, at Broadway, 1-312 744 1139). All are open 9am-9pm Monday to Thursday, 9am-5pm on Friday and Saturday. For other locations, see www.chipublib.org.

Harold Washington Library Center *400 S State Street, at W Congress Parkway, the Loop (1-312 747 4300, www.chipublib.org). El: Blue or Red to Jackson; Brown, Orange, Pink or Purple to Library.* **Open** 9am-9pm Mon-Thur; 9am-5pm Fri, Sat; 1-5pm Sun. **Map** p309 H13.

The main branch of the Chicago Public Library, the second largest library in the world, houses two million volumes, plus a theatre, meeting rooms and a large number of free-access computer terminals.

LOST PROPERTY

Airports

If you lose an item at either Chicago airport near the ticket counters or close to the gates, contact your airline. If you lose anything in other areas, call the numbers below.

Airport public areas *O'Hare* 1-773 686 2385. *Midway* 1-773 838 3003.
Airport transit system *O'Hare* 1-773 601 1817.
Food courts *O'Hare* 1-773 686 6148.
Parking facilities *Both airports* 1-773 686 7532.
Security checkpoints *O'Hare* 1-773 894 8760. *Midway* 1-773 498 1308.

Public transport

If you lose something on public transport, contact the relevant company (*see p286*).

Taxis

If you lose something in a cab, call the taxi company (there are several different firms in the city). You'll need the number of the cab.

MEDIA

Home to the country's third-largest media market, with a newspaper heritage to rival that of New York, Chicago is a media big hitter.

Daily newspapers

Chicago Tribune
www.chicagotribune.com.
Founded in 1847, the *Tribune* is the most powerful paper in Illinois. Its strengths include sports and Friday's entertainment supplement. However, thanks to cost-cutting and questionable editorial decisions, it's not the paper it once was. Under owner Sam Zell, the paper's parent company filed for Chapter-11 bankruptcy protection in 2008, and its future still appears uncertain.

The *Tribune* also publishes **RedEye**, a flimsy morning tabloid comprised of articles from that morning's paper and entertainment pieces. It's available for free at or near most El stations.

Chicago Sun-Times
www.suntimes.com.
The *Sun-Times* is the *Trib*'s tabloid competitor. Though it offers gritty reporting and good coverage of Chicago sports, in-depth news is largely absent.

Daily Herald & SouthtownStar
www.dailyherald.com & *www.southtownstar.com.*
The *Daily Herald* and *Southtown Star* cover the suburbs. The *Herald* publishes zoned suburban editions, while the *Star* concerns itself with the southernmost area of the city.

Magazines

Time Out Chicago
www.timeoutchicago.com.
Obviously we're biased, but we think TOC is essential for locals and visitors wanting to know what's going on in town. While the weekly print edition came to a halt in spring 2013, the robust website is updated daily and covers every corner of the city's arts and entertainment scene, with substantial coverage of shopping, eating and drinking.

Chicago Reader
www.chicagoreader.com.
Now under the ownership of the Sun-Times, the *Reader* is the city's dominant free weekly, though it no longer carries the gravitas with which it made its name. It does still carry some good writing, and includes Dan Savage's notorious 'Savage Love' sex advice column.

The Onion *www.theonion.com.*
In addition to the satire for which it's best known, *The Onion* offers coverage of music and movies, and (like the *Reader*) the 'Savage Love' column. It's available free every week in bars and some stores.

Other publications

Other streetcorner boxes are filled with a variety of freesheets. A few are specific to the area in which they're found; others, such as the **Windy City Times** (www.wctimes.com) and the **Chicago Free Press** (www.chicagofreepress.com), are targeted at the gay community. **Newcity** (www.newcity.com) is a scrappy culture rag. Paid-for monthlies include the surprisingly cultured **Chicago** magazine (www.chicagomag.com), and **Where** (www.wheretraveler.com), tilted at the tourist market.

Radio

The more interesting sounds on Chicago's dial emanate from college

ESSENTIAL INFORMATION

stations: Northwestern's **WNUR** (89.3 FM, www.wnur.org); Columbia College's **WCRX** (88.1 FM, www.wcrx.net); **WDCB** (90.9 FM, www.wdcb.org) from the College of DuPage; Loyola's **WLUW** (88.7 FM, www.wluw.org); the University of Chicago's **WHPK** (88.5 FM, http://whpk.org); and St Xavier University's **WXAV** (88.3 FM, www.wxav.com). Pick of the pack is **WBEZ** (91.5 FM, www.wbez.org), the city's public radio station.

The major FM rock stations, like **WXRT** (93.1 FM, wxrt.cbslocal.com), alternative stations like **WKQX** (101.1 FM, www.q101.com), and top 40 stations like **WTMX** (101.9 FM, www.wtmx.com), are generally pretty bland. Pop kids may like **WKSC** (103.5 FM, www.kisschicago.com) and **WBBM** (96.3 FM, www.b96.cbslocal.com), while those after classic rock should head to **WLUP** (97.9 FM, www.wlup.com).

Sports-wise, **WBBM** (780 AM, www.wbbm780.com) is the home of the Bears; **WGN** (720 AM, www.wgnradio.com) broadcasts Cubs and Blackhawks games; and **WSCR** (670 AM, www.670thescore.com) broadcasts the White Sox.

Television

In addition to local affiliates of major networks – **CBS2** (aka WBBM, www.chicago.cbslocal.com), **NBC5** (aka WMAQ, www.nbcchicago.com), **ABC7** (aka WLS, www.abclocal.go.com/wls) and **Fox** (channel 32, aka WFLD, www.myfoxchicago.com) – the biggest station is **WGN-9** (www.wgntv.com).

MONEY

The US dollar ($) is divided into 100 cents (¢). Coins run from the copper penny (1¢) to the silver nickel (5¢), dime (10¢), quarter (25¢), less-common half-dollar (50¢) and very rare dollar. Green notes or 'bills' come in denominations of $1, $5, $10, $20, $50 and $100.

Bring at least one major credit card: they are accepted at nearly all hotels, restaurants and shops. The most widely accepted cards are American Express (AmEx), Diners Club (DC), Discover (Disc), MasterCard (MC) and Visa (V); in our listings, we've indicated where a venue accepts cards.

Banks & ATMs

Most banks are open 9am-5pm during the week. You'll need photo ID to cash travellers' cheques. Not

all banks offer currency exchange. There are ATMs throughout the city: in banks, stores and even bars. ATMs accept Visa, MasterCard and AmEx, as well as other cards, but may charge a usage fee. If you've forgotten your PIN, most banks will dispense cash to cardholders.

Bureaux de change

Try and travel with some US dollars. You can change money at the airport, but the rates may not be great. If you want to cash travellers' cheques at a shop, note that some require a minimum purchase.

Stores that bill themselves as 'currency exchanges' will not help you exchange your currency: they're basically cheque-cashing services and don't accept foreign funds. Instead, try an AmEx office.
American Express *605 N Michigan Avenue, at E Ohio Street, Magnificent Mile (1-312 943 7840). El: Red to Chicago.* **Open** 9am-5.30pm Mon-Fri; 10am-4pm Sat. **Map** p310 J10.
Other locations 55 W Monroe Street, at N Dearborn Street, the Loop (1-312 541 5440).

Lost or stolen credit cards

American Express *Cards* 1-800 992 3404. *Travellers' cheques* 1-800 221 7282.
Diners Club 1-800 234 6377.
Discover 1-800 347 2683.
MasterCard *Cards* 1-800 622 7747.
Visa *Cards* 1-800 847 2911. *Travellers' cheques* 1-800 227 6811.

Tax

In Chicago, standard sales tax is a huge 10.25 per cent. The tax isn't included in the marked price of goods and will be added at the till. For hotel rooms and services, the tax rate is a nasty 16.4 per cent.

OPENING HOURS

For banks, *see left*; for post offices, *see right*; for public transport, *see p286*. General office hours in the city are 9am to 5pm during the week. Most bars are open until 2am, or 3am on Saturday.

POLICE

For emergencies, call **911**. You don't have to report non-emergency crimes in person: phone them in on **311** (or, from out of town, 1-312 746 6000). The details will be taken and paperwork can be sent to you. The

city's most central police station is at 1718 S State Street (1-312 745 4290); for others, see www.cityofchicago.org/police.

POSTAL SERVICES

Post offices in Chicago are usually open 9am to 5.30pm Monday to Friday; most are closed on Sundays. Phone 1-800 275 8777 or check www.usps.com for locations.

Stamps can be bought at any post office and at some hotels, vending machines and drugstores. Stamps for postcards within the US cost 33¢; for Europe, the charge is 98¢. A regular stamp is 46¢. For couriers and shippers, *see p289.*
Main Chicago Post Office *433 W Harrison Street, at S Canal Street, West Loop. El: Blue to Clinton.* **Open** 8.30am-midnight Mon-Fri; 9am-11pm Sat; 10am-9pm Sun. **Map** p309 G13.
The Loop *211 S Clark Street, at W Adams Street. El: Blue or Red to Jackson; Brown, Orange, Pink or Purple to Quincy.* **Open** 7am-6pm Mon-Fri. **Map** p309 H12.
River North *540 N Dearborn Street, at W Grand Avenue. El: Red to Grand.* **Open** 8.30am-6pm Mon-Fri; 9am-3pm Sat; 9am-2pm Sun. **Map** p311 H10.
Lincoln Park *2405 N Sheffield Avenue, at N Fullerton Avenue. El: Brown, Purple or Red to Fullerton.* **Open** 9am-6.30pm Mon-Fri; 9am-3pm Sat. **Map** p312 E5.
Lakeview *1343 W Irving Park Road, at N Southport Avenue. El: Red to Sheridan.* **Open** 8.30am-6.30pm Mon-Fri; 8.30am-3pm Sat.

RELIGION

Baptist

Unity Fellowship Missionary Baptist Church *211 N Cicero Avenue, at W Maypole Avenue, West Side (1-773 287 0267). El: Green to Cicero.* **Services** 7.30am, 11am Sun.

Buddhist

Buddhist Temple of Chicago *1151 W Leland Avenue, at N Racine Avenue, Uptown (1-773 334 4661, www.budtempchi.org). El: Red to Lawrence.* **Services** 11am Sun. **Map** p310 G9.

Catholic

Holy Name Cathedral *735 N State Street, at E Superior Street, River North (1-312 787 8040,*

ESSENTIAL INFORMATION

www.holynamecathedral.org). El: Red to Chicago. **Services** 6am, 7am, 8am, 12.10pm, 5.15pm Mon-Fri; 8am, 12.10pm, 5.15pm, 7.30pm Sat; 7am, 8.15am, 9.30am, 11am, 12.30pm, 5.15pm Sun. **Map** p310 H10.

Old St Mary's Church *1500 S Michigan Avenue, at S State Street, the Loop (1-312 922 3444, www. oldstmarys.com). El: Green, Orange or Red to Roosevelt.* **Services** 8.30am, noon Mon-Fri; noon, 5pm Sat; 8.30am, 11.30am, 6pm Sun. **Map** p309 H13.

Eastern Orthodox

St George Orthodox Cathedral *917 N Wood Street, at W Iowa Street, West Town (1-312 666 5179, www.saintgeorgecathedral. net). El: Blue to Division.* **Services** 9.30am Sun. **Map** p315 C9.

Episcopal

St James Cathedral *65 E Huron Street, at N Wabash Avenue, Magnificent Mile (1-312 787 7360, www.saintjamescathedral.org). El: Red to Chicago.* **Services** 5.30pm Wed; 12.10pm Thur, Fri; 8am, 9am, 11am Sun. **Map** p310 H10.

Jewish

Chicago Loop Synagogue *16 S Clark Street, at W Madison Street, the Loop (1-312 346 7370, www. chicagoloopsynagogue.org). El: Blue or Red to Monroe.* **Services** 7.45am, 1.30pm, 4.45-5pm (depends on sunset) Mon-Fri; 9am, 3.45-4.30pm, 4.45-5.30pm (depends on sunset) Sat; 9.30am, 4.30-4.45pm (depends on sunset) Sun. **Map** p309 H11.

Chicago Sinai Congregation (Reform) *15 W Delaware Place, at N State Street, Gold Coast (1-312 867 7000, www.chicagosinai.org). El: Red to Chicago.* **Services** 6.15pm Fri; 10.30am Sun. **Map** p310 H9.

Lutheran

First St Paul's Evangelical Lutheran Church *1301 N LaSalle Street, at W Goethe Street, Gold Coast (1-312 642 7172, www. fspauls.org). El: Red to Clark/ Division.* **Services** 7am, 7pm Wed; 9.30am, 10.45am Sun. **Map** p311 H8.

Methodist

First United Methodist Church at the Chicago Temple *77 W Washington Boulevard, at N Clark Street, the Loop (1-312 236 4548, www.chicagotemple.org). El: Blue,*

Brown, Green, Orange, Pink or Purple to Clark/Lake. **Services** 7.30am, 12.10pm Wed; 5pm Sat; 8.30am, 11am Sun. **Map** p309 H12.

Muslim

Downtown Islamic Center *231 S State Street, at E Jackson Boulevard, the Loop (1-312 939 9095, www. dic-chicago.org). El: Brown, Green, Orange, Pink or Purple to Adams/ Wabash; Red to Jackson.* **Open** 9am-5pm Mon-Fri. **Map** p309 H12.

Presbyterian

Fourth Presbyterian Church *126 E Chestnut Street, at N Michigan Avenue, Magnificent Mile (1-312 787 4570, www.fourthchurch.org). El: Red to Chicago.* **Services** 8am, 9.30am, 11am, 4pm Sun. **Map** p310 J9.

SAFETY & SECURITY

Follow the same precautions as you would in any urban area. Don't draw attention to yourself by unfolding a huge map and looking lost, and do beware of hustlers. Don't leave your purse or wallet in a place where it could easily be pickpocketed; leave valuables in a hotel safe if possible, and don't carry too much cash. And try to avoid deserted areas late at night. Potentially dangerous parts of town include parts of the West Side and, especially, parts of the South Side.

SMOKING

Smoking is outlawed in Chicago's restaurants and bars.

STUDY

The most prestigious of Chicago's many educational establishments is the **University of Chicago** in Hyde Park (1-773 702 1234, www. uchicago.edu). Other prominent institutions include the **University of Illinois at Chicago** (UIC) in the West Loop (1-312 996 7000, www.uic.edu); **Loyola University** (1-773 274 3000, www.luc.edu) and **Northwestern University** (1-847 491 3741, 1-312 503 8649, www.northwestern.edu), both split over big campuses on the Far North Side and smaller downtown set-ups; and **DePaul University** (1-312 362 8000, www.depaul.edu). And then there are numerous specialist establishments, such as the **School of the Art Institute** and **Columbia College Chicago**.

US universities are more flexible about part-time study than their European equivalents. Stipulations for non-English-speaking students might include passing the TOEFL; most students also have to give proof of financial support.

TELEPHONES

Dialling & codes

There are five area codes in the Chicagoland area. **312** covers downtown Chicago (roughly as far north, west and south as 1600 on the street grid); **773** covers the rest of the city; **847** serves the northern suburbs; **708** covers the southern and western suburbs; and the areas to the far west are served by **630**. Numbers beginning **1-8—** (eg 1-800, 1-888) are toll-free within the US. Numbers prefaced with **1-900** are charged at premium rates.

If you're dialling outside your area code, dial 1 + area code + seven-digit number. On payphones, an operator or recording will tell you how much money to add.

For collect or when using a phone card, dial 0 + area code + phone number and listen for the operator or recorded instructions.

For international calls, dial the US international access code (011) or the '+' symbol (from a mobile phone), then the country code (*see below*), then the number.

Australia 61.
Germany 49.
Japan 81.
New Zealand 64.
UK 44 (omit first '0' of area code).

Mobile phones

Chicago operates on the 1900 GSM frequency. Travellers from Europe with tri-band phones should be able to connect to one or more of the networks, assuming their home provider has an arrangement with a local network; check before leaving.

Check the price of calls before you depart. Rates may be hefty and, unlike in the UK, you'll probably be charged for receiving as well as making calls. It might be cheaper to rent or buy a phone while you're in town; for phone rentals, *see p166*.

Operator services

Operator 0.
Emergencies (ambulance, fire, police) 911.
Local and long-distance directory enquiries 411.

Public phones

Payphones are pretty hard to find. But if you do come across one, it'll accept nickels, dimes and quarters. Check for a dialling tone before adding change. Local calls usually cost 35¢. The rate rises steeply as the distance between callers increases (an operator or recorded message will tell you how much to add).

TIME

Chicago operates under US Central Standard Time (CST), six hours behind Greenwich Mean Time (GMT) and one hour behind Eastern Standard Time (EST). The border between Eastern and Central Standard Times is just to the east: Michigan and much of Indiana are on EST. From the second Sunday in March until the first Sunday in November, Daylight Saving Time puts the clocks forward an hour.

TIPPING

Waiters, bellhops and the like are paid a menial wage, and depend on tips to get by. In general, tip cab drivers, wait staff, hairdressers and food delivery people 15-20 per cent of the total tab. Tip bellhops and baggage handlers $1-$2 a bag. And in bars, bank on tipping a buck a drink.

TOILETS

Public toilets are few and far between. Head to a mall, hotel, department store, shop with a café attached (such as Barnes & Noble) or fast food outlet. Bars and restaurants can be a little on the sniffy side unless you buy something first.

TOURIST INFORMATION

The **Chicago Office of Tourism** dispenses information about the city online at www.choosechicago.com, by phone on 1-877 244 2246 (within the US) and 1-312 201 8847 (outside the US), and via three visitor centres.

The **Chicago Cultural Center** is the most useful of the three.

Chicago Cultural Center *77 E Randolph Street, at N Michigan Avenue, the Loop (1-312 744 6630, 1-877 244 2246, www. choosechicago.com). El: Blue to Washington; Brown, Green, Orange, Pink or Purple to Randolph/Wabash; Red to Lake.* **Open** 8am-7pm Mon-Thur; 8am-6pm Fri; 9am-6pm Sat; 10am-6pm Sun. **Map** p309 J12.
Chicago Water Works *163 E Pearson Street, at N Michigan Avenue, Magnificent Mile (1-312 744 8783, 1-877 244 2246, www.choosechicago.com). El: Red to Chicago.* **Open** 9.30am-6pm Mon-Sat; 10am-5pm Sun. **Map** p310 J9.
Millennium Park *201 E Randolph Street, in Northwest Exelon Pavilion, the Loop (1-312 742 1168, 1-877 244 2246, www.millenniumpark. org). El: Blue or Red to Washington; Brown, Green, Orange, Pink or Purple to Randolph/Wabash.* **Open** 6am-11pm daily. **Map** p309 J12.

VISAS & IMMIGRATION

Under the **Visa Waiver Scheme**, citizens of 27 countries, including the UK, Ireland, Australia and New Zealand, don't need a visa for stays of less than 90 days (for business or pleasure) as long as they have a machine-readable passport (e-passport) valid for the full 90-day period, a return ticket, and authorisation to travel through the ESTA (Electronic System for Travel Authorization) scheme. Apply online at www.cbp.gov/xp/cgov/travel/id_visa/esta/.

Mexicans and Canadians don't usually need visas but must have legal proof of citizenship. All other travellers must have visas. Visa applications can be obtained from the nearest US embassy or consulate, or online. Apply at least three weeks before you plan to travel. UK citizens should call the Visa Information Line: 0904 2450 100 (£1.50/min) or see www.usembassy.org.uk.

Immigration regulations apply to all visitors, regardless of visa status. During the flight, you'll be issued with an immigration form, which you must complete and present to an official on the ground. You'll have your fingerprints and photograph taken as you pass through immigration.

WHEN TO GO

For average temperatures, *see left*. Summer can be very humid, winter brings 40 inches of snow and, year-round, there's the wind. In other words, prepare for anything.

Public holidays

New Year's Day (1 Jan); **Martin Luther King Jr Day** (3rd Mon in Jan); **President's Day** (3rd Mon in Feb); **Memorial Day** (last Mon in May); **Independence Day** (4 July); **Labor Day** (1st Mon in Sept); **Columbus Day** (2nd Mon in Oct); **Veterans' Day** (11 Nov); **Thanksgiving Day** (4th Thur in Nov); **Christmas Day** (25 Dec).

WOMEN

When walking at night, take plenty of care: avoid unlit, deserted streets, and be alert for people trailing you. When travelling on trains at night, always try to pick a busy carriage.

WORKING IN THE US

Foreigners must find a US company to sponsor their application for an **H-1 visa**, which permits work in the country for up to five years. For the H-1 visa to be approved, the employer must convince the Immigration Department that there is no American citizen qualified to do the job as well. UK students can contact the **British Universities North America Club** (BUNAC) for help in arranging a temporary visa and, perhaps, a job (www.bunac.org/uk).

THE LOCAL CLIMATE

Average temperatures and monthly rainfall in Chicago.

	High (°C/°F)	Low (°C/°F)	Rainfall (mm/in)
Jan	0 / 32	-8 / 18	56 / 2.2
Feb	3 / 38	-4 / 24	46 / 1.8
Mar	8 / 47	0 / 32	76 / 3.0
Apr	15 / 59	6 / 42	93 / 3.6
May	21 / 70	11 / 51	94 / 3.7
June	27 / 80	16 / 61	109 / 4.3
July	29 / 84	19 / 66	94 / 3.7
Aug	28 / 83	18 / 65	98 / 3.9
Sept	24 / 76	14 / 57	81 / 3.2
Oct	18 / 64	8 / 46	69 / 2.7
Nov	9 / 49	2 / 35	84 / 3.3
Dec	3 / 37	-4 / 24	67 / 2.6

ESSENTIAL INFORMATION

Further Reference

BOOKS

Fiction

Nelson Algren *The Neon Wilderness* (1947)
This collection of short stories set the scene for novels such as *The Man with the Golden Arm* (1949).
Saul Bellow *The Adventures of Augie March* (1953)
A coming-of-age tale of sorts, and one of several Chicago novels by Bellow; also check out the magisterial *Humboldt's Gift* (1975).
Sandra Cisneros
Loose Woman (1994)
Poems by the author of the fine *A House on Mango Street*.
Theodore Dreiser
Sister Carrie (1900)
Perhaps the first great Chicago novel, a tale of the corruption of a young woman in the big bad city.
James T Farrell
Studs Lonigan (1935)
Farrell's three Lonigan stories tell of the coming of age of an Irish American in the early 20th century.
Sara Paretsky
Indemnity Only (1982)
The first outing for Paretsky's 'tec VI Warshawski, now a veteran of a dozen hard-boiled whodunnits.
Upton Sinclair *The Jungle* (1906)
Sinclair's masterpiece is set in the Chicago stockyards.
Scott Turow *The Laws of Our Fathers* (1996)
One of many page-turners from the Chicago lawyer turned author.
Richard Wright *Native Son* (1940)
A prescient tale of murder and racial issues in Chicago.

Non-fiction

Eliot Asinof *Eight Men Out* (1963)
The story of how the Chicago White Sox threw the 1919 World Series; later adapted for cinema.
Richard Cahan & Michael Williams
Richard Nickel's Chicago (2006)
This paean to Nickel, who fought an often solitary battle to save the city's architecture, is packed with beautiful photography.
Adam Cohen & Elizabeth Taylor *American Pharaoh* (2000)
It's lazily written, but this biography of Mayor Daley keeps the reader interested.

Nadine Cohodas *Spinning Blues into Gold* (2000)
The story of Chess Records has been waiting to be told for years; Cohodas does a fine job telling it.
Robert Cromie *The Great Chicago Fire* (1958)
How the city lost its innocence. And most of its buildings too.
Peter Golenbock
Wrigleyville (1996)
Golenbock's history of the Chicago Cubs is a highly entertaining read.
James R Grossman, Ann Durkin Keating & Janice L Reiff (eds) *The Encyclopaedia of Chicago* (2004)
Incomplete, but still a treasure trove of history, conjecture and anecdote.
LeAlan Jones & Lloyd Newman *Our America* (1997)
Subtitled 'Life and Death on Chicago's South Side', *Our America* tells of life in Chicago's ghettos through the eyes of two teenagers.
Erik Larson *The Devil in the White City* (2004)
An imaginative jaunt around the 1893 World's Columbian Exposition in the company of architect Daniel Burnham and murderer HH Holmes.
Richard Lindberg *To Serve and Collect* (1991)
A splendidly titled survey of police corruption in Chicago, between 1855 and 1960.
David Garrard Lowe
Lost Chicago (rev.2000)
A wonderful book detailing some marvellous Chicago buildings that didn't survive the wrecking ball.
Elizabeth McNulty
Chicago Then and Now (2000)
Containing some beautiful old photographs, this book places the emphasis firmly on the 'then'.
Donald L Miller
City of the Century (1996)
'The epic of Chicago', reads the appropriate subtitle for the definitive history of the city.
Mike Royko
One More Time (1999)
A collection of articles by the grand old man of Chicago journalism. Also worth a look: his biography of Richard J Daley, *Boss* (1971).
Richard Schneirov et al (eds) *The Pullman Strike and the Crisis of the 1890s* (1999)
One of the city's defining moments gets the essay treatment in this surprisingly engrossing book.

Alice Sinkevitch (ed)
AIA Guide to Chicago (2004)
'AIA' stands for the American Institute of Architects, which, with the Chicago Architecture Foundation, is behind this excellent survey of the city's buildings.
Carl Smith *The Plan of Chicago: Daniel Burnham and the Remaking of the American City* (2006)
How Daniel Burnham went about rebuilding Chicago.
Studs Terkel
Division Street: America (1967)
One of many worthwhile books from the late local legend: others include *Working* (1974).
Bill Veeck with Ed Linn
Veeck As in Wreck (1962)
The autobiography of the one-legged baseball executive who planted the ivy at Wrigley Field.
Lynne Warren et al (eds)
Art in Chicago 1945-1995 (1996)
A survey of more than 100 artists.

Poetry & drama

Gwendolyn Brooks
Selected Poems (1963)
Poetry from the first African American to win the Pulitzer prize.
Ben Hecht & Charles MacArthur *The Front Page* (1928)
A classic stage work co-authored by Ben Hecht, a notable local hack.
David Mamet
Mamet Plays 1 (1994)
Stage works, including *Sexual Perversity in Chicago* (1977) and *American Buffalo* (1976).
Carl Sandburg
Selected Poems (1996)
This collection includes the classic *Chicago Poems* (1916).

FILMS

About Last Night…
dir. Edward Zwick (1986)
The singles scene on Division Street forms the basis for this lame 1980s flick based on David Mamet's play *Sexual Perversity in Chicago*.
Backdraft *dir. Ron Howard* (1991)
Fire in Chicago, albeit 120 years after the biggest fire of them all.
The Blues Brothers
dir. John Landis (1980)
Feeble sketch extended to breaking point, or riotous romp? Either way, Chicago should get a credit alongside Belushi and Aykroyd.

The Break-Up
dir. Peyton Reed (2006)
Jennifer Aniston and Vince Vaughn
try to resolve their differences in
this romantic comedy.
Chicago *dir. Rob Marshall* (2002)
A massively popular adaptation
of the roaring '20s musical.
The Color of Money
dir. John Hughes (1986)
Paul Newman and Tom Cruise shoot
some stick on the North Side.
The Dark Knight
dir. Christopher Nolan (2008)
Batman comes to Chicago.
Eight Men Out
dir. John Sayles (1988)
Sayles' retelling of the Black Sox
tale, adapted from Eliot Asinof's
book, succeeds despite its treacle-
thick sympathies for 'Shoeless' Joe.
Ferris Bueller's Day Off
dir. John Hughes (1986)
Matthew Broderick skips school
to hit countless local landmarks.
'Bueller? Bueller...? *Bueller!*'
The Fugitive
dir. Andrew Davis (1993)
Harrison Ford on the run.
Go Fish *dir. Rose Troche* (1994)
A winning Chicago-set romantic
comedy with a twist: it's set on
the lesbian scene.
Hardball *dir. Brian Robbins* (2001)
Keanu Reeves stars as a bum who
takes over a Little League team
from the projects of Cabrini-Green.
**Henry: Portrait of a Serial
Killer** *dir. John McNaughton* (1986)
If you see anyone on Lower Wacker
Drive claiming their car has broken
down, keep driving.
High Fidelity
dir. Stephen Frears (2000)
Successful translation of Nick
Hornby's London novel to Chicago.
Hoop Dreams
dir. Steve James (1994)
Enthralling documentary following
two young MJ wannabes.
The Lake House
dir. Alejandro Agresti (2006)
Strained supernatural romance
with an architectural undertone
and some nice on-location shots.
My Best Friend's Wedding
dir. PJ Hogan (1997)
Julia Roberts and Cameron Diaz
find love (kinda) in the Windy City.
Risky Business
dir. Paul Brickman (1983)
A ludicrous plot – Tom Cruise is a
teenager on the make, Rebecca de
Mornay his hooker acquaintance –
is saved by sharp scripting.
Road to Perdition
dir. Sam Mendes (2002)
Tom Hanks plays a mob enforcer,
and Chicago plays itself, in this dark
period drama set in the '30s.

Running Scared
dir. Peter Hyams (1986)
Billy Crystal stars with Gregory
Hines in this comic cop flick.
The Untouchables
dir. Brian de Palma (1987)
Competent, Costner-starring
retelling of the Capone-Ness battles.

MUSIC

Patricia Barber
Mythologies (2006)
A song cycle based on the 2,000-
year-old works of Roman poet Ovid.
The Cole Porter Mix (2008) may
prove an easier way into the works
of this intriguing singer-pianist.
Big Black
Songs About Fucking (1987)
Grim and grubby, fierce and
fearsome. Leader Steve Albini has
gone on to engineer a staggering
number of indie notables.
Cheap Trick *Cheap Trick* (1977)
The debut set from the local kings
of power-pop, formed in Rockford
but relocated to Chicago.
Chicago Transit Authority
Chicago Transit Authority (1969)
After a name change, they carved
out a career as cheesy soft rockers.
But Chicago's debut is a peach.
Common *Be* (2006)
Lonnie Lynn, Jr's breakthrough
album, co-produced by fellow local
Kanye West.
Bobby Conn *Homeland* (2004)
Playful – or, perhaps, just plain
silly – alt-pop.
Felix da Housecat
Kittenz and Thee Glitz (2001)
As a teenager, Felix Stallings, Jr
was a protégé of DJ Pierre.
Robbie Fulks
Country Love Songs (1996)
Fulks defies categorisation, but this
record – on local label Bloodshot –
is an alt.country landmark.
Howlin' Wolf
The Genuine Article (1951)
The best of Chester Arthur Burnett.
Ahmad Jamal *At the Pershing:
But Not for Me* (1958)
A jazz classic, recorded at the now-
defunct Pershing Hotel on the city's
South Side.
R Kelly *R* (1998)
Sprawling double-disc set from the
now-disgraced singer.
The Jesus Lizard *Goat* (1991)
The best record by the recently
reformed quartet, released on local
label Touch & Go.
Curtis Mayfield *Curtis* (1970)
Mayfield's stunning debut contains
'Move on Up'.
Liz Phair *Exile in Guyville* (1993)
A startling rethink of the Stones'
Exile On Main Street.

Tortoise *TNT* (1998)
The most accessible album from
the post-rock doyennes.
Muddy Waters
The Anthology 1947-1972 (2001)
Two discs cover the essential cuts
of the pioneering bluesman.
Kanye West
Late Registration (2005)
Dazzling 21st-century hip hop.
Waco Brothers
Freedom and Weep (2005)
The most recent album from the
rabble-rousing troupe.
Wilco *Yankee Hotel
Foxtrot* (2002)
The disc that saw Jeff Tweedy
shed the alt.country tag. The cover
shot stars the Marina City towers.
Various Artists
The Sound of Chicago House (2006)
Marshall Jefferson, Sterling Void
and others appear on this 2-CD set,
a summary of the scene that
revolutionised dance in the '80s.
Various Artists
The Chess Story 1947-1975 (1999)
15 CDs, 335 tracks, and everything
you ever wanted to know about
Chess Records but were afraid to
ask. Plenty of smaller compilations
do a decent job for less money.

WEBSITES

www.chicagoist.com
Pithy, searching and occasionally
laugh-out-loud news and comment
on what's happening in town.
www.chicagoparkdistrict.com
Details on where to find the city's
500-plus parks, along with
information on their amenities.
www.chicagotribune.com
The local news.
www.choosechicago.com
Masses and masses of information
for visitors to the city, including
maps and details of guided tours.
**www.encyclopedia.chicago
history.org**
The content of this vast book (*see
p295*), compiled by the Newberry
Library and the Chicago Historical
Society, is available online.
www.cityofchicago.org
The city's homepage needs an
overhaul. However, if you've got
the patience to wade through
it, you'll eventually find what
you need.
www.timeoutchicago.com
Listings, previews, reviews, features
and plenty more. Your one-stop
guide to what's on in the city.
www.transitchicago.com
Everything you ever wanted to
know about the Chicago Transit
Authority, including downloadable
system maps and timetables.

Index

INDEX

INDEX

INDEX

INDEX

INDEX

Maps

Chicago Overview

See p319

See p314

See pp312-313

See pp310-311

See p315

See p314

See pp308-309

See p316

Lake

Michigan

PETERSON AVE 6000N
W FOSTER AVE 5200N
W LAWRENCE AVE 4800N
W MONTROSE AVE 4400N
W IRVING PARK RD 4000N
W ADDISON ST 3600N
W BELMONT AVE 3200N
W DIVERSEY PKWY 2800N
W DIVERSEY AVE
W FULLERTON AVE 2400N
W ARMITAGE AVE 2000N
W NORTH AVE 1600N
W DIVISION ST 1200N
W CHICAGO AVE 800N
W LAKE ST
W WASHINGTON BLVD
W MADISON ST 1N
S OGDEN AVE W
W ROOSEVELT RD 1200S
W 16TH ST 1600W
W 16TH PL
W OGDEN AVE
W 18TH ST
W CERMAK RD 2200S
W 26TH ST
W 31ST ST
W 35TH ST
W PERSHING RD
W 43RD ST
W 47TH ST
W 51ST ST
W 55TH ST
W GARFIELD BLVD
W 59TH ST
W 63RD ST

Belmont Harbor
Lincoln Park
Humboldt Park
Garfield Park
Douglas Park
Grant Park
North Branch Chicago River
Washington Park
Hyde Park
Jackson Park

CANADA
Winnipeg
Ottawa
Québec
Montreal
Minneapolis
Toronto
Buffalo
Boston
Detroit
Pittsburg
New York
Philadelphia
Chicago
Washington
Kansas City
St Louis
USA
Oklahoma City
Memphis
Atlanta
Charleston
Dallas
Houston
New Orleans
Miami
CUBA

Time Out Chicago 307

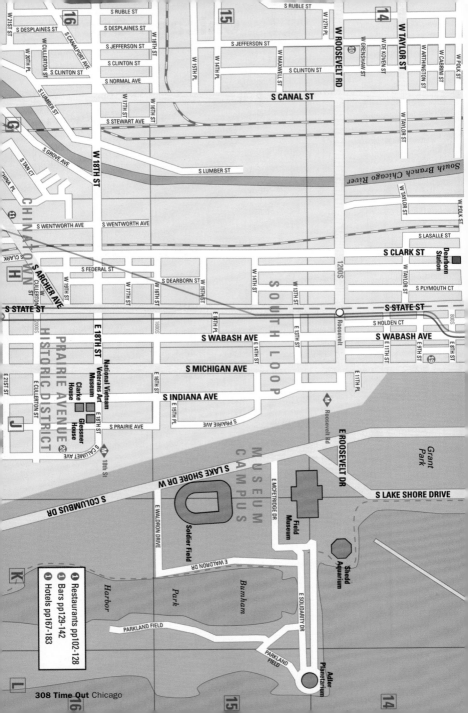

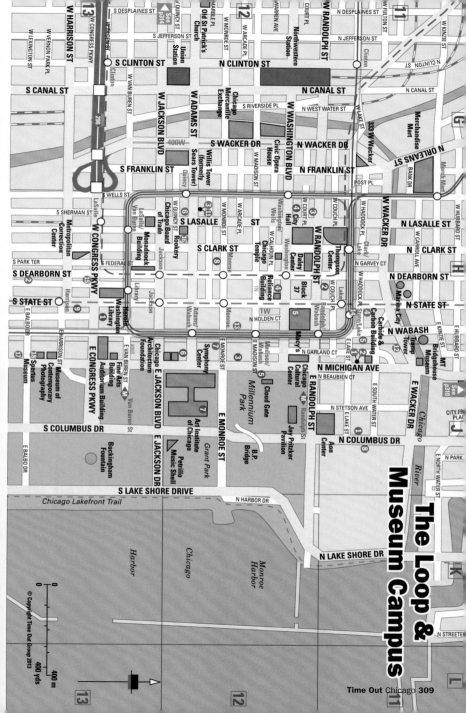

The Loop & Museum Campus

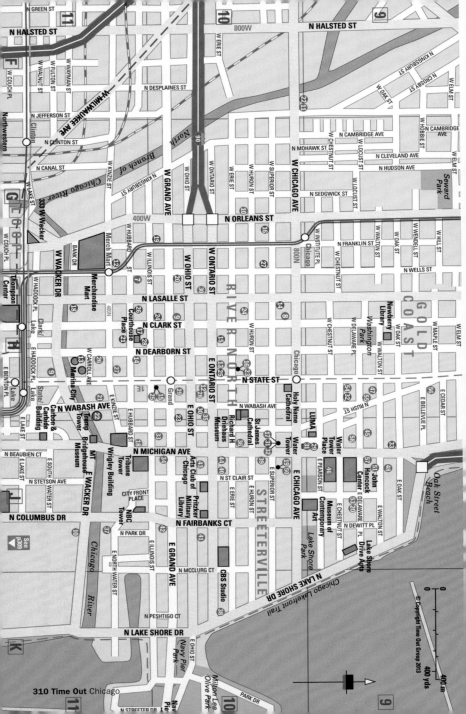

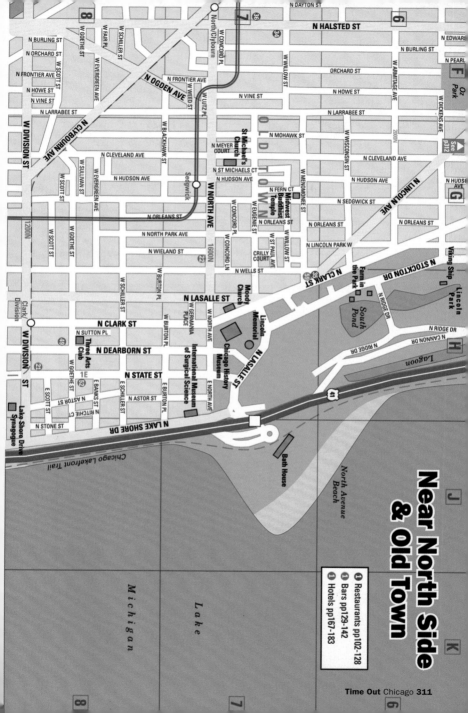

Near North Side & Old Town

- **1** Restaurants pp102-128
- **1** Bars pp129-142
- **1** Hotels pp167-183

Wicker Park
& Bucktown

❶ Restaurants pp102-128
❶ Bars pp129-142
❶ Hotels pp167-183

Holstein Park

BUCKTOWN

Vestern

WICKER
PARK

Flatiron
Building

Padrewski House

Gingerbread
House

Wicker
Park

Division Street
Russian & Turkish
Bath House

Holy Trinity
Orthodox Cathedral

St Volodymyr
Ukranian Orthodox
Cathedral

UKRAINIAN
VILLAGE

North Branch of Chicago River

0 400 m
0 400 yds

© Copyright Time Out Group 2013

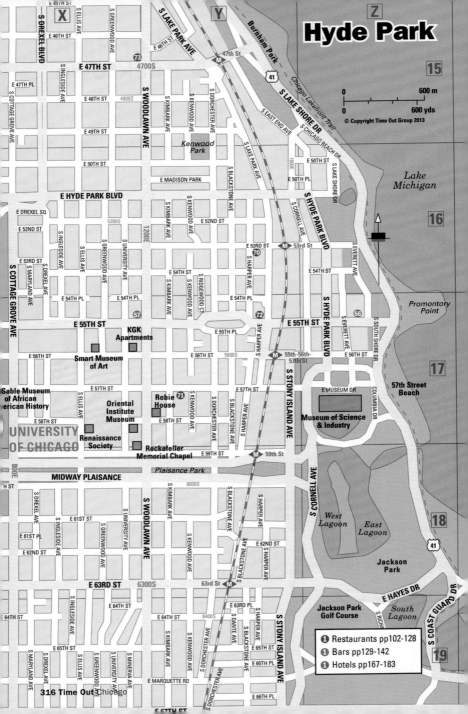

Hyde Park

X   Y   Z

15

16

17

18

19

0   600 m
0   600 yds

© Copyright Time Out Group 2013

Lake Michigan

Burnham Park

Chicago Lakefront Trail

Promontory Point

57th Street Beach

S LAKE PARK AVE
47th St
4700S
E 47TH ST
S DREXEL BLVD
S ELLIS AVE
S GREENWOOD AVE
E 46TH ST
S LAKE PARK AVE
E 47TH PL
E 48TH ST
4800S
S COTTAGE GROVE AVE
S INGLESIDE AVE
S WOODLAWN AVE
S KIMBARK AVE
S KENWOOD AVE
S DORCHESTER AVE
E 49TH ST
Kenwood Park
S LAKE PARK AVE
S EAST END AVE
S CHICAGO BEACH DR
E 50TH ST
E 50TH PL
180E
S HYDE PARK BLVD
S LAKE SHORE DR
E MADISON PARK
E HYDE PARK BLVD
E DREXEL SQ
5200S
1200E
E 52ND ST
S CORNELL AVE
S EVERETT AVE
E 53RD ST
53rd St
70
E 54TH ST
E 54TH ST
S RIDGEWOOD CT
E 54TH PL
56
E 55TH ST
57
KGK Apartments
E 55TH PL
S HARPER AVE
E 55TH ST
55th–56th–57th St
72
E 56TH ST
5600S
Smart Museum of Art
E 57TH ST
S STONY ISLAND AVE
E MUSEUM DR
Robie House 71
Oriental Institute Museum
Museum of Science & Industry
Renaissance Society
Rockefeller Memorial Chapel
E 58TH ST
E 59TH ST
59th St
Sable Museum of African American History
UNIVERSITY OF CHICAGO
800E
MIDWAY PLAISANCE
Plaisance Park
Columbia Dr
S SOUTH SHORE DR
S LAKE SHORE DR
6000S
West Lagoon
East Lagoon
Jackson Park
S CORNELL AVE
S DREXEL AVE
S INGLESIDE AVE
S GREENWOOD AVE
S UNIVERSITY AVE
S WOODLAWN AVE
S KIMBARK AVE
S KENWOOD AVE
S BLACKSTONE AVE
S HARPER AVE
E 61ST ST
E 61ST PL
E 62ND ST
E 62ND ST
41
E 63RD ST
6300S
63rd St
E 63RD PL
S DANTE AVE
6400S
E 64TH ST
Jackson Park Golf Course
E HAYES DR
South Lagoon
S COAST GUARD DR
S RICHARDS DR
E 65TH ST
S MARYLAND AVE
S DREXEL AVE
S ELLIS AVE
S GREENWOOD AVE
S UNIVERSITY AVE
S MINERVA AVE
S KIMBARK AVE
S KENWOOD AVE
S DORCHESTER AVE
S BLACKSTONE AVE
S HARPER AVE
S STONY ISLAND AVE
E MARQUETTE RD
E 65TH PL
E 66TH PL
E 67TH ST

❶	Restaurants pp102-128
❶	Bars pp129-142
❶	Hotels pp167-183

Street Index

For ease of use, all streets in this index are listed alphabetically without their various N, S, E or W prefixes.